ARNOLD READERS IN HISTORY

TITLES IN THE
arnold readers in history SERIES

ALREADY PUBLISHED

THE ENGLISH CIVIL WAR
Edited by Richard Cust and Ann Hughes

THE FRENCH REVOLUTION IN SOCIAL AND
POLITICAL PERSPECTIVE
Edited by Peter Jones

INTERNATIONAL FASCISM
Edited by Roger Griffin

THE IMPACT OF THE ENGLISH REFORMATION 1500–1640
Edited by Peter Marshall

THE ORIGINS OF THE SECOND WORLD WAR
Edited by Patrick Finney

THE TUDOR MONARCHY
Edited by John Guy

IN PREPARATION

BRITISH POLITICS AND SOCIETY 1906–1951
Edited by John Stevenson

WOMEN'S WORK: THE ENGLISH EXPERIENCE 1650–1914
Edited by Pamela Sharpe

GENDER AND HISTORY IN WESTERN EUROPE

Edited by

ROBERT SHOEMAKER
AND
MARY VINCENT

Lecturers in History, University of Sheffield

A member of the Hodder Headline Group
LONDON • SYDNEY • AUCKLAND

First published in Great Britain in 1998 by
Arnold, a member of the Hodder Headline Group,
338 Euston Road, London NW1 3BH

http://www.arnoldpublishers.com

Co-published in the United States of America by
Oxford University Press Inc.,
198 Madison Avenue, New York, NY 10016

British Library Cataloguing in Publication Data
A catalogue record for this book is available from the British Library

Library of Congress Cataloging-in-Publication Data
A catalog record for this book is available from the Library of Congress

ISBN 0 340 67694 9 (pb)
ISBN 0 340 67693 0 (hb)

Production Editor: Wendy Rooke
Production Controller: Priya Gohil

Typeset in 10/12pt Sabon by
J&L Composition Ltd, Filey, North Yorkshire
Printed and bound in the United Kingdom by
MPG Books Ltd, Bodmin, Cornwall

Contents

Preface   vii

Acknowledgements   viii

Introduction   1

SECTION I THEORY AND METHOD

Introduction   23

1 Women's history and gender history: aspects of an
   international debate
   Gisela Bock   25

2 Gender: a useful category of historical analysis
   Joan W. Scott   42

3 What should historians do with masculinity? Reflections on
   nineteenth-century Britain
   John Tosh   65

4 'Adam spoke first and named the orders of the world': masculine
   and feminine domains in history and sociology
   Leonore Davidoff   85

SECTION II THE BODY AND SEXUALITY

Introduction   107

5 Orgasm, generation, and the politics of reproductive biology
   Thomas Laqueur   111

6 Extracts from *Oedipus and the Devil: Witchcraft, sexuality and
   religion in early modern Europe*
   Lyndal Roper   149

7   The birth of the queen: sodomy and the emergence of gender
     equality in modern culture, 1660–1750
     Randolph Trumbach   161

             SECTION III SEPARATE SPHERES?

Introduction   177
8   The early formation of Victorian domestic ideology
     Catherine Hall   181
9   Golden age to separate spheres? A review of the categories and
     chronology of English women's history
     Amanda Vickery   197

                 SECTION IV RELIGION

Introduction   229
10   Talking back: women as prophets during the Civil War and
     Interregnum, 1640–1655
     Phyllis Mack   233
11   Immaculate and powerful: the Marian revival in the nineteenth
     century
     Barbara Corrado Pope   260

                 SECTION V POLITICS

Introduction   281
12   Women on top
     Natalie Zemon Davis   285
13   Marianne's citizens? Women, the Republic and universal suffrage
     in France
     Siân Reynolds   306
14   Womanly duties: maternalist politics and the origins of welfare
     states in France, Germany, Great Britain, and the United States,
     1880–1920
     Seth Koven and Sonya Michel   319

                  SECTION VI WORK

Introduction   349
15   Women's work, gender conflict, and labour markets in Europe
     1500–1900
     Katrina Honeyman and Jordan Goodman   353

     Index   377

Preface

Gender is a large (and growing) area of historical interest, and it has proved possible to provide only a very limited sample of the most stimulating work on this subject in this reader. For reasons of space, we have been unable to include any articles on periods before 1500, or on areas outside Western Europe, and even within these limits we have had to be very selective. We have tried to include important and path-breaking articles which were published in less easily accessible places, and to choose articles which illustrate the wide range of historical subjects affected by gender. Readers should be aware that, also for reasons of space, most of the articles have been subject to some editorial pruning. This applies particularly to the notes, where references to foreign language publications and manuscript sources, which students are unlikely to need, as well as some discursive notes, have been omitted. Those wishing to follow up the full references given in any of these articles are urged to consult the original versions. Location and full publication details are given at the start of each reading.

This Reader arose out of a course on 'Gender in European History, 1600–1950', which we have been teaching in the Department of History at the University of Sheffield since 1993. All of the pieces collected here (and many more) have been used in seminars, and we owe a debt to our students as these discussions have helped us greatly in deciding which articles to include. For assistance in the selection of articles, we are also grateful to Tim Hitchcock, Ludmilla Jordanova and Stephanie McCurry. Thanks are due to all the authors who kindly gave permission for their works to be reproduced here, and we are especially grateful to Siân Reynolds for providing a new introduction to her piece. The comments made by three anonymous referees on the original proposal helped us to sharpen up the final version. Finally, we would like to thank Wendy Bracewell, Linda Edmondson, Paul Heywood and John Tosh for reading various drafts of the introduction and making valuable suggestions.

RBS/MMTV
Sheffield, August 1997

Acknowledgements

The editors and the publisher would like to thank the following for permission to use copyright material:

Gisela Bock: 'Women's history and gender history: aspects of an international debate', from *Gender and History* 1 (1989), 7–30. Reprinted by permission of Blackwell Publishers Limited.

Joan W. Scott: 'Gender: a useful category of historical analysis', from *American Historical Review* 91: 5 (1986). Reprinted by permission of the author.

John Tosh: 'What should historians do with masculinity?', from *History Workshop Journal* 38 (1994). Reprinted by permission of Oxford University Press Limited.

Leonore Davidoff: '"Adam Spoke First and Named the Orders of the World": masculine and feminine domains in history and sociology', from H. Corr and L. Jamieson (eds), *The Politics of Everyday Life* (1990). Copyright © Corr and Jamieson. Reprinted by permission of Macmillan Press Limited and St Martin's Press, Incorporated.

Thomas Laqueur: 'Orgasm, generation and the politics of reproductive biology' from C. Gallagher and T. Laqueur (eds), *The Making of the Modern Body*. Copyright © 1986 The Regents of the University of California. Reprinted by permission of the author and the University of California Press.

Lyndal Roper: Selection from *Oedipus and the Devil* by Lyndal Roper (1994). Reprinted by permission of the author and Routledge Limited.

Randolph Trumbach: 'The birth of the queen: sodomy and the emergence of gender equality in modern culture, 1660–1750', from M. Duberman, M. Vicinus and G. Chauncey Jr (eds), *Hidden from History: Reclaiming the*

Gay and Lesbian Past (Penguin, 1991). Reprinted by permission of the author.

Catherine Hall: 'The early formation of Victorian domestic ideology' in *White, Male and Middle Class: Explorations in Feminism and History* by Catherine Hall (Polity Press, 1992). Reprinted by permission of Blackwell Publishers Limited and Routledge Incorporated.

Amanda Vickery: 'Golden age to separate spheres? A review of the categories and chronology of English women's history', from *Historical Journal* 36 (1993), 383–414. Reprinted by permission of the author and Cambridge University Press.

Phyllis Mack: 'Talking back: women as prophets during the Civil War and Interregnum' from *Visionary Women: Ecstatic Prophecy in Seventeenth-Century England* by Phyllis Mack. Copyright © 1992 The Regents of the University of California. Reprinted by permission of the author and the University of California Press.

Barbara Corrado Pope: 'Immaculate and powerful: the Marian revival in the nineteenth century', from C.W. Atkinson, C.H. Buchanan and M.R. Miles (eds), *Immaculate and Powerful: The Female in Sacred Image and Social Reality*. Copyright © 1985 by Clarissa W. Atkinson, Constance H. Buchanan and Margaret R. Miles. Reprinted by permission of Beacon Press.

Natalie Zemon Davis: 'Women on top' from *Society and Culture in Early Modern France* by Natalie Zemon Davis. © 1975 by the Board of Trustees of the Leland Stanford Junior University. Reprinted by permission of Blackwell Publishers Limited and Stanford University Press.

Siân Reynolds: 'Marianne's citizens? Women, the Republic and universal suffrage in France' in S. Reynolds (ed.), *Women, State and Revolution* (Harvester Press, 1986). Reprinted by permission of the author.

Seth Koven and Sonya Michel: 'Womanly duties: maternalist politics and the origins of welfare states in France, Germany, Great Britain and the United States, 1880–1920', from *American Historical Review* 95: 4 (1990). Reprinted by permission of the authors.

Katrina Honeyman and Jordan Goodman: 'Women's work, gender conflict and labour markets in Europe 1500–1900', from *Economic History Review* 44 (1991). Copyright © 1991 Economic History Society. Reprinted by permission of Blackwell Publishers Limited.

Every effort has been made to trace all copyright holders of material. Any rights not acknowledged here will be acknowledged in subsequent printings if sufficient notice is given to the publisher.

Introduction

Gender history: the evolution of a concept

Teachers of history have long impressed upon their students the importance of defining the terms they use in historical analysis. 'Class' is a case in point; 'gender' is another. As a relatively new term, gender does not yet have the same acreage of explanation attached to it as does class, but the word has still attracted an extraordinary amount of scholarly attention. Originally used in English as a grammatical term, it was adopted by feminist scholars of the 1970s to describe and analyse sexual difference.[1] For many, 'gender' allowed scholars to theorize masculinity and femininity as social constructions, separate from – if, in some sense, related to – anatomical sex. In 1972, the sociologist Ann Oakley argued that

> 'Sex' is a word that refers to the biological differences between male and female. . . . 'Gender', however, is a matter of culture: it refers to the social classification into 'masculine' and 'feminine'. . . . The constancy of sex must be admitted, but so also must the variability of gender.[2]

While, as we shall see, such an unproblematized view of biological sex would subsequently be challenged, historians had acquired a term which encouraged them to investigate the historical construction of sex roles.

When the term 'gender' began to enter into common scholarly usage, the great bulk of the work to which it was applied concerned women. Stimulated on the one hand by the growing interest of historians in 'history from below', and on the other by the women's movement in the United States and Europe, the 1970s and 1980s witnessed an explosion of scholarship on the history of women, with many important monographs and articles published which were dedicated to making women 'visible' in the past.[3] Like social and labour history before it, women's history recovered the voice of the voiceless, making the study of subjects as diverse as midwifery, prostitution, the romantic novel and criminal slander legitimate and rewarding areas of investigation for the historian. Not only did this body of work dramatically enhance and expand the subject matter of history, it also challenged conventional periodization. For example, Joan Kelly's pioneering investigation of women in the Renaissance concluded that they were not part of 'events that further the historical development of men': they did not experience a renaissance, 'at least not during the Renaissance'.[4] In this and other cases, women's history forced 'mainstream' historians to question traditional assumptions about the practice of history.

By the time historians began to use gender in the 1980s some dissatisfaction had been expressed with the direction women's history had taken, and gender provided the opportunity of a new approach. Despite a plethora of often very technically accomplished, empirical studies of women's past lives, there was frustration that the new subject matter had rarely succeeded in changing the way traditional, men-centred history was practised. The problem, as characterized by Elizabeth Fox-Genovese in 1982, was that most women's history implicitly accepted the 'dominant male view' that women were 'other', that their aims and concerns were not those of men, and that their history, therefore, lay apart. Pointing out that adopting such an approach did not challenge mainstream history but rather left it more or less intact – 'adding women to history is not the same as adding women's history' – Fox-Genovese called for women's historians to leave what threatened to become a ghetto and begin investigating gender systems that operated within wider society, and governed the lives of both women and men.[5]

One of the results of applying the theoretical ideas associated with the concept of gender to women's history was an interrogation of the category 'woman'. Building on the findings of a now academically established generation of women's historians, above all in the United States, younger scholars, influenced in part by linguistic critical theory and deconstruction techniques and very conscious of the later, more fractured history of the feminist movement, began to question the very idea of 'women' as a historically constant collectivity. How, asked Denise Riley, do we (or our historical subjects) answer the question 'at this instance, am I a woman as distinct from a human being?'[6] In posing this question, and calling for the deconstruction of what was meant by both 'woman' and 'women', Riley made explicit what she regarded as a tension at the very heart of both feminist politics and feminist scholarship. Working through the polarity of 'equality' and 'difference', she demonstrated the essentially competing claims of evaluating women simply as human beings or citizens, and the claim to a unique female nature which gave women a special understanding or even superiority in fields such as pacifism, education or social work. Battles such as the suffrage – won by female and often feminist protagonists, and now studied by female and often feminist scholars – had seen women's rights defined and defended both as human rights denied women simply through prejudice and inequality, and as 'natural' qualities which only women could bring to politics.[7]

Questioning the category 'woman' was the result of the influence not only of linguistic philosophy and deconstruction techniques (discussed below in the next part of this Introduction), but also of work being done within women's history itself. Marxist feminists – a much more influential school in Britain than in the United States – had always been as concerned with class as they were with gender and the work of sympathetic historians examined the often complex relationship between the two.[8] For those concerned with class oppression, women's oppression could be neither simple nor universal. Crudely put, women in a hegemonic class position were both oppressors (of working-class men and women) and oppressed (by more powerful male members of their own class). Similarly, Black and Asian historians, especially in the United States, disputed the universality of female experience as reconstructed by women's history, pointing out that both the object of enquiry and the enquirers were invariably white and usually middle-class. For these scholars, 'race, gender and class are interlocking and interdependent formations of domination, and . . . these dimensions of social life are experienced simultaneously'.[9]

Among the most dramatic examples of the rethinking of the category of 'women' has been the question of agency under the Third Reich: were women victims of Nazism or its perpetrators?[10] This has generated a far-reaching and at times acrimonious debate. The fate of Jewish and gypsy women was clearly determined on the grounds of race rather than gender. But even among ethnic German women the claim that some were perpetrators and others victims is no less compelling for being prosaic. To make such a claim is not to abandon the use of gender as an analytical tool: although gender is not an all-encompassing force, it is ever-present. The fact that as many men as women were affected by the regime's sterilization laws does not, for instance, invalidate the argument that these laws were principally directed against women, who were defined as reproducers in a way which men were not.[11]

In sum, the ideological framework within which many women's historians initially operated had led to a focus on women's collective historical experience rather than their diverse experiences. In contrast, gender provided a way of conceptualizing the relationship between the two. The emphasis on collective experience had also led women's historians to emphasize continuity rather than change in the history of women's subordination. As discussed in the introduction to Section VI of this reader, for example, it has been argued that women's work opportunities and conditions of work have been inferior to those of men for most of Western European history. The search for explanation led to an emphasis on universals: the cross-cultural and, it is claimed, ever-present tendency to associate the female with nature while men are linked with culture, or to associate women with the private sphere of domestic and reproductive duties and men with the public world outside the home.[12]

The most influential universal was the concept of patriarchy. The literal meaning of the term as rule by the father was widened by many early feminist historians to refer more generally to men's persistent domination over women. In the late 1970s and early 1980s, however, the term was criticized for being ahistorical (in that it implied that male domination was permanent and immutable), and too simplistic (in the sense that it failed to account for the many positive and uncontentious relationships which occur between the sexes), and it treated women solely as victims.[13] According to Linda Gordon, the goal of feminists ought to be 'to advance a theoretical framework to our scholarship that transcends the victim/heroine, domination/resistance dualism and incorporates the varied experiences of women'.[14] By 1989, according to Judith Bennett, 'the term "patriarchy" [had] all but disappeared from most women's history'. Bennett defended the term on the grounds that 'patriarchy highlights the pervasiveness and durability of women's oppression', though she claimed this does not imply that it is unchanging. Together with a number of other historians and sociologists, she argued that the term *can* be seen as historically variable, taking different forms in different times and places. A. J. Hammerton, for example, has shown how men in Victorian England were increasingly censured for cruelty to their wives, which led men's marital conduct to be subject to increasing surveillance. Although this led to a 'chipping away at the edges of patriarchy', men adapted to the new climate; Hammerton argues that the term patriarchy is valuable 'for understanding ways in which [male] power was modified without being abandoned'. For Bennett, the highest priority of women's historians should be to identify the 'workings' of patriarchy, to understand 'how it has managed to survive and endure'.[15]

The debate over patriarchy has thus forced historians to recognize the historical variability of male power, and to explore its workings. Patriarchy is no longer seen as an *explanation* for women's oppression, and is more often seen as a *problem*, for which the answers are complex and lie in a study of the relationships between men and women, and in an investigation of masculinity. Thus in his manifesto for the history of masculinity reproduced in Section I of this reader, John Tosh argues that a central task for historians of masculinity is to examine the ways in which men aggrandize power at the expense of women, at both a psychic and a social level; 'that . . . is what patriarchy means'.

Gender not only answered some of the theoretical issues raised by women's history, it also opened up the history of masculinity as a new area of enquiry. In an early and important consideration of the 'sub-discipline' of women's history (published in 1976), Natalie Zemon Davis called for the 'record of female activity in the past' no longer to operate in isolation either from men or from its historical context. Calling for a consideration of 'the significance of sex roles in social life and historical change', Davis outlined an approach which would soon be characterized as 'gender history'. For her, it was self-evident that 'we should not be working only on the subjected sex any more than an historian of class can focus exclusively on peasants'. Addressing the relations between the sexes, 'gender groups in the historical past', would enable the historian of women directly to address some of the central concerns of the discipline as a whole – power, periodization, social structure and symbolic systems. Such an approach would, the article implied, integrate women's history into the disciplinary mainstream, so widening the audience for work on women and changing the nature of history itself.[16]

Interest in the history of masculinity evolved from work on women's history, but it was also stimulated by other contemporary concerns. In the late 1970s and early 1980s in Britain, the 'men's movement' questioned modern patriarchal gender roles, arguing that society's expectations imprisoned men and prevented them from expressing their emotions. Just as some women had done since the late 1960s, some men began to search the historical record in the hopes of finding alternative, more positive conceptions of masculinity.[17] Although the questions were similar, writing about the history of men proved in some ways methodologically more problematic than writing women's history. As John Tosh's piece in the first section of this reader explains, masculinity has proved resistant to historical analysis. Of course, history writing has until very recently overwhelmingly been about men, but it has tended to assume that men were an unproblematic norm, and that, unlike women, they were never in any way *limited* by their sex. Historians have rarely analysed ideas about men and patterns of male behaviour in terms of changing constructions of masculinity. Not only has the historiography obscured this issue, but the very primary sources historians rely upon embody similar assumptions, by not differentiating between men acting individually and men acting jointly with their wives or families, for example when listing occupations or memberships of voluntary societies. An example of the difficulties involved in studying the history of masculinity can be found in the chapter entitled 'Men in the Third Reich' in Michael Burleigh and Wolfmann Wippermann's study of Nazi Germany, *The Racial State*. Although the authors begin by asking why so little has been written about men as a separate 'anthropological' category in Hitler's Germany, the chapter moves on almost immediately to consider racial, occupational and class groups and the SS, but nowhere offers any consideration of understandings of masculinity in Nazi Germany. Indeed, men, either as a category or as individuals, are, paradoxically, rendered almost invisible in the course of the discussion.[18]

One of the distinctive issues historians of masculinity must confront is the significance of the specific socialization processes experienced by boys as they grow up. According to feminist psychoanalytic theory the transformation of boys into men is a more difficult process than that of girls into women due to the fact that boys must reject the early 'feminine' influence of their mother, and that this forces men to work harder to assert and defend their masculinity.[19] This argument may seem unprovable and unhistorical, but in fact historically in Europe far greater effort has been devoted to the socialization of young men than young women in homosocial environments such as journeymen's associations, schools and youth groups: boys are frequently expected to pass some kind of test (such as a school initiation rite) in order to be considered 'real' men (with those who fail branded 'effeminate'). Subordinate forms of masculinity are also subjected to greater repression than their feminine counterparts. It has been argued that, whereas women are typically under the control of men, 'men . . . are not always under the domination of others and are therefore harder to control socially'.[20] Instead, men's behaviour is regulated by what have been termed 'hegemonic' definitions of masculinity, which marginalize and repress 'unmanly' forms of behaviour.[21] In nineteenth-century Britain and the United States, for example, the dominant form was the ideal of 'manliness', which emphasized the qualities of moral and physical courage and Christian virtue; by the end of the century greater emphasis was placed on physical endurance and stoicism. George Mosse has identified the nineteenth and early twentieth centuries as a period when an 'all-embracing male stereotype' emerged, which saw a similar direct connection between men's physical strength and appearance and their internal moral virtues of honour, courage and self-control.[22] Concurrently, nonconformist forms of male behaviour were repressed. Homosexuality was subject to increasing intolerance, as the homosexual man was labelled as a distinct type, a deviant or subordinate form of masculinity. The consequent repression of any homosexual tendencies in 'normal' men has been associated with the new importance placed on confining sexual activity within marriage at this time, thus illustrating the important point that definitions of masculinity can only be fully understood in the 'context of a whole structure of gender relations'. Dominant forms of masculinity were used to reinforce hierarchies of power: the subordination of both working-class and non-white men was justified by such men's allegedly 'effeminate' lack of control over their own lives.[23]

Despite men's superior position in the gender hierarchy, historians have thus tended to see masculinity as inherently unstable, and have focused their attention on the processes by which masculine identities are constructed, and acquire 'hegemonic' status at the expense of marginalizing other types of behaviour. This helps explain why the earliest studies in the field focused on deviant and contested notions of masculinity, notably homosexuality (see Section II). Recent work, however, has focused on dominant forms of masculinity, and on how such codes of conduct typically involve the assertion of difference from, and power over, both women and 'abnormal' men. In researching what are essentially the workings of patriarchy, these investigations have led historians of masculinity into more 'mainstream' topics. Through studying subjects as diverse as adolescence, popular literature, the history of science, nationalism and imperialism, warfare, international relations, and attitudes towards technology, these historians have added force to the argument that gender is relevant to virtually any conceivable topic of historical analysis.[24] Their research has shed light on a number of conceptual gender issues, notably the ways in which gender identities and hierarchies are constructed, both within and between sexes.

Both because gender history often involves the study of masculinity and because gender historians have tended to problematize some of the fundamental assumptions of women's historians, gender history is sometimes seen as a rejection of women's history. It has been suggested that '[s]ome people (mostly men, but some women too) prefer "gender" because it can include men and is thus more polite than other feminist terms'.[25] Thus, gender can be seen as a way of neutralizing the radical feminist agenda of women's history. This perception has often been compounded by the institutional threat, perceived by many in the USA, that in replacing 'women's studies' with 'gender studies' women were being pushed aside by male scholars interested in men's studies and gay studies. To many outside the USA, this possible colonization is a worrying but essentially parochial issue, yet it underlies nearly all the published debates or dialogues between supporters of women's and proponents of gender history.[26] This in turn, of course, reflects the pioneering role played by American feminist scholars in both these fields, and the early institutional recognition women's history obtained in US academe. But it is unlikely to have the same resonance among gender historians in Europe who, by and large, earn their living in traditional academic departments (often history but also sociology, literature and language departments) or among younger scholars whose personal and intellectual development took place in the wake of the feminist movement rather than in the thick of it.

Such essentially political concerns should not obscure the fact that, as demonstrated above, gender history grew out of women's history, and that many, perhaps most, of the historians who use the term 'gender' identify themselves as feminists. Gender was neither imposed on nor foreign to the original enterprise of women's history. Indeed, some of the earliest published work reproduced in this book clearly illuminates the ways in which gender relations develop and alter over time. Although they do not employ the language of gender, Natalie Zemon Davis's article 'Women on Top' and Siân Reynolds's piece on 'universal' suffrage in Section V (published in 1975 and 1986 respectively) discuss and illuminate both relationships between women and men and the presence, rather than the assumed absence, of the feminine in political activity. A desire for development within the field of women's history led many of its leading protagonists to begin exploring ideas of gender: a desire which sprang, in part, from a sensitivity towards the criticisms levelled at universalist claims and an increasingly problematized understanding of the category 'women'. For example, Joan Scott's early work concerned the relationship between economic change and women's work, and she later went on to publish the influential manifesto for gender history included in Section I of this reader.[27] None the less, despite the calls for women's history to incorporate gender and increase its impact on mainstream history, some feminist historians have continued to argue that women's history will and should remain distinct, that it is inevitably in opposition to male or official history.[28]

Theoretical approaches

Historians of gender need not only to document the history of sex roles, but also to explain why differences between (and within) the sexes have existed, changed, or often persisted despite concurrent dramatic historical transformations. A full range of the possible explanatory factors of gender difference have been investigated – material forces, language, anatomical and psychological qualities. In this discussion we will assess the debates over each of these approaches, with a view to documenting the range of theoretical perspectives available to gender historians.

There have been two phases in the short historiography of gender: early work took place within the framework of social scientific history, while more recent work has been influenced by other disciplines, notably literary and cultural theory and psychoanalysis. In the 1970s and 1980s, gender historians tended to look at the historically contrasting material situations of men and women, and how these varied according to economic and social status, and to examine how, correspondingly, cultural definitions of masculinity and femininity have varied in different times and places. Gender was perceived as central to any social system, along with race and class, and many historians (and other social scientists) devoted considerable efforts to ascertaining the relationships between this 'holy trinity'. In a European (as opposed to American) context, race arguably was much less important until the period of imperial expansion in the nineteenth century, and has featured less prominently in the historiography: the focus has been on the intersection of gender and class. Perhaps the best and most influential example of this approach is Leonore Davidoff and Catherine Hall's book, *Family Fortunes: Men and Women of the English Middle Class* (1987), which linked changing gender roles to the formation of a distinct middle-class identity at that time.

But as the theoretical interests of many historians shifted in the 1980s, the history of gender changed too. Because, as Joan Scott points out, gender 'is absent from the major bodies of social theory articulated from the eighteenth to the early twentieth century', it was arguably more susceptible than most historical approaches to the influence of new theoretical developments from other disciplines.[29] In her article reproduced in Section I, Scott outlines the intellectual journey which led her to reject Marxist and psychoanalytic approaches and adopt the ideas of linguistic and critical theory (often subsumed today under the shorthand of 'postmodernism').

Pointing to the deconstruction techniques of Jacques Derrida, Scott called upon historians to focus their attention on language and, in particular, the way in which language constructs meaning. Criticizing both the largely descriptive thrust of women's history and the naive way in which most historians approached language, Scott looked towards the ways in which meanings were constructed at given moments in the past. Like many others, Scott called for a proper awareness of the historical nature of gender, a rejection of 'fixed' or 'naturalized' binary oppositions between female and male, and a recognition that concepts of masculinity and femininity are not necessarily correspondingly linked to biological men and women. Her work pointed to the all-pervasiveness of gender, the way in which it had symbolized and represented power relations. Gender, for Scott, was 'a primary way of signifying relationships of power'. Thus, it could be seen to operate in areas traditionally closed to women (and their historians), notably labour politics, high politics, diplomacy and warfare.[30]

Unsurprisingly, Scott's call for new methods, and her explicit rejection of the old, have caused considerable controversy, and her article became part of a much wider debate about the value and relevance of postmodern, linguistic techniques to historians.[31] Some have rejected her stance completely; others defend it enthusiastically.[32] Some distinguished feminists have been perturbed by what they see as a potential eclipsing of women in postmodernist scholarship. Christine Stansell, for instance, in her reply to Joan Scott, suggested that privileging terms such as 'gender' and 'language' over and above 'women' 'is to give up ground in a field of discursive conflict'.[33] The implicit danger was that, once again, women would be rendered invisible to history, not least because historically women have written far fewer texts (the primary source material for discursive deconstruction) than men.[34] On a broader scale many non-gender, as well as gender, historians worried about the 'historical nihilism' of postmodernism – with its insistence on the construction of meaning through language (an approach shared by hermeneutics), the absence of either objective truth or an autonomous self (or subject), and the reduction of historical writing to a series of competing narratives which have more in common with fiction than with 'truth'.[35] As we shall see, others worried about the priority given to ideas at the expense of the material forces which shape men's and women's lives. The counterclaims of Marxist and social history techniques were all explored in print.[36]

Although the possibilities Scott's deconstructionist technique opened up for an 'unlocking' of the gender system were greeted with some excitement, even sympathetic observers expressed some criticisms.[37] Louise Tilly, for instance, who had worked extensively with Scott in the past,[38] argued that her emphasis on textual and linguistic analysis, together with the postmodern emphasis on the decoding of binary oppositions, downplayed the role of human agency and risked over-emphasizing cultural constraints on human actions. Seeing deconstruction as 'a method of exposing hidden meanings, not constructing new ones', Tilly cast doubt on the explanatory force of the technique, pointing out its 'scant regard for time or context'.[39] It has become commonplace for historians to highlight the danger of discourse theory creating and employing an idea of language as somehow outside history – 'a structure prior to and independent of material context', 'a thing in itself, a pattern of understanding that evolves according to its own internal laws and shapes human experience according to its formal demands'.[40] This separation of language and material or social context leads on to the problem of whether such an approach denies the agency of historical actors, a problem which is, perhaps, still more intractable. Agency has become a central focus of the debates on history and postmodernism, whether or not they are concerned with gender.

The problem is raised in responses to an exploration of language and gender in Chartism, which Scott first published in 1987, in part as a critique of Gareth Stedman Jones's analysis of Chartist language. While Stedman Jones had argued that the fact that Chartist language was essentially political reflected the movement's fundamentally political, rather than social, character, Scott complained that he had failed to pay sufficient attention to the way language constructs meaning. For Scott, because the Chartist vision of class rested on conceptions of property which were 'indisputably gendered', an exploration of Chartist language reveals the close relationship between class and gender.[41] Christine Stansell agreed that language – though, like Anna Clark, she demonstrated a preference for the more precise term 'rhetoric' – 'transports the invisible presence of the feminine into the smoky taverns and coffee-houses packed with declaiming and petitioning Chartist men'. Yet, while language shaped the ideas of those who followed Chartism and other forms of political radicalism, Stansell argues its constituency was formed elsewhere, 'in the realm of a social experience quite distinct from the realm of speech and text'. By itself, she argued, language would not bring gender into sight in the way Scott claimed: 'it is ultimately the activities of real women which press gender into the service of rhetoric'. Historical subjectivity – 'the conscious activity of people in making and remaking the world' – was missing from Scott's analysis. The task of surviving in early industrial England, of providing for families and caring for children, also shaped working-class life. '[N]o text . . . can subsume social experience.'[42]

A similar critique was made by Anna Clark. The postmodern view of power being dispersed throughout society and exercised through networks in which 'subjects are constructed through discourses' rarely, she argued, answered the question of who exercised that power. Such questions were obviously of prime importance to those whose principal interest lay in investigating women's oppression, but Clark's point was not that power relations were fixed or patriarchal, but rather that they were constantly in flux, 'shifting . . . because real political actors, including women, negotiated and contested them'. For Scott, the important point about Chartism is that its adherents defined citizenship in masculine terms: the participation, or not, of women in this process is irrelevant. For Clark, on the other hand, such a definition was the outcome of struggles both 'between working-class men and women and between working-class men and the state'. Chartists chose the rhetoric of domesticity as a means of uniting working-class men and women, at the cost of excluding women from most forms of work and politics. Clark rejected the postmodernist tendency – which undoubtedly builds on the long-established tradition of dichotomous thought in the West – to see binary oppositions between masculine/feminine, public/private, individual/community, as constructing meaning. In contrast, she sees no fixed correlation between such pairs of opposites, believing that gender dichotomies are 'historically constructed, yet repeatedly contested'.[43] In her book on 'Gender and the Making of the British Working Class', Clark attempted to weave the analysis of discourse with an examination of the struggles for power of working-class men and women. None the less, the emphasis given to male working-class rhetoric in her argument has led her, too, to be accused of paying insufficient attention to women's agency in her study. In part, this may be due to the relative paucity of texts which embody female working-class voices in this period. Yet, in another recent review of scholarship influenced by the work of Joan Scott, the point is made that, for many historians, the analysis of discourse has not eclipsed an established mode of research, which privileges social experience and material reality.[44]

The problem of agency also arises in conflicts over the distinction between 'sex' and 'gender' which have divided gender historians. The apparently easy distinction made between unchanging 'sex' and historically changing 'gender' in the quote from Ann Oakley on the first page of this Introduction – a distinction which characterized the language of gender on its initial adoption by the scholarly community – has come under increasing challenge, as is evident in Gisela Bock's article in the first section of this reader. As a historian of Nazi Germany, Bock demonstrates a particular sensitivity towards notions of 'biology', which she sees as 'a static reductionist model'. She finds the distinction between sex and gender most troubling, arguing that this 'problematic reduction' actually confirms traditional notions of unchanging sex differences precisely because it 'reduces sex to a "biological" category'. Biology is thus 'a modern metaphor for the old assumption that men are ungendered and women are gendered beings'.[45] While many historians working outside modern German history continue to use the terms 'biological' and 'anatomical' as synonyms, Bock's acute scrutiny of the sex/gender dichotomy has found considerable support from historians looking at the history of the body. Many of these scholars work within a tradition of the history of medicine or the history of science (usually biology) and they are often concerned with representation, or how the body was understood and depicted in metaphorical as well as descriptive terms.[46] Thomas Laqueur's article in Section II of this reader shows how scientific understandings of anatomical sex differences changed over time. In the twentieth-century West, of course, physical anatomy has also changed as improved nutrition and health care has led to human beings living longer, growing taller and, at the extremes, achieving standards of physical prowess (for example, in athletics) unimaginable in previous eras. With an earlier age of menarche, and a later age of menopause, reproductive lives have been elongated, although the development of efficient and easily available contraception has had the effect of actually decreasing levels of reproduction. While some aspects of human life – the facts of birth, maturity, ageing and death, the need to satisfy bodily requirements such as hunger, and the existence of anatomical sex – remain historical constants, it is important to recognize that both the understanding and the experience of 'biology' varies widely, across both time and space.

The sex/gender dichotomy poses a further problem. Bock's article in Section I also points to the international nature of developments in gender history. However, this multicultural, multilinguistic existence creates difficulties. Bock, a German working on German history, has pointed out that the distinction, both linguistic and methodological, between sex and gender works best in English. The meaning of the word 'gender' has, of course, changed in many languages, including English where it was originally a grammatical term, and the new usage has been imported into Romance languages. *Género* is increasingly used in Spanish; *genre* has become the equivalent in French. Bock points out, however, that the 'linguistic dynamics and connotations' of these terms may vary in different languages. Italian, for example, continues to use *essere sessuato* for 'gendered being', despite a distinction now being made between *sesso* [sex] and *genere* [gender].[47] German provides a still more complex case, as the language has a single term, *Geschlecht*, for the concepts of both sex and gender. This linguistic trope obviously means that German-speaking historians are used to conceptualizing gender in a rather different way from English-speaking ones. It is surely no coincidence that several German historians reject the sex/gender dichotomy, while Bock herself has called for a comprehensive use of the term 'gender' which would include both 'gender' and 'sex'.[48]

The influential French thinker Luce Irigaray similarly rejects any distinction between sex and gender. But for Irigaray, the goal is to emphasize, rather than problematize, the sexed nature of gender. A Lacanian psychoanalyst by training, she employs a powerful analysis of the gendered nature of Romance languages which, she argues, routinely render women and the feminine invisible (as in the simple plural which takes the masculine form, or the possessive which, in French, agrees with the object being possessed) or inferior (as in the differential values ascribed to male and female gendered words).[49] Irigaray seeks to prevent the feminine from becoming obliterated or neutralized by incorporation into or acceptance of the masculine, either in language or elsewhere. Her quest is for a 'sexed subjectivity', a distinct female identity within society, discourse and human relations.

'Humanity is comprised of two different subjective identities and their respective objects or objectives.' Her emphasis on the imperative need to recognize the separate female 'I' has meant that Irigaray, like Julia Kristeva, is primarily a theorist of difference.[50]

This approach to theorizing sexual difference has proved immensely influential although, as Linda Gordon has observed, it has not had the same impact on all academic disciplines. Both Kristeva and Irigaray work within a tradition of psychoanalytic thought, and what Gordon calls 'the difference motif' has proved more dominant in linguistics, literature and philosophy than in history or sociology. This may, in part, be due to the different use historians and psychoanalysts make of evidence. Irigaray supports her reading of the human condition by reference to historical periods which are, in fact, mythological ones – 'the cleavages in History in the gynocratic, matriarchal, patriarchal, phallocratic eras'.[51] Such interpretations have been a mainstay of psychoanalytic analysis since Freud and have done much to illuminate the workings of the human psyche, an area which has only very recently begun to receive attention from historians, who are inevitably sceptical of eternal truths and cross-cultural constants. None the less, its influence is growing. Historians of patriarchy have looked to psychic processes to explain men's tendency to assert power over women.[52] Lyndal Roper's work on women and witchcraft in early modern Germany, an excerpt of which is reproduced in Section II of this reader, is based on the premise that 'bodies are not merely creations of discourse . . . what we need is a history that can problematise the relation between the psychic and the physical'. We cannot understand why sexual fantasies of witchcraft concentrated on female bodies, imagining 'the loss of boundaries altogether, the filling of the body with evil substances and the elision of the gap between one's own body and the maternal body', without a recognition that such images were shaped by the unconscious. While the argument is compelling, Roper herself admits that historians have not yet succeeded in integrating the physicality of male and female bodies, and their role in shaping the unconscious, with historically changing social and cultural forces.[53]

In attempting to understand why gender roles have historically taken the form that they have, and to explain why they change much more slowly than other socially defined roles, historians of gender have been forced to engage with some of the central dilemmas which confront students of the humanities: the role played by biology and psychology in motivating human action; the relative importance of ideological and material forces in causing historical change; and the role that current political agendas should play in shaping scholarship. An examination of the debates currently taking place in gender history illustrates how historical research reveals a richly complex picture which points to the dangers of prioritizing any one historical methodology over another.[54] Despite ideological efforts stressing distinct gender roles, often based on suppositions of 'natural' difference, men's and women's lives have alternately overlapped and diverged in complicated ways. While the theoretical insights of other disciplines have provided enormously important conceptual approaches for gender historians, detailed historical research is still needed to test and examine their application to the past.

Topics of investigation

As we have seen, debates within gender history mobilize similar questions to those currently preoccupying historians across the discipline. There could be few clearer indications of the way in which gender history has become integrated into the disciplinary mainstream. Textbooks and outline national history courses now routinely consider (if often only briefly) gender relations and the position and role of women. The painstaking research and monographic publication which has been built up since the 1970s means that there is now a substantial body of historical knowledge about gender relations in the past which simply did not exist before. This corpus is the foundation for the many more specialist courses and publications which are available both to students and to scholars, not just in Women's or Gender Studies departments but also in many established, conventional History departments. Gender history has, it would seem, finally arrived.

But what has it achieved? In the remainder of the Introduction we will briefly survey the topics of historical research where gender has made a significant impact, reserving more detailed discussion of the topics covered in the rest of the reader to the introductions to each section. Needless to say, the subjects of investigation have been wide-ranging, and very much influenced by the theoretical perspectives historians have adopted. Early, social scientific, research on gender tended to focus on work, and the extensive historiography on this subject is discussed in the introduction to Section VI of this reader. With the 'linguistic turn', historians began to investigate how language and other representations construct gender differences. Just how influential this approach has been is evident in the fact that examples can be found throughout this reader. Leonore Davidoff's article in Section I argues that, from the seventeenth century, influential concepts in science, medicine, political theory, economics and law were imbued with ideas of gender difference which have come to dominate our culture and institutions. In Section II, Thomas Laqueur's article examines how conceptions of gender were mapped onto medical understandings of the differences between male and female bodies. Section III includes Catherine Hall's account of the origins of key aspects of the ideology of separate spheres in late eighteenth-century England. In Section IV, the articles by Phyllis Mack and Barbara Corrado Pope examine the gendered nature of religious language, symbolism and imagery. And in Section V, the articles by Natalie Davis and Siân Reynolds show a similar interest in the gendered nature of political language.

These articles, however, represent only a selection of the types of discourse and subject matter which gender historians have analysed with a view towards identifying the intellectual and cultural sources of gender difference. Most obviously, literature, both elite and popular, has proved a fertile ground. Historians, as well as literary critics, have analysed everything from popular ballads to drama, poetry and novels for their representations of gender, and the material they have found has been so rich that they have linked the rise of entire new genres, such as the English periodical and the novel, with important transformations in gender roles.[55] Others have analysed conduct books for prescriptions of appropriate behaviour for men and women.[56] The visual arts have also been analysed for the often complicated gendered meanings they convey.[57] Historians of philosophy and science have studied some of the issues raised by Davidoff's article in this reader, in particular exploring how in the seventeenth and eighteenth centuries rationality and science came to be seen as masculine qualities, opposed to feminine nature, morality and sensibility.[58] Another subject of discourse where the concepts have been found to be fundamentally gendered has been political theory, an aspect of politics which has been particularly receptive to a gendered analysis. The writings of political theorists from the Greeks to the twentieth century have been shown to promote gender difference by directly or indirectly privileging what were perceived to be male values, frequently by making a fundamental distinction between the (male) public sphere (which was seen to be political) and the (female) private sphere (which was not).[59] Historians influenced by psychoanalysis have analysed support for imperialism, militarism and fascism through an analysis of men's fantasies, both in their writings and as stimulated by the heroic narratives that they read.[60]

To what extent, however, have these gendered discourses identified by scholars actually shaped the gender roles as lived by men and women? Those working from a linguistic or psychoanalytic perspective argue that language shapes social reality, but they do not always examine the intersection between the two. With the exception of the introductory section on theory and method, the articles selected for this reader do just that. Arguably it is this approach which offers the prospect of the most exciting work on gender at the moment, as is evident, for example, in research on the interrelationships between war and gender.[61] Subjects long thought to be immune to gender analysis, such as war, diplomacy and high politics, are being reevaluated from this perspective.

Probably the most promising area of current research, however, concerns the very process by which gender differences are acquired in the first place, the socialization process of individuals from birth to adulthood. For historians working on the 'construction' of masculinity and femininity, this is an obvious, but rather neglected, subject of investigation. Cultural history, psychoanalysis and social history come together in the analysis of the relationship between cultural norms and childrearing practices. Although the family has been the subject of sustained investigation by social historians since the 1970s, existing writing has insufficiently explored the notions of masculinity and femininity embedded in the roles played by husbands and wives, and fathers and mothers. Even less has been written about the different childhood experiences of boys and girls, despite the key role, as noted earlier, the early years are alleged to play in rendering the construction of gender identity a more problematic experience for men than for women.[62] More work has been done on adolescence. Several historians have written about the role that apprenticeship, school, youth groups and other male adolescent 'rites of passage' have played in the construction of masculine identities.[63] Female adolescence has been less well served, with the exception of domestic service, that common employer of young women (and some men) which, despite their subordination to a master or mistress, allowed such women a period of unaccustomed semi-independence before marriage.[64] Other historians are turning to education, both formal and informal, as an inculcator of gendered values.[65] These topics require much more attention if we are to understand fully the processes by which gender roles have been historically constructed and perpetuated, not only in discourse but also in social practice.

Notes

1 A usage pioneered by sociologists and social anthropologists: Ann Oakley, *Sex, Gender and Society* (London, 1972); Sherry Ortner, 'Is Female to Male as Nature is to Culture?' in Michele Zimbalist Rosaldo and Louise Lamphere (eds), *Women, Culture, and Society* (Stanford, CA, 1974); Gayle Rubin, 'The Traffic in Women: Notes on the Political Economy of Sex' in Rayna R. Reiter (ed.), *Towards an Anthropology of Women* (New York, 1975).
2 Oakley, *Sex, Gender and Society*, p. 16.
3 For bibliographical guides, see Karen Offen, Ruth Roach Pierson and Jane Rendall (eds), *Writing Women's History: International Perspectives* (London, 1991) and Gayle V. Fischer (comp.), *Journal of Women's History Guide to Periodical Literature* (Bloomington, IN, 1992). See also Natalie Zemon Davis and Joan Scott, 'Women in History', *Past and Present* 101 (1983), pp. 125–57, as well as the following pioneering collections of essays: Renate Bridenthal, Claudia Koonz and Susan Stuard (eds), *Becoming Visible: Women in European History* (Boston, MA, 1976; 2nd edn, 1987) and Mary S. Hartman and Lois Banner (eds), *Clio's Consciousness Raised* (New York, 1974).
4 Joan Kelly-Gadol, 'Did Women Have a Renaissance?' in Bridenthal *et al.*, *Becoming Visible*, pp. 175–201; *idem*, 'The Social Relation of the Sexes: Methodological Implications of Women's History', *Signs* 1 (1976), pp. 809–23.
5 Elizabeth Fox-Genovese, 'Placing Women's History in History', *New Left Review* 133 (1982), pp. 5–29.
6 Denise Riley, *'Am I That Name?': Feminism and the Category of 'Women' in History* (London, 1988), p. 6 and *passim*. See also Judith Butler, *Gender Trouble: Feminism and the Subversion of Identity* (London and New York, 1990) and Mary Poovey,

'Feminism and Deconstruction', *Feminist Studies* 14:1 (1988), pp. 51–65. These and other developments within women's history are mapped chronologically in Joan Scott, 'Women's History' in Peter Burke (ed.), *New Perspectives on Historical Writing* (Cambridge and Oxford, 1991), pp. 42–66.

7 Riley, *Am I That Name?*, esp. chs 1 and 4.

8 This is evident, for example, in the work of Sheila Rowbotham and Catherine Hall. See Sheila Rowbotham, *Hidden from History: Rediscovering Women in History from the Seventeenth Century to the Present* (London, 1974) and Catherine Hall, *White, Male and Middle Class: Explorations in Feminism and History* (Cambridge and Oxford, 1992).

9 Sonya O. Rose, 'Gender History/Women's History: Is Feminist Scholarship Losing its Critical Edge?', *Journal of Women's History* 5:1 (1993), p. 91. See also Scott, 'Women's History' pp. 55–9 on the 'pluralizing' of the category 'women' as a result of work done in the social sciences, including history. The forceful critiques of race have had most impact on American history, but European historians should look to recent work being done on empire and the experience of colonization, as well as to the flourishing school of Indian gender history: see, e.g., Kumkum Sangari and Sudesh Vaid (eds), *Recasting Women: Essays in Colonial History* (New Brunswick, NJ, 1989) and Nupur Chadhuri and Margaret Strobel (eds), *Western Women and Imperialism: Complicity and Resistance* (Bloomington, Indiana, 1992). A pioneering attempt to interrogate 'whiteness' is incorporated in Catherine Hall, '"From Greenland's Icy Mountains . . . to Afric's Golden Sands": Ethnicity, Race and Nation in Mid-Nineteenth-Century England', *Gender and History* 5:3 (1993).

10 For introductions to the debate, see Atina Grossman, 'Feminist Debates about Women and National Socialism', *Gender and History* 3:3 (1991), pp. 350–8 and Mary Nolan, 'Work, Gender and Everyday Life: Reflections on Continuity, Normality and Agency in Twentieth-Century Germany' in Ian Kershaw and Moshe Lewin (eds), *Stalinism and Nazism: Dictatorships in Comparison* (Cambridge, 1997), pp. 329–37.

11 See the work by Gisela Bock. Her articles in English include 'Racism and Sexism in Nazi Germany: Motherhood, Compulsory Sterilisation and the State', *Signs* 8:3 (1983) pp. 400–21; 'Antinatalism, Maternity and Paternity in National Socialist Racism' in Gisela Bock and Pat Thane (eds), *Maternity and Gender Politics: Women and the Rise of the European Welfare States* (London, 1991), pp. 233–55; 'Equality and Difference in National Socialist Racism', in Gisela Bock and Susan James (eds), *Beyond Equality and Difference: Citizenship, Feminist Politics and Female Subjectivity* (London and New York, 1992), pp. 89–109.

12 Ortner, 'Is Female to Male'; Michele Z. Rosaldo, 'The Use and Abuse of Anthropology: Reflections on Feminism and Cross-cultural Understanding', *Signs* 5 (1980), pp. 389–417.

13 Sheila Rowbotham, 'The Trouble with "Patriarchy"' (1979) and Sally Alexander and Barbara Taylor, 'In Defence of "Patriarchy"', reprinted in Raphael Samuel (ed.), *People's History and Socialist Theory* (London, 1981), pp. 364–73. A summary of some of these debates is provided in Judith Bennett, 'Feminism and History', *Gender and History* 1:3 (1989), pp. 251–72.

14 Linda Gordon, 'What's New in Women's History' in Teresa de Lauretis (ed.), *Feminist Studies/Critical Studies* (Madison, WI, 1986), p. 25.

15 Bennett, 'Feminism and History', pp. 254, 266; A. J. Hammerton, *Cruelty and Companionship: Conflict in Nineteenth-Century Married Life* (London, 1992), p. 7; Sylvia Walby, 'Theorising Patriarchy', *Sociology* 23:2 (1989), pp. 213–34. Other historians who incorporate patriarchy in their analyses include Anthony Fletcher, *Gender, Sex and Subordination in England, 1500–1800* (New Haven, CT, and London, 1995), and Honeyman and Goodman (see their article in Section VI of this reader).

16 Natalie Zemon Davis, '"Women's History" in Transition: The European Case', *Feminist Studies* 3:3/4 (1976), pp. 83–103.

17 Michael Roper and John Tosh (eds), 'Introduction', in *Manful Assertions: Masculinities in Britain since 1800* (London, 1991), p. 6.

18 Michael Burleigh and Wolfmann Wippermann, *The Racial State: Germany 1933–1945* (Cambridge, 1991), pp. 267–303. A more focused gender analysis of Nazi

racial policy (i.e. one which considers the roles of both women and men) is begun in Bock, 'Equality and Difference'.

19 David Gilmore, *Manhood in the Making: Cultural Concepts of Masculinity* (New Haven, CT, 1990), pp. 27–9; Nancy Chodorow, 'Family Structure and Feminine Personality', in Rosaldo and Lamphere (eds), *Women, Culture, and Society*, pp. 43–66.

20 Gilmore, *Manhood in the Making*, p. 221.

21 R. W. Connell, *Masculinities* (Oxford, 1995), pp. 76–81.

22 Norman Vance, *The Sinews of the Spirit: The Ideal of Christian Manliness in Victorian Literature and Religious Thought* (Cambridge, 1985); David Newsome, *Godliness and Good Learning: Four Studies on a Victorian Ideal* (London, 1961); J. A. Mangan and James Walvin (eds), *Manliness and Morality: Middle-Class Masculinity in Britain and America, 1800–1940* (Manchester, 1987); George L. Mosse, *The Image of Man: The Creation of Modern Masculinity* (Oxford, 1996).

23 Jeffery Weeks, *Coming Out: Homosexual Politics in Britain from the Nineteenth Century to the Present* (London, 1977) and his *Sex, Politics and Society: The Regulation of Sexuality since 1800* (London, 1981), esp. p. 107; Connell, *Masculinities*, p. 185; Catherine Hall, 'Competing Masculinities: Thomas Carlyle, John Stuart Mill, and the case of Governor Eyre' in her *White, Male and Middle Class*, pp. 255–95; John C. Fout (ed.), *Forbidden History: The State, Society and the Regulation of Sexuality in Modern Europe* (Chicago and London, 1992); Robert A. Nye, *Masculinity and Male Codes of Honor in Modern France* (Oxford, 1993).

24 Examples are given in the notes to the third part of this Introduction.

25 Mariana Valverde, 'Dialogue', *Journal of Women's History* 5:1 (1993), p. 122.

26 E.g. Louise Tilly, 'Gender, Women's History and Social History', Gay L. Gullickson, 'Comment on Tilly: Women's History, Social History, and Deconstruction', Judith M. Bennett, 'Comment on Tilly: Who Asks the Questions for Women's History' and a final response by Tilly, *Social Science History* 13:4 (1989), pp. 439–80; Sonya Rose, 'Gender History/Women's History', with separate comments by Kathleen Canning, Anna Clark, Mariana Valverde and Marcia R. Sawyer, *Journal of Women's History* 5:1 (1993), pp. 89–128.

27 Louise A. Tilly and Joan W. Scott, *Women, Work and the Family* (New York, 1978).

28 See, e.g., Gordon's claim that 'Women's history is not just different, it is critical; it is against men's history': 'What's New in Women's History', p. 28.

29 Scott, 'Gender: A Useful Category of Historical Analysis', *American Historical Review* 91:5 (1986), p. 1066.

30 Ibid., p. 1069. Power in this sense is understood by Scott in the Foucaultian sense of 'dispersed constellations of unequal relationships, discursively constituted in social "fields of force"'.

31 These debates – which are about both Scott's work and the wider questions raised by postmodernism – may be followed in Tilly *et al.*, 'Gender, Women's History and Social History', Rose, 'Gender History/Women's History' and Joan W. Scott, 'On Language, Gender and Working-Class History', with responses by Bryan D. Palmer, Christine Stansell and Anson Rabinbach, *International Labor and Working-Class History* 31 (1987), 1–36. Scott's most important essays on gender – including 'Gender: A Useful Category' and 'On Language, Gender, and Working-Class History' – have been collected in Joan Wallach Scott, *Gender and the Politics of History* (New York, 1988); there are critiques of her approach in the reviews by Linda Gordon (published with a response from Scott in *Signs* 15:1 [1990], pp. 853–60), Catherine Hall ('Politics, Poststructuralism and Feminist History', *Gender and History* 3 [1991], pp. 204–10) and Claudia Koonz (in *Women's Review of Books* 6:4 [1989], pp. 19–20). See also Louise M. Newman, 'Critical Theory and the History of Women: What's at Stake in Deconstructing Women's History', *Journal of Women's History* 2:3 (1991), pp. 58–68.

32 For the extremes of the debate see Joan Hoff, 'Gender as a Postmodern Category of Paralysis', *Women's History Review* 3 (1994), pp. 149–68 and, subsequently, June Purvis, 'Women's History and Poststructuralism', Susan Kingsley Kent, 'Mistrials and Diatribulations: A Reply to Joan Hoff', Caroline Ramazanoglu, 'Unravelling Postmodern Paralysis: A Response to Joan Hoff' and Joan Hoff, 'A Reply to My Critics', all in *Women's History Review* 5:1 (1996), pp. 5–30.

33 Stansell in *International Labor and Working-Class History*, p. 29.
34 See, e.g., Kathleen Canning (citing Gisela Bock), 'German Particularities in Women's History/Gender History', *Journal of Women's History* (1993), p. 103.
35 Attention tends to focus on the works of Hayden White in this context. See his 'The Historical Text as Literary Artefact' in Hayden White, *Tropics of Discourse: Essays in Cultural Criticism* (Baltimore and London, 1978), pp. 81–100.
36 See, e.g, Palmer in *International Labor and Working-Class History* (1987); Hall, 'Politics, Poststructuralism and Feminist History'; Tilly, 'Gender, Women's History and Social History'; Bennett, 'Feminism and History'.
37 E.g. Gullickson, 'Women's History, Social History, and Deconstruction', pp. 465-9.
38 Tilly and Scott, *Women, Work and the Family*.
39 Tilly, 'Gender, Women's History and Social History', pp. 452–3.
40 See Palmer and Stansell in *International Labor and Working-Class History*, quotes at pp. 16, 27.
41 Gareth Stedman Jones, *Languages of Class: Studies in English Working Class History, 1832–1982* (Cambridge, 1983); Scott, 'On Language, Gender and Working-Class History'.
42 Stansell in *International Labor and Working-Class History*, esp. pp. 26–9.
43 Clark in *Journal of Women's History*, pp. 118, 115–18.
44 Anna Clark, *The Struggle for the Breeches: Gender and the Making of the British Working Class* (Berkeley, CA, 1995); review by Tim Hitchcock in *Albion* 28 (Spring 1996), pp. 123–4; Theodore Koditschek, 'The Gendering of the British Working Class', *Gender and History* 9 (1997), pp. 333–63.
45 See Bock, 'Challenging Dichotomies: Perspectives on Women's History' in Karen Offen *et al.* (eds), *Writing Women's History*, pp. 7–9.
46 See Roy Porter, 'History of the Body' in Burke (ed.), *New Perspectives on Historical Writing*, pp. 206–32 and Ludmilla Jordanova, *Sexual Visions: Images of Gender in Science and Medicine between the Eighteenth and Twentieth Centuries* (Hemel Hempstead, 1989).
47 Bock, 'Challenging Dichotomies', p. 9.
48 Ibid.; see also Canning, 'German Particularities', p. 102, fn 4.
49 Luce Irigaray, 'A Personal Note', 'Women's Discourse and Men's Discourse' and 'Linguistic Sexes and Genders', collected in Luce Irigaray, *je, tu, nous: Toward a Culture of Difference* (New York and London, 1993), pp. 9–14, 29–36, 67–74.
50 Irigaray, *je, tu, nous*, p. 105 and *passim*; Julia Kristeva, 'Women's Time', *Signs* 7:1 (1981), pp. 13–35.
51 Irigaray, *je, tu, nous*, p. 12 and *passim*.
52 See the article by John Tosh in Section I and Alexander and Taylor, 'In Defence of "Patriarchy"'.
53 Lyndal Roper, *Oedipus and the Devil: Witchcraft, Sexuality and Religion in Early Modern Europe* (London, 1994), pp. 21, 26.
54 See, for example, debates over the merits of the metaphor of separate spheres, discussed in the Introduction to Section III of this reader.
55 See, e.g., Anna Clark, 'The Politics of Seduction in English Popular Culture, 1748–1848' in Jean Radford (ed.), *The Progress of Romance: The Politics of Popular Fiction* (London, 1986), pp. 47–70; Catherine Belsey, *The Subject of Tragedy: Identity and Difference in Renaissance Drama* (London, 1985); Nancy Armstrong, *Desire and Domestic Fiction: A Political History of the Novel* (Oxford, 1987); Susan Morgan, *Sisters in Time: Imagining Gender in Nineteenth-Century British Fiction* (Oxford, 1989); Katherine Shevelow, *Women and Print Culture: The Construction of Femininity in the Early Periodical* (London, 1989).
56 Fletcher, *Gender, Sex and Subordination in England*, esp. chs 16 and 19; Robert Shoemaker, *Gender in English Society, 1650–1850: The Emergence of Separate Spheres?* (London, 1998), pp. 21–36.
57 See, e.g., Marcia Pointon, 'Liberty on the Barricades: Women, Politics and Sexuality in Delacroix' in Siân Reynolds (ed.), *Women, State and Revolution* (Brighton, 1986), pp. 25–43; Marina Warner, *Joan of Arc: The Image of Female Heroism* (London, 1991). Such work may be usefully compared to studies of iconography and symbol-

ism which conspicuously fail to introduce a gender analysis, e.g. Maurice Agulhon, *Marianne into Battle: Republican Imagery and Symbolism in France, 1789–1880* (Cambridge and Paris, 1977) and Martha Hanna, 'Iconography and Ideology: Images of Joan of Arc in the Idiom of the Action Française, 1908–31', *French Historical Studies* 14:2 (1985), pp. 215–39.

58 Susan Bordo, 'The Cartesian Masculinization of Thought', *Signs* 11:3 (1986), pp. 439–56; Jordanova, *Sexual Visions* and her 'Gender and the Historiography of Science', *British Journal for the History of Science* 26 (1993), pp. 469–83; Londa Schiebinger, 'Why Mammals are Called Mammals: Gender Politics in Eighteenth-Century Natural History', *American Historical Review* 98 (1993), pp. 382–411.

59 Susan Moller Okin, *Women in Western Political Thought* (Princeton, 1979); Jean Bethke Elshtain, *Public Man, Private Woman: Women in Social and Political Thought* (Princeton, 1981).

60 Klaus Theweleit, *Male Fantasies* (2 vols, Oxford, 1987–9); Graham Dawson, *Soldier Heroes: British Adventure, Empire and the Imagining of Masculinities* (London, 1994); John M. MacKenzie, 'The Imperial Pioneer and Hunter and the British Masculine Stereotype in late Victorian and Edwardian Times' in Mangan and Walvin (eds), *Manliness and Morality*, pp. 176–98.

61 Margaret R. Higonnet *et al.* (eds), *Behind the Lines: Gender and the Two World Wars* (New Haven, CT, and London, 1987); Joanna Bourke, *Dismembering the Male: Men's Bodies, Britain and the Great War* (London, 1996).

62 On marriage, motherhood and fatherhood, see L. Roper, *The Holy Household: Women and Morals in Reformation Augsburg* (Oxford, 1989), and the work of John Tosh (see references in the introduction to Section I).

63 John Springhall, 'Building Character in the British Boy: The Attempt to Extend Christian Manliness to Working Class Adolescents, 1880–1914' and Allen Warren, 'Popular Manliness: Baden Powell, Scouting and the Development of Manly Character', both in Mangan and Walvin (eds), *Manliness and Morality*, pp. 52–74 and 199–219; Merry Wiesner, '*Wandervogels* and Women: Journeymen's Concepts of Masculinity in Early Modern Germany', *Journal of Social History* 24 (1991), pp. 767–82; John Gillis, *Youth in History* (2nd edn, New York, 1984).

64 Bridget Hill, *Servants: English Domestics in the Eighteenth Century* (Oxford, 1996); Patty Seleski, 'Women, Work, and Cultural Change in Eighteenth- and Early Nineteenth-Century London', in T. Harris (ed.), *Popular Culture in England 1500–1850* (Basingstoke, 1995), pp. 143–67; Teresa McBride, 'The Modernisation of Women's Work', *Journal of Modern History* 49:2 (1977), pp. 231–45.

65 Fletcher, *Gender, Sex and Subordination in England*, chs 15, 18; Michèle Cohen, *Fashioning Masculinity: National Identity and Language in the Eighteenth Century* (London, 1996); Sharif Gemie, *Women and Schooling in Nineteenth-Century France 1815–1914: Gender, Authority and Identity in the Female Schooling Sector* (Keele, 1995).

THEORY AND METHOD

Introduction

Gender is a subject which has generated considerable theoretical discussion, among both historians and non-historians, and it is impossible fully to understand historical writing on this subject without being aware of these debates. The articles in this section – all of which were written by practising historians – address some of the most important theoretical and methodological issues raised by gender, while the debates to which they contribute are surveyed in more detail in the Introduction to this reader.

The selections start with Gisela Bock's introduction to the subject of gender history which addresses the question of how it is different from women's history, and looks in particular at how 'biological' factors shape gender roles. Bock's interest in how ideas of biology are socially constructed arises, at least in part, from her work on the Third Reich. A leading historian of Nazi Germany – whose work has, on occasion, provoked controversy – she has also helped to pioneer the comparative study of gender history in twentieth-century Europe.[1] Bock's article is followed by Joan Scott's influential manifesto on gender, which not only stakes important claims for the wider significance of gender history, but also introduces a postmodernist perspective. Scott began her career writing about the history of women's work in France, though her interests have subsequently broadened. She has increasingly engaged with historiographical and methodological issues, and has published articles on a number of subjects, notably on the importance of gendered language to the development of class in the nineteenth century. It is possible to trace the evolution of her approach through the articles collected in her *Gender and the Politics of History* (1988).[2]

John Tosh's article in this section clearly sets out the conceptual issues raised by the new field of the history of masculinity. A historian of nineteenth-century England, Tosh's primary interest is in the domestic lives of middle-class men, investigating the apparent contradiction between their public roles and responsibilities and their attraction to domesticity, an attraction which existing historical work on 'separate spheres' tends to obscure.[3] Finally, Leonore Davidoff's essay not only demonstrates the importance of a historical perspective in understanding how gender identities are constructed, but its analysis of the gendered origins of modern social theory provides a compelling example of the potential of gender as an analytical tool. She is perhaps best known for the book she co-wrote with Catherine Hall, *Family Fortunes: Men and Women of the English Middle Class, 1780–1850* (1987), which provided a fundamental contribution to the debate over 'separate spheres'. However, Davidoff has also published widely on aspects of women's and men's domestic lives, work and sociability in nineteenth-century England, focusing especially on contexts, such as relations between masters and servants or landladies and lodgers, where the two sexes interacted.[4]

Notes

1 See, in particular, the collections she has edited with Pat Thane, *Maternity and Gender Politics: Women and the Rise of the European Welfare States 1880s–1950s* (London and New York, 1991) and Susan James, *Beyond Equality and Difference: Citizenship, Feminist Politics and Female Subjectivity* (London and New York, 1992). For references to her work on gender in Nazi Germany, see the Introduction.
2 Further references are given in the discussion of Scott's work in the Introduction.
3 John Tosh, 'From Keighly to St. Denis: Separation and Intimacy in Victorian Bourgeois Marriage', *History Workshop Journal* 40 (1995), pp. 193–206 and 'Domesticity and Manliness in the Victorian Middle Class: The Family of Edward White Benson' in Michael Roper and John Tosh (eds), *Manful Assertions: Masculinities in Britain since 1800* (London, 1991). These issues are also examined in his forthcoming book, *Men at Home: Domesticity and the Victorian Middle Class*.
4 A major contributor to the *Cambridge Social History of Britain,* her most important essays have recently been collected in Leonore Davidoff, *Worlds Between: Historical Perspectives on Gender and Class* (Cambridge, 1995).

1

Women's history and gender history: aspects of an international debate

GISELA BOCK

A few years ago, the question, 'Is there a history of women?' was far from being a rhetorical one. Traditional historiography has excluded women not only inadvertently, but sometimes programmatically from 'universal' or 'general' history.[1] Meanwhile, the question has been answered in part by an expansion of research and by the impact, though still modest, which women's history and women historians have had on the historical profession. Some well-established historical journals in the United States, Switzerland, Italy, Sweden and Denmark have even risked the double step of dedicating issues to women's history and to a new generation of women historians.[2] We have discovered that women's history has not only emerged in the last two decades, but that there has been a long tradition of female historians studying the history of women, a tradition which had been extinguished or pushed into the background by the academic establishment of the historical profession.[3] The search for women's history has encouraged reflection on what such history could be, what implications it holds for the rest of historiography, and what its relationship to a truly general history should be, a history in which women and men equally have a place.

The pursuit of 'restoring women to history' soon led to that of 'restoring history to women'.[4] Women and female experience have a history which, though not independent from men's history, is nonetheless a history of its own, of women as women. To explore it, the hierarchies between the historically important and unimportant had to be overturned. What women have done, should do and want to do is being scrutinized and re-evaluated. Despite the numerous, heterogeneous and sometimes controversial results, there are two common features which have recently been pointed out by Maïté Albistur: 'There is no doubt that the plot of women's history is no less complex than that of men's. But we may assume that time as lived by the female part of humanity does not pass according to the same rhythms and that it is not perceived in the same way as that of men.'[5] The history of women equals that of men insofar as it is just as rich and complicated, and that it is not linear, logical or cohesive. On the other

Reprinted from *Gender and History* 1:1 (1989), pp. 7–30. Reprinted by permission of Blackwell Publishers Ltd.

hand, it is different from the history of men, and it is precisely because of this difference that it deserves to be studied – a difference that may embrace not only the contents of historical experience, but also the experience of time itself.[6]

The autonomous character of women's history, its difference from the history of men, does not mean it is less important or just a 'special' or 'specifically female' problem.[7] Rather, we must recognize that, on the one hand, general history has up to now essentially been male-specific, and on the other hand, that the history of women must count as just as general as that of the 'other' sex. But more than this, the difference between women's and men's history does not imply that the history of women is identical for all women: women do not all have the same history. Awareness of the otherness, the difference, the inequality between female and male history has been complemented by an awareness and historical study of the otherness, the differences and inequalities among women themselves. In this vein, the Italian journal for women's history, *Memoria*, devoted an issue to the subject *'piccole e grandi diversità'* (small and great differences).[8]

The diversity of female experiences and situations which has been brought to light has resulted, among other things, from the fact that women's history has dealt with virtually all domains of society: with areas where only women are present (such as women's organizations, women's culture, modern housework), those where women make up the majority (such as the objects of witch hunts and poor relief), those where women existed in equal numbers to men (families, sexual relations, classes, ethnic minorities), those domains where women made up a minority in relation to men (such as factory work or historiography), and those where they were absent altogether (such as 'universal' suffrage in the nineteenth and large parts of the twentieth century). In other words, the history of women can only be grasped in the plural, not in the singular, but its variety exists in the context of the complex history of the entire female sex.

Women's history has used all methods and approaches available to historians, including biography, cultural, anthropological, economic and political history, history of mentalities and of ideas, oral history and the methods preferred in social history, such as the study of mobility, historical demography and family history. In fact, the originality of women's and gender history lies not so much in its methods, or in any single method, as in the questions it asks and in its perspectives. As in the rest of history, questions and perspectives are not neutral, and their choice is based on preliminary, conscious or unconscious, political or theoretical decisions; it is in reference to them that the sources begin to speak to us.

Women's history is influenced by feminist experience and thought, often by the desire to contribute to social change. Such motives are a source of illumination, but they can sometimes, in regard to history, also be a weakness, namely when today's ideals and values are simply projected back into

the past, as an anachronism. As one historian has warned us, we may suc-
cumb to the professional vice of many historians when we see the past only
as a function of, and as an instrument for, the present, thus preventing 'a
true dialogue with the women of the past'.[9]

In keeping with this diversity of groupings and diversity of methods, let us
take an example which highlights the difference between women's history
and that of men, as well as the differences among women themselves. In early
modern Italy, particularly in the sixteenth and seventeenth centuries, new
forms of poor relief emerged, promoted by periods of economic crisis, plagues
and urban overpopulation. Begging was rigorously prohibited within the
cities, and new institutions were created to incarcerate the poor. In traditional
historiography this has been viewed as a *grand renfermement*, 'Great
Confinement' (Foucault) which created the basis for the rise of capitalism and
the male labour-force it needed, by terrorizing those who refused to work or
were thought to refuse and by labelling the undeserving poor. On closer
inspection, however, it has become clear that the great majority of those shut
in were women who were traditionally considered part of the deserving
poor. Indeed, some of the more important of those institutions soon came to
be exclusively reserved for women, such as the *Ospedale dei Mendicanti* in
Florence. Whereas male poverty, particularly male begging, was considered a
refusal to work, female poverty and begging was defined as a loss or a threatening loss of 'female honour'. This *onore femminile* was understood as sexual integrity, a social criterion which also applied to all other women.

An ever more differentiated network of convent-like institutions was
established in the cities, where 'irregular' women – battered, abandoned and
unruly wives, adulteresses, ex-prostitutes, widows, old women, female
orphans and daughters of poor parents – sought shelter or were forced to
enter for varying periods of time. Often, and particularly in the case of
young women, the institutions admitted only the beautiful, since the sexual
honour of crippled, ill or ugly women seemed not to be threatened: 'The
poor girls who had no other dowry or support than their beauty', noted an
author in 1674, should not have to 'sell their only capital, their chastity, for
a miserable prize just in order to survive for a day.'[10] The task of those institutions was to preserve or restore female honour – hence the title, *conserva-
tori* – substituting the family which should have acted as the protector of
honour, and to assist the inmates in finding the means to return to a normal life: a dowry for marriage or for entering a nunnery, or help in finding
a job as domestic servant. In Florence in 1632, three-quarters of the inmates
of all poor relief institutions were women, and these constituted about one-
twentieth of the female population. Hence, the female experience of
poverty and poor relief was different from that of men; it was an experience
not of all women, but of a minority. Yet, the experience of this female
minority was connected to the image and reality of the female sex as a
whole.

Gender as a social, cultural, historical category

In studying women's past, one important point of departure has been the observation that women are half of humankind and in some countries and times, even more than half; indeed, an important and influential contribution bears the title *The Majority Finds Its Past*.[11] In conceptual terms, this observation implies the following principle: it is no less problematic to separate the history of women from history in general than to separate the history of men – and even more so, truly general history – from the history of women. Women's history concerns not merely half of humankind, but all of it.

The most important step in efforts to link the history of one half to the other half, and both to history in general, has been to conceptualize women as a sociocultural group, i.e. as a sex. As a result, men also become visible as sexual beings, so that the new perspective turns out to be not just about women and women's issues but about all historical issues.[12] Since the mid-1970s, gender (*Geschlecht, genere, genre, geslacht*) has been introduced as a fundamental category of social, cultural and historical reality, perception and study, even though the new terminology, which in some languages indicates a shift from a grammatical concept to a broader sociocultural one, has different linguistic and cultural connotations in different tongues.[13] One of the major reasons for the introduction of the term 'gender' in this broader sense as well as for its relatively rapid diffusion in place of the word 'sex' (at least in English), has been the insistence that the 'woman question', women's history and women's studies, cannot be reduced solely to sex in the sense of sexuality, but must embrace all areas of society including the structures of that society. Hence the concept gender implies that history in general must also be seen as the history of the sexes: as gender history (*Geschlechtergeschichte, storia di genere* or *storia sessuata, histoire sexuée*).

To the same extent that the need to study gender has for many people become self-evident, gender or the sexes are no longer perceived as something self-evident: neither as an obvious matter nor as an *a priori* given. It is now clear that the concepts, the underlying assumptions and the consequences of historical research in gender terms, must be created, conceived and investigated anew, since they have not been part of the historiographic vocabulary. Thus, for instance, in the important multi-volume *Geschichtliche Grundbegriffe* (Fundamental Historical Concepts), the entry *Geschlecht* does not appear alongside such other terms as 'work', 'race' or 'revolution', nor does 'woman', let alone 'man'. Despite centuries of philosophical speculation about the sexes, *Geschlecht* likewise fails to appear in the *Historisches Wörterbuch der Philosophie* (Historical Dictionary of Philosophy), and under the entry *Geschlechtlichkeit* (sexuality) we find cell plasma, genes, and hormones.[14]

But gender history rejects both these approaches: the omission of gender and its reduction to an object of apparently natural science. We have learned to see that, on the one hand, all known societies have gender-based spaces, behaviours, activities and that gender-based differentiation exists everywhere. On the other hand, the concrete manifestations of gender difference are not the same in all societies; they are not universal, and the variations within the status of the female sex are just as manifold as those within the status of the male sex. Secondly, we have learned to separate the question of gender-based difference from the question of gender-based hierarchies, i.e. the power relations between men and women. The differentiation and the hierarchies are not always necessarily connected with one another, nor are they identical: for instance, a sexual division of labour does not necessarily imply a sexual division of social rewards and of power. Thirdly, it has become clear that the perception of male and female scholars, most of whom are West Europeans or North Americans, is often profoundly shaped by the gender relations of their own culture, by widespread ethno- or Euro-centrism, and by differing assumptions about the status and the emancipation of women. The current perceptions of the sexes and the terms used to describe them are to a large extent a product of the history of culture, science and of gender relations themselves, particularly since the eighteenth century.[15] Therefore, the sexes and their relations must be perceived as social, political and cultural entities. They cannot be reduced to factors outside of history, and still less to a single and simple, uniform, primal or inherent cause or origin.

When we speak of gender as a 'category' in this context, the term refers to an intellectual construct, a way of perceiving and studying people, an analytic tool that helps us to discover neglected areas of history. It is a conceptual form of sociocultural inquiry that challenges the sex-blindness of traditional historiography. It is important to stress that the category gender is, and must be perceived as, context-specific and context-dependent.[16] While it does offer fundamental possibilities for a more profound understanding of virtually all historical phenomena, it should not be used as a static pattern, a myth of origins for explaining the panorama of historical events. Its power is not one of elimination – by reducing history to a model – but of illumination, as a means to explore historical variety and variability. Gender is a 'category', not in the sense of a universal statement but, as the Greek origin of the word suggests, in the sense of public objection and indictment, of debate, protest, process and trial.

This public objection is directed above all at the category 'biology', a static, reductionistic model, and thus a major obstacle to historical understanding. In order to take gender as a sociocultural category seriously, historians must above all do away with the sociocultural category 'biology' and abandon the notions attached to it. For a common language among historians who study women in culture and society, this means doing without the word biology.

Mireille Laget's book, *Naissances*, is one example of how to treat a subject eminently bound up with the female body without reverting to biology.[17] Critical studies of precisely those historical figures and processes that made use of 'biology' (such as, for instance, German National Socialism), should analyse, translate and not simply repeat the term.

On the level of conceptualization, it must be recognized that 'biology', as commonly used in historical writing, usually does not really refer – as the term is meant to suggest – to something non-social, pre-social, and even less to an object of natural science, but is itself a sociocultural category which has marked and distorted the perception and relation of the sexes, as well as other groups. The word *biology* was invented by German and French male scholars in the early nineteenth century, later acquiring many diverse meanings, some of which no longer exist. It came into circulation and common use at the turn of the century, earlier in the German- and English-speaking world, later in the Romance languages, particularly in and through the 'nature vs. nurture' debate of that period.[18] Previously, biology did not exist, and the terms used to describe the female sex were of a different kind and context than the later gender-linked biology. In the twentieth century, the word *biology* became part of the common language of the right as well as of the left. Yet, the earlier women's movement, significantly, did not use this word and usually expressed visions of gender, including ideas on motherhood, in cultural terms.

Today, biology has such a variety of meanings that the use of the term by historians is more confusing than explanatory. It may mean a natural science, especially genetics, with which historians do not deal professionally. It also means the objects of this science, ranging from life and death to anatomy and bodies, to genes and brains, from plants and biological food to animals and human beings. Today the question even arises as to whether a biological mother is the genetic or the pregnant mother. Biology may refer to a way of thinking and acting upon human and other beings, matters and activities, ranging from physiological determinism to physiological change. Since the period when the term *biology* came to be commonly used, particularly in the latter sense, it referred to an inherent, unchanging constant behind cultural phenomena (as was often, but not always the case with the concept *nature*). Possibly even more often, it also implies a perspective of social change through 'biological', meaning bodily, intervention.

The sociocultural character of the idea of 'biology' is visible on various levels. It carries a clear gender bias, since it is regularly used in speaking about the female sex, but not about the male sex. Long before biology existed, Jean-Jacques Rousseau, for example, made a similar point, but in exclusively cultural terms: 'The male is male only at certain moments, the female is female all her life' (he was cautious enough to add a small but revealing reservation: '. . . or at least during her youth').[19] Biology is a modern metaphor for the old assumption that men are ungendered and women are gendered beings, that men are the 'one' and women the 'other sex' or even, as in the nineteenth century, 'the sex'.

Most importantly, this assumption implies a value judgement. Biology can be loaded with hopes and fears, can be viewed as an obstacle and as a resource; it has specific, though varying contents. The content which has been historically and politically the most powerful is one which carries a negative judgement on human value; here, biology is a metaphor for the lack of value, for inferiority (*Minderwertigkeit*). This is why it has been used for those areas and activities of women's lives which are assigned less value than male areas and activities, such as child-bearing, child-raising and housework, which do not usually count as work, even though *Gebärarbeit* ('bearing work') was a common term in traditional German gynaecology, and in English, French and Italian giving birth is referred to as work (*labour, travail, travaglio*).

This use of the term *biology* is based on the notion that physical differences among persons justify social and political inequality, and that such equality should be granted only to those who are physically equal. The problem of biology proves to be one of economic, social and cultural relations between the sexes: 'the peculiar arrangement whereby many women receive economic rewards for their social contribution (in child care, home-making, and community work) only indirectly, via their husband's income, is neither morally nor practically required by the fact (if indeed it were a fact) that women are biologically better parents than men'.[20] It is not anatomy that brings inferior rewards to those women, but culture in the form of *biology*, of biological value judgements.

That biology is above all a value judgement is also visible in the fact that thinking in terms of biology did not initially relate only to women, but also to other social phenomena which came to be excluded from the social: for instance, the issue of the insane and the feeble-minded, the ill, of life and death, of (genetic or other) hereditary traits, of the body and of embodiment, of ethnic groups and races. One might say that the emergence of biology as a sociocultural category and perspective of social intervention since the end of the nineteenth century extended to all those phenomena which transcended the traditional 'social question' and those objects which could be grasped within traditional social science and policy. In this context, the racist notion of biology is particularly illuminating about its sexist version, for both developed simultaneously and overlapped.

It is self-evident that black people are not physically equal to whites in all respects, but are different in one respect. It is self-evident that women are physically not equal to men in all respects, but rather, different in four or five respects. But this partial and physical difference is neither the cause nor an explanation for the relation between whites and 'alien' races or between one and the 'other' sex: 'Biology itself is mute'.[21] Sexism and racism are not derived from physical differences. Rather, certain physical

differences are used to legitimate pre-existing social relations and, in particular, power relations. So-called biological differences become metaphors for
actual or alleged different lifestyles. Both modern racism and modern sexism classify the 'alien' or the 'other' group as inferior, denying not only the
right of such groups to be equal, but also – and probably more important –
the right to be different without being punished for it. In other words, they
discriminate against those who actually or allegedly live, must live, want to
live in a different way – regarding body, mind, emotions, i.e. culture – from
that group which sets the cultural norms and values.[22]

There are various and recent attempts by historians and (socio-)biolo-
gists to search and, of course, find biology in history, and again by no means
only on the part of conservatives or reactionaries.[23] In women's and feminist
studies also, it has become common to identify the female body, its activities and those surrounding it, as biology. Most often, such biology refers
simply to maternity, as in the vision of doing away with female biology, particularly in the form of test-tube babies, in order to achieve an assumed
equality between the sexes.[24] Historians, too, use the language and the concept, as in the assertion that the main obstacle to women's liberty is in their
'fatalités biologiques', on which male dominance is supposedly founded,
and that women must somehow emancipate themselves from their biology.[25]
However, such values and notions are problematic, partly because female
'biology' may in fact soon be dispensed with all too easily through the modern science of biology. One might recall Hannah Arendt's comment of 1972
on such emancipation or equality: 'The real question to ask is, what do we
lose if we win?'[26]

Even more important for historical thought, however, is the problem that
such notions and values, when projected back into the past, are anachronistic and fail to do justice to women's actual experiences in and of history. For
instance, the 200,000 women sterilized in National Socialist Germany by no
means experienced this removal of their 'fatalités biologiques' as a liberation. Their case, and that of many other victims of National Socialism,
demonstrates clearly that sexist and racist biology was a perspective of
social change through biological measures, through intervention in body
and life. Moreover, the fact that some thousands of women died as a result
of compulsory sterilization was not due to female biology. Instead, it was
the result of the power relations between the predominantly male agents of
Nazi racism and their victims, half of whom were women.[27] And if in such
cases, historians should not attribute childlessness and death to biology, in
other cases it is child-bearing that should not be attributed to biology, but
to gender relations.[28]

The frequent reduction, by feminists as well as non-feminists, of (female)
embodiedness, and specifically of maternity, to 'biology' or 'biological sex' is
misleading because it obscures what women's and gender history is attempting to render visible: the concrete, manifold and changing forms of women's

and men's bodily experience, activity and representation, which is not neatly separable from other kinds of experience, activity and representation.[29]

This same problematic reduction is put forward and theorized in the dichotomy proposed between '(biological) sex' and '(social) gender', and in the hypothesis of the 'transformation of raw biological sex into gender' including the ensuing debate about what and how much is to be attributed to the one or to the other.[30] This sex/gender distinction does not resolve, but only restates, for the sexes, the controversy 'nature vs. nurture', a more embracing opposition. It is ambivalent and problematic because, while postulating gender as a sociocultural category, it simultaneously reduces sex to a 'biological' category and thereby confirms traditional visions of gender. Often, and for good reasons, the dichotomy has been found to be analytically and empirically false. Even eminent theoreticians of gender realize this but insist that it cannot be dismissed because of politically inspired fears of biologically deterministic backlash.[31] Political motives, however, that lead us to refuse important intellectual insights may not lead to the best political results for women. Perhaps it is time to realize – particularly in view of an ever better-known past – that sociocultural conditions are by no means easier and faster to change than those which are called biological. Indeed, it should be realized that the sex/gender dichotomy as well as the biologically deterministic backlash are both rooted in the opposite assumption, that sociocultural conditions are amenable to change while biology remains immutable.

In any case, political motives which block theoretical insights do not lead to historical insights. As to the study of the past in a gender perspective, it seems more useful to do without 'biology' and to use gender in a comprehensive way: comprehending not only that part of women's and men's life which is proven to be culturally constructed, but also that part which falls, or is assumed to fall, outside it. Only then can gender become a historical category in the full sense.

As to the impact and power of the material and bodily world inside and outside of us which may seem to defy human reason and historical reasoning, we should be able to find other words than those dictated by the biological tradition. Some of these words can be found in precisely those historical studies which sometimes are perceived as focusing on women's biology (such as the history of maternity, child-bearing, midwives, wet-nurses, prostitutes) and which have demonstrated that the female (as well as the male) body is shaped by culture and history. Here, surely, is a domain not of biology, but of women's and gender history.

Gender as social, cultural, historical relations

Gender or the sexes refer neither to an object, nor to various objects; rather, they refer to a complex set of relations and processes. 'Thinking in relations'[32] is needed in order to understand gender as an analytical category as well as a cultural reality, in the past as well as in the present. Such a vision of gender has implications for all forms of history as they are now practiced:

Women's history as gender history

Perceiving gender as a complex and sociocultural relation implies that the search for women in history is not simply a search for some object which has previously been neglected. Instead, it is a question of previously neglected relations between human beings and human groups. In the words of the late anthropologist Michelle Zimbalist Rosaldo, 'Women must be understood . . . in terms of relationship – with other women and with men – (not) of difference and apartness'.[33] Rosaldo pointed to an important and often ignored dimension which goes beyond the now obvious insistence that women's history be integrated into general history through the study of relations between women and men. Not only must we study the relations *between* the sexes, but also the relations *within* the sexes, not only those of women to men, and of men to women, but also relations among women and among men.

Many relations among men have been the focus of historical writing, those emerging in the political, military, economic and cultural realms, and those between kin and friends, but rarely have they been studied as intra-gender relations or as to their impact on women. On the other hand, it is also vital to look at women's relationships with each other: between house-wives and female servants, between mothers and daughters, between mothers, wet-nurses and midwives, between social workers and poor women, between female missionaries and the women of colonized peoples, among women in the professions and in politics, and to be aware of relations of conflict as well as solidarity. The history of female kin, friendship and love between women has become an important area of research.[34] Such studies have usually focused strongly on intra-gender relations as well as on their significance to men.

Insisting on the importance of studying the relations within the sexes and particularly between women becomes all the more crucial in the 1980s as the concept of *gender, Geschlecht, genere, genre* threatens to become high fashion, which seeks to soften the challenge of women's history by developing a kind of gender-neutral discourse on gender.[35] But if it is forgotten that the discovery of the social, cultural and historical relations between and within the sexes was the result of women studying women and men, we have fallen far short of our goal: not a gender-neutral but a gender-encompassing approach to general history. Women's history is gender history *par excellence*.

The fact that it is still not evident for scholars to view gender history, particularly in respect to women, also as a history within the sexes was recently shown by the eminent British historian Lawrence Stone. Expert on, among other areas, *Family, Sex and Marriage*, he has studied a field where gender relations are of conspicuous importance and where women are half of the group to be examined.[36] In his article, 'Only Women', he set himself up as a historians' god and handed down 'Ten Commandments' for the writing of women's history which – surprising for a historian – were to apply 'at any time and in any place'. The first of them: 'Thou shalt not write about women except in relation to men and children'. Whereas the author correctly recognized that the new approaches deal essentially with relations and their history, he failed to see that women are not conditioned solely by their relations to men, that the relations of women to other women are just as important as those of women to men, that children are not genderless beings, and that the history of men should also include their relations to women.

Gender history as men's history

Examining men's relations to women means viewing what previously counted as an object of 'history in general' in gender-conscious and thus 'male-specific' terms: the history of men as men. Questions about gender have mainly focused on the female sex, on 'the woman question'. Men appear to exist beyond gender relations to the same degree that they dominate them. While the imperative that women's history always be related to men's has become commonplace, up to now the reverse has hardly been true.

Military history and the history of warfare are a case in point. They have dealt exclusively with men – and for good reason, since warfare in the Western world (at least within Europe) has generally been a form of direct confrontation between groups of men. Nonetheless, explicitly male-specific issues have not been raised in this field, for example its connection with the history of masculinity. Furthermore, wars have had an enormous significance for women and for the relations between and within the sexes. We need only think of the strongly gender-based and sexual war symbols and language in wars of liberation as well as in civil wars, in aggressive as well as in defensive wars, of women camp followers in the early modern armies, of the women's peace movement before, during and after the First World War or of the new forms of prostitution which appear in the First and Second World Wars.[37]

The past few years have seen a rise of 'men's studies', mainly carried out by men, which deal with the relations between men and women, and among men. Some authors have examined the relation between war and the social construction of masculinity, and they have underlined that the latter should not be understood as a 'biological given'. What women's studies have shown is now being confirmed by men's studies: gender norms and gender realities are not identical and they are subject to historical change. According to a French historian, masculinity meant not only power but also grief and suffering for nineteenth-century men. Fatherhood has also become a focus of interest for historians. Some of these studies – those being done by men – draw inspiration from a current call for male participation in female experiences and work ('Pregnant Fathers: How Fathers can Enjoy and Share the Experiences of Pregnancy and Childbirth') or for 'men's rights', a tendency not merely corresponding to feminist demands for women's rights, but – as might be expected – also at odds with them. Although these men's studies have illuminated some topics, much remains to be done, particularly in the field of history.

An issue which is still often considered as 'women's history', namely the ways in which famous – that is, male – philosophers and other thinkers have thought about women, the sexes, sexuality and the family, must in fact be viewed as men's history. It is men's, not women's history for reasons which have been discussed in various contexts, i.e. the fact that these writings present primarily men's views on women, that their image of the sexes is rarely descriptive but normative and proscriptive, and that the norms for women are usually not only different from the norms for men, but also from the realities of women's lives. The study of men's thinking on gender has come to be very diversified and it has brought to light many and unexpected complexities and contradictions, between different philosophers as well as within individual men's thought.[38]

Such studies have also promoted the awareness of a specifically historical question of method: the problematic character of a historiography which limits itself to the presentation and repetition of the misogynous pronouncements which were said and written by men over the centuries. This often leads from outrage and denunciation to a kind of fascination. It risks becoming anachronistic as it neglects the analysis of such texts against the background of their historical context and significance, of their role within the complete works of an author and how they were judged by their female contemporaries.[39]

Studies in intellectual history which turn to the fewer and often less known female philosophers or to the thought and judgements of other women regarding gender as well as other relations, often uncover important differences from male thinking. Here one might consider Hannah Arendt's central concept of political thought, 'natality' – the principle and capacity of human beings to act in new ways, beyond whatever happened in history, by virtue of their being born – and her notion of human plurality which she saw symbolized in the plurality of the sexes; or Carol Gilligan's insights into women's 'different voice' in moral judgements.[40] Thus, intellectual history also demonstrates that the history of men as men becomes visible only when seen in relation to women's history and women's thought and hence in a perspective of gender history.

[. . .]

Gender relations and other sociocultural relations

Looking at gender as a sociocultural relation enables us to see the links between gender and numerous other sociocultural relations in a fresh light; there are, for example, class, race, age, sexuality, culture, language, freedom, religion, family, economy. Often, for instance in the debate 'class vs. gender', a kind of competition has been set up between gender and other dimensions, so that it is not the interaction of different relations that is sought, but rather, which is considered as more fundamental, more real, more important. For instance, in Stone's Seventh Commandment: 'Thou shalt not exaggerate the importance in the past of gender over that of power, status, and wealth, even if all women experienced the same biological destiny'.

However, the assertion that (apparently) gender-neutral factors carry more weight than gender-based ones ('biological' ones according to Stone), disregards the fact that each such factor has historically meant something different for women than for men. This is obvious, for instance, in the case of power and of wealth. In the case of power not just because men have usually had more power than women, and power over women at that. Under the surface of formal cleavages of power between the sexes, women have also had their own forms of power, often of a more informal kind, power – or rather, as French historians say, 'powers' – of various kinds, such as participation in men's power, power vis-à-vis other women, self-assertion as women. Gender studies have contributed to seeing the phenomenon of power as highly differentiated, and one of the forms of legitimization of power has been gender.[41]

The gender dimensions in the case of wealth are strikingly clear. Women as a social group have had a smaller income than men and namely – at least in the nineteenth and twentieth centuries – in three respects: as houseworkers or homemakers, they had no income, as lower- and middle-class wage earners they had a smaller income than the men of their class, and in higher income brackets they represent only a small proportion (for instance, making up four per cent of history professors at West German universities today).

Hence, each sociocultural relation means something different for women and for men. We must, however, go beyond even this insight and recognize that each one of the apparently gender-neutral relations between human beings is *also* conditioned by gender relations; gender is one constituent factor of all other relations. The history of religion, from the ancient gods to those of the twentieth century, is incomprehensible if treated as gender-neutral. The same is true of ethnic minorities, whose gender history has been studied particularly in the United States; more recently, the history of Jewish and Gypsy women as well as of other women who have suffered racist discrimination has been taken up in Germany. These women differ not only from those of the majority, but also from men in their respective minority groups.[42]

On the other hand, the language of racism is obsessed with the sexes and sexuality, and it contains a characteristic mixture of sexuality, blood and violence. Contemporaries rightly diagnosed National Socialist anti-Judaism as also being 'sexual anti-semitism'. Historians of European and particularly German racism – more specifically, men who belonged to its victims – have shown that in the racist world view, the 'Aryan' or 'Nordic' person was a 'Westerner of the male sex'. Racism cannot be understood without understanding its gender dimension, which is one of its constituent factors. And if, conversely, the analysis of gender relations or sexism includes an analysis of race relations or racism, we may arrive at new and unexpected results. One of these might be the insight that the specifically National Socialist policy towards women did not consist – as is usually assumed – in 'pronatalism and a cult of motherhood'. Rather, it was antinatalism, a cult of fatherhood, virility and mass extermination of women as well as men.[43]

History, then, is not only of male, but also of female, experience. It should not be studied only in male or apparently gender-neutral perspectives, but also in female and gender-encompassing perspectives. This should not mean a simple inversion of the traditional postulate that other human relations are more important than gender relations, by setting up a counter-claim that gender is more important than everything else, although it is clear that inversion first opened our senses to many historical discoveries. Rather, it means that gender relations are equally as important as all other human relations, and that gender relations contribute to and affect all other human relations. Conversely, all other human relations contribute to and affect gender relations.

To insist on the hypothesis that other relations are more fundamental than gender relations is both ideological and historically unproductive. It recalls the situation of Cassandra, the king's daughter, in Christa Wolf's narrative.[44] Cassandra dreamt that she had to judge as to whether 'the moon or the sun could shine brighter'. A humble and wise woman taught her that this was a misguided 'attempt to find an answer to a completely absurd question'. When Cassandra finally understood that she 'had the right, perhaps even the duty to reject it' she had taken a crucial and liberating step in comprehending her own history.

Notes

1 Carl N. Degler, *Is There a History of Women?* (Oxford University Press, Oxford, 1975); Michelle Perrot, ed., *Une histoire des femmes est-elle possible?* (Editions Rivages, Paris, 1984).

2 *American Historical Review*, 89/3 (1984); *Schweizerische Zeitschrift für Geschichte*, 34/3 (1984); *Quaderni storici*, 44 (1980); *Historisk tidsskrift*, 3 (1980) and 1 (1987); *Den jyske Historiker*, 18 (1980); *Historievidenskab*, 21 (1980).

3 Kathryn Kish Sklar, 'American Female Historians in Context, 1770–1930', *Feminist Studies*, 3/1–2 (1975), pp. 171–84; Natalie Z. Davis, 'Gender and Genre: Women as Historical Writers, 1400–1820', in *Beyond Their Sex: Learned Women of the European Past*, ed. Patricia H. Labalme (New York University Press, New York/London, 1980), pp. 153–82; Bonnie G. Smith, 'The Contribution of Women to Modern Historiography in Great Britain, France, and the United States, 1750–1940', *American Historical Review*, 89 (1984), pp. 709–32; id., 'Seeing Mary Beard', *Feminist Studies*, 10/3 (1984), pp. 399–416; Joan Thirsk, Foreword, in *Women in English Society 1500–1800*, ed. Mary Prior (Methuen, London/New York, 1985), pp. 1–21; Karen Offen, 'The Beginnings of "Scientific" Women's History in France 1830–1848', in *Proceedings of the 11th Annual Meeting of the Western Society for French History*, 3–5 November 1983 (University of Kansas, Lawrence/Kansas, 1984), pp. 255–71.

4 Joan Kelly-Gadol, 'The Social Relation of the Sexes: Methodological Implications of Women's History', *Signs*, 1 (1976), pp. 809–24, esp. p. 809; rpt. in Joan Kelly, *Women, History and Theory* (University of Chicago Press, Chicago/London, 1984).

5 Maïté Albistur, 'Catalogue des archives Marie-Louise Bouglé à la Bibliothèque historique de la ville de Paris', typescript, p. 2.

6 Natalie Zemon Davis, 'Women's History as Women's Education', in Natalie Zemon Davis and Joan W. Scott, *Women's History as Women's Education* (Smith College, Northampton, Mass., 1985), p. 16; Hester Eisenstein and Alice Jardine, eds, *The Future of Difference* (G.K. Hall and Barnard Women's College, Boston, 1980), p. XVIII; Kelly-Gadol, 'Social Relation', pp. 810–12.

7 This 'special case' approach is apparent in the pervasive use of terms such as 'frauenspezifisch', '"specifically" female', 'la "spécificité" féminine', 'la "specificità" femminile'.

8 *Memoria: Rivista di storia delle donne*, 2 (1981); see also Paola Di Cori, Introd. to *Memoria*, 15 (1985): 'Culture del femminismo'.

9 Gianna Pomata, in *La ricerca delle donne*, Maria Cristina Marcuzzo and Anna Rossi-Doria, eds (Rosenberg and Sellier, Torino, 1987), pp. 119–20.

10 Quoted in Luisa Ciammitti, 'Quanto costa essere normali. La dote nel Conservatoria femminile di Santa Maria del Baracano (1630–1680)', *Quaderni storici*, 53 (1983), p. 470.

11 Gerda Lerner, *The Majority Finds Its Past: Placing Women in History* (Oxford University Press, New York, 1979).

12 Elizabeth Gross, 'What is Feminist Theory?', in *Feminist Challenges*, Carole Pateman and Elizabeth Gross, eds (Allen and Unwin, Sydney, 1986), p. 194.

13 Joan W. Scott, 'Gender: A Useful Category of Historical Analysis', *American Historical Review*, 91 (1986), pp. 1053–75, esp. pp. 1053–4; Paola Di Cori, 'D'alla storia delle donne a una storia di genere', *Rivista di storia contemporanea*, 16 (1987), pp. 548–59, esp. pp. 554–7 for a comparison of 'gender' and the Italian *genere*. The German *Geschlecht* means sex, grammatical gender, sexual physiology, but also 'generation' and 'lineage' or 'kinship' and, as *Menschengeschlecht*, 'human race' or 'humankind'. In French, *sexe* has remained the only concept, but is now complemented, in analogy to the Italian development, by *genre*; see *Les Cahiers du Grif*, 37–38 (Spring 1988), special issue on 'Le genre de l'histoire' (ed. Tierce).

14 Otto Brunner, Werner Conze, and Reinhart Koselleck, eds, *Geschichtliche Grundbegriffe* (Klett Verlag, Stuttgart, 1972–1984), Vols I–V; Joachim Ritter, ed., *Historisches Wörterbuch der Philosophie* (Wissenschaftliche Buchgesellschaft, Darmstadt, 1974), p. 443.

15 Carol MacCormack and Marilyn Strathern, eds, *Nature, Culture and Gender* (Cambridge University Press, Cambridge, 1980); Sherry B. Ortner and Harriet Whitehead, eds, *Sexual Meanings: The Cultural Construction of Gender and Sexuality* (Cambridge University Press, Cambridge, 1981); Martine Segalen, *Mari et femme dans la société paysanne* (Flammarion, Paris, 1980); Rayna Rapp, 'Anthropology', *Signs*, 4

(1979), pp. 497–513; Louise Lamphere and Michelle Z. Rosaldo, eds, *Woman, Culture and Society* (Stanford University Press, Stanford, 1974); Nicole-Claude Mathieu, *Ignored by Some, Denied by Others: The Social Sex Category in Sociology* (Women's Research and Resources Centre, London, 1978); Gianna Pomata, 'La storia delle donne: una questione di confine', in *Il mondo contemporaneo: Gli strumenti della ricerca*, Giovanni de Luna et al., eds (La Nuova Italia, Florence, 1983), pp. 1434–69; Susan Carol Rogers, 'Woman's Place: A Critical Review of Anthropological Theory', *Comparative Studies in Society and History*, 20 (1978), pp. 1223–62.

16 Jane Flax, 'Gender as a Problem: In and For Feminist Theory', *Amerikastudien/ American Studies*, 31 (1986), pp. 193–213; Scott, 'Gender' (note 13 above); special issue of *Nuova donnawomanfemme*, 22 (1983), pp. 12, 43, 131; Sandra Harding, 'The Instability of the Analytical Categories of Feminist Theory', *Signs*, 11 (1986), pp. 645–64.

17 Mireille Laget, *Naissances: L'accouchement avant l'âge de la clinique* (Seuil, Paris, 1982).

18 The latter expression had been coined by Francis Galton as well as the term 'eugenics'.

19 Jean-Jacques Rousseau, *Emile ou De l'éducation*, in *Oeuvres complètes*, Vol. III (Seuil, Paris, 1971), p. 245.

20 Helen H. Lambert, 'Biology and Equality', *Signs*, 4 (1978), pp. 97–117, esp. pp. 115–6.

21 Rapp, 'Anthropology' (note 15 above), p. 503.

22 See Margaret Wright, 'I Want the Right to be Black and Me', in *Black Women in White America*, ed. Gerda Lerner (Random House, New York, 1972), p. 608: 'In black women's liberation we don't want to be equal with men, just like in black liberation we're not fighting to be equal with the white man. We're fighting for the right to be different and not be punished for it.' The German Jewish women's movement fought not only for equality as Jews and as women, but also for their right to be different both as Jews and as women; see Marion Kaplan, *The Jewish Feminist Movement in Germany. The Campaigns of the Jüdischer Frauenbund, 1904–1938* (Greenwood Press, Westport, 1979).

23 The 1984 conference of the Association of German Historians in Berlin hosted a panel of (male) historians on 'History and Biology'. In their attempts at biological explanation, they touched upon perceptions of time and space, 'negative reactions towards people of a "different kind"', the 'sexual dualism' of society, the women's peace movement around World War I, emotions and intellect, the subjective dimension of history, 'body language' and even same-sex relationships among women. The conference also hosted a panel of (female) historians of women's history (the first of its kind at the association's meetings), but it did not deal with biology. The contributions on women's history are published in *Journal für Geschichte*, 2 (1985), the 'biological' contributions in *Saeculum*, 36/1 (1985).

24 Shulamith Firestone, *The Dialectic of Sex. The Case for Feminist Revolution* (Bantam, Toronto and New York, 1970); anything that has to do with the female body is called 'biology' for instance by Sayers, *Biological Politics* (Tavistock, London, 1982).

25 Yvonne Knibiehler, 'Chronologie et Histoire des femmes', in *Histoire des femmes* (note 1 above), p. 55.

26 Quoted in Elisabeth Young-Bruehl, *Hannah Arendt. For Love of the World* (Yale University Press, New Haven, 1982), p. 523.

27 Gisela Bock, *Zwangssterilisation im Nationalsozialismus: Studien zur Rassenpolitik und Frauenpolitik* (Westdeutscher Verlag, Opladen, 1986), esp. Ch. VII.

28 Nuto Revelli, *L'anello forte. La donna: storie di vita contadina* (Einaudi, Torino, 1985), an excellent example of oral history, presents interviews with peasant women from North Western Italy; many of them tell how they have been forced by their husbands to bear more children than they wanted, because having children was considered part of male honour.

29 See, for example, Susan R. Suleiman, ed., *The Female Body in Western Culture* (Harvard University Press, Cambridge, 1986); 'The Making of the Modern Body: Sexuality and the Social Body in the 19th Century', special issue of *Representations*, 14 (1986); Gisela Bock and Giuliana Nobili, eds, *Il corpo delle donne: immagini e realta*

storiche (Il lavoro editoriale, Ancona, 1987); Julia Epstein, *The Woman in the Body: A Cultural Analysis of Reproduction* (Beacon Press, Boston, 1987); Elizabeth Spelman, 'Woman as Body: Ancient and Contemporary Views', *Feminist Studies*, 8 (1982), pp. 109–31; Elizabeth Spelman, 'Theories of Race and Gender/The Erasure of Black Women', *Quest*, 5, No. 4 (1982), pp. 36–62.

30 Quotes from Gayle Rubin, 'The Traffic in Women', in *Toward an Anthropology of Women*, ed. Rayna R. Reiter (Monthly Review Press, New York, 1975), pp. 157–210.

31 Harding, 'Instability' (note 16 above), p. 662. It should also be taken into consideration that many languages do not have a vocabulary for the English sex/gender distinction (see note 13 above).

32 Flax, 'Gender' (note 16 above), p. 199; Scott, 'Gender' (note 13 above).

33 Michelle Z. Rosaldo, 'The Use and Abuse of Anthropology', *Signs*, 5 (1980), p. 409.

34 Carroll Smith-Rosenberg, *Disorderly Conduct: Visions of Gender in Victorian America* (Knopf, New York, 1985); Martha Vicinus, *Independent Women: Work and Community for Single Women* (University of Chicago Press, Chicago, 1985); Lillian Faderman, *Surpassing the Love of Men. Romantic Friendship and Love between Women from the Renaissance to the Present* (William Morrow, New York, 1981); Leila J. Rupp, '"Imagine My Surprise": Women's Relationships in Historical Perspective', *Frontiers. A Journal of Women's Studies*, 5/3 (1980), pp. 61–70; special issue of *Signs*, 9/4 (1984), and *Nuova donnawomanfemme*, 10–11 (1979), 23–24 (1985); Christine Stansell, 'Revisiting the Angel in the House: Revisions of Victorian Womanhood', *The New England Quarterly*, Vol. LX, No. 3 (1987), pp. 466–83.

35 See Scott, 'Gender' (note 13 above), p. 1056.

36 Nonetheless, only the entry 'Women' appears in the index, not the entry 'Men', for men count as the general case, women as the special one: Lawrence Stone, *Family, Sex and Marriage in England 1500–1800* (Penguin, Harmondsworth, 1979; 1st edn 1977), p. 447. The article mentioned is Lawrence Stone, 'Only Women', in the following: *The New York Review of Books*, 32/6 (11 April, 1985), p. 21.

37 Sandra M. Gilbert, 'Soldier's Heart: Literary Men, Literary Women, and the Great War', *Signs*, 8 (1983), pp. 422–50; also in Margaret R. Higonnet et al., eds, *Behind the Lines: Gender and the Two World Wars* (Yale University Press, New Haven, 1987). Lela B. Costin, 'Feminism, Pacifism, Internationalism and the 1915 International Congress of Women', *Women's Studies International Forum*, 5 (1982), 301–15; Anne Wiltsher, *Most Dangerous Women: Feminist Peace Campaigners of the Great War* (Pandora, Henley-on-Thames, 1985); Carol R. Berkin and Clara M. Lovett, eds, *Women, War and Revolution . . .* (Holmes and Meier, New York, 1980); Margaret R. Higonnet et al., eds, as above; Barton C. Hacker, 'Women and Military Institutions in Early Modern Europe', *Signs*, 6 (1981), pp. 643–71; Lise Hirshberg, *Women, War and Peace: A Selected Bibliography and Filmography* (Institute for Research on Women, New Brunswick, 1986).

38 Susan M. Okin, *Women in Western Political Thought* (Princeton University Press, Princeton, 1979); Jean Bethke Elshtain, ed., *The Family in Political Thought* (Harvester, Brighton, 1982); Raoul Mortley, *Womanhood: The Feminine in Ancient Hellenism, Gnosticism, Christianity, and Islam* (Delacroix, Sydney, 1981); Ian Maclean, *The Renaissance Notion of Woman: A Study in the Fortunes of Scholasticism and Medical Science in European Intellectual Life* (Cambridge University Press, Cambridge, 1980); Arlene W. Saxonhouse, *Women in the History of Political Thought: Ancient Greece to Machiavelli* (California University Press, Berkeley, 1984); Linda J. Nicholson, *Gender and History. The Limits of Social Theory in the Age of the Family* (Columbia University Press, New York, 1986).

39 Arlette Farge, 'Pratique et effets de l'histoire des femmes', in *Histoire des femmes* (note 1 above), pp. 30–1.

40 Jean Bethke Elshtain, *Meditations on Modern Political Thought: Masculine/Feminine Themes from Luther to Arendt* (Praeger, New York, 1986), pp. 110–12; Hannah Arendt, *The Human Condition* (University of Chicago Press, Chicago, 1958), pp. 7–15, 177–8, 247; Carol Gilligan, *In a Different Voice: Psychological Theory and Women's Development* (Harvard University Press, Cambridge, 1982).

41 Scott, 'Gender' (note 13), p. 1073; Michelle Perrot, 'Les femmes, le pouvoir, l'his-
    toire', in *Histoire des femmes* (note 1), pp. 205–22; Susan Carol Rogers, 'Female
    Forms of Power and the Myth of Male Dominance', *American Ethnologist*, 2 (1975),
    pp. 727–56; Ruth Bordin, *Women and Temperance: The Quest for Power and Liberty
    1873–1900* (Temple University Press, Philadelphia, 1981); Nancy F. Cott, *The Bonds
    of Womanhood* (Yale University Press, New Haven, 1977); Mary Ryan, *Cradle of the
    Middle Class* (Cambridge University Press, Cambridge, 1981).
42 Caroline Walker Bynum, *Jesus as Mother. Studies in the Spirituality of the High
    Middle Ages* (University of California Press, Stanford, 1982); Aviva Cantor, *The Jew-
    ish Woman, 1900–1985: A Bibliography* (Biblio Press, Fresh Meadows, 1987); Jacque-
    line Jones, *Labor of Love, Labor of Sorrow: Black Women, Work and the Family
    from Slavery to the Present* (Basic Books, New York, 1985); Catriona Clear, 'Walls
    Within the Walls: Nuns in 19th-century Ireland', in *Gender in Irish Society* (Galway
    University Press, Galway, 1987); Maxine S. Seller, *Immigrant Women* (Temple Uni-
    versity Press, Philadelphia, 1981).
43 Quotes from Comité des délégations juives, ed., *Die Lage der Juden in Deutschland*
    (Ullstein, Frankfurt, 1983, 1st edn 1934), p. 468; George L. Mosse, *Toward the Final
    Solution: A History of European Racism* (Howard Fertig, London, 1978).
44 Christa Wolf, *Kassandra* (Luchterhand, Darmstadt, 1983), pp. 100–1 (my transla-
    tion).

2
Gender: a useful category of historical analysis

JOAN W. SCOTT

> *Gender. n. a grammatical term only. To talk of persons or creatures of
> the masculine or feminine gender, meaning of the male or female sex,
> is either a jocularity (permissible or not according to context) or a
> blunder.*
>
> (Fowler's *Dictionary of Modern English Usage*, Oxford, 1940)

Those who would codify the meanings of words fight a losing battle, for
words, like the ideas and things they are meant to signify, have a history.
Neither Oxford dons nor the Académie Française have been entirely able to
stem the tide, to capture and fix meanings free of the play of human invention and imagination. Mary Wortley Montagu added bite to her witty
denunciation 'of the fair sex' ('my only consolation for being of that gender
has been the assurance of never being married to any one among them') by
deliberately misusing the grammatical reference.[1] Through the ages, people
have made figurative allusions by employing grammatical terms to evoke
traits of character or sexuality. For example, the usage offered by the

Reprinted from *American Historical Review* 91:5 (1986). Reprinted by permission of the
author.

Dictionnaire de la langue française in 1876 was, 'On ne sait de quel genre il est, s'il est mâle ou femelle, se dit d'un homme très-caché, dont on ne connait pas les sentiments.'[2] And Gladstone made this distinction in 1878: 'Athene has nothing of sex except the gender, nothing of the woman except the form.'[3] Most recently – too recently to find its way into dictionaries or the *Encyclopedia of the Social Sciences* – feminists have in a more literal and serious vein begun to use 'gender' as a way of referring to the social organization of the relationship between the sexes. The connection to grammar is both explicit and full of unexamined possibilities. Explicit because the grammatical usage involves formal rules that follow from the masculine or feminine designation; full of unexamined possibilities because in many Indo-European languages there is a third category – unsexed or neuter.

In its most recent usage, 'gender' seems to have first appeared among American feminists who wanted to insist on the fundamentally social quality of distinctions based on sex. The word denoted a rejection of the biological determinism implicit in the use of such terms as 'sex' or 'sexual difference.' 'Gender' also stressed the relational aspect of normative definitions of femininity. Those who worried that women's studies scholarship focused too narrowly and separately on women used the term 'gender' to introduce a relational notion into our analytic vocabulary. According to this view, women and men were defined in terms of one another, and no understanding of either could be achieved by entirely separate study.

[. . .]

In addition, and perhaps most important, 'gender' was a term offered by those who claimed that women's scholarship would fundamentally transform disciplinary paradigms. Feminist scholars pointed out early on that the study of women would not only add new subject matter but would also force a critical reexamination of the premises and standards of existing scholarly work. 'We are learning,' wrote three feminist historians, 'that the writing of women into history necessarily involves redefining and enlarging traditional notions of historical significance, to encompass personal, subjective experience as well as public and political activities. It is not too much to suggest that however hesitant the actual beginnings, such a methodology implies not only a new history of women, but also a new history.'[4] The way in which this new history would both include and account for women's experience rested on the extent to which gender could be developed as a category of analysis. Here the analogies to class (and race) were explicit; indeed, the most politically inclusive of scholars of women's studies regularly invoked all three categories as crucial to the writing of a new history.[5] An interest in class, race, and gender signaled first, a scholar's commitment to a history that included stories of the oppressed and an analysis of the meaning and nature of their oppression and, second, scholarly understanding that inequalities of power are organized along at least three axes.

The litany of class, race, and gender suggests a parity for each term, but, in fact, that is not at all the case. While 'class' most often rests on Marx's elaborate (and since elaborated) theory of economic determination and historical change, 'race' and 'gender' carry no such associations. No unanimity exists among those who employ concepts of class. Some scholars employ Weberian notions, others use class as a temporary heuristic device. Still, when we invoke class, we are working with or against a set of definitions that, in the case of Marxism, involve an idea of economic causality and a vision of the path along which history has moved dialectically. There is no such clarity or coherence for either race or gender. In the case of gender, the usage has involved a range of theoretical positions as well as simple descriptive references to the relationships between the sexes.

Feminist historians, trained as most historians are to be more comfortable with description than theory, have nonetheless increasingly looked for usable theoretical formulations. They have done so for at least two reasons. First, the proliferation of case studies in women's history seems to call for some synthesizing perspective that can explain continuities and discontinuities and account for persisting inequalities as well as radically different social experiences. Second, the discrepancy between the high quality of recent work in women's history and its continuing marginal status in the field as a whole (as measured by textbooks, syllabi, and monographic work) points up the limits of descriptive approaches that do not address dominant disciplinary concepts, or at least that do not address these concepts in terms that can shake their power and perhaps transform them. It has not been enough for historians of women to prove either that women had a history or that women participated in the major political upheavals of Western civilization. In the case of women's history, the response of most non-feminist historians has been acknowledgment and then separation or dismissal ('women had a history separate from men's, therefore let feminists do women's history, which need not concern us'; or 'women's history is about sex and the family and should be done separately from political and economic history'). In the case of women's participation, the response has been minimal interest at best ('my understanding of the French Revolution is not changed by knowing that women participated in it'). The challenge posed by these responses is, in the end, a theoretical one. It requires analysis not only of the relationship between male and female experience in the past but also of the connection between past history and current historical practice. How does gender work in human social relationships? How does gender give meaning to the organization and perception of historical knowledge? The answers depend on gender as an analytic category.

For the most part, the attempts of historians to theorize about gender have remained within traditional social scientific frameworks, using long-standing formulations that provide universal causal explanations. These theories have been limited at best because they tend to contain reductive or overly simple generalizations that undercut not only history's disciplinary sense of the complexity of social causation but also feminist commitments to analyses that will lead to change. A review of these theories will expose their limits and make it possible to propose an alternative approach.[6]

The approaches used by most historians fall into two distinct categories. The first is essentially descriptive; that is, it refers to the existence of phenomena or realities without interpreting, explaining, or attributing causality. The second usage is causal; it theorizes about the nature of phenomena or realities, seeking an understanding of how and why these take the form they do.

In its simplest recent usage, 'gender' is a synonym for 'women.' Any number of books and articles whose subject is women's history have, in the past few years, substituted 'gender' for 'women' in their titles. In some cases, this usage, though vaguely referring to certain analytic concepts, is actually about the political acceptability of the field. In these instances, the use of 'gender' is meant to denote the scholarly seriousness of a work, for 'gender' has a more neutral and objective sound than does 'women.' 'Gender' seems to fit within the scientific terminology of social science and thus dissociates itself from the (supposedly strident) politics of feminism. In this usage, 'gender' does not carry with it a necessary statement about inequality or power nor does it name the aggrieved (and hitherto invisible) party. Whereas the term 'women's history' proclaims its politics by asserting (contrary to customary practice) that women are valid historical subjects, 'gender' includes but does not name women and so seems to pose no critical threat. This use of 'gender' is one facet of what might be called the quest of feminist scholarship for academic legitimacy in the 1980s.

But only one facet. 'Gender' as a substitute for 'women' is also used to suggest that information about women is necessarily information about men, that one implies the study of the other. This usage insists that the world of women is part of the world of men, created in and by it. This usage rejects the interpretive utility of the idea of separate spheres, maintaining that to study women in isolation perpetuates the fiction that one sphere, the experience of one sex, has little or nothing to do with the other. In addition, gender is also used to designate social relations between the sexes. Its use explicitly rejects biological explanations, such as those that find a common denominator for diverse forms of female subordination in the facts that women have the capacity to give birth and men have greater muscular strength. Instead, gender becomes a way of denoting 'cultural constructions' – the entirely social creation of ideas about appropriate roles for women and men. It is a way of referring to the exclusively social origins of the subjective identities of men and women. Gender is, in this definition, a social category imposed on a sexed body.[7] Gender seems to have become a particularly useful word as studies of sex and sexuality have proliferated, for it offers a way of differentiating sexual practice from the social roles assigned to women and men. Although scholars acknowledge the connection between sex and (what the sociologists of the family called) 'sex roles,' these scholars do not assume a simple or direct linkage. The use of gender emphasizes an entire system of relationships that may include sex, but is not directly determined by sex or directly determining of sexuality.

These descriptive usages of gender have been employed by historians most often to map out a new terrain. As social historians turned to new objects of study, gender was relevant for such topics as women, children, families, and gender ideologies. This usage of gender, in other words, refers only to those areas – both structural and ideological – involving relations between the sexes. Because, on the face of it, war, diplomacy, and high politics have not been explicitly about those relationships, gender seems not to apply and so continues to be irrelevant to the thinking of historians concerned with issues of politics and power. The effect is to endorse a certain functionalist view ultimately rooted in biology and to perpetuate the idea of separate spheres (sex or politics, family or nation, women or men) in the writing of history. Although gender in this usage asserts that relationships between the sexes are social, it says nothing about why these relationships are constructed as they are, how they work, or how they change. In its descriptive usage, then, gender is a concept associated with the study of things related to women. Gender is a new topic, a new department of historical investigation, but it does not have the analytic power to address (and change) existing historical paradigms.

Some historians were, of course, aware of this problem, hence the efforts to employ theories that might explain the concept of gender and account for historical change. Indeed, the challenge was to reconcile theory, which was framed in general or universal terms, and history, which was committed to the study of contextual specificity and fundamental change. The result has been extremely eclectic: partial borrowings that vitiate the analytic power of a particular theory or, worse, employ its precepts without awareness of their implications; or accounts of change that, because they embed universal theories, only illustrate unchanging themes; or wonderfully imaginative studies in which theory is nonetheless so hidden that these studies cannot serve as models for other investigations. Because the theories on which historians have drawn are often not spelled out in all their implications, it seems worthwhile to spend some time doing that. Only through such an exercise can we evaluate the usefulness of these theories and, perhaps, articulate a more powerful theoretical approach.

Feminist historians have employed a variety of approaches to the analysis of gender, but they come down to a choice between three theoretical positions.[8] The first, an entirely feminist effort, attempts to explain the origins of patriarchy. The second locates itself within a Marxian tradition and seeks there an accommodation with feminist critiques. The third, fundamentally divided between French post-structuralist and Anglo-American object-relations theorists, draws on these different schools of psychoanalysis to explain the production and reproduction of the subject's gendered identity.

Theorists of patriarchy have directed their attention to the subordination of women and found their explanation for it in the male 'need' to dominate the female. In Mary O'Brien's ingenious adaptation of Hegel, she defined male domination as the effect of men's desire to transcend their alienation from the means of the reproduction of the species. The principle of generational continuity restores the primacy of paternity and obscures the real labor and the social reality of women's work in childbirth. The source of women's liberation lies in 'an adequate understanding of the process of reproduction,' an appreciation of the contradiction between the nature of women's reproductive labor and (male) ideological mystifications of it.[9] For Shulamith Firestone, reproduction was also the 'bitter trap' for women. In her more materialist analysis, however, liberation would come with transformations in reproductive technology, which might in some not too distant future eliminate the need for women's bodies as the agents of species reproduction.[10]

If reproduction was the key to patriarchy for some, sexuality itself was the answer for others. Catherine MacKinnon's bold formulations were at once her own and characteristic of a certain approach: 'Sexuality is to feminism what work is to marxism: that which is most one's own, yet most taken away.' 'Sexual objectification is the primary process of the subjection of women. It unites act with word, construction with expression, perception with enforcement, myth with reality. Man fucks woman; subject verb object.'[11] Continuing her analogy to Marx, MacKinnon offered, in the place of dialectical materialism, consciousness-raising as feminism's method of analysis. By expressing the shared experience of objectification, she argued, women come to understand their common identity and so are moved to political action. For MacKinnon, sexuality thus stood outside ideology, discoverable as an unmediated, experienced fact. Although sexual relations are defined in MacKinnon's analysis as social, there is nothing except the inherent inequality of the sexual relation itself to explain why the system of power operates as it does. The source of unequal relations between the sexes is, in the end, unequal relations between the sexes. Although the inequality of which sexuality is the source is said to be embodied in a 'whole system of social relationships,' how this system works is not explained.[12]

Theorists of patriarchy have addressed the inequality of males and females in important ways, but, for historians, their theories pose problems. First, while they offer an analysis internal to the gender system itself, they also assert the primacy of that system in all social organization. But theories of patriarchy do not show how gender inequality structures all other inequalities or, indeed, *how* gender affects those areas of life that do not seem to be connected to it. Second, whether domination comes in the form of the male appropriation of the female's reproductive labor or in the sexual objectification of women by men, the analysis rests on physical difference. Any physical difference takes on a universal and unchanging aspect, even if theorists of patriarchy take into account the existence of changing forms and systems of gender inequality.[13] A theory that rests on the single variable of physical difference poses problems for historians: it assumes a consistent or inherent meaning for the human body – outside social or cultural construction – and thus the ahistoricity of gender itself. History becomes, in a sense, epiphenomenal, providing endless variations on the unchanging theme of a fixed gender inequality.

Marxist feminists have a more historical approach, guided as they are by a theory of history. But, whatever the variations and adaptations have been, the self-imposed requirement that there be a 'material' explanation for gender has limited or at least slowed the development of new lines of analysis. Whether a so-called dual-systems solution is proffered (one that posits the separate but interacting realms of capitalism and patriarchy) or an analysis based more firmly in orthodox Marxist discussions of modes of production is developed, the explanation for the origins of and changes in gender systems is found outside the sexual division of labor. Families, households, and sexuality are all, finally, products of changing modes of production. That is how Engels concluded his explorations of the *Origins of the Family*;[14] that is where economist Heidi Hartmann's analysis ultimately rests. Hartmann insisted on the importance of taking into account patriarchy and capitalism as separate but interacting systems. Yet, as her argument unfolds, economic causality takes precedence, and patriarchy always develops and changes as a function of relations of production. When she suggested that 'it is necessary to eradicate the sexual division of labor itself to end male domination,' she meant ending job segregation by sex.[15]

Early discussions among Marxist feminists circled around the same set of problems: a rejection of the essentialism of those who would argue that the 'exigencies of biological reproduction' determine the sexual division of labor under capitalism; the futility of inserting 'modes of reproduction' into discussions of modes of production (it remains an oppositional category and does not assume equal status with modes of production); the recognition that economic systems do not directly determine gender relationships, indeed, that the subordination of women pre-dates capitalism and continues under socialism; the search nonetheless for a materialist explanation that excludes natural physical differences.[16] An important attempt to break out of this circle of problems came from Joan Kelly in her essay, 'The Doubled Vision of Feminist Theory,' where she argued that economic and gender systems interacted to produce social and historical experiences; that neither system was causal, but both 'operate simultaneously to reproduce the socioeconomic and male-dominant structures of [a] particular social order.' Kelly's suggestion that gender systems had an independent existence provided a crucial conceptual opening, but her commitment to remain within a Marxist framework led her to emphasize the causal role of economic factors even in the determination of the gender system: 'The relation of the sexes operates in accordance with, and through, socioeconomic structures, as well as sex/gender ones.'[17] Kelly introduced the idea of a 'sexually based social reality,' but she tended to emphasize the social rather than the sexual nature of that reality, and, most often, 'social,' in her usage, was conceived in terms of economic relations of production.

The most far-reaching exploration of sexuality by American Marxist feminists is in *Powers of Desire*, a volume of essays published in 1983.[18] Influenced by increasing attention to sexuality among political activists and scholars, by French philosopher Michel Foucault's insistence that sexuality is produced in historical contexts, and by the conviction that the current 'sexual revolution' required serious analysis, the authors made 'sexual politics' the focus of their inquiry. In so doing, they opened the question of causality and offered a variety of solutions to it; indeed, the real excitement of this volume is its lack of analytic unanimity, its sense of analytic tension. If individual authors tend to stress the causality of social (by which is often meant 'economic') contexts, they nonetheless include suggestions about the importance of studying 'the psychic structuring of gender identity.' If 'gender ideology' is sometimes said to 'reflect' economic and social structures, there is also a crucial recognition of the need to understand the complex 'link between society and enduring psychic structure.'[19] On the one hand, the editors endorse Jessica Benjamin's point that politics must include attention to 'the erotic, fantastic components of human life,' but, on the other, no essays besides Benjamin's deal fully or seriously with the theoretical issues she raises.[20] Instead, a tacit assumption runs through the volume that Marxism can be expanded to include discussions of ideology, culture, and psychology and that this expansion will happen through the kind of concrete examination of evidence undertaken in most of the articles. The advantage of such an approach lies in its avoidance of sharp differences of position, the disadvantage in its leaving in place an already fully articulated theory that leads back from relations of the sexes to relations of production.

A comparison of American Marxist-feminist efforts, exploratory and relatively wide-ranging, to those of their English counterparts, tied more closely to the politics of a strong and viable Marxist tradition, reveals that the English have had greater difficulty in challenging the constraints of strictly determinist explanations. This difficulty can be seen most dramatically in the recent debates in the *New Left Review* between Michèle Barrett and her critics, who charged her with abandoning a materialist analysis of the sexual division of labor under capitalism.[21] It can be seen as well in the replacement of an initial feminist attempt to reconcile psychoanalysis and Marxism with a choice of one or another of these theoretical positions by scholars who earlier insisted that some fusion of the two was possible.[22] The difficulty for both English and American feminists working within Marxism is apparent in the works I have mentioned here. The problem they face is the opposite of the one posed by patriarchal theory. Within Marxism, the concept of gender has long been treated as the by-product of changing economic structures; gender has had no independent analytic status of its own.

A review of psychoanalytic theory requires a specification of schools, since the various approaches have tended to be classified by the national origins of the founders and the majority of the practitioners. There is the Anglo-American school, working within the terms of theories of object-relations. In the U.S., Nancy Chodorow is the name most readily associated with this approach. In addition, the work of Carol Gilligan has had a far-reaching impact on American scholarship, including history. Gilligan's work draws on Chodorow's, although it is concerned less with the construction of the subject than with moral development and behavior. In contrast to the Anglo-American school, the French school is based on structuralist and post-structuralist readings of Freud in terms of theories of language (for feminists, the key figure is Jacques Lacan).

Both schools are concerned with the processes by which the subject's identity is created; both focus on the early stages of child development for clues to the formation of gender identity. Object-relations theorists stress the influence of actual experience (the child sees, hears, relates to those who care for it, particularly, of course, to its parents), while the post-structuralists emphasize the centrality of language in communicating, interpreting, and representing gender. (By 'language,' post-structuralists do not mean words but systems of meaning – symbolic orders – that precede the actual mastery of speech, reading, and writing.) Another difference between the two schools of thought focuses on the unconscious, which for Chodorow is ultimately subject to conscious understanding and for Lacan is not. For Lacanians, the unconscious is a critical factor in the construction of the subject; it is the location, moreover, of sexual division and, for that reason, of continuing instability for the gendered subject.

In recent years, feminist historians have been drawn to these theories either because they serve to endorse specific findings with general observations or because they seem to offer an important theoretical formulation about gender. Increasingly, those historians working with a concept of 'women's culture' cite Chodorow's or Gilligan's work as both proof of and explanation for their interpretations; those wrestling with feminist theory look to Lacan. In the end, neither of these theories seems to me entirely workable for historians; a closer look at each may help explain why.

My reservation about object-relations theory concerns its literalism, its reliance on relatively small structures of interaction to produce gender identity and to generate change. Both the family division of labor and the actual assignment of tasks to each parent play a crucial role in Chodorow's theory. The outcome of prevailing Western systems is a clear division between male and female: 'The basic feminine sense of self is connected to the world, the basic masculine sense of self is separate.'[23] According to Chodorow, if fathers were more involved in parenting and present more often in domestic situations, the outcome of the oedipal drama might be different.[24]

This interpretation limits the concept of gender to family and household experience and, for the historian, leaves no way to connect the concept (or the individual) to other social systems of economy, politics, or power. Of course, it is implicit that social arrangements requiring fathers to work and mothers to perform most child-rearing tasks structure family organization. Where such arrangements come from and why they are articulated in terms of a sexual division of labor is not clear. Neither is the issue of inequality, as opposed to that of asymmetry, addressed. How can we account within this theory for persistent associations of masculinity with power, for the higher value placed on manhood than on womanhood, for the way children seem to learn these associations and evaluations even when they live outside nuclear households or in households where parenting is equally divided between husband and wife? I do not think we can without some attention to symbolic systems, that is, to the ways societies represent gender, use it to articulate the rules of social relationships, or construct the meaning of experience. Without meaning, there is no experience; without processes of signification, there is no meaning (which is not to say that language is everything, but a theory that does not take it into account misses the powerful roles that symbols, metaphors, and concepts play in the definition of human personality and human history).

Language is the center of Lacanian theory; it is the key to the child's induction into the symbolic order. Through language, gendered identity is constructed. According to Lacan, the phallus is the central signifier of sexual difference. But the meaning of the phallus must be read metaphorically. For the child, the oedipal drama sets forth the terms of cultural interaction, since the threat of castration embodies the power, the rules of (the father's) law. The child's relationship to the law depends on sexual difference, on its imaginative (or fantastic) identification with masculinity or femininity. The imposition, in other words, of the rules of social interaction is inherently and specifically gendered, for the female necessarily has a different relationship to the phallus than the male does. But, gender identification, although it always appears coherent and fixed, is, in fact, highly unstable. Like words themselves, subjective identities are processes of differentiation and distinction, requiring the suppression of ambiguities and opposite elements in order to assure (and create the illusion of) coherence and common understanding. The idea of masculinity rests on the necessary repression of feminine aspects – of the subject's potential for bisexuality – and introduces conflict into the opposition of masculine and feminine. Repressed desires are present in the unconscious and are constantly a threat to the stability of gender identification, denying its unity, subverting its need for security. In addition, conscious ideas of masculine or feminine are not fixed, since they vary according to contextual usage. Conflict always exists, then, between the subject's need for the appearance of wholeness and the imprecision of terminology, its relative meaning, its dependence on repression.[25] This kind of interpretation makes the categories of 'man' and 'woman' problematic by suggesting that masculine and feminine are not inherent characteristics but subjective (or fictional) constructs. This interpretation also implies that the subject is in a constant process of construction, and it offers a systematic way of interpreting conscious and unconscious desire by pointing to language as the appropriate place for analysis. As such, I find it instructive.

I am troubled, nonetheless, by the exclusive fixation on questions of 'the subject' and by the tendency to reify subjectively originating antagonism between males and females as the central fact of gender. In addition, although there is openness in the concept of how 'the subject' is constructed, the theory tends to universalize the categories and relationship of male and female. The outcome for historians is a reductive reading of evidence from the past. Even though this theory takes social relationships into account by linking castration to prohibition and law, it does not permit the introduction of a notion of historical specificity and variability. The phallus is the only signifier; the process of constructing the gendered subject is, in the end, predictable because always the same. If, as film theorist Teresa de Lauretis suggests, we need to think in terms of the construction of subjectivity in social and historical contexts, there is no way to specify those contexts within the terms offered by Lacan. Indeed, even in de Lauretis's attempt, social reality (that is, 'material, economic and interpersonal [relations] which are in fact social, and in a larger perspective historical') seems to lie outside, apart from the subject.[26] A way to conceive of 'social reality' in terms of gender is lacking.

The problem of sexual antagonism in this theory has two aspects. First, it projects a certain timeless quality, even when it is historicized as well as it has been by Sally Alexander. Alexander's reading of Lacan led her to conclude that 'antagonism between the sexes is an unavoidable aspect of the acquisition of sexual identity . . . If antagonism is always latent, it is possible that history offers no final resolution, only the constant reshaping, reorganizing of the symbolization of difference, and the sexual division of labor.'[27] It may be my hopeless utopianism that gives me pause before this formulation, or it may be that I have not yet shed the episteme of what Foucault called the Classical Age. Whatever the explanation, Alexander's formulation contributes to the fixing of the binary opposition of male and female as the only possible relationship and as a permanent aspect of the human condition. It perpetuates rather than questions what Denise Riley refers to as 'the dreadful air of constancy of sexual polarity.' She writes: 'The historically constructed nature of the opposition [between male and female] produces as one of its effects just that air of an invariant and monotonous men/women opposition.'[28]

It is precisely that opposition, in all its tedium and monotony, that (to return to the Anglo-American side) Carol Gilligan's work has promoted. Gilligan explained the divergent paths of moral development followed by boys and girls in terms of differences of 'experience' (lived reality). It is not surprising that historians of women have picked up her ideas and used them to explain the 'different voices' their work has enabled them to hear. The problems with these borrowings are manifold, and they are logically connected.[29] The first is a slippage that often happens in the attribution of causality: the argument moves from a statement such as 'women's experience leads them to make moral choices contingent on contexts and relationships' to 'women think and choose this way because they are women.' Implied in this line of reasoning is the ahistorical, if not essentialist, notion of woman. Gilligan and others have extrapolated her description, based on a small sample of late twentieth-century American schoolchildren, into a statement about all women. This extrapolation is evident especially, but not exclusively, in the discussions by some historians of 'women's culture' that take evidence from early saints to modern militant labor activists and reduce it to proof of Gilligan's hypothesis about a universal female preference for relatedness.[30] This use of Gilligan's ideas provides sharp contrasts to the more complicated and historicized conceptions of 'women's culture' evident in the *Feminist Studies* 1980 symposium.[31] Indeed, a comparison of that set of articles with Gilligan's formulations reveals the extent to which her notion is ahistorical, defining woman/man as a universal, self-reproducing binary opposition – fixed always in the same way. By insisting on fixed differences (in Gilligan's case, by simplifying data with more mixed results about sex and moral reasoning to underscore sexual difference), feminists contribute to the kind of thinking they want to oppose. Although they insist on the revaluation of the category 'female' (Gilligan suggests that women's moral choices may be more humane than men's), they do not examine the binary opposition itself.

We need a refusal of the fixed and permanent quality of the binary opposition, a genuine historicization and deconstruction of the terms of sexual difference. We must become more self-conscious about distinguishing between our analytic vocabulary and the material we want to analyze. We must find ways (however imperfect) to continually subject our categories to criticism, our analyses to self-criticism. If we employ Jacques Derrida's definition of deconstruction, this criticism means analyzing in context the

way any binary opposition operates, reversing and displacing its hierarchical construction, rather than accepting it as real or self-evident or in the
nature of things.[32] In a sense, of course, feminists have been doing this for
years. The history of feminist thought is a history of the refusal of the hierarchical construction of the relationship between male and female in its
specific contexts and an attempt to reverse or displace its operations. Feminist historians are now in a position to theorize their practice and to develop
gender as an analytic category.

Concern with gender as an analytic category has emerged only in the late
twentieth century. It is absent from the major bodies of social theory articulated from the eighteenth to the early twentieth centuries. To be sure, some
of those theories built their logic on analogies to the opposition of male and
female, others acknowledged a 'woman question,' still others addressed the
formation of subjective sexual identity, but gender as a way of talking about
systems of social or sexual relations did not appear. This neglect may in
part explain the difficulty that contemporary feminists have had incorporating the term gender into existing bodies of theory and convincing adherents of one or another theoretical school that gender belongs in their
vocabulary. The term gender is part of the attempt by contemporary feminists to stake claim to a certain definitional ground, to insist on the inadequacy of existing bodies of theory for explaining persistent inequalities
between women and men. It seems to me significant that the use of the word
gender has emerged at a moment of great epistemological turmoil that takes
the form, in some cases, of a shift from scientific to literary paradigms
among social scientists (from an emphasis on cause to one on meaning,
blurring genres of inquiry, in anthropologist Clifford Geertz's phrase[33]),
and, in other cases, the form of debates about theory between those who
assert the transparency of facts and those who insist that all reality is construed or constructed, between those who defend and those who question
the idea that 'man' is the rational master of his own destiny. In the space
opened by this debate and on the side of the critique of science developed
by the humanities, and of empiricism and humanism by post-structuralists,
feminists have not only begun to find a theoretical voice of their own but
have found scholarly and political allies as well. It is within this space that
we must articulate gender as an analytic category.

   What should be done by historians who, after all, have seen their discipline dismissed by some recent theorists as a relic of humanist thought? I do
not think we should quit the archives or abandon the study of the past, but
we do have to change some of the ways we have gone about working, some
of the questions we have asked. We need to scrutinize our methods of analysis, clarify our operative assumptions, and explain how we think change
occurs. Instead of a search for single origins, we have to conceive of
processes so interconnected that they cannot be disentangled. Of course, we

identify problems to study, and these constitute beginnings or points of entry into complex processes. But it is the processes we must continually keep in mind. We must ask more often how things happened in order to find out why they happened; in anthropologist Michelle Rosaldo's formulation, we must pursue not universal, general causality but meaningful explanation: 'It now appears to me that woman's place in human social life is not in any direct sense a product of the things she does, but of the meaning her activities acquire through concrete social interaction.'[34] To pursue meaning, we need to deal with the individual subject as well as social organization and to articulate the nature of their interrelationships, for both are crucial to understanding how gender works, how change occurs. Finally, we need to replace the notion that social power is unified, coherent, and centralized with something like Foucault's concept of power as dispersed constellations of unequal relationships, discursively constituted in social 'fields of force.'[35] Within these processes and structures, there is room for a concept of human agency as the attempt (at least partially rational) to construct an identity, a life, a set of relationships, a society with certain limits and with language – conceptual language that at once sets boundaries and contains the possibility for negation, resistance, reinterpretation, the play of metaphoric invention and imagination.

My definition of gender has two parts and several subsets. They are interrelated but must be analytically distinct. The core of the definition rests on an integral connection between two propositions: gender is a constitutive element of social relationships based on perceived differences between the sexes, and gender is a primary way of signifying relationships of power. Changes in the organization of social relationships always correspond to changes in representations of power, but the direction of change is not necessarily one way. As a constitutive element of social relationships based on perceived differences between the sexes, gender involves four interrelated elements: first, culturally available symbols that evoke multiple (and often contradictory) representations – Eve and Mary as symbols of woman, for example, in the Western Christian tradition – but also, myths of light and dark, purification and pollution, innocence and corruption. For historians, the interesting questions are, which symbolic representations are invoked, how, and in what contexts? Second, normative concepts that set forth interpretations of the meanings of the symbols, that attempt to limit and contain their metaphoric possibilities. These concepts are expressed in religious, educational, scientific, legal, and political doctrines and typically take the form of a fixed binary opposition, categorically and unequivocally asserting the meaning of male and female, masculine and feminine. In fact, these normative statements depend on the refusal or repression of alternative possibilities, and, sometimes, overt contests about them take place (at what moments and under what circumstances ought to be a concern of historians). The position that emerges as dominant, however, is stated as the only possible one. Subsequent history is written as if these normative positions were the product of social consensus rather than of conflict. An example of this kind of history is the treatment of the Victorian ideology of domesticity as if it were created whole and only afterwards reacted to instead of being the constant subject of great differences of opinion. Another kind of example comes from contemporary fundamentalist religious groups that have forcibly linked their practice to a restoration of women's supposedly more authentic 'traditional' role, when, in fact, there is little historical precedent for the unquestioned performance of such a role. The point of new historical investigation is to disrupt the notion of fixity, to discover the nature of the debate or repression that leads to the appearance of timeless permanence in binary gender representation. This kind of analysis must include a notion of politics as well as reference to social institutions and organizations – the third aspect of gender relationships.

Some scholars, notably anthropologists, have restricted the use of gender to the kinship system (focusing on household and family as the basis for social organization). We need a broader view that includes not only kinship but also (especially for complex, modern societies) the labor market (a sex-segregated labor market is a part of the process of gender construction), education (all-male, single-sex, or coeducational institutions are part of the same process), and the polity (universal male suffrage is part of the process of gender construction). It makes little sense to force these institutions back to functional utility in the kinship system, or to argue that contemporary relationships between men and women are artifacts of older kinship systems based on the exchange of women.[36] Gender is constructed through kinship, but not exclusively; it is constructed as well in the economy and the polity, which, in our society at least, now operate largely independently of kinship.

The fourth aspect of gender is subjective identity. I agree with anthropologist Gayle Rubin's formulation that psychoanalysis offers an important theory about the reproduction of gender, a description of the 'transformation of the biological sexuality of individuals as they are enculturated.'[37] But the universal claim of psychoanalysis gives me pause. Even though Lacanian theory may be helpful for thinking about the construction of gendered identity, historians need to work in a more historical way. If gender identity is based only and universally on fear of castration, the point of historical inquiry is denied. Moreover, real men and women do not always or literally fulfill the terms of their society's prescriptions or of our analytic categories. Historians need instead to examine the ways in which gendered identities are substantively constructed and relate their findings to a range of activities, social organizations, and historically specific cultural representations. The best efforts in this area so far have been, not surprisingly, biographies: Biddy Martin's interpretation of Lou Andreas-Salomé, Kathryn Sklar's depiction of Catharine Beecher, Jacqueline Hall's life of Jessie Daniel Ames, and Mary Hill's discussion of Charlotte Perkins Gilman.[38] But collective treatments are also possible, as has been shown in studies of the terms of construction of gender identity for British colonial administrators in India and British-educated Indians who emerged as anti-imperialist, nationalist leaders.

The first part of my definition of gender consists, then, of all four of these elements, and no one of them operates without the others. Yet they do not operate simultaneously, with one simply reflecting the others. A question for historical research is, in fact, what the relationships among the four aspects are. The sketch I have offered of the process of constructing gender relationships could be used to discuss class, race, ethnicity, or, for that matter, any social process. My point was to clarify and specify how one needs to think about the effect of gender in social and institutional relationships, because this thinking is often not done precisely or systematically. The theorizing of gender, however, is developed in my second proposition: gender is a primary way of signifying relationships of power. It might be better to say, gender is a primary field within which or by means of which power is articulated. Gender is not the only field, but it seems to have been a persistent and recurrent way of enabling the signification of power in the West, in Judeo-Christian as well as Islamic traditions. As such, this part of the definition might seem to belong in the normative section of the argument, yet it does not, for concepts of power, though they may build on gender, are not always literally about gender itself. French sociologist Pierre Bourdieu has written about how the 'di-vision du monde,' based on references to 'biological differences and notably those that refer to the division of the labor of procreation and reproduction,' operates as 'the best-founded of collective illusions.' Established as an objective set of references, concepts of gender structure perception and the concrete and symbolic organization of all social life.[39] To the extent that these references establish distributions of power (differential control over or access to material and symbolic resources), gender becomes implicated in the conception and construction of power itself. The French anthropologist Maurice Godelier has put it this way: 'It is not sexuality which haunts society, but society which haunts the body's sexuality. Sex-related differences between bodies are continually summoned as testimony to social relations and phenomena that have nothing to do with sexuality. Not only as testimony to, but also testimony for – in other words, as legitimation.'[40]

The legitimizing function of gender works in many ways. Bourdieu, for example, showed how, in certain cultures, agricultural exploitation was organized according to concepts of time and season that rested on specific definitions of the opposition between masculine and feminine. Gayatri Spivak has done a pointed analysis of the uses of gender in certain texts of British and American women writers.[41] Natalie Davis has shown how concepts of masculine and feminine related to understandings and criticisms of the rules of social order in early modern France.[42] Historian Caroline Bynum has thrown new light on medieval spirituality through her attention to the relationships between concepts of masculine and feminine and religious behavior. Her work gives us important insight into the ways in which these concepts informed the politics of monastic institutions as well as of individual believers.[43] Art historians have opened a new territory by reading social implications from literal depictions of women and men.[44] These interpretations are based on the idea that conceptual languages employ differentiation to establish meaning and that sexual difference is a primary way of signifying differentiation.[45] Gender, then, provides a way to decode meaning and to understand the complex connections among various forms of human interaction. When historians look for the ways in which the concept of gender legitimizes and constructs social relationships, they develop insight into the reciprocal nature of gender and society and into the particular and contextually specific ways in which politics constructs gender and gender constructs politics.

Politics is only one of the areas in which gender can be used for historical analysis. I have chosen the following examples relating to politics and power in their most traditionally construed sense, that is, as they pertain to government and the nation-state, for two reasons. First, the territory is virtually uncharted, since gender has been seen as antithetical to the real business of politics. Second, political history – still the dominant mode of historical inquiry – has been the stronghold of resistance to the inclusion of material or even questions about women and gender.

Gender has been employed literally or analogically in political theory to justify or criticize the reign of monarchs and to express the relationship between ruler and ruled. One might have expected that the debates of contemporaries over the reigns of Elizabeth I in England and Catharine de Medici in France would dwell on the issue of women's suitability for political rule, but, in the period when kinship and kingship were integrally related, discussions about male monarchs were equally preoccupied with masculinity and femininity.[46] Analogies to the marital relationship provide structure for the arguments of Jean Bodin, Robert Filmer, and John Locke. Edmund Burke's attack on the French Revolution is built around a contrast between ugly, murderous *sans-culottes* hags ('the furies of hell, in the abused shape of the vilest of women') and the soft femininity of Marie-Antoinette, who escaped the crowd to 'seek refuge at the feet of a king and husband' and whose beauty once inspired national pride. (It was in reference to the appropriate role for the feminine in the political order that Burke wrote, 'To make us love our country, our country ought to be lovely.'[47]) But the analogy is not always to marriage or even to heterosexuality. In medieval Islamic political theory, the symbols of political power alluded most often to sex between man and boy, suggesting not only forms of acceptable sexuality akin to those that Foucault's last work described in classical Greece but also the irrelevance of women to any notion of politics and public life.[48]

Lest this last comment suggest that political theory simply reflects social organization, it seems important to note that changes in gender relationships can be set off by views of the needs of state. A striking example is Louis de Bonald's argument in 1816 about why the divorce legislation of the French Revolution had to be repealed:

> Just as political democracy 'allows the people, the weak part of political society, to rise against the established power,' so divorce, 'veritable domestic democracy,' allows the wife, 'the weak part, to rebel against marital authority' . . . 'In order to keep the state out of the hands of the people, it is necessary to keep the family out of the hands of wives and children.'[49]

Bonald begins with an analogy and then establishes a direct correspondence between divorce and democracy. Harking back to much earlier arguments about the well-ordered family as the foundation of the well-ordered state, the legislation that implemented this view redefined the limits of the marital relationship. Similarly, in our own time, conservative political ideologues would like to pass a series of laws about the organization and behavior of the family that would alter current practices. The connection between authoritarian regimes and the control of women has been noted but not thoroughly studied. Whether at a crucial moment for Jacobin hegemony in the French Revolution, at the point of Stalin's bid for controlling authority, the implementation of Nazi policy in Germany, or the triumph in Iran of the Ayatollah Khomeni, emergent rulers have legitimized domination, strength, central authority, and ruling power as masculine (enemies, outsiders, subversives, weakness as feminine) and made that code literal in laws (forbidding women's political participation, outlawing abortion, prohibiting wage-earning by mothers, imposing female dress codes) that put women in their place.[50] These actions and their timing make little sense in themselves; in most instances, the state had nothing immediate or material to gain from the control of women. The actions can only be made sense of as part of an analysis of the construction and consolidation of power. An assertion of control or strength was given form as a policy about women. In these examples, sexual difference was conceived in terms of the domination or control of women. These examples provide some insight into the kinds of power relationships being constructed in modern history, but this particular type of relationship is not a universal political theme. In different ways, for example, the democratic regimes of the twentieth century have also constructed their political ideologies with gendered concepts and translated them into policy; the welfare state, for example, demonstrated its protective paternalism in laws directed at women and children.[51] Historically, some socialist and anarchist movements have refused metaphors of domination entirely, imaginatively presenting their critiques of particular regimes or social organizations in

terms of transformations of gender identities. Utopian socialists in France
and England in the 1830s and 1840s conceived their dreams for a harmo-
nious future in terms of the complementary natures of individuals as
exemplified in the union of man and woman, 'the social individual.'[52] European anarchists were long known not only for refusing the conventions of
bourgeois marriage but also for their visions of a world in which sexual
difference did not imply hierarchy.

These examples are of explicit connections between gender and power,
but they are only a part of my definition of gender as a primary way of signifying relationships of power. Attention to gender is often not explicit, but
it is nonetheless a crucial part of the organization of equality or inequality.
Hierarchical structures rely on generalized understandings of the so-called
natural relationship between male and female. The concept of class in the
nineteenth century relied on gender for its articulation. When middle-class
reformers in France, for example, depicted workers in terms coded as feminine (subordinated, weak, sexually exploited like prostitutes), labor and
socialist leaders replied by insisting on the masculine position of the working class (producers, strong, protectors of their women and children). The
terms of this discourse were not explicitly about gender, but they relied on
references to it, the gendered 'coding' of certain terms, to establish their
meanings. In the process, historically specific, normative definitions of gender (which were taken as givens) were reproduced and embedded in the culture of the French working class.[53]

The subject of war, diplomacy, and high politics frequently comes up
when traditional political historians question the utility of gender in their
work. But here, too, we need to look beyond the actors and the literal
import of their words. Power relations among nations and the status of
colonial subjects have been made comprehensible (and thus legitimate) in
terms of relations between male and female. The legitimizing of war – of
expending young lives to protect the state – has variously taken the forms of
explicit appeals to manhood (to the need to defend otherwise vulnerable
women and children), of implicit reliance on belief in the duty of sons to
serve their leaders or their (father the) king, and of associations between
masculinity and national strength.[54] High politics itself is a gendered concept, for it establishes its crucial importance and public power, the reasons
for and the fact of its highest authority, precisely in its exclusion of women
from its work. Gender is one of the recurrent references by which political
power has been conceived, legitimated, and criticized. It refers to but also
establishes the meaning of the male/female opposition. To vindicate political power, the reference must seem sure and fixed, outside human construction, part of the natural or divine order. In that way, the binary
opposition and the social process of gender relationships both become
part of the meaning of power itself; to question or alter any aspect threatens the entire system.

If significations of gender and power construct one another, how do things change? The answer in a general sense is that change may be initiated in many places. Massive political upheavals that throw old orders into chaos and bring new ones into being may revise the terms (and so the organization) of gender in the search for new forms of legitimation. But they may not; old notions of gender have also served to validate new regimes.[55] Demographic crises, occasioned by food shortages, plagues, or wars, may have called into question normative visions of heterosexual marriage (as happened in some circles, in some countries in the 1920s), but they have also spawned pro-natalist policies that insist on the exclusive importance of women's maternal and reproductive functions.[56] Shifting patterns of employment may lead to altered marital strategies and to different possibilities for the construction of subjectivity, but they can also be experienced as new arenas of activity for dutiful daughters and wives.[57] The emergence of new kinds of cultural symbols may make possible the reinterpreting or, indeed, rewriting of the oedipal story, but it can also serve to reinscribe that terrible drama in even more telling terms. Political processes will determine which outcome prevails – political in the sense that different actors and different meanings are contending with one another for control. The nature of that process, of the actors and their actions, can only be determined specifically, in the context of time and place. We can write the history of that process only if we recognize that 'man' and 'woman' are at once empty and overflowing categories. Empty because they have no ultimate, transcendent meaning. Overflowing because even when they appear to be fixed, they still contain within them alternative, denied, or suppressed definitions.

Political history has, in a sense, been enacted on the field of gender. It is a field that seems fixed yet whose meaning is contested and in flux. If we treat the opposition between male and female as problematic rather than known, as something contextually defined, repeatedly constructed, then we must constantly ask not only what is at stake in proclamations or debates that invoke gender to explain or justify their positions but also how implicit understandings of gender are being invoked and reinscribed. What is the relationship between laws about women and the power of the state? Why (and since when) have women been invisible as historical subjects, when we know they participated in the great and small events of human history? Has gender legitimated the emergence of professional careers?[58] Is (to quote the title of a recent article by French feminist Luce Irigaray) the subject of science sexed?[59] What is the relationship between state politics and the discovery of the crime of homosexuality?[60] How have social institutions incorporated gender into their assumptions and organizations? Have there ever been genuinely egalitarian concepts of gender in terms of which political systems were projected, if not built?

Investigation of these issues will yield a history that will provide new perspectives on old questions (about how, for example, political rule is imposed, or what the impact of war on society is), redefine the old questions in new terms (introducing considerations of family and sexuality, for example, in the study of economics or war), make women visible as active participants, and create analytic distance between the seemingly fixed language of the past and our own terminology. In addition, this new history will leave open possibilities for thinking about current feminist political strategies and the (utopian) future, for it suggests that gender must be redefined and restructured in conjunction with a vision of political and social equality that includes not only sex, but class and race.

Notes

1 *Oxford English Dictionary* (1961 edn), vol. 4.
2 E. Littré, *Dictionnaire de la langue française* (Paris, 1876).
3 Raymond Williams, *Keywords* (New York, 1983), 285.
4 Ann D. Gordon, Mari Jo Buhle, and Nancy Shrom Dye, 'The Problem of Women's History,' in Berenice Carroll, ed., *Liberating Women's History* (Urbana, Ill., 1976), 89.
5 The best and most subtle example is from Joan Kelly, 'The Doubled Vision of Feminist Theory,' in her *Women, History and Theory* (Chicago, 1984), 51–64, especially 61.
6 For a review of recent work on women's history, see Joan W. Scott, 'Women's History: The Modern Period,' *Past and Present*, 101 (1983): 141–57.
7 For an argument against the use of gender to emphasize the social aspect of sexual difference, see Moira Gatens, 'A Critique of the Sex/Gender Distinction,' in J. Allen and P. Patton, eds, *Beyond Marxism? Interventions after Marx* (Sydney, 1983), 143–60.
8 For a somewhat different approach to feminist analysis, see Linda J. Nicholson, *Gender and History: The Limits of Social Theory in the Age of the Family* (New York, 1986).
9 Mary O'Brien, *The Politics of Reproduction* (London, 1981), 8–15, 46.
10 Shulamith Firestone, *The Dialectic of Sex* (New York, 1970). The phrase 'bitter trap' is O'Brien's, *Politics of Reproduction*, 8.
11 Catherine MacKinnon, 'Feminism, Marxism, Method, and the State: An Agenda for Theory,' *Signs*, 7 (Spring 1982): 515, 541.
12 Ibid., 541, 543.
13 For an interesting discussion of the strengths and limits of the term 'patriarchy,' see the exchange between historians Sheila Rowbotham, Sally Alexander, and Barbara Taylor in Raphael Samuel, ed., *People's History and Socialist Theory* (London, 1981), 363–73.
14 Frederick Engels, *The Origins of the Family, Private Property, and the State* (1884; reprint edn, New York, 1972).
15 Heidi Hartmann, 'Capitalism, Patriarchy, and Job Segregation by Sex,' *Signs*, 1 (Spring 1976): 168. See also 'The Unhappy Marriage of Marxism and Feminism: Towards a More Progressive Union,' *Capital and Class*, 8 (Summer 1979): 1–33; 'The Family as the Locus of Gender, Class, and Political Struggle: The Example of Housework,' *Signs*, 6 (Spring 1981): 366–94.
16 Discussions of Marxist feminism include Zillah Eisenstein, *Capitalist Patriarchy and the Case for Socialist Feminism* (New York, 1979); A. Kuhn, 'Structures of Patriarchy and Capital in the Family,' in A. Kuhn and A. Wolpe, eds, *Feminism and Materialism* (London, 1978); Rosalind Coward, *Patriarchal Precedents* (London, 1983); Hilda Scott, *Does Socialism Liberate Women?* (Boston, 1974); Jane Humphries, 'Working Class Family, Women's Liberation and Class Struggle: The

Case of Nineteenth-Century British History,' *Review of Radical Political Economics*, 9 (1977): 25–41; Jane Humphries, 'Class Struggle and the Persistence of the Working Class Family,' *Cambridge Journal of Economics*, 1 (1971): 241–58; and see the debate on Humphries's work in *Review of Radical Political Economics*, 12 (Summer 1980): 76–94.

17 Kelly, 'Doubled Vision of Feminist Theory,' 61.

18 Ann Snitow, Christine Stansell, and Sharon Thompson, eds, *Powers of Desire: The Politics of Sexuality* (New York, 1983).

19 Ellen Ross and Rayna Rapp, 'Sex and Society: A Research Note from Social History and Anthropology,' in *Powers of Desire*, 53.

20 'Introduction,' *Powers of Desire*, 12; and Jessica Benjamin, 'Master and Slave: The Fantasy of Erotic Domination,' *Powers of Desire*, 297.

21 Johanna Brenner and Maria Ramas, 'Rethinking Women's Oppression,' *New Left Review*, 144 (March–April, 1984): 33–71; Michèle Barrett, 'Rethinking Women's Oppression: A Reply to Brenner and Ramas,' *New Left Review*, 146 (July–August 1984): 123–28; Angela Weir and Elizabeth Wilson, 'The British Women's Movement,' *New Left Review*, 148 (November–December 1984): 74–103; Michèle Barrett, 'A Response to Weir and Wilson,' *New Left Review*, 150 (March–April 1985): 143–47; Jane Lewis, 'The Debate on Sex and Class,' *New Left Review*, 149 (January–February 1985: 108–20.

22 For early theoretical formulations, see *Papers on Patriarchy: Conference, London 76* (London, 1976). For an attempt to get beyond the theoretical impasse of Marxist feminism, see Coward, *Patriarchal Precedents*. See also the brilliant American effort in this direction by anthropologist Gayle Rubin, 'The Traffic in Women: Notes on the "Political Economy" of Sex,' in Rayna R. Reiter, ed., *Towards an Anthropology of Women* (New York, 1975): 167–68.

23 Nancy Chodorow, *The Reproduction of Mothering: Psychoanalysis and the Sociology of Gender* (Berkeley, Calif., 1978), 169.

24 Ibid., 166.

25 Juliet Mitchell and Jacqueline Rose, eds, *Jacques Lacan and the Ecole Freudienne* (London, 1983); Sally Alexander, 'Women, Class and Sexual Difference,' *History Workshop*, 17 (Spring 1984).

26 Teresa de Lauretis, *Alice Doesn't: Feminism, Semiotics, Cinema* (Bloomington, Ind., 1984), 159.

27 Alexander, 'Women, Class and Sexual Difference,' 135.

28 Denise Riley, 'Summary of Preamble to Interwar Feminist History Work,' unpublished paper, presented to the Pembroke Center Seminar, May 1985, p. 11.

29 Carol Gilligan, *In a Different Voice: Psychological Theory and Women's Development* (Cambridge, Mass., 1982).

30 Useful critiques of Gilligan's book are: J. Auerbach, *et al.*, 'Commentary on Gilligan's *In a Different Voice*,' *Feminist Studies*, 11 (Spring 1985); and 'Women and Morality,' a special issue of *Social Research*, 50 (Autumn 1983).

31 *Feminist Studies*, 6 (Spring 1980): 26–64.

32 By 'deconstruction,' I mean to evoke Derrida's discussion, which, though it surely did not invent the procedure of analysis it describes, has the virtue of theorizing it so that it can constitute a useful method. For a succinct and accessible discussion of Derrida, see Jonathan Culler, *On Deconstruction: Theory and Criticism after Structuralism* (Ithaca, N.Y., 1982), especially 156–79. See also Jacques Derrida, *Of Grammatology* (Baltimore, 1976); Jacques Derrida, *Spurs* (Chicago, 1979); and a transcription of Pembroke Center Seminar, 1983, in *Subjects/Objects* (Fall 1984).

33 Clifford Geertz, 'Blurred Genres,' *American Scholar*, 49 (October 1980): 165–79.

34 Michelle Zimbalist Rosaldo, 'The Use and Abuse of Anthropology: Reflections on Feminism and Cross-Cultural Understanding,' *Signs*, 5 (Spring 1980): 400.

35 Michel Foucault, *The History of Sexuality*, vol. I, *An Introduction* (New York, 1980); Michel Foucault, *Power/Knowledge: Selected Interviews and Other Writings, 1972–77* (New York, 1980).

36 For this argument, see Rubin, 'Traffic in Women,' 199.

37 Rubin, 'Traffic in Women,' 189.

38 Biddy Martin, 'Feminism, Criticism and Foucault,' *New German Critique*, 27 (Fall 1982): 3–30; Kathryn Kish Sklar, *Catharine Beecher: A Study in American Domesticity* (New Haven, Conn., 1973); Mary A. Hill, *Charlotte Perkins Gilman: The Making of a Radical Feminist, 1860–1896* (Philadelphia, 1980).

39 Pierre Bourdieu, *Le Sens Pratique* (Paris, 1980), 246–47, 333–461, especially 366.

40 Maurice Godelier, 'The Origins of Male Domination,' *New Left Review*, 127 (May–June 1981): 17.

41 Gayatri Chakravorty Spivak, 'Three Women's Texts and a Critique of Imperialism,' *Critical Inquiry*, 12 (Autumn 1985): 243–46. See also Kate Millett, *Sexual Politics* (New York, 1969). An examination of how feminine references work in major texts of Western philosophy is carried out by Luce Irigaray in *Speculum of the Other Woman* (Ithaca, N.Y., 1985).

42 Natalie Zemon Davis, 'Women on Top,' in her *Society and Culture in Early Modern France* (Stanford, Calif., 1975), 124–51.

43 Caroline Walker Bynum, *Jesus as Mother: Studies in the Spirituality of the High Middle Ages* (Berkeley, Calif., 1982); Caroline Walker Bynum, 'Fast, Feast, and Flesh: The Religious Significance of Food to Medieval Women,' *Representations*, 11 (Summer 1985): 1–25; Caroline Walker Bynum, 'Introduction,' *Religion and Gender: Essays on the Complexity of Symbols* (Beacon Press, 1987).

44 See, for example, T.J. Clarke, *The Painting of Modern Life* (New York, 1985).

45 The difference between structuralist and post-structuralist theorists on this question rests on how open or closed they view the categories of difference. To the extent that post-structuralists do not fix a universal meaning for the categories or the relationship between them, their approach seems conducive to the kind of historical analysis I am advocating.

46 Rachel Weil, 'The Crown Has Fallen to the Distaff: Gender and Politics in the Age of Catharine de Medici,' *Critical Matrix* (Princeton Working Papers in Women's Studies), 1 (1985). See also Louis Montrose, 'Shaping Fantasies: Figurations of Gender and Power in Elizabethan Culture,' *Representations*, 2 (Spring 1983): 61–94; and Lynn Hunt, 'Hercules and the Radical Image in the French Revolution,' *Representations*, 2 (Spring 1983): 95–117.

47 Edmund Burke, *Reflections on the French Revolution* (1892; reprint edn, New York, 1909), 208–209, 214. See Jean Bodin, *Six Books of the Commonwealth* (1606; reprint edn, New York, 1967); Robert Filmer, *Patriarcha and Other Political Works*, ed. Peter Laslett (Oxford, 1949); and John Locke, *Two Treatises of Government* (1690; reprint edn, Cambridge, 1970).

48 I am grateful to Bernard Lewis for the reference to Islam. Michel Foucault, *Historie de la Sexualité*, vol. 2, *L'Usage des plaisirs* (Paris, 1984). One wonders in situations of this kind what the terms of the subject's gender identity are and whether Freudian theory is sufficient to describe the process of its construction.

49 Cited in Roderick Phillips, 'Women and Family Breakdown in Eighteenth Century France: Rouen 1780–1800,' *Social History*, 2 (May 1976): 217.

50 On the French Revolution, see Darlene Gay Levy, Harriet Applewhite, and Mary Johnson, eds, *Women in Revolutionary Paris, 1789–1795* (Urbana, Ill., 1979), 209–20; on Soviet legislation, see the documents in Rudolph Schlesinger, *The Family in the USSR: Documents and Readings* (London, 1949), 62–71, 251–54; on Nazi policy, see Tim Mason, 'Women in Nazi Germany,' *History Workshop*, 1 (Spring 1976): 74–113, and Tim Mason, 'Women in Germany, 1925–40: Family, Welfare and Work,' *History Workshop*, 2 (Autumn 1976): 5–32.

51 Elizabeth Wilson, *Women and the Welfare State* (London, 1977); Jane Lewis, *The Politics of Motherhood: Child and Maternal Welfare in England 1900–1939* (Montreal, 1980); Mary Lynn McDougall, 'Protecting Infants: The French Campaign for Maternity Leaves, 1890s–1913,' *French Historical Studies*, 13 (1983): 79–105.

52 On English utopians, see Barbara Taylor, *Eve and the New Jerusalem* (New York, 1983); on France, Joan W. Scott, 'Men and Women in the Parisian Garment Trades: Discussions of Family and Work in the 1830s and 40s,' in Pat Thane, *et al.*, eds, *The Power of the Past: Essays for Eric Hobsbawm* (Cambridge, 1984), 67–94.

53 Louis Devance, 'Femme, famille, travail et morale sexuelle dans l'idéologie de 1848,' in *Mythes et représentations de la femme au XIXᵉ siècle* (Paris, 1976); Jacques Rancière and Pierre Vauday, 'En allant à l'expo: l'ouvrier, sa femme et les machines,' *Les Révoltes Logiques*, 1 (Winter 1975): 5–22.

54 Gayatri Chakravorty Spivak, ' "Draupadi" by Mahasveta Devi,' *Critical Inquiry*, 8 (Winter 1981): 381–402; Homi Bhabha, 'Of Mimicry and Man: The Ambivalence of Colonial Discourse,' *October*, 28 (Spring 1984): 125–33; Karin Hausen, 'The Nation's Obligations to the Heroes' Widows of World War I,' in Margaret R. Higonnet, *et al.*, eds, *Women, War and History* (New Haven, Conn., 1986).

55 On the French Revolution, see Levy, *Women in Revolutionary Paris*; on the American Revolution, see Mary Beth Norton, *Liberty's Daughters: The Revolutionary Experience of American Women* (Boston, 1980); Linda Kerber, *Women of the Republic* (Chapel Hill, N.C., 1980); Joan Hoff-Wilson, 'The Illusion of Change: Women and the American Revolution,' in Alfred Young, ed., *The American Revolution: Explorations in the History of American Radicalism* (DeKalb, Ill., 1976), 383–446. On the French Third Republic, see Steven Hause, *Women's Suffrage and Social Politics in the French Third Republic* (Princeton, N.J., 1984).

56 On pro-natalism, see Denise Riley, *War in the Nursery* (London, 1984). On the 1920s, see the essays in *Strategies des Femmes* (Paris, 1984).

57 For various interpretations of the impact of new work on women, see Louise A. Tilly and Joan W. Scott, *Women, Work and Family* (New York, 1978); Thomas Dublin, *Women at Work: The Transformation of Work and Community in Lowell, Massachusetts, 1826–1860* (New York, 1979); and Edward Shorter, *The Making of the Modern Family* (New York, 1975).

58 See, for example, Margaret Rossiter, *Women Scientists in America: Struggles and Strategies to 1914* (Baltimore, 1982).

59 Luce Irigaray, 'Is the Subject of Science Sexed?' *Cultural Critique*, 1 (Fall 1985): 73–88.

60 Louis Crompton, *Byron and Greek Love: Homophobia in Nineteenth-Century England* (Berkeley, Calif., 1985). This question is touched on in Jeffrey Weeks, *Sex, Politics and Society* (New York, 1983).

3

What should historians do with masculinity? Reflections on nineteenth-century Britain

JOHN TOSH

Any call for historians to take masculinity seriously is exposed to objection on three fronts. It can be seen as an unwelcome take-over bid, as unacceptably subversive, or as a modish irrelevance. Though none of these objections has produced an articulate critique, they are no less powerful for that; together I suspect they account for most of the reluctance of the historical profession to explore the potential of this new perspective.

Reprinted from *History Workshop Journal* 38 (1994). Reprinted by permission of Oxford University Press Ltd.

The first position is taken by those who see the history of masculinity as a not-so-subtle attempt to infiltrate women's history and blunt its polemical edge. The appropriate response was given as long ago as 1975 by Natalie Zemon Davis. Addressing a feminist audience, she remarked

> It seems to me that we should be interested in the history of both women and men, that we should not be working only on the subjected sex any more than an historian of class can focus entirely on peasants. Our goal is to understand the significance of the *sexes*, of gender groups in the historical past.[1]

This analogy is not to do with symmetry or balance, but about the need to understand a system of social relations *as a whole* – class in the first instance, gender in the second. Davis was arguing that unless the field of power in which women have lived is studied, the reality of their historical situation will always be obscured. On those grounds alone, the gendered study of men must be indispensable to any serious feminist historical project. There are still no doubt students who object to the inclusion of masculinity in women's studies courses, but within academia Davis's point has been repeatedly made by feminist historians in recent years.[2]

One reason why feminists have come to feel happier with the study of masculinity is that its full subversive potential is becoming visible. It is this realization which shapes the second line of attack. One of the problems of women's history has been that so much of its output has concerned areas like family, philanthropy and feminist politics which can be shrugged off by mainstream historians as a minority pursuit with no bearing on their work (they are of course mistaken). But the history of masculinity cannot be cordoned off in this way. It must either be rejected, or incorporated into the traditional heartland. In an edited collection, *Manful Assertions*, which appeared in 1991, Michael Roper and I brought together essays on labour, business, religion, education and national identity in Britain over the past 200 years, and were we assembling the volume now we would be able to include material on institutional politics too.[3] In other words, historians of masculinity are in a strong position to demonstrate (not merely assert) that gender is inherent in all aspects of social life, whether women are present or not.

Perhaps the commonest response among historians is an all-too-familiar weary scepticism. Masculinity according to this view is merely the latest in a series of ideological red-herrings which will add nothing to what we already know about identity, social consciousness and social agency in the past – and indeed will probably obscure what we *do* know. It's easy to write off this attitude as a symptom of intellectual fatigue. But in fact it relates to a crucial feature of masculinity in most societies that we know about, and certainly modern Western ones, namely its relative invisibility. Men were the norm against which women and children should be measured. Women were 'carriers' of gender, because their reproductive role was held to define their place in society and their character. Masculinity remained largely out of sight since men as a sex were not confined in this or any other way: as Rousseau bluntly put it, 'The male is only a male at times; the female is a female all her life and can never forget her sex'.[4] This view proved remarkably enduring. Even in the late Victorian heyday of scientific belief in sexual difference, little was made of men's distinctive biology and the character traits that might flow from it, compared with the volume of comment on women.[5] Men's nature was vested in their reason not their bodies. A profound dualism in Western thought has served to keep the spotlight away from men. In the historical record it is as though masculinity is everywhere but nowhere.

[. . .]

What then is the historical connection between patriarchy[6] and masculinity? [. . .] The answer offered by recent work on manliness is: not much. To move beyond that rather bland disclaimer, we have to turn from masculinity as a set of cultural attributes to consider masculinity as a social status, demonstrated in specific social contexts. I say 'demonstrated' because public affirmation was, and still is, absolutely central to masculine status. Here it is worth taking note of some of the earlier findings of feminist anthropology. Michelle Rosaldo pointed to a critical distinction between the upbringing of boys and girls in almost all societies. Whereas girls are expected to graduate to womanhood in a largely domestic setting under a mother's tutelage, boys have to be prepared for a more competitive and demanding arena. Their qualification for a man's life among men – in short for a role in the public sphere – depends on their masculinity being tested against the recognition of their peers during puberty, young adulthood and beyond. As Rosaldo put it,

> A woman becomes a woman by following in her mother's footsteps, whereas there must be a break in a man's experience. For a boy to become an adult, he must prove himself – his masculinity – among his peers. And although all boys may succeed in reaching manhood, cultures treat this development as something that each individual has achieved.[7]

What precisely has to be achieved varies a lot between cultures, but in modern Western societies the public demonstration of masculinity occurs in three linked arenas – home, work and all-male associations. I would like to dwell on the gendered meaning of each of these contexts in nineteenth-century Britain, because I think that together they account for much of the reason why masculinity should matter to social historians.

In most societies that we know of, setting up a new household is the essential qualification for manhood. The man who speaks for familial dependents and who can transmit his name and his assets to future generations is fully masculine. The break is all the clearer when it is recognized that marriage requires setting up a new household, not forming a sub-unit within the parental home. In the nineteenth century this was a governing condition of the transition to adult life. Bachelorhood was always an ambivalent status, though its cultural appeal was greater at some times than others – particularly at the end of the century. Once established, a household had to be sustained by the man's productive activities. In the eighteenth century this condition was met in many areas by household production, with the man directing the labour of family members and other dependents.[8] As this pattern declined during the following century, increasing emphasis was placed on the man's unaided labours. Notwithstanding the prevalence of women's employment in the working class, the cultural weight attached to the *male* breadwinner was overwhelming. It was reflected positively in the demand for a 'family wage', and negatively in the humiliation of the unemployed man obliged to depend on his wife's earnings, and in the anger of the skilled artisan displaced by female labour. 'What is the feeling of a man in this position?' asked a Kidderminster carpet weaver in 1894. 'Has it not a tendency to reduce him and create a *littleness* when he is no longer the bread-winner of the family?' (emphasis added).[9]

The location of authority within the household was the other key determinant of masculine status here. The power of the *paterfamilias* is most assured when he controls the labour of household members, which is why household production is usually taken to imply a patriarchal family. By the mid-nineteenth century economic organization had moved sharply away from this pattern, but patriarchal values still held sway. The belief in the household as a microcosm of the political order, vigorously re-stated by Evangelicals, underlined the importance of the man being master in his own home.[10] The law remained pretty unyielding. The husband was legally responsible for all members of the household, including servants, and only in cases of extreme cruelty (mental or physical) was his authority over wife or children at risk. In cultural terms, up-to-date notions of domesticity and companionate marriage may have carved out a more autonomous sphere for the wife, especially in middle-class families, but the ultimate location of authority was seldom in doubt. Indeed, as Jim Hammerton has recently pointed out, companionate marriage often led the husband to be *more* assertive and heavy-handed, not less.[11] Home might be the 'woman's sphere', but the husband who abdicated from his rights in the cause of a quiet life was in common opinion less than a man, and he was a common butt of music-hall humour.[12]

Maintenance of a household at a level of comfort appropriate to one's social status presupposed an income from work – the second leg of masculine reputation. But not just *any* work. It wasn't enough that the work be dependable or even lucrative – it had to be dignified, and the wide currency of this notion is one of the most distinctive features of the nineteenth-century gender regime. For middle-class work to be dignified, it had to be absolutely free from any suggestion of servility or dependence on patronage. 'Look not for success to favour, to partiality, to friendship, or to what is called interest', declared William Cobbett; 'write it on your heart that you will depend solely on your own merit and your own exertions.'[13] Neither the practice of a profession nor the running of a business was represented as a mere burden. It might become so in particular instances, – if one found oneself in the wrong occupation, or wrecked one's constitution through overwork, but fundamentally a man's occupation in life was his 'calling', often seen as subject to the workings of Providence. The idea that what a man did in his working life was an authentic expression of his individuality was one of the most characteristic – and enduring – features of middle-class masculinity.[14]

Inevitably the scope for these values in the working class was limited. But the idea that the working man's property lay in his skill, acquired by apprenticeship or training under his father's eye, carried a comparable load of moral worth, and it was the basis on which craft unions demanded the continuation of traditional labour relations based on respect for the masculine skills of the men.[15] Among the manual working class, it seems highly likely that the aggressive celebration of physical strength as an exclusive badge of masculinity, described by Paul Willis in the 1970s,[16] prevailed in Victorian times too. The hapless office clerk fell between two stools: in middle-class terms his occupation was servile, while the labourer despised his soft hands and poor physique.[17] In each case masculine self-respect demanded the exclusion of women. The gender coding of the world of work could accept the reality of women's labour in the domestic setting as servants or homeworkers. But the entry of women into formal paid work out of the home – whether it was mill-girls at the beginning of the century or female office-clerks at the end – always occasioned strain, not only because there might be less work (or less well-paid work) for men, but because their masculine identity as the working sex was at stake.[18]

The third leg of men's social identity is less familiar, and certainly much less developed in the theoretical literature. But all-male associations are integral to any notion of patriarchy beyond the household. They embody men's privileged access to the public sphere, while simultaneously reinforcing women's confinement to household and neighbourhood. This perception has made little impact on historical work on modern Western societies. 'Male bonding' would be a handy label, if it did not suggest something primal and trans-historical.[19] For we are dealing here with quite a wide variety of social forms. Some, like craft guilds or chambers of commerce or professional bodies, existed to promote the pursuit of business, and might therefore be subsumed under my second heading of work. But there were far too many men's associations which had little or nothing to do with work. I am thinking of the voluntary associations and pressure groups whose voices together made up 'public opinion', and the clubs, taverns and bars which oiled the wheels of friendship, politics and leisure (as well as business).

The salience of these groups is partly determined by the life cycle. The appeal of all-male conviviality is probably greatest among young unmarried men who are temporarily denied the full privileges of masculinity: the journeyman's association, the street gang, the sports club. Schooling often intensifies it. In the second half of the nineteenth century the public schools were patriarchal institutions not only because they excluded women, but because they instilled an enduring preference for all-male sociability. But the appeal of associational life goes well beyond youth. In the nineteenth century this was most evident in the United States, where the hold of fraternal lodges over the leisure-time and the purses of urban men of all classes in the generation after the Civil War was truly remarkable.[20] Britain boasted an array of institutions for men of all ages, ranging from the pub, the friendly society and the working men's club through to the middle-class voluntary association and the West End club.[21] All of these arenas were at one time or another correctly perceived by women as contributing to the edifice of male exclusionary power. They sustained the powerful myth that masculinity is about the exclusive company of men, and of course most work settings reinforced this. What the literary critic Eve Sedgwick has dubbed the 'homosocial alliance' is fundamental to masculine privilege. At the same time, as she points out, it operates within clear limits, for in the interests of protecting the key patriarchal institution of marriage, desire between males is inadmissible; camaraderie must remain just that. So while male bonding is prescribed, homosexuality is proscribed.[22] It was no coincidence that the first modern homosexual panic occurred in the 1880s, when the clubability of the propertied classes was particularly pronounced and their age of marriage (around thirty for men) unprecedentedly late. Any hint of erotic charge or emotional excess between men, such as had been commonplace in polite society a generation earlier, now aroused suspicion. W.T. Stead's remark to Edward Carpenter in 1895 that 'a few more cases like Oscar Wilde's and we should find the freedom of comradeship now possible to men seriously impaired'[23] proved all too accurate. All-male associations sustained gender privilege, while at the same time imposing a discipline on individuals in the interests of patriarchal stability.

In dwelling on the importance of home, work and association as minimal components of masculine identity, I have doubtless laboured the obvious. My reason for doing so is that I have wanted to prepare the ground for the more interesting claim that the precise character of masculine formation at any time is largely determined by the balance struck *between* these three components. I think it's now widely recognized that constant emphasis on the 'separation of spheres' is misleading, partly because men's privileged ability to pass freely between the public and the private was integral to the social order. And some notion of complementarity is always implied by that key nineteenth-century indicator of masculinity achieved, 'independence', combining as it did dignified work, sole maintenance of the family, and free association on terms of equality with other men. But it's much rarer to see these elements considered as a linked system – characterized, as any such system must be, by contradiction and instability. Yet this, it seems to me, is one of the most promising ways of pinning down the social dynamics of masculinity.

Consider, first of all, the Victorian middle class. Any notion of a solid bourgeois masculinity is not tenable. The balance between my three components was inherently unstable and often gave visible signs of strain. Essentially this was because the ideology of domesticity raised the profile of home life far beyond its traditional place in men's lives, and hence posed in an acute form the conflict between the private and public constituents of masculinity. Already in Cobbett's writings one can see the tensions between family life and 'the gabble and balderdash of a club or pot-house company'.[24] By mid-century, when middle-class mores placed the tavern off-limits, this conflict was less stark. The decorous entertainment of lectures and concerts, not to mention collective action in the public interest, appeared to be in less conflict with domestic values, though real devotees of domestic comfort had to be reminded that duty in the public sphere might require some personal sacrifice.[25] More fundamental was the clash between work and home. In which sphere was a man really himself? The implications of the work ethic, in its unyielding Victorian form, were clear, and in spelling them out Carlyle had immense and enduring influence. But there was a strong current running the other way. The adage 'an Englishman's home is his castle', which enjoyed wide currency by the 1850s,[26] conveyed a double meaning of possession against all comers, and of refuge or retreat from the world beyond. This second meaning spoke with special force to those middle-class men who experienced the world of work as alienating or morally undermining. From Froude through Dickens to William Hale White, Victorian fiction propounds the notion that only at home can a man be truly himself; as Froude put it in *The Nemesis of Faith* (1849), 'we lay aside our mask and drop our tools, and are no longer lawyers, sailors, soldiers, statesmen, clergymen, but only men'.[27] And, lest you should suppose that historians were above this alienation, Coventry Patmore (writing in the same vein) specifically included the scholar 'wearying his wits over arid parchments'.[28] By the 1880s the balance had shifted. For the professional classes at least, domesticity was increasingly associated with ennui, routine and feminine constraint.[29] The result was a higher rate of male celibacy, rising club membership, and a vogue for 'adventure' – both in the real-life hazards of mountaineering and the rougher sports, and in what Sir Arthur Conan Doyle admiringly called 'the modern masculine novel' of Robert Louis Stevenson and Rider

Haggard.[30] For middle-class men at the turn of the century the respective
pulls of home and the homosocial world were much more evenly matched
than they had been for their grandfathers. Perhaps no clearer evidence
could be found than the enormous appeal of Scouting to boys and scout-
masters alike: the camp-fire was all that the domestic hearth was not.

In the working class men's commitment to home was more problematic
still. In most cases there was of course far less to hold the working man
there. If his home served also as a workshop it was unlikely to boast the
modicum of amenities which might draw him to his own fireside. If he was
an employee on average earnings or less, his wife's work at home combined
with domestic overcrowding were likely to increase the attractions of the
pub. There were plenty of people within the working class who deplored
this state of affairs. Anna Clark has drawn attention to that strand within
Chartism which advocated a domesticated manhood, like the London
Working Men's Association which denied 'the attributes and characters of
men' to those who were forgetful of their duties as fathers and husbands.[31]
By the 1870s the claim to a dignified home life was part of the stock-in-trade
of trade union leaders.[32] It seems clear that in the late Victorian period there
was a growing minority of comparatively well-paid skilled workers who
entirely supported the household and spent much of their leisure-time there.
Yet the reality could be very different outside this privileged group. Both
Ellen Ross and Carl Chinn describe an urban working-class world from
which private patriarchy had almost disappeared. The husband was often
made to feel a bull-in-a-china-shop, excluded from the emotional currents
of the family. More likely than not, as a boy he would have developed
domestic and nurturing skills, but an important part of his growing up to
manhood was to 'forget' these skills. The wife, on the other hand, was the
one who maintained vital neighbourhood support, who negotiated with
landlords and welfare workers, and who supervised the children's schooling.
Even moving house was often her decision. London magistrates sometimes
spoke of the wife's 'headship of the home'. This was in the context of
domestic assault – surely a symptom of the acute masculine ambivalence
experienced by men married to women who so effectively controlled the
domestic sphere.[33] One can argue whether working men's attachment to
convivial drinking was cause or effect of their discomfort in the home, but
cutting a figure in the pub was clearly a far less equivocal sign of masculine
status than presiding over the home. Charting the ebb and flow of men's commitment to domestic life, whether in the working class or the bourgeoisie,
has much to reveal about the dynamics of masculinity – then and now.

Although this is far from being a comprehensive account, it should be clear
that in the nineteenth century masculinity had multiple social meanings.
Citing this kind of historical material has become a standard procedure for
students of gender who wish to emphasize masculinity as multiform.[34] It is

obviously important to dispose once and for all of the argument that masculinity is 'natural' and thus beyond history. But well-documented diversity
raises the opposite problem that masculinity may be merely a second-order
feature, contingent on other social identities: teasing out the play of masculinity in Chartism or the bourgeois work ethic may add colour to our
understanding, but it does not introduce a new dynamic.

There is some truth in this. For example, it is a fair inference from Davidoff and Hall's *Family Fortunes* that domesticated manliness was essentially
the character-set of a more devout and materially confident middle class
expressed in gender terms. Particular classes are sometimes associated with
a distinctive masculinity. In the nineteenth century upwardly mobile men
had to adapt themselves to different masculine expectations, like the artisan
rising into 'respectability',[35] or the young Thomas Carlyle railing against the
enfeebled masculinity of the London men of letters whose ranks he sought
to join.[36] There is a sense, too, in which ruling classes may propagate their
distinctive masculine codes to the society at large, just as they disseminate
their political values. It has often been pointed out, for example, that Baden-
Powell's intention in setting up the Boy Scouts was to introduce boys from
the lower-middle and working classes to public-school manliness, as the best
basis for physical fitness, an ethic of service, and patriotism. (It should be
noted that the exercise was selective: while the public schools aimed to train
boys in obedience and then command, the second stage was played down in
the Scouts.[37])

But gender status cannot be reduced to class status. Even when the two
are running in parallel, so to speak, interpretation of experience and action
is likely to be significantly modified by taking masculinity into account. It
makes a difference to recognize that unemployment not only impoverished
workers but gravely compromised their masculine self-respect (including
their ability to demand respect from women). In late nineteenth-century
London the industrialization of traditional workshop trades not only made
earnings more precarious; it also destroyed the father's ability to endow his
son with a craft or a job, and was resented for this reason.[38] Again, if domestic violence is placed in the context of a volatile power relationship between
the sexes at home, we can move beyond trite commonplaces about the
power of cheap liquor. In short, consideration of masculinity (like femininity) enlarges the range of factors relevant to the historian of social identity
or social change. It is precisely because Davidoff and Hall structure *Family
Fortunes* around masculinity and femininity that we now have a different
view of the middle class in the early nineteenth century; their achievement
is not to fill out the gender attributes of a class we already know about, but
to place gender at the centre of class formation itself.

But there is a further reason why masculinity is resistant to incorporation
within other social categories. It has its own pecking order which is ultimately to do with upholding patriarchal power rather than a particular

class order. Ruling groups do not only valorize particular features of their own masculine code; they often marginalize or stigmatize other masculine traits in a way which cuts across more familiar social hierarchies. This will be clear if we look at the two categories most often repressed, young bachelors and homosexuals. In most societies the energy of young men who are physically mature but not yet in a position to assume the full duties or privileges of an adult is combustible, to say the least. Much of the offence that they give is because they precociously affect fully adult modes of masculine behavior in exaggerated or distorted forms. Since the heyday of the disorderly apprentice, young men have been a by-word for brawling, drunkenness, sexual experiment and misogyny (the last two being entirely compatible of course). Lyndal Roper's recent work vividly evokes this aspect of sixteenth-century Augsburg.[39] In the modern period, societies have varied greatly in how they have approached this issue, sometimes allowing the breathing-space of a Bohemian life-style as in France, sometimes employing a combination of control and diversion as in middle-class Britain.[40]

The targeting of social control at homosexuals was of course historically much more specific. Only in the late nineteenth century did the now familiar polarization between 'normal' heterosexual and 'deviant' homosexual finally take shape. Just when homosexuality (as distinct from homosexual behavior) 'emerged' has become a contentious area of scholarship in recent years. There can be little doubt that a vigorous gay sub-culture existed in early eighteenth-century London, or that 'molly-houses' periodically attracted draconian repression.[41] But the stigmatization of homosexuals as an aberrant category of men set apart from the 'normal' seems only to have fully developed at a highly specific conjuncture in the late nineteenth century: when medical theory identified a congenitally defective 'third sex', when a strident Social Purity movement seized on homosexuality as a metaphor for national decline, and when homosexuals themselves developed an emancipatory 'Uranian' identity. From then on the figure of the homosexual was established as a patriarchal scapegoat – someone who struck at the roots of the family, flouted the work ethic, and subverted the camaraderie of all-men association.[42]

One can say, therefore, that the dominant masculinity is constructed in opposition to a number of subordinate masculinities whose crime is that they undermine patriarchy from within or discredit it in the eyes of women. Sometimes an entire persona is demonized, as in the case of the homosexual; sometimes specific forms of male behavior are singled out. A good example of this second category is wife-beating. In the course of the nineteenth century domestic violence became increasingly unacceptable to 'respectable' opinion. As is well known, the campaign which culminated in the Matrimonial Causes Act of 1878 was headed by Frances Power Cobbe. But the fight in Parliament was led by Henry Labouchere who saw in wife-beating a damnable slur on the honour of the male sex.[43]

Both the disciplining of subordinate masculinities and the modification of gender norms imposed on the majority of men illustrate the workings of what is sometimes called 'hegemonic masculinity'. This concept has been developed by the sociologist R.W. Connell in order to explain the gender structure of contemporary societies. Connell maintains that one neglected explanation for patriarchy's successful survival and adaptation is the solidarity of men in upholding it – in not 'rocking the boat'. 'Hegemonic masculinity' denotes those expressions of masculinity – like exclusive heterosexuality or the double standard or the assumption that paid work is a male birthright – which serve most effectively to sustain men's power over women in society as a whole. From this perspective, the dominant forms of masculinity are those which marshal men with very different interests behind the defence of patriarchy.[44] The historical application of Connell's theory is limited by the central role he accords to the powerful images of mainstream masculinity put out by the modern mass media, but it becomes increasingly relevant from the 1880s, when the role of the stage and the printed word in shaping gender identification was already in evidence.[45] 'Hegemonic masculinity' is a convenient phrase because it reminds us that masculinity carries a heavy ideological freight, and that it makes socially crippling distinctions not only between men and women, but between different categories of men – distinctions which have to be maintained by force, as well as validated through cultural means.

Once we are clear about the ways in which masculine identities diverge from – and in some contexts overlay – class identities, it is easier to understand why masculine insecurity has had such wide social ramifications in the past, as today. Masculinity is insecure in two senses: its social recognition depends on material accomplishments which may not be attainable; and its hegemonic form is exposed to resistance from both women and subordinated masculinities. (There is a third sense in which masculinity tends to insecurity, arising out of its psychic constitution, to which I turn in the next section.)

In discussing the three foundations of work, home and association, I showed how the social definition of masculinity was determined by the balance between them – and how that balance was inherently variable. However, my argument needs to be taken one stage further. Each of these bases of masculine identification was itself uncertain. This was particularly true of the first two. A proper job and a viable household were highly vulnerable to the vicissitudes of the economic cycle. Individual men might experience acute loss of masculine self-respect through a lack of housing, a shortage of apprenticeships, being thrown out of work, and so on. It is to the credit of recent historians like Sonya Rose and Keith McClelland that we can now grasp the gender implications of these familiar vicissitudes of working-class life.[46] The argument here is not that masculinity was *always* experienced as something contingent and vulnerable. It is not difficult to think of categories of men who never had any reason to doubt their social qualifications for manhood once they had attained adulthood. Nor should one forget those men who were able to make a virtue of their gender non-conformity – the Bohemian, the club *habitué*, the member of a homosexual coterie.[47] My point is rather that, for the majority of men who wielded comparatively little social and economic power, loss of masculine self-respect was as much an occupational hazard as loss of income.

As for hegemonic masculinity, any system of hegemony is by definition liable to insecurity. Holding the line on forms of masculinity intended to uphold patriarchy is always open to the danger of contestation and subversion. This, after all, was the thrust of much action by women in the public sphere – notably successive campaigns for marriage-law reform, and the crusade for Social Purity.[48] The New Woman was, of course, widely construed as a threat to the patriarchal order. Of greater substance perhaps were the female plaintiffs in the post-1857 Divorce Court, whose courage in exposing their painful circumstances to the glare of publicity brought (as Hammerton has shown) the long-term benefit of raising socially acceptable standards of men's marital conduct.[49] At various times during the nineteenth century the subordinated masculinities whom I mentioned earlier were also seen as a threat. In his various manifestations as the lout, the loafer and the hooligan, the unmarried youth was consistently condemned – either as a threat to patriarchal order in the present, or (by the turn of the century) as a degenerate who threatened the manly vigour of future generations.[50] During the nineteenth century the ability of homosexual men to achieve changes in the organization of patriarchy was much less than has been the case in the last thirty years, but it was in the 1880s that the typecasting of gays as everything that the front-line troops of patriarchy are not began to assume its modern shape.

This is the context in which to consider the idea of a 'crisis in masculinity'. As used by present-day theorists, the term denotes a situation in which the traditionally dominant forms of masculinity have become so blurred that men no longer know what is required to be a 'real man' – either because of structural changes or because of challenging critique, or both.[51] There is the drawback that, if we speak of 'crisis', we imply stability the rest of the time. But there is a difference between the individual's insecurity and the undermining of masculinity across a swathe of society, especially when this is articulated and acted upon.

Elaine Showalter has popularized the notion of a 'masculine crisis' in *fin de siècle* Britain, mostly on the strength of the cultural challenge posed by the New Woman and the visible homosexual.[52] I would like to offer a brief example which pays more attention to shifts in the social underpinnings of masculinity in the same period – namely, popular support for imperialism. This is a promising context, because the empire's masculine associations were so strong, and so much of its significance to the British represented a displacement of domestic concerns. An important strand of jingo sentiment was the male clerical workers of the lower middle class, noted for their uninhibited participation in Mafeking night, their enlistment in volunteer army units – and also their taste for imperial adventure fiction.[53] They are of course a classic example of a marginal class, balanced precariously between the workers and the bourgeoisie, and hence likely to make a very public avowal of what they perceived to be respectable or patriotic values. But we must also take note of their masculine job anxieties. From the 1880s onwards, more and more clerical work was being given to women – up to a quarter in some cities – and male clerks protested at this slur on their manhood.[54] A hearty, and above all a *physical* identification with the quintessentially masculine ethos of empire was one very effective way in which that slur could be countered. On this reading, male clerks were a class fraction undergoing acute gender insecurity at this time, and they grasped the most easily improvised way of re-affirming their masculinity. As a form of political identification (and also, it might be said, as a career choice[55]) the empire served to underpin beleaguered masculinities at home. The components of masculine status have, I would argue, been too long taken for granted as a fixture largely outside the narratives of social change. As this neglect is rectified, other features of the historical landscape, no less familiar than imperialism, are likely to change their configuration too.[56]

So far, in treating masculinity as a social identity – as an aspect of the structure of social relations – I have reflected the dominant trend in Britain in historical writing about gender. But of course this is not the only approach, nor the most challenging one. Masculinity is more than social construction. It demands to be considered also as a *subjective* identity, usually the most deeply experienced that men have. And this brings into play the early formation of the gendered personality in the intimate relations of family life. What men subsequently seek to validate through recognition of their peers has been shaped in infancy and childhood in relations of nurture, desire and authority. It is therefore a mistake to treat masculinity merely as an outer garment or 'style', adjustable according to social circumstances. Nor does it make much sense baldly to equate masculinity with the reflexes which serve to maintain gender inequality. Subjectivity is the other, indispensable part of the picture. This is where the problems of conceptualization and analysis are most acute. For all the gaps and speculations in my discussion of masculinity and patriarchy, the issues I raised were at least issues of social and intellectual history, to be addressed by well-tried research methods. Masculinity as subjective identity, on the other hand, has received far less attention and raises much greater scepticism in the profession. The quicksand of psychoanalytic theory, combined with serious technical problems of sources and sampling, has undoubtedly been a deterrent to historians in Britain, where these matters have tended to be left to cultural studies.

This is not the place to enter a discussion of the subtleties of competing interpretations within the psychoanalytic tradition – for which I am anyway not qualified – but I do want to stress the key psycho-dynamics of masculinity which feature in most variants of the tradition. All gender identities are unstable and conflictual because the growing infant has to negotiate a path through a dual identification – with both parents (or their surrogates) – and because so much of his/her adult identity is formed in this way (rather than through biological endowment, or cultural influences). The outcome of this process of growth is that men have feminine bits of themselves (just as women have masculine bits). Peer-group pressure among men in the public arena requires them to disown their feminine side, in the process setting very rigid boundaries for the self. And the unacknowledged feminine within is disposed of by being projected onto other categories of men, often with socially repressive results, as in the case of homosexuals. Men's conflict with the feminine within is sometimes treated as a psychic universal, with the kind of baleful consequences that make it hard to have any optimism about a more equitable gender order in the future. To the extent that all boys have to go through a separation from infant identification with the mother which can never be fully accomplished, there is a universal pattern here. But what this perspective loses sight of is that cultures vary immensely in how much significance they accord to mothering, how far they permit men to express feminine qualities, and how far they insist that masculinity should, so to speak, be all of a piece. These questions are the realm of the historian *par excellence*.[57]

We are a long way from approaching these questions in a systematic way. But I would like to discuss two contrasted contexts where the benefits of a psychically informed approach are beginning to come into view. The first takes me back to the subject of manliness with which I began. Here we have a code of masculinity which demands to be treated as a *public* code – a guide to masculine performance in the public sphere. The mistake is to regard such codes as pertaining to the public sphere alone. We need to ask the question, who taught young men about manliness? – and to go further than the more obvious answers. There has been much emphasis on the public schools.[58] But what is often forgotten is that the public school-boy was not a *tabula rasa* at thirteen; he was someone whose formative years had been spent in an upper- or middle-class home, and who continued to spend considerable stretches of each year there. His first and most enduring instructors in manliness were his parents.

A good deal turns on which parent took the lead. And here the vital context is the relatively recent elevation of the mother's role. Whereas in the eighteenth century mothers had been thought of as too indulgent to be trusted with their sons for long, by the 1830s moral motherhood was well into its stride, at least in middle-class circles. Wives were increasingly seen as morally superior to their husbands and as the conscience of the home.[59] Their role as guide and teacher of the young, especially boys, was accordingly extended. Fathers might continue to engage in 'serious talk' with their sons on the quandaries of adult life, but mothers, particularly those married to remote aristocratic husbands or to over-worked middle-class ones, now had control over a large area of moral education, and it is clear that this included 'manliness'. Mary Benson was married to a bishop who regarded himself as an expert on the subject (having been a public-school headmaster for thirteen years); but it was she who urged on their twelve-year old son in 1879 with these words: 'I want you to be manly and all that we have ever talked of tends to this. . . . Stir yourself up then, my boy, and be a man.'[60]

Middle-class males in late Victorian Britain thus tended to face a difficult transition to an adult masculine identity. Not only did they have to deal with an infant separation trauma enhanced by a pronounced emphasis on maternal nurture; they also had the unsettling awareness that what they knew of manliness had, to some degree at least, been filtered through a feminine sensibility. Their own code of manliness was accordingly more brittle and less tolerant of the 'feminine' within. Thus, whereas young men earlier in the century were often able to express intense feelings in public – in tears, hugs and so forth – this became increasingly rare in their sons and grandsons. The dominant code of manliness in the 1890s, so hostile to emotional expression and so intolerant of both androgyny and homosexuality, can be interpreted as a by-product of a raised imperial consciousness – especially with regard to the imperial frontier and the manly qualities required there.[61] But this is to see manliness as rooted only in the public sphere. I am suggesting that its late nineteenth-century version was also the outward symptom of a need to repress the feminine within – a psychic universal maybe, but one which had been greatly exacerbated by the distinctive domestic regime of the middle and upper classes over the previous generation or so. Psychic and social were inextricably intertwined in this, as in so many other aspects of gender.

My second example takes us beyond the world of home and school and considers some of the wide-ranging implications of projection. I say 'wide-ranging' because it is this aspect which best explains why gender identities rooted in intimate experience spill over into social consciousness and sometimes political action. Any identity, and especially an insecure one, is partly constructed in juxtaposition to a demonized 'other' – an imagined identity composed of all the relevant negatives, and pinned onto its nearest approximation in the real world. This aspect of masculine identity is now best recognized in historical studies of culture conflict and colonialism, and the explanation is straightforward enough. Confronted by forms of racism which strike us in retrospect as bizarre in the extreme, we are more likely to take seriously a framework of explanation which moves beyond instrumental rationality. For it is clear that the deep investment of British society in empire arose not just from profit and career but from compelling fantasies of mastery. And these appealed not only to colonial whites who had face-to-face contact with other races, but to men in Britain who had never travelled beyond Europe. Thomas de Quincey's violent racial fantasies (as analysed by John Barrell) are a telling instance of this, and on a broader canvas Catherine Hall's current work (though less psychoanalytic) is intended to show how English national identities were constructed through powerful notions of sexual and racial difference.[62] The production of images of Africa, India or the Caribbean shifted the meanings attached to being white and male (and female too).

The psychic structure of colonial discourse was certainly not uniform. On one level, it was about idealized masculinities like those of the so-called 'martial races' – embodying desirable qualities which had been 'lost' or marginalized by the British and might now be repossessed through imperial control – a theme which runs through Baden-Powell's *Scouting for Boys* (1908) and was to account for much of T.E. Lawrence's popular appeal.[63] Alternatively colonial subjects were viewed as children – a popular fantasy with paternalistic officials and missionaries, despite the long-term implications of equality and displacement. But most powerful of all was the projection of femininity, because this combined disparagement and desire in a heady mixture. What white men thought they recognized in the Other reflected both the compulsion to disown their own feminine and their attraction to those same feminine qualities. Sometimes the feminine was ascribed to whole regions, as in the allure of the Dark Continent awaiting penetration and mastery. More often it was attached to colonized men specifically. Colonial discourse was full of the effeminate and devious Bengali, or the docile and affectionate slave in the West Indies. Sexual expression was more relaxed overseas, the work ethic often non-existent. Local life-styles which for the Englishman in the tropics were the road to a ruined career could appeal as unrestrained fantasy back home, one moment speaking to hidden desires, and the next moment informing violently punitive impulses.[64]

This is the point at which to re-introduce masculinity as cultural representation. For the power of these images of the Other to shape masculine identities in Britain itself (as distinct from the colonies) depended on their presence in visual and literary culture. By 'culture' here I don't of course mean the explicit and self-conscious culture of manliness, but rather the contingent and contradictory meanings inscribed in the culture at large, where gendered distinctions abound in popular forms, ranging from missionary magazines through travel writing and adventure fiction to popular ballad and music hall. Here one certainly finds the portrayal of imperial paragons and heroes, like Henty's boy adventurers or the figure of Allen

Quartermain. But I suspect that the strongest hold was exercised by the evocation of the Other, especially the negative racial stereotypes I've just mentioned. The artisan, the clerk and the shop-worker were invited to participate in imperial fantasies of mastery and thereby find new ways of expressing (and perhaps containing) the tensions in their own gender identity.[65] The popular assumption of superiority over other races in the empire operated at a much deeper level than a complacent comparison of material circumstances. It follows that the questions we have to ask about the quickening of imperial consciousness in late Victorian Britain include not only how it was affected by changes in the social underpinnings of masculinity at home, but what changes occurred in the imagined relationship between masculinities in Britain and the empire overseas.

Masculinity as I have analysed it in this paper is both a psychic and a social identity: psychic, because it is integral to the subjectivity of every male as this takes shape in infancy and childhood; social, because masculinity is inseparable from peer recognition, which in turn depends on performance in the social sphere. It is the uneasy and complex relation between these two elements which explains masculinity's power to shape experience and action, often in ways beyond the conscious grasp of the participants. At one and the same time, men pursue practical goals of gender aggrandizement and are guided by unacknowledged fantasies designed to defend the psyche.[66] That, it seems to me, is what patriarchy means. Most patriarchal forms in history have arisen from psychic needs combined with a perception of the material advantage to be derived from power over women. Tracing the inter-connections and weighing their social impact is clearly a major task for historians. The challenge was thrown down over a decade ago by Sally Alexander and Barbara Taylor,[67] and it must be said that only very slow progress has so far been made.

The other task which I would highlight relates to my discussion of masculine hierarchies. It is certainly vital to establish that these hierarchies had a life of their own, not reducible to distinctions of class, ethnicity or religion. This is why, when we bring gender into social history, we aren't simply contextualizing people's reactions more richly – we are shifting the weight of explanation. But that makes the question of determination all the more pressing. What was the dynamic behind the fluctuating balance between work, home and association which I have identified as the key arenas of masculine recognition? What shaped the dominant or hegemonic practices of masculinity in any given society? And how should we conceive of the relation between the discursive and the social when dealing with structures of power that often remained hidden? All the resources of the cultural and social historian will surely be needed in these endeavors. The answers, I suggest, will not be the province of yet another sub-specialism, but will be central to how we as historians think about our subject.

Notes

Place of publication is London unless otherwise stated.

1 Natalie Zemon Davis, '"Women's History" in Transition: the European Case', *Feminist Studies* 3, 1976, p. 90.

2 See for example Jane Lewis, *Labour and Love: Women's Experience of Home and Family, 1850–1940*, Oxford, 1986, editor's introduction, p. 4; Gisela Bock, 'Women's History and Gender History: Aspects of an International Debate', *Gender and History* 1, 1989, p. 18.

3 Michael Roper and John Tosh (eds), *Manful Assertions: Masculinities in Britain since 1800*, 1991. For masculinity and institutional politics, see Jon Lawrence, 'Class and Gender in the Making of Urban Toryism, 1880–1914', *English Historical Review* 108, 1993, pp. 629–52.

4 William Boyd (ed. and trans.), *Émile for Today: The Émile of Jean Jacques Rousseau*, 1956, p. 132.

5 Cynthia Eagle Russett, *Sexual Science: The Victorian Construction of Womanhood*, Cambridge MA, 1989.

6 I use the term 'patriarchy' aware of the misgivings which its use has recently aroused. I make no assumptions about the biological or trans-historical character of men's power over women; nor am I concerned to identify a specifically patriarchal mode of production at a given time. I use the term descriptively to indicate those areas of life where men's power over women and children constitutes a significant form of stratification. The broader debate can still be usefully followed in the exchange between Sheila Rowbotham, Sally Alexander and Barbara Taylor, in Raphael Samuel (ed.), *People's History and Socialist Theory*, 1981. See also Michael Roper and John Tosh, 'Historians and the Politics of Masculinity', in Roper and Tosh, *Manful Assertions*, pp. 8–11.

7 Michelle Z. Rosaldo, 'Woman, Culture and Society: a Theoretical Overview', in M.Z. Rosaldo and L. Lamphere (eds), *Woman, Culture and Society*, Stanford, 1974, p. 28. For a plethora of ethnographic examples, see David D. Gilmore, *Manhood in the Making: Cultural Concepts of Masculinity*, New Haven, 1990.

8 Maxine Berg, *The Age of Manufactures, 1700–1820*, 1985, ch. 6 and 9; Bridget Hill, *Women, Work and Sexual Politics in Eighteenth-Century England*, Oxford, 1989.

9 Sonya Rose, *Limited Livelihoods: Gender and Class in Nineteenth-Century England*, 1992, p. 128.

10 Leonore Davidoff and Catherine Hall, *Family Fortunes: Men and Women of the English Middle Class, 1780–1850*, 1987, ch. 1–2.

11 A. James Hammerton, *Cruelty and Companionship: Conflict in Nineteenth-Century Married Life*, 1992, ch. 3–4.

12 J.S. Bratton, *The Victorian Popular Ballad*, 1975, pp. 184–8.

13 William Cobbett, *Advice to Young Men* (1830), 1926, p. 10.

14 Davidoff and Hall, *Family Fortunes*, pp. 229–34.

15 Keith McClelland, 'Some Thoughts on Masculinity and the "Representative Artisan" in Britain, 1850–1880', *Gender and History* 1, 1989, pp. 164–77 (reprinted in Roper and Tosh, *Manful Assertions*, pp. 74–91).

16 Paul Willis, *Learning to Labour: How Working-Class Kids Get Working-Class Jobs*, 1977, pp. 52, 148.

17 Gregory Anderson, *Victorian Clerks*, Manchester, 1976.

18 On the mill-girls, see Ivy Pinchbeck, *Women Workers and the Industrial Revolution, 1750–1850*, 1930, and Jane Rendall, *Women in an Industrializing Society, 1750–1880*, Oxford, 1990. On women office clerks, see Anderson, *Victorian Clerks*.

19 Merry E. Wiesner, 'Guilds, Male Bonding and Women's Work in Early Modern Germany', *Gender and History* 1, 1989, p. 125.

20 Mary Ann Clawson, *Constructing Brotherhood: Class, Gender and Fraternalism*, Princeton NJ, 1989; Mark C. Carnes, *Secret Ritual and Manhood in Victorian America*, New Haven, 1989.

21 Not all of these institutions were the exclusive preserve of men throughout the period: for example, women did appear in pubs and they had their own friendly

society lodges in the early nineteenth century. But by the second half of the century the exceptions to male control were relatively few. See R.J. Morris, 'Clubs, Societies and Associations', in F.M.L. Thompson (ed.), *The Cambridge Social History of Britain 1750–1950*, Cambridge, 1990, vol. 3, pp. 430–6.

22 Eve K. Sedgwick, *Between Men: English Literature and Male Homosocial Desire*, New York, 1985, ch. 1.

23 Quoted in Jeffrey Weeks, *Coming Out: Homosexual Politics in Britain From the Nineteenth Century to the Present*, 1977, p. 21.

24 Cobbett, *Advice to Young Men*, p. 170.

25 See for example, John Angell James, *The Family Monitor, or a Help to Domestic Happiness*, Birmingham, 1828, p. 22.

26 Frances Armstrong, *Dickens and the Concept of Home*, Ann Arbor, 1990, p. 155, fn. 1.

27 J.A. Froude, *The Nemesis of Faith* (1849), as quoted in Walter E. Houghton, *The Victorian Frame of Mind, 1830–1870*, New Haven, 1957, pp. 345–6.

28 [Coventry Patmore], 'The Social Position of Women', *North British Review* 14 (1851), pp. 521–2.

29 For a preliminary sketch of this interpretation, see John Tosh, 'Imperial Masculinity and The Flight From Domesticity in Britain, 1880–1914', in T. Foley *et al.*, *Gender and Colonialism*, (Galway, 1995) 72–85.

30 A. Conan Doyle, quoted in J.A. Hammerton (ed.), *Stevensoniana*, 1903, p. 243. On the appeal of adventure as a counterpoint to domesticity, see Martin Green, *Dreams of Adventure, Deeds of Empire*, New York, 1979.

31 Anna Clark, 'The Rhetoric of Chartist Domesticity: Gender, Language and Class in the 1830s and 1840s', *Journal of British Studies* 31, 1992, pp. 70–1.

32 McClelland, 'Masculinity and the "Representative Artisan".'

33 Carl Chinn, *They Worked All Their Lives*, Manchester, 1988; Ellen Ross, *Love and Toil: Motherhood in Outcast London, 1870–1918*, New York, 1993. See also Nancy Tomes, 'A "Torrent of Abuse": Crimes of Violence Between Working-Class Men and Women in London, 1840–1875', *Journal of Social History* 11, 1978, pp. 328–45. A striking account of the twentieth century is Pat Ayers and Jan Lambertz, 'Marriage Relations, Money and Domestic Violence in Working-Class Liverpool, 1919–39', in Lewis, *Labour and Love*, pp. 195–219.

34 E.g. Lynne Segal, *Slow Motion: Changing Masculinities, Changing Men*, 1990.

35 For an unusual and illuminating instance, see Pamela Walker, '"I Live But Not Yet I For Christ Liveth in Me": Men and Masculinity in the Salvation Army, 1865–90', in Roper and Tosh, *Manful Assertions*, pp. 92–112.

36 Norma Clarke, 'Strenuous Idleness: Thomas Carlyle and the Man of Letters as Hero', in Roper and Tosh, *Manful Assertions*, pp. 25–43.

37 See especially Michael Rosenthal, *The Character Factory: Baden-Powell and the Origins of the Boy Scout Movement*, 1984, ch. 3. Also Robert H. MacDonald, *Sons of the Empire: The Frontier and the Boy Scout Movement, 1890–1918*, Toronto, 1993, pp. 159–62.

38 Ross, *Love and Toil*.

39 Lyndal Roper, 'Blood and Cod-pieces', in her *Oedipus and the Devil: Witchcraft, Sexuality and Religion in Early Modern Europe*, 1994.

40 John R. Gillis, *Youth and History*, 2nd edn, New York, 1981.

41 Alan Bray, *Homosexuality in Renaissance England*, 1982, ch. 4; Rictor Norton, *Mother Clap's Molly House: Gay Subculture in England 1700–1830*, 1992, esp. ch. 3–5.

42 The notion of a distinctive construction of homosexuality in the late nineteenth century may have been overstated by recent historians following in the wake of Foucault, but a qualitative change at that time seems undeniable. The evidence is marshalled in Weeks, *Coming Out*, ch. 1–6, 10, and Weeks, *Sex, Politics and Society*, 2nd edn, 1989, ch. 6.

43 Hammerton, *Cruelty and Companionship*, pp. 65–7.

44 R.W. Connell, *Gender and Power*, Oxford, 1987, esp. pp. 183–8; Tim Carrigan, Bob Connell and John Lee, 'Toward a New Sociology of Masculinity', in Harry Brod (ed.), *The Making of Masculinities*, Boston, 1987, pp. 63–100.

45 See especially Judith Walkowitz, *City of Dreadful Delight: Narratives of Sexual Danger in Late-Victorian London*, 1992.

46 Rose, *Limited Livelihoods*; McClelland, 'Masculinity and the "Representative Artisan".'

47 These examples tend to presuppose a good income and social position. Working-class instances are more difficult to find. We need to know much more about those communities where almost all the available paid work was for women and the men performed the domestic labor. For suggestive comment on the Potteries at the turn of the century, see Margaret Hewitt, *Wives and Mothers in Victorian Industry*, 1958, p. 193.

48 Mary L. Shanley, *Feminism, Marriage and the Law in Victorian England, 1850–1895*, Princeton NJ, 1989; Sheila Jeffreys, *The Spinster and Her Enemies: Feminism and Sexuality 1880–1930*, 1985, pp. 6–26; Frank Mort, *Dangerous Sexualities: Medico-Moral Politics since 1830*, 1987, pp. 103–36.

49 Hammerton, *Cruelty and Companionship*, pp. 82–133.

50 Geoffrey Pearson, *Hooligan: A History of Respectable Fears*, 1983. More generally, see Gillis, *Youth and History*.

51 Connell, *Gender and Power*, pp. 158–63; Michael S. Kimmel, 'The Contemporary "Crisis" of Masculinity in Historical Perspective', in Brod, *Making of Masculinities*, pp. 121–53; Arthur Brittan, *Masculinity and Power*, Oxford, 1989, pp. 25–35.

52 Elaine Showalter, *Sexual Anarchy: Gender and Culture at the Fin de Siècle*, 1991, esp. pp. 9–15.

53 Richard N. Price, 'Society, Status and Jingoism: the Social Roots of Lower Middle-Class Patriotism, 1870–1900', in Geoffrey Crossick (ed.), *The Lower Middle Class in Britain*, 1977.

54 Anderson, *Victorian Clerks*, pp. 56–60; Meta Zimmeck, 'Jobs for the Girls: The Expansion of Clerical Work for Women, 1850–1914', in Angela John (ed.), *Unequal Opportunities*, 1986, pp. 153–77.

55 For the argument that a reduction of sexual opportunity for young men in late Victorian Britain increased the flow of recruits to the colonies, see Ronald Hyam, *Empire and Sexuality: The British Experience*, Manchester, 1990.

56 Chartism is a good example. See Clark, 'Rhetoric of Chartist Domesticity'.

57 A very influential account of the psychic foundations of masculinity has been Nancy Chodorow, *The Reproduction of Mothering: Psychoanalysis and the Sociology of Gender*, Berkeley, 1978. For a general survey, see Segal, *Slow Motion*, esp. ch. 4 and 5.

58 See especially David Newsome, *Godliness and Good Learning*, 1961, and J.R. de S. Honey, *Tom Brown's Universe: The Development of the Victorian Public School*, 1977.

59 Jane Rendall, *The Origins of Modern Feminism*, 1985, esp. ch. 2–3. See also Ruth Bloch, 'American Feminine Ideals in Transition: the Rise of the Moral Mother, 1785–1815', *Feminist Studies* 4, 1978, pp. 101–26.

60 Quoted in Geoffrey Palmer and Noel Lloyd, *E. F. Benson As He Was*, Luton, 1988, p. 22.

61 H. John Field, *Toward a Programme of Imperial Life: The British Empire at the Turn of the Century*, Oxford, 1982.

62 John Barrell, *The Infection of Thomas de Quincey: A Psychopathology of Imperialism*, New Haven, 1991. Catherine Hall, *White, Male and Middle Class*, Cambridge, 1992, ch. 9–10, and '"From Greenland's Icy Mountains . . . to Afric's Golden Sand": Ethnicity, Race and Nation in Mid-Nineteenth-Century England', *Gender and History* 5, 1993, pp. 212–43.

63 Graham Dawson, 'The Blond Bedouin: Lawrence of Arabia, Imperial Adventure and the Imagining of English-British Masculinity', in Roper and Tosh, *Manful Assertions*, pp. 113–44.

64 Barrell, *Infection of Thomas de Quincey*.

65 See Joseph Bristow, *Empire Boys: Adventures in a Man's World*, 1991, esp. pp. 130–46.

66 Or, as Joanna de Groot has put it, men's power 'should be understood not just as a practical function but also as a process of defining the self and others'. Joanna de Groot, '"Sex" and "Race": the Construction of Language and Image in the

Nineteenth Century', in Susan Mendus and Jane Rendall (eds), *Sexuality and Subordination*, 1989, p. 100.

67 Sally Alexander and Barbara Taylor, 'In Defence of "Patriarchy"', in Samuel (ed.), *People's History and Socialist Theory*, p. 372.

4

'Adam spoke first and named the orders of the world': masculine and feminine domains in history and sociology

LEONORE DAVIDOFF

Gender categories generate social relations which, partially at least, constitute all other social relations and activities. As a basic axis of society, gender forms the social as well as linguistic air we breathe. A focus on gender illuminates the relationship between history and sociology and confirms Philip Abrams' dictum that in some fundamental respect, the two disciplines are trying to do the same thing and are employing the same logic of explanation to do so (Abrams, 1982, p. ix).

Our world has been constructed along gender lines at every level. Our everyday language, images and expressions carry a tint of oppositional masculinity and femininity but so, too, do concepts used in scholarly analysis. How can this fundamental pattern, now haltingly and laboriously uncovered by feminist thinkers, have been hidden for so long? A simplified answer to such a complicated question must include the fact that sexual categories are built in terms of super- and sub-ordination. It is the agency given to the powerful which has written the scores within which we produce our harmonies – and even our discordancies. Gendered ideas become themselves instruments of control over resources, over people, and things and, especially, over the drawing of boundaries: between people, between things and between people and things. Those in positions of control have had no reason to look behind generalized 'given' categories, so often categories based on covert masculine identification. They have no motivation to seek out the supplementary, shadowy presences without which not only their working concepts but their whole cosmology would melt away (Scott, 1989).

Simmel long ago compared the power position between modern men and women to that of master and slave:

One of the privileges of the master [is] that he does not always need
to think about the fact that he is the master . . . there is no doubt that
the woman loses a conscious sense of her being as a female much more
rarely than holds true for the man and his being as a male.

(Oaks, 1984, p. 103)

The derivation of the word 'gender', its relation to 'gens' or orders, indicates its centrality to classification systems depending on notions of difference. Gender, therefore, operates as a fundamental organizing category, but
also at the level of social relations and the structure of personal identity
(Haraway, 1987). Given this range, it would be surprising if ideas about gender could be contained within a single disciplinary framework. On the other
hand, feminist thinkers have recently turned from striving to build a monolithic grand theory and now emphasize the historically specific. In practice,
historical research has been one of the most fruitful areas of feminist analysis (Gerson and Peiss, 1985; Stacey and Thorne, 1985).

There seem to be a number of reasons for this. As we have seen, recent
social history has rejected static categorizing; in particular it has abjured
dichotomous models in favour of greater complexity. When historians have
avoided functionalist explanations this leaves open a space to consider the
role of the powerful and challenges to that power. It is perhaps easier to
observe in the past how the living through of gender relationships is a
process of negotiation, of contradiction between thought systems and
between these systems and consequent behaviours. Like anthropologists,
historians can reflect on their own categories when seen in an unfamiliar
context. But more than anthropologists, they can then observe how these
categories have been inherited and reworked in their own society.

No matter what the discipline, from the very nature of its subject matter,
all feminist scholarship has tended to be more self conscious about the
'object of analysis', to break the subject/object dichotomy of the social,
indeed all sciences (*Signs*, 1987). Feminist thinkers have had to live with a
certain *inherent instability* in their categories (Harding, 1986). They have
had to pay particular attention to boundaries, both the permeability and the
limits of categories. In particular they have stressed the shifting definitions
of identities, seeing the individual self as constantly reconstructed in various contexts and by various relationships (de Lauretis, 1986). For example,
family, marriage, kinship, sexuality and gender are seen as mutually constructed but also understood as drawn from a range of 'cultural domains',
including the political/jural and economic (Landes, 1984). In turn these
'public spheres' cannot be understood without recognizing their grounding
in gender relations.

As if grasping these hidden interconnections were not arduous enough,
the picture is further complicated by the fact that gender categories are so
often 'embodied'. That is, they make use of putative characteristics of the

body for signification, they use a language of the body. For example, building on the older notion of a 'body politic', literate English Victorians constantly spoke of their society as Head (man), Heart (women) and Hands
(ungendered workers). Such conceptualizations carry powerful messages;
gender and power are experienced through and by the body not only in
appearance but also in stance, gait and even the physical space occupied
(Connell, 1987).

Coming to terms with the flux and variation in gender relationships has
not come easily. It has to be understood that boundaries and locations can
shift, yet a system of masculine superordination remains intact. For example, it has begun to be recognized that the shift of women into or out of
wage work has made only marginal differences to their life chances since the
structure and meaning of wage work itself is already gendered.

Unfortunately, feminists ourselves have not always followed the logic of
these insights. Understandably, most started where women were found – in
the family, kinship, questions about sexuality – in other words, what was
already defined as the private sphere. But in continuing to concentrate on
these locations, masculine privilege as unproblematic, as somehow exempt
from determination by gender, has been perpetuated (Flax, 1987). To put it
at its starkest formulation, in our concentration on making clear that
women's connection with the private, the identification of women with the
'natural', has been socially constructed, we have risked the nonsense of
allowing men to be regarded as 'naturally cultural', as 'naturally rational'
beings (Mathieu, 1978).

On the contrary, masculinity, in particular full adult masculine status,
has always been defined in relation to women (as well as in relations
between different categories of men). Far from being the ungendered norm,
a whole range of structures, ideas and individual attributes in the economic,
political, religious, moral as well as domestic domains have been gendered
territories staked out and fiercely contested, a process in which the creation
and maintenance of masculine identity has often played a central role (Morgan, 1987; Hearn, 1987). Masculinity, like femininity, comes in a variety of
contradictory forms. For example, the manliness of the early nineteenth-
century middle class embraced the man so easily moved to tears while simultaneously acting as household head and as 'fit and proper person' to hold
public office. In the words of a contemporary, a 'real manliness as consisting of all that is pure and true and strong and tender' (Davidoff and Hall,
1987, p. 110).

It is in historical examples such as these that the links between categories
of 'men' and 'women', 'masculinity' and 'femininity' and their intermesh-
ing with other categories of class, ethnicity and race will be discerned. The
effort to conceive gender as an abstract logical grid, without a notion of historical process, is doomed for the categories are only worked out during
that process. The links, even at the conceptual level, have to be considered

as emergent in social practices, gender groups 'as they are constituted and as they constitute themselves' (Connell, 1983, p. 37).

One of the most important of such constitutions was the seventeenth-century formulation which cast sexual difference as the basis of political definition, crediting a masculine capacity to active agency with political rights including rights over the persons of others (Pateman, 1989). Here it was not so much that women were omitted entirely as that they were placed at the farthest end of a continuum of sociality (Riley, 1988, p. 15). This idea of masculine potency and enactment was central to the trans-formations of the seventeenth and eighteenth centuries and forms the her-itage of both history and sociology today. Building on that heritage, even the assumed division between abstract concepts and accounts of the every-day has its roots in a gendered epistemology (Caplan, 1988; Smith, 1988; Stinchcombe, 1984).

In this chapter, in brief and schematic form, I will look first at a series of concepts related by a core of unacknowledged, gendered assumptions which came to dominate the thought and institutions of powerful literate élites in Western thought from the seventeenth to the nineteenth century. But I also call attention to alternative voices which have been almost completely silenced in our twentieth century inheritance.

The final section situates these thought patterns in the early and mid-nineteenth century, the period when sociology was being formed as a disci-pline. In bringing out the centrality of gender to this story, I shall deliberately concentrate on the moulding of masculine identities since, paradoxically, this has been the unnamed premise on which the whole saga has rested.

A number of related ideas and practices had emerged from pre-nineteenth century developments and centred in the concepts of *rationality, the indi-vidual, the market* and *property*. To each of these I will briefly turn, keep-ing in mind that such ideas and their practical implementation were embedded in a prior culture, a culture already deeply imbued with gender differentiations.

The sixteenth and seventeenth centuries had witnessed a gradual shift from the idea that good or bad fortune, white witches and wizards or evil agencies, resided in people to a realization that what befell individuals and groups might be due to environmental effects. Here is found the 'nascent statistical sense' which saw patterns in seemingly random behaviours (Thomas, 1971, p. 656).

This emerging objectivity in scientific, commercial and other bodies of knowledge claimed a universality, but as Simmel has said, in actual his-torical configurations the idea of rationality was masculine throughout (Oaks, 1984). The dichotomous categories of science and nature, of ratio-nal thought and morality/spirituality flooded the world view of literate

European élites, oppositions which were used and transformed in many contexts over the next two centuries but whose dualistic form remained.

Rational expertise as in science, medicine and the legal system gradually became the major source of intellectual authority using a statement of universal laws to draw ever further from what was seen as the ignorance of 'Old Wives Tales' (sic), while in the economic sphere, the rational calculation of income was torn away from the moral community.

The effort to maintain such dualities raised many contradictions. One of the most important was the jostling together of an idea of the feminine as both natural *and* moral in its role as 'other' to the masculine educated knower (Jordanova, 1989). The feminine became identified with all that enlightened knowledge had left behind as well as the object of scientific enquiry as in a feminized concept of 'Nature' (Brown and Jordanova, 1981). But men, too, were both a-moral operators in the economy *and* represented the highest form of morality as free citizens of the polity.

In these oppositions, adult rational masculinity withdrew from the body. And with its disembodiment went a casting off of sexuality so that by the early nineteenth century, only women were constituted as sexual beings. Indeed in Victorian parlance, women were THE SEX. As we shall see, men's sexuality was then reincarnated in a naturalized biology (Bock, 1989).

Max Weber, the greatest student of rationality, who was more insightful, if more troubled, about such matters, stated the opposition with its implied gender connotations:

> Rational ascetic alertness, self-control and methodical planning of life are threatened most by the peculiar irrationality of the sexual act which is ultimately and uniquely unsusceptible to rational organization.
> (Weber, 1968, vol. II, p. 603)

The importance of meanings assigned to the body can be followed into the political arena. The eighteenth-century tradition of civic humanism was concerned with obligations of citizens to a political community and implied the ultimate defence of that community through the ability to bear arms (Hont and Ignatieff, 1983). Such a contribution was, by deep seated custom, denied to women who were only recognized in a narrow inferior form as mothers, through the bearing of new citizens. As Carole Patemen argues, it was not the fact of physical birth which created this difference but rather that no recognition, no 'political significance', was given to this particular ability of women which men lacked (Pateman, 1988, p. 96).

The core idea associated with the drive to rationality was *the individual*, the self conceived as the source of knowledge and meaning. It was only individuals who could enter into civil and commercial contracts; it was the individual, rational and free, who represented both political and moral authority. The individual, however, had by definition to focus on *difference*; individuality was predicated on the idea of a 'dichotomous other' which carried a covert dimension of power (Luhman, 1986). Down through the nineteenth century, the 'otherness' of designated non-individuals can be traced in the construction of class and racial categories as well as gender.

Rational individuals through their free status and power of knowledge were independent of other men's will or influence. And the public domain was defined by the presence of such individuals. That domain was now firmly also where 'the economy' was placed (Appleby, 1978). It must follow that the private domain would be where the category 'women' would be found. Nevertheless, the exact equation of the public with the masculine and the private with the feminine is too simplistic. Aside from other considerations, in both ideal and practice, men were able to move between both spheres, while in fact, many women glided into the public from time to time although their legitimacy was always questioned – note the term 'public women' or 'women of the streets' for prostitutes (Stacey, 1986).

The masculinity of the individual rested on the double meaning contained in the concept of *subject*. The subject could be an initiator, the subject who acts, but that actor needed a subject upon which to act, who was subjected to his authority. It is as if a man's self-fabricated subjecthood could only be attained at the cost of another – so often a feminine other's – subjection, 'of the realization of her nature in the private realm' (Landes, 1984, p. 29). Individuality implied mastery over others conceived as objects and dependants. Thus, the two meanings of subject were fractured along gender lines from the start.

It was above all within marriage that women's subjecthood was evident, both symbolically and in action. Married women, under the doctrine of *coveture* died a kind of civil death, losing any capacity for active agency in either civil or commercial life (Pateman, 1988; Davidoff and Hall, 1987).

By the 1820s when the term 'individualism' had come into more general use, the idealized individual subject, the maker of the world, the genius and extramundane of the Romantic hero, was conceived as transcendent to particular milieu or even physical space. Framed in these terms, it was evident that he could only be masculine whether he appeared in 'ethical responsibility, civic identity, artistic representation or economic behaviour' (Heller and Wellberry, 1986, p. 1).

The core notion of independent integrity from subjection to the will of others is evident in concomitant discussions about the meaning of childhood and adult status. These discussions, too, reveal a deep unease about dealing with embodied, live human beings who are yet often treated as commodities (Jordanova, 1987). But whatever defined the individuality of the child, if a boy, time would bring full adulthood. Coleridge, significantly, claimed that the obverse of manliness was childishness (Conder, 1857). It may be of some significance that boys who spent their first five or six years wearing little skirts with leading strings tied to their shoulders were ceremonially 'breeched' into adult masculine garb when they passed out of the hands of mothers and nurses to masculine instructors while girls remained in petticoats all their years. Another group where dependence and gender were increasingly at odds was the nineteenth-century male domestic servant who displayed his master's authority in the ribbons on his shoulders and the colours of his livery. He had an image of being both sexually disruptive and effeminate; the bird in a cage (an image also applied to wives), he was derogated as 'the flunkey', opposite to the manly independent worker.

From such examples it may be seen how ideas about dependence and gender ran deep into the consciousness, the mental maps, of the articulate and powerful. It was the collection of masculine personas, the individuals inhabiting a range of domains, which made up the potential public of the community and the nation. Women, children, servants, the poor, were seen as having no community; they were mobile as they followed their natural masters.

But the relationship of gender to the concept of self was more complicated than in formulations of political theory or classical economics. Alongside the rational masculine individual, there followed a shadowy figure based on a different order of morality, an a-political, less bounded, self associated with personal emotion, parenthood and increasingly with notions of good taste. Its highest expression came to be the bodily incarnation of delicate Victorian womanhood. Exponents of classical liberalism and utilitarian thinkers alike were happy to leave the sphere of 'moral or domestic economy' to the natural order of the family or the still powerful order of religious institutions (Jaggar, 1984). Indeed it is within the radical proselytizing language of the late eighteenth-century Evangelical movement that some of the most intense and revealing contradictions about the notion of self appear. An apotheosis of selflessness in the service of God demanded constant examinations *of* the self. Men, in particular, were under great tension between the demands of masculine self-assertion and agency on the one hand and the obliteration of self in the service of Jesus Christ. Religion embraced both public and private spheres (Davidoff and Hall, 1987, Part I).

By the early nineteenth century, however, the religious domain was firmly excluded from the ideas and institutions which above all validated the rational individual, that of *the market*. Before the seventeenth century, the periodic chaos and uncontrollability, the 'fickleness', of commercial transactions had at times been associated with femininity. But as more commercial links were made the key relationship between production and consumption was removed from everyday, literal market place transactions to more abstract forces and symbolic representations. Price rates and credit began to stand in for the *personal* contact of bargain and exchange of material goods (Appleby, 1978).

There was still much suspicion about the growing 'paper screen' of credit mechanisms and a fierce antagonism to the new breed of agents, 'factors' and money men who operated the system. Nevertheless, a conception of inexorable laws, cast more like the mechanical laws of gravity – rational, immutable and masculine, only open to interpretation and manipulation by the knowing subject – developed alongside institutions such as banks, stock exchanges, corn and other commodity markets. Such laws were predicated on quantitative properties in people as well as land and moveable goods; all included a common denominator of price. The assignment of a calculable value to more and more areas of lived experience grew with the increase in the circulation of money throughout the eighteenth century. Money was becoming a currency to measure all value but what could not (or, it was thought, should not) be so measured, what did not have a price, now seemed to have no value (Appleby, 1978). The private sphere was outside the possibility of such value; that was its attraction, even its justification (Davidoff, 1990). As for the woman embedded in the domesticity coming to epitomize the private domain, her 'price was above rubies'.[1]

The discussion of the market and its relationship to morality became – as it has remained to this day – a 'matter of continuing contention' (Gray, 1987, p. 178). As Robert Gray has shown, a-moral liberal economics remained tied to a moral social organicism, echoed in the struggle to divide production and consumption, commerce and philanthropy. These sets of gendered dualisms were evident in early nineteenth-century iconography of the pitiless employer exploiting the defenceless female factory child. Here, too, were echoes of earlier representations of exploitation in the sexual seduction of the poor rural maiden by the aristocratic rake, a convention often used in political struggles (Clark, 1987).

But adult married women, too, were seen as marginal to production (although of course they actually continued to act as 'producers'). They could not make binding contracts, could not sue or be sued. They could only enter the economic circuit as consumers or in the specialized 'business' of philanthropy (Prochaska, 1980; Ryan, 1981).

A world divided between production and consumption could not have been assembled without changes in the fundamental institutions of *property*. In the seventeenth century the conception of property began to shift from a set of rights to a thing. Rights to property were now seen as 'unlimited in amount, unconditional in the performance of social functions and freely transferable' (Sugarman and Rubin, 1984, p. 27). By the eighteenth century, absolute property, originally conceived as land, extended to the growing forms of liquid capital in real estate, stock and plant, bonds and shares.

Property relations, too, were firmly based on the idea of a rational, free individual acting through contract and thus, by definition, excluding women. But women, via the family and as producers of male children, played a vital role as *conduits* of property. Despite their grave legal disabilities, they did have certain, highly circumscribed, rights as property owners.

Paradoxically, hiding behind the paper screen of credit and market mechanisms, female capital could circulate widely. However, by the nineteenth century, new forms of middle class property organization, in particular the revamping of the aristocratic trust, made certain that women's property ownership remained primarily in the form of consumption, making 'women's active generation of lasting wealth virtually impossible' (Davidoff and Hall, 1987, p. 451). Since in Britain citizenship, the inclusion in the body politic rested on an independence given by the ownership of property, these initial limitations created a built-in stumbling block to women's claims for full civil participation.

In popular mythology as well as legal conception, the single, individualistic and self-generated entrepreneur came to embody the man of property. These features became the essence of that quintessentially Victorian concept, 'Character'. His supporting network of female kin, their labour and the contribution of their property were obliterated (Davidoff and Hall, 1987, Part II).

The original formulation of a free, rational individual gave men one further vital capacity – property in their own labour and in their own skill. Indeed, this capacity highly coloured definitions of skill. Women, subordinated by personal bonds to father, brother or husband, could never alienate their labour in this way. To a certain extent they resembled paupers, those outside the labour contract. Within the growing sphere of waged labour, wages not only gave means of subsistence but were the 'true sign of exchange' between employer and workman (sic) rather than a relationship of master and servant (husband and wife) (Pateman, 1988; Davidoff, 1986a).

The father, as value creator and as supporter/protector of his dependants, became the legitimate worker entitled to a 'family wage'. These capacities were used by working class men to override the powerful derogation of manual work. The ambivalences as well as gendered overtones gathered around the concept of *work* in the Victorian period are evident in elaborate meanings ascribed to hands – their whiteness, smoothness or roughness and dirt – as visible signs of non-labour but also of femininity (Davidoff, 1983).

If we accept the premise that the individual self was based on difference, in particular sexual difference, then it follows that views of sexuality must also have changed during this period. From the limited attention paid to this question so far, it would seem that in the seventeenth century, it was recognized that both women and men had carnal appetites, but sexuality was not yet an entity divorced from other parts of life. Within this view, however, women were held to be especially sexually voracious, their appetites especially threatening (Porter, 1982). At the end of the eighteenth century an idea of 'sexuality' as a separate entity began to appear, yet 'sex expanded differently into the old fields of body and soul' for women than for men (Riley, 1988, p. 104).

By the beginning of the nineteenth century, lines of sexual identity were hardening. Femininity – at least for the literate classes – had evolved into a passionless maternity or weak sensuality, only roused by men's action. Such a view may seem to sit strangely with the positing of women as 'the sex'. The key to such an involuted construction lies in the disembodied masculinity we have been examining. Rational, individual man had become a 'Cartesian mind that happened to be located in biological matter in motion' (Harding, 1986, p. 661). Male sexuality was banished to a naturalized 'biological' realm and was often visualized as a hydraulic model or, in keeping with the dominant market metaphor, a spermatic economy of saving and spending (Barker-Benfield, 1973).

During the nineteenth century, for men, the location and timing of work processes and sexuality became more compartmentalized. Play and leisure were now the opposite of *occupation*, ergo, sexuality was equated with the frivolous, the childish, the feminine. Beauty and desire were confined to women's bodies and if promoted by men's bodies, such desire transmuted to a fascination with muscularity or romanticized physical strength.

The interplay of views about individuality, rationality and sexuality can be followed in the complicated tapestry of gendered meanings mapped out on the grid of the human body (Connell, 1987). Like the prototypical 'other', woman might not only be the tender heart to man's cool directing head, but sometimes was cast along with social outcasts such as paupers and gypsies in unsavoury nether regions below the waist (Himmelfarb, 1971).

The placing of these groups was also fixed in geographical space which took on bodily overtones. For example, there were the men-only public arenas of office and club as well as wealthy homes divided between lady's boudoir, gentleman's smoking room or study and the back passages or basements inhabited by servants (Davidoff, 1983; Davidoff, 1986b). Such subliminal imagery of hierarchy could arouse strong emotions of power and desire, repugnance and fascination, which can be sensed in the intricate social metaphors of dirt and pollution which exude from so many Victorian texts (Stallybrass and White, 1986). Beyond even this shadowy realm of symbol and image which reflected, but also sometimes fractured, the conception of rational individuality, there were echoes of other voices telling other stories or reworking elements of the dominant narrative.

The alternatives posed by Owenite socialists, including a questioning of gender patterns, have been given some attention (Taylor, 1983). But there were other, still less audible opinions from non-literate peoples among the urban poor as well as in rural areas, cultures with their own, sometimes very different, gender cosmologies (Phythian-Adams, 1980). It has been argued, for example, that working class women held a notion of self which created mutuality as a form of individuality based on interdependence, the recognition of other agents as part of one's own agency (Smith and Valenze, 1988, p. 296). But these expressions had no significance from the perspective of the authoritative centre; they have been given little historical credence or moral status.

The faintness of contesting views from the periphery alerts us to the power abrogated by the numerous 'Adams' over the years in the naming of the social world. The fictions of disembodied actors, the fable of capacity to sell labour away from the person – and the body – of the labourer, gained a currency by the third quarter of the nineteenth century which has provided the architecture of our thoughts about the social world. These ideas were inevitably carried forward by the discipline which was formulated in that period – sociology.

Nevertheless, the constructors of high theory did not succeed completely in framing the social world. A detailed examination of the varieties of masculinities in the early and mid-nineteenth century brings out some unacknowledged contradictions which historians as well as sociologists must confront.

From the 1830s, in Britain, the themes of work and sexuality were endlessly sought out, defined and debated. Some of these discussions can be read through developments in state engrossment, in the Factory Acts, and above all, in that extraordinary scheme of legislation, the New Poor Law of 1834. It was particularly here that the ideal of a male breadwinner working a fully defined day/week and the dependence of wives and children was made manifest. Respectable sexual mores, too, permeated ordinances of Workhouse administration, out-relief and the notorious Bastardy Clause.

The step towards Civil Registration of births, death and marriages in 1837, the closing off of opportunities for more loosely defined plebian marriages chronicled by John Gillis, as well as moves to control if not eradicate non-familial households through the lodging house legislation of the 1840s and 1850s reflect the way definitions of individuality filtered through the framing of family, kinship and work (Gillis, 1985; Davidoff, 1979).

By and large, these were the products of middle class men's beliefs and actions. By the late 1830s, both symbolized and reinforced by the 1832 Reform Act, a middle class conception of masculinity began to permeate large parts of British society. From the late eighteenth century middle class claims had been directed against both aristocratic status flowing from land ownership and the culture of an emergent working class. Middle class efforts instead focused on religious redemption – 'the aristocracy of the saved' – and the independence gained through ownership and manipulation of liquid capital or professional expertise.

The particular task confronting middle class men was to redefine the notion of work, with its demeaning connotations of subordination. This they vigorously accomplished within the evangelical religious dimension but also within the newly minted individuality of political economy. Gradually what middle class men did to gain a livelihood shifted from a *situation* under clientage, to an *occupation*. Occupation was, and has remained, quintessentially masculine. It called forth qualities regarded as opposite to the feminine in a conception of *Manhood* which was at the furthest remove from the dependency of women through marriage.

But, as we have seen, Manhood, in fact, vitally depended on female support. The struggle to differentiate the masculine arena from the feminized was, thus, intense and appears in many guises. It is evident in the dramatic shift in middle class men's clothing. In the eighteenth century, the ideal for male attire included ruffled shirts, lace, silks and bright colours. Close fitting stockings and knee breeches showed off shapely limbs and gave a hint of sexual display, hair was long and curled, cheeks smooth shaven. Within a generation, a radical transformation took place leading to the dark, shapeless and utilitarian trousered suit, tall hat and heavy whiskers of the 1850s in deliberate strong contrast to the bell-shaped crinolined, ringleted, colourful female image (Davidoff and Hall, 1987). Yet these changes were accompanied by a wave of pseudo-chivalric masculine fantasies of combat and honour far removed from the daily world of counting house or office (Girouard, 1981).

By mid-century, the belief in an individual as captain of his fate bit deeper into the social fabric. Some working class men had begun to repudiate notions of manhood based on physical prowess or honour and focused on control of passion, sobriety and a form of domesticity which even among radicals, cast women as sisters and wives to the artisan community rather than actors in their own right (Clark, 1987).

As Barbara Taylor has shown, the short-lived Owenite feminist effort was superseded by men eager to defend their honourable status from cheap female and juvenile labour as well as to create a standard of domestic comfort based on wives' home-making commensurate with their status in the working class community (Taylor, 1983). Gradually the notion of *competence* changed its meaning from a man's ability to earn a comfortable subsistence for self and family through the practice of an entire craft, to simply the ability lodged in an *individual's* labour (Baron, 1990). For the notion of the male breadwinner was not only imposed from above. Rather a negotiated version of middle class domesticity was adopted within large sections of the working class despite the fact that only a narrow stratum could afford to put it into practice (McClelland, 1989; Danon, 1985).

Numerous nineteenth-century struggles over control of the labour process, the ability of working men to set the price and conditions of their labour, were also regarded as fighting off attempts to degrade and insult Manhood. The all-male experience of apprenticeship had taught the boy to be a man in class terms and to be a worker in gender terms (Baron,

1990). Men engaged with tools and materials in the workplace. Long experience of work processes shaped their 'property in skill' which underlay claims to masculine exclusivity (Rule, 1987). The very products of manufacture were coloured by gender connotations, most explicitly in entirely masculine arenas such as metal working, engineering and the railway which had evolved from the closed crafts of smiths, wheelwrights and millwrights. But even in workshops or factories where both men and women were employed, men usually made large or elaborated goods, women the plain and small. Men made outer garments, women underclothing and children's wear.

By the 1880s more men were claiming a property in work, and on this basis entry into the political community, pushed forward in the awarding of the franchise to successive waves of working class men in 1867 and 1884. Their claim to citizenship was on the basis of a manhood which refused to be judged less of a man because of differences in wealth (Tholfsen, 1976). In their case, collective organization rather than thrusting entrepreneurship underpinned masculine independence so vital to this property in labour (McClelland, 1989, p. 150; Rose, 1988). The male domestic servant, that 'creature' of his master, was the last to gain full citizenship; only he had not been transformed by the labour contract which had culminated in the 1870s Employers and Workmen's Acts which had replaced that of Master and Servant.

It should come as no surprise, then, that by the later nineteenth century, the designation *working woman* has an uneasy, contradictory sound (Papanek, 1979). To many, women, by definition, were incapable of creating the same kind of value as men and thus could never be 'workers' (Scott, 1987a). Historians have begun to recognize how these formulations have affected their basic data such as the construction of census categories (Higgs, 1987). Working class women may have known that they must be at least self supporting during much of the life cycle, but they too gained from pinning at least part of that support on the breadwinning family members (Osterud, 1986). And in a labour market framed by these assumptions, the threat of the unattached working woman, the 'independent factory girl', so often seen by middle class observers as one step from the prostitute, was also a potential hazard to working men (Cockburn, 1989).

If this were the only form in which masculinity appeared in nineteenth-century society, our understanding would be relatively straightforward. But older traditions, other groups, offered a range of competing masculinities. There was, for example, also a romanticized anti-work, anti-domestic ethos centred on the public house, the race course and the prize fight. (The whole area of sport and its relationship to masculinity has hardly been recognized.) Admiration for physical prowess and sexual adventuring did not simply disappear in the face of middle class proselytizing. A myth of coalition between the aristocrat and the working class man − 'nature's gentleman' – which ridiculed the sedentary, hen-pecked middle class homebody dies hard. It was reincarnated in more democratic myths of mateship in the homosocial ambience of the Australian outback and the American West (Lake, 1986).

Even middle class men, however, with their devotion to Hearth and Home, joined in the many extra-familial all-male locations where their identities were also forged, from the West End Club to the voluntary society, from the nascent public schools to the Oxford Movement within the Anglican Church. Spaces for male bonding removed from feminine influence abounded in what by the late nineteenth century was a highly sexually segregated society. Such organizations as the Freemasons and other fraternal orders specifically claimed a brotherhood overarched by masculine hierarchy. In some cases these became a pseudo-family of brothers joined together in 'bonds of sentiment, loyalty and obligation' (Clawson, 1986, p. 689). It is significant that, once again, male domestic servants were pointedly excluded from the Freemasons.

We have followed the creation of a masculine identity, or rather identities, through a variety of settings. We have seen how these culminated in the claims – not necessarily the actual exercise – of manhood suffrage and a citizenship based on men's property in their labour, their self-defined role in the production of wealth. These rights, accruing to men, implied negative qualities in women. Just as women's dependency was sometimes portrayed as a brake on progress in the middle class, so among radical working men, women's putative ignorance and involvement in the minutiae of the domestic were seen as a drag on the politically conscious working class.

The late nineteenth-century feminist movement, for all the progress made in the quality of women's lives, was never able to come to terms with the deeply masculine concept of citizenship which set the terms for the 60-year-long struggle for women's suffrage. In the same period and with a mutual influence not often recognized, a rising militarism brought to the surface implicit, taken for granted, ideas about the relationship of gender, citizenship and its ultimate expression – war.

As a feminist theorist has pointed out, belief in the masculinity of war was created precisely by leaving that which was seen as feminine behind, by the putative capacity to rise above what femaleness symbolically represented. In this conception, men in war moved into the universal and truly ethical because they transcended 'womanhood'. Women were seen as the embodiment (sic) of the individual body, of natural feelings and private interests. They were only able to serve their nation by negation, by giving up what was most precious in the private sphere (Lloyd, 1986). Thus, in the famous recruiting poster which became an enduring image of the Great War of 1914–18, the women of England were urged to say 'GO' to their menfolk. It was only by giving the fruits of their bodies, their sons, that women could achieve a kind of patriotism, although one utterly different from that of men. It was on the basis of this exclusion from full membership in the community and its centres of wealth and power that some women opposed war, not only on some mystical attachment to the giving and preserving of life (Pierson, 1987).

This cursory survey has examined some core ideas of our Western heritage and the consequent view of masculinity deriving from them. It has briefly touched on some of the institutions in which they were embedded and by which they were modified. It has indicated alternate visions extant in our recent past and now silenced.

The concept of the rational individual and his domain, the category of public sociality, became not only an idealization of nineteenth-century society in general but the primary orientation of social scientific enquiry (Yeatman, 1984b). The fledgling discipline of sociology was moulded during the volatile decades of the early nineteenth century, coterminous with and contributing to the struggles for dominance of these concepts. The keystone of the sociological edifice, the concept of *class*, was based on the premise of a totally separate productive order. Family and kinship were taken as necessary but natural corollaries of this order and were constructed around a similar concept of the individual self (Collier and Yanagisako, 1987). Within the construct of family the category 'woman' was explicitly located just as 'man' was assumed within the economy, polity and the realms of knowledge. Sociologists (and historians influenced by them) have assumed the family as secondary and peripheral, always responsive to changes in the public sphere although some latter-day social historians have begun to argue that in special cases, lines of influence might have run the other way.

Both assumptions rest on the original gendered dualisms going back to the seventeenth century. The proliferation of 'hyphen solutions' to bind together the separate spheres such as Marxist-feminism has not proved very satisfactory. It is increasingly evident that the most valiant attempts to extend concepts of rationality or universalism to women, to embrace them in the class system, are bound to founder on the fact that, as Joan Scott reminds us, these 'languages' are already dualistic and already gendered (Scott, 1987b, p. 44).

Acknowledging the need to find a different language, to seek a variety of approaches, to admit permeable and pervasive relationships, should not be seen as failure but as the possibility of new beginnings (Flax, 1987). Here the sociologist's drive towards parsimony may have to be balanced by a nodding towards the more descriptive seamless web of the historian.

The effort to rise above the notion of the unitary individual self and give genuine recognition to the 'other', to the periphery, may break the rational mode. In the long run, however, it could provide a 'more inclusive, more democratic, less monovocal analysis which will capture the irregularities, particularities and contradictions which make up the whole of social life' (Yeatman, 1987, pp. 7–9).

Philip Abrams, echoing C. Wright-Mills, called for a sociology which would 'enable all men (sic) to become aware of historical structures and of their own place within them' (Abrams, 1982, p. 17). But such a call must be based on a genuine recognition of those whose place up to now has been in the shadows of the non-social, a designation which may lead all too easily into the darkness of the non-human.

Notes

1 Early nineteenth-century clergymen such as the Anglican, Richard Cobbol, and his City of London Independent colleague, Thomas Binney, reinterpreted these Biblical views to emphasize that modern British wives were not expected to 'labour in the vineyards'. The timing of these conceptual shifts, starting in the early seventeenth century, has often been confused with the actual separation of home and workplace, a development which became widespread only in the early nineteenth century.

References

Abrams, P. (1982), *Historical Sociology* (Shepton Mallet, Somerset, England: Open Books Publishing).

Appleby, J.O. (1978), *Economic Thought and Ideology in 17th Century England* (Princeton N.J.: Princeton University Press).

Barker-Benfield, B. (1973), 'The Spermatic Economy: A Nineteenth-Century View of Sexuality' in M. Gordon (ed.), *The American Family in Social-Historical Perspective* (New York: St Martin's Press).

Baron, A. (1990), 'An "Other" Side of Gender Antagonism at Work: Men, Boys and the Remasculinization of Work in the Printing Trade 1880–1920' in A. Baron (ed.), *Work Engendered: Towards a New Understanding of Men, Women and Work* (Ithaca, New York: Cornell University Press).

Bock, G. (1989), 'Women's History and Gender History: Aspects of an International Debate', *Gender and History*, vol. 1, no. 1, Spring.

Brown, P. and Jordanova, L. (1981), 'Oppresive Dichotomies: the Nature/Culture Debate', Cambridge Women's Studies Group, *Women in Society: Interdisciplinary Essays* (London: Virago).

Caplan, P. (1988), 'Engendering Knowledge: The Politics of Ethnography', *Anthropology Today*, vol. 14, nos. 5 & 6.

Clark, A. (1987), *Women's Silence, Men's Violence: Sexual Assault in England 1770–1840* (London: Pandora).

Clawson, M.A. (1986), 'Nineteenth-Century Women's Auxiliaries and Fraternal Orders', *Signs: Journal of Women in Culture and Society*, vol. 12, no. 1, Autumn.

Cockburn, C. (1989), 'Formations of Masculinity – Introduction', *Gender and History,* vol. 1, no. 2, Autumn.

Collier, J.F. and Yanagisako, S. (eds) (1987), 'Introduction', *Gender and Kinship: Essays Toward a Unified Analysis* (Stanford: Stanford University Press).

Conder, E. (1857), *Josiah Conder: A Memoir* (London: John Snow).

Connell, R.W. (1983), 'How Should We Theorise Patriarchy?' in R.W. Connell (ed.), *Which Way is Up? Essays on Class, Sex and Culture* (Sydney: Allen & Unwin).

Connell, R.W. (1987), *Gender and Power* (Cambridge: Polity Press).

Danon, R. (1985), *Work in the English Novel: the Myth of Vocation* (London: Croom Helm).

Davidoff, L. (1979), 'The Separation of Home and Work? Landladies and Lodgers in Nineteenth and Twentieth Century England' in S. Burman (ed.), *Fit Work For Women* (London: Croom Helm).

Davidoff, L. (1983), 'Class and Gender in Victorian England' in J. Newton *et al.* (eds), *Sex and Class in Victorian Britain* (London: Routledge).

Davidoff, L. (1986a), 'Mastered for Life: Servant and Wife in Victorian and Edwardian England' in P. Thane and A. Sutcliffe (eds), *Essays in Social History,* vol. II (Oxford: Oxford University Press).

Davidoff, L. (1986b), *The Best Circles: 'Society', Etiquette and the Season* (London: Hutchinson).

Davidoff, L. (1990), 'The Rationalization of Housework' in D. Leonard and S. Allen (eds), *Sexual Divisions Revisited* (London: Macmillan).

Davidoff, L. and Hall, C. (1987), *Family Fortunes: Men and Women of the English Middle Class, 1780–1850* (London: Hutchinson).

De Lauretis, T. (1986), *Feminist Studies/Critical Studies* (Bloomington, Indiana: Indiana University Press).

Flax, J. (1987), 'Postmodernism and Gender Relations in Feminist Theory', *Signs: Journal of Women in Culture and Society,* vol. 12, no. 4, Summer.

Gerson, S. and Peiss, K. (1985), 'Boundaries, Negotiation, Consciousness: Reconceptualising Gender Relations', *Social Problems,* vol. 32, no. 4, April.

Gillis, J. (1985). *For Better For Worse: British Marriages 1600 to the Present* (Oxford: Oxford University Press).

Girouard, M. (1981), *The Return to Camelot: Chivalry and the English Gentleman* (New Haven: Yale University Press).

Gray, R. (1987), 'The Languages of Factory Reform in Britain, c. 1830–1860' in P. Joyce (ed.), *The Historical Meaning of Work* (Cambridge: Cambridge University Press).

Haraway, D. (1987), 'Geschlecht' in W.F. Haug (ed.), *Kritisches Wörterbuch des Marxismus,* vol. I (Berlin).

Harding, S. (1986), 'The Instability of the Analytical Categories of Feminist Theory', *Signs: Journal of Women in Culture and Society,* vol. II, no. 4, Summer.

Hearn, J. (1987), *The Gender of Oppression: Men, Masculinity and the Critique of Marxism* (Brighton: Wheatsheaf).

Heller, T., Sosha, M. and Wellberry, D.E. (eds) (1986), *Restructuring Individualism: Autonomy, Individuality and the Self in Western Thought* (Stanford: Stanford University Press).

Higginbotham, E.B. (1989), 'Beyond the Sound of Silence: Afro-American Women's History', *Gender and History*, vol. I, no. 1, Spring.

Higgs, E. (1987), 'Women, Occupations and Work in the 19th Century Census', *History Workshop Journal*, no. 23, Spring.

Himmelfarb, G. (1971), 'Mayhew's Poor: A Problem of Identity', *Victorian Studies*, vol. 14, March.

Hont, I. and Ignatieff, M. (1983), *Wealth and Virtue* (Cambridge: Cambridge University Press).

Jaggar, A.M. (1984), *Feminist Politics and Human Nature* (Brighton: Wheatsheaf).

Jordanova, L. (1987), 'Conceptualizing Childhood in the 18th Century: The Problem of Child Labour', *British Journal for Eighteenth Century Studies*, vol. 10.

Jordanova, L. (1989), *Sexual Visions: Images of Gender in Science and Medicine Between the Eighteenth and Twentieth Centuries* (Hemel Hempstead, England: Harvester Wheatsheaf).

Lake, M. (1986), 'The Politics of Respectability: Identifying the Masculinist Context', *Historical Studies*, vol. 22, no. 86, April.

Landes, J. (1984), 'Women and the Public Sphere: A Modern Perspective', *Social Analysis: Journal of Cultural and Social Practice*, no. 15, August.

Lloyd, G. (1986), 'Selfhood, War and Masculinity' in C. Pateman and E. Gross (eds), *Feminist Challenges* (Sydney: Allen & Unwin).

Luhman, N. (1986), 'The Individuality of the Individual: Historical Meanings and Contemporary Problems' in T. Heller, M. Sosha and D. Wellberry (eds), *Reconstructing Individualism: Autonomy, Individuality and the Self in Western Thought* (Stanford: Stanford University Press).

Mathieu, N.C. (1978), 'Man-Culture and Woman-Nature?', *Women's Studies International Quarterly*, vol. 1, no. 1.

McClelland, D. (1989), 'Some Thoughts on Masculinity and the "Representative Artisan" in Britain 1850–1880', *Gender and History*, vol. 1, no. 2, Summer.

Morgan, D. (1987), *It Will Make A Man of You: Notes on National Service, Masculinity and Autobiography* (Manchester: Studies in Sexual Politics, University of Manchester), no. 17.

Oaks, G. (1984), *Georg Simmel: On Women, Sexuality and Love* (New Haven: Yale University Press).

Osterud, N.G. (1986), 'Gender Divisions and the Organization of Work in the Leicester Hosiery Industry' in A.V. John (ed.), *Unequal Opportunities: Women's Employment in England 1800–1918* (Oxford: Blackwell).

Papanek, H. (1979), 'Family Status Production: The Work and Non-Work of Women', *Signs: Journal of Women in Culture and Society*, vol. 4, no. 4.

Pateman, C. (1988), *The Sexual Contract* (Cambridge: Polity Press).

Pateman, C. (1989), 'The Paradox of Women's Citizenship', paper delivered at the Swedish Collegium for Advanced Study in the Social Sciences, Uppsala, Sweden, April.

Phythian-Adams, C. (1980), 'Rural Culture' in G. Mingay (ed.), *The Victorian Countryside*, vol. II (London).

Pierson, R. (1987), '"Did Your Mother Wear Army Boots?": Feminist Theory and Women's Relation to War, Peace and Revolution' in S. Macdonald *et al.*, *Images of Women in Peace and War: Cross-Cultural and Historical Perspectives* (London: Macmillan).

Porter, R. (1982), 'Mixed Feelings: The Enlightenment and Sexuality in Eighteenth Century Britain' in P.-G. Bouce (ed.), *Sexuality in Eighteenth Century Britain* (Manchester: Manchester University Press).

Prochaska, F.K. (1980), *Women and Philanthropy in 19th Century England* (Oxford: Oxford University Press).

Riley, D. (1988), *'Am I that Name?': Feminism and the Category of 'Women' in History* (London: Macmillan).

Rose, S. (1988), 'Gender Antagonism and Class Conflict: Exclusionary Tactics of Male Trade Unionists in 19th Century Britain', *Social History*, vol. 13, no. 2, May.

Rule, J. (1987), 'The Property of Skill' in P. Joyce (ed.), *The Historical Meaning of Work* (Cambridge: Cambridge University Press).

Ryan, M. (1981), *Cradle of the Middle Class: The Family in Oneida County, New York 1790–1865* (Cambridge: Cambridge University Press).

Scott, J. (1987a), '"L'ouvriere! Mot impie, sordide . . . " Women Workers in the Discourse of French Political Economy 1840–1860' in P. Joyce (ed.), *The Historical Meaning of Work* (Cambridge: Cambridge University Press).

Scott, J. (1987b), 'A Reply to Criticism', *International Labour and Working Class History*, no. 32, Fall.

Scott, J. (1989), 'Women's History' in P. Burke (ed.), *New Perspectives on Historical Writing* (Cambridge: Polity Press)

Signs: Journal of Women in Culture and Society (1987), 'Editorial Introduction', vol. 12, no. 4, Summer.

Smith, D. (1988), *The Everyday World as Problematic: A Feminist Sociology* (Milton Keynes: Open University Press).

Smith, R.L. and Valenze, D.M. (1988), 'Mutuality and Marginality: Liberal Moral Theory and Working Class Women in 19th Century England', *Signs: Journal of Women in Culture and Society*, vol. 13, no. 2, Winter.

Stacey, J. and Thorne, B. (1985), 'The Missing Feminist Revolution in Sociology', *Social Problems*, vol. 32, no. 4, April.

Stacey, M. (1986), 'Gender and Stratification: One Central Issue or Two' in

R. Crompton and M. Mann (eds), *Gender and Stratification* (Cambridge: Polity Press).

Stallybrass, P. and White, A. (1986), *The Politics and Poetics of Transgression* (Cambridge: Cambridge University Press).

Stinchcombe, A.L. (1984), 'The Origins of Sociology as a Discipline', *ACTA Sociologica*, vol. 27, no. 1.

Sugarman, D. and Rubin, G.R. (eds) (1984), 'Introduction', *Law, Economy and Society: Essays in the History of English Law* (London: Professional Books).

Taylor, B. (1983), *Eve and the New Jerusalem. Socialism and Feminism in the 19th Century* (London: Virago).

Tholfsen, T.R. (1976), *Working Class Radicalism in Mid-Victorian England* (London: Croom Helm).

Thomas, K. (1971), *Religion and the Decline of Magic* (London and New York).

Weber, M. (1968), 'Religious Ethics and the World: Sexuality and Art' in G. Roth and C. Wittich (eds), *Economy and Society*, vol. II (Berkeley and Los Angeles).

Yeatman, A. (1984a), 'Introduction', 'Gender and Social Life', Special Issue, *Social Analysis: Journal of Cultural and Social Practice*, Number 15, August.

Yeatman, A. (1984b), 'Gender Differentiation of Social Life in Public and Domestic Domains', *Social Analysis: Journal of Cultural and Social Practice*, Number 15, August.

Yeatman, A. (1987), 'A Feminist Theory of Social Differentiation', paper presented at the American Sociological Association Conference, August.

THE BODY AND
SEXUALITY

Introduction

Conceptions about the different bodies, reproductive roles, and sexual pleasure accorded to each sex are fundamental to any understanding of gender. Modern thinking on this subject owes much to the work of Michel Foucault, who, in his three-volume *History of Sexuality*, argued that sexual desire is historically constructed, and pointed to the nineteenth century as an important period for the creation of discourses around sex which served to police it.[1] Deviant sexuality, notably homosexuality, was the first aspect of this subject studied by gender historians. Work on this topic, notably by Randolph Trumbach, the author of the third article reproduced below, showed that male homosexual behaviour, and attitudes towards it, have changed considerably since the seventeenth century, and Trumbach argued that such changes were the product of broader transformations in gender roles. His theory that it was the eighteenth century which first witnessed the formation of a distinct homosexual identity has been disputed by historians who argue that it was only created by medical and social theorists at the end of the nineteenth century, but it is clear that the 'molly house' culture of early eighteenth-century London *did* represent a distinctive break with seventeenth-century manifestations of homo-eroticism.[2] Trumbach's arguments concerning the wider context of this change have also been challenged. His attempt to link this change with the growth of gender equality as manifested in the growth of companionate marriage in this period has fallen foul of recent revisionist work which emphasizes continuities in the history of the family; others have argued that he overstates the role sexual identity played in eighteenth-century conceptions of masculinity.[3] Work on other sexual orientations from a gendered perspective is at a less advanced stage. Towards the end of his article Trumbach points to the fact that a parallel change did not occur in the history of lesbianism at this time; work by him and others has shown that female homosexuality has a different history because it was perceived to be less threatening to dominant conceptions of both femininity and masculinity.[4] With some notable exceptions, still less work has been done on heterosexuality.[5]

More recently, attention has shifted from sexuality to the body itself as a marker of gender difference. The ideas of Thomas Laqueur, first published in the article reproduced below and subsequently developed in his book *Making Sex: Body and Gender from the Greeks to Freud* (1990), have been enormously influential. Just as it has been argued that gender differences construct sexual desire, so Laqueur argued that they shaped medical conceptions of the difference between male and female bodies and their roles in the reproductive process. He argued that a fundamental alteration in those medical understandings, from a paradigm of the 'one sex' body to the 'two sex' body, took place in the late eighteenth century as a result, not of scientific 'discoveries', but of the 'political, economic, and cultural transformations' of the period which promoted theories of gender difference. The idea that science and medicine were acutely gendered has been supported by work on scientific language and representations, notably that by Ludmilla Jordanova, but Laqueur's clear argument of changing paradigms has had unusually wide impact.[6] It has, however, provoked a number of critical responses, which we can only briefly summarize here. It is argued that the transformation that Laqueur documents started earlier, in the sixteenth century, and lasted for a longer period than he suggests; that neither the 'one sex' nor the 'two sex' model was dominant to the exclusion of other theories in their respective periods; that the cultural change which occurred in the eighteenth century was not so much an exacerbation of gender difference as a change in the ideas which justified that difference; that his arguments are based on a study of elite, male, medical discourse and it is not explained how these ideas reached a wider audience; that his explanation for why this change occurred is too limited, and more attention should be paid to other cultural developments, including the changing understandings of gender roles embodied in the growth of domestic ideology; that Laqueur only examines female bodies to the exclusion of the male, which remains an unexamined norm; and, as Lyndal Roper argues in the second article in this section, that Laqueur denies entirely the actual physicality of male and female bodies.[7]

Most of these points seek only to qualify or develop Laqueur's argument, rather than undermine it, a sign of just how important and influential his work has been. Roper's critique, however, is more fundamental. Challenging the basic assumption of Laqueur and other gender historians that sexual difference can be understood at a purely discursive or social level, Roper seeks to reintroduce the corporeality of men's and women's bodies, and their psychic experiences, into the analysis. Like most arguments deriving from a psychoanalytic perspective, however, it is not yet clear how historians can actually do this, given the limitations both of our understanding of how the unconscious works and of available evidence which sheds light on these problems. The excerpt reprinted here constitutes most of the introduction to her book *Oedipus and the Devil*, a collection of case studies on sexuality, magic, witchcraft and religion in early modern Germany, in which she developed her arguments. Roper herself recognizes that this approach is still in its infancy, and 'the book represents a journey, not an arrival'.[8] None the less, the challenge she poses to gender historians – for whom the problem of how to conceptualize anatomical difference is ever-present – is crucial.

Notes

1 Michel Foucault, *The History of Sexuality* (3 vols: English translation, Harmondsworth, 1979–86).
2 Ibid.; Jeffery Weeks, *Sex, Politics and Society: The Regulation of Sexuality since 1800* (2nd edn, London, 1989); John C. Fout, *Forbidden History: The State, Society and the Regulation of Sexuality in Modern Europe* (Chicago and London, 1992). For the period before 1700, see Alan Bray, *Homosexuality in Renaissance England* (London, 1982) and his 'Homosexuality and the Signs of Male Friendship in Elizabethan England', *History Workshop Journal* 29 (1990).
3 Robert B. Shoemaker, *Gender in English Society, 1650–1850: The Emergence of Separate Spheres?* (London, 1998), pp. 101–13; Philip Carter, 'Men about Town: Representations of Foppery and Masculinity in Early Eighteenth-Century Urban Society'

in H. Barker and E. Chalus (eds), *Gender in Eighteenth-Century England* (London, 1997).

4 See R. Trumbach, 'London's Sapphists: From Three Sexes to Four Genders in the Making of Modern Culture' in J. Epstein and K. Straub (eds), *Body Guards: The Cultural Politics of Gender Ambiguity* (London, 1991); Judith Brown, *Immodest Acts: The Life of a Lesbian Nun in Renaissance Italy* (Oxford, 1986); T. Castle, *The Apparitional Lesbian: Female Homosexuality and Modern Culture* (New York, 1993); E. Donaghue, *Passions Between Women: British Lesbian Culture 1688–1801* (London, 1993); L. Faderman, *Surpassing the Love of Men* (London, 1981).

5 Tim Hitchcock, 'Redefining Sex in Eighteenth-Century England', *History Workshop Journal* 41 (1996), pp. 72–90; Lesley A. Hall, *Hidden Anxieties: Male Sexuality, 1900–1950* (Cambridge, 1991); Robert A. Nye, *Masculinity and Male Codes of Honor in Modern France* (Oxford, 1993), chs 3–6; Carol Smart, 'Disruptive Bodies and Unruly Sex: The Regulation of Reproduction and Sexuality in the Nineteenth Century' in Carol Smart (ed.), *Regulating Womanhood: Historical Essays on Marriage, Motherhood and Sexuality* (London, 1992), pp. 7–32.

6 Ludmilla Jordanova, *Sexual Visions: Images of Gender in Science and Medicine between the Eighteenth and Twentieth Centuries* (Hemel Hempstead, 1989).

7 Katherine Park and Robert A. Nye, 'Destiny is Anatomy', *The New Republic*, 18 February 1991; Tim Hitchcock, *English Sexualities, 1700–1800* (Basingstoke and London, 1997), pp. 45–9; Robert Martensen, 'The Transformation of Eve: Women's Bodies, Medicine and Culture in Early Modern England', in Roy Porter and M. Teich (eds), *Sexual Knowledge, Sexual Science: The History of Attitudes to Sexuality* (Cambridge, 1994), pp. 107–33; Anthony Fletcher, *Gender, Sex and Subordination in England, 1500–1800* (New Haven, CT, and London, 1995), ch. 2.

8 Lyndal Roper, *Oedipus and the Devil: Witchcraft, Sexuality and Religion in Early Modern Europe* (London, 1994), p. 27.

5

Orgasm, generation, and the politics of reproductive biology

THOMAS LAQUEUR

Sometime in the late eighteenth century human sexual nature changed, to paraphrase Virginia Woolf. This essay gives an account of the radical eighteenth-century reconstitution of female, and more generally human, sexuality in relation to the equally radical Enlightenment political reconstitution of 'Man' – the universalistic claim, stated with starkest clarity by Condorcet, that the 'rights of men result simply from the fact that they are sentient beings, capable of acquiring moral ideas and of reasoning concerning these ideas. [And that] women, having these same qualities, must necessarily possess equal rights.'[1]

Condorcet moves immediately to biology and specifically to reproductive biology. Exposure to pregnancy, he says, is no more relevant to women's political rights than is male susceptibility to gout. But of course the facts or supposed facts of female physiology were central to Condorcet, to Mill, to feminists as well as antifeminists, to liberalism in its various forms and also to its enemies. Even the political pornography of Sade is grounded in a theory of generation. The body generally, but especially the female body in its reproductive capacity and in distinction from that of the male, came to occupy a critical place in a whole range of political discourses. It is the connection between politics and a new disposition of male and female that concerns me here.[2]

Near the end of the century of Enlightenment, medical science and those who relied upon it ceased to regard the female orgasm as relevant to generation. Conception, it was held, could take place secretly, with no tell-tale shivers or signs of arousal. For women the ancient wisdom that 'apart from pleasure nothing in mortal kind comes into existence' was uprooted. We ceased to regard ourselves as beings 'compacted in blood, of the seed of man, and the pleasure that [comes] with sleep.' We no longer linked the loci of pleasure with the mysterious infusing of life into matter. Routine accounts, like that in a popular Renaissance midwifery text of the clitoris as that organ 'which makes women lustful and take delight in copulation,' without which they 'would have no desire, nor delight, nor would they ever conceive,' came to be regarded as controversial if not manifestly stupid.[3]

Sexual orgasm moved to the periphery of human physiology. Previously a deeply embedded sign of the generative process – whose existence was no more open to debate than was the warm, pleasurable glow that usually accompanies a good meal – orgasm became simply a feeling, albeit an enormously charged one, whose existence was a matter for empirical inquiry or armchair philosophizing. Jacques Lacan's provocative characterization of female orgasm, 'la jouissance, ce qui ne sert a rien,' is a distinctly modern possibility.[4]

The new conceptualization of the female orgasm, however, was but one formulation of a more radical eighteenth-century reinterpretation of the female body in relation to that of the male. For several thousand years it had been a commonplace that women have the same genitals as men, except that, as Nemesius, bishop of Emesa in the sixth century, put it: 'Theirs are inside the body and not outside it.' Galen, who in the second century A.D. developed the most powerful and resilient model of the homologous nature of male and female reproductive organs, could already cite the anatomist Herophilus (third century B.C.) in support of his claim that a woman has testes with accompanying seminal ducts very much like the man's, one on each side of the uterus, the only difference being that the male's are contained in the scrotum and the female's are not.[5]

For two millennia the organ that by the early nineteenth century had become virtually a synecdoche for woman had no name of its own. Galen refers to it by the same word he uses for the male testes, *orchis*, allowing context to make clear with which sex he is concerned. Regnier de Graaf, whose discoveries in 1672 would eventually make the old homologies less plausible, continues to call the ovaries he is studying by their old Latin name, *testiculi*. A century later the Montpelierian physiologist Pierre Roussel, a man obsessed with the biological distinctiveness of women, notes that the two oval bodies on either side of the uterus 'are alternatively called ovaries or testicles, depending on the system which one adopts.' As late as 1819, the *London Medical Dictionary* is still somewhat muddled in its nomenclature: 'Ovaria: formerly called female testicles; but now supposed to be the receptacles of ova or the female seed.' Indeed, doggerel verse of the nineteenth century still sings of these hoary homologies after they have disappeared from learned texts:

> . . . though they of different sexes be,
> Yet on the whole they are the same as we,
> For those that have the strictest searchers been,
> Find women are but men turned outside in.

By 1800 this view, like that linking orgasm to conception, had come under devastating attack. Writers of all sorts were determined to base what they insisted were fundamental differences between male and female sexuality, and thus between man and woman, on discoverable biological distinctions. In 1803, for example, Jacques Moreau de la Sarthe, one of the founders of 'moral anthropology,' argued passionately against the nonsense written by Aristotle, Galen, and their modern followers on the subject of women in relation to men.[6] Not only are the sexes different, they are different in every conceivable respect of body and soul, in every physical and moral aspect. To the physician or the naturalist the relation of woman to man is 'a series of oppositions and contrasts.' Thus the old model, in which men and women were arrayed according to their degree of metaphysical perfection, their vital heat, along an axis whose telos was male, gave way by the late eighteenth century to a new model of difference, of biological divergence. An anatomy and physiology of incommensurability replaced a metaphysics of hierarchy in the representation of women in relation to men.[7]

But neither the demotion of female orgasm nor the biology of incommensurability of which it was a part follow simply from scientific advances. True, by the 1840s it had become clear that, at least in dogs, ovulation could occur without coition and thus presumably without orgasm. And it was immediately postulated that the human female, like the canine bitch, was a 'spontaneous ovulator,' producing an egg during the periodic heat that in women was known as the menses. But the available evidence for this half truth was at best slight and highly ambiguous. Ovulation, as one of the pioneer twentieth-century investigators in reproductive biology put it, 'is silent and occult: neither self-observation by women nor medical study through all the centuries prior to our own era taught mankind to recognize it.' Indeed until the 1930s standard medical advice books recommended that to *avoid* conception women should have intercourse during the middle of their menstrual cycles – i.e., during days twelve through sixteen, now known as the period of *maximum* fertility. Until the 1930s even the outlines of our modern understanding of the hormonal control of ovulation were unknown. Thus, while scientific advances might in principle have caused a change in the understanding of the female orgasm, in fact the reevaluation of pleasure occurred a century and a half before reproductive physiology came to its support.[8]

The shift in the interpretation of the male and female body, however, cannot have been due, even in principle, primarily to scientific progress. In the first place the 'oppositions and contrasts' between the female and the male have been self-evident since the beginning of time: the one gives birth and the other does not, to state the obvious. Set against such momentous truths, the discovery, for example, that the ovarian artery is not, as Galen would have it, the homologue of the vas deferens is of relatively minor significance. Thus, the fact that at one time male and female bodies were regarded as hierarchically, that is vertically, ordered and that at another time they came to be regarded as horizontally ordered, as opposites, as incommensurable, must depend on something other than one or even a set of real or supposed 'discoveries.'

In addition, nineteenth-century advances in developmental anatomy (germ-layer theory) pointed to the common origins of both sexes in a morphologically androgynous embryo and thus not to their intrinsic difference. Indeed the Galenic homologies were by the 1850s reproduced at the embryological level: the penis and the clitoris, the labia and the scrotum, the ovary and the testes shared common origins in fetal life. Finally, and most tellingly, no one was very interested in looking at the anatomical and concrete physiological differences between the sexes until such differences became politically important. It was not, for example, until 1797 that anyone bothered to reproduce a detailed female skeleton in an anatomy book so as to illustrate its difference from the male. Up to this time there had been one basic structure for the human body, the type of the male.[9]

Instead of being the consequence of increased scientific knowledge, new ways of interpreting the body were rather, I suggest, new ways of representing and indeed of constituting social realities. As Mary Douglas wrote, 'The human body is always treated as an image of society and . . . there can be no natural way of considering the body that does not involve at the same time a social dimension.' Serious talk about sexuality is inevitably about society. Ancient accounts of reproductive biology, still persuasive in the early eighteenth century, linked the experiential qualities of sexual delight to the social and indeed the cosmic order. Biology and human sexual experience mirrored the metaphysical reality on which, it was thought, the social order too rested. The new biology, with its search for fundamental differences between the sexes and its tortured questioning of the very existence of women's sexual pleasure, emerged at precisely the time when the foundations of the old social order were irremediably shaken, when the basis for a new order of sex and gender became a critical issue of political theory and practice.[10]

The anatomy and physiology of hierarchy

The existence of female sexual pleasure, indeed the necessity of pleasure for the successful reproduction of humankind, was an unquestioned commonplace well before the elaboration of ancient doctrines in the writings of Galen, Soranus, and the Hippocratic school. Poor Tiresias was blinded by Juno for agreeing with Jove that women enjoyed sex *more* than men. The gods, we are told in the *Timaeus*, 'contrived the love of sexual intercourse by constructing an animate creature of one kind in us men, and another in women'; only when the desire and love of the two sexes unite them are these creatures calmed. Galen's learned texts, *On the Seed* and the sections on the reproductive organs in *On the Usefulness of the Parts of the Body*, are intended not to query but rather to explain the obvious: 'why a very great pleasure is coupled with the exercise of the generative parts and a raging desire precedes their use.'[11]

Heat is of critical importance in the Galenic account. It is, to begin with, the sign of perfection, of one's place in the hierarchical great chain of being. Humans are the most perfect of animals, and men are more perfect than women by reason of their 'excess of heat.' Men and women are, in this model, not different in kind but in the configuration of their organs; the male is a hotter version of the female, or to use the teleologically more appropriate order, the female is the cooler, less perfect version of the male.[12]

Understanding the machinery of sex thus becomes essentially an exercise in topology: 'Turn outward the woman's, turn inward, so to speak, and fold double the man's, and you will find the same in both in every respect.' Galen invites his readers to practice mentally the admittedly difficult inversions.

> Think first please, of the man's [external genitalia] turned in and extending inward between the rectum and the bladder. If this should happen, the scrotum would necessarily take the place of the uterus with the testes lying outside, next to it on either side.

The penis in this exercise becomes the cervix and vagina; the prepuce becomes the female pudenda and so forth, continuing on through the various ducts and blood vessels. Or, he suggests, try it backwards:

> Think too, please, of the converse, the uterus turned outward and projecting. Would not the testes [ovaries] then necessarily be inside it? Would it not contain them like a scrotum? Would not the neck [the cervix], hitherto concealed inside the perineum but now pendant, be made into the male member?[13]

In fact, Galen argues, 'You could not find a single male part left over that had not simply changed its position.' And, in a blaze of rhetorical virtuosity, he elaborates a stunning and unsuspected simile to make all this more plausible: the reproductive organs of women are like the eyes of the mole. Like other animals' eyes, the mole's have 'vitreous and crystalline humors and the tunics that surround [them]'; yet, they do not see. Their eyes do not open, 'nor do they project but are left there imperfect.' Likewise, the womb itself is an imperfect version of what it would be were it projected outward. But like the eyes of a mole, which in turn 'remain like the eyes of other animals when these are still in the uterus,' the womb is forever as if still in the womb![14]

If the female is a replica of the male, with the same organs inside rather than outside the body, why then, one might ask, are women not men? Because they have insufficient heat to extrude the organs of reproduction and, as always for Galen, because form befits function. Nature in her wisdom has made females cooler, allowing their organs to remain inside and providing there a safe, guarded place for conception and gestation. More-over, if women were as hot as men, semen planted in the womb would shrivel and die like seed cast upon the desert; of course, the extra nutriment needed by the fetus would likewise burn off. The fact remains that women, whatever their special adaptations, are but variations of the male form, the same but lower on the scale of being and perfection.[15]

In this model, sexual excitement and the 'very great pleasure' of climax in both men and women are understood as signs of a heat sufficient to con-coct and commingle the seed, the animate matter, and create new life. Fric-tion heats the body as it would two objects rubbing together. The chafing of the penis, or even its imagined chafing in a nocturnal emission, warms the male organ and, through its connections to veins and nerves, every other part of the body. As warmth and pleasure build up and diffuse, the increas-ingly violent movement of the whole man causes the finest part of the blood to be concocted into semen, a kind of foam that finally bursts forth power-fully and uncontrollably like an epileptic seizure, to use the analogy Galen borrowed from Democritus.[16]

In women, the rubbing of the vagina and the neck of the womb performs the same function though, some writers would argue, with a somewhat dif-ferent rhythm of delight. The author of the Hippocratic treatise *The Seed* maintains, for example, that heat in women builds up more gradually, resulting in a pleasure at once more sustained and less intense than the male's. Though her orgasm occurs whether she emits before or after the man, it is most intense if it occurs at the moment the sperm and its heat touches the womb. Then, like a flame flaring when wine is sprinkled on it, the woman's heat blazes most brilliantly. The nuances of the orgasm thus represent the inner workings of the body as well as the cosmic order of per-fection. Orgasm's crescendo bears witness to the Galenic-Hippocratic two-seed model of conception in which women, contra Aristotle, actually 'seminate' at the peak of their sexual raptures. Like men, women also give forth their semen in response to imaginary friction in the heat of youth or in the quiet of the night. The limbs and back of a widow who had not been with a man for some time ache, Galen reports, from the build-up of semen until she discharges a viscous semen and feels the kind of physical pleasure she would have experienced in intercourse. Others, similarly situated, dis-charge a thinner more urine-like liquid – one presumes the secretion of the paraurethral glands.[17]

Galen elaborates metaphors linking friction, chafing, and itching with the production of the generative substance in considerable detail. Semen, in addition to being the product of genital heat, is also thought to produce spe-cific local effects. Its fluid parts constitute an acrid humor that accumulates under the skin and causes an itch that, he reminds his readers, is enormously pleasurable to relieve. Avicenna, through whose widely influential *Canon* Galen came to be known in the medieval West, elaborates this image even further: an 'itching,' a 'pruritus' in the mouth of the womb, accompanied by its inflammation or erection, are taken to be the physical signs in women of the desire for intercourse. The skin of the genital area, Galen argues, is more sensitive than other skin, the desire to scratch it more vehement, and the resulting pleasure more intense. Finally, semen as a local irritant during coition opens up and straightens the mouth of the womb, making it receptive to the male semen.[18]

Like a great steam generator, the whole body warms up to produce the seed; the sensations of intercourse and the orgasm itself indicate that everything is working as it should. But in this model sexual pleasure is not specifically genital, despite the fact that intercourse is viewed as the relieving of a localized itch and the organs of copulation as sources, through friction, of heat. Orgasm's warmth, though more vehement and exciting, is in kind no different from other warmth and can be produced in some measure by food, wine, or the power of imagination.

Ancient medicine bequeathed to the Renaissance a physiology of flux and corporeal openness, one in which blood, mother's milk, and semen were fungible fluids, products of the body's power to concoct its nutriment. Thus, not only could women turn into men, as writers from Pliny to Montaigne testified (see below), but bodily fluids could turn easily into one another. This not only explained why pregnant women, who, it was held, transformed food into nourishment for the fetus, and new mothers, who transformed the catamenial elements into milk, did not menstruate; it also accounted for the observation that obese women, who transformed the normal plethora into fat, and dancers, who used up the plethora in exercise, did not menstruate either and were thus generally infertile. Menstrual blood and menstrual bleeding were, moreover, regarded as no different than blood and bleeding generally. Thus Hippocrates views nosebleed and the onset of menstruation as equivalent signs of the resolution of fevers. A woman vomiting blood will stop if she starts to menstruate, and it is a good sign if epistaxis occurs in a woman whose courses have stopped. Similarly, bleeding in men and in women is regarded as physiologically equivalent. If melancholy appears 'after the suppression of the catamenial discharge in women,' argues Araeteus the Cappadocian, 'or the hemorrhoidal flux in men, we must stimulate the parts to throw off their accustomed evacuation.'[19]

Indeed, the menses, until one hundred years before its phantasmagoric nineteenth-century interpretations by Michelet and others, was still regarded, as it had been by Hippocrates, as but one form of bleeding by which women rid themselves of excess materials. Brazilian Indian women 'never have their flowers,' writes an eccentric seventeenth-century English compiler of ethnographic curiosities, because 'maids of twelve years old have their sides cut by their mothers, from the armpit down unto the knee . . . [and] some conjecture they prevent their monthly flux in this manner.' Albrecht von Haller, the great eighteenth-century physiologist, argues that

in puberty the plethora 'in the male, vents itself frequently through the nose
. . . but in the female the *same* plethora finds a more easy vent downward.'
Herman Boerhaave, the major medical teacher of the generation before
Haller, cites a number of cases of men who bled regularly through the hemorrhoidal arteries, the nose, or the fingers or who, if not bled prophylacti-
cally, developed the clinical signs, the tenseness of the body, of amenorrhea.
Even the enlightened Frederick the Great had himself bled before battle to
relieve tension and facilitate calm command.[20]

The fungibility of fluids thus represented in a different register the
anatomical homologies described earlier. The higher concoction of male
semen with respect to that of the female and the fact that males generally
rid themselves of nutritional excesses without frequent bleeding bore witness both to the essential homology between the economies of nutrition,
blood, and semen in men and women, and to the superior heat and greater
perfection of the male. Sexual heat was but an instance of the heat of life
itself, and orgasm in both sexes the sign of warmth sufficient to transform
one kind of bodily fluid into its reproductively potent forms and to assure a
receptive place for the product of their union. In this context, it is not difficult to see why Galen's clinical judgments on the relationship between pleasure and fertility, or between the absence of pleasure and barrenness, should
have become commonplace in both learned and popular Renaissance medical literature.

Avicenna, the eleventh-century Arab writer who served as a conduit to
the West for much ancient medicine, writes in some detail of how a woman
may not 'be pleased by' the smallness of her mate's penis 'wherefore she
does not emit sperm; and when she does not emit sperm a child is not
made.' 'Pleasure induces a hasty emission of sperm'; conversely, if women
delay in emitting 'and do not fulfill their desire . . . the result is no generation.' The midwife and physician Trotulla in the twelfth century describes
how barrenness can well be the sad consequence of too little or too much
heat, though she does not distinguish sexual heat from its more mundane
varieties. Of course, it is argued in a great body of Renaissance literature
that barrenness might well be due to anatomical defects and arguably to
witchcraft, but either a lack of passion or an excess of lust had to be considered in any differential diagnosis. In men, insufficient heat manifested by
a lack of sexual desire could be remedied by rubbing the loins with heat-
producing drugs. Still other drugs – in addition to lascivious talk, coquetry,
and the like – could cure 'defect of spirit,' the inability to have an erection
when desire was present. In women adversity and indisposition 'to the pleasures of the lawful sheets' or 'no pleasure and delight' in intercourse, along
with a slow pulse, little thirst, thin urine, scant pubic hair, and similar signs,
were almost certain indicators of insufficient heat of the testicles to concoct
the seed. As Jacob Rueff puts it in discussing the problem of cold, 'The
fruitfulness of man and wife may be hindered very much for want of desire

to be acquainted with Venus.' Conversely, too much desire (prostitutes were thought seldom to conceive); curly, dark, and plentiful hair (marks of the virago, the virile, unnaturally warm woman); a short or absent menses (the hot body burning off the excess materials that in normal women were eliminated through the monthly courses) indicated excessive heat, which will consume or shrivel up the seed.[21]

Thus, to ensure 'generation in the time of copulation,' the right amount of heat, made manifest by normal sexual pleasure and in the end by orgasm, must be produced. Talk and teasing, several books suggest, were the first resort. Women should be prepared with lascivious words, writes John Sadler, having pointed out earlier the importance of mutual orgasm; sometimes the problem is neither the womb nor other impediments in either spouse,

> except only in the manner of the act as when in the emission of the seed, the man is quicke and the woman too slow, whereby there is not a concourse of both seeds at the same instant as the rules of conception require.

He further recommends wanton behavior, 'all kinde of dalliance' and 'allurement to venery.' Then, if the man still found his mate 'to be slow, and more cold, he much cherish, embrace and tickle her.' He must

> handle her secret parts and dugs, that she may take fire and be enflamed in venery, for so at length the wombe will strive and waxe fervent with desire of casting forth its own seed, and receiving the man's seed to be mixed together therein.

The womb, as another writer notes almost a century later, 'by Injoyment Naturally receives Seed for Generation . . . as Heat [attracts] Straws or Feathers.' Be careful, warn Ambroise Pare and others, not to leave a woman too soon after her orgasm, 'lest aire strike the open womb' and cool the seeds so recently sown.[22] If all this fails, the Renaissance pharmacopoeia was full of useful drugs that worked either directly or by sympathetic magic. Pare recommends 'fomenting her secret parts with a decoction of hot herbes made with muscadine, or boiled in other good wine,' and rubbing civet or muske into the vagina. Submerge the privates in a warm sitz bath of junipers and chamomile, advises another authority. The heart of a male quail around the neck of a man and the heart of a female around the neck of a woman were said to enhance love, presumably because of the lecherous character of birds generally and perhaps of quails in particular; a concoction of ale hoof and pease straw was also indicated.[23]

In the Renaissance, as in late antiquity, an unbreakable bond between orgasm and fulfillment of the command to be fruitful and multiply linked personal experience to a greater social and cosmic order. On the one hand concupiscence and the irresistible attractions of sexual rapture stood as

marks in the flesh of mankind's fall from grace, of the essential weakness of
the will. But on the other hand pleasure was construed as precisely what compelled men and women to reproduce themselves, despite what prudence or
individual interest might dictate. The import of the *Timaeus*'s account of creation was that in both men and women brazenly *self-willed* genitals assured
the propagation of the species through their love of intercourse even if reason might urge abstinence. This notion is elaborated with an especial
poignancy for women in the popular Renaissance literature. Only 'ardent
appetite and lust' prevent the 'bitter decay in short time of mankind'; only the
fact that a mercifully short memory and an insatiable desire made women
forget the dangerous agonies of childbirth allowed the human race to continue. Women, with clinched fists 'in the great pain and intolerable anguish'
of the time of their travail, 'forswear and bind themselves never to company
with a man again.' Yet time after time, the 'singular natural delight between
men and women' causes them to forget 'both the sorrow passed and that
which is to come.' If the bearing of children was God's offer of consolation
for the loss of eternal life, the lethean pleasures of sex were a counterweight
to its pain. The biological 'invisible hand' of delight made them cooperate in
assuring the immortality of the species and the continuity of society.[24]

Male and female bodies in these Renaissance accounts were, as is perhaps
obvious, still very much those of Galen. Consider Leonardo's drawings, or
the far more influential engravings in Andreas Vesalius' epoch-marking *De
humani corporis fabrica* and his more popular *Tabulae sex*, all of which
reinforce the hoary model through striking new representations. When
Vesalius is self-consciously trying to emphasize the homologies between
male and female organs of generation (fig. 5.1) and, even more telling, when
he is not (fig. 5.2), he is firmly in the camp of the 'ancients,' however much
he might rail against the authority of Galen in other contexts. But the
anatomical accuracy of Galen is not what is at issue here. The female reproductive system can be, and indeed on occasion was still in the late nineteenth century, 'accurately' rendered in the manner of Vesalius long after the
old homologies had lost their credibility. But after the late seventeenth century and the collapse of the hierarchical model there was, in general, no
longer any reason to draw the vagina and external pudenda in the same
frame with the uterus and the ovaries. Bodies did not change, but the meanings of the relationship between their parts did.[25]

Seventeenth-century audiences still gave credence to a whole collection of
tales, going back at least to Pliny, that illustrate the structural similarities
and thus the mutability of male and female bodies. Sir Thomas Browne, in
his *Enquiries into Vulgar and Common Errors* (1646), devotes an entire
chapter to the question of whether 'every hare is both male and female.' He
concludes that 'as for the mutation of sexes, or transition of one into
another, we cannot deny it in Hares, it being observable in Man.' Some
pages later, in an exegesis of Aristotle and the schoolmen, he continues on

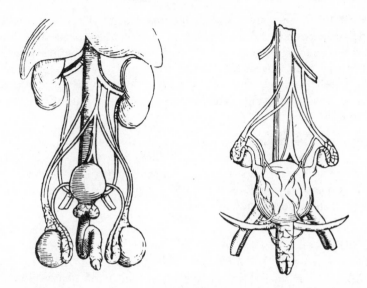

Figure 5.1 Andreas Vesalius, male and female reproductive organs, *Tabulae Sex*. From *The Anatomical Drawings of Andreas Vesalius*, ed. Charles D. O'Malley and J.B. de C.M. Saunders (New York, 1982).

Figure 5.2 Vesalius, uterus, vagina, and external pudenda from a young woman, *De humani corporis*. This illustration was not made to illustrate homologies with the male organ. From *Anatomical Drawings of Vesalius*.

this subject: 'As we must acknowledge this Androgynal condition in Man, so can we not deny the like doth happen in beasts.' Ambroise Pare, the great sixteenth-century surgeon, recounts the case of one Germain Garnier, christened Marie, who was serving in the retinue of the king. Germain was a well-built young man with a thick, red beard who until he was fifteen had lived and dressed as a girl, showing 'no mark of masculinity.' But then, in the heat of puberty,

> as he was in the fields and was rather robustly chasing his swine, which were going into a wheat field, [and] finding a ditch, he wanted to cross over it, and having leaped, at that very moment the genitalia and the male rod came to be developed in him, having ruptured the ligaments by which they had been held enclosed.

Marie, soon to be renamed, hastened home to his/her mother, who consulted physicians and surgeons, all of whom assured her that her daughter had become her son. She took him to the bishop, who called an assembly that decided that indeed a transformation had taken place. 'The shepard received a man's name: instead of Marie . . . he was called Germain, and men's clothing was given him.' (Some persisted in calling him Germain-Marie as a reminder that he had once been a girl.) Montaigne tells the same story, 'attested to by the most eminent officials of the town.' There is still, he reports, in the area 'a song commonly in the girls' mouths, in which they warn one another not to stretch their legs too wide for fear of becoming males, like Marie Germaine.'[26]

How were transformations like Marie's possible? Pare offers the following account:

> The reason why women can degenerate into men is because women have as much hidden within the body as men have exposed outside; leaving aside, only, that women don't have so much heat, nor the ability to push out what by the coldness of their temperament is held bound to the interior. Wherefore if with time, the humidity of childhood which prevented the warmth from doing its full duty being exhaled for the most part, the warmth is rendered more robust, vehement, and active, then it is not an unbelievable thing if the latter, chiefly aided by some violent movement, should be able to push out what was hidden within.

The learned Caspar Bauhin explains more succinctly how 'women have changed into men', namely, 'The heat having been rendered more vigorous, thrusts the testes outward.' Such transformations, however, seem to work only up the great chain of being.

> We therefore never find in any true story that any man ever became a woman, because Nature tends always toward what is most perfect and

not, on the contrary, to perform in such a way that what is perfect should become imperfect.[27]

Moreover, the Galenic structure survived the discovery of a new, and one would think totally incompatible, homology: that of the clitoris to the penis. This organ first was described accurately by Renaldus Colombus, Vesalius' successor in the chair at Padua, and was called in various six-teenth-century learned texts the *mentula muliebris* (female penis or woman's yard, to use the English vernacular), *columnella* (column), *crista* (cock's comb), *nympha* (the term used by Galen presumably to refer to this organ), *dulcedo amoris* or *oestrum veneris* (*taon de Venus* in French, refer-ring to a frenzy, the *oestrum* metaphorically linked to the *taon*, i.e., 'gadfly' or 'oxfly'). Jane Sharp, whose 1671 midwifery guide was last reprinted in 1728, could happily argue at one point in her work that the vagina, 'which is the passage for the yard, resembleth it turned inward,' while arguing two pages later and with no apparent embarrassment, that the clitoris is the female penis. 'It will stand and fall as the yard doth and makes women lust-ful and take delight in copulation,' thus helping to assure the conditions necessary for conception. The labia thus fit nicely into both systems of analogies. They give women great pleasure in copulation and, as the ancients said, defend the matrix from outward violence, but they are also, as John Pechey puts it, 'that wrinkled membranous production, which clothes the Clitoris like a foreskin.' This left open the question of whether the vagina or the clitoris were to be thought of as the female penis, though both could be regarded as erectile organs. One midwifery manual notes that 'the action of the clitoris is like that of the yard, which is erection' and, on the very same page, that 'the action of the neck of the womb [the vagina and cervix] is the same with that of the yard; that is to say, erection.' Thus, until the very end of the seventeenth century there seemed no difficulty in hold-ing that women had an organ homologous, through topological inversion, to the penis inside their bodies, the vagina, and another one morphologi-cally homologous to the penis, outside, the clitoris.[28]

Perhaps the continued power of the systemic, genitally unfocused account of sex inherited by Renaissance writers from antiquity – the view of the sexually excited body as a great boiler heating up to blow off steam – explains why mutually incompatible interpretations of male and female genitals caused so little consternation. Seventeenth-century writers seem to have welcomed the idea that male and female pleasure was located in essen-tially the same kind of organ. They remain undisturbed by the clitoris's sup-posed dual function – licit pleasure in heterosexual intercourse and illicit pleasure in 'tribadism.' They elaborate the penis/clitoris homology with great precision: the outward end of the clitoris, one physician writes, is like the glans of the penis, and like it 'the seat of the greatest pleasure in copu-lation in women.' According to another, the tip of the clitoris is, therefore, also called the 'amoris dulcedo.' They would have found very curious Marie Bonaparte's contention that 'clitoroidal women' suffer from one of the stages of frigidity or protohomosexuality. Rather, as Nicholas Culpepper writes without the fanfare of controversy: 'It is agreeable both to reason and authority, that the bigger the clitoris in a woman, the more lustful they are.'[29]

The ancient account of bodies and sexual pleasures was not ultimately dependent for its support simply on facts or supposed facts about the body, even though it was articulated in the concrete language of anatomy and physiology. Were it otherwise, the system of homologies would have fallen well before its time from the sheer weight of readily apparent difficulties. The recognition of the clitoris is a case in point. The word *clitoris* makes its first known English appearance in 1615 when Helkiah Crooke argues that it *differs* from the yard: '[It] is a small body, not continued at all with the bladder, but placed in the height of the lap. The clitoris hath no passage for the emission of seed; but the virile member is long and hath a passage for seed.' Yet, one can easily set beside this quite correct list of facts equally unexceptional observations supporting the contrary view. The clitoris, for example, is called the *tentigo* in Thomas Vicary's enormously popular *The Anatomie of the Body of Man* (1586), a term borrowed from the eleventh-century Arab medical writer Albucasis meaning in Latin 'a tenseness or lust; an erection.' It is, of course, erectile and erotogenous, and thus a 'counterfeit yard,' if one chooses to emphasize these features.[30]

The homological view survived not only the potential challenge posed by the anatomist Colombus's discovery of the clitoris, but other expressions of scepticism as well. Crooke, in the text cited above, attacks the Galenic homologies in general, pointing out that the scrotum of a man is thin-skinned while the base of the womb, its homologue, is 'a very thicke and tight membrane.' Again, this is scarcely a telling point when compared with the self-evident fact that the womb carries a baby while the penis does not. Moreover, the topological inversions suggested by Galen are, and were known to be, manifestly implausible if taken literally. Recall the mind-bending metaphor of the womb as a penis inside itself, like the eyes of a mole, or perfectly formed but hidden within, like the eyes of other animals *in utero*. Jacques Duval, another seventeenth-century physician, proposes trying Galen's 'thought experiment' and concludes quite rightly that it does not work: 'If you imagine the vulva completely turned inside out . . . you will have to envisage a large-mouth bottle hanging from a women, a bottle whose mouth rather than base would be attached to the body and which would bear no resemblance to what you had set out to imagine.' But in fact, a bottle shaped like the vagina and womb hanging by its mouth does resemble a penis; indeed it is the precise form of the codpiece.[31]

The fact that criticisms of the Galenic model are not only self-evident but were also sprinkled throughout the literature is a reminder that the cultural construction of the female in relation to the male, while expressed in terms of the body's concrete realities, was more deeply grounded in assumptions about the nature of politics and society. It was the abandonment of these assumptions in the Enlightenment that made the hierarchically ordered system of homologies hopelessly inappropriate. The new biology, with its search for fundamental differences between the sexes and between their desires, emerged at precisely the time when the foundations of the old social order were irremediably shaken. Indeed, as Havelock Ellis discovered, 'It seems to have been reserved for the nineteenth century to state that women are apt to be congenitally incapable of experiencing complete sexual satisfaction and are peculiarly liable to sexual anaesthesia.' But what happened to the old biology, to its complex of metaphors and relations? In some respects nothing happened to it; or, in any case, nothing happened very fast.[32]

Politics and the biology of sexual difference

When in the 1740s the young Princess Maria Theresa was worried because she did not immediately become pregnant after her marriage to the future Hapsburg emperor, she asked her physician what she ought to do. He is said to have replied:

> Ceterum censeo vulvam Sanctissimae Majestatis ante coitum esse titillandum [Moreover I think the vulva of Her Most Holy Majesty is to be titillated before intercourse].

The advice seems to have worked as she bore more than a dozen children. Similarly, Albrecht von Haller, one of the giants of eighteenth-century biological science, still postulated an erection of both the external and the internal female reproductive organs during intercourse and regarded women's orgasm as a sign that the ovum has been ejaculated from the ovary. Although he is well aware of the existence of the sperm and the egg and of their respective origins in the testes and ovaries, and has no interest in the Galenic homologies, the sexually aroused female in his account bears a remarkable resemblance to the male under similar circimstances.

> When a woman, invited either by moral love, or a lustful desire of pleasure, admits the embraces of the male, it excites a convulsive constriction and attrition of the very sensible and tender parts; which lie within the contiguity of the external opening of the vagina, after the same manner as we observed before of the male.

The clitoris grows erect, the nymphae swell, venous blood flow is constricted, and the whole external genitalia become turgid as the system works 'to raise the pleasure to the highest pitch.' A small quantity of lubricating mucous is expelled in this process, but the same action which, by increasing the heights of pleasure, causes a greater conflux of blood to the whole genital system of the female, occasions a much more important alteration in the interior parts.

The uterus becomes turgid with inflowing blood; likewise the fallopian tubes become erect 'so as to apply the ruffle or fingered opening of the tube to the ovary.' Then, at the moment of mutual orgasm, the 'hot male semen' acting on this already excited system causes the extremity of the tube to reach still further until, 'surrounding and compressing the ovarium in fervent congress, [it] presses out and swallows a mature ovum.' The extrusion of the egg, Haller points out finally to his learned readers, who would probably have read this torrid account in the original Latin,

> is not performed without great pleasure to the mother, nor without an exquisite unrelatable sensation of the internal parts of the tube, threatening a swoon or fainting fit to the future mother.[33]

The problem with which this essay began thus remains. Neither advances in reproductive biology nor anatomical discoveries seem sufficient to explain the dramatic revaluation of the female orgasm that occurred in the late eighteenth century and the even more dramatic reinterpretation of the female body in relation to that of the male. Rather, a new model of incommensurability triumphed over the old hierarchical model in the wake of new political agendas. Writers from the eighteenth century onward sought in the facts of biology a justification for cultural and political differences between the sexes that were crucial to the articulation of both feminist and antifeminist arguments. Political theorists beginning with Hobbes had argued that there is no basis in nature for any specific sort of authority – of a king over his people, of slaveholder over slave, nor, it followed, of man over woman. There seemed no reason why the universalistic claims made for human liberty and equality during the Enlightenment should exclude half of humanity. And, of course, revolution, the argument made in blood that mankind in all its social and cultural relations could be remade, engendered both a new feminism and a new fear of women. But feminism itself, and indeed the more general claims made by and for women to public life – to write, to vote, to legislate, to influence, to reform – was also predicated on difference.

Thus, women's bodies in their corporeal, scientifically accessible concreteness, in the very nature of their bones, nerves, and, most important, reproductive organs came to bear an enormous new weight of cultural meaning in the Enlightenment. Arguments about the very existence of female sexual passion, about women's special capacity to control what desires they did have, and about their moral nature generally were all part of a new enterprise seeking to discover the anatomical and physiological characteristics that distinguished men from women. As the natural body itself became the gold standard of social discourse, the bodies of women became the battleground for redefining the most ancient, the most intimate, the most fundamental of human relations: that of woman to man.

It is relatively easy to make this case in the context of explicit resistance to the political, economic, or social claims of women. Prominent male leaders in the French Revolution, for example, strenuously opposed increased female participation in public life on the grounds that women's physical nature, radically distinguished from that of men and represented most powerfully in the organs of reproduction, made them unfit for public life and better suited to the private sphere. Susanna Barrows maintains that fears born of the Paris Commune and of the new political possibilities opened up by the Third Republic generated an extraordinarily elaborate physical anthropology of sexual difference to justify resistance to change. In the British context the rise of the women's suffrage movement in the 1870s elicited a similar response. Tocqueville argues that in the United States democracy had destroyed the old basis for patriarchal authority and that consequently it was necessary to trace anew and with great precision 'two clearly distinct lines of action for the two sexes.' In short, wherever boundaries were threatened arguments for fundamental sexual differences were shoved into the breach.[34]

But reinterpretations of the body were more than simply ways of reestablishing hierarchy in an age when its metaphysical foundations were being rapidly effaced. Liberalism postulates a body that, if not sexless, is nevertheless undifferentiated in its desires, interests, or capacity to reason. In striking contrast to the old teleology of the body as male, liberal theory begins with a neuter body, sexed but without gender, and of no consequence to cultural discourse. The body is regarded simply as the bearer of the rational subject, which itself constitutes the person. The problem for this theory then is how to derive the real world of male dominion of women, of sexual passion and jealousy, of the sexual division of labor and cultural practices generally from an original state of genderless bodies. The dilemma, at least for theorists interested in the subordination of women, is resolved by grounding the social and cultural differentiation of the sexes in a biology of incommensurability that liberal theory itself helped bring into being. A novel construal of nature comes to serve as the foundation of otherwise indefensible social practices.

For women, of course, the problem is even more pressing. The neuter language of liberalism leaves them, as Jean Elshtain recently argues, without their own voice. But more generally the claim of equality of rights based on an essential identity of the male and female, body and spirit, robs women both of the reality of their social experience and of the ground on which to take political and cultural stands. If women are indeed simply a version of men, as the old model would have had it, then what justifies women writing, or acting in public, or making any other claims for themselves as

women? Thus feminism, too – or at least historical versions of feminisms –
depends upon and generates a biology of incommensurability in place of
the teleologically male interpretation of bodies on the basis of which a feminist stance is impossible.[35]

Rousseau's essentially antifeminist account is perhaps the most theoreti-
cally elaborated of the liberal theories of bodies and pleasures, but it is only
one of a great many examples of how deeply a new biology is implicated in
cultural reconstruction. In the state of nature, as he imagined it in the first
part of *A Discourse on Inequality*, there is no social intercourse between the
sexes, no division of labor in the rearing of young, and, in a strict sense, no
desire. There is, of course, brute physical attraction between sexes, but it is
devoid of what he calls 'moral love,' which 'shapes this desire and fixes it
exclusively on one particular object, or at least gives the desire for this chosen object a greater degree of energy.' In this world of innocence there is no
jealousy or rivalry, no marriage, no taste for this or that woman; to men in
the state of nature 'every woman is good.' Rousseau is remarkably concrete
in specifying the reproductive physiology of women that must, in his view,
underlie this condition. Hobbes, he argues, erred in using the struggle of
male animals for access to females as evidence for the natural combativeness
of the primitive human state. True, he concedes, there is bitter competition
among beasts for the opportunity to mate, but this is because for much of
the year females refuse the male advance. Suppose they were to make themselves available only two months out of every twelve: 'It is as if the population of females had been reduced by five-sixth.' But women, he points out,
have no such periods of abstinence and are thus not in short supply:

> No-one had ever observed, even among savages, females having like
> those of other species fixed periods of heat and exclusion. Moreover,
> among several of such animals, the whole species goes in heat at the
> same time, so that there comes a terrible moment of universal passion,
> a moment that does not occur in the human species, where love is
> never seasonal.

Reproductive physiology and the nature of the menstrual cycle bear an
enormous weight here; the state of nature is in large measure conceptualized as dependent on the supposed biological differences between women
and beasts.[36]

But what happened to this primitive state of desire? Rousseau gives an
account of the geographical spread of the human race, of the rise of the
division of labor, of how in developing a dominion over animals man
'asserted the priority of his species, and so prepared himself from afar to
claim priority for himself as an individual.' But the individuation of desire,
the creation of what he calls the moral part of love ('an artificial sentiment'), and the birth of imagination ('which causes such havoc amongst us')
are construed as the creation of women and, specifically, as the product of

female modesty. The *Discourse* presents this modesty as volitional, as instrumental: '[It is] cultivated by women with such skill and care in order to establish their empire over men, and so make dominant the sex that ought to obey.' But in *Emile* modesty is naturalized: 'While abandoning women to unlimited desires, He [the Supreme Being] joins modesty to these desires in order to constrain them.' And somewhat later in a note Rousseau adds: 'The timidity of women is another instinct of nature against the double risk they run during their pregnancy.' Indeed, throughout *Emile* he argues that natural differences between the sexes are represented and amplified in the form of moral differences that society erases only at its peril.[37]

Book 5 begins with the famous account of sexual difference and sameness. 'In everything not connected with sex, woman is man . . . In everything connected with sex, woman and man are in every respect related but in every respect different.' But, of course, a great deal about women *is* connected with sex: 'The male is male only at certain moments. The female is female her whole life . . . Everything constantly recalls her sex to her.' 'Everything,' it turns out, is everything about reproductive biology: bearing young, suckling, nurturing, and so on. Indeed the chapter becomes a catalogue of physical and consequently moral differences between the sexes; the former, as Rousseau says, 'lead us unawares to the latter,' Thus, 'a perfect woman and a perfect man ought not to resemble each other in mind any more than in looks.' From the differences in each sex's contribution to their union it follows that 'one ought to be active and strong, the other passive and weak.' 'One must necessarily will and be able; it suffices that the other put up little resistance.' The problem with Plato, Rousseau argues, is that he excludes 'families from his regime and no longer knowing what to do with women, he found himself *forced to make them men.*' It is precisely this sameness of 'the exercises' Plato gives men and women, this 'civil promiscuity which throughout confounded the two sexes in the same employments and the same labors and which cannot fail to engender the most intolerable abuses,' to which Rousseau objects. But what are these objectionable abuses?

> I speak of that subversion of the sweetest sentiments of nature, sacrificed to an artificial sentiment which can only be maintained by them
> – as though there were no need for a natural base on which to form conventional ties; as though the love of one's nearest were not the principle of the love one owes the state; as though it were not by means of the small fatherland which is the family that the heart attaches itself to the large one; as though it were not the good son, the good husband, and the good father [all males of course] who make the good citizen.

Finally, returning to the ostensible subject of the book, Rousseau concludes that 'once it is demonstrated that man and woman are not and ought not to be constituted in the same way in either their character or temperament, it follows that they ought not to have the same education.'[38]

For Rousseau a great deal depends, it turns out, on the natural modesty of women and on their role, distinct from the male's, in reproducing the species. Indeed, all of civilization seems to have arisen in consequence of the secular fall from innocence when the first woman made herself temporarily unavailable to the first man. But Rousseau is simply pushing harder on a set of connections that are commonplace in the Enlightenment – although by no means always so antifeminist in their interpretation. In his article on 'jouissance,' Diderot locates the creation of desire, of marriage and the family if not of love itself, at the moment *women* first came to withhold themselves from just any man and chose instead one man in particular:

> when women began to discriminate, when she appeared to take care in choosing between several men upon whom passion cast her glances . . . Then, when the veils that modesty cast over the charms of women allowed an inflamed imagination the power to dispose of them at will, the most delicate illusions competed with the most exquisite of senses to exaggerate the happiness of the moment . . . two hearts lost in love vowed themselves to each other forever, and heaven heard the first indiscreet oaths.[39]

Most prominently among the figures of the Scottish Enlightenment, John Millar argues for the critical role of women and their virtues in the progress of civilization. Far from being lesser men, they are treated in his *Origin of the Distinctions of Ranks* as both a moral barometer and as an active agent in the improvement of society. Millar's case begins with the claim that sexual relations, being most susceptible 'to the peculiar circumstances in which they are placed and most liable to be influenced by the power of habit and education,' are the most reliable guide to the character of a society. In barbarous societies, for example, women accompanied men to war and were scarcely different from them; in peaceful societies that had progressed in the arts, a woman's 'rank and station' were dictated by her special talents for rearing and maintaining children and by her 'peculiar delicacy and sensibility,' whether these derived from her 'original constitution' or her role in life. Thus civilization in Millar's account leads to an increasing differentiation of male and female social roles; this greater differentiation of roles – and specifically what he takes to be improvements in the lot of women – are signs of moral progress. But women themselves in more civilized societies are also the engines of further advance. 'In such a state, the pleasures which nature has grafted upon love between the sexes, become the source of an elegant correspondence, and are likely to have a general influence upon the commerce of society.' In this, the highest state – he is thinking of French salon society and of the *femme savant* –

[women are] led to cultivate those talents which are adapted to the intercourse of the world, and to distinguish themselves by polite accomplishments that tend to heighten their personal attractions, and to excite those peculiar sentiments and passions of which they are the natural objects.

Thus, desire among civilized men, and indeed modern civilization, is inextricably bound up in Millar's moral history with feminine accomplishment.[40]

It is hardly surprising in the context of Enlightenment thought that the moral and physical differentiation of women from men is also critical to the political discourse of women writers – from Anna Wheeler and early socialists at one end of the political spectrum through the radical liberalism of Mary Wollstonecraft to the domestic ideology of Hannah More and Sarah Ellis. For Wheeler and others, as Barbara Taylor argues, the denial or devaluation of female passion is to some degree part of a more general devaluation of passion. Reason, they dare to hope, would be triumphant over the flesh. Wheeler and early utopian socialists are, after all, writing out of the tradition that produced William Godwin's argument that civilization would ultimately eliminate destructive passions, that the body finally would be curbed by Enlightenment and be subsumed under the captaincy of the mind. It is against this view, as Catherine Gallagher argues, that Thomas Malthus rehabilitates the body and insists upon the absolute irreducibility of its demands, especially its sexual demands.[41]

But the nature of female passion and of the female body is unresolved in Wheeler's work. Her book, *An Appeal of One-Half the Human Race, Women, Against the Pretensions of the Other Half, Men, to Retain Them in Political and Thence in Civil and Domestic Slavery*, jointly written with William Thompson, is a sustained attack on James Mill's argument that the interests of women and children are subsumed – i.e., are virtually represented by – the interests of husbands and fathers. This 'moral miracle,' as they call it, would be credible were Mill right in holding that women are protected against abuse because men 'will act in a kind way toward women in order to procure from her those gratifications, the zest of which depends on the kindly inclinations of one party yielding them.' Since women are themselves free from sexual desire, they are in an excellent bargaining position vis à vis men, who are decidedly not liberated from their bodies. Nonsense, say Wheeler and Thompson. If women are 'like the Greek Asphasia,' cold and sexless, the argument might have force. But not only are they, like men, sexed and desirous but, in the current state of affairs, 'Woman is more the slave of man for gratification of her desires than man is to woman.' The double standard allows men to seek gratification outside of marriage but forbids it to women.[42]

Both Wheeler and Thompson's analysis of the sorry shape of the male world and their need to claim some political ground for women lead them dramatically to change their emphasis and make almost the opposite case as well. In a chapter entitled 'Moral Aptitude for Legislation More Probable in Women than Men,' woman is represented not as equally passionate as man but as more moral, more empathetic, and generally better able to act in accord with the common interest and not merely out of self-interest. Whether women had these traits in some hypothetical state of nature or acquired them through a kind of moral Lamarckianism is unclear, but in the modern world they demonstrate a great susceptibility to pain and pleasure, a more powerful desire to promote the happiness of others, and a more developed 'moral aptitude' than men. These, Wheeler and Thompson argue, are the most important qualities in a legislator. It is, moreover, precisely women's inferior strength and her inability to oppress others through superior force as men are wont to do that will ensure that they rule fairly and justly. Moreover, women as mothers and as the weaker sex need a world at peace far more than men, and they would thus be constitutionally more likely to legislate ways to obtain it. Wheeler and Thompson's arguments are more poignantly put than this summary suggests, but they contribute to a construction of woman not very different from that of the domestic ideologists. Whether through inherent nature – because they have more sensitive nervous systems, as many eighteenth- and nineteenth-century doctors held – or through centuries of suffering, women are construed as less passionate and hence morally more adept than men.[43]

As a radical liberal, Mary Wollstonecraft is caught in much the same dilemma. On the one hand, liberal theory pushes her to declare that the neutral, rational subject has in essence no sex. On the other hand, she was in her own life only too aware of the power, indeed the destructive violence, of sexual passion. Moreover she seems to have held, with Rousseau, that civilization increases desire and that 'people of sense and reflection are most apt to have violent and constant passions and to be preyed on by them.' Finally, as Zillah Eisenstein argues, for Wollstonecraft to subscribe to the notion of the subject as genderless would be to deny what to her were manifestly present, the particular qualities of women's experiences.[44]

Her solution was to take for women the moral high ground. Blessed with a unique susceptibility 'of the attached affections,' women's special role in the world is to civilize men and raise up children to virtue. In the *Female Reader*, Wollstonecraft lays on a heavy dose of religion, which she says will be 'the solace and support' of her readers when they find themselves, as they often will, 'amidst the scenes of silent unobserved distress.' 'If you wish to be loved by your relations and friends,' she counsels without detectable irony, 'prove that you can love them by governing your temper.' Good humor, cheerful gaity, and the like are not to be learned in a day. Indeed, as Barbara Taylor argues, Wollstonecraft shares with early socialist feminists a commitment to 'passionlessness,' whether out of some sense of its political possibilities, an acute awareness of passion's dangers, or a belief in the special undesiring qualities of the female body.[45]

In any case, Wollstonecraft's arguments for the differences between the sexes begin to sound very much like Sarah Ellis's, however profound the political chasm that divided the two women. In *Wives of England*, one of the canonical works of domestic ideology, Ellis argues that from the wife and mother, 'as head of a family and mistress of a household, branch off in every direction trains of thought, and tones of feeling, operating upon those more immediately around her, but by no means ceasing there . . . extending outwards in the same manner, to the end of all things.' This influence is born of the heightened moral sensibilities with which the female organism seems blessed. Though women are to have no role in the world of mundane politics, they are to confront issues

> such as extinction of slavery, the abolition of war in general, cruelty to animals, the punishment of death, temperance, and many more, on which, neither to know, nor to feel, is almost equally disgraceful.

In short, women's politics must be the politics of morality.[46]

All of this is not intended as an argument that writers from Hobbes, through Sade and Rousseau, and on to Ellis were all engaged in precisely the same theoretical or political undertaking. Rather, I have sought to display the wide range of apparently unrelated political agendas in which a new differentiation of the sexes occupied a critical place. Desire was given a history, and the female body distinguished from the male's, as the seismic transformations of European society between the seventeenth and the nineteenth centuries put unbearable pressure on old views of the body and its pleasures. A biology of hierarchy grounded in a metaphysically prior 'great chain of being' gave way to a biology of incommensurability in which the relationship of men to women, like that of apples to oranges, was not given as one of equality or inequality but rather as a *difference* whose meaning required interpretation and struggle.

Reproductive biology and the cultural reconstruction of women

I want now to turn from political and moral theory to the sciences of reproductive biology, to the seemingly unpromising domain of ovarian and uterine histology and the clinical observation of menstruation and fertility. Aldous Huxley's remark that 'the sciences of life can confirm the intuitions of the artist, can deepen his insights and extend the range of his vision' could as well be said of those who produced what he takes to be a prior and culturally pure knowledge. The dry and seemingly objective findings of the laboratory and the clinic become, within the disciplines practiced there, the stuff of art, of new representations of the female as a creature profoundly different from the male. And this 'art,' clothed in the prestige of natural science, becomes in turn the specie, the hard currency of social discourse.[47]

But I do not want to give the impression that reproductive biology or clinical gynecology are simply exercises in ideology. I will therefore begin by describing a critically important discovery of the early nineteenth century: that some mammals – nineteenth-century researchers believed all mammals – ovulate spontaneously during regularly recurring periods of heat, independently of intercourse, conception, pleasure, or any other subjective phenomena. Until the early 1840s the question of when and under what conditions ovulation took place was as obscure as it had been in 1672 when de Graaf argued that what he called the female testicle actually produced eggs. In the first place no one had observed a mammalian egg until 1827, when Karl Ernst von Baer, in a brilliant piece of research, definitively demonstrated its existence, first in the ovarian follicle and subsequently in the fallopian tubes of a dog. Until then, direct evidence for ovulation was lacking. At the time of his great discovery, von Baer still believed that an animal ovulated only when sexually stimulated; he therefore used a bitch that he knew to have quite recently mated. This was only reasonable, since the late eighteenth-century researches of the Englishmen William Cruickshank and John Haighton, on which von Baer relied, had shown that rabbits do *not* generally ovulate without intercourse; indeed they had claimed that ovulation is dependent on conception.[48]

In humans, the evidence for spontaneous ovulation was, in the early nineteenth century, highly ambiguous. Numerous anecdotal clinical reports, based on increasingly available autopsy material, claimed that cicatrices – scars remaining after a wound, sore, or ulcer has healed – can be demonstrated on ovaries of virgins and that these are left there by the release of an ovum and, more to the point, by the release of numerous ova corresponding to the number of menstrual cycles that the woman had had. But what, if anything, did this prove? Very little. Johann Friedrich Blumenbach, professor of medicine at Göttingen and one of the most distinguished physicians of Europe, for example, had been among the first to notice by the late eighteenth century that ovarian follicles burst without the presence of semen or even 'without any commerce with the male.' But he concluded from these cases only that, on occasion, 'venereal ardour alone ... could produce, among the other great changes in the sexual organs, the enlargement of the vesicles' and even their rupture.

> On this point I find it difficult in the present state of knowledge to make up my mind; but I think it pretty evident that, although semen has no share in bursting the ovarium, the high excitement that occurs during the heat of brutes and the lascivious states of the human virgin

is sufficient frequently to effect the discharge of the ova. It is perhaps impossible otherwise to explain the fact that ova are so commonly expelled from the ovaria, and impregnated whenever a connection is arbitrarily or casually brought about.

Johannes Muller, professor of physiology at Berlin, a leading proponent of biological reductionism, concludes that scars on the ovaries of virgins mark anomalous ovulations. Thus, while the exact forces causing the egg to be thrust into the fallopian tube remained unknown, the evidence until the 1840s was by no means sufficient to establish the normal occurrence of ovulation independent of coition, venereal arousal, or even conception.[49]

The critical experiment establishing spontaneous ovulation in dogs and by extension other mammals was elegantly simple. In the novelistic style that characterizes so much early nineteenth-century scientific reporting, Theodor L.W. Bischoff tells his reader that on 18 and 19 December 1843 he noted that a large bitch in his possession had begun to go into heat. On the 19th he allowed her contact with a male dog, but she refused its attentions. He kept her securely imprisoned for two more days and then brought on the male dog again; this time she was interested but the animals were separated before coition could take place. At ten o'clock two days later, i.e., on the morning of the 23rd, he cut out her left ovary and fallopian tubes and carefully closed the wound. The Graafian follicles in the excised ovary were swollen but had not yet burst. Five days later he killed the dog and found in the remaining ovary four developing corpus lutei filled with serum; careful opening of the tubes revealed four eggs. He concludes:

> I do not think it is possible to demonstrate with any more thoroughness the whole process of the ripening and expulsion of the eggs during heat, independently of coition, than through this dual observation on one and the same animal.

And of course if ovulation occurs independently of coition it must also occur independently of fecundation. Indeed, F.A. Pouchet considered the later discovery in itself so major that he formulated it as his 'fifth' and critical law of reproductive biology, 'le point capital' of his 476-page *magnum opus*. The historian Michelet was enraptured and hailed Pouchet for having formulated the entire science of reproductive biology in a definitive work of genius, a monument of daring grandeur.[50]

Granted that dogs and pigs go into heat and during this period ovulate whether they mate or not, what evidence was there that women's bodies behave in a similar manner? No one prior to the early twentieth century had claimed to have seen a human egg outside the ovary. Bischoff admitted that, in the absence of such a discovery, there was no direct proof for the extension of his theory to women, but he was sure that an egg would be found soon enough. In 1881, V. Hensen, professor of physiology at Kiel,

notes in L. Hermann's standard *Handbuch der Physiologie* that except for
two probably spurious reports, human eggs still eluded investigators,
though he adds, in a curiously optimistic footnote, that 'it can not be so
difficult to find a [human] egg in the [fallopian] tubes.' In fact, an unfer-
tilized egg was not reported until 1930, and then in the context of an argument against the nineteenth-century view relating heat to menstruation.
Thus, the crucial experimental link – the discovery of the egg – between
menstruation on the one hand and the morphology of the ovary on the
other was lacking in humans. Investigators could only note in the cases
that came their way that women were menstruating or that they were at
some known point in their menstrual cycles and then attempt to correlate
these observations with the structural characteristics of the ovary removed
in surgery or autopsy. They lacked as a biological triangulation point the
actual product of the ovary, and the results of their studies were manifestly
unsatisfactory. Evidence for the timing of ovulation based on pregnancy
from a single coition whose occurrence in the menstrual cycle was supposedly known was likewise increasingly ambiguous. The role of the ovaries
in the reproductive cycle of mammals was very imperfectly understood
until the publication of a series of papers beginning in 1900, while the
hormonal control of ovulation by the ovary and the pituitary remained
unknown until the 1930s.[51]

But despite the paucity of evidence in humans, the discovery of spontaneous ovulation in dogs and other mammals was of enormous importance
in the history of representing women's bodies. Beginning in the middle of
the nineteenth century, the ovaries came to be regarded as largely
autonomous control centers of reproduction in the female animal, and in
humans they were thought to be the essence of femininity itself. 'Propter
solum ovarium mulier est id quod est,' as the French physician Achilles
Chereau puts it; it is only because of the ovary that woman is what she is.
Moreover, menstruation in women came to be interpreted as the precise
equivalent of the heat in animals, marking the only period during which
women are normally fertile. Widely cited as Pouchet's eighth law, the view
was that 'the menstrual flow in women corresponds to the phenomena of
excitement which manifests itself during the rut [*l'époque des amours*] in a
variety of creatures and especially in mammals.' The American physician
Augustus Gardner drew out the implications of the menstruation/rut analogy less delicately: 'The bitch in heat has the genitals tumified and red-
dended, and a bloody discharge. The human female has nearly the same.'
'The menstrual period in women,' announces the *Lancet* in 1843, 'bears a
strict physiological resemblance' to the heat of 'brutes.'[52]

With these interpretations of spontaneous ovulation the old physiology
of pleasure and the old anatomy of sexual homologies were definitively
dead. The ovary, whose distinction from the male testes had only been recognized a century earlier, became the driving force of the whole female

economy, with menstruation the outward sign of its awesome power. As the distinguished British gynecologist Mathews Duncan put it, in an image too rich to be fully teased apart here: 'Menstruation is like the red flag outside an auction sale; it shows that something is going on inside.' And that something, as will become clear, was not a pretty sight; the social characteristics of women seemed writ in blood and gore. The silent workings of a tiny organ weighing on the average seven grams in humans, some two to four centimeters long, and the swelling and subsequent rupture of the follicles within it, came to represent synecdochically what it was to be a woman.[53]

But why would anyone believe that menstruation was in women what heat was in the dog? The answer lies outside the bounds of science in a wide range of cultural demands on the enterprise of interpretation. Consider, for example, the answer Bischoff himself offers: the equivalence of menstruation and heat is simply common sense. If one accepts spontaneous ovulation during periods of heat in mammals generally, it 'suggests itself.' In any case there is much indirect evidence for the equation of heat and menstruation, in addition to the authority of the 'most insightful physicians and naturalists' from the earliest times on.

In fact the analogy was far from evident, and most of those from antiquity to Bischoff's day who gave their views on the subject repudiated it. Haller's *Physiology* is quite explicit on the point that, while there are 'some animals, who, at the time of their venal copulation, distil blood from their genitals,' menstruation is peculiar 'to the fair sex [of] the human species.' Moreover, in contrast to bleeding in animals, menstruation for Haller is quite independent of the periodicity of sexual desire. Intercourse neither increases nor decreases the menstrual flux: women deny a heightened 'desire of venery' during their periods and report rather being 'affected by pain and languor.' Finally, sexual pleasure is localized 'in the entrance of the pudendum' and not in the uterus, from which the menses flow. Blumenbach, among the most widely reprinted and translated texts of the next generation, joins Pliny in arguing that only women menstruate, though cautioning his readers that the investigation of the 'periodical nature of this hemorrhage is so difficult that we can obtain nothing beyond probability' and should thus be careful not to offer mere conjecture as fact.[54]

What scant facts there were seemed more anthropological than biological, and these came under severe attack. In a masterful review of the literature up to 1843, Robert Remak, professor of neurology at Posen, argues that even if one grants that, as do healthy women, all or some mammals have regularly recurring periods of bleedings and that the bleeding in animals originates in the uterus and not from the turgescent external genitalia – neither concession being warranted by the evidence – there remains 'one further circumstance on which to ground the most radical difference between menstruation and the periodical flow of blood from the genitals of animals':

In female animals the bleeding accompanies heat [*brunst*], the period
of the most heightened sexual drive, the only time the female will
allow the male access, and the only time she will conceive. Quite to the
contrary, in women the menstrual period is scarcely at all connected to
increased sexual desire nor is fecundity limited to its duration; indeed
a kind of instinct keeps men away from women during the menses –
some savage people like certain African and American tribes isolate
menstruating women in special quarters – and experience shows that
there is no time during the inter-menstrual period when women can
not conceive. It follows therefore that the animal heat is totally missing in women . . . Indeed the absence of menstruation in animals is
one of the features that distinguish man from the beasts.

Johannes Muller, in his 1843 textbook, comes to similar conclusions. He
modestly points out that neither the purposes nor the causes of the periodical return of the menses are known. Quite probably, however, it exists to
'*prevent* in the human female the periodical return of sexual excitation
[*brunst*]' that occurs in animals. Common sense, in short, does not explain
why nineteenth-century investigators would want to view the reproductive
cycle of women as precisely equivalent to that of other animals.[55]
    Professional politics and the imperatives of a particular philosophy of
science offer perhaps part of an answer. As Jean Borie points out, Pouchet's
is 'une gynaecologie militante'; the same can be said of that of many of his
colleagues, especially his French ones. Their mission was to free women's
bodies from the stigma of clerical prejudice and centuries of popular superstition and, in the process, to substitute the physician for the priest as the
moral preceptor of society. Sexuality would shift from the realms of religion
to those of science triumphant. At the heart of the matter lay the faith that
reproduction, like nature's other mysteries, was in essence susceptible to
rational analysis. Thus, in the absence of specific evidence of human ovulation, 'logic' for Pouchet would dictate that women functioned no differently
from the bitch, sow, or female rabbit, who in turn followed the same fundamental laws as mollusks, insects, fishes, or reptiles. He explicitly calls his
readers' attention to the pristinely scientific, experimentally grounded,
character of his work and its avoidance of metaphysical, social, and religious concerns. Thus, there were considerable professional and philosophical attractions to the position that menstruation was like heat and that a
sovereign organ, the ovary, ruled over the reproductive processes that made
women what they were.[56]
    But this radical naturalization, this reduction of women to the organ that
differentiates them from men, was not in itself a claim for their association
with nature as against culture and civilization. The argument for the equation of heat and menstruation could be just as easily used to prove women's
moral elevation as to prove the opposite. Indeed the very fact that women,

on account of their recurrent cycles of rut, were more bound to their bodies than were men was evidence on some accounts for their superior capacity to transcend the brutish state. Arguing against those who held that the lack of animal-like lust or behavioral disturbances in women belied the new theory of spontaneous ovulation, one noted authority draws attention to 'the influence exercised by moral culture on the feelings and passions of humanity.' Observe 'the marvellous power exercised by civilization on the mind of her who, from her social position, is rendered the charm of man's existence.' Is it a wonder that the creature who can subjugate her own feelings, simulate good cheer when her heart is rent in agony, and in general give herself up to the good of the community can exercise control 'the more energetically, at a time [menstruation] when she is taught that a stray thought of desire would be impurity, and its fruition pollution.' But then, as if to back off from this model of woman as being simultaneously a periodically excited time bomb of sexuality and a model for the power of civilization to keep it from exploding, G.F. Girdwood concludes that 'to aid her in her duty, nature has wisely provided her with the sexual appetite slightly developed.'[57]

The interpretive indigestion of this passage, its sheer turning in on itself, bears witness to the extraordinary cultural burden that the physical nature of women – the menstrual cycle and the functions of the ovaries – came to bear in the nineteenth century. Whatever one thought about women and their rightful place in the world could, it seemed, be mapped onto their bodies, which in turn came to be interpreted anew in the light of these cultural demands. The construal of the menstrual cycle dominant from the 1840s to the early twentieth century rather neatly integrates a particular set of discoveries into a biology of incommensurability. Menstruation, with its attendant aberrations, became a uniquely and distinguishingly female process. Moreover, the analogy now assumed between heat and menstruation allowed evidence hithertofore used against the equivalence of the reproductive cycles of women and brutes to be reinterpreted to mean the opposite. Behavior hidden in women, just as ovulation is hidden, could be made manifest by associating it with the more transparent behavior of animals.

Thus, for example, the author of one of the most massive compilations of moral physiology in the nineteenth century could argue that the quite mad behavior of dogs and cats during heat, their flying to satisfy the 'instinct which dominates all else,' leaping around an apartment and lunging at windows, repeated 'so to speak indefinitely' if the venereal urge were not satisfied, is but a more manifest version of what the human female too experiences. Since both women and brutes are thought to be subject to the same 'orgasme de l'ovulation,' and since the bursting of the ovarian follicle was marked by the same deluge of nervous excitement and bleeding in both, whatever discomfort adolescent girls might feel at the onset of menstruation and whatever irritability or tension a woman might experience during her

menses could be magnified through the metaphors of this account and reinterpreted as but the tip of a physiological volcano. Menstruation, in short,
was a minimally disguised heat. Women would behave like brutes were it
not for the thin veneer of civilization. Language, moreover, adjusted to the
new science. The whole cultural baggage of *brunst, rut, heat* – words hithertofore applied only to animals – and the neologism *estrous*, derived from
the Latin *oestrum*, 'gadfly,' meaning a kind of frenzy and introduced to
describe a process common to all mammals, was subtly or not so subtly
laden on the bodies of women.[58]

Menstrual bleeding thus became the sign of a periodically swelling and
ultimately exploding ovarian follicle whose behavioral manifestation is an
'estrous,' 'brunst,' or 'rut.' But what one saw on the outside was only part
of the story; the histology of the uterine mucosa and of the ovary revealed
much more. Described in seemingly neutral scientific language, the cells of
the endometrium or corpus luteum became re-presentations, rediscriptions
of the social theory of sexual incommensurability. Walter Heape, the militant antisuffragist and reader in zoology at Cambridge University, for example, is absolutely clear on what he thinks of the female in relation to the
male body. Though some of the differences between men and women are
'infinitely subtle, hidden' and others 'glaring and forceful,' the truth of the
matter, he argues, is that

> the reproductive system is not only structurally but functionally fun-
> damentally different in the Male and the Female; and since all other
> organs and systems of organs are affected by this system, it is certain
> that the Male and Female are essentially different throughout.

They are, he continues, 'complementary, in no sense the same, in no sense
equal to one another; the accurate adjustment of society depends on proper
observation of this fact.' A major set of these facts were evident, for Heape
and many others, in the uterus. It should be noted, however, that the basic
histology of menstruation – let alone its causes – was not established until
the classic 1908 paper of L. Adler and F. Hitschmann. Previous descriptions,
as these two young Viennese gynecologists noted, were demonstrably inadequate. The point here is less that so little was known about menstruation
than that it was described in a way that created, through an extraordinary
leap of the synecdochic imagination, a cellular correlative to the socially
distinguishing characteristics of women. Histology mirrored with uncanny
clarity what it meant to be female.[59]

Today, the uterus is described as passing through two stages, rather col-
orlessly designated 'secretory' and 'proliferative,' during each menstrual
cycle. In the nineteenth and early twentieth centuries it was said to proceed
through a series of at least four and as many as eight stages. Its 'normal'
stage was construed as 'quiescence,' followed by 'constructive' and 'destructive' stages and a stage of 'repair.' Menstruation, as one might surmise, was

defined as occurring at the destructive stage, when the uterus gave up its lining. As Heape puts it, in an account redolent of war reportage, the uterus during the formation of the menstrual clot is subject to 'a severe, devastating, periodic action.' The entire ephithelium is torn away at each period,

> leaving behind a ragged wreck of tissue, torn glands, ruptured vessels, jagged edges of stroma, and masses of blood corpuscles, which it would seem hardly possible to heal satisfactorily without the aid of surgical treatment.

Mercifully, this is followed by the recuperative stage and a return to normalcy. Little wonder that Havelock Ellis, steeped in this rhetoric, would conclude that women live on something of a biological roller coaster. They are, 'as it were, periodically wounded in the most sensitive spot in their organism and subjected to a monthly loss of blood.' The cells of the uterus are in constant, dramatic flux and subject to soul-wrenching trauma. Ellis concludes, after ten pages of still more data on the physiological and psychological periodicity in women, that the establishment

> of these facts of morbid psychology, are very significant; they emphasize the fact that even in the healthiest woman a worm however harmless and unperceived, gnaws periodically at the roots of life.[60]

A gnawing worm is by no means the only metaphor of pain and disease employed to interpret uterine or ovarian histology. The bursting of the follicle is likened by Rudolph Virchow, the father of modern pathology, to teething, 'accompanied with the liveliest disturbance of nutrition and nerve force.' For the historian Michelet, woman is a creature 'wounded each month,' who suffers almost constantly from the trauma of ovulation, which in turn is at the center, as Thérèse Moreau has shown, of a physiological and psychological phantasmagoria dominating her life. Less imaginatively, a French encyclopedia likens follicular rupture to 'what happens at the rupture of an acute abscess.' The German physiologist E.F.W. Pfluger likens menstruation to surgical debridement, the creation of a clean surface in a wound, or alternatively, to the notch used in grafting a branch onto a tree, to the 'innoculationschnitt.' Imperatives of culture or the unconscious, not positive science, informed the interpretations of the female body more or less explicitly in these accounts.[61]

While all of the evidence presented so far is by men and produced in a more or less antifeminist context, image making, the construction of the body through science, occurs in feminist writers as well. Mary Putnam Jacobi's *The Question of Rest for Women During Menstruation* (1886), for example, is a sustained counterattack against the view that 'the peculiar changes supposed to take place in the Graafian vesicles at each period . . . involve a peculiar expenditure of nervous force, which was so much dead loss to the individual life of the woman.' Women were therefore unfit for higher education, a variety of jobs, and other activities that demand large expenditures of the mental and physcial energy that was thought to be in such short supply. Since the 'nervous force' was commonly associated in higher animals and in women with sexual arousal, Jacobi's task becomes one of severing the sexual from the reproductive life of women, of breaking the ties between the two postulated in the ovarian theory of Bischoff, Pouchet, Adam Raciborski, and others.[62]

Much of her book is taken up with a compilation of the real or supposed empirical failings of this view. Neither menstruation nor pregnancy, she argues for example, are tied to the time of ovulation; indeed as several hundred cases of vicarious menstruation in women suggest, menstruation itself is only statistically, not in any more fundamental way, bound to ovulation and thus to reproduction. The amount of blood that flows to the uterus even in women who feel particular pelvic heaviness is but a tiny proportion of the body's blood and far less than the proportion transferred to the stomach and intestines during the obviously normal daily processes of digestion. There is no evidence, Jacobi continues, that the uterus, ovaries, or their appendages become turgid during the menstrual period, and thus the effort to link a sort of histological tension of the reproductive organs to sexual tension, to the excitement of heat, must come to naught. But though many of her criticisms are well taken, she neither offers a more compelling new theory of the physiology of ovulation nor gives a clearer picture of cellular changes in the uterine mucosa during the menstrual cycle than do those she is arguing against.[63]

Jacobi does, however, offer a new metaphor: 'All the processes concerned in menstruation converge, not toward the sexual sphere, but the *nutritive*, or one department of it – the reproductive.' The acceleration of blood flow to the uterus 'in obedience to a *nutritive* demand' is precisely analogous to the 'afflux of blood to the muscular layer of the stomach and intestines after a meal.' Jacobi, like her opponents, tended to reduce woman's nature to woman's reproductive biology. But for her, the essence of female sexual difference lay not in periodically recurring nervous excitement nor in episodes of engorgement, rupture, and release of tension but rather in the quiet processes of nutrition. Far from being periodical, ovulation in Jacobi's account is essentially random: 'The successive growth of the Graafian vesicles strictly resembles the successive growth of buds on a bough.' Buds, slowly opening into delicate cherry or apple blossoms and, if fertilized, into fruit, are a far cry from the wrenching and sexually intense swellings of the ovary imagined by the opposing theory.[64]

Indeed, Jacobi's woman is in many respects the inverse of that of Pouchet, Raciborski, or Bischoff. For these men the theory of spontaneous ovulation demanded a woman shackled to her body, woman as nature, as physical being, even if the tamed quality of her modern European avatar spoke eloquently of the power of civilization. For Jacobi, on the other hand, spontaneous ovulation implied just the opposite. Biology provides the basis for a radical split between woman's mind and body, between sexuality and reproduction. The female body carries on its reproductive functions with no mental involvement; conversely, the mind can remain placidly above the body, free from its constraints. Jacobi's first effort at a metaphorical construction of this position uses fish whose ova are extruded without 'sexual congress, and in a manner analogous to the process of defecation and micturation.' In higher animals sexual congress is necessary for conception, but ovulation remains spontaneous and independent of excitement. From this, it follows, according to Jacobi, that *'the superior contribution of the nutritive element of reproduction made by the female is balanced by an inferior dependence upon the animal or sexual element: in other words, she is sexually inferior.'*[65]

Of course, Jacobi cannot deny that in lower animals female sexual instinct is tied exclusively to reproduction and that a ruptured follicle or follicles are invariably found during the rut. She nevertheless maintains that there is no proof of anything but a coincidental relationship between the state of the ovaries and the congested state of the external and internal genitalia that seems to signal sexual readiness. But in women, she adamantly maintains, 'the sexual instinct and reproductive capacity remain distinct; there is no longer any necessary association between sexual impulse, menstruation, and the dehiscence of ova.' Indeed, her entire research program is devoted to showing that the menstrual cycle may be read as the ebb and flow of female nutritive rather than sexual activity, that its metabolic contours are precisely analogous to those of nutrition and growth. And this brings one back to the metaphor of the ovary as fruit blossom. The woman buds as surely and as incessantly as the 'plant, continually generating not only the reproductive cell, but the nutritive material without which this would be useless.' But how, given that women generally eat less than men, do they obtain a nutritive surplus? Because 'it is the possibility of making this reserve which constitutes the *essential peculiarity* of the female sex.'[66]

The point here is not to belittle Jacobi's scientific work but rather to emphasize the power of cultural imperatives, of metaphor, in the production and interpretation of the rather limited body of data available to reproductive biology during the late nineteenth century. At issue is not whether Jacobi was right in pointing out the lack of coincidence between ovulation and menstruation in women and wrong in concluding that there is therefore no systematic connection between the two. Rather, both she and her opponents emphasized some findings and rejected others on largely extrascientific considerations. In the absence of an accepted research paradigm, their criteria were largely ideological – seeing woman either as civilized animal or as mind presiding over a passive, nutritive body.

But perhaps even the accumulation of fact, even the coherent and powerful modern paradigm of reproductive physiology in contemporary medical texts, offers but slight restraint on the poetics of sexual difference. Indeed, the subject itself seems to inflame the imagination. Thus, when W.F. Ganong's 1977 *Review of Medical Physiology*, a standard reference work for physicians and medical students, allows itself one moment of fancy it is on the subject of women and the menstrual cycle. Amidst a review of reproductive hormones, of the process of ovulation and menstruation described in the cold language of science, one is quite unexpectedly hit by a rhetorical bombshell, the only lyrical moment linking the reductionism of modern biological science to the experiences of humanity in 599 pages of compact, emotionally subdued prose:

> Thus, to quote an old saying, 'Menstruation is the uterus crying for lack of a baby.'

Cultural concerns have free license here, however embedded they may be in the language of science. As in nineteenth-century texts, synecdochic leaps of the imagination seem to view woman as the uterus, which in turn is endowed, through the by now familiar turn of the pathetic fallacy, with feelings, with the capacity to cry. The body remains an arena for the construction of gender even though modern research paradigms do, of course, isolate the experimental and interpretive work of reproductive biology from extrascientific pressures far more than was possible in the essentially pre-paradigmatic research of the nineteenth century.[67]

Scientific advances, I have argued, did not destroy the hierarchical model that construed the female body as a lesser, turned-inward version of the male, nor did they banish female orgasm to the physiological periphery. Rather, the political, economic, and cultural transformations of the eighteenth century created the context in which the articulation of radical differences between the sexes became culturally imperative. In a world in which science was increasingly viewed as providing insight into the fundamental truths of creation, in which nature as manifested in the unassailable reality of bones and organs was taken to be the only foundation of the moral order, a biology of incommensurability became the means by which such differences could be authoritatively represented. New claims and counterclaims regarding the public and private roles of women were thus contested through questions about the nature of their bodies as distinguished from those of men. In these new discursive wars feminists as well as antifeminists sacrificed the idea of women as inherently passionate; sexual pleasure as a sign in the flesh of reproductive capacity fell victim to political exigencies.

Notes

1 Condorcet, 'On the Admission of Women to the Rights of Citizenship' (1791), in *Selected Writings*, ed. Keith Michael Baker (Indianapolis, 1976), 98.

2 Ibid., 98; see, for example, Sade's *Philosophy in the Bedroom*, trans. Richard Seaver and Austryn Wainhouse (New York, 1965), 206 and *passim.*
3 Wisdom of Solomon 7.2 and Philo, *Legum allegoriae* 2.7, cited in Peter Brown, 'Sexuality and Society in the Fifth Century A.D.: Augustine and Julian of Eclanum,' in *Tria corda: Scritti in onore di Arnaldo Momigliano*, ed. E. Gabba (Como, 1983), 56; Mrs. Jane Sharp, *The Midwives Book* (1671), 43–44.
4 'There is a *jouissance* proper to her, to this "her" which does not exist and which signifies nothing'; Jacques Lacan, 'God and the *Jouissance* of ~~The~~ Woman,' in *Feminine Sexuality*, ed. Juliet Mitchell and Jacqueline Rose (New York, 1982), 145.
5 Nemesius of Emesa, *On the Nature of Man* (Philadelphia, 1955), 369; Galen, *De semine* 2.1, in *Opera omnia*, ed. C.G. Kuhn, 20 vols. (1821–33), 4: 596.
6 Regnier de Graaf, *A New Treatise Concering the Generative Organs of Women*, translation of *De mulierum organis generationi inservientibus tractatus novus* (1672) by H.D. Jocelyn and B.P. Setchell, *Journal of Reproduction and Fertility*, suppl. no. 17 (1972), 131–35; Pierre Roussel, *Système physique et moral de la femme* (1775; Paris, 1813), 79–80; Bartholomew Parr, ed., *The London Medical Dictionary*, vol. 2 (Philadelphia, 1819), 88–89; *Aristotle's Masterpiece* (1803; reprint edn, New York, 1974), 3.
7 Jacques Moreau de la Sarthe, *Histoire naturelle de la femme*, vol. 1 (Paris, 1803), 15, which sounds the theme of the entire volume.
8 George W. Corner, 'The Events of the Primate Ovarian Cycle,' *British Medical Journal* no. 4781 (23 August 1952): 403.
9 For an early and clearly presented table of embryological homologies, see Rudolf Wagner, ed., *Handwörterbuch der Physiologie*, vol. 4 (Braunschweig, 1853), s.v. 'Zeugung,' 763. Regarding skeletons, see Londa Schiebinger, 'Skeletons in the Closet: The First Illustrations of the Female Skeleton in Eighteenth-Century Anatomy,' in Catherine Gallagher and Thomas Laqueur, eds, *The Making of the Modern Body* (Berkeley, 1987). 1759 is an alternative date for the first representation of the female skeleton; see ibid.
10 Mary Douglas, *Natural Symbols* (New York, 1982), 70.
11 Plato, *Timaeus* 91A–C, Loeb Classical Library, ed. R.G. Bury (Cambridge, Mass., 1929), 248–50; Galen, *On the Usefulness of the Parts of the Body*, ed. and trans. Margaret May, 2 vols. (Ithaca, N.Y., 1968), 2: 640.
12 Ibid., 1: 382 and n. 78; 2: 628, 630.
13 Ibid., 2: 628–29.
14 Ibid., 2: 629.
15 Ibid., 2: 630–31 and, more generally, 636–38.
16 Ibid., 2: 640–43.
17 Hippocrates, *The Seed*, in *Hippocratic Wrirings*, ed. G.E.R. Lloyd (London, 1978), 319; for Galen on wet dreams in women see *De semine* 2.1, in *Opera omnia*, 4: 599. There is no space in this paper to argue for the basic compatibility of Aristotle's views with what became the dominant Galenic model. See Michael Boylan, 'The Galenic and Hippocratic Challenges to Aristotle's Conception Theory,' *Journal of the History of Biology* 17, no. 1 (Spring 1984): 83–112.
18 Galen, *On the Usefulness of Parts*, 2: 640–44; Avicenna, *Libri in re medica omnes . . . id est libri canonis* (Venice, 1564), 3.21.1.25.
19 This is all quite commonplace in classical medicine. See, for examples, Aristotle, *Generation of Animals* 727a3–15, 776a15–33 on milk and *History of Animals* 581b30–583b2 on semen and menstrual blood as plethora and on menstrual blood finding its way to the breasts and becoming milk (*The Complete Works of Aristotle*, ed. Jonathan Barnes, 2 vols, Princeton, N.J., 1984); Aetius of Amida, *Tetrabiblion*, trans. James V. Ricci (Philadelphia, 1950); Hippocrates, *Aphorisms* 32 and 33 and *Epidemics* 1.16, in *The Medical Works of Hippocrates*, ed. and trans. John Chadwick and W.N. Mann (Oxford, 1950). Renaissance texts, both popular and learned, repeated much of this lore; see, for example, Patricia Crawford, 'Attitudes to Menstruation in Seventeenth-Century England,' *Past and Present*, no. 91 (1981): 48–73.
20 The earliest version of the hemorrhoidal bleeding/menstruation equivalency I have encountered is in Aristotle, *Generation of Animals* 27a10, where he notes that

women in whom the menstrual discharge is normal are not troubled with hemorrhoidal bleeding or nosebleeds. See J.B. [John Bulwer], *Anthropometamorphosis:
Man Transformed of the Artificial Changling* (1653), 390; and Albrecht von Haller,
Physiology: Being a Course of Lectures, vol. 2 (1754), paragraph 816, p. 293, my
emphasis.

21 Avicenna, *Canon* 3.20.1.44; Trotulla of Salerno, *The Diseases of Women*, ed. Eliza-
beth Mason-Huhl (Los Angeles, 1940), 16–19; on witchcraft and barrenness see
Nicholas Fontanus, *The Woman's Doctour* (1652), 128–37; Jacob Rueff, *The Expert
Midwife* (1637), book 6, p. 16 (on witchcraft) and p. 55 (quote).

22 John Sadler, *The Sicke Woman's Private Looking Glass* (1636), 118 and 110–18 more
generally: Pierre Dionis, *A General Treatise of Midwifery* (1727, from a late seventeenth-century French text), 57 (on the importance of the imagination); Ambroise
Pare, 'Of the Generation of Man,' in *The Workes of the Famous Chirurgion . . .* ,
trans. Thomas Johnson (1634), book 24, pp. 889–90; Robert Barrett, *A Companion
for Midwives* (1699), 62.

23 Pare, 'Of the Generation of Man,' 889; Trotulla, *Diseases of Women*, 16; William
Sermon, *The Ladies Companion or the English Midwife* (1671), 13; Sadler, *Looking
Glass*, 118ff.

24 Euchar Roesslin, *The Byrth of Mankynde* (1545), fol. 28.

25 J.B. de C.M. Saunders and Charles D. O'Malley, *The Anatomical Drawings of
Andreas Vesalius* (New York, 1982), point out that fig. 5.1 was drawn to illustrate
the Galenic homologies while the penis-like vagina in fig. 5.2 is simply an artifact of
having to remove the organs in a great hurry.

26 Sir Thomas Browne, *Pseudodoxia Epidemica or Enquiries into Very Many Received
Tenents and Commonly Presumed Truths*, vol. 2 of *The Works of Sir Thomas
Browne*, ed. Geoffrey Keynes (London, 1928), book 3, chap. 17, pp. 212–13, 216;
Browne denies the vulgar belief in the annual alteration of sex in hares; Ambroise
Pare, *On Monsters and Marvels*, ed. and trans. by Janis L. Pallister (Chicago, 1982),
32; *Montaigne's Travel Journal* (San Francisco, 1983), 6.

27 Pare, *On Monsters*, 32–33; Caspar Bauhin, *Theatrum Anatomicum* (Basel, 1605), as
cited in William Harvey, *Lectures on the Whole Anatomy* (1616), ed. and trans. C.D.
O'Malley, F.N.L. Poynter, and K.F. Russell (Berkeley, 1961), 132 and 467n.

28 On the discovery of the clitoris see Renaldo Colombo, *De re anatomica* (1572), book
2, chap. 16, pp. 447–48; for synonyms see Joseph Hyrtl, *Onomatologia anatomica*
(Vienna, 1880), s.v. 'clitoris'; Sharp, *Midwives Book*, 44–45; John Pechey, *Complete
Midwives Practice* (London, 1698), 49.

29 Thomas Gibson, *The Anatomy of Humane Bodies Epitomized* (4th edn, 1694), 99;
Marie Bonaparte, *Female Sexuality* (New York, 1953), 3, 113–15; for more recent
psychoanalytic thought on this subject see *Journal of the American Psychoanalytic
Institute* 14 (1966): 28–128 and 16 (1968): 405–612; Nicholas Culpepper, *A Dictionary for Midwives; or A Guide for Women* (1675), part 1, p. 22.

30 Helkiah Crooke, *A Description of the Body of Man* (1615), 250; Thomas Vicary's
work is also known as *The Englishman's Treasure* (1585), 53.

31 Crooke, *Description*, 250; Jacques Cuval, *Des Hermaphrodites, accouchemens des
femmes . . .* (1612), 375, cited in Stephen Greenblatt, 'Fiction and Friction,' an
unpublished paper he has generously let me read.

32 Havelock Ellis, *Studies in the Psychology of Sex*, vol. 3 (Philadelphia, 1923), 194; the
phenomenon Ellis observes is, I suggest, of eighteenth-century origins.

33 Cited in V.C. Medvei, *A History of Endocrinology* (Boston, 1982), 357; Haller, *Physiology*, paragraphs 823–26, pp. 301–3. Haller, at the time he wrote these passages,
was an ovist; that is, he believed that the egg contained the new life and that the
sperm merely activated its development. But the same sorts of accounts were also
written by spermaticists.

34 See for examples Jane Abray, 'Feminism in the French Revolution,' *American Historical Review 80*, no. 1 (February 1975): 43–62; Susanna Barrows, *Distorting Mirrors*
(New Haven, 1981), chap. 2; Susan Sleeth Mosedale, 'Science Corrupted: Victorian
Biologists Consider "The Woman Question,"' *Journal of the History of Biology* 11,
no. 1 (Spring 1978): 1–55; Elizabeth Fee, 'Nineteenth-Century Craniology: The Study

of the Female Skull,' *Bulletin of the History of Medicine* 53, no. 3 (Fall 1979): 915–33; Lorna Duffin, 'Prisoners of Progress: Women and Evolution,' in Sara Delamont and Lorna Duffin, eds, *Woman: Her Cultural and Physical World* (New York, 1978), 56–91; Alexis de Tocqueville, *Democracy in America*, ed. Phillips Bradley, vol. 2 (New York, 1945), 223.

35 Jean Elshtain, *Public Man, Private Woman* (Princeton, N.J., 1981), chap. 3.

36 Jean-Jacques Rousseau, *A Discourse on Inequality*, trans. Maurice Cranston (Harmondsworth, 1984), 104.

37 Ibid., 102–3, 110; *Emile; or, On Education*, trans. Allan Bloom (New York, 1979), book 5, pp. 359 and 362n.

38 Ibid., 357–58, 362–63.

39 Denis Diderot, *Encyclopédie*, s.v. 'Jouissance'; I have taken the translation with some modifications from *The Encyclopedia*, ed. and trans. Stephen J. Gendzier (New York, 1967), 96; *jouissance* is translated here as 'enjoyment,' but it is perfectly clear that Diderot means by it sexual pleasure and passion.

40 John Millar, *Origin of the Distinctions of Ranks* (Basel, 1793), 14, 32, 86, 95–96.

41 Barbara Taylor, *Eve and the New Jerusalem: Socialism and Feminism in the Nineteenth Century* (New York, 1983), esp. chap. 2 and *passim*; Catherine Gallagher, 'The Body Versus the Social Body in the Works of Thomas Malthus and Henry Mayhew,' in Gallagher and Laqueur, eds, *Making of the Modern Body*.

42 Anna Wheeler and William Thompson, *An Appeal of One-Half the Human Race, Women, Against the Pretensions of the Other Half, Men, to Retain Them in Political and Thence in Civil and Domestic Slavery* (London, 1825), 60–61.

43 Ibid., 145 and part 2, question 2, generally.

44 Zillah Eisenstein, *The Radical Future of Liberal Feminism* (New York, 1981), chap. 5, pp. 89–112; Mary Wollstonecraft, *Thoughts on the Education of Daughters . . .* (1787), 82.

45 Ibid., *Female Reader* (1789), vii; Taylor, *Eve*, 47–48. I take the term *passionlessness* and an understanding of its political meaning in the early nineteenth century from Nancy Cott's pioneering article 'Passionlessness: An Interpretation of Victorian Sexual Ideology, 1790–1850,' *Signs* 4, no. 21 (1978): 219–36.

46 Sarah Ellis, *The Wives of England* (London, n.d.), 345; and *The Daughters of England, Their Position in Society, Character & Responsibilities* (London, 1842), 85, Mitzi Myers, 'Reform or Ruin: A Revolution in Female Manners,' *Studies in the Eighteenth Century* 11 (1982): 199–217, makes a persuasive case for considering writers as far apart politically as the domestic ideologists and Mary Wollstonecraft as engaged in the same moral enterprise.

47 Aldous Huxley, *Literature and Science* (New York, 1963), 67; quoted in Peter Morton, *The Vital Science: Biology and the Literary Imagination, 1860–1900* (London, 1984), 212.

48 Karl Ernst von Baer, 'On the Genesis of the Ovum of Mammals and of Man,' trans. C.D. O'Malley, *Isis* 47 (1956): 117–53, esp. 119; John Haighton, 'An Experimental Inquiry Concerning Animal Impregnation,' reported by Maxwell Garthshore, *Philosophical Transactions of the Royal Society of London* 87, part 1 (1797): 159–96; and William Cruickshank, 'Experiments in Which, on the Third Day After Impregnation, the Ova of Rabbits Were Found in the Fallopian Tubes . . . ,' reported by Everard Home, ibid., 197–214, esp. 210–11; on the difficulties of discovering the mammalian ovum see A.W. Meyer, *The Rise of Embryology* (Stanford, Calif., 1939), chap. 8.

49 For references to some of the English and French clinical reports see William Baly, *Recent Advances in the Physiology of Motion, the Senses, Generation, and Development* (London, 1848), 46n; Johann Friederich Blumenbach, *The Elements of Physiology*, trans. John Elliotson (1828), 483–84; Johannes Muller, *Handbuch der Physiologie des Menschen*, vol. 2 (Coblenz, 1840), 644–45 and 643–49 generally on the release of the ovum.

50 Theodor L.W. Bischoff, *Beweis der von der Begattung unabhängigen periodischen Reifung und Loslösung der Eier der Säugethiere und des Menschen* (Giesen, 1844), 28–31; F.A. Pouchet, *Théorie positive de l'ovulation spontanée et de la fécondation*

des Mammifères et de l'espèce humaine (Paris, 1847), 104–67 (for the evidence supporting this claim), 452; Jules Michelet, *L'Amour* (Paris, 1859), xv.

51 Bischoff, *Beweis*, 43; V. Hensen, in L. Hermann, *Handbuch der Physiologie*, vol. 6 (Leipzig, 1881), part 2, p. 69; Q.U. Newell, *et al.*, 'The Time of Ovulation in the Menstrual Cycle as Checked by Recovery of the Ova from the Fallopian Tubes,' *American Journal of Obstetrics and Gynaecology* 19 (February 1930): 180–85.

52 Achilles Chereau, *Memoires pour servir a l'étude des maladies des ovaires* (Paris, 1844), 91; Pouchet, *Théorie positive*, 227; Augustus Gardner, *The Causes and Curative Treatment of Sterility, with a Preliminary Statement of the Physiology of Generation* (New York, 1856), 17; *Lancet*, 28 January 1843, 644.

53 Duncan, 'The Changes That Take Place in the Non-Pregnant Uterus During the Oestrous Cycle,' in F.H.A. Marshall, *The Physiology of Reproduction* (New York, 1910), 75.

54 Bischoff, *Beweis*, 40 and 40–48 generally on this point; Haller, *Physiology*, paragraph 812, p. 290 (p. 419 of the 1803 English edition); Blumenbach, *Elements*, 461–62; the oft-repeated allusion to Pliny is from his *Natural History* 7.15.63.

55 Robert Remak, 'Über Menstruation und Brunst,' *Neue Zeitschrift für Geburtskunde* 3 (1843): 175–233, esp. 176; Muller, *Handbuch*, 640.

56 Jean Borie, 'Une Gynecologie passionée,' in Jean-Paul Aron, ed., *Misérable et glorieuse: La Femme du XIX siècle* (Paris, 1980), 164ff.; Angus McLaren, 'Doctor in the House: Medicine and Private Morality in France, 1800–1850,' *Feminist Studies* 2, no. 3 (1974–75): 39–54: Pouchet, *Théorie positive*, introduction, 12–26 (on the use of 'logic' in the absence of hard evidence see his discussion of the first law, esp. 15), 444–46 (summary of his programmatic statement).

57 G.F. Girdwood, 'On the Theory of Menstruation,' *Lancet*, 7 October 1844, 315–16.

58 Adam Raciborski, *Traité de la menstruation* (Paris, 1868), 46–47 and 43–47 generally.

59 Walter Heape, *Sex Antagonism* (London, 1913), 23; F. Hitschmann and L. Adler, 'Der Bau der Uterusschleimhaut des geschlechtsreifen Weibes mit besonderer Berucksichtigung der Menstruation,' *Monatsschrift für Geburtshulfe und Gynäkologie* 27, no. 1 (1908): 1–82, esp. 1–8, 48–59.

60 Walter Heape's account of the stages of menstruation is in his 'The Menstruation of *Semnopithecus entellus*,' *Philosophical Transactions of the Royal Society of London*, ser. B. 185, part 1 (1894): 411–66 plus plates, esp. 421–40; the quotation is from Marshall's summary *Physiology*, 92; Havelock Ellis, *Man and Woman: A Study of Human Secondary Sexual Characteristics* (London, 1904), 284, 293.

61 Rudolph Virchow, *Der puerperale Zustand: Das Weib und die Zelle* (1848), 751, as cited in Mary Jacobi, *The Question of Rest for Women During Menstruation* (New York, 1886). 110. According to Michelet (*L'Amour*, 393), the ovary was of course not the only source of woman's fundamental sickness: 'Ce siècle sera nommé celui des maladies de la matrice,' he argues, having identified the fourteenth century as that of the plague and the sixteenth as that of syphilis (iv). See Thérèse Moreau, *Le Sang de l'histoire* (1982); A. Charpentier, *Cyclopedia of Obstetrics and Gynaecology*, trans. Egbert H. Grandin (New York, 1887), part 2, p. 84; for Pfluger see Hans H. Simmer, 'Pfluger's Nerve Reflex Theory of Menstruation: The Product of Analogy, Teleology and Neurophysiology,' *Clio Medica* 12, no. 1 (1977): 57–90, esp. 59.

62 Jacobi, *Question of Rest*, 1–25, 81, and 223–32 *passim*.

63 Ibid., section 3, pp. 64–115, is devoted to laying out and criticizing the so-called ovarian theory of menstruation.

64 Ibid., 98–100.

65 Ibid., 83, 165; emphasis is in the text.

66 Ibid., 99, 167–68.

67 W.F. Ganong, *Review of Medical Physiology*, 8th edn (Los Altos, Calif., 1977), 332 and 330–44 *passim*.

6

Extracts from *Oedipus and the Devil: Witchcraft, sexuality and religion in early modern Europe*

LYNDAL ROPER

For many historians, feminists and non-feminists alike, 'gender' was the category through which it looked as if women's history might have the potential not only to enter history as a respectable historical field, but to reshape the historical narratives themselves. The axiom that gender identity was not a biological given but a historical creation was immensely liberating: the historian's task was to lay bare the precise historical meaning of masculinity and femininity in the past, thus relativizing the content of these constructs in the present. We were able to show, for instance, that early modern men delighted in fashion and clothes, that medieval women were to be found working in practically all sectors of the economy, that motherhood, when infants were sent to wet-nurses, must have constituted a different bond from the relationship we know today.

[...]

When the so-called new cultural history broke with the idea of linear narratives, disrupting the unity of culture, it seemed to offer a new space for feminist history. If our cultural heritage was necessarily fragmented, if the fiction of a unified culture could be surrendered, then women were guaranteed a voice in the story. (Paradoxically, in fact, some of even the new cultural history does rely in the end on a unity of culture, based on the shared nature of language: a solution which simply replicates the problem of women's relation to culture at another, more intractable level.[1]) For feminist historians, the lure of cultural anthropology and discourse theory was its organizing power. If gender was created through discourse, or through social behaviour and interaction, the substance of sexual difference was historical – and therefore, it was something we could change. Gender as a concept consequently seemed to offer a way of giving feminists access both to anthropological history and to discourse history. Joan Scott's 1985 article resoundingly affirmed not only that gender *was* a historical category

Reprinted from Lyndal Roper, *Oedipus and the Devil* (Routledge, 1994). Reprinted by permission of the author and Routledge Ltd.

but that it was a category of historical analysis.[2] Deconstruction allowed feminists to juggle with the reversals and inversions, hidden meanings and endless contradictions of sexual difference – as if sexual difference were no longer a prison from which one could not escape but an ethereal substance, an endless play of light and shadow in which the intellect could delight.

Applied historically, however, deconstruction has the tendency to reproduce its own tricks and paradoxes. The contradictions of femininity in sixteenth-century Germany bear an uncanny resemblance to those of twentieth-century Britain. Indeed, Scott herself remains tantalizingly vague about the sense in which gender *is* a historical category. For while we have learnt to discern the effects of gender in politics, war and business history – all the historical territories which historians once used to believe to be the preserve of real male history – what remains less clear is how gender itself effects historical change. Instead, we borrow from the state- and class-based narratives of historical transformation, leaving it vague what causal difference gender makes. Gender appears more often to be a matter of key, transposing the old familiar historical songs into soprano or bass registers: the tunes, however, remain the same.

If gender is to be a category of social explanation, it must bridge the gap between discourse, social formation and the individual sexed subject.[3] Just as cultural anthropological approaches and discourse theory seemed, in the end, to offer a somewhat flat account of subjectivity, so also, feminist history, because of its symbiotic critical relationship with these intellectual developments, remained caught in the limitations of the terms it criticized. In the final analysis, gender, for all its splendid play of discursive variegation, remains a category whose content proves elusive, and whose causal claims are a cypher.

Recently, feminist writers, too, have rejected the comfortable orthodoxy of the distinction between sex and gender.[4] Judith Butler has pointed out that the sex/gender distinction naturalizes sex, itself the product of culture, while reinstating the very binary distinction between nature and culture which we need to question.[5] This move robs historians of the sociological tools we once used to present sexual identity as a historical and social product. It turns out that the part of sexual identity which could once be neatly isolated as social creation, distinct from the 'givenness' of biological sex, reveals itself to be no more a creation than sex itself. 'Gender' as a sociological category is an illusion created by the terms of its own delimitation.

Yet history has not been done out of a job by post-modernism. Ironically, history and historians are very important to post-structuralist sceptics. For if sex, the person and sexual identities are contingent creations, not just at the level of detail, but as ontological categories, then it becomes crucial that there be 'other worlds' in which these categories did not organize experience. History seems to offer both such other possible worlds and an account of how we came by the categories with which we now live. Butler's demolition of 'sex' and 'person' proceeds by demonstrating the contingency of those very categories and their embeddedness in the binary divisions they seek to critique. But it is an irony of her position that she introduces the very same pattern at the historical level, as she aims to 'expose the contingent acts that create the appearance of a naturalistic necessity'.[6] There is an implicit historical 'before' and 'after', defined by the presence or absence of the binary oppositions her argument reifies; the moment *before* 'the category of "women", the subject of feminism, is produced and restrained by the very structures of power through which emancipation is sought'.[7] Historians, who are equally complicit in the search for grand moments of transformation around which to create narrative suspense – how, after all, do you organize a gripping history of emotion if you have no historical epochs around which to group your chapters? – then often reach for the chestnuts: it must be the Renaissance, the Reformation or Absolutism which explains change. The problem with this kind of work is that too much is made to follow from the historical. That a distinction looks different in different historical periods does not show that it is entirely contingent. History itself plays too great and yet too little a role in this kind of work: too much, because an overemphasis is placed on the degree to which human beings change; too little, because the stress on discursive creation oversimplifies subjectivities and foreshortens the range and complexity of historical determinants.

Surrendering the distinction between sex and gender has certainly brought gains. There have been explorations of the history of biological sex itself. Thomas Laqueur has argued that until the eighteenth century, a one-sex model of the body predominated in which sexual difference was a matter of degree, not of two distinct sexes.[8] This is a powerful synthesis, which challenges our most basic assumptions about the naturalness of sexual distinction. Yet what Laqueur is actually describing is the discourse of medical theory. It is not apparent that it was by means of such theory that early modern people understood their bodies. Rather, their culture rested on a very deep apprehension of sexual difference as an organizing principle of culture – in religion, work, magic and ritual. It is a far easier task to investigate literate discourse on sexual difference than it is to get at the way early modern people actually conceived of sexual difference, because such structures are not fully conscious, and cannot be articulated with the same transparency as medical theory. Randolph Trumbach has argued for the rapidly shifting nature of the relationship between the categories of sex and gender: eighteenth-century Londoners, he claims, had a model of three sexes – man, woman, and hermaphrodite – and three genders, the third 'illegitimate gender' being 'the adult passive transvestite effeminate male or molly who was supposed to desire men exclusively'. By the late nineteenth century there were two sexes and four gender roles, 'man, woman, homosexual man, and lesbian woman'.[9] In much of this writing, sexual identity becomes a kind of masquerade for which the

early modern period is the theatre; as if to have a sexual identity in early
modern Europe was to participate in a permanent cross-dressing party.
Indeed, by a curious sleight of hand, cross-dressers and transsexuals are
often the examples to which historians turn when they consider the problem of individual subjectivity in general in early modern Europe.[10]

The challenge of the history of the body to discourse theory is that it
confronts discursive creationism with the physical, with a reality that is only
in part a matter of words. So, for instance, while Londa Schiebinger's fascinating account of the development of the science of anatomy in the eighteenth century is able to show how gendered notions became written into
perceptions of skeletal difference, one wonders naggingly whether there
may not actually be differences between the skeletons of the two sexes
which are not a creation of eighteenth-century science.[11] It is of course true
that we experience the body through mediations of various kinds, and,
because we want to emphasize the way notions of the body are constructed,
the temptation is to write as if there were nothing *but* a historically constructed body. Our own terminology does not help: 'the body', after all, is
itself an irritatingly non-physical abstraction.

Sexual difference is not purely discursive nor merely social. It is also
physical. The cost of the flight from the body and from sexual difference is
evident in what much feminist historical writing has found it impossible to
speak about; or indeed, in the passionate tone of the theoretical work which
most insists on the radically constructed nature of sexual difference. In my
own work, this gap is most evident in [. . .] an essay about the social construction of gender through language and social practice – but its sources
tell another story about the pain and pleasure of love. At its heart there is
an absence: bodies. How indeed can there be a history of sex which is purely
about language and which omits bodies?

I do not think I was untypical in seeking to escape femininity by a flight
from the body and a retreat to the rational reaches of discourse. The pain,
the frustration and the rage of belonging to the sex which does not even
yet have its own history, and which is so often in the role of outsider in any
intellectual context, make it tempting to deny sexual difference altogether
– or to attempt to design one's sexual identity in any way one chooses.
This is a wild utopianism. As Barbara Taylor has shown, it has its roots in
the very beginnings of feminism, in the passionately ambivalent, even
misogynist rhetoric of Mary Wollstonecraft, for example, about the failings of 'systematically voluptuous' women.[12] It is also a deeply creative
force. It has enabled both men and women to envisage new ways of organizing relations between the sexes, and new fields of action for women and
for men. Yet when utopianism becomes intellectual, and loses its imaginative relation to the givenness of bodies, it does so at great cost. We need an
understanding of sexual difference which will incorporate, not fight
against, the corporeal.

[...]

I have been arguing that both social constructionism and linguistic con-structionism short-circuited the realm between language and subjectivity, as if there were no space here to be bridged. Language, by means of its social character, simply impressed a social construction of gender upon the wax of the individual psyche. Or, in the social constructionist version of this theory, collective rituals, performances, habits of work or sociability are seen to imprint themselves upon the individual psyche. When the variable of gender is added, the effect is barely more than to inflect the kind of subjectivity the group mediates: masculinity and femininity themselves are both collectively created. Theories of these kinds link individual and collective psychology. They supply an account of subjectivity which is inherently, though superfi-cially, historical; for as social conditions change, so also will individual con-sciousness. And as discourses become transformed, so too must the linguistic expressions of the individual be transformed.

But one further consequence of this vision of the subject and the social is to reinstate the division between the mental and the corporeal. For the early modern period this ought to make us pause, for this was the period *before* our familiar vision of the division between mind and body – our Cartesian heritage – was articulated. An engagement with pre-modern soci-ety, with its magical world-view and its belief in the demonic, with its assumption that emotions can cause harm in others or its conviction that sanctity can be seen and felt in the uncorrupted body of the saint itself, offers us the chance of rethinking our own habitual classifications of men-tal and corporeal. Our nineteenth-century heritage is a conception of the rational which banishes witchcraft, spells, the demonic and the popular to the margins of society, the underworld or the rural. Or, as one might cari-cature this, it was as we grew enlightened that the world became disen-chanted.[13] But looking at the early modern world can allow us to suspend the distinction between the rational and the irrational, thus helping us to understand our own intuition of the mind–body relation in new ways. As my essays in *Oedipus and the Devil* argue, magic, exorcisms and sexual utopianism, so far from being exotic manifestations of the pre-modern, were central to early modern society – and, as Eva Labouvie has demon-strated in a suggestive reconstruction of the logic of early modern peasant sorcery, to rationality itself.[14] It is in the arena of the magical, the irrational, in witch-trials that – paradoxically enough – the individual subject of the early modern period unfolds.

Bodies have materiality, and this too must have its place in history. The capacity of the body to suffer pain, illness, the process of giving birth, the effects on the body of certain kinds of exercise such as hunting or riding – all these are bodily experiences which belong to the history of the body and are more than discourse. We are familiar with the idea that culture shapes how we experience bodily events, and we have learnt from Norbert Elias how social structure impacts on bodily comportment – we are less ready to admit, or to explore historically, how particular patterns of movement, clothes, illnesses in turn influence culture and subjectivity.

Bodies are not merely the creations of discourse. What we have is a history of discourses about the body; what we need is a history that can problematize the relation between the psychic and the physical. Indeed, the beginnings of psychoanalysis lie in the fascination with the juncture between the physical and the psychic. In Freud's essay on *Senatspräsident* Dr Daniel Paul Schreber, it is the physical dimension of Schreber's paranoid illness which captures Freud's attention: Schreber's retention of his faeces or his belief that his body was turning into that of a woman.[15] Psychic disturbance takes physical form; distorted body images are among the most important features of the illness and offer the clues to its healing. In part because of its interest in sexuality, the paradigmatic area where imagination and physiology coincide, psychoanalysis has offered a powerful way of understanding how bodily experience must of necessity be connected with mental life. One might argue that there can be no experience of the body which is not also psychic, no way of grasping the body without the mediation of mental representations and, therefore, no 'body' which is not historically constructed. But this is only half the story.

What we lack is a fully developed theoretical account of how the physical flows back into the psychic. In Freud, the physical is supplied through a partially biologistic understanding of the drives, but this is about physical functioning rather than bodies themselves. In the work of the psychoanalyst Melanie Klein, bodies dissolve into body images, as if there is nothing that holds together the disembodied breasts, penises and corporeal interiors which populate the psychic imagination.[16] Because of the importance of articulation in psychoanalysis, the so-called 'talking cure', psychoanalysis can sometimes seem to be itself a kind of drama involving the production of a certain kind of text, so that the connection between psyche and body can seem to be just discourse. But this would be to leave out the interconnection between the psychic and the somatic, the problematic which animates so much of Freud's writing and which was the source of many of the theoretical breakthroughs as well as many of the splits within the psychoanalytic movement in its early years. Indeed, it still today remains a vexed area.

The body as we experience it is more than the sum of tactile and kinetic impressions. Our experience of the body is organized by body images. These are in part culturally created, and to that extent they have a collective history. We gain access to these only partially through language, and it is misleading, I think, to equate them with discourse or language.[17] In searching for the body images of the sixteenth century, I am looking for something more than the ways the body was talked about; I want to delineate the only partially conscious images of the body which lie below the surface of language. Body images, bodily malfunction or even what the psychoanalyst Joyce McDougall calls somatic expression, can be a kind of mute communication, a pre-linguistic resource to which we resort when language dries up in inexpressible psychic pain.[18] The body rears its head, so to speak, often only when we are ill, or in agony – a restriction of bodily expression to the pathological. But bodily expression can also be integrated in positive experience, for example, in the pleasure of dance or in sexual delight. And since we are our bodies (more so than we like to admit), bodily symbolism belongs to the deepest religious tools we have.[19] It can convey what we find impossible to put into words.

This was particularly so in the sixteenth century. It is no accident that it should have been the issue of communion which so inflamed passions and divided early modern people. Communion, after all, is far more than a metaphor. Taking communion is a physical process, and the ingestion of the Host, the drinking of the wine, was a physical act through which community and the relationship with God was consummated. Theologically, the issue for reformers was how to understand Christ's incarnation, for the ritual posed the question of the relationship between the divine and the human. The issue around which battle was joined was not only how one should understand the corporeality of the divine, but how this ritual should be carried out: should both elements or only one be received? Should one receive the elements from the hands of the priest? Could one touch the Host? That is, the question of the body, and the boundaries between human and divine, lay at the very heart of the Reformation.[20]

How did early modern Germans visualize the body? What conscious and unconscious imagery lies beneath their language? [. . .] Early modern German culture furnishes a variety of ways of grasping the body. In the literature of excess, the body is imagined as a container for a series of processes: defecation, sexual pollution, vomiting. Fluids course about within the body, erupting out of it, leaving their mark on the world outside. The body is not so much a collection of joints and limbs, or a skeletal structure, as a container of fluids, bursting out in every direction to impact on the environment.[21] This vision of the body as a container of evil fluids is reminiscent of what the psychoanalyst Melanie Klein has to say about the child's conceptualization of the mother's body as a vessel containing evil and dangerous substances,[22] or what the French theorist Julia Kristeva describes as 'abjection', a state which is also related to the tie with the maternal body.[23] But what is different is that the accent is not so much on the badness of the fluids contained in the body as in the pleasure of release. What in Klein and Kristeva is viewed as a negative, pathological imagination – to be sure, part of the psychic heritage we all share – is in this writing a source of pleasure. This is a particular way of eroticizing bodily openings – mouth, anus, penis – as if the operation of the muscles could be simply enjoyed, as if there could be a world where no inhibitions operated to curb the free exchange of fluids between inner and outer, as if the enjoyment of simple release, simple expulsion, is the transgression – a conception which derives its imaginative pull from the literature of repression, of muscular control. This is a world which recalls that of the infant who does not have to control his or her defecation or excretion. And it is also a state in which the boundaries between the self and others, the bounded self and the fluids which spill into the surrounding world, have become melted, as if one could approach the state in which there is no longer distinction between self and world, mother and baby. Yet the literature of excess is anything but a regression *tout court*. Its preoccupations were highly literate, framed within a Latinate, written culture, and it constituted a linguistically sophisticated, controlled cultural creation.[24]

The matching half of this imagistic set is to be found in the literature of discipline: the sets of ordinances, proclamations and mandates which secular authorities promulgated with increasing elaboration from the late fifteenth century, reaching a first full expression in the years of the Reformation, and continuing well into the seventeenth century. This is a literature which crosses the Catholic/Protestant divide. And it was accompanied by a moralistic literature, reaching its high point in the Devil books of the mid-sixteenth century. This, too, conceives of vices as a kind of inner fluid, constantly threatening to burst the bounds of discipline. It is as if the individual is a shapeless collection of active sins constantly threatening to burst through the musculature of morals. Discipline is a kind of 'fence', to use the metaphor of the Augsburg councillors, which has but little strength against the untameable brute force of the lusts within.[25] This literature cannot best be understood, I think, on the repression/release model, for once again, the body is conceived of as a kind of vessel barely able to contain the forces inside it, all of which are imagined in highly active terms as physical activities: gluttony, fighting, fornicating, blaspheming. Even the house, the basic unit of social organization, is conceived of as a skin so thin that it can hardly hold its murderous denizens together: the master patriarch, most likely to fall prey to every kind of vice, the mistress, only too ready to surrender herself to concupiscence, the children, servants and apprentices, naturally inclined to disorder and disrespect for parental authority. A vision of the house, then, which conceives of *disorganization*, anarchy rather than articulation as the natural state.

Another corporeal map, this time a Catholic one, is evident in exorcism, a practice which enjoyed a renewed vogue in the second half of the sixteenth century as Catholics aimed to prove the superiority of their religion over Protestants.[26] Here again, the *insides* of the body are of crucial importance, for it is in the bodily interior that the demons are housed. The demon must be brought out of the body and into the light, expelled from the bodily cavity, if the sufferer is to be cured. This time, however, the expulsion is an unmistakably good thing, while the passage of demons out of the body is painful not pleasurable, producing bodily writhings and contortions. The openings of the body take on especial significance: the devils often leave via the mouth, and bodily orifices such as the ears and nose play an important role. Unpleasant sensual experience plays a powerful role in exorcism: the audience smell a foul, diabolic sulphurous stench, as if we are not very far from the man of excess, the audience are riveted by sounds, by the utterances of the hidden devils speaking from within the body of the possessed woman, sometimes with a man's voice, the hum of prayer and invocation which, like repeated formulae, comforts through sensual rather than linguistic means, through touch, as the audience hold the possessed woman in their laps, grasp her and can feel for themselves the strength of the diabolic forces which thrust her about.

There is certainly a sexual undertow in this imagination. It is no coincidence that exorcisms took place on beds, nor that the spectacle involved the woman rolling about on the ground, her dress askew and her shame uncovered. Nor was it an accident that exorcisms also demonstrated the honour due to Mary, who is at once both mother and virgin. If we ask what map of the body Mary might represent on this grid, then we can speculate that although as a mother, she might potentially be a container of all these terrifying and dangerous substances that inhabit maternal bodies, sexually she is a sealed body, pierced only by the Holy Ghost. She might represent a femininity which is safe and impossible. In terms of bodily imagery, it may be that, imaginatively, Mary offers a counter-resolution to the spectacle of possessed femininity as the exorcist frees the victim with her aid. But it is a resolution which provokes the repetition of the drama, precisely because the resolution is impossible.[27]

The sexual fantasies of witchcraft draw on similar visions of a body which can lose its organization, and in which liquids within the body become poisonous, killing instead of nourishing. The most common form such fantasies took was apparently to cluster around the ideas of feeding and nourishment of babies in the first six weeks of life. Sexual fantasies to which witches give voice often also display a similar vision of a disorganized body: in English witch fantasies, teats appear not confined to the breast, but all over the body as the Devil's mark; they are often to be found near the anus or vagina, as if the bodily orifices had become interchangeable.[28] Sexual activity, when it takes place at the witches' sabbath, is imagined as an orgy in which 'sodomy', that medieval catch-all, becomes an imprecise term for every kind of unorthdox sexual coupling, imprecise because what it refers to cannot quite be named or imagined. That is to say, I do not think that sexual intercourse at the witches' sabbath is just a 'reversal' of normal sexual behaviour, an inversion which 'turns the world upside down' for a moment, but which leaves its categories intact.[29] Rather, what we encounter here is a disordered imagination in which anal and oral sex *don't* reinstate the heterosexual norm of which they are the inverse, but dissolve the categories of the discrete, functioning body altogether. Something much more primary is at work here, fantasies to do with sex and death, with non-reproductive intercourse, sexual union as an engulfment which destroys the identity, and behind this, the horror of sex with the mother herself, the return to the death of the womb. In this sense, I think the fantasies of witchcraft are heir to these earlier visions of the body, but now their maternal content becomes much more manifest. They, too, give voice to very primitive kinds of mental distress, to the moment when distinctions between oneself and others seem to elide, when the shape of the body seems to blur and utter helplessness and terror result.

It is easier to delineate the kinds of semi-conscious imaginings of the body that are at work here than it is to explain, historically, why they should have proved particularly compelling at certain historical moments. If I were to hazard a chronological chain of imaginative connection, I would speculate that the image of the excessive body which constantly breaks out of its own boundaries – the preoccupation with the processes of excreting – and the fascination with muscular control acted in vortex fashion, pulling some kinds of imagination back towards earlier scenes from childhood. The transition from a vision of the body which was primarily of a male body, but which could also be applied to female bodies (the grotesque excessive comic figure Grobian had his female equivalent Grobiana[30]), to a concentration on the female body alone, which we find in images of witchcraft, is important.[31] Fascination with boundaries, control and the substances within the body allowed one to imagine and indeed experience the loss of boundaries altogether, the filling of the body with evil substances and the elision of the gap between one's own body and the maternal body. These terrifying spectres nourished the corporeal imagination of the witch-craze. Why and how these spectres seized the minds of individuals and groups of people at some times and some places will require a detailed compilation of social factors, and an exploration of the relation between judicial process and political power [. . .] Part of the answer must lie in the psychic and corporeal realms, and we neglect these at our peril.

I have been advocating an approach to early modern subjectivities which will recognize the collective elements of culture without trivializing individual subjectivity. I have been arguing that gender cannot be understood as the social acquisition of an unproblematic sexual identity. Sexual difference has a bodily dimension. Sexual identity can never be satisfactorily understood if we conceive it as a set of discourses about masculinity or femininity. Nor can the individual subject be adequately understood as a container of discourse – a conception which evacuates subjectivity of psychology. We are very far from knowing how such discourses relate to people's own sexual identities, which nearly always lack the coherence – or even the comforting contradictions – of discourse. Understood as a discursive creation alone, gender is not a category of historical analysis because, lacking an account of the connections between social and psychic, it cannot adequately conceptualize change.

It is far easier to insist on the need for a history of early modern culture which will incorporate the subjective, the psychic and the corporeal than it is to show how that history will look. [. . .] But I am convinced that unless history and cultural anthropology – and we ourselves – can learn to admit the psychic and the corporeal, we shall never truly encounter the past.

Notes:

1 See, for instance, David Sabean's path-breaking *Power in the Blood. Popular culture and village discourse in early modern Germany*, Cambridge 1984.
2 Joan W. Scott, 'Gender: A useful category of historical analysis', reprinted in *idem*, *Gender and the Politics of History*, New York 1988.
3 Here see Sally Alexander's important exploration of this point in 'Women, Class and Sexual Differences in the 1830s and 1840s. Some reflections on the writing of feminist history', *History Workshop Journal*, 17, 1984, pp. 125–49.
4 See, in particular, Denise Riley, *'Am I that Name?' Feminism and the category of 'Women' in history*, London 1988.
5 Judith Butler, *Gender Trouble. Feminism and the subversion of identity*, New York and London 1990.
6 Ibid., p. 33.
7 Ibid., p. 2.
8 Thomas Laqueur, *Making Sex. Body and gender from the Greeks to Freud*, Cambridge, Mass. 1990; and for different views, see Evelyne Berriot-Salvadore, 'The Discourse of Medicine and Science', in Natalie Zemon Davis and Arlette Farge (eds), *A History of Women in the West*, vol. 3, *Renaissance and Enlightenment Paradoxes*, Cambridge, Mass. 1993; and Gianna Pomata, 'Uomini mestruanti: somiglianze e differenze fra i Sessi in Europa in età moderna', *Quaderni Storici*, 79, 1992, pp. 51–103.
9 Randolph Trumbach, 'London's Sapphists: From three sexes to four genders in the making of modern culture', in Julia Epstein and Kristina Straub (eds), *Body Guards. The cultural politics of gender ambiguity*, New York and London 1991, pp. 112, 113; 'Sex, Gender and Sexual Identity in Modern Culture: Male sodomy and female prostitution in Enlightenment London', in John C. Fout (ed.), *Forbidden History: The state, society, and the regulation of sexuality in modern Europe. Essays from the Journal of the History of Sexuality*, Chicago, Ill. 1992.
10 Rudolf Dekker and Lotte C. van de Pol, *The Tradition of Female Transvestism in Early Modern Europe*, trans. Judy Marcure and Lotte C. van de Pol, Basingstoke 1989.
11 Londa Schiebinger, 'Skeletons in the Closet: The first illustrations of the female skeleton in eighteenth-century anatomy', in Catherine Gallagher and Thomas Laqueur (eds), *The Making of the Modern Body. Sexuality and society in the nineteenth century*, Berkeley, Calif. 1987. I am grateful to Peter Lake for pointing this out.
12 Mary Wollstonecraft, *A Vindication of the Rights of Woman*, London 1992, introduction by Barbara Taylor, p. xxiv.
13 For a powerful critique of this view, see Bob Scribner, 'The Reformation, Popular Magic and the "Disenchantment of the World"', *Journal of Interdisciplinary History*, 23, 1993, pp. 475–94.
14 Eva Labouvie, *Zauberie und Hexenwerk. Ländlicher Hexenglaube in der frühen Neuzeit*, Frankfurt am Main 1991; *idem*, *Verbotene Künste. Volksmagie und ländlicher Aberglaube in den Dorfgemeinden des Saarraumes (16.–19. Jahrhundert)*, St Ingbert 1992.

15 Sigmund Freud, 'Psychoanalytische Bemerkungen über einen autobiographisch beschriebenen Fall von Paranoia (Dementia paranoides)', *Sigmund Freud. Studienausgabe*, Frankfurt am Main 1969–75, vol. 7, pp. 133–203.

16 Melanie Klein, *Love, Guilt and Reparation and Other Works 1921–45*, new edn, London 1988; *idem, Envy and Gratitude and Other Works 1949–63*, new edn, London 1988; *idem, Narrative of a Child Analysis*, new edn, London 1989; *idem, The Psychoanalysis of Children*, London 1989.

17 Compare, here, Barbara Maria Stafford, *Body Criticism. Imaging the unseen in Enlightenment art and medicine*, Cambridge, Mass. and London 1991, on what she terms 'nondiscursive articulations' in the eighteenth century (p. 6), and see Sharon Fermor, 'Movement and Gender in Sixteenth-Century Italian Painting', in Kathleen Adler and Marcia Pointon (eds), *The Body Imaged. The human form and visual culture since the Renaissance*, Cambridge 1993.

18 Joyce McDougall, *Theatres of the Mind: Illusion and Truth on the Psychoanalytic Stage*, New York 1985.

19 See Caroline Walker Bynum, *Fragmentation and Redemption. Essays on gender and the human body in medieval religion*, New York 1992, esp. the introductory essay, 'History in the Comic Mode'.

20 Miri Rubin, *Corpus Christi. The Eucharist in late medieval culture*, Cambridge 1991; Michel de Certeau, *The Mystic Fable: vol. 1, The Sixteenth and Seventeenth Centuries*, trans. Michael B. Smith, Chicago, Ill. 1992, pp. 79ff.; Natalie Zemon Davis, 'Missed Connections: *Religion and Regime*', *Journal of Interdisciplinary History*, 1, 1971, pp. 38–94; and Guy Swanson, 'Systems of Descent and Interpreting the Reformation', *Journal of Interdisciplinary History*, 1, 1971, pp. 419–46.

21 On the 'bodiliness' of early modern culture, see Norbert Schindler, 'Karneval, Kirche und verkehrte Welt. Zur Funktion der Lachkultur im 16. Jahrhundert', in *idem, Widerspenstige Leute*, Frankfurt am Main 1992, esp. pp. 159–67.

22 Melanie Klein, *The Psychoanalysis of Children*.

23 See, for example, Julia Kristeva, *Powers of Horror. An essay on abjection*, trans. Leon S. Roudiez, New York 1982; *idem, Desire in Language. A semiotic approach to literature and art*, ed. Leon S. Roudiez, trans. Thomas Gora, Alice Jardine and Leon S. Roudiez, London 1980.

24 Michael Screech, *Rabelais*, London 1979; Erich Auerbach, *Mimesis. The representation of reality in western literature*, trans. Willard Trask, Princeton, NJ 1953, pp. 262–84.

25 Lyndal Roper, *The Holy Household. Women and morals in Reformation Augsburg*, Oxford 1989, pp. 57ff.

26 See H.C. Erik Midelfort, 'Sin, Melancholy, Obsession: Insanity and culture in 16th century Germany', in S.L. Kaplan (ed.), *Understanding Popular Culture*, Berlin 1984; and on Protestant understandings, Stuart Clark, 'Protestant Demonology: Sin, superstition, and society (c. 1520–c. 1630)', in Bengt Ankarloo and Gustav Henningsen (eds), *Early Modern European Witchcraft. Centres and peripheries*, Oxford 1990.

27 Marina Warner, *Alone of all Her Sex: The myth and cult of the Virgin Mary*, London 1976.

28 See Jim Sharpe, 'Witchcraft and Women in Seventeenth-Century England: Some northern evidence', *Continuity and Change*, 6, 1991, pp. 179–200; and Marianne Hester, *Lewd Women and Wicked Witches. A study of the dynamics of male domination*, London 1992, esp. pp. 161–97.

29 On inversion in witchcraft, see the classic article by Stuart Clark, 'Inversion, Misrule and the Meaning of Witchcraft', *Past and Present*, 87, 1980, pp. 98–127.

30 Friedrich Dedekind, *Grobianus und Grobiana*, trans. C. Scheidt, Frankfurt 1567.

31 Exorcism is interesting here, since both men and women may be possessed. H.C. Erik Midelfort, 'The Devil and the German People: Reflections on the popularity of demon possession in sixteenth-century Germany', in Steven Ozment (ed.), *Religion and Culture in the Renaissance and Reformation* (Sixteenth-Century Essays and Studies, 11), Kirksville, Mo. 1989, p. 110.

7

The birth of the queen: sodomy and the emergence of gender equality in modern culture, 1660–1750

RANDOLPH TRUMBACH

In probably all human societies other than those under the influence of the Christian religion, it has been legitimate for two males to have sexual relations with each other. There have been only two restrictions: that the adult men who had sexual relations with males also marry women and produce families; that the adult male in the sexual act always take the active or penetrator's role. The second point was guaranteed in one of two ways. In the first pattern (as in Japan, China, New Guinea, Australia, some tribal African societies, in Islam, and in the classical Mediterranean world), the adult male had sexual relations with an adolescent boy who might be his wife, his concubine, his lover, or his whore. In the second pattern (to be found in southern Asia from Polynesia to Madagascar, among the North American Indians, and among some African tribes), the adult male had sexual relations with a small minority of adult males who had permanently adopted many (but not all) of the characteristics of women in speech, gesture, clothes, and work. Christian Europe, by contrast, had since the twelfth century made illicit all sexual relations between two persons of the same gender. Such sexual relations nonetheless occurred. And when they did so they were enacted within the framework of the two worldwide human patterns.

In traditional European societies, men who did not restrict their sexual experience to marriage usually had sex with both adolescent boys and female whores. But as modern Western societies emerged in the late seventeenth century this pattern began to change. By 1700 there were appearing in the cities of northern Europe, especially in those like London, Paris, and Amsterdam, which had populations of half a million, a minority of markedly effeminate men whose most outstanding characteristic was that they desired to have sex only with other males. These men either seduced males from the majority who were not effeminate and thereby ran the risks of arrest and punishment, or of blackmail; or they safely had relations with each other inside a protective subculture. It looks as though Europe was

Reprinted from Duberman, Vicinus and Chauncey Jr (eds), *Hidden from History: Reclaiming the Gay and Lesbian Past* (Penguin, 1991). Reprinted by permission of the author.

switching from one world pattern to another – from men having sex with boys to men having sex with transvestite adult males. But it was not quite that, for at the same moment it began to be felt that it was impossible for the average, normal male to feel any sexual desire for another male of any age or condition. To be masculine was to experience sexual desire only for women. Europe was switching from adult male libertines who had sex with boys and with women to a world divided between a majority of men and women who desired only the opposite gender and a minority of men and women who desired only the same gender. It is the purpose of this essay to show this change happening in a single European society between 1660 and 1750, in England, and especially in London. The conclusion of the essay will consider why this great change occurred.[1]

Part I: The sodomite as rake

The behavior of the relatively small circle of aristocratic libertines in the 1660s and 1670s provides the best, if fragmentary, evidence of bisexual libertinism. These libertines can be found in three kinds of material: in letters and diaries; in the trials for sodomy; and in the imaginative literature of the stage and of the new pornographic genre. In this world the love of boys certainly did not exclude the love of women; but the love of boys was seen as the most extreme act of sexual libertinism; and it was often associated, as well, with religious skepticism, and even republican politics. It is as though sodomy were so extreme a denial of the Christian expectation that all sexual acts ought to occur in marriage and have the potential of procreation, that those who indulged in it were likely also to break through all other conventions in politics and religion. The unconventionality of that minority of rakes who were sodomitical was therefore frightening to society at large; but they were not held in contempt. It was, instead, that they were secretly held in awe for the extremity of their masculine self-assertion, since they triumphed over male and female alike. Most men who did not keep within the bounds of matrimony indulged in a more quotidian fornication. But in the *Wandering Whore* (1660), the anonymous author explained that there were men who 'will not be contented with doing the business.' One man, for instance wanted to be under a table snarling as if he would bite off the 'whibb-bobs' of the half-dozen girls who stood around him; another 'will needs shite in one of our wenches mouth's'; a third 'will needs be whipt to raise lechery and cause a standing P——.' But it was the fourth who would 'fayn be buggering some of our wenches, if the Matron could get their consent, but had rather be dealing with smooth-fac'd prentices.' Anal intercourse was the most extreme of sexual acts, and the libertine desired to perform it either with a woman or with an adolescent boy whose beard had not begun to grow.[2]

It was in this libertine world that the twenty-four-year-old Sir Charles Sedley stood naked on the balcony of an inn and in full daylight, 'showed his nakedness,' 'acting all the postures of lust and buggery that could be imagined,' abused the Scriptures, and preached that he had such a powder to sell 'as should make all the cunts in town run after him.' He was punished by the magistrate. But when Pepys discussed the story in 1663, what stood out was the buggery – two of Pepys' acquaintances declaring that 'buggery is now almost grown as common among our gallants as in Italy, and that the very pages of the town begin to complain of their masters for it.' The supposed Italian origins of this act long continued to be a familiar way for Englishmen to distance themselves from it. Pepys' alarm at this aristocratic vice made him piously conclude that 'blessed be God, I do not to this day know what is the meaning of this sin, nor which is the agent nor which the patient.' But all the Restoration sources (except Pepys) took for granted that the boy was passive.[3]

This was the presumption that Lord Rochester made when he sang to his mistress:

> Nor shall our love-fits, Chloris, be forgot,
>   When each the well-looked link boy strove t'enjoy,
> And the best kiss was the deciding lot
>   Whether the boy fucked you, or I the boy.

But both Rochester and the boy were interested in Chloris as well as in each other. Rochester's letters to Henry Savile confirm that this and the other references in his poems were genuine reflections of Rochester's taste. Once he sent Savile a young Frenchman, his valet, of whom he said, 'The greatest and gravest of this court of both sexes have tasted his beauties.' It is possible that the valet later tried to blackmail his master. For despite the public bravado of the libertine's statements, the law could exact a harsh price if an actual act could be proven.[4]

The lawyer John Hoyle, for instance, was arrested and indicted for buggering William Bristow, a poulterer. Hoyle is one of the clearest examples of the bisexual libertine, but not surprisingly, it has been very difficult for this to be seen by twentieth-century readers who are committed to the presumption of mutually exclusive conditions of homosexuality and heterosexuality. Hoyle moved in libertine circles. Sir Charles Sedley described his republican conversation in a tavern, and his lover Aphra Behn wrote of his fondness for Lucretius. Whitelocke Bulstrode went further and called him an 'atheist, a sodomite professed, a corrupter of youth, and a blasphemer of Christ.' Hoyle had a number of women lovers in addition to Mrs. Behn; but Behn also gave the name of at least one of his male lovers. Behn's twentieth-century biographers, however, simply label Hoyle 'a homosexual' and take this as the cause of the failure of his affair with Behn. They presume that a man who had sex with males must be *really* interested only in men, even though he also had affairs with women. There is no room in their philosophy for the bisexual libertine. But Hoyle escapes their net, as he escaped the charge before the grand jury. He died, instead, in a drunken brawl that he had begun by 'railing against all government.'[5]

Other libertine rakes did not escape the law as easily as Hoyle, as the case of Lord Castlehaven illustrates. In 1631 Castlehaven was found guilty and executed for promoting a rape on his wife and for sodomy with his young male pages. He took the boys to bed with his wife, and after he had watched them entering her, he sodomized them by coming between their thighs. He was also fully capable of relations with a woman, having had several children by a first wife. In libertine fashion, he was a skeptic in religion.[6]

The life of the rake sometimes made it into the plays of the Restoration stage – even if less often than is sometimes thought – and mainly in the 1670s. But the bisexual libertine made it there even less often.[7]

Aphra Behn (1671), Thomas Otway (1680), and Nathanial Lee (1680) did each write a play in which it was indicated that one of their rakes (who was shown mainly in hot pursuit of women) was also interested in boys. Behn's Lorenzo looks at a woman who in her disguise he thinks a male page, and says 'this stripling may chance to mar my market of women now – 'tis a fine lad, how plump and white he is; would I could meet him somewhere i' th' dark, I'd have a fling at him, and try whether I were right Florentine.' He later asks the 'smooth-fac'd boy' how long he has 'been set up for thy self' (as a prostitute), and advises him to leave women alone, as wenching will 'spoil a good face and mar your better market of the two.' Otway's Sir Jolly Jumble tickles Beaugard's legs and calls him 'my Ganimede'; he calls Courtine a pretty fellow and tries to kiss him; but he then moves on to romp with his three (female) whores. Lee's Nemours similarly calls Bellamore his 'sweet-fac'd pimp' and later 'thou dear soft rogue, my spouse, my Hephestion, my Ganymed'; but Bellamore is as interested as his master in women and guarantees where Nemours will be able to meet the Duchess of Cleves by saying that he has it from 'one of her women whom I have debauched.'[8]

What is missing in all this material is the adult, effeminate, exclusively homosexual male who seeks an adult male partner. I have found only one possible reference to such men in the *Wandering Whore*: 'There are likewise hermaphrodites, effeminate men, men given to much luxury, idleness, and wanton pleasures, and to that abominable sin of sodomy, wherein they are both active and passive in it, whose vicious actions are onely to be whispered amongst us.' These men are deviant, however, not so much because of their sodomy, but because they were adult males who sometimes played the passive role. But hermaphrodites were also actual people who possessed sexually ambiguous genitalia – a child, for instance, on whom Robert Wittie reported to the Royal Society in 1672: assigned to the female gender at birth by the midwives but thought by Wittie to be a boy. Canonical tradition had required such persons to permanently choose one gender or another and had held them guilty of sodomy if they alternated in their sexual behavior. For this reason, perhaps, 'hermaphrodite' could be used to refer to adult men who switched from active to passive without being biological hermaphrodites. But such men were presumably interested in taking the active role with women. There is also no suggestion that they engaged in cross-dressing. We must therefore distinguish their effeminacy from the predominating effeminacy of the adult male fop.[9]

Part II: Fops and beaus: effeminacy and sodomy

The fop is often misinterpreted by the twentieth-century reader of Restoration plays to be a 'homosexual.' But in an important essay, Susan Staves has pointed out that fops, while effeminate in manner from their contemporaries' point of view, were also presumed to be sexually interested in women. That interest, however, was differently expressed from the rake's. Maiden in Thomas Baker's *Tunbridge-Walks* (1703) confides that 'I never keep company with lewd rakes that go to nasty taverns, talk smuttily, and get fuddl'd; but visit the ladies, and drink tea, and chocolate.' In the three generations between 1660 and 1750, public attitudes toward the fop changed dramatically by generation. Between 1660 and 1690, Restoration drama firmly rejected the fop in favor of the rake. After 1690, however, the rake himself fell to the power of romantic marriage on the stage, and the fop's domesticated interests came to be more highly valued. But between 1720 and 1750 the fop's effeminacy came under a new kind of criticism (and this is the point at which Staves does not fully see the significance of her evidence), which by the late eighteenth century made the fop a character appropriate only to low farce and exiled him from high comedy.[10]

After 1720 the fop's effeminacy, in real life and on the stage, came to be identified with the effeminacy of the then emerging role of the exclusive male sodomite – known in the ordinary language of his day as a *molly*, and later as a *queen*. The meaning of the word *effeminate* consequently changed. In the seventeenth century it had been used to describe one of two types: the smooth-faced Ganymedes who might even be transvestite to attract their adult male partners; or the adult male obsessed with women – 'thou call'st me effeminate,' wrote Donne, 'for I love women's joys.'[11] But by the early eighteenth century, the second of these two meanings had disappeared; by then an adult effeminate male was likely to be taken to be an exclusive sodomite. Consequently when Garrick in 1747 wrote the role of Fribble in *Miss in Her Teens*, a critic could see that he was attempting 'to laugh out of countenance that *mollifying elegance* which manifests itself with such bewitching grace in the *refined* youths of this *cultivated age*.' And to be mollified was to adopt the manners of the molly.[12]

The transformation of the fop into the molly can clearly be seen in the way in which Smollett in his novel *Roderick Random* (1748) treated his source for the figure of Captain Whiffle. The character was based on the 'finical sea fop' in Charles Shadwell's *The Fair Quaker of Deal* (1710), about whom there is no hint of sodomitical desires. But Whiffle comes on board in the most extravagant garb with a 'crowd of attendants, all of whom . . . seemed to be of their patron's disposition'; and the ship's gossip soon accuses him of 'maintaining a correspondence with his surgeon, not fit to be named.' When, therefore, the late eighteenth century developed a male gender role that eschewed the violence of the rake for the domesticity of the faithful husband, who avoided smut, drunkenness, and violence, it was a role that had also put aside those extravagances of the fop that were now associated with the molly.[13]

Among those extravagances were elaborate clothes and enthusiastic forms of greeting. Consequently men's clothes were simplified. And they gave up kissing each other. By 1749 it could be said that when males kissed each other in greeting, it was the 'first inlet to the detestable sin of sodomy'; and that the same thing was true of extravagant male dress. But kissing was, of 'all the customs effeminacy has produced,' the most 'hateful, predominant, and pernicious.' It was a custom brought over, of course, 'from Italy (the mother and nurse of sodomy); where the master is oftener intriguing with his page, than a fair lady.' It was better to shake hands – 'more manly; more friendly, and more decent.' A society of men was formed who vowed never to kiss any man, and they kept their rule 'many times at the expense of a quarrel.' Even brothers ceased to kiss: 'I saw myself two brothers take a very solemn leave of each other without one kiss, though not without tears.' By contrast two men in a private room in a tavern in 1727 were identified by the waiter as sodomites because 'he heard them kissing each other.' At the end of the eighteenth century, Continental visitors had to be warned that kissing between men had unacceptable connotations: Only handshaking or a civil bow were allowed.[14]

It should now be clear that the effeminacy of the fop was not associated before the 1690s with the practice of adult male sodomy. Such reckless sexual practices as sodomy were the province instead of the abandoned rake. In the mid-1680s, however, the new role of the beau emerged; he mediated between the fop and the rake and he made it possible for foppish effeminacy by the end of the 1690s to become associated with sodomy. *Fop* had been a derogatory epithet applied by others. *Beau* was used by some men as a term of self-description for the overdressed man who had taken on some of the splash of the old-style rake. And part of that splash was sodomy with boys.[15]

This is the context that gives meaning to the trial for sodomy in 1698 of Captain Rigby, and it helps to explain why the case was so much discussed. Rigby was a beau who attempted to seduce a boy he had met in the park. One of his critics blamed his actions on his 'effeminate madness' as a fop, though the critic presumed that as a fop he was still interested in women as well, since he 'manages his whore.' This is one of the very earliest attempts to tie effeminacy to sodomy, and it was clearly inspired by the elaborate way Rigby dressed. Rigby himself gave a quite different motive for his actions. When the boy had complained that 'a woman only was fit' to raise a man's lust to the highest degree (as Rigby said the boy had done for him), Rigby replied that the women were all diseased: 'D—mn 'em, they are all pox'd, I'll have nothing to do with them.' Other men, according to John Dunton in 1710, followed a similar course: Prostitutes had 'burnt so many beaus, that now he-whores are coming in use.' These men were to him, however, 'a new society . . . call'd S—d——ites; men worse than goats, who dressed themselves in petticoats.' But Rigby was a beau whose elaborate male clothes were still quite different from those of a woman.[16]

Part III: The sodomite as he-whore

It is almost certainly the case that the effeminate manner of a beau like Rigby was seen in 1699 as the cause of his sodomy, only because there had begun to appear a new kind of sodomite who was identified principally by his effeminate manner. Consequently, by the 1720s a complete lack of interest in women, and male transvestism, had become in the public mind the accompaniments of sexual desire between two adult males. But it is very hard to find this new sodomite in the sources prior to 1707. There are only hints. There were arrests of groups of sodomites (as opposed to the usual single individual) at London and at Windsor in 1699. In 1704 John Norton took hold of the privates of John Coyney, 'putting them in his mouth and sucking them.' Now, the mouth is an ambiguous sexual organ when it comes to the question of who is in control, but it is probably safe to see Norton's action as evincing a desire on the part of one adult man to be sexually submissive to another.[17] But it was dangerous to attempt to seduce men who did not share such tastes. Such relations could be more safely pursued in a subculture of the like-minded where men who could be both active and passive sought each other. This begins to appear clearly three years later, in 1707, with the arrests of sodomites in a number of known meeting places, which could not suddenly have come into existence in that year. The further arrests and commentary in 1709 reinforce this and document groups of effeminate adult males who were interested in men or in boys, but not at all in women; these men had sexual relations with each other, and sometimes with males who were not effeminate sodomites.

In 1707 the Societies for the Reformation of Manners sent its agents into the recognized meeting places on London-bridge and around the arcades of the Royal Exchange. Two of the younger men who made passes at the agents had been seduced previously for money by older men. But William Huggins, who was a porter and had been married for a year to a young wife who was pregnant, confessed when apprehended that 'he had heard there were such sort of persons in the world, and he had a mind to try.' The boghouses, or public latrines, of London provided a third meeting place where old and new sodomites intermingled. An apothecary in the Strand picked up Thomas Vaughan in the piazzas of Covent Garden – another arcade (like that of the Exchange) that was ideal for sauntering – and took Vaughan to the boghouse in the Savoy and asked him 'to bugger him.' Vaughan also forced a confession out of another man, William Guilham, 'a person that frequently committed frigging' (i.e., masturbation – the word sodomy is deliberately crossed out in the deposition). Guilham had made an attempt on a boy in the Temple bog-house. The question for us, though, is whether the apothecary who wanted to be buggered by an adult man belonged to the same world as the one who masturbated boys. It may be that in the boghouses the old rakish sodomites intermingled with the new, more passive kind.

The popular literature that the trials produced certainly presumed that the passive adult male was something new. A broadside ballad called 'The Women-hater's Lamentation' was published on the occasion of the suicide in jail of three of the arrested men. It claimed that nearly a hundred more were 'accused for unnatural deprising the fair sex, and intriguing with one another.' It sported three woodcuts with a picture of two adult men embracing in the middle, and the three suicides on either side. The ballad called them a 'club' and a 'gang.' Lady Cowper noted in her diary that one of the suicides left a note claiming his innocence, and that this indicated to many that there existed an extensive trade in the blackmailing of timid men who could not manage their defense, even if innocent of the charge. She was very likely right, since throughout the rest of the century the odium attached to the new role of the effeminate sodomite, and the difficulty of disproving the charge, led to a great many blackmail cases.[18]

The material from 1709 makes it even clearer that contemporaries were beginning to see a kind of sodomite different from the men who frigged and sodomized boys and advised them to try lewd women. The new sodomites met as clubs in taverns, and they called themselves (according to Ned Ward) *mollies*. It is a word probably related to *molly*, which meant a female prostitute; it starts a long tradition in English language usage whereby the slang terms for prostitutes in one generation subsequently are appropriated for sodomites (e.g., queen, punk, gay, faggot, fairy, and fruit). It makes clear that the sodomite viewed himself, and was seen by others, no longer as a rake but as a species of outcast woman. One sodomite could later say to another, 'Where have you been, you saucy Queen?' (When queen still meant prostitute.) 'If I catch you strolling and caterwauling I'll beat the milk out of your breasts, I will so.' Dunton called them 'he-whores.' Jonathan Wild recalled that William Hitchen, the London Under-Marshal and himself a sodomite, had offered to 'introduce him to a company of he-whores.' When Wild, 'not apprehending rightly his meaning, asked if they were hermaphrodites,' Hitchen replied, 'No ye fool . . . they are sodomites, such as deal with their own sex instead of females.' Dunton added that 'some doat on men, and some on boys.'[19]

Inside the tavern or molly-house, as the sources from 1709 to 1730 testify, the mollies enacted the rituals of their new identity. (There are four principal sources: Ned Ward in 1709; Wild in 1718 describing an event in 1714; the trials of 1726; and James Dalton in 1728.[20]) In the safety of their clubs, which (as Dalton noted) lessened the likelihood of blackmail, they greeted each other as Madam and Your Ladyship, as Wild discovered when he entered with Hitchen: 'calling one another my dear, hugging and kissing, tickling and feeling each other, as if they were a mixture of wanton males and females; and assuming effeminate voices, female airs'; with some mollies evidently taking the active role and some the passive. There were ceremonies mocking the connection of sex to marriage and childbearing; these might be seen as suggestions of religious skepticism, but their principal purpose is more likely to have been the imitation of the lives of women. Dalton was present at a wedding between a man called 'Moll Irons and another Molly' who was a butcher; two other butchers stood as bridesmaids. One of them was the Princess Seraphina, who by a trial four years later is confirmed as a real enough person. There were mock deliveries of children, complete with the groaning mother, the midwife, and a baby in the form of a wooden doll, which both Ward and Dalton described. The actual sexual encounters in the molly-houses in 1725 and 1726 occurred in this same context of mock marriage. In Mother Clap's house in Field Lane in Holborn, after 'kissing, hugging, and making love (as they called it),' they went into another room where there were beds, 'which, in their dialect, they called *Marrying*.' Edward Courtney claimed (though the jury did not believe him) that George Whitle's alehouse had a room with a bed for couples who had a mind to be married and that it was called the chapel.

Dalton was taken to molly-houses by a man whom he always called Sukey or Susanna Haws, who specialized in blackmailing his fellow sodomites. Dalton noted the female names that most mollies used in the houses were taken to conceal their true identities, but these names probably also allowed them to take on a second effeminate identity. There was Garter Mary, 'a man who sells garters about the streets'; and Nurse Ashcroft and Fish Hannah, who were both fishmongers; and Aunt Mug, who kept a molly-house. The trials of 1726 yield a rich crop of pseudonyms. York Horner was Pru, John Towleton was Mary Magdalen, Thomas Mugg was Judith, and Samuel Roper (who was married to a woman) was Plump Nelly. All of these kept molly-houses. Samuel Gadiger alias Miss Rose, Thomas Wareham alias Miss Wareham, William Gent alias Mademoiselle Gent, John Whale alias Margaret or Peggy Whale, and Martin McIntosh alias Orange Dib, were all charged with sodomy.[21]

Occasionally a group of mollies went dancing, with many of them dressed as women. Wild recalled that Hitchen, the sodomitical Under-Marshal, had arrested (in revenge for being ignored by some young men) a group of mollies as they returned home from a ball in Holborn. Some had 'gowns, petticoats, headcloths, fine laced shoes, furbelow scarves, masks and complete dresses for women; others had riding hoods; some were dressed like shepherdesses; others like milkmaids with fine green hats, waistcoats, and petticoats; and others had their faces painted and patched and very extensive whoop petticoats which were then very lately introduced.'

There were men who when on their own dressed as women, like the lone footman arrested late at night in the street in 1727. More revealingly, there were cases of men like Dalton's acquaintances Sukey Haws and the Princess Seraphina, who seem to have spent most of their time in women's clothes and to have been referred to by their ordinary acquaintances almost entirely as *she* and *her*. John Cooper was the Princess Seraphina. Margaret Holder described him as a Mollycull, 'one of the runners that carries messages between gentlemen . . . going of sodomitical errands.' Mary Poplet said she had 'never heard she [sic] had any other name than the Princess Seraphina'; she had 'seen him [sic] several times in women's clothes, she [sic] commonly used to wear a white gown and a scarlet cloak with her hair frizzled and curled all around her forehead; and then she would so flutter her fan and make such fine curtsies that you would not have known her from a woman: she takes great delight in balls and masquerades.' Even the Princess, however, sometimes dressed as a man, as the evidence comes from a case in which she had charged Thomas Gordon with forcing her to undress in Chelsea Fields in order to exchange her fine male clothes for his. But Gordon insisted that the clothes had been given in the expectation that he would allow Seraphina to bugger him.[22]

Seraphina establishes the extent to which effeminacy could be taken. Even his identity was not entirely feminine, however, but a combination of both genders: He sometimes dressed as a male, and he had proposed to take the active or penetrator's role with Gordon. On the other hand, even the men who were married to women adopted female names once inside the molly-house. It had become the case that after 1700 most adult sodomites were both active and passive, whereas before 1700 only a minority of sodomites had been so. But in a parallel way, there existed after 1700 a minority of adult sodomites (like sailors in the navy) who would refer to a boy as 'cunt,' and were presumably exclusively active.[23] In other words, every predominant system produces its variant.

Those sailors at sea, and the married men in the molly-houses, would, however, have caused great difficulty for the common belief that the majority of men could feel no interest at all in other men. Because of this belief many men accused of sodomy attempted to disprove the charge by showing that they were either married or had 'loved a girl too well to be concerned in other affairs'; and sometimes they succeeded. The sodomites who picked up boys therefore faced a new level of hostility both from the boys and their friends, since it was no longer possible, as it had been in the seventeenth century, for a boy to pass from the passive to the active role at manhood. All males now needed to be active at every stage of life in order to establish a masculine status.[24]

It was not yet the case, however, that women were obliged to disavow all sexual interest in women to establish a feminine status. There was as yet no lesbian role to be avoided, though men were aware that some women desired women. Women's gender role revolved, instead, around the avoidance of the prostitute's identity. The differences between male and female identity can be seen in the attitude toward male and female cross-dressing in the theater. Until 1660, all female roles on the English stage were played by cross-dressing boys, with many suggestions made as to their sexual passivity with the older actors. (It partly accounts for the libertine behavior of Marlowe and Shakespeare.) At the Restoration, actresses began to share the female roles with boy actors, and probably by the end of the century had replaced them. But there then grew up instead a convention by which actresses played male roles in male attire; this continued in popularity throughout the eighteenth century. There were limits to this public female transvestism. Charlotte Charke made a reputation playing these 'breeches parts,' as her father Colley Cibber had made his reputation playing fops. But when Charke took to dressing as a man in the London streets, and toured the provinces with an actress who passed as her wife, it caused a break with her family. On the other hand, she published an account of her behavior and was never arrested for it.[25]

The final task is to ask why the great transition should have occurred. In most other cultures that produce an adult male transvestite group – whether the North American *berdache*, the Polynesian *mahu*, or the Omani *xanith* – this role usually serves as bridge between the male and female roles in societies where those roles are not radically differentiated.[26] The appearance of the English molly and his European counterparts would therefore indicate that male and female roles had begun to grow more nearly equal. This is confirmed by the development at that time of the companionate marriage and the domesticated family.[27] But the older European tradition that all sexual acts must be procreative – which had partly produced the older system of illicit relations between men and boys – now guaranteed that the molly could not find licit partners among the majority of adult males. The molly was therefore a wall of separation between the genders rather than a bridge. But he was a wall that perhaps made possible an unprecedented development of equality between the other two genders, since it was now the case that there would remain a radical separation of male and female experience, no matter how far equality might go in other ways. Men would never know what it was like to desire men: Only women knew that. And the molly's outcast status was the demonstration of what awaited a man who tried to cross the boundary between sexual desire in the two legitimated genders.

Notes

1 The summary statements of the introduction are more fully documented in Randolph Trumbach, 'London's Sodomites: Homosexual Behavior and Western Culture in the Eighteenth Century,' *Journal of Social History* 11 (1977): 1–33; 'Sodomitical Subcultures, Sodomitical Roles and the Gender Revolution of the Eighteenth Century: The Recent Historiography,' *Eighteenth-Century Life* 9 (1985): 109–21, reprinted in *'Tis Nature's Fault: Unauthorized Sexuality during the Enlightenment*, ed. R.P. Maccubin (New York, 1987).
2 *The Wandering Whore* (London, 1660–1663), 6 parts, part 3, p. 9; ed. Randolph Trumbach (reprint ed., New York: Garland, 1986).
3 *The Diary of Samuel Pepys*, ed. Robert Latham and William Matthews (London, 1971), 4: 209–10.
4 David M.Vieth, *The Complete Poems of John Wilmot, Earl of Rochester* (New Haven, 1978), pp. 117, 51, 53; Jeremy Treglown, *The Letters of John Wilmot, Earl of Rochester* (Chicago, 1980), pp. 230, 243, 160, 25–6.
5 Angeline Goreau, *Reconstructing Aphra* (New York, 1980), pp. 189–206; George Woodcock, *The Incomparable Aphra* (London, 1948), pp. 105–16.
6 *The Tryal and Condemnation of Mervin, Lord Audley, Earl of Castlehaven* (London, 1699), pp. 14–19, in *Sodomy Trials*, ed. Trumbach (reprint ed., New York, 1986). A more detailed narrative: Caroline Bingham, 'Seventeenth-Century Attitudes Toward Deviant Sex,' *Journal of Interdisciplinary History* 1 (1971): 446–68.
7 D.C. Clark, 'The Restoration Rake in Life and Comedy' (Ph.D. thesis, Florida State University, 1963); R.D. Hume, *The Development of English Drama in the Late Seventeenth Century* (Oxford, 1976), and *The Rakish Stage* (Carbondale, Ill., 1983).
8 Aphra Behn, 'The Amorous Prince,' in *Works*, ed. Montague Summers, 6 vols. (reprint ed., New York, 1967), 4: 186, 196–7, 210–11; Thomas Otway, 'The Souldiers Fortune,' in *Works*, ed. J.C. Ghosh, 2 vols. (reprint ed., Oxford, 1968), 2: 103–7; Nathaniel Lee, 'The Princess of Cleve,' in *Works*, ed. T.B. Strong and A.L.Cooke, 2 vols. (reprint ed., Metuchen N.J., 1968), 2: 157, 177–8.
9 *The Wandering Whore* (1660), part 4, p. 5; A.P. Hall and M.B. Hall, eds., *Correspondence of Henry Oldenburg* (Madison, Wis., 1973), 9: 298–302; Pierre Darmon, *Trial by Impotence* (London, 1985), pp. 40–51; J.M. Saslow, *Ganymede in the Renaissance* (New Haven, 1986), pp. 75–90, 220 n. 29, 222 n. 44.
10 Susan Staves, 'A Few Kind Words for the Fop,' *Studies in English Literature*, 22 (1982): 413–28.
11 Alan Bray, *Homosexuality in Renaissance England* (London: 1982), pp. 130–1 n. 77.
12 [Nathaniel Lancaster?], *The Pretty Gentleman* (London, 1747), p. 6, quoted in Staves, 'Kind Words,' p. 419.
13 Staves, 'Kind Words,' pp. 421–8 (which I have modified); Tobias Smollett, *The Adventures of Roderick Random* (1748), ed. P.-G. Boucé (New York, 1981), pp. 194–9; Boucé, *The Novels of Tobias Smollett* (London, 1976), pp. 267–8.
14 *Satan's Harvest Home* (London, 1749), pp. 50–4; ed. Trumbach (reprint ed., New York, 1985); *Proceedings at . . . Old Bailey*, 22–25 February 1727: Richard Skekos; Louis Crompton, *Byron and Greek Love* (Berkeley, 1985), pp. 295–6 n. 26.
15 L.D. Potter, 'The Fop and Related Figures in Drama from Johnson to Cibber' (Ph.D. thesis, Cambridge University, 1965), pp. 159–61.
16 *A Compleat Collection of Remarkable Tryals . . . in the Old Bailey*, 2 vols. (London, 1718), 1: 236–42; Bray, *Homosexuality*, pp. 98, 139; A.G. Craig, 'The Movement for the Reformation of Manners, 1688–1715' (Ph.D. thesis, University of Edinburgh, 1980), pp. 168–75; John Dunton, *Athenianism*, 2 vols. (London, 1710), 2: 94.
17 *Tryal of Castlehaven*, preface; Greater London R.O.: MJ/SR/2028, Recog. 9.

18 *The Tryal and Conviction of several reputed Sodomites . . . 20th day of October 1707* (British Library: 515. 1. 2 (205)); Greater London R.O.: MJ/SP/Sept. 1707; *The Woman-Hater's Lamentation* (London, 1707), in *Sodomy Trials*, ed. Trumbach; Hertfordshire Record Office: D/EP/F32, vol. 4, 10 October 1707.

19 *A full and true account of the discovery and apprehending a notorious gang of sodomites in St. James's* (London, 1709) (British Library: 515. 1. 2 (209)); Edward Ward, *The Secret History of Clubs* (London, 1709), pp. 284–300, *recte* 290; Oxford English Dictionary, molly; Wayne Dynes, *Homolexis* (New York, 1985), *passim*, for faggot as early-nineteenth-century West Country for prostitute: Polly Morris, 'Sexual Reputation in Somerset, 1733–1850' (Ph.D. thesis, University of Warwick, 1985); *Hell Upon Earth* (London, 1729), p. 43; ed. Trumbach (reprint ed., New York, 1985): This is preceded by an account of fops and beaus, who are presented as silly, but interested in women (pp. 32–41); Dunton, *Athenianism*, pp. 94–9; [Jonathan Wild], *An Answer to a Late Insolent Libel* (London, 1718), p. 30.

20 Ward, *History of Clubs*; Wild, *Answer*, pp. 30–2, reprinted in F.S. Lyons, *Jonathan Wild* (London, 1936), pp. 278–81, and on which see Gerald Howson, *Thief-Taker General* (New York, 1970), pp. 60–5, *et passim*; *Select Trials at . . . the Old Bailey*, 4 vols. (London, 1742), 2: 362–72; ed. Trumbach (reprint ed., New York, 1985), 4 vols., in 2; James Dalton, *A Genuine Narrative . . . since October Last* (London, 1728), pp. 31–43.

21 Greater London R.O.: MJ/SR/2459: Newgate Calendar, #57, 60, MJ/SR/2461: New Prison List; *The London Journal*, 23, April 1726, 17 December 1726.

22 *St. James Evening Post*, 3–5 Oct. 1727; *Proceedings . . . Old Bailey* (1732), no. 6, pp. 166–70).

23 A.N. Gilbert, 'Buggery and the British Navy, 1700–1861,' *Journal of Social History* 10 (1976–7): 72–98, at p. 75.

24 Trumbach, 'London's Sodomites,' p. 18; 'Sodomitical Assaults, Gender Role, and Sexual Development in Eighteenth-Century London,' *Journal of Homosexuality* 16 (1988): 407–29.

25 Trumbach, 'London's Sodomites,' p. 13; 'Modern Prostitution and Gender in *Fanny Hill*,' *Sexual Underworlds of the Enlightenment*, ed. G.S. Rousseau and Roy Porter (Manchester, 1987); J.H. Wilson, *All the King's Ladies* (Chicago, 1958), pp. 67–86; Pat Rogers, 'The Breeches Part,' in *Sexuality in Eighteenth-Century Britain* (Manchester, 1982), ed. P.G. Boucé, pp. 244–58; Charlotte Charke, *A Narrative of the Life* (London, 1755), reprint ed. L.R.N. Ashley (Gainesville, 1969); Lois Potter, 'Colley Cibber: The Fop as Hero,' *Augustan Worlds*, ed. J.C. Hilton et al. (New York, 1978), pp. 153–64; and see Lynne Friedl, 'Passing Women,' in *Underworlds*, ed. Porter and Rousseau.

26 W.L. Williams, *The Spirit and the Flesh* (Boston, 1986); R.I. Levy, 'The Community Function of Tahitian Male Transvestism,' *Anthropological Quarterly* 44 (1971): 12–21; Unni Wikan, *Behind the Veil in Arabia* (Baltimore, 1982), chap. 9; R.L. Munroe, J.W.M. Whiting, D.J. Hally, 'Institutionalized Male Transvestism and Sex Distinctions,' *American Anthropologist* 71 (1969): 87–90.

27 Lawrence Stone, *The Family, Sex and Marriage in England, 1500–1800* (New York, 1977); Randolph Trumbach, *The Rise of the Egalitarian Family* (New York, 1978).

SEPARATE SPHERES?

Introduction

'Separate spheres' is the most common metaphor used to characterize gender roles, and an examination of it illustrates how some of the theoretical debates in gender history affect its practice. A term used since the early nineteenth century, 'separate spheres' was adopted by historians in the 1970s to characterize the accentuation of gender difference among the middle classes which took place in the late eighteenth and early nineteenth centuries, stimulated by the evangelical revival. As explained in the article by Catherine Hall, reproduced below, while public life was increasingly seen as an exclusively male domain, domesticity came to be the sphere of activity in which women's moral virtues could and should be most fully developed. Although these ideas were first expressed in England by a small group of evangelicals, the Clapham Sect, Hall argues that they were so suited to the values of the emerging middle class that they became a central plank of the distinct middle-class identity which formed in the nineteenth century, an argument further developed in the book she co-wrote with Leonore Davidoff, *Family Fortunes* (1987).

Historians have since used the concept of separate spheres to describe gender relations in many times and places, particularly in the nineteenth century, but they have interpreted its significance for women differently. While in Britain the 'cult of domesticity' has been interpreted largely as confining women's opportunities, in the United States and France historians, especially feminist historians, have seen the emergence of a distinct sphere of activity for women as providing them with an opportunity to create their own culture and to assert the value of distinctly female skills and virtues. Martine Segalen, for example, characterized peasant marriages in nineteenth-century France as symmetrical unions in which men and women possessed equally important, if distinct, functions in the running of the household and family farm. In a different context, that of bourgeois ladies excluded from their husbands' businesses in late nineteenth-century northern France, Bonnie Smith has demonstrated how the wives constructed a distinct set of values, summed up in the phrase 'Christian feminism', which privileged domestic virtues over the corruption and ambition of the male public sphere.[1]

However, the use of separate spheres as a way of characterizing gender difference has come under attack. In a wide-ranging review of American women's historiography, Linda Kerber deconstructed this metaphor and showed how, despite its limitations, it has been adopted by feminists 'of every generation' for what she implies are political reasons. In a parallel critique of English women's historiography reproduced below, Amanda Vickery complains that historians have tended to confuse prescriptive ideology with actual practice, and suggested that they have ignored alternative, dissenting, points of view. More fundamentally, Vickery argues that separate spheres in the nineteenth century was neither as new nor as clear-cut as historians have suggested, nor was it restricted to a single social class, a point reinforced by the work of Segalen. Historians of France have, however, questioned the image of complementarity and equality in the two spheres documented in Segalen's work. Noting that she 'depict[s] a society without conflict', it has been

argued that Segalen ignores the crucial fact that the women's sphere was not isolated from male domination, as enforced through ideology and the threat of violence. Women's actions on the family farm, for example, were fundamentally
constrained by the expectation that women, but not necessarily men, must sacrifice
their personal interests to those of the family as a whole.[2]

Historians have paid less attention to what separate spheres meant for men,
who were expected not only to play an important role in public life, but also to
exercise their authority in the domestic sphere, where their participation could
conflict with women's attempt to carve out their own sphere of influence. In Victorian England men's authority at home was threatened on the one hand by their
absence while at work, and on the other by a companionate ideal of marriage and
the great moral and spiritual importance accorded to women by evangelical religion. As a refuge from the harsh world of work, domesticity was attractive to men,
who depended on their wives not just for material, but also for spiritual and emotional comforts, but it also potentially undermined their patriarchal authority.[3] These
interrelationships between men's and women's lives tend to be obscured by the
uncritical use of a metaphor which emphasizes the separation of men's and
women's spheres of activity.

In defence of separate spheres, it has been argued that it *is* appropriate to
describing gender roles at certain moments in time, notably the nineteenth century. Noting the 'peculiar . . . firmness' of the boundaries of separate spheres in
Germany, some historians have argued that the concept is particularly relevant to
that country's history. The idea that gender difference was determined by nature
became widespread from the late eighteenth century and subsequently women
were completely excluded from political life. Such ideas were not peculiar to
Germany, however, as is evident from Thomas Laqueur's study of European-wide
changes in anatomical understandings of the body at this time, leading to the 'two
sex' model of sexual difference summarized in his piece in Section II of this reader.
As Leonore Davidoff has reasserted, even in England the ideology of domesticity
in the nineteenth century rested on an assertion that the '"Home" [was] the natural place for women'.[4] Although Vickery was right to point out that ideas of
gender difference along a separate spheres model were not new in the nineteenth century, the important point is that such ideas were articulated in new
ways. Not only was the term 'separate spheres' actually used for the first time, but
the character of the arguments (based on 'natural' difference) used to reinforce
this separation, and the degree of moral value that was placed on its maintenance,
were also new.

None the less, it is important to recognize that social practice rarely conforms
to the strict difference dictated by ideologies. In practice, men and women in the
nineteenth century often occupied the same geographical spaces and even, especially at work, performed some similar tasks. In England, the 'separation' of responsibilities that did exist, especially among the middle class, took place not along public/
private boundaries, but according to type of activity: women were concerned, at
home and abroad, with issues of maternity, morality, religiosity and philanthropy,

while men dominated 'high' politics, institutional management, and most forms of paid employment which did not involve domestic skills.[5] These boundaries were the subject of continual negotiation: women's lives were lived in continual interaction with men, and vice versa. All these points are obscured by the mechanistic use of the metaphor of separate spheres, and historians would do well to use this term with care, or even think of a different metaphor altogether. And although it is true that historically far more effort has been devoted to the maintenance and reinforcement of gender boundaries than the reverse, historians should also be open to the possibility that some historical periods (not least, our own) have witnessed a convergence, rather than a separation, of spheres.

Notes

1 Martine Segalen, *Love and Power in the Peasant Family: Rural France in the Nineteenth Century* (English edition [trans. by Sarah Matthews]: Oxford, 1983); Bonnie Smith, *Ladies of the Leisure Class: The Bourgeoises of Northern France in the Nineteenth Century* (London, 1981). For the United States, see the literature discussed in Linda Kerber, 'Separate Spheres, Female Worlds, Woman's Place: The Rhetoric of Women's History', *Journal of American History* 75 (1988), pp. 11–17.
2 Kerber, 'Separate Spheres'; Cécile Dauphin *et al.*, 'Women's Culture and Women's Power: Issues in French Women's History' in Karen Offen *et al.* (eds), *Writing Women's History: International Perspectives* (London, 1991), pp. 107–33; Michelle Perrot, 'Women, Power and History: The Case of Nineteenth-Century France' in Siân Reynolds (ed.), *Women, State and Revolution: Essays on Power and Gender in Europe since 1789* (Brighton, 1986), pp. 44–59; Tessie Liu, 'Le Patrimonie Magique: Reassessing the Power of Women in Peasant Households in Nineteenth-Century France', *Gender and History* 6 (1994), pp. 13–36.
3 Leonore Davidoff and Catherine Hall, Family Fortunes: Men and Women of the English Middle Class, 1780–1850 (London, 1987), pp. 324, 329–32; A. J. Hammerton, *Cruelty and Companionship: Conflict in Nineteenth-Century Married Life* (London, 1992), pp. 166–7; John Tosh, *Men at Home: Domesticity and the Victorian Middle Class* (forthcoming).
4 Eve Rosenhaft, 'Women, Gender and the Limits of Political History in the Age of "Mass" Politics' in L. E. Jones and J. Retallack (eds), *Elections, Mass Politics, and Social Change in Modern Germany* (Cambridge, 1992), p. 150; Lynn Abrams and Elizabeth Harvey, 'Introduction: Gender and Gender Relations in German History' to their edited collection *Gender Relations in German History: Power, Agency and Experience from the Sixteenth to the Twentieth Century* (London, 1996), pp. 16–27; Robert A. Nye, *Masculinity and Male Codes of Honor in Modern France* (Oxford, 1993), ch. 4; Leonore Davidoff, *Worlds Between: Historical Perspectives on Gender and Class* (Cambridge, 1995), p. 8.
5 Robert B. Shoemaker, *Gender in English Society, 1650–1850: The Emergence of Separate Spheres?* (London, 1998).

8

The early formation of Victorian domestic ideology

CATHERINE HALL

The Victorian middle-class ideal of womanhood is one that is well documented – the 'angel in the house', the 'relative creature' who maintained the home as a haven, is familiar from novels, manuals and even government reports. There is plenty of evidence to suggest that by the 1830s and 1840s the definition of women as primarily relating to home and family was well established. But what were the origins of the ideal? 1780–1830 has been called the period of the making of the industrial bourgeoisie. That class defined itself not only in opposition to the new proletariat, but also the classes of landed capitalism – the gentry and the aristocracy. Their class definition was built not only at the level of the political and the economic – the historic confrontations of 1832 and 1846 – but also at the level of culture and ideology. The new bourgeois way of life involved a recodification of ideas about women. Central to those new ideas was an emphasis on women as domestic beings, as primarily wives and mothers. Evangelicalism provided one crucial influence on this definition of home and family. Between 1780 and 1820, in the Evangelical struggle over anti-slavery and over the reform of manners and morals, a new view of the nation, of political power and of family life was forged. This view was to become a dominant one in the 1830s and 1840s. The Evangelical emphasis on the creation of a new lifestyle, a new ethic, provided the framework for the emergence of the Victorian bourgeoisie.

It has been argued that Evangelical morality was probably the single most widespread influence in Victorian England.[1] Evangelicals were staunch members of the Church of England who believed in reform from within rather than in following the example of John Wesley, who in the 1780s had in effect seceded from the established Church to form the Methodist sect. The crucially important position of the Clapham Sect, as leaders of the Evangelicals, and their influence on nineteenth-century England has long been recognized. They occupy a position of distinction in Whig history, but have been less revered by radicals.[2] The Whig interpretation sees the Sect as

Reprinted from Catherine Hall, *White, Male and Middle Class: Explorations in Feminism and History* (Polity Press, 1992). Reprinted by permission of Blackwell Publishers Ltd and Routledge Incorporated.

having played a vital role, not only in establishing the great nineteenth-century tradition of extra-Parliamentary agitation, but also as a group marked by moral superiority and freedom from self-interest. The origins of the group lay in Henry Thornton's house at Clapham and the focus which that provided for a number of prominent Evangelicals at the end of the eighteenth century. The Thornton family were prosperous bankers and John Thornton, Henry's father, was an influential Evangelical. Clapham became a centre for a number of families who were united in their interests and interconnected by marriage. The major figures were Henry Thornton, William Wilberforce, Zachary Macaulay (who was Editor of the Evangelical *Christian Observer* and did much of the research and writing on the slavery issue), James Stephen (a barrister) and Lord Teignmouth (who was Governor General of India for five years). All of them lived in Clapham for long periods, where an Evangelical, John Venn, held the living. In addition, there were other people who were very closely associated and paid frequent visits – Thomas Gisborne, for example, a country gentleman, cleric and author; Hannah More, the celebrated author; and Charles Simeon, who was the Evangelical leader in Cambridge. The Sect's work was primarily devoted to the furtherance of Evangelical principles in various political and social fields. They are best known for their contributory effort to the abolition of the slave trade and of slavery, their missionary activities both within and beyond England, and their influence on the foundation of Sunday schools and many other philanthropic and reforming institutions. In a much quoted entry in his diary in 1787, Wilberforce wrote that his mission was to abolish the slave trade and reform the manners and morals of the nation; virtually all the activities of the Clapham Sect sprang from these two commitments.

The Sect's second campaign – the attempt to transform national morality – had less clear legislative goals than the anti-slavery movement. Its concern was to redefine the available cultural norms and to encourage a new seriousness and respectability in life. The Clapham Sect aimed to provide a new model that would displace the licentiousness and immorality which they saw around them. This *modus vivendi* would be widely propagated by means of pamphlets, manuals, sermons, and as many other media as could be utilized. At the same time it would be reinforced institutionally by getting legislation passed on such issues as public amusements, sabbatarianism and obscene publications. The onslaught on morality was a highly organized campaign, and although it did not fire the national imagination in the same way that the anti-slavery issue had, it nevertheless had an important impact on manners at the beginning of the nineteenth century.[3]

The Evangelical concern with national morality had, as its premiss, the belief of the Sect that religion should be a daily rule of life rather than a question of doctrinal purity. Like the Methodists, they emphasized the importance of a well-ordered daily routine. Their overwhelming sense of sin necessitated the formulation of rules for daily life, in an attempt to reduce the possibilities of collapse into the natural condition. Hannah More and Wilberforce wrote journals which give us considerable insight into the practices of Evangelical living. Both of them see self-examination as absolutely central in their attempt to live according to God. Passivity and obedience were demanded in relation to God's word. A vital distinction was made between nominal and real Christianity: the nominal Christian accepts only the forms. The eighteenth-century religious revival was concerned with an attempt to get beneath the forms, to transform the meaning of religion *from within*. The Evangelical decision to stay inside the established Church meant that pressure for internal reconstruction was perhaps even stronger on them than on the Methodists – since the latter were creating new external forms of religious organization as well.

Wilberforce's immensely influential *Practical Christianity* gives us one of the clearest statements of Evangelical views. He insisted on the distinction between real and nominal belief. Christianity, he argued, 'is a state into which we are not born, but into which we must be translated; a nature which we do not inherit, but into which we are to be created anew . . . This is a matter of labour and difficulty, requiring continual watchfulness, and unceasing effort, and unwearied patience.'[4] Life is a journey towards salvation and the image of the pilgrim is constantly there. Wilberforce and Hannah More both experienced conversion in adulthood and, as a result, reconstructed their lives. Wilberforce aimed to live by rule and to subject his life to constant scrutiny in an attempt to be of the greatest productive use to others. He believed that an individual's only strength sprang from a deep and abiding sense of his own weakness and inadequacy – hence the constant need for self-criticism and self-examination. Criticism, moreover, should be not just an individual practice but a mutual practice amongst the believers. Self-discipline was therefore a *sine qua non* in the Evangelicals' philosophy. Their letters and diaries bear constant witness to the difficulties of achieving it. It is important not to read back into this early phase of Evangelicalism the critique of its aspects in Victorian England with which we are familiar from Dickens, Thackeray or Butler. Between 1790 and 1820 the movement was in struggle, constantly on the attack against the evils it saw surrounding it, and attempting to transform English life. After 1820 Evangelicalism increasingly established itself as a part of the dominant culture. It lost its early purity and could justly be accused of priggishness, conventionality, hypocrisy and conservatism. But the first generation of the Clapham Sect were unceasingly diligent in their efforts to behave properly, to live as *real* Christians should, and to change their way of life.

In the 1780s the Evangelicals were convinced of the necessity for a national reform of manners. They wanted to attack the aristocracy's laxness and impose a new rule of life. In current political weakness they saw a reflection of moral depravity. It seemed clear that moral reform was impossible without the support of the ruling class and the established Church – and those were their initial constituencies. If – as they believed – Wesley's attempt at it had been doomed from the start by his reliance on preaching the Word, then they instead would exploit any political channels open to them. Society was seen to be in need of effective leadership and guidance. The growth of the middle class made this particularly urgent because it was in danger of adopting the lax principles of those of higher rank; furthermore, the commercial spirit did not appear naturally favourable to the maintenance of religious principles.

The attack on manners and morals was initially organized mainly around producing propaganda aimed at the upper classes.[5] It took the French Revolution to transform a modest campaign into a major national force. In the dangerous years of the 1790s a simple, repressive policy was not enough; an active regeneration was also necessary in support of England. As Lady Shelley wrote in her diary: 'The awakening of the labouring classes after the first shocks of the French Revolution, made the upper classes tremble. Every man felt the necessity for putting his house in order.' E.P. Thompson had added to this: 'To be more accurate, most men and women of property felt the necessity for putting the houses of the poor in order.'[6] But to put the houses of the poor in order was only one part of the Evangelical campaign. They believed in self-regeneration as well as the proper instruction of the poor, and it was this duality which gave their movement such power. Their position cannot be equated with Toryism – they were subject to vitriolic attacks from sections of the ruling class as well as from radicals. The Evangelicals only ever had a limited amount of support from aristocratic and landed circles. Their major support, despite the intentions of the Clapham Sect, came from the middle ranks.

Between 1780 and 1832 England was in a period of transition – from an aristocratic and mercantile capitalist society, where land was still the major source of power, to an industrial capitalist society with a large and influential bourgeoisie. The Evangelicals were able to play a mediating role in this transition. They neither unquestioningly supported the old society nor uncritically welcomed the new. Their religious position drew on some of the same criticisms of established religious forms as had the Methodists, yet they remained staunch Anglicans; and unlike the Methodists, they never developed a popular base amongst the labouring classes. They insisted on the possibility of reform from within, rather than by creating new structures. Similarly, in political terms, they advocated transformation from within, rather than a direct change in the distribution of political power. They believed in the traditional power of the aristocracy and appealed to the old ruling groups, yet their desire for particular kinds of change drove them to seek support from the expanding middle class. In order to achieve the abolition of the slave trade and of slavery, for example, they needed pressure group organization on a massive scale - yet they still believed in the absolute power of an unreformed House of Commons to make legislative decisions. The success of the anti-slavery campaign marked an important transitional moment on the way to a full demand for recognition of middle-class power.[7]

The religious base of the Evangelicals allowed them to insist that the issues they took up were moral, not political. Anti-slavery came to be seen as 'above politics'. Their solution to the political problems facing England in the wake of the French Revolution was declared to be a religious solution – not a political one. It was the religious consciousness of England, they argued, which determined her political condition.

> To the decline of Religion and morality our national difficulties must both indirectly and directly be chiefly ascribed ... My only solid hopes for the well-being of my country depend not so much on her fleets and armies, not so much on the wisdom of her rulers, or the spirit of her people, as on the persuasion that she still contains many, who in a degenerate age, love and obey the Gospel of Christ; on the humble trust that the intercession of these may still be prevalent, that for the sake of these Heaven may still look upon us with an eye of favour.[8]

Real Christianity must be cultivated to arrest the progress of political decay.

The Clapham Sect members were neither old-style aristocrats nor new-style manufacturers. Yet they came to be seen as representing the interests of England and of sections of the middle classes. The major interests of the Sect were in financial and mercantile capital. The Wilberforce family money came from the Baltic trade and by the 1770s had been partly invested in land. The Thorntons were well-established bankers. Macaulay's money derived from African trade. There were remarkably few manufacturers involved. The Evangelicals always looked for wealthy and aristocratic support; they believed in the importance of influencing the great, and rejoiced in titled and royal backing. Wilberforce was one of Pitt's closest friends and mixed regularly with the governing elite. Nevertheless, this group was associated from its early days with the new middle-class culture of industrial England. The Clapham Sect came to articulate and represent the needs and changing consciousness of a new society. Their own links with the old mercantile bourgeoisie and the landed aristocracy enabled them to form a bridge between the old ruling groups and the aspirant middle classes. Organizations like the anti-slavery movement created a forum where these different class fractions could meet and cooperate. The Evangelicals were able to bridge class divisions because they had a strikingly new view of desirable life-styles and political responsibilities. Their great influence lay not only in their own power, but also in having the ear of others in authority. An important geographical factor was also involved in their potential to form a link between classes: London was the capital and the centre of political life, and the Sect was effectively based there. London was also a major centre of middle-class life. It was, however, not an expanding area for the factory system – and it remained the heartland of financial and commercial capitalism where the Evangelicals were so well represented. When manufacturers and industrialists came to London, they did so partly to enjoy metropolitan life and to engage in London politics. Consequently it was possible for the Sect to bridge the gap in London more easily than in Manchester or Rochdale, where the balance of class forces was different.

It is important to take account of the hostility of sections of the ruling class to Evangelicalism and the attempted reforms. Once the first fury of the French Revolution was over, with its initial effect of binding all property owners together, the High Church began to attack the Evangelicals. In the Evangelical campaign, 1797 had been a crucial year – a year of moral panic in England.[9] There were mutinies in the fleet, fears of a French invasion and of rebellion in Ireland, and a widespread belief in a conspiracy to undermine religion and morality. The fears about internal conditions had been manageable until there was also a serious threat from outside. Then the combination of the threat both from without and within England provoked a grave crisis of confidence; it was in this context that Wilberforce published *Practical Christianity*, with such immediate success. Moral and sexual subversion seemed to many to be the greatest dangers facing the country. But a High Church/Evangelical alliance over the moral dangers confronting the nation was not to last. High Churchmen associated immorality with French influence and mismanagement. The Evangelicals saw it as the result of the lack of true religion and the sinful heart of man. This marked a fundamental disagreement and the High Church inaugurated a campaign against the attempted Evangelical infiltration of the seats of power.[10] This was a struggle within sections of the ruling class and the Evangelicals were increasingly forced to look for support to the middle ranks.

In the wake of the French Revolution England was split politically. Evangelicalism provided a rallying point against Jacobinism. The beliefs and values of the truly religious were totally opposed to those of Godwin and the Jacobin circles. Because they regarded themselves as a campaigning movement engaged in struggle, the Evangelicals built a network and an organization across the country which permeated English life. By means of the anti-slavery associations, the Cheap Repository Tracts, the Sunday schools and many other societies, they penetrated aspects of daily life and provided a politics and morality that recognized the power of the French and industrial revolutions and responded to that challenge. That response was in open conflict with both new working-class organization and consciousness, and with Old Corruption. It is not that the Clapham Sect simply represented and reflected the interests of the new capitalist class: at a particular historical moment a particular class fraction or group can represent the interests of other factions or classes and can embody ideas and practices which have repercussions far beyond them. It is in this sense that the Clapham Sect spoke for others and, therefore, came to be seen as something other than what it was. It was understood selectively and taken up in part.

Central to the Evangelicals' attempt to reconstruct daily life and create a new morality with liberal and humanist parameters on the one hand (the attack on slavery), yet buttressed by social conservatism on the other (the reform of manners and morals), was the redefinition of the position of the woman in the family. The Evangelical attempt to transform daily life was based on the belief in the universality of sin and the need for constant struggle against it. A primary arena of this struggle must be the home and family. The Evangelical ideal of the family and the woman at home was developed well before the French Revolution. Cowper, for example, 'the poet of domesticity', was writing in the 1780s. But it was the debate about the nature and the role of women, produced by the Revolution, which opened the floodgates of manuals from Evangelical pens. Mary Wollstonecraft's *Vindication of the Rights of Woman* was first published in 1792 – before the tide had really been turned in England by the Terror. Hannah More was appalled by the book and she became the major protagonist of an alternative stance.

The *Vindication* is basically a plea for equality with bourgeois men – educational, legal and political equality. It is also an attack on the idea of femininity. Wollstonecraft was fired by the example of the Revolution to demand an extension of the rights of men to women. She saw women's inferior status as resulting from their environment – not from a lack of natural abilities. She argued for better education for women, to equip them for the world.[11] The Evangelicals started from a fundamentally different position: men and women are not equal; the sexes are naturally distinct; women should be better educated, but only to make them better wives and mothers. The 1790s saw a flood of writing defining, arguing and extending this position. The feminist belief in the equality of the sexes was absolutely rejected. Thomas Paine was dangerous in that he proposed equality between men, but if that argument were to be extended to women the whole social fabric would be under attack. At least it could be demonstrated that there was a *natural* division between the sexes. Arguments about social hierarchies also began with assumptions about nature, but less easily gained acceptance: the ideological underpinning of the 'natural constitution' was more apparent than beliefs in the inevitable concomitants of the sexual division. The debate on women, the family and the sexual division of labour was thus an integral part of the 1790s discussions about the organization of society. The Evangelical beliefs in the special and important duties of women in the home again played a mediating role between Radicals and Old Corruption. It is dependence which binds people together, argues More, both in the family and in the social hierarchy.

> Now it is pretty clear, in spite of modern theories, that the very frame and being of societies, whether great or small, public or private, is jointed and glued together by dependence. Those attachments which arise from, and are compacted by, a sense of mutual wants, mutual affection, mutual benefit, and mutual obligation, are the cement which secures the union of the family as well as of the State.[12]

The Evangelicals pilloried aristocratic ideals of women – they attacked as inadequate the way in which women were educated and the refusal to take them seriously. They denounced the double standard and championed the value of a good marriage. They drew on the eighteenth-century debate about women – they admired Richardson and agreed with the early Cobbett about, for example, the unfortunate aping of their betters by aspirant farmers' wives. They were responding again to the major social transformation which was taking place in England as a result of the development of capitalism. They were concerned with the problem of defining for the middle ranks a way of life best suited to their affluence and leisure. By the 1780s, existing material conditions enabled many more women to forgo employment – and a 'lady of leisure' enjoyed the hallmark of gentility. As Pinchbeck has demonstrated, the number of well-to-do women in mercantile and commercial ventures was dropping.[13] How were these women, with their new-found wealth and time, to behave? And who was to provide the model? Hannah More, Gisborne, Wilberforce, Mrs West, Mrs Sherwood and many others were adept and successful in assuming the role of mentors.

Evangelicalism has been described as 'the religion of the household' and it is clear that the notion of home and family was central to their religious views. Cowper refers to

> Domestic happiness, thou only bliss
> Of paradise that has survived the Fall.[14]

Home was one place where attempts could be made to curb sin – in the world outside it was obviously far more difficult. The household was seen as the basis for a proper religious life – morality began at home. The Clapham Sect were champions of family life themselves and in many ways lived like a large extended family. They lived with each other (often for long periods), they intermarried, they went on holiday together, and the men worked together. The values of domestic life were highly prized. Stephen, in his essay on the Sect, takes the unusual step of including domestic portraits of the key members as well as a discussion of their public contributions. He sees Wilberforce as at his best in the home and argues that the example of his household was a wonderful incentive to the practice of religion. 'There is something peculiar in Wilberforce's character and situation,' he writes, 'that seems to point it out as the design of Providence, that he should serve his Master in this high and special walk, and should have, so to speak, a kind of *domestic publicity* – that he should be at home a candle set on a candlestick as well as abroad a city built upon a hill.'[15]

Hannah More, in her novel *Coelebs*, offers the ideal example of the religious home. Set in their country house, the Stanley family are presented as the epitome of a religious household, living out their Evangelical and Utilitarian practice on a daily basis.[16] The country ambience is important. More, like Gisborne and other Evangelicals, believed that the ideal of a new-style benevolent paternalism was more viable in a rural than in an urban environment. Religious and domestic virtues were linked in the concept of a religious household. Sunday abstinence, for example, acquired significance when Sunday was defined as a family day. This linking of the religious with the domestic was extended to the division between the public and the private sphere, and was crucial to Evangelical thinking about the home. The basic split was between the world as hostile and the home as loving – a split that became commonplace in Victorian England.

The Evangelical movement was both intensely public and intensely private. The emphasis on the individual religious life came from a view of the world as immoral and distracting. But once people had been converted, they were needed in that world as moral missionaries. They were fired by the most private of passions – for sincerity and terrible truthfulness, with great emotional warmth on moral issues – and they had to carry all this with them into a public sphere which might be indifferent, cynical or hostile. 'They' were all men (except in philanthropy, where women were allowed a supporting role); consequently, the split between the private and the public spheres became a split between the sexes of a peculiarly exaggerated kind. Home became the sphere of women and the family; the world outside became the sphere of men. Wilberforce's letters abound with the imagery of conflict and trouble in the world, peace and calm at home. When away from his family on business, he wrote to his wife very regularly. 'Pray for me,' he wrote just before Parliament reassembled, 'that I may be enlightened and strengthened for the duties of this important and critical session. Hitherto God has wonderfully supported and blessed me; oh how much beyond my deserts! It will be a comfort to me to know that you all who are, as it were, on the top of the mountain, withdrawn from and above the storm, are thus interceding for me who am scuffling in the vale below.'[17] This idealized view of the home was common to the Clapham Sect. Family prayers became a symbol of the togetherness. Cowper evokes the warmth and cosiness of an Evangelical family evening:

Now stir the fire and close the shutters fast,
Let fall the curtains, wheel the sofa round,
And, while the bubbling and loud hissing urn
Throws up a steaming column, and the cups
That cheer but not inebriate, wait on each
So let us welcome peaceful evenings in.[18]

Within the household it was quite clearly established that men and
women had their separate spheres. Hannah More defined certain qualities
and dispositions as 'peculiarly feminine'. Cultural differences were seen as
natural. Women were naturally more delicate, more fragile, morally weaker,
and all this demanded a greater degree of caution, retirement and reserve.
'Men, on the contrary, are formed for the more public exhibition on the
great theatre of human life';[19] men had grandeur, dignity and force; women
had ease, simplicity and purity. This absolute distinction between men and
women is repeated time and again in Evangelical writing.

Evangelicals expected women to sustain and even to improve the moral
qualities of the opposite sex. It is at this level that the Evangelicals offered
women an area of importance which, therefore, holds within itself considerable contradictions. Women, it was believed, could act as the moral regen-
erators of the nation. They occupied a key position in the struggle to reform
and revive the nation. Women in the home could provide, as it were, a revolutionary base from which their influence could shine forth: 'If our women
lose their domestic virtues, all the charities will be dissolved, for which our
country is a name so dear. The men will be profligate, the public will be
betrayed, and whatever has blessed or distinguished the English nation on
the Continent will disappear,' wrote a friend to More, congratulating her on
her book on female education.[20] That book, published in 1799 in the wake
of the moral panic, exhorted women to play their part in the struggle for
national survival. They were being offered a field where they could be
allowed to wield some power and influence within the moral sphere. They
could play an important part in the reform of manners and morals. Wilberforce made a similar plea for women's support in *Practical Christianity*. He
argued that women were especially disposed to religion; this was partly
because their education was limited and they were not exposed to the moral
dangers of the classics. The woman, therefore, had the particular duty of
encouraging her husband's religious sensibilities: 'when the husband should
return to his family, worn and harassed by worldly cares or professional
labours, the wife, habitually preserving a warmer and more unimpaired
spirit of devotion, than is perhaps consistent with being immersed in the
bustle of life, might revive his languid piety.' Women had open to them a
most noble office: 'we would make them as it were the medium of our intercourse with the heavenly world, the faithful repositories of the religious
principle, for the benefit both of the present and the rising generation.'[21]

Because the major problem in England was seen by the Evangelicals as being the prevalent state of religious and moral decadence, this emphasis on the religious power of the woman considerably modified their emphasis elsewhere on subordination. In a later period, Victorian feminists like Mrs Jameson were to build on this contradiction.

The good Evangelical woman had recognizable characteristics: she was modest, unassuming, unaffected and rational. ('Rational' was used as the opposite to 'sentimental' or 'subject to violent feeling'.) Babington, a prominent figure in the Clapham Sect, wrote to Macaulay on the eve of his marriage in 1799, detailing the distinction between the male and female spheres:

> You have been a grave and active African governor, surrounded by business and difficulties and dangers, and enjoying little affectionate and no female society. Selina has been entirely with females, and her companions have been her near relations and friends. Under these circumstances you meet as man and wife, with habits of domestic life more different than those of men and women, who act on the same principle, generally are. She must endeavour to assimilate herself to you, and you to her, without either of you departing from your proper sphere . . . Hours of relaxation are among the most useful, as well as most pleasant seasons of matrimonial life, if they do not recur too frequently, and if the source of enjoyment be pure and hallowed . . . In general you should lead her through cheerful cornfields, and pastures, and when opportunity offers go out of your way a little to show a flowery meadow or a winding stream.[22]

The implication is clear that the man is wiser and will guide the woman into the area appropriate to her, occasionally introducing her to new ideas.

The right choice in marriage was seen as vital to a good Evangelical life. Since the religious household was the basis of Christian practice, it was essential to find the right partner. *Coelebs* is structured around the hero's search for a wife:

> In such a companion I do not want a Helen, a Saint Cecilia, or a Madame Dacier; yet she must be elegant or I should not love her; sensible, or I should not respect her; prudent, or I should not confide in her; well-informed, or she could not educate my children; well-bred, or she could not entertain my friends; consistent, or I should offend the shade of my mother; pious, or I should not be happy with her.[23]

The striking feature of this passage is that the woman is seen only in relation to the man. She is, in Mrs Ellis's later phrase, a 'relative creature'. Hannah More, although herself an independent and unmarried woman, consistently relegated women to a dependent role. There can be no higher praise for a woman than that she is worthy of her husband, whose happiness she creates. As Coelebs puts it, 'It appears to me that three of the great inducements in the choice of a wife are, that a man may have a directress for his family, a preceptress for his children, and a companion for himself.'[24] There is no suggestion of what the woman might want for *herself*. The letters and diaries of the Clapham Sect demonstrate the degree to which these views were lived through – they were not simply presented in manuals for others. Women were both central to, and absent from, the Clapham Sect. They were central in that the definition of their position constituted a major area of Evangelical thought and writing. They were absent in that the absolute assumption of their subordination meant that their activities were hidden. Apart from Hannah More, the majority of writing about the Sect was by men. This was no doubt partly because the women's letters were not seen as worth keeping. Halévy describes More as 'one of the great men of the party'[25] – since she does not fit the stereotypes of what an Evangelical woman, or indeed any woman, should be, she is presented as exceptional. When Stephen described the domestic lives of the Sect, the wives were there as supportive backcloth, helpmeets to their husbands. Wilberforce frequently gave an account of family parties and documented all those present, except his wife. It is tempting to assume that this was because she was so taken for granted that she did not have to be mentioned. The woman, after all, was private property. Gisborne saw the duties of the woman as threefold: first, to look after husbands, parents, children, relatives and friends; second, to set a good example to men and improve manners by that example; third, to care for children.[26] The whole notion of duty was, of course, central to Evangelicalism.

The unmarried woman had to do what she could; basically, Evangelical writing on women assumed marriage and the family. Within marriage it was quite clear that the wife was subordinate to her husband – it was not a question open to 'speculative arguments'. Faithful and willing obedience on the part of the wife was essential, even in cases of domestic management. The first set of duties – looking after the home and family – was, in St Paul's terms, 'guiding the house'. The superintendence of domestic management is clearly demarcated from doing the work itself; there was an absolute assumption that servants would be available. Domestic management required regularity of accounts and the proper care of money. Home should be seen as the wife's centre. There she could influence to the good her children, her servants, and her neighbours. It is in the home that 'the general character, the acknowledged property, and the established connections of her husband, will contribute with more force than they can possess elsewhere, to give weight and impressiveness to all her proceedings'.[27] Women were consequently advised not to leave home too much – it was only there that they could achieve moral excellence.

A great deal of emphasis was placed by the Evangelicals on the power of women to demonstrate by example. Daily practice in the home must be an attempt to live out principles. The letters and journals of the Clapham Sect would suggest that their daughters and wives did try to do this. But there was also one public arena open to them and that was philanthropy. The activities of women in charitable organizations between 1790 and 1830 give us the most concrete evidence so far available of the power of the Evangelical example on women's lives.[28] Charity was seen as the proper activity of a lady. 'I have often heard it regretted,' says Mrs Stanley in *Coelebs*, 'that ladies have no stated employment, no profession. It is a mistake. Charity is the calling of a lady; the care of the poor is her profession.'[29] More argued that women were peculiarly suited to philanthropic activities – they had leisure, an acquaintance with domestic wants and more sympathy with female complaints. Charity should become a part of daily life. Being philanthropic was, of course, both a reflection of virtue and a relief from a life bounded by the home.

If women were to be able to exercise a proper moral influence, they must be well educated. A clear distinction was made between the education of the daughters of the poor and those of the upper and middle classes. The daughters of the poor should be trained as servants or as good wives; the emphasis in their schooling should be on industry, frugality, diligence and good management. The daughters of the well-to-do, on the other hand, should be educated for moral excellence, and that meant that the traditional girls' training which they had been receiving was quite inadequate. To be able to dress well, to dance and play the piano, was not enough. 'The profession of ladies,' wrote More, 'is that of daughters, wives, mothers and mistresses of families.'[30] They should, therefore, be trained for that. Given these considerations, there was much to be said for educating girls at home. A mother was the best person to train her daughter. The purpose of that training was not to enable women to compete with men, but to prepare them in the best possible way for their relative sphere. Mothers were responsible for the children of both sexes in infancy, for their daughters until they left home. The Evangelicals stressed the importance of parental responsibility and the religious implications of good motherhood. The fathers took especial responsibility for their sons, but often had very close domestic ties with their daughters as well.

The Evangelical ideology of domesticity, it has been argued here, was not an ideal constructed for others, but an attempt to reconstruct family life and the relations between the sexes on the basis of 'real' Christianity. The Puritans had developed many similar views on marriage in an earlier period. The two groups shared the experience of living through a period of very rapid social, political and economic change; the articulation of their response was in religious terms, but it cannot be understood outside the particular historical conjuncture. Changing ideas about women and the family must be seen in relation to changes in the mode of production and in the social relations of production and reproduction. The Puritans and the Evangelicals shared a need to build a protected space in a hostile world, from which the great campaign of evangelization could be securely launched. The home was an area which could be controlled and which was relatively independent of what went on outside. The home did provide a haven. The expansion of capitalist relations of production in the late eighteenth century meant that homes were increasingly separated from workplaces, although this was a lengthy process and, in some trades, family workshops survived for a very long time. It has also been suggested that domestic demand for such items of household utility as china provided one of the main factors in the industrial 'take-off' at the end of the eighteenth century.[31] In other words, the emergence of a particular kind of home was directly related to the expansion of productive forces. But the way that home was realized, lived in and experienced within the middle ranks was crucially mediated by Evangelicalism.

The Clapham Sect, as we have seen, set some of the boundaries for public and domestic life in Victorian England. Their ideas were not, however, always understood in the way that they would have wished. They were benevolent paternalists but they were understood as the precursors of Utilitarianism and the power of the bourgeoisie. They were mercantile princes and clerics but they ushered in the machine age. They were a group with aristocratic connections, some of them belonging to the governing elite of England, yet they paved the way for the alliance between that old ruling class and the manufacturers. Their importance lies in the mediating role which they were able to play, by virtue of their class position, in the transitional period between the era of mercantile capitalism and the recognized dominance of industrial capitalism. They belonged to neither side and so were able to speak to both.

The campaign on slavery gave the Sect national status; it established the claim to represent the middle classes and articulate their demands. The campaign in itself was massively influential in shaping those demands – steering the 'middling ranks' towards liberalism and a national consensus rather than towards a more radical perspective and an alliance with the new industrial proletariat. The campaign on manners and morals would undoubtedly have been far less effective if the anti-slavery movement had not been such a success. The religious principles of the Evangelicals drove them from within. They became moral entrepreneurs committed to struggling for widescale conversion to their views. Their evangelizing campaign gained massive support, but only up to a certain point. Anti-slavery became identified as the British way. England claimed moral superiority in her style of colonization. Respectability and decorum ruled, but the double standard reigned supreme in Victorian England. The split between the public and the private sphere, the subordination of the woman in the family, and the protection of private property were key features of nineteenth-century England; but the truly religious households remained a minority phenomenon.

The forms, shaped by the Evangelicals for one purpose, were moulded to another. Just as the Puritan notion of the family was partly a response to the development of productive forces and partly an ideological form that must be understood in terms of its own logic, so was the Evangelical. But the Evangelical capacity to respond to the changing social relations of industrial capitalism and redefine the family form ensured that notions of home and domesticity in the nineteenth century would be heavily influenced by the Mores, Gisbornes, and Thorntons of this world.

Inside that dynamic, the bourgeois ideal of the family became a part of the dominant culture and, by the 1830s and 1840s, was being promoted through propaganda as the only proper way to live.[32] In the government reports of that period, working wives and mothers are presented as something unnatural and immoral. Working-class women were castigated for being poor housewives and inadequate mothers. If married women were to enter paid employment, they should not be seen; they should work at home. They should not flaunt their independence as the mill girls did. It is worth noting that the early campaigns to improve the working conditions of women focused on the factory system and the mines and did not come to grips with more hidden areas, such as the sweated trades. The bourgeois family was seen as the proper family, and that meant that married women should not work. The ideology of the family thus obscured class relations, for it came to appear above class. That ideology also obscured the cultural definition of sexual division of labour, since the split between men and women came to be seen as naturally ordained. Nature decreed that all women were first and foremost wives and mothers.

Notes

1 E.g. Noel Annan, *Leslie Stephen* (Macgibbon & Kee, London, 1951).
2 Cf. George O. Trevelyan, *The Life and Letters of Lord Macaulay* (Longmans, Green & Co., London, 1876). A more recent version is E.M. Howse, *Saints in Politics* (Allen & Unwin, London, 1953). For a contemporary radical critique, see William Cobbett, *Political Register*, 3 October 1818.
3 The most helpful secondary source on this is Maurice Quinlan, *Victorian Prelude: A History of English Manners 1700–1830* (Columbia University Press, London, 1941).
4 William Wilberforce, *A Practical View of the Prevailing Religious System of Professed Christians in the Higher and Middle Classes in this Country Contrasted with Real Christianity* (T. Cadell Jun. and W. Davies, London, 1797), p. 298.
5 The first major statement was Hannah More, *Thoughts on the Importance of the Manners of the Great to General Society* (T. Cadell Jun. and W. Davies, London, 1788).
6 E.P. Thompson, *The Making of the English Working Class* (Penguin, Harmondsworth, 1968), p. 60.
7 For an interesting discussion of the importance of the anti-slavery agitation in terms of a political transition, see David Brion Davis, *The Problem of Slavery in the Age of Revolution* (Cornell University Press, London, 1975).
8 R.I. and S. Wilberforce, *The Life of William Wilberforce*, vol. 3 (John Murray, London, 1838), p. 487.

9 For a good account of 1797, see Eric Trudgill, *Madonnas and Magdalens* (Heinemann, London, 1976).

10 One of the best examples of this division is the Blagdon Controversy over Hannah More's running of Sunday schools. Cf. W. Roberts (ed.), *The Life and Correspondence of Mrs Hannah More* (R.B. Seeley and W. Burnside, London, 1834), and Ford K. Brown, *Fathers of the Victorians* (Cambridge University Press, Cambridge, 1961).

11 For an interesting discussion of Wollstonecraft from a feminist perspective, see Margaret Walters, 'The Rights and Wrongs of Women: Mary Wollstonecraft, Harriet Martineau, Simone de Beauvoir', in Juliet Mitchell and Ann Oakley (eds), *The Rights and Wrongs of Women* (Penguin, Harmondsworth, 1976).

12 Hannah More, *Strictures on the Modern System of Female Education*, vol. 2 (T. Cadell Jun. and W. Davies, London, 1799), pp. 186–7.

13 Ivy Pinchbeck, *Women Workers and the Industrial Revolution 1750–1850* (Frank Cass, London, 1969).

14 William Cowper, *The Task*, in W. Benham (ed.), *Selected Works of William Cowper* (Macmillan & Co., London, 1889).

15 James Stephen, *Essays in Ecclesiastical Biography* (Longman, Brown, Green & Longman, London, 1845), p. 510.

16 E. Halévy was one of the first to discuss the connections between Evangelicalism and Utilitarianism in *England in 1815* (Ernest Benn, London, 1913). That discussion is developed in Davis, *The Problem of Slavery*.

17 Wilberforce, *The Life of William Wilberforce*, vol. 5, p. 77.

18 Cowper, *The Task*, Bk 4.

19 Hannah More, *Essays Principally Designed for Young Ladies* (R.B. Seeley and W. Burnside, London, 1777), p. 5.

20 In a letter to Hannah More, in Roberts (ed.), *Life and Correspondence*, vol. 3, p. 453.

21 Wilberforce, *A Practical View*, p. 453.

22 Viscountess Knutsford, *Life and Letters of Zachary Macaulay* (Edward Arnold, London, 1900), p. 234.

23 Hannah More, *Coelebs in Search of a Wife*, vol. 1 (R.B. Seeley and W. Burnside, London, 1809), p. 23.

24 More, *Coelebs*, p. 78.

25 Halévy, *England in 1815*.

26 Thomas Gisborne, *Duties of the Female Sex* (T. Cadell Jun. and W. Davies, London, 1801).

27 Gisborne, *Duties*.

28 Cf. F.R. Prochaska, 'Women in English Philanthropy 1790–1830', *International Review of Social History*, vol. 19, pt 3, 1974; Brown, *Fathers of the Victorians*.

29 More, *Coelebs*, vol. 2, p. 20.

30 More, *Coelebs*, vol. 2, p. 20.

31 Neil McKendrick, 'A New Look at the Contribution of the Employment of Women and Children to the Industrial Revolution', in Neil McKendrick (ed.), *Historical Perspectives: Studies in English Thought and Society in Honour of J.H. Plumb* (Europa, London, 1974).

32 Cf. Sally Alexander, 'Women's Work in Nineteenth-Century London' in Mitchell and Oakley (eds), *The Rights and Wrongs of Women*.

9

Golden age to separate spheres? A review of the categories and chronology of English women's history

AMANDA VICKERY

I

'Public and private', 'separate spheres', and 'domesticity' are key words and phrases of academic feminism. The dialectical polarity between home and world is an ancient trope of western writing; the notion that women were uniquely fashioned for the private realm is at least as old as Aristotle. But the systematic use of 'separate spheres' as *the* organizing concept in the history of middle-class women is of more recent vintage. Formative for American feminist historians in the 1960s and 1970s was the idea that gender oppression, the experience of sisterhood and a feminist consciousness have a natural, evolving relationship. Resulting studies undertook a quasi-marxist search for this developing consciousness. Nineteenth-century advice books, women's magazines, evangelical sermons and social criticism provided chapter and verse on the bonds of womanhood at their most elaborate, although such literature was prescriptive rather than descriptive in any simple sense. Thus a particularly crippling ideology of virtuous femininity was identified as newly-constructed in the early to mid-nineteenth century. What Barbara Welter dubbed the 'cult of true womanhood' prescribed the attributes of the proper American female between 1820 and 1860. She was to be pious, pure, submissive and domesticated, for the true woman turned her home into a haven for all that was civilized and spiritual in a materialistic world.[1] The assumption that capitalist man needed a hostage in the home was endorsed by subsequent historians who linked the cult of true womanhood to a shrinkage of political, professional and business opportunities for women in the years 1800–40.[2] In this way, the glorification of domestic womanhood became associated with the deterioration of women's public power, which was itself presented as a function of industrialization. Consequently, the early nineteenth century assumed

Reprinted from *Historical Journal* 36:2 (1993), pp. 383–414. Reprinted by permission of the author and Cambridge University Press.

its present status as one of the key, constitutive periods in the history of gender.

[. . .]

Although the foundation of the separate spheres framework was established through a particular reading of didactic and complaint literature, ensuing primary research was rarely designed to test the reliability or significance of this sort of evidence. Many women's historians neglected to ask the questions posed by early modern family historians: Did the sermonizers have any personal experience of marriage? Did men and women actually conform to prescribed models of authority? Did prescriptive literature contain more than one ideological message? Did women deploy the rhetoric of submission selectively, with irony, or quite cynically? And to quote Keith Wrightson, did 'theoretical adherence to the doctrine of male authority and *public* female subordination' mask 'the *private* existence of a strong complementary and companionate ethos'?[3] Those modernists who reminded us that 'the attitudes of ordinary people are quite capable of resisting efforts to reshape or alter them' had little impact on the development of the field.[4] Instead, research confidently built on the sands of prescription. The old sources predetermined the questions asked of the new. The process is here illuminated by Nancy Cott describing the evolution of the historical characterization of the 'woman's sphere' from domestic cage, to ambivalent arena of both constraint and opportunity, to the safe haven of a loving female subculture:

> The three interpretations primarily derived from three different kinds of sources; the first from published didactic literature about woman's place and the home, the second from the published writings of women authors, and the third from the private documents of non-famous women. It is worth pointing out that the more historians have relied on women's personal documents the more positively they have evaluated woman's sphere.[5]

However different these successive interpretations might seem, the conceptual importance of a constraining 'women's sphere' is constant. Rather than conclude from positive female testimony that women were not necessarily imprisoned in a rigidly defined private sphere, the dominant interpretation simply sees the private sphere in a better light. Moreover, the assumption prevails that it is helpful and appropriate to examine culture and society in terms of intrinsically male and female spheres.

And indeed the dichotomy between the home and the world continued to structure the bulk of the work on nineteenth-century American women until the mid to late 1980s. Recently, however, crucial criticisms of the American historiography have been offered by Linda Kerber, leading her to ask 'why speak of worlds, realms, spheres at all?' and American research now in progress seems more sceptical in its approach.[6] Yet this interpretive tradition was by no means restricted to American women's history, having predetermined the way historians have conceptualized the experience of middle-class women in England.[7] And as British historians were slower to elaborate this conceptual framework, so now they are slower to abandon it.

Of course, elements of the interpretations were hardly new in British historiography. After all, in popular understanding 'Victorian' has long served as a general synonym for oppressive domesticity and repressive prudery. But more specifically, as early as the 1940s and 1950s cultural historians such as Walter Houghton, Maurice Quinlan and Muriel Jaeger had seen the assertion of a new model of femininity as a central component in the rise of Victorianism – a shift in standards and behaviour which Quinlan and Jaeger saw in process from the closing decades of the eighteenth century.[8] Using the same sources (the sanctimonious novels and sermons of Evangelicals like Hannah More, Mrs Sherwood and Mrs Trimmer, the didactic manuals of Sarah Stickney Ellis and her ilk, and the sentimental or chivalric fantasies of Coventry Patmore, John Ruskin, Alfred Lord Tennyson, and so on), a younger generation of women's historians told essentially the same story but with greater rhetorical flourish, arguing that a new ideology of ultra-femininity and domesticity had triumphed by the mid-Victorian period. The first studies painted a highly-charged picture of the typical woman of the nineteenth-century middle class. A near prisoner in the home, Mrs Average led a sheltered life drained of economic purpose and public responsibility. As her physicality was cramped by custom, corset and crinoline, she was often a delicate creature who was, at best, conspicuously in need of masculine protection and, at worst, prey to invalidism. And yet she abjured self-indulgence, being ever-attentive and subservient to the needs of her family. Only in her matronly virtue and radiant Christianity did she exercise a mild authority over her immediate circle. She was immured in the private sphere and would not escape till feminism released her.[9]

Thereafter, the rise of the ideology of domesticity was linked, as in the American case, to the emergence of middle-class cultural identity. It was separate gender spheres which allegedly put the middle in the middle class.

> Definitions of masculinity and femininity played an important part in marking out the middle class, separating it off from other classes and creating strong links between disparate groups within that class – Nonconformists and Anglicans, radicals and conservatives, the richer bourgeoisie and the petite bourgeoisie. The separation between the sexes was marked out at every level within the society in manufacturing, the retail trades and the professions, in public life of all kinds, in the churches, in the press and in the home. The separation of spheres was one of the fundamental organizing characteristics of middle-class society in late eighteenth and early nineteenth-century England.[10]

Of course, as organizing characteristics go, class had long been seen as central to the history of nineteenth-century England. In adding gender to the picture of class society, historians of women confirmed a vision of the past shared by most social historians in England in the 1960s and 1970s. And indeed class was to remain a more powerful category in English women's history than in its American counterpart, and as a result the notion of a universal sisterhood which triumphantly bridged the gulf between mistress and servant, prosperous philanthropist and poor recipient never took a firm hold in English historiography.

Less pronounced in the English literature than in the American was the argument that life in a confined sphere could be emotionally enriching for early Victorian women, although there is some work on the support networks and intense friendships of late Victorian rebels.[11] However, the argument that women in prosperous families were robbed of economic and political function and incarcerated in a separate private sphere in the early years of the century came to serve as useful prelude to accounts of feminist assault on public institutions in the later period. Implicit and sometimes explicit in such accounts was the assumption that the private sphere operated as a pressure cooker generating pent-up frustrations which eventually exploded as mass female politics.[12] Revealingly, the first significant history of the English women's movement, written by the activist Ray Strachey in 1928, had opening chapters entitled: 'The prison house of home, 1792–1837', 'The stirring of discontent, 1837–1850', 'The widening circle, 1837–1850' and 'The demand formulated, 1850–1857'.[13]

As Ray Strachey's subtitles suggest, support for the argument that feminism was a reaction to a new regime of domestic incarceration was found in the protests of the late Victorian and Edwardian feminists themselves. Many of them called from the soap-box for a female invasion of the male public sphere and used metaphors of confinement, restriction, stunting and belittlement to convey the frustrations of their girlhoods.[14] The literary children of the Victorians, such as Vera Brittain and Virginia Woolf, who penned graphic portraits of stuffy parental mores, have also lent useful support to the familiar account of nineteenth-century women languishing or raging within an upholstered cage. Of course, in their efforts to debunk the reputation of the preceding generation, female critics were not alone. Convinced that they had thrown off the fetters of the nineteenth century (a conviction that became even more pronounced after the Great War), several early twentieth-century rebels turned a scathing eye on their parents' shortcomings, and thus it is to the likes of Lytton Strachey, Samuel Butler, Edmund Gosse and so on that we owe the enduring caricature of the hidebound and home-loving Victorians.[15]

Buttressed therefore by three types of evidence – didactic literature, contemporary feminist debate and post-Victorian denunciations – the separate spheres framework has come to constitute one of the fundamental organizing categories, if not *the* organizing category of modern British women's history. Moreover, through the medium of women's studies, the orthodoxy has been communicated to adjacent disciplines, where 'public and private', 'separate spheres', and 'domesticity' are rapidly becoming unquestioned key words.[16]

Of course, interpretations have developed over time. Proponents of the British separate spheres framework have revised many of their early generalizations. Sceptics have debated particular aspects of the framework, with varying degrees of effectiveness. Most are now at pains to present women as sentient, capable beings rather than as passive victims, emphasizing the ways in which women shaped their own lives within a male-dominated culture. The Angel-in-the-House model of Victorian ladyhood has proved most vulnerable to criticism. Using household manuals aimed at the lower middle-class wife managing on about £200 a year, Patricia Branca contested the representativeness of the pure and passive stereotype. Only prosperous upper middle-class ladies, she argued, idly received callers and supervised staff with cool aplomb. The vast majority of middle-class housewives coped with heavy housework and quarrelsome servants, while simultaneously struggling with the nervous art of creative accounting.[17] Meanwhile, using the manuscripts of the wealthy, professional Paget family, Jeanne Peterson disputed the usefulness of the model for even the privileged few.

> According to the received wisdom, Victorian ladies cared for nothing but homes and families, their education was 'decorative adornment' and they submitted to fathers and husbands. Three generations of Paget women do not conform to this. Their education was more than decorative, their relationship to money less distant than we thought, their physical lives more vigorous, expansive and sensual than either scholars today or some Victorians have led us to believe.[18]

The breathless inadequacy model of bourgeois femininity has also been questioned in studies of intrepid emigrants, formidable travellers and driven philanthropists. Feeble females would simply not have been capable of the courageous enterprise and conscientious administration that recent work reveals.[19] In fact, as Pat Thane has astutely argued, it is actually rather difficult to reconcile the 'strong sense of social responsibility, purpose and commitment to hard work with which Victorians of both sexes and all classes were socialized' with the conventional story of *increasing* female passivity.[20]

In fact, where historians have researched the activities of particular individuals and groups, rather than the contemporary social theories which allegedly hobbled them, Victorian women emerge as no less spirited, capable, and, most importantly, diverse a crew as in any other century.[21] Not that diversity should surprise us. Early modern family historians have long stressed the unique role of character and circumstance in shaping a woman's freedom of manoeuvre in marriage. Assuredly, stern patriarchs

sometimes married biddable girls,[22] but by the same token strong women
sometimes married weak men. Martin Pugh, for example, in an analysis of
four elite Victorian marriages, the duke and duchess of Marlborough, Lord
and Lady Londonderry, the earl and countess of Jersey, and Lord and Lady
Knightley, observes: 'each of these husband and wife teams included a partner who tended to be home-loving, unambitious and easily exhausted by the
stress of public life; in every case it was the male'.[23] As women in the past
have varied in strong-mindedness and the ability to exert influence, so
brains, force of character and a lofty indifference to persuasion have not
been equally distributed amongst the male population – a fact which novel-
ists have noted even if historians have not:

> The theory of man and wife – that special theory in accordance with
> which the wife is to bend herself in loving submission before her hus-
> band is very beautiful; and would be good altogether if it could only
> be arranged that the husband should be the stronger and greater of the
> two. The theory is based upon that hypothesis and the hypothesis
> sometimes fails of confirmation.[24]

The endless permutations in matrimonial power relations that can result
from the accidents of circumstance and character have led some scholars to
argue for the unpredictable variety of private experience, in any given
period, whatever the dominant ideology.[25] But even if we reject such extreme
particularism, the history of ideas tell us that in every era alternative 'ideologies' are usually on offer. Another look at Victorian sexual debate, for
instance, reveals that it may not have been so universally 'Victorian' as we
have been led to believe.[26] Wherever angelic uniformity was to be found, it
was not in Victorian sitting rooms, despite the dreams of certain poets,
wistful housewives, and ladies' advice books.

Most historians now concede that few women actually lived up to the
fantasies of Ruskin and Patmore, but still differ as to how seriously the Victorians took their didactic medicine. Martha Vicinus, for instance, reflects
that if 'nineteenth-century women were not always the passive, submissive
and pure creatures of popular idealizations . . . neither were they completely free from this stereotype'.[27] However, much recent scholarship has
refused to see the domestic ideal as a force which, in and of itself, severely
limited a woman's freedom of manoeuvre. Most vehement in this vein is
Jeanne Peterson, who concludes that the ideal of the domesticated
Madonna was simply an irrelevance in upper middle-class households. The
imposition of such a constraining behavioural model, she suspects, would
have made rebellious New Women of an entire generation. 'Instead the freedom, the adaptability, the choices inherent in genteel family life laid the
basis for a profound conservatism.'[28] In parallel, Martin Pugh's study of
aristocratic women and conservative politics signals the important possibility that ladies paid only lip-service to formal subservience in order to spare

their husbands' flimsy egos or perhaps the censure of posterity. Certainly, the memoirs of many late Victorian female politicians seem contrived to convey a suitably unthreatening picture of satisfied maternity and genteel leisure, so much so that they sometimes contain no reference whatsoever to a customary gruelling work-load of canvassing, committees and public speaking which can be substantiated from other sources.[29] Similarly, a thorough conversance with conservative assessments of woman's proper place (worried over in her diary) failed to keep Lady Charlotte Guest from translating the Mabinogian from medieval Welsh and managing the Dowlais iron works after her husband's death, while simultaneously mothering her ten children.[30] Of course, these particular examples are culled from the records of the socially exalted, who were better placed than most to flout convention or indulge exciting enthusiasms if they chose, nevertheless their experience still serves to remind us of the elementary, but crucial, point that women, like men, were eminently capable of professing one thing and performing quite another. Just because a volume of domestic advice sat on a woman's desk, it does not follow that she took its strictures to heart, or whatever her intentions managed to live her life according to its precepts.

Nevertheless, faith in the constitutive power of domestic precepts still lingers in the explanation of the achievements of mid-Victorian heroines. The heroic narrative assumes that a model of domestic femininity was *actively imposed* on women, who experienced feelings of entrapment of such strength that they were led fiercely to resist their containment, resulting in a glorious escape from the private sphere. To be sure, extraordinary women like Florence Nightingale have left passionate writings which ask us to see public heroism as an inevitable reaction to a previous period of mind-numbing cloistration. However, while Nightingale felt her early career aspirations cruelly thwarted, she herself had been taught Latin and Greek by her father, and was expected to engage in a ceaseless round of good works and charitable visiting in young adulthood.[31] Although Nightingale undoubtedly lacked scope for her great ambitions, she was hardly locked in the parlour with nothing but advice books for nourishment.

The power of domestic ideology as a catalyst is an implicit argument in Jane Rendall's thoughtful micro-study of female aspirations and activity amongst the fortunate. As young women in the 1840s and 50s, Bessie Parkes and Barbara Leigh Smith both resented and complained of their limited horizons.[32] By extension, Rendall implies that their subsequent formidable careers as managers, campaigners, essayists, travellers and energetic participants in radical and bohemian London Society should be seen as a reaction to this stultifying containment, rather than evidence that domestic prescripts had limited purchase in certain circles. Interestingly, however, both Parkes and Leigh Smith, like many of their confederates in the Victorian women's movement, hailed from radical political backgrounds. Of course, the importance of the radical inheritance has long been acknowledged (and not least by Rendall),[33] yet few have reflected on the possibility that equal rights feminism was less a reflex response to a newly imposed model of stifling passivity, than the fruition of a political tradition.[34] Privileged women saw social and political freedoms newly won by their fathers and brothers, while their own rights as citizens languished. Liberal feminists borrowed the rhetoric of unjust exclusion and applied it to their own case. But a feminist consciousness of educational disadvantage, virtually non-existent career structure, and exclusion from the major institutions of state is not, in itself, proof that the majority of women in comfortable households had no engagement with the world outside their front door. Nor, when exploring the question of causation and chronology, need a flowering of female politics be read as evidence that the preceding years had witnessed the social internment of middle-class women.

In consequence of recent work both theoretical and empirical, doubts now circulate within women's history about the conceptual usefulness of the separate spheres framework. As Jane Lewis remarked in 1986: 'while such a separation of spheres appears to fit the recent historical experience of western women well, anthropologists have found, first that the dichotomy conflates too easily with public/private and reproduction to be a useful conceptual tool and second that it has more descriptive than analytical power'.[35] But despite the dissenting voices, the questions, focus and chronology of the separate spheres framework still holds an uneasy sway. At conferences and seminars, participants raise queries and criticisms, while defendants of 'separate spheres' acknowledge the weaknesses of many aspects of the framework, yet still 'separate spheres' is believed to be of central importance in the history of nineteenth-century women and remains the model taught to students. To add to the confusion, the vocabulary of separate spheres also overlaps with that deployed by political historians to rather different ends; specifically, in the argument that the eighteenth century saw the creation, through the market in print, of a public sphere of politics, in contrast to the previously closed political world of Westminster and the royal court.[36] A major study by Leonore Davidoff and Catherine Hall has tried to take account of recent doubt and debate, but still asserts the historical significance of the ideology of separate spheres.[37] As a result, *Family fortunes: men and women of the English middle class* offers the most complex use of separate spheres as an organizing concept to date. Indeed, many see the book as the last word on the subject. Unquestionably, therefore, a landmark of English women's history, *Family fortunes* is an appropriate focus of detailed critical attention.

The explicit aim of *Family fortunes* is to insert an awareness of the constitutive role of gender into 'the main agenda of social and historical analysis'.[38] This is achieved by bringing the analysis of gender relations to bear on the question of mid-Victorian class formation. To this end, *Family fortunes* offers an account of the economic, associational, religious and domestic lives of middle-class families in Birmingham, Essex and Suffolk, between the years 1780 and 1850. And indeed the study impresses as a massively detailed and richly elaborated account of gender relations in a certain religious and institutional milieu. It offers much invaluable illumination of the complexities which lie beneath the stereotypes: the hidden investment of female knowledge, labour and capital in apparently male-only enterprises; the varying organization of the different churches and religious associations which offered women a place, albeit circumscribed; the role of wider kin in the life of the supposedly intensely nuclear bourgeois family; and the contradictory nature of middle-class taste and aspiration – even in the papers of the pious families studied, the scandalous Lord Byron was cited almost as often as the unexceptionable William Cowper and Hannah More. If anything, however, the richness and singularity of the picture Davidoff and Hall reconstruct refuses the general structure they seek to impose. The picture still stands although the claims they make for it, in my opinion, do not. In brief, they argue that gender played a crucial role in the structuring of an emergent, provincial, middle-class culture, for it was the ideology of domesticity and separate gender spheres which gave distinctive form to middle-class identity. Yet this claim rests upon a series of problematic assumptions which must be explored if women's historians are truly to assess the usefulness of the modified separate spheres framework and to build on the research of Davidoff and Hall in creative ways.

First and foremost, *Family fortunes* rests on the conviction that a class society emerged between 1780 and 1850. For many historians of women, E.P. Thompson's inspirational masterpiece, *The making of the English working class* celebrated the making of a class with the women left out. *Family fortunes*, by contrast, presents the making of the middle class with women and the family emphatically in the spotlight. Without reference to the ever-growing literature on the culture and consequence of the early-modern middling sort, Davidoff and Hall assert that the provincial middle class took shape in the late eighteenth and early nineteenth centuries. Set apart from aristocracy and gentry by virtue of evangelized religion, a domestic value-system and non-landed wealth, the middle classes experienced a 'growing desire for independence from the clientage of landed wealth and power' which culminated in the political incorporation of the first reform act. Despite internal differences in income and outlook, the nineteenth-century middle class were bound together by a distinctive culture; moderate, rational and commercial, but above all moral and domesticated. These cultural values stood in marked contrast to the lavish and licentious mores of the aristocracy and gentry, although eventually the middle-class world view would become 'the triumphant common sense of the Victorian age'.[39]

This account, however, begs many questions. The last decade has witnessed a massive rethinking of Marxian categories and narratives, particularly in the context of early nineteenth-century England. Yet despite all the recent scholarship, both theoretical and empirical, the old theories about class-making remain fundamental to *Family fortunes*, and surprisingly are not open to debate. Their picture of a mid-Victorian bourgeois triumph does not account for new research and novel interpretations. Nineteenth-century historians have re-emphasized the resilience of landed power in government, economy and society, the strength of vertical allegiances up and down the social structure as a whole, and the internal divisions among the commercial classes themselves.[40] Meanwhile seventeenth- and eighteenth-century historians might ask what was so novel about men of middling wealth enjoying both political power in urban institutions and a sense of moral purpose from a cosy home life?[41] And indeed *exactly* how and why the transition from a 'middling sort' to the archetypal 'middle class' is made between 1688 and 1850 has not yet been elucidated.[42]

[. . .]

In the assertion that modern class and gender relations were made in the period from 1780 to 1850, Davidoff and Hall call into play vintage assumptions about the impact of economic change. The period from 1780 to 1850 is a conventional choice for nineteenth-century historians and in characterizing these seventy years as formative, Davidoff and Hall are not unusual. They do not aim to examine the late eighteenth century in any detail; in fact their close focus is saved for the period 1820–50. Again the eighteenth century is the sketchy before-picture, the primeval sludge out of which modern, industrial society emerges. There seems to be a consensus in the literature about nineteenth-century society that 1780 is a key social and economic moment. Implicitly this derives from an old idea of a late eighteenth-century industrial 'take-off',[43] which enabled historians to cite the industrial revolution as the *deus ex machina* accounting for most social developments. But in the light of a revised economic history which has variously stressed the vigour of seventeenth-century and early eighteenth-century international commerce and domestic manufacturing, and/or down-played the socio-economic contrast between 1750 and 1850 in England as a whole,[44] it is surprising that social historians should continue to present, with relatively little qualification, an apocalyptic industrial revolution, 1780–1850, as the midwife of modernity. After all, seventeenth- and early eighteenth-century wealth creation was sufficiently impressive for there to be plenty of commercial families supporting non-earning wives, prospering long before Hannah More and William Wilberforce took up their campaigns. Similarly, the ideas and institutions which allegedly defined both economic man and a manly economy: accounting, banking, an investment market, a complex retail network and so on were also well-established before 1780.[45]

If the economic changes of the period 1780 to 1850 were not as dramatic as *Family fortunes* implies, it cannot be said that the same years were unmomentous in terms of politics. Davidoff and Hall stress the role of the shock-waves of the French revolution and the campaigning zeal of the evangelicals in creating a new moral climate in English social and political life discernible from the 1790s. In the turbulent decades ahead, it is argued, the image of pure womanhood unsullied by public cares was to offer the English middle class a vision of harmony and security in an uncertain world. What should we make of this version of events? Firstly, it is clear that texts extolling domestic virtue and a clear separation of the realms of men and women circulated long before 1789, so it cannot be the case that political fears begat this particular theory of social organization.[46] Secondly, while no-one would deny that evangelicalism was a crucial force in nineteenth-century society, the extent to which evangelicalism was an exclusive middle-class project is unclear: the Clapham sect themselves hailed from lesser gentry, while the appeal of methodism was obviously felt far down the social hierarchy. Thirdly, it would be mistaken to see evangelical enthusiasm thriving in every middle-class home, just because the history of the tepid, the backsliding and the utterly indifferent nineteenth-century household remains to be written. And fourthly, the extent to which shifts in public morality actually stripped women of important powers and freedoms is also obscure. Of course, it is beyond question that the Victorians were different from the mid Georgians in their public reactions to sex. Moreover, many early nineteenth-century commentators believed that manners and mores had undergone a transformation in their lifetime. Witness Emily, Duchess of Leinster musing in retrospect in 1804 on the explicit writing style of Mary Wortley Montagu:

> Lady Mary's are certainly not hints, but very plain speaking, and I am apt to think that want of delicacy was very much the fashion in those days [i.e. 1720–40]. It was going off in my times [i.e. 1750–65], but I still remember it was retained by all those women who were [regarded?] *wits* among the old ones, and there was always a fan held up to the face when their jokes were repeated before any young people by those middle age. Lady Townshend went on with it for many years when quite out of fashion, but she was singular.[47]

Similarly, looking back on his youth in 1827, Sir Walter Scott reflected that elite men no longer dared 'to insult decency in the public manner then tolerated' although he was undecided as to whether a profound transformation of values had occurred or merely a change in outward appearances: 'we are not now, perhaps, more moral in our conduct than men of fifty years ago, but modern vice pays a tax to appearances, and is contented to wear a mask of decorum'.[48] Assuredly, the behaviour of both women *and* men became more constrained in certain public contexts. Yet does the onset of prudishness necessarily signal the haemorrhage of important powers for women? That so many of us have presumed it does, *ipso facto*, is perhaps more of a testimony to the continuing strength of the 1960s belief that sexual adventure and social liberation are synonymous, than the result of research on early nineteenth-century social practices. Still, evangelical fervour *may* have resulted in the discrediting of certain public arenas within which privileged women had once been active, like the theatre auditorium, the assembly room and the pleasure garden, although research on this issue is in its infancy. Nevertheless, if evangelized religion took from some women's public lives with one hand, it undoubtedly gave with the other in the burgeoning of religious associations, moral campaigns and organized charity. Certainly, this was Wilberforce's rather self-serving conclusion:

> There is no class of persons whose condition has been more improved in my experience than that of unmarried women. Formerly there seemed to be nothing useful in which they could naturally be busy, but now they may always find an object in attending the poor.[49]

Moreover, Linda Colley has recently argued that the conservative backlash of the 1790s offered opportunities for *greater* female participation in a new public life of loyalist parades, petitions and patriotic subscriptions. Viewed from this angle, in fact, reactionary politics offered these 'angels of the state' a higher public profile, not an upholstered private cage.[50]

And this brings us back to the vexed question of separate spheres. Taking account of feminist revisionism, Davidoff and Hall recognize that the prescriptions of sermons and conduct books can never offer a perfect design for living. (In fact, Davidoff herself suggested in an important essay in 1977 that the ideal system laid out in sermons and manuals was belied by the complexity of lived experience.[51]) Davidoff and Hall argue that the spheres could never be truly separate and that it was impossible for Victorians to live as if that separation was absolute. Nevertheless, they still assert that the ideology of separate spheres had a powerful hold on the imagination of the Victorian bourgeoisie and that negotiating this ideology was a central middle-class concern. It was the middle-class belief in appropriate spheres which shaped the formal organization (if not the day-to-day running) of their emergent institutions. Their argument for the ideological significance of 'separate spheres' rests upon the existence of a large body of nineteenth-century texts extolling the strict separation of the public and private, and the fact that religious institutions tended to segregate the formal activities of men and women. But does this juxtaposition offer sufficient proof that the Victorians exerted themselves to live up to the rhetoric of separate spheres? Davidoff and Hall do not offer evidence from personal manuscripts of a constant dialogue between precept and practice. Instead, they detail the attempts of churchmen of all denominations to ensure a proper division of labour between the sexes: women were allotted subsidiary roles, directed to single-sex committees and for the most part expected to content themselves dispensing liquid and emotional refreshment.[52] However, this raises a crucial question – is the maintenance of a sexual division of labour within institutions *the same thing as* the separation of public and private spheres? If we decide it is, then we must conclude that the drive to create separate spheres is universal, transcending class and time, for throughout history and across cultures there are virtually no institutions which have not differentiated between men and women when it comes to dispensing power and prestige. Of course, if the segregation of men and women within church organization can be shown to be a novel development, then it might be read as another manifestation of the forces that spawned the separate spheres literature, thereby confirming the status of 'separate spheres' as a powerful ideology. And in this vein, Davidoff and Hall assume: 'as so often, increased formality led to the increasing marginalization of women'.[53] Yet, few eighteenth-century historians would claim that women enjoyed an institutional heyday in their period. If anything, the early nineteenth-century growth of female committee work and the like looks like an expansion of the female role, not a diminution. Indeed, one might go further and argue that the stress on the proper female sphere in Victorian discourse signalled a growing concern that more women were seen to be active *outside* the home rather than proof that they were so confined. In short, the broadcasting of the language of separate spheres looks like a conservative response to an unprecedented *expansion* in the opportunities, ambitions and experience of late Georgian and Victorian women.

In questioning the ideological power of the separate spheres rhetoric in the making of the middle class, or the confinement of women, this essay does not argue that the vocabulary of public and private spheres had no currency in nineteenth-century society. Linda Colley's female patriots used the rhetoric of separate spheres to legitimize their actions. 'Posing as the pure-minded Women of Britain was, in practice, a way of insisting on the right to public spirit.'[54] Equally, philanthropists deployed this rhetoric to justify their non-domestic activities. That they should call on the language of true womanly duty is hardly surprising. After all, even St Paul conceded that good works became good women. Moreover, sentimentalists like Ruskin handed rhetorical success on a plate when they mused: 'a woman has a personal work or duty, relating to her own home, and a public work and duty which is also the expansion of that' and 'wherever a true wife comes, [home] is always around her'.[55] In arguing that organized charity represented an altogether natural extension of female domestic duties, a form of 'social housekeeping', activists defeated the opposition with its own weapons. Demonstrably, also, the language of separate spheres was deployed in the late Victorian controversy about women's citizenship. Numerous campaigners stated categorically that they wanted access to the public sphere, by which they clearly meant the universities, the professions, local and central government. Gissing's fictional New Women called for 'an armed movement, an invasion by women of the spheres which men have always forbidden us to enter' and categorically rejected 'that view of us set forth in such charming language by Mr Ruskin'.[56] As the reference to John Ruskin suggests, feminist speeches were tactically contrived to argue with those who contended that women ought to return to their traditional responsibilities and stay out of institutional life.[57] Feminist polemic was designed to convert and galvanize an audience; it did not pretend to be a nuanced account of women's everyday lives and informal powers. Of course, to stress the debating role of feminist rhetoric is to labour the blindingly obvious, but the proselytizing function is worth remembering, before we assume firstly that the well-reproduced speeches offer a simple description of the daily reality of life in domestic prison and secondly that what campaigners meant by the public and the private coincides with what those words mean to historians.

It should be emphasized that none of this is to argue that Victorian women had a fine time of it. It is beyond question that they laboured under great disadvantages: legal, institutional, customary, biological and so on. Nor should one suppose that all was happiness and harmony in the middle-class family. Clearly, if a husband was deaf to persuasion, resolved to push his prerogatives to the utmost, then marriage could mean miserable servitude for his unlucky wife. But it is to say that the metaphor of separate spheres fails to capture the texture of female subordination and the complex interplay of emotion and power in family life, and that the role of an ideology of separate spheres in the making of the English middle class, 1780–1850, has not been convincingly demonstrated. It is also to suggest that our preoccupation with the ideology of separate spheres may have blinded us to the other languages in play in the Victorian period. As a sociological study of a particular set of gender relations at a particular historical moment, *Family fortunes* has much to offer to the next generation of women's historians, but the overarching historical narrative it seeks to tell should be discussed and debated, not given the unwarranted status of holy writ.

II

The unquestioned belief that the transition to industrial modernity robbed women of freedom, status and authentic function underlies most modern women's history. One can hardly pick up a text on women's lives in the nineteenth century which is not founded on the conviction that things ain't what they used to be. But were the work opportunities and public liberties enjoyed by propertied women before the factory so much greater than those of the Victorian period? Much of the literature on early modern women's work and social lives would have us believe so. The second major account of change in the history of middle-class women rests on a tale of female marginalization resulting from early modern capitalism. Like so many theories in social and economic history, the intellectual origins of this story lie in the nineteenth century. Socialist writers, particularly Friedrich Engels and the first generation of female professionals, were preoccupied with the idea that women were infinitely better off before the coming of commerce. The overthrow of capitalist society, Engels confidently predicted, would see a return to the traditional equality of the sexes. Political democracy would not crumble if women were admitted as full citizens, implied the first female historians, since reforming legislation would simply restore the status quo ante.[58] In so arguing, however, these pioneer thinkers engendered a compelling vision of a pre-capitalist utopia, a golden age, for women, which shapes the writing of history to this day. At the same time, they sketched a social, cultural and economic transformation so abstract that it could be applied to almost any region or historical period.

And indeed it has. Countless historians follow Engels by presenting women as valued and productive on page one of their study, but then ultimately devalued and redundant by the conclusion, usually fifty years later. Take two classics of English economic history: Alice Clark's *Working life of women in the seventeenth century* (1919) and Ivy Pinchbeck's *Women workers and the Industrial Revolution* (1930). These historians held differing views on the quality of industrial life and the implications of female exclusion from it. Nevertheless, both saw the declining role of the woman worker and the associated rise of the male breadwinner as a consequence of capitalism in various guises, although for Alice Clark the *key* period of loss was the late seventeenth century, while for Pinchbeck the crucial decades fell between 1790 and 1840. Despite the chronological inconsistencies, however, Clark and Pinchbeck share many assumptions about the character and consequences of economic change which have been assimilated to a generalized narrative.

According to customary wisdom, sometime between 1600 and 1800 a wholesome 'family economy' wherein men, women and children shared tasks and status gave way to an exploitative wage economy which elevated the male breadwinner and marginalized his dependants. The commercialization of agriculture and the enclosure movement strangled the informal livelihood contrived by many labouring families on the land. The housewife lost her ability to contribute through husbandry, while female field workers who had previously worked shoulder to shoulder with their menfolk were suddenly marginalized in sporadic, demeaning and low-paid agricultural occupations. Meanwhile, the mechanization of industrial processes took manufacturing out of the early modern home and into the modern factory, separating for ever after the home and workplace.[59]

Thus, in brief, the orthodox version. However, there is now a growing chorus of heretical voices. In 1983, Olwen Hufton questioned the validity of the decline and fall model of women's work in early modern Europe, since it rests on the dubious assumption of a lost egalitarian Eden, which has proved elusive to empirical research. The more research that is done, concluded Hufton, the more the vision of the *bon vieux temps* recedes into an even more distant past. In parallel, Judith Bennett argued in 1988 that if women's work was 'low-skilled, low-status and low-paying' in the nineteenth century then it always had been. Thus the basic continuities in women's work between 1200 and 1900 must render inadequate the conventional explanation of female subordination in terms of capitalism and industrialization.[60] Along with general criticisms of the master narrative, the last few years have also seen the publication of case studies which undermine particular aspects of the story for early modern England. Unfortunately for our purposes, most of this work concentrates on the experience of labouring women; however, it is useful briefly to summarize some of the new findings here as they have important implications for the discussion of the wealthier women that follows.

The saga of the good old days and their sorry demise has been problematized by new work on agriculture, rural manufacturing and urban labour. When it comes to women's work in agriculture, the universal narrative fails to capture the different histories of sheep-corn and wood-pasture farming, the contrast between the well-studied South-East and the under-researched North-West, and the different experiences of families with a skilled and unskilled head.[61] Moreover, even for the corn belt, the notion of a sudden metamorphosis of the sturdy independent small-holder into the landless proletarian is belied by the long, drawn-out history of enclosure. After all, there had been waged day labour on the land since at least the sixteenth century. And most significantly, there is little convincing evidence that men and women's agricultural work had ever been interchangeable. Certainly, one of the few substantial case studies, a recent examination of Norfolk farming in the late sixteenth century, convincingly demonstrates that men's and women's work was clearly differentiated in terms of tasks, status and remuneration. Unless old, feeble, or simple, men rarely did jobs like weeding or picking over corn, 'any more than women built houses, hewed timber, ploughed, harrowed, threshed, carted hay and corn, dug ditches or cut hedges'.[62] But if early modern agriculture was no bed of roses for women, was rural industry any better? While it is undoubtedly the case that women experienced substantial losses in this sector due to the mechanization of handspinning in the late eighteenth century, it is not clear that women's non-agricultural paid labour was especially rewarding before the factory. The received picture of a self-sufficient, non-alienating family enterprise is not supported by the available case studies. In fact, production by the family as a unit was far from being the norm. For example, for the vast majority of the worsted handspinners of Yorkshire and the lacemakers of Devon, their work was not a complement to their husband's trade, but an entirely separate form of waged employment.[63] Emphatically, waged work was no invention of nineteenth-century industrialists, nor was work before the factory as household-centred and as communitarian as has been suggested. But even where men and women did work alongside each other on a shared project, in the classic proto-industrial family, for example, a sexual division of labour usually prevailed. Furthermore it is not clear that a woman's industrial work was any more agreeable when directed by a husband, rather than a formal employer, or that her obvious contribution to the family's manufacturing output necessarily translated into higher status. Indeed the belief that a heavy workload automatically translates into power and prestige is a curious one for women's historians to espouse.

Yet even if the history of the textile industry *could* be made to fit the conventional chronology of economic decline, an all-inclusive chronology for women's labour should not be derived from textiles alone. Firstly, women had a different experience in other rural industries. In metalwares and the smaller domestic industries mechanization only reinforced a pre-established division of labour, and women's labour remained paramount throughout the nineteenth century.[64] Secondly, whatever the change over time in women's work roles in the countryside, there was virtually none in the city. Peter Earle's recent comparison of female employment in London in 1700 and in 1851 reveals that domestic service, charring, laundry, nursing, and the making and mending of clothes were the most common occupations in both periods. While participation rates declined, the general structure of the female labour market remained the same. There was no systematic reduction in the range of employments available to labouring women over the period.[65] So while the end of the eighteenth century was distinctive in the history of women's work insofar as this period witnessed the grievous loss of remunerative employment in one important sector of the economy, the domestic manufacture of textiles, the decline of handspinning is not sufficient in itself to support a theory of absolute and comprehensive decline for every working woman in everything from economic power and legal independence to public assertiveness and sexual respect.[66]

It is against this background of scepticism about a history which blindly insists that women's status had deteriorated from a past golden age that we should assess the parallel arguments about wealthier women. Here the central tragic theme is the much-lamented metamorphosis of the seventeenth-century business woman or diligent housekeeper into the nineteenth-century parasite. In the sixteenth and early seventeenth centuries, so Alice Clark famously argued, the wives of craftsmen and manufacturers made a substantial contribution to the family enterprise since the home and workplace were usually one. Women at all social levels were true partners to their husbands, demonstrated a capacity for business and their engagement in commercial life aroused no comment. It was usual for gentlewomen to be active in household and estate management, public affairs and even government. But as the century wore on the rapid increase of wealth permitted the wives of prosperous men to withdraw from all forms of productive activity. In parallel, the spread of 'capitalistic organization' ensured that manufacturing became concentrated on central premises. Once production left the home, the wife was divorced from her husband's trade and lost the informal opportunity to learn his skills. Creative housekeeping fell into decay. In contrast to their hardy and resourceful Elizabethan grandmothers, the moneyed ladies of the Restoration were distinguished only by their 'devotion to idle graces'.[67]

This resonant tale of a female descent into indolence and luxury has been frequently reiterated.[68] Moreover, it is tacit in most accounts that the female liberation from manual labour is *ipso facto* disempowering. Lawrence Stone, for instance, leaves us in no doubt about the frivolousness and futility of a woman's life once she had vacated the dairy and laid down the distaff.

> Wives of the middle and upper classes increasingly became idle drones. They turned household management over to stewards, reduced their reproductive responsibilities by contraceptive measures, and passed their time in such occupations as novel reading, theatre going, card playing and formal visits . . . The custom of turning wives into ladies 'languishing in listlessness' as ornamental status objects spread downwards through the social scale.[69]

Some have built on the tale of women's divorce from useful labour, to assert that the 'new domestic woman' was the inevitable bride of the new economic man.

> [With the] eighteenth-century glorification of 'Man' came a radical narrowing of women's participation in and contribution to productive and social life, and a drastic diminution of women's stature. It was not merely a relative decline. Pre-capitalist woman was not simply relatively eclipsed by the great leap forward of the male achiever; she suffered rather an absolute setback.[70]

Echoing nineteenth-century preoccupations, scholars of English literature have tried to chart the construction of domesticated femininity, although there is a certain confusion as to whether the new domestic woman was the epitome of bourgeois personality, or was an ornament shared by the middling ranks and the landed. But whatever her social background, it is agreed that the sweet domesticate was created 'in and by print'. Kathryn Shevelow's study of early eighteenth-century periodicals leads her to conclude that 'during the eighteenth century, as upper and middle-class Englishwomen increasingly began to participate in the public realm of print culture, the representational practices of that print culture were steadily enclosing them within the private sphere of the home'.[71] But for all the stress on the constitutive power of language in the emergence of homely virtue, most of the literary studies take on trust the prior existence of an entirely new breed of bored, housebound, cultural consumers created at a particular historical moment by capitalism.[72] Therefore, whether informed by Foucault, Lacan or

Greenblatt, recent feminist literary criticism still depends ultimately on a narrative of social and economic change which has barely changed since 1919.

So on what basis did Alice Clark found her original argument? In fact, her evidence for change over time was remarkably slight. She used diaries, letters and depositions to establish the courage and capability of ladies in the late sixteenth century and early to mid-seventeenth century, but to demonstrate that 'their contact with affairs became less habitual as the century wore away' she relied on a different order of source material.[73] She cited unflattering comparisons of the inadequate English lady with her sober Dutch counterpart, Mary Astell's sorrowful criticisms of the 'Ladies of Quality', the stock characters of restoration drama, and the fact that Samuel Pepys was surprised and pleased to hear a friend's wife talk like a merchant. (In addition to such commentary, she cited the declining number of women who were named as sole executrix of their husband's will as proof of a withering female ability. However, whether it is possible to detect a single pattern of testamentary practice over the centuries and to attribute any change in practice to a growing perception of feminine inconsequence remains a very open question.[74]) But it is undeniably the case that the late seventeenth century saw a steady increase in texts grumbling about unemployed womanhood, a muttering which grew to a clamour from the 1690s. A new character graced the pages of plays, commentaries and complaint literature, the London woman who scorned productive labour for the sake of consumerism and pleasure. Most critical and subsequently most quoted was Daniel Defoe: 'As ladies now manage', he remarked, they 'scorn to be seen in the compting house, much less behind the counter; despise the knowledge of their husband's business, and act as if they were ashamed of being tradesmen's wives, and never intended to be tradesmen's widows.' Instead she will 'sit above in the parlour, receive visits, drink tea and entertain her neighbours, or take a coach and go abroad'.[75] However, the redundant woman of the Augustan period, languishing on her sofa, may not have been as novel a creature as the indictments suggest. Perhaps it was her flamboyant habits that were new and public, rather than her actual lack of occupation. It could even be argued that such criticism was merely another symptom of the general moral panic in the late seventeenth century about the decline of spartan virtue and the rise of luxurious corruption, rather than evidence of any new social group or practice. After all, in their fears about the vicious consequences of wealth, writers fell back upon stereotypical images of devouring, unreasonable womanhood, images that were as old as Eve herself – something which suggests we might better view such accusations as testimony to the persistence of *male* anxieties, rather than a simple guide to *female* behaviour.[76] And of course, scholars of print might suggest that the rising tide of complaint and conduct literature owes far more to the relaxation of censorship after the failure to renew the licensing act in 1695 than it does to the outbreak of a new disease called female parasitism.

But if this flowering of public discussion was not necessarily a simple reaction to the mass female abandonment of active enterprise, was it subsequently responsible for the creation of an entirely new model of feminine behaviour? Did the *grand peur* about female ostentation and publicity lead to the inscription of a new pattern of virtuous, domesticated womanhood? To be sure, many scholars have detected a growing emphasis on women's innate moral superiority and a declining preoccupation with uncontrollable female sexuality in Augustan literature. Backed by an impressive survey of courtesy literature written between 1670 and 1750, Fenela Childs argues that cloying idealization set in from 1700, although she stresses the obvious but important point that visions of female nature had for centuries oscillated between impossibly pure and irredeemably depraved.[77] Similarly, Marlene Legates suggests that we should not overestimate the novelty of eighteenth-century views of women. She argues that chastity and obedience were ancient pre-requisites of the ideal woman, that a belief in woman as redeemer was as old as courtly love, that positive views of marriage had coexisted with explicit misogyny in classical and humanist thought, and that even the sentimental themes of love, marriage and virtue under siege had a long pedigree. Legates concludes that the eighteenth century saw not so much a dramatic break with past assumptions about the good woman, as a compelling dramatization of her traditional predicament.[78] Evidently, eighteenth-century literature contained much that nineteenth-century historians might identify as 'domestic ideology', yet these themes were far from revolutionary. Moreover, periodicals, novels, sermons and conduct books undoubtedly contained many other ideological messages besides and were probably subject to multiple and/or selective readings. Indeed, as this essay has frequently implied, we should not presume without evidence that women (or men) mindlessly absorbed a particular didactic lesson like so many pieces of blotting paper.[79]

In any case, research on the seventeenth and early eighteenth-century economy raises doubts about the conviction that female enterprise decayed substantially between 1700 and 1850. Firstly, it is clear that the explanatory power given to the notion of the separation of the home and workplace is unwarranted. Of course, if industrial change had involved a simple linear transition from family workshop to factory this process could have had a devastating impact across the board. But as D.C. Coleman remarked in another context, there were many key early modern enterprises which simply could not be performed in a cottage by husband, wife and children. In mining, ship-building, iron smelting, pottery firing, glass blowing, paper making, soap boiling, fulling wool and so on, the place of work was of necessity divorced from bed and board from the very inception of the industry. Moreover, the factory was far from being the normal unit of production in the mid-nineteenth century.[80] Economic change followed many roads and did not arrive at a single destination. And secondly when we consider those businesses that women pursued in their own right, continuity is more apparent than change. Peter Earle's study of late seventeenth-century London reveals women *already* clustered in the so-called feminine trades: petty retail, food and drink, and textiles. (In fact, women's businesses in York were concentrated in petty retail, food and drink, and textiles *as far back as the fifteenth century*.[81]) Widows had long been unwilling to pursue their late husband's business if it was an uncongenial trade. They tended either to remarry a journeyman, or sell up. Moreover, single women were prominent in the London rental and investment market, as they were in rural moneylending, suggesting that the economic choices of wealthier women were already biased against active, risky business.[82] It was probably considerably easier for an heiress to operate as a landlady, money-lender, rentier, or investor than to run a male business in a male world. Indeed, it could be argued that a female withdrawal from active enterprise was essentially a function of increasing wealth. Therefore *any* study of an expanding business, be it in fourteenth-century York, seventeenth-century London, or nineteenth-century Birmingham, would be likely to show a reduction over three generations in the formal participation of female members of the owning family. In determining the incidence of female withdrawal from business over the long term, what may be crucial is not the growth of capitalism as such, but increases in the number of businesses generating sufficient wealth to allow such withdrawal. What we need are careful comparisons across time and space of the role of women in enterprises of a similar scale. Yet even at this early stage of research, it is already clear that many centres of commerce and manufacturing had boasted a select population of non-earning ladies long before the flowering of literature advocating domestic womanhood – a fact which must be taken on board when making large statements about causation and chronology in the lives of wealthier women.

[. . .]

The wives of the merchants and manufacturers I have studied were definitely not idle, but it cannot be said that they enjoyed extensive commercial opportunities which their Victorian equivalents subsequently lost. Nor should the eighteenth century be seen as a golden age of female public life. And this point takes us back to my earlier discussion of separate spheres. In no century before the twentieth did women enjoy the public powers which nineteenth-century feminists sought – the full rights of citizenship. Public life for the gentlemen I have studied invariably incorporated some form of office, but there was no formal place for their wives in the machinery of local administration. Customarily, a wealthy woman wielded power as a mother, kinswoman, housekeeper, consumer, hostess and arbiter of polite

sociability. If all this adds up to a separation of the public sphere of male
power and the private sphere of female influence, then this separation was
an ancient phenomenon which certainly predated the misogyny of the
1690s, evangelicalism, the French revolution and the factory.

The public/private dichotomy may, therefore, serve as a loose description
of a very long-standing difference between the lives of women and men.
What is extremely difficult to sustain, however, is the argument that sometime between 1650 and 1850 the public/private distinction was constituted
or radically reconstituted in a way that transformed relations between the
sexes. The shortcomings of the public/private dichotomy as an analytical
framework are many, but most obviously there is little unanimity among
historians as to what public and private should be held to mean in this context. Current interpretations of 'the public' vary enormously. In a historian's
hands, a public role can mean access to anything from politics, public office,
formal employment, opinion, print, clubs, assembly, company, the neighbourhood, the streets, or simply the world outside the front door. However,
we should take care to discover whether our interpretation of public and
private marries with that of historical actors themselves. Take the excel-
lently documented experience of Elizabeth Shackleton of Alkincoats. She
resorted often to the 'publick papers', perpetuated her dead husband's 'publick spirit' by selling his famous rabies medicine at an affordable price, witnessed her second husband's 'publick humiliation' in the house of a tenant,
and saw her own kitchen become 'very publick' with a stream of unexpected
visitors. Doubtless, the likes of Mrs Shackleton figured in that 'publick'
addressed by both the *Ladies Magazine* and the *Leeds Intelligencer*.[83] Most
of her labour took place within the house, yet from her medicine room she
traded with men throughout the north, and from her writing desk wrote
business letters to a national network. Evidently, her public and private cannot be mapped on to the physical home and the external world. The 'publick' for Elizabeth Shackleton was inextricably bound up with company,
opinion and information. She had access to all of these. For Bessy Ramsden
going out 'in publick' in the 1760s and 1770s meant a visit to the theatre, the
assembly, the pleasure garden or a trial. Another wife of a London professional, the diarist Anna Larpent, listed all 'the publick places and private
entertainments' she visited and enjoyed between 1773 and 1787. Public
places listed in 1773 included the play, the opera, Richmond assembly and
Ranelagh – all venues which could be penetrated for the price of a ticket and
where visitors could see and be seen. Private entertainments were exclusive
gatherings entered by invitation only. So, while women such as Elizabeth
Shackleton, Bessy Ramsden and Anna Larpent were obviously severely dis-
abled when it came to institutional power, they did not lack access to the
public sphere, *as they understood it*. It seems likely that eighteenth-century
conceptions of publicity were different from those of nineteenth-century
feminists and twentieth-century historians. All of which underlines the

deficiencies in our knowledge of the distinctions between public and private in language, never mind as social practice.

III

This, then, is the contradictory inheritance of seventeenth- and nineteenth-century women's history. In essence, the rise of the new domestic woman (whether in her seventeenth- or nineteenth-century guise), the separation of the spheres, and the construction of the public and private are all different ways of characterizing what is essentially the same phenomenon: the marginalization of middle-class women. Like the insidious rise of capitalism, the collapse of community, the nascent consumer society and the ever-emerging middle class, it can be found in almost any century we care to look. When confronted with the numerous precedents, nineteenth-century historians of this phenomenon may claim that early modern developments represent only the *germ* of what was to come on a grand scale for the Victorian middle class. But the obvious problems of periodization which result cannot be brushed aside with the explanatory catch-all of 'uneven development'. The problem is exemplified if we try to reconcile Susan Amussen's work on early-modern Norfolk and Leonore Davidoff's on nineteenth-century Suffolk. Are we to believe that women were driven out of a public sphere of production and power in one district in the seventeenth century, while just over the county border the same development was delayed by well over a hundred years? Surely uneven development of this magnitude would have raised some contemporary comment, or at the very least female migration.

As a conceptual device, separate spheres has also proved inadequate. The economic chronologies upon which the accounts of women's exclusion from work and their incarceration in domesticity depend are deeply flawed. At a very general level, eighteenth- and early nineteenth-century women were associated with home and children, while men controlled public institutions, but then this rough division could be applied to almost any century or any culture[84] – a fact which robs the distinction of analytical purchase. If, *loosely speaking*, there have always been separate spheres of gender power, and perhaps there still are, then 'separate spheres' cannot be used to explain social and political developments in a particular century, least of all to account for Victorian class formation.

To conclude, this paper suggests that the orthodox categories of both seventeenth-century and nineteenth-century women's history must be jettisoned if a defensible chronology is to be constructed. Of course, such a renunciation carries a cost. A belief in the wholesale transformation wrought by capitalism on the economic role of women has provided early-modern women's history with an alluring big picture. Without that faith, we must accept a less heroic and more provisional chronology. Nevertheless, the notion of separate spheres in particular has done modern women's history a great service. With this conceptual framework women's history moved beyond a whiggish celebration of the rise of feminism, or a virtuous rediscovery of those previously hidden from history. In asserting the instrumental role of the ideology of separate spheres in modern class formation, historians asserted the wider historical significance of gender. Thereby the interpretation offered powerful justification for the study of women when the field was embattled. Yet strategic concerns do not in themselves justify the development of an artificial and unwieldy conceptual vocabulary. In the attempt to map the breadth and boundaries of female experience, new categories and concepts must be generated, and this must be done with more sensitivity to women's own manuscripts.

The burden of this piece has not been to argue that the discourses of femininity and masculinity, space and authority, found in printed literature are not important. Yet their power to shape female language and behaviour needs to be demonstrated, not taken as read. Otherwise virtually any printed text we come across can be deemed to have ideological potency regardless of the form of the publication, its popularity with the readers, or the currency of the ideas contained within it. In short, 'intertextuality' must be researched, not simply asserted in the abstract. Case studies are needed of the economic roles, social lives, institutional opportunities and personal preoccupations of women from the seventeenth to the nineteenth centuries. In parallel, we need a long span, but integrated, history of the full range of debates about women's proper role covering the same period. (For too long it has been assumed that domestic ideology hogged the discursive stage unchallenged.) All this needs to be undertaken with especial sensitivity to changes in the range of language and categories employed. Only then will we establish with any precision the extent to which women accepted, negotiated, contested or simply ignored, the much quoted precepts of proper female behaviour in past time. Only then will we establish whether the rhetoric of domesticity and private spheres contributed to female containment, or instead was simply a defensive and impotent reaction to public freedoms already won.

Notes

1 B. Welter, 'The cult of true womanhood, 1820–60', *American Quarterly*, XVIII (1966), 151–74.
2 See especially G. Lerner, 'The lady and the mill girl: changes in the status of women in the age of Jackson', *Midcontinent American Studies Journal*, X (1969), 5–15.
3 K. Wrightson, *English society 1580–1680* (1982), p. 92.
4 C.N. Degler, 'What ought to be and what was: women's sexuality in the nineteenth century', *American Historical Review*, LXXIX (1974), 1490. Another widely cited, but apparently unheeded, article has stressed the possible difference between what a woman was told to do, what she thought she was doing and what she actually did: J.

Mechling, 'Advice to historians or advice to mothers', *Journal of Social History*, IX (1979), 44–63.

5 N.F. Cott, *The bonds of womanhood: woman's sphere in New England, 1780–1835* (New Haven, 1977), p. 197.

6 L. Kerber, 'Separate sphere, female worlds, woman's place: the rhetoric of women's history', *Journal of American History*, LXXV (1988), 9–39.

7 The argument has its analogue for working-class women in the debates around the rise of the male breadwinner and the family wage; E. Roberts, *Women's work, 1840–1940* (Basingstoke, 1988).

8 W.E. Houghton, *The Victorian frame of mind, 1830–1870* (New Haven, 1957), pp. 341–93; Muriel Jaeger, *Before Victoria: changing standards and behaviour, 1787–1837* (London, 1956), pp. 113–30; Maurice Quinlan, *Victorian prelude: a history of English manners, 1700–1830* (New York, 1941), pp. 139–59.

9 The classic work on vulnerable and cloistered femininity is M. Vicinus (ed.), *Suffer and be still: women in the Victorian age* (Bloomington, Indiana, 1972).

10 C. Hall, 'Gender divisions and class formation in the Birmingham middle class, 1780–1850', in R. Samuel (ed.), *People's history and socialist theory* (1981), p. 174.

11 See M. Vicinus, 'One life to stand beside me: emotional conflicts in first generation college women in England', *Feminist Studies*, VIII (1982), 603–28, and *idem*, 'Distance and desire: English boarding school friendships', *Signs*, IX (1984), 600–22.

12 M. Vicinus, *Independent women: work and community for single women, 1850–1920* (1985), p. 3; M. Shanley, *Feminism, marriage and the law in Victorian England* (1989), pp. 6–7; J. Horowitz, *Strong-minded women: and other lost voices from nineteenth-century England* (Harmondsworth, 1984), p. 5.

13 R. Strachey, *The cause: a short history of the women's movement in Great Britain* (1978).

14 For a brief, but suggestive, discussion of the vocabulary of feminist autobiography, see C. Dyhouse, *Feminism and the family in England, 1880–1939* (Oxford, 1989), pp. 14–16.

15 Carol Dyhouse observes that Vera Brittain's retrospective autobiography written in 1933 attributes much more pent-up frustration to her younger self growing up in Edwardian Buxton, than was ever expressed in the diary written at the time: C. Dyhouse, 'Mothers and daughters in the middle class home, c. 1870–1914', in J. Lewis (ed.), *Labour and love: women's experiences of home and family, 1850–1940* (Oxford, 1986), p. 42. For a cautionary note about over-reliance on those writings shaped by the fashion for looking back in anger, see J. Tosh, 'Domesticity and manliness in the Victorian middle-class', in M. Roper and J. Tosh (eds), *Manful assertions: masculinities in Britain since 1800* (1991), pp. 60–1.

16 Particularly striking in this vein is work of the so-called 'new' art historians. On the nineteenth-century ideology of domesticity, read D. Cherry, 'Picturing the private sphere', *Feminist Art News*, V (1982), 5–11, L. Nead, *Myths of sexuality: representations of women in Victorian Britain* (Oxford, 1988), especially pp. 12–47, and R. Parker, *The subversive stitch: embroidery and the making of the feminine* (1984).

17 See P. Branca, 'Image and reality: the myth of the idle Victorian woman', in M. Hartman and L. Banner (eds), *Clio's consciousness raised: new perspectives on the history of women* (New York, 1974), 179–91 and *idem*, *Silent sisterhood: middle-class women and the Victorian home* (1975).

18 M.J. Peterson, 'No angels in the house: the Victorian myth and the Paget women', *American Historical Review*, LXXXIX (1984), 693.

19 The earnest enterprise and managerial skill of which Victorian women were capable is amply demonstrated by F.K. Prochaska, *Women and philanthropy in nineteenth-century England* (Oxford, 1980) and A. Summers, 'A home from home: women's philanthropic work in the nineteenth century', in S. Burman (ed.), *Fit work for women* (1977), pp. 33–63.

20 P. Thane, 'Late Victorian women', in T.R. Gourvish and A. O'Day (eds), *Later Victorian Britain, 1867–1900* (Basingstoke, 1988), pp. 175–208.

21 See P. Jalland, *Women, marriage and politics, 1860–1914* (Oxford, 1986); B. Caine, *Destined to be wives: the sisters of Beatrice Webb* (Oxford, 1988); Peterson, *Family,*

love and work in the lives of Victorian gentlewomen (Bloomington, Indiana, 1989). And despite the authors' assumptions, the following contain copious evidence of female diversity: P. Rose, *Parallel lives: five Victorian marriages* (New York, 1983), and Horowitz, *Strong-minded women*.

22 Tosh, 'Domesticity and manliness', pp. 50–1.

23 M. Pugh, *The Tories and the people, 1880–1935* (Oxford, 1985), p. 48.

24 A. Trollope, *The Belton estate* (1865; Oxford, 1991), p. 132.

25 V. Larminie, 'Marriage and the family: the example of the seventeenth century Newdigates', *Midland History*, IX (1984), p. 18.

26 Consider F.B. Smith, 'Sexuality in Britain, 1800–1900: some suggested revisions', in M. Vicinus (ed.), *A widening sphere: changing roles of Victorian women* (Bloomington, Indiana, 1977), pp. 182–98.

27 M. Vicinus, 'Introduction', in M. Vicinus (ed.), *A widening sphere*, p. xix.

28 Peterson, 'No angels', p. 708.

29 Pugh, *Tories and the people*, p. 47.

30 See R. Guest and A. John, *Lady Charlotte: a biography of the nineteenth century* (1989).

31 See Florence Nightingale, *Cassandra*, republished in Ray Strachey, *The cause*.

32 J. Rendall, 'Friendship and politics: Barbara Leigh Smith Bodichon (1827–91) and Bessie Rayner Parkes (1829–1925)', in S. Mendus and J. Rendall (eds), *Sexuality and subordination: interdisciplinary studies of gender in the nineteenth century* (1989), pp. 136–70.

33 The importance of the radical political heritage in the world view of Parkes and Leigh Smith is elaborated in J. Rendall, 'A moral engine? Feminism, liberalism and the English woman's journal', in J. Rendall (ed.), *Equal or different: women's politics, 1800–1914* (Oxford, 1987), pp. 112–38.

34 In a similar vein, Sally Alexander has reflected that 'we come closer to the terrain of feminist grievance and capture a decisive moment in its political temporality if we examine the forms of working-class politics themselves in the 1830s and 40s, and their language of demand and aspiration': 'Women, class and sexual differences in the 1830s and 40s: some reflections on the writing of a feminist history', *History Workshop Journal*, XVIII (1984), 130.

35 J. Lewis, 'Reconstructing women's experience', in Lewis (ed.), *Labour and love*, p. 20.

36 The *locus classicus* is J. Brewer, *Party, ideology and popular politics at the accession of George III* (Cambridge, 1976).

37 L. Davidoff and C. Hall, *Family fortunes: men and women of the English middle class, 1780–1850* (1987).

38 Ibid. p. 29.

39 Ibid. p. 28.

40 F.M.L. Thompson, *The rise of respectable society: a social history of Britain, 1830–1900* (1988).

41 A wealth of data on the early modern middling sort is in P. Earle, *The making of the English middle class: business, society and family life in London, 1660–1730* (1989).

42 Davidoff and Hall drew heavily on the then unpublished work of R.J. Morris. This has since appeared as R.J. Morris, *Class, sect and party: the making of the British middle class, Leeds 1820–50* (Manchester, 1990), which stresses the role of voluntary associations, while underestimating their significance in the seventeenth and eighteenth centuries.

43 W.W. Rostow, 'The take-off into self-sustained growth', *Economic Journal*, LXVI (1956), 25–48.

44 Read M. Fores, 'The myth of a British industrial revolution', *History*, LXVI (1981), 181–98 and D. Cannadine, 'The present and the past in the English industrial revolution, 1880–1980', *Past and Present*, CIII (1985), 131–72. Recently, however, there has been an attempt to resurrect the idea of economic transformation, see M. Berg and P. Hudson, 'Rehabilitating the industrial revolution', *Economic History Review*, 2nd ser., XLV (1992), 24–50.

45 For Davidoff and Hall's account of the construction of the independent economic man, see *Family fortunes*, pp. 198–271.

46 For example, Dod and Cleaver's *Household government* (1614) made it clear that while a husband was to 'Travel, seek a living . . . get money and provisions . . . deal with many men . . . dispatch all things outdoor', a wife's duties were to 'keep the house . . . talk with few . . . boast of silence . . . be a saver . . . oversee and give order within.' (I am indebted to Susan Lippit for this reference.) The notion of women as guardian of the family's heart and virtue was also well-established. In 1697, Mary Astell cited the mother's crucial influence over men in childhood as reason enough to support any scheme to improve female education: M. Astell, *A serious proposal to the ladies, for the advancement of their true and greatest interest by a lover of her sex* (1697), p. 97. Addison, Steele and many other writers of courtesy literature glamorized the pure domestic woman in the early decades of the eighteenth century. At mid-century Thomas Marriott praised women for their superior purity, their crucial role as mothers and their smiling guardianship of the sanctuary of the home. Women's virtue, he asserted, was vital to the preservation of the state and the British race. This exemplary virtue justified female efforts to reform society's morals: T. Marriott, *Female conduct, being an essay on the art of pleasing the fair sex* (1759).

47 British Library, HHMS (1804), Letter from Emily Duchess of Leinster to Hon. Caroline Fox. (I am indebted to Stella Tillyard for this reference.)

48 Quoted in Quinlan, *Victorian prelude*, p. 255.

49 Quoted in Jaeger, *Before Victoria*, p. 37.

50 L. Colley, *Britons: forging the nation, 1707–1837* (New Haven, 1992), pp. 237–81.

51 Davidoff, 'The separation of home and work? Landladies and lodgers in the nineteenth and twentieth centuries', in Burman (ed.), *Fit work*, pp. 64–97. This study serves as a reminder 'that there is no natural or fixed separation between a private and public sphere' (at p. 93).

52 Davidoff and Hall, *Family fortunes*, pp. 107–48.

53 Ibid. p. 119.

54 Colley, *Britons*, p. 281.

55 J. Ruskin, 'Of Queens' Gardens', in *Sesame and lilies* (1907), pp. 71, 60.

56 G. Gissing, *The odd women* (1893; 1980), p. 135.

57 Consider the contemporary arguments relayed in J. Lewis (ed.), *Before the vote was won: arguments for and against women's suffrage* (1987) and B. Harrison, *Separate spheres: the opposition to women's suffrage in Britain* (1978).

58 See F. Engels, *Origin of the family, private property and the state* (1972), *passim*, and the introduction by M. Chaytor and J. Lewis to the 1982 Routledge edition of A. Clark, *Working life of women in the seventeenth century*, pp. ix–xliii.

59 For a summary of orthodox views on this topic, see B. Hill, *Women, work and sexual politics in the eighteenth century* (Oxford, 1990), pp. 24–68.

60 O. Hufton, 'Women in history: early modern Europe', *Past and Present*, CI (1983), 126; J. Bennett, 'History that stands still: women's work in the European past', *Feminist Studies*, XIV (1988), 269–83.

61 The different economic experiences of families headed by specialist and non-specialist rural labourers is suggested by the excellent article by A. Hassell Smith, 'Labourers in late sixteenth-century England: a case study from north Norfolk, parts one and two', *Continuity and Change*, IV (1989), 11–52, 367–94. Much less work has been done on pastoral regions, which is ironic since these were traditional areas of high female employment. Nevertheless, even at this stage of research it seems unlikely that female predominance in the dairy was seriously threatened until the rise of big commercial dairies in the later nineteenth century. See D. Valenze, 'The art of women and the business of men: women's work and the dairy industry, c. 1740–1840', *Past and Present*, CXXX (1991), 142–69.

62 Hassell Smith, 'Labourers', p. 377.

63 The vast majority of the worsted handspinners of Yorkshire and the lacemakers of Devon were not married to men in textile-related trades. For the Devon findings, see P. Sharpe, 'Literally spinsters: a new interpretation of local economy and demography in Colyton in the seventeenth and eighteenth centuries', *Economic History Review*, 2nd ser., XLIV (1991), 46–65. The Yorkshire findings are those of John Styles.

64 M. Berg, 'Women's work, mechanisation and the early phase of industrialisation in England', in P. Joyce (ed.), *The historical meanings of work* (Cambridge, 1987), pp. 64–98.
65 P. Earle, 'The female labour market in London in the late seventeenth and early eighteenth centuries', *Economic History Review*, 2nd ser., XLII (1989), 328–52.
66 Nor should the particular marginalization of the late eighteenth century be seen as a unique cataclysm, *the* moment when capitalism tossed labouring women aside. Rather, there were several moments in the last millennium when women were drawn into the formal economy in enormous numbers only to be dispensed with when demographic conditions or technological innovations rendered their contribution less vital. S.C. Ogilvie, 'Women and proto-industrialisation in a corporate society: Wurtenberg woollen weaving, 1590–1760', in P. Hudson and W.R. Lee (eds), *Women's work and the family economy in historical perspective* (Manchester, 1990), pp. 76–103.
67 See Clark, *Working life*, pp. 14, 41, 296.
68 Consider S. Amussen, *An ordered society: gender and class in early modern England* (Oxford, 1988), 187; C. Hall, 'The history of the housewife', in *idem, White, male and middle class: explorations in feminism and history* (Oxford, 1992), pp. 43–71; M. George, *Women in the first capitalist society: experiences in seventeenth-century England* (Brighton, 1988), pp. 1–10; Hill, *Women, work and sexual politics*, pp. 49–52, 78–80, 126–9, 245–9. On 'the restriction of women's professional and business activities at the end of the nineteenth century', see Pinchbeck, *Women workers*, pp. 303–5. And on the ambition of the wealthier farmer's wife to achieve 'gentility' by having 'nothing to do', see pp. 33–40.
69 L. Stone, *The family, sex and marriage in England, 1500–1800* (1977), p. 396.
70 M. George, 'From goodwife to mistress: the transformation of the female in bourgeois culture', *Science and Society*, XXXVII (1973), 6.
71 K. Shevelow, *Women and print culture: the construction of femininity in the early periodical* (1989), pp. 5 and 1.
72 N. Armstrong, 'The rise of the domestic woman', in *idem, Desire and domestic fiction: a political history of the novel* (Oxford, 1987), pp. 59–95; V. Jones (ed.), *Women in the eighteenth century: constructions of femininity* (1990), pp. 10–11; R. Ballaster, M. Beetham, E. Frazer and S. Hebron, 'Eighteenth-century women's magazines', in *idem, Women's worlds: ideology, femininity and the women's magazine* (Basingstoke, 1991), pp. 43–74; Shevelow, *Women and print culture*, pp. 53–7.
73 Clark, *Working life*, pp. 35–41.
74 On English traditions, consult Amy Erickson, 'Common law versus common practice: the use of marriage settlements in early modern England', *Economic History Review*, 2nd ser., XLIII (1990), 21–39.
75 D. Defoe, *The complete English tradesman* (1726), p. 348. On the 'displeasing spectacle of idle womanhood', see also P. Earle, *The world of Defoe* (1976), pp. 244–5, and George, 'Goodwife to mistress', pp. 157–9. Much useful material is in F. Nussbaum, *The brink of all we hate: satires on women, 1660–1750* (Lexington, Kentucky, 1984).
76 See J. Sekora, *Luxury: the concept in western thought, Eden to Smollett* (Baltimore, 1977).
77 F. Childs, 'Prescriptions for manners in English courtesy literature, 1690–1760, and their social implications' (unpublished D.Phil. thesis, Oxford University, 1984), pp. 285–7.
78 M. Legates, 'The cult of womanhood in eighteenth-century thought', *Eighteenth-Century Studies*, I (1976), 21–39.
79 A salutary development in this context is the attempt to recover the history of the reader herself. Two essays which contest the conventional image of the leisured reader passively ingesting eighteenth-century text in private are N. Tadmor, 'Household reading and eighteenth-century novels', and J. Brewer, 'Anna Larpent: representing the reader', both in J. Raven, N. Tadmor and H. Small (eds), *The practice and representation of reading in England* (New York, 1996). An important study of the modern reader is J.A. Radway, 'Women read the romance: the interaction of text and context', *Feminist Studies*, LX (1983), 53–78.

80 D.C. Coleman, 'Proto-industrialization: a concept too many', *Economic History Review*, 2nd ser., XXXVI (1983), 435–48.

81 See Earle, 'Female labour market'.

82 On the generation of income, see P. Earle, *The making of the English middle class: business, society and family life in London, 1660–1730* (1989), pp. 158–74, and B.A. Holderness, 'Credit in a rural community, 1660–1800', *Midland History*, III (1975), 94–115.

83 Jasper Goodwill, *The Ladies Magazine or Universal Entertainer* (London, 1750), no. I for Saturday 18 Nov. 1749, vol. I, preface.

84 See M.Z. Rosaldo, 'The use and abuse of anthropology: reflections on feminism and cross-cultural understanding', *Signs*, V (1980), 389–417; and Kerber, 'Rhetoric of women's history', pp. 18–19.

SECTION IV

RELIGION

Introduction

At the beginning of the 1980s, virtually no work existed on gender and religion, although the sustained preference for religious activity and devotion shown by women over men had long been a commonplace observation of both religious and social historians. This key area of sexual difference – acute in the modern period but observable long before – was becoming increasingly well documented as part of the growing interest in the social history of religion. Institutional structures – for so long the staple of ecclesiastical history – were obviously not going to provide an answer to the question why women went to mass and, apparently, believed in God more than men any more than they were going to explain why anybody went to church at all. Instead, social historians of religion became increasingly influenced by anthropological and sociological findings and techniques. They examined popular piety, pilgrimages and parish confraternities rather than church–state relations, and were interested above all in the individual experience of belief.

These studies of popular piety soon began to explore the question of why women believed more than men, and how their beliefs differed. The whole question of belief underwent some evaluation, and the phenomenon of religious faith was no longer seen as explicable by simple assumptions of 'false consciousness' on the part of feminist and socialist historians for whom religion was a traditional enemy.[1] Rather, the role of religion as a source of individual and communal identities was emphasized, and a vision of an 'unofficial', popular religion emerged, a religion which was largely conducted away from the supervision of the clergy. Such studies of popular religion focused on village communities, where religious activity was customarily segregated by gender, in terms of both what the two sexes were allowed to do and what they chose to do. Explicitly female devotions and religious practices were also revealed, bearing witness to a consistent female presence in the Christian churches which, in both the early modern and the modern periods, often numerically exceeded that of men.[2]

The increasing interest shown by historians influenced by postmodernism in the analysis of text, language and discourse had a profound effect on the work being done on gender and religion. The findings of social historians with regard to popular religious practices, such as visits to shrines and communal rituals, were now complemented by studies of theological understandings and beliefs, as well as of liturgy and spirituality. This analysis of language and symbolism revealed a profoundly gendered tradition of Christian thought, which affected both the Catholic and Protestant traditions. Established, clerical churches, particularly those with celibate male priesthoods, were shown to have been consistently misogynistic, and women were entirely excluded from both the ministry and ecclesiastical decision-making (even in the Protestant UK, the first woman minister, a Congregationalist, was ordained only in 1919). However, the offer of salvation was the same for both men and women, who were both able to engage in individual relationships with God. Women were even widely credited with greater moral fortitude than men, in part as compensation for a supposed lack of intellectual vigour. The presence of the feminine in imagery, language and symbolism was also often pronounced.[3]

Women could, therefore, act as mouthpieces for the divine, whether as prophets or as visionaries, as the pieces collected below demonstrate. Phyllis Mack considers a time of political, social and theological upheaval, in this case, the English Civil War. Prophecy, especially female prophecy, is particularly associated with such periods of social and millenarian uncertainty. Women prophets, drawing their authority from their role as passive vessels for the divine word, created their own prophetic voice by using the language and imagery of their own domestic and spiritual experiences: a point Mack establishes with fascinating comparisons between male and female prophetic rhetoric. A similar kind of distinctive female authority, which rarely threatened the established order, was established by the apparitions of the Virgin Mary which occurred in Europe from the 1830s and which are discussed by Barbara Corrado Pope. These visions gave a new prominence to female saints and symbols in a conservative and clerical church as the favoured visionaries – often later canonized as saints – were invariably children and young girls.

While the voices and actions of prophets and visionaries can provide remarkable insight into male and female spirituality, such people are obviously exceptional. Historians have become increasingly interested in the opportunities religion offered ordinary women and men. Religious faith and practice has consistently been more common in the countryside than in the city, and among the haves rather than the have-nots. However, even if found predominantly among the ranks of peasant and bourgeois women, the 'Godly woman' or *beata* was common and recognized throughout western Europe, at least since the Reformation period. How much scope the Reformation offered to women has been the subject of some debate. Natalie Zemon Davis, for instance, pointed to the way in which city women in Protestant France began to explore new avenues such as Bible study. The emphasis on moral domestic virtue allowed a new evaluation of the role of married women in Protestant societies, though for the Reformation period itself, this appears to have gone hand in hand with a reassertion of patriarchal authority within the household.[4] As the article by Catherine Hall in Section III of this reader shows, however, the Protestant tradition retained an idea of the moral virtue of the married state. Although this allowed an intensely positive evaluation of female domesticity, this could only occur within a properly ordered patriarchal household.

The opportunities offered to women in Catholic Europe were, of course, rather different. Convents provided a channel for female religious devotion and, importantly, an alternative to marriage. However, only really in the nineteenth century did they become a unique source of professional occupations for women. The dramatic explosion of women's religious congregations in late nineteenth-century Europe, which far outnumbered their male counterparts, was directly related to their new involvement in teaching, nursing and social work. Though more reliant on the voluntary tradition, religious philanthropy also provided an outlet for women's energies in Protestant Europe, as well as for married bourgeois women throughout the continent.[5]

The existence of unaccustomed career opportunities for women has been one of the more prosaic reasons advanced by historians in explanation of what is often perceived to be a 'feminization' of religion from the mid-nineteenth century. While it was often the case in earlier periods that women were more heavily involved in religious activity than were men,[6] only now did men actively seem to be leaving the Church in large numbers. Religion and the structures provided by the Christian churches are always likely to have provided women with rare opportunities for sociability and philanthropic employment, as well as for emotional release and consolation and, importantly, access to the power of the divine. Historians of modern Europe have also cited the greater reluctance of men to submit to clerical authority in an age when the Church was retrenching and its authority emphasized.[7] The crucial question is not why so many women stayed loyal to the churches, but why so many men did not. Unlike the 'feminization of religion', this remains largely unexplored, although historians both of gender and of religion are now turning their attention to men, not only to those concerned to establish manly, non-feminine religious identities but also those who rejected religion in favour of an often violent anti-clericalism.[8]

Notes

1 Jim Obelkevich, Lyndal Roper and Raphael Samuel (eds), *Disciplines of Faith: Studies in Religion, Politics and Patriarchy* (London and New York, 1987), pp. 3–9.
2 See, e.g., William A. Christian Jr, *Person and God in a Spanish Valley* (revised edn: Princeton, NJ, 1989) and Clarissa W. Atkinson, '"Your Servant My Mother": The Figure of Saint Monica in the Ideology of Christian Motherhood' in Clarissa W. Atkinson, Constance H. Buchanan and Margaret R. Miles (eds), *Immaculate and Powerful: The Female in Sacred Image and Social Reality* (Boston, MA, 1985), pp. 139–72.
3 The work of Caroline Walker Bynum is of immense importance here. See her 'Introduction: The Complexity of Symbols' in C. W. Bynum, S. Harrell *et al.*, *Religion and Gender: Essays on the Complexity of Symbols* (Boston, 1987), pp. 1–20 as well as her *Jesus as Mother: Studies in the Spirituality of the High Middle Ages* (Berkeley, CA, 1982). The Marian tradition in the Catholic church is also important; see Marina Warner, *Alone of All Her Sex: The Myth and the Cult of the Virgin Mary* (London, 1976).
4 Natalie Zemon Davis, 'City Women and Religious Change' in Zemon Davis (ed.), *Society and Culture in Early Modern France* (Stanford, CA, 1975), pp. 65–96; Diane Willen, 'Godly Women in Early Modern England: Puritanism and Gender', *Journal of Ecclesiastical History* 43 (1992), pp. 561–80; Lyndal Roper, *The Holy Household: Women and Morals in Reformation Augsburg* (Oxford, 1989).
5 Frances Lannon, *Privilege, Persecution, and Prophecy: The Catholic Church in Spain 1875–1975* (Oxford, 1987), ch. 3; Caitriona Clear, *The Nun in Nineteenth-Century Ireland* (Washington DC, 1988); Susan O'Brien, '*Terra Incognita*: The Nun in Nineteenth-Century England', *Past and Present* 121 (1988), pp. 110–40; Mary Vincent, *Catholicism in the Second Spanish Republic: Religion and Politics in Salamanca, 1930–36* (Oxford, 1996), ch. 2. On philanthropy see e.g. Anne Summers, 'The Costs and Benefits of Caring: Nursing Charities, c.1830–c.1860' in Jonathan Barry and Colin Jones (eds), *Medicine and Charity before the Welfare State* (London, 1991), pp. 133–48 and Bonnie Smith, *Ladies of the Leisure Class: The Bourgeoises of Northern France in the Nineteenth Century* (London, 1981).

6 Clive D. Field, 'Adam and Eve: Gender in the English Free Church Constituency', *Journal of Ecclesiastical History* 44 (1993), pp. 63–79; Patricia Crawford, *Women and Religion in England, 1500–1720* (London and New York, 1993).
7 Hugh McLeod, *Religion and the People of Western Europe, 1789–1945* (Oxford, 1981), pp. 28–35; Ralph Gibson, *A Social History of French Catholicism, 1789–1914* (London, 1989), pp. 180–90; Lannon, *Privilege, Persecution, and Prophecy*, pp. 53–8; James F. McMillan, 'Religion and Gender in Modern France: Some Reflections' in F. Tallett and N. Atkin (eds), *Religion, Society and Politics in France since 1789* (London and Rio Grande, 1991).
8 Pamela J. Walker, '"I Live but Not Yet I for Christ Liveth in Me": Men and Masculinity in the Salvation Army' in Michael Roper and John Tosh (eds), *Manful Assertions: Masculinities in Britain since 1800* (London, 1991), pp. 92–112.

10

Talking back: women as prophets during the Civil War and Interregnum, 1640–1655

PHYLLIS MACK

Introduction

[...]

Did the female prophet have an authentic religious sensibility? Most observers, from seventeenth-century Puritans to the nineteenth-century puritan Max Weber, have agreed that women are particularly prone to the expression of an ardent, even passionate religiosity. Yet the vast majority of historians observing the women prophets of the 1640s and early 1650s have been inclined to discuss their work from every perspective *except* that of religion. Adopting the feminine stereotypes of seventeenth-century writers but not their spirituality, some have viewed the ecstatic preaching of visionary women as a form of emotional catharsis and a symptom of women's fundamental psychic instability, a view stated explicitly by Alfred Cohen, who calls his essay on female visionaries 'Prophecy and Madness.' Other scholars have expressed the same negative perception in more subtle, possibly unconscious ways. Thus, David Lovejoy remarked that Anne Hutchinson did not *think* about religious issues; she 'soaked up' antinomianism, while in Christopher Hill's now classic work, *The World Turned Upside Down*, the sympathetic discussion of women in the radical sects occurs only in the chapters on insanity and free love.[1]

Historians of women generally disagree with these perceptions of the causes of women's emotional frustration, but they tend to agree that religious women preached in order to fulfill nonreligious needs, whether emotional, material, or sexual. Confined to an obscure existence, without property, official power, or political status, visionary women supposedly experienced a sense of freedom and self-realization when they spoke in public. 'In a world where female freedom was carefully curbed,' writes one historian, 'to be free to believe was the first step in becoming free to do as one wished.'[2]

In short, historians appear to be united in treating women's spirituality as a metaphor for something else; what divides them is the question whether the woman prophet actually had a mind. Most attribute no agency whatsoever to visionary women, no consciousness of their own or the world's problems and of their role in solving them, while others say they had too much. The former have been remarkably credulous in treating contemporary pamphlet literature as objective historical evidence and accepting accusations of women's hysteria and rampant sexuality at absolutely face value, while the latter have simply ignored the cultural discourse that affected visionary women's self-perception and have celebrated the assertive strategies of prophets who did not even claim to be awake during the time they preached. Perhaps these analyses tell us more about their creators' own preoccupations and experiences than they do about the historical reality of women as prophets.

This essay will address the issues of women's freedom and religiosity by posing a series of specific and (I hope) productive questions: How did visionary women replicate the discourse on womanhood that formed such an important part of their cultural environment, and how did they seek to shape that discourse to their own ends or, rather, to godly, spiritual ends? Did they constitute a genuine threat to social order? Did the atmosphere of religious freedom, that atmosphere that gave her audience the freedom to attend to lay prophets and preachers, also give the prophet the freedom to speak her own thoughts, or were women as prophets attempting to say something that even the most admiring of their contemporaries could not hear?

Talking back

[. . .]

Who were the women prophets of the 1640s and early 1650s, and how did they view themselves? Popular imagination portrayed the female visionary as a human transmitter of divine knowledge, a sort of spiritual battery, humming with the energy of the universe. Prophecy and witchcraft, or prophecy and possession by diabolical powers, were often conflated, not only because the external behavior of both these types was similar but because, in both cases, the woman's body and behavior frequently exhibited tangible signs (catatonia, witches' marks) that betrayed her as a being whose fragile mental and moral powers had been submerged beneath a tidal wave of occult energy.

The visionaries of the Civil War and Interregnum did not share this traditional definition of female prophecy. They saw themselves as seekers embarked on a quest for moral perfection. They frequently experienced a transformation from an obsession with guilt and suicide to an assurance of salvation and of a social mission. Their confessional experiences led them directly into the act of prophecy and to membership in a congregation.[3] Thus, Mary Cary formulated a new, moral definition of prophecy that universalized the experience of communication with the divine:

> Every saint in a sense, may be said to be a prophet . . . for when the Lord hath revealed himself unto the soul and discovered his secrets to it, . . . the soul cannot choose but declare them to others. . . . He that speaketh to edification, exhortation and consolation, though with much weakness, doth as truly prophesy as he that hath greatest abilities.[4]

Anna Trapnel, who had her first vision at the age of nine, was certain that she was damned, was tempted by suicide, and sought for salvation in several Puritan congregations before emerging as a Fifth Monarchist prophet. Trapnel's prophetic work, *A Legacy for Saints*, included a preface by her new congregation that affirmed her high regard for scripture, her respect for the ministry, her beautiful and blameless conversation, and her 'sweet, meek, sober, exemplary temper.' The preface also noted that Trapnel wished the work to be published posthumously but deferred to their decision.[5]

The female visionary was not only a self-motivated seeker after moral truth; she was also self-educated. Mary Cary, a young woman of London, maintained that her understanding of divine commands did not come from 'any immediate revelation – or that she had been told it by an Angel'; it was the fruit of a twelve-year study of scripture, which she had begun in 1636 at the age of fifteen.[6] [. . .] Eleanor Davies was exceptional in that she never displayed much interest in the working of divine moral power in herself or in her own moral or spiritual condition, nor did she ally herself with any of the religious tendencies that arose as a challenge to the Anglican hierarchy, despite the fact that she condemned Archbishop Laud as a rapist and murderer. Yet even Lady Eleanor saw herself less as a sibyl than as a biblical scholar working to decipher and interpret her own divine messages. After one cataclysmic experience in which she was anointed as the handmaid of Daniel, she devoted her life to writing glosses on her own visions, one of which predicted the discovery of a new hemisphere having 'magnificent libraries with printed books.' She showed particular interest in the numerology and arcane symbolism of Daniel and Ezekiel; indeed, she perceived these prophets as intervening directly in her own personal affairs. The night she received a writ denying her the tithes she was owed on one of her estates, 'a bold star facing the moon passed through her body,' and she knew that she must speak as Ezekiel.[7]

In short, the mentality of the most eminent female prophets was not, in their view, radically dissimilar to that of male ministers, many of whom also surmounted suicidal impulses, heard voices, and attended to the spiritual import of their own dreams. Indeed, in a different world some of these

women might have become ministers.[8] Katherine Chidley and Mary Cary
actually insisted that they *were* ministers, not prophets; that is, they spoke
out of their own conviction and learning, not involuntarily as the transmit-
ters of specific angelic messages. Even those visionaries who entered trance
states sometimes counseled visitors and family members in a pastoral mode.
So Mrs. Joan Drake, following several days and nights of visionary ecstasy,
advised her husband on household management, while the adolescent Sarah
Wight offered consolation and reasonable counsel to visitors who suffered
from depression: 'In preaching the Gospel,' she told her audience, 'light,
motion, and power goes out to all: which men resist, and such are destroyed,
not because they could not believe; but because they resist, and will not
obey, and so die.'[9]

What *did* distinguish these female visionaries from male clergymen,
besides the obvious disparities in education and background, was their location of spiritual transformation and creativity in the mother/child relationship. Anna Trapnel attributed her prophetic gifts to the words of her
mother, 'Lord! Double thy spirit upon my child,' uttered three times before
her death.[10] Sixteen-year old Sarah Wight berated herself in her trances for
harsh words and thoughts about her mother, confessing that '*If any one see
and feel what I have seen and felt they would take heed of murmuring
against God and a parent. You never murmured so much against God, and
against my mother, as I have done*; Ah, ah, ah, sighing and weeping as she
spoke.'[11] At one moment she contemplated offering herself to the wild dogs
at Moorfield 'that her mother might never hear of her more,' and when she
lost her sight and hearing, a neighbor bathed her eyes and held them open
so that 'she saw and knew her mother.'[12] [. . .] Elizabeth Avery wrote that
before her enlightenment she had lost three children and with them all
meaning in life. '[I was left] in a horror, as if I were in hell, none could comfort me, nothing could satisfy me, no friends, nothing.' Katherine Chidley,
mother of seven children, made her first public protest in 1626, when she
joined with other women in refusing to be churched after childbirth; she and
Mary Pope both collaborated with their sons, to whom they dictated their
works.[13]

[. . .]

One does not need to posit the existence of an innate female nature in
order to understand why the prophets' locus of spiritual pain and transformation was the experience of motherhood and daughterhood. One need
only remember the social preoccupations of women and conventions of
female spirituality that pervaded seventeenth-century culture. Puritan good-
wives, Baptist women, and great ladies like Mary, Countess of Warwick, all
saw, and were taught to see, moral and spiritual significance in childbirth
and in the mother/child relationship.[14]

If women as prophets understood themselves as mothers, daughters, readers, and seekers after truth, one might speculate that, in a culture in which spiritual suffering and communication with the divine were viewed as real, indeed normative experiences, then far from being a marginalized, hysterical fringe group in seventeenth-century society, women like Grace Cary and Anna Trapnel were the ones whose spiritual sicknesses were healed, for the numerous other wives, daughters, and new mothers who succumbed to despair, refused to eat, or dreamed of Jesus as they lay in their beds either died at home (like Joan Drake, who was visited by nine different ministers and numerous physicians and who expired after ten nights of visionary ecstasy) or simply disappeared from view, at peace or not at peace, and resumed their domestic responsibilities (like Martha Hatfield, a young girl whose seizures and trances were recorded by her uncle, the vicar of Sheffield, and who later married and bore a child).[15] Prophetic women, however, translated their sense of personal guilt into a vision of external evil, of a society corrupted by sin, and embraced the challenge of expelling that evil from the world. So Grace Cary, a respectable widow from Bristol, after a period of deep internal conflict, had an initial dream that blossomed into a series of visions inviting her to approach the throne of grace, through 'glorious shining lights accompanied with vehement rushing winds,' finally culminating in a full-blown apparition of 'a king's head and face without a body, which looked very pale and wan: it had a crown upon it and the crown was all bloody in a circle about.' The message: treason and death, which, after a further period of prayer and fasting, she translated into a public plea for a reconciliation between king and Parliament.[16]

One might also speculate that what distinguished the prophet from the young women and matrons who struggled for their salvation behind closed doors was that they were deprived of the compassionate yet repressive attentions of male family members. For whatever their class background – and women prophets ranged from the impoverished countrywoman Elinor Channel to the aristocrat Eleanor Davies – several who achieved eminence were either single, widowed, or orphaned. Anna Trapnel, the unmarried daughter of a London shipwright, lost her father when she was a child, and when her mother died she lived with two different older women before joining the Fifth Monarchist sect. When a magistrate interrogating her remarked, 'I understand you are not married,' she replied, 'Then having no hindrance, why may not I go where I please, if the Lord so will?'[17]

[...]

Those women who were married frequently had to resist the opposition of their spouses. Elinor Channel was forbidden by her husband to prophesy, whereupon she became dumb until he relented. Eleanor Davies prophesied against the wishes of *her* two husbands (her second husband was an insane

invalid at the time she published her first work). She also made it clear that
she considered her domestic responsibilities less significant than her
prophetic calling. Describing popular suspicions that the prophetic boy she
took into her house was a witch, she wrote, 'immediately upon this, the
spirit of prophecy falling likewise upon me, then were all vexed worse than
ever, ready to turn the house upside down, . . . when *laying aside household*
cares all, and having no conversation with any but the word of God . . . I
found out this place.' Only two women, Katherine Chidley and Dorothy
Hazzard, received their husbands' active support, though Chidley's activities were chiefly in collaboration with her son.[18]

The prophet's spiritual independence may have also been assisted by the
fact that she was often economically independent as well. Anna Trapnel
defended herself to magistates as an independent, tax-paying citizen.
Katherine Chidley was a businesswoman, supplying the government's
troops in Ireland with five thousand pairs of stockings in 1650–51. Elizabeth
Poole and Elizabeth Warren lived by their own labor as seamstress and
school teacher, respectively. Mary Pope inherited her husband's salting business and paid the costs of her tracts herself. So did Lady Eleanor, whose
entire career was punctuated by lawsuits as well as prophecies, as she
doggedly defended her rights to her jointure and to the financial benefits
attached to the ownership of her estates.[19]

[. . .]

Clearly women were dependent on men for patronage once they began to
prophesy in public. Indeed, no woman presuming to address a mixed audience on political issues could have survived without male allies, either as
editors, apologists, ministers, or, in a very few cases, lovers. Excepting Lady
Eleanor, every important prophet belonged to a congregation that was
supervised by male ministers, and most (again excepting Lady Eleanor)
were dependent on male editors who bracketed their texts by salutations
that affirmed their piety and respectability, inserted supporting biblical cita-
tions, and added substantive arguments; most strikingly is this so in the case
of Elinor Channel, whose vague prophecies were transformed into a Royalist polemic by her editor, Arise Evans.

Yet women also exhibited remarkable initiative and persistence in using
or ignoring the patronage system for their own purposes. Grace Cary consulted some divines from Bristol, who could neither confirm nor deny the
authenticity of the visions she had written down and attempted to dissuade
her from further action. She then decided for herself that the visions were
genuine, traveled to London, and gained the intercession of the Lord Marquis of Hambleton, who obtained an audience with the king, to whom she
communicated her message of reconciliation.[20] Mary Pope asked members
of Parliament to correct the flaws in her treatise before she printed it. When

they ignored her, she printed it herself and hired someone to present copies at the doors of both houses of Parliament. Mary Cary withheld publication of one of her tracts for seven years, until she felt there was greater general receptivity to prophecies.[21]

[. . .]

Women also appear to have made a distinction between the men to whom they turned for patronage and the women who provided them with emotional support. When Anna Trapnel was about to embark on a dangerous mission to Cornwall, she discussed the project with her 'sisters,' ten of whom sat up with her all night to pray for a good outcome. After her arrest she was visited in Bridewell by a group of women, one of whom moved into prison with her, staying for seven of the eight weeks of her incarceration. [. . .] When Elizabeth Poole's Baptist minister expelled her and circulated a letter condemning her 'immoral' behavior, the wife of another minister intercepted it and wrote her own letter of support. Sarah Jones was a friend of the preacher Katherine Chidley and the visionary Sarah Wight. Anna Trapnel also knew Sarah Wight and visited her shortly before the beginning of her own quite similar visions.[22]

[. . .]

Visions and wise counsel

[. . .]

When we examine the substance of these visionaries' published writings, we find them collectively contradicting a fundamental female stereotype, that of woman as a figure of disorder, an enemy of structured, civilized existence. Indeed, a primary characteristic of many women's visionary pronouncements, whether Royalist or radical, was their tone of moderation and restraint. Sarah Wight, member of a Baptist congregation, counseled visitors from within the moral and scriptural traditions of orthodox Calvinism.[23] Grace Cary followed the king to York to warn him about the evils of Archbishop Laud and Queen Henrietta Maria and pleaded with Parliament to reconcile with the king and tolerate Puritans but not Independents or any radical groups, be they 'Prelates, Anabaptists, Antinomians, Adamites, Familists . . . Papists and Arminian Innovators.' She also decided not to publish her vision, despite the pleas of friends, but to circulate it in manuscript, thereby keeping God's word out of the hands of 'the meaner sort, of vulgar people,' whose conversation might discredit it.[24] Elizabeth Poole criticized the king when she appeared before the Council chamber in 1649 but counseled Oliver Cromwell against regicide, asserting that all the 'glorious glittering images of state policies, religious ordinances, orders, faiths, lights, knowledges . . . drawn over [with] beautiful pretenses' could not hide the 'worldly dark part' in the king's executioners. Ultimately, only fear and self-interest and a thirst for blood were satisfied. Poole compared the duty of Parliament to that of a loyal wife who bears the pain of her husband's guilt:

> a just woman must deliver up her husband to the just claim of the law, though she might not accuse him to the law, nor yet rejoice over him to see his fall, for all that pass by and behold her, will say this was a strumpet, and not a faithfull wife, that rejoiceth at the fall of her husband; and contrariwise the faithful wife mourneth in secret for him: . . . you owe him all that you have and are, and although he would not be your father and husband, . . . yet know that you are for the Lord's sake to honor his person. For he is the father and husband of your bodies.[25]

[. . .]

Other visionaries were equally restrained in their criticism of the monarchy. Eleanor Davies defied episcopal authority but was apparently an orthodox Anglican in every other respect. Elizabeth Warren counseled men to stay within their stations and women to follow the opinions of their husbands, defended the necessity of traditional learning for the ministry, and condemned the Civil War as punishment for the people's greed. Mary Pope reminded Parliament that the brunt of the war had been borne by 'the middle rank of people, that are the chief upholders of the highest rank, and of the lowest,' and urged that the poor be relieved and soldiers be paid on time.[26] For all these women, the natural law that justified the king's survival was presented as more fundamental than the specific misdeeds and oversights of which the king was guilty.

Elizabeth Avery, Mary Cary, Anna Trapnel, and Katherine Chidley *were* radicals: Avery, Cary, and Trapnel supportive of the millennarian Fifth Monarchist sect, which rejected the legality of the Protectorate; Chidley a supporter of the Levelers. Cary was one of the few women prophets who supported the execution of the king: 'when the late King was in his height, I declared my confidence, that the Parliament should prevail over him, and at last destroy him.'[27] She envisioned a world turned upside down:

> They that seek not [salvation] . . . but that do covet to treasure up most riches for themselves, and to poll, and rob, and cheat the people, to enhance their own estates, and make themselves great in the world, and their children gay and splendid among men . . . these shall become the basest and the vilest among men. . . . There must be such a time, when the saints must be so lifted up out of the dust, as they must be

the top and the head of all nations: and whatsoever kingdom and nation will not serve them must perish.[28]

Yet her visionary program was more concerned with poverty and education than with the violent victory of the saints. Her utopia was a world without poverty or famine, in which men and women no longer lived in enmity with nature or each other, and where wild animals were not enemies of men and women but served them. [. . .] The pleasures and creature comforts of the world would become innocent, being the fruit of the people's own labor. Clothing would be beautiful but not gaudy. Society would be ordered, for the godly magistrate would still wield the sword, punishing drunkards, whoremasters, and swearers, yet the full potential of a renovated human nature would be released.[29] [. . .] Cary was one of only two writers, male or female, to propose a scheme of university reform, using colleges as the basis for evangelizing the world. She was also unique in proposing to extend toleration to papists and atheists.[30]

Anna Trapnel held similar views of human renovation, education, and religious toleration: 'that [all] might be of one heart and one mind; and that knowledge might cover the earth, as water the sea; . . . and the kingdom restored to this old *Israel*, which was the first married wife.' She originally prophesied in favor of the Protectorate, seeing Cromwell as Gideon 'going before Israel, blowing the trumpet of courage and valor.'[31] Later, as a Fifth Monarchist, she became more radical, condemning the Protectorate as illegitimate and unlawful and predicting that the saints would become earls and potentates. Yet she was also a pacifist and condemned Thomas Venner's abortive plot to forcibly install King Jesus on the throne of England.[32]

[. . .]

Above all, and regardless of their political and religious position, women prophets saw the ravaged political edifice of the monarchy less in terms of a conflict among institutions or theological positions than in terms of concrete human suffering, expressed most powerfully by Mary Cary's poignant utopian vision:

> No infant of days shall die; none shall die while they are young; all shall come to a good old age. They shall not be afflicted for the loss of their children; for they shall live till they be an hundred years old. . . . The streets shall be full of boys and girls playing . . . and old men and old women shall live till they come to a good old age, till they walk with a staff in their hand for age.[33]

Cary was unique among members of the sect in her concern for the helpless poor, criticizing those members of Parliament who would consider a poor relief act and then lay it aside for three, six, or twelve months. She suggested a postage fee, to be used for support of those who could not work or had too many children to feed.[34] Katherine Chidley [. . .] argued that ministers should earn their bread by their own manual labor. She further argued that independent sects be tolerated because they maintain all of their own poor 'as well as any other man,' while Mary Pope inveighed against the materialism of shopkeepers who trade until the last possible moment on Saturday night; she also suggested a program to relieve the poor in individual parishes. The Leveler women's petition of April 1649 was written entirely in Chidley's style:

> Considering, that we have an equal share and interest with men in the commonwealth, and it cannot be laid waste, (as now it is) and not we be the greatest and most helpless sufferers therein; and considering that poverty, misery, and famine, like a mighty torrent, is breaking in upon us, . . . and we are not able to see our children hang upon us, and cry out for bread, and not have wherewithall to feed them, we had rather die than see that day.[35]

In short, however radical their proposals for social and spiritual reform, and however strident the tone of those proposals, women's programs were less destructive of the established social order than those of their male counterparts. Moreover, the tone of their remonstrances against the king was far less hyperbolic and emotional than the contemporary pamphlet literature that presented Charles as a doting husband, a pathetic weakling, and a depraved lover of the Anglican church.[36] The personal claims made by women to be handmaids or spouses of the Holy Spirit were also far less grandiose than those of the male pseudo-messiahs who preached alongside them. Mary Gadbury, who called herself 'the bride of the lamb,' was completely overshadowed by the Ranter William Franklin, with whom she traveled and preached and who claimed to be a reincarnation of Jesus Christ; she was also a nearly isolated case.[37] Eleanor Davies announced herself proudly as the 'handmaiden of the most high God of heaven, this book brought forth by Her, fifth Daughter of George Lord of Castlehaven.'[38] But for sheer arrogance or self-delusion, even Lady Eleanor could not hold a candle to Lodowijk Muggleton and John Reeve, who said they were the two Witnesses of the Spirit in Revelation and cursed to eternity anyone who opposed them; or John Rogers, 'the Shakers' God,' who claimed to be the messiah; or John Moore, who said he was Christ; [. . .] or Miles Fry, alias Emmanuel Plantagenet, the son of Queen Elizabeth by God the Father.[39] Many female prophets compared themselves to famous biblical figures, but these male prophets believed they *were* famous biblical figures. The introductions to women's tracts, soothing the reader with an excess of deferential disclaimers, certainly could not be more different from the 'divine fireworks' presented by Abiezer Coppe: 'Read [my tract] through, and laugh not at it; if thou dost I'll destroy thee, and laugh at thy destruction.' Nor did any woman's behavior compare to that of Coppe, who expressed his spiritual fervor in an extravagance of indiscriminate kissing.[40]

Clearly, many women had both the spiritual and the intellectual capacity to contribute to the political discourse that dominated the Civil War period, and, clearly, their political intention was not to subvert all traditional morality or destroy every vestige of established authority. However, regardless of the substantive content of women's visionary writings and pronouncements and the relative restraint with which they were presented, their overall effect on most observers was probably to reinforce traditional preconceptions of the volatile, essentially uncivilized nature of all womanhood. The reason for this was not simply a preconceived prejudice against women on the part of their audience. It was also the result of visionary women's own affective and literary style, for if respectable women were constrained by convention to behave with humility and modesty, the female visionary was constrained to behave as though she were literally out of her mind.

Visionary expression and the gender order

[. . .]

To the magistrates and congregations who listened to women's accounts of their visionary experiences, the female prophet's right to exercise public authority was not based on the recognition that she possessed qualities of leadership that had previously gone unnoticed. On the contrary, we have seen that beliefs about the traditional and quite familiar qualities of passivity, irrationality, and passion that had justified women's *absence* from the political arena were used to justify their visionary activities as well. 'As for . . . Anna Trapnel,' wrote a contemporary witness of her trances,

> it is, (to be plain) to me a very strange dispensation, yet I am persuaded she hath communion with God in it. . . . If she did continue in it but for one or two days, I should be apt to think she might do it when she would . . . save for two things. First, she is so stiffened in her God that were she not warm, one would think her dead. Secondly: Because she cannot make a verse when she is her self. But it is strange to me she should continue for eight days.[41]

In one London Baptist church, Anne Harriman threatened to leave the congregation because a male member had said he would not walk with those who gave women liberty to speak in church, and she would not walk where she had not got this right. The church, untypically, acceded to her demand, stating that 'a woman . . . being a prophetess . . . may speak, prophesy, pray, with a veil. Others may not.'[42] Even radical sectarians insisted on making a distinction between authority that was spiritual and communal and authority that was political and hierarchical. The Fifth Monarchists, who allowed women to testify, vote, act as spies, and even meet separately from men, insisted on a distinction not only between preaching and prophesying but between prophesying as a leader of the church and as a 'mere' vessel of God. Thus, John Rogers argued that women 'keep from public preaching, or prophesying, or teaching as officers or ministers do. . . . Now we plead not for this; but for the common ordinary liberty due to them as members of the Church, viz. to speak, object, offer, or vote with the rest.'[43] Rogers's admonition to his women congregants, urging them to be both courageous and deferential, painfully conveys the awkwardness of his, and their, position:

> To women, I wish ye be not too forward, and yet not too backward, but hold fast your liberty . . . keep your ground which Christ hath won and got for you; maintain your right, defend your liberty, even to the life, lose it not, but be courageous, and keep it. And yet be cautious too. . . . Your silence may sometimes be the best advocate of your orderly liberty, and the sweetest evidence of your prudence and modesty. . . . And yet ye ought not by your silence to betray your liberty, trouble your consciences, lose your privileges and rights; or see the truth taken away or suffer before your eyes; but I say, be not too hasty nor too high.[44]

Thus, the image of women's essential liminality was given added resonance even by those writers who were most supportive of women's improved opportunities. And for them, as for their less sympathetic contemporaries, a woman who interrupted a parliamentary meeting by babbling or singing, her eyes glazed, would probably seem less of an anomaly than one who tried to appear as a concerned citizen or minister engaging in public theological debates or rational biblical exegesis. One aristocratic lady learned this to her cost when she tried to address a Separatist congregation in London in 1645. After apologizing for 'some bodily indispositions,' she began speaking in a low voice on the nature of love. Being urged to speak louder, she became confused and was finally shouted down. 'In brief, there was such laughing, confusion and disorder at the meeting, that the minister professed he never saw the like.'[45] A woman who disturbed the public peace by singing or mumbling prophecies risked imprisonment or worse, but her audience was far less likely to laugh.

Thus, the prophet's only means of establishing her credibility in a public forum was to present herself as a defender of the natural order in which she was subservient while simultaneously affirming that she had transcended that natural order. She had to convince her audience that she was both less and more than human. So Mary Pope, 'finding God over-powering my spirit, and as it were forcing of me on,' admonished wives to render unto husbands only what husbands were due and defended her right to speak as a prophet:

Whatsoever governors we are under, whether magistrates, ministers, husbands, fathers, or masters, we should not obey them . . . farther than is according to God's commission . . . seeing David held it no disparagement, though a king, to take the advice of a woman, (I Sam. 25.33) and seeing that God himself, hath in many great acts honored women as well as men, and above men.[46]

Yet she professed herself to be appalled by the specter of social breakdown that followed upon the claims of a woman's individual conscience:

Principles of nature, vary not as languages do, and if principles of nature be inviolable, and indispensible, much more is divinity. Opinions ought not to be the rule of things, but the nature of the things it self. . . . In the prophet Jeremiah's time, the women did not bake cakes to the queen of heaven without their husbands (Jer. 44.19). But now in our time there be some teachers that have taught our women to follow their new found out truths, without their husbands: and I think in some families there are as many opinions as people. . . . When we see such division come to pass, we shall know the end of the world is near.[47]

We find this disjunction between women's portrayal of themselves as supernatural and as human beings – or more abstractly, their rendering of the discourses of religion and politics – permeating the very grammar of their visionary texts. Eleanor Davies's visions were conveyed in fractured feminine images that, to many readers, went well beyond the limits of sane discourse:

Where belonging to passages of *inns*; the one frequented all hours, and drinking, not more free than the others darksom *grates close*; famished there no few. But requisit *bridges*, and the like, the true *narrow way* (by suffering) that leads *to life*; From him a proper *passage* or mention. Straits of the *virgins-womb* had passed; besides seafaring-persons his followers in that way not unexperienced, afore arrive the *welcome haven*.[48]

[. . .] Yet this arrogant woman, who viewed the deaths of her two husbands as vindications of her spiritual calling and who lathered her prophetic texts with accounts of family grievances, also chose the institution of patriarchal marriage as one of her most sustained metaphors for true piety. Interestingly, the moment Lady Eleanor portrayed the voice of a jealous God as that of a husband, she also assumed a syntactically straightforward prose style, expressing herself in quite respectable discursive language:

Suppose a man after his marriage to a young virgin, should say, my experience is more than yours, I cannot always walk hand in hand with you, neither may I keep you in a cloister that will not be for your health or my profit, neither must you forget your covenant to be subject to my desires not tending to the harm of either of us; . . . many strangers will strive to be your servants; not all for your beauty but some for malice and envy to me: Though your intent be good in all things, yet because I am very jealous of mine honor, entertain none in that manner; . . . in the end they will draw your affection from me; Besides, much resort though she be never so chaste, is dalliance the mark of a known harlot, which sort of woman I would have you differ from. . . . Yes doubtless I am the Lord thy God.[49]

Similarly, Anna Trapnel, who delivered her public prophecies in a trance state, as if inundated by the spirit, combined biblical themes with images of women's fluidity in order to validate her own authority to prophesy. 'Then the Lord made His rivers flow,' she wrote,

which soon broke down the banks of an ordinary capacity, and . . . mounted my spirits into a praying and singing frame. . . . The Lord [will] be . . . a place of broad rivers and streams, . . . these are rivers that the waters rise up to the ankles, yea to the knees, and so to the loins, and at length they become a flowing high spring, . . . this is water of Life, it recovers the dying vitals, and fainting spirits, the which none of men's strong liquors of arts and sciences can do, neither can any compounded water of human invention.[50]

This was language and behavior quite unlike her reasoned declaration that she should be respected as an adult, taxpaying citizen. 'You call me vagabond,' she wrote to the magistrates who attempted to discredit her,

but how will you make that good? . . . I lived with my mother till she died, . . . then I kept house with the means my mother left me, and payed taxes toward maintaining of the army then in the field; and this I did not grudgingly, but freely and willingly; I sold my plate and rings, and gave the money to the public use; you did not call me vagabond then.[51]

Anna Trapnel was well aware of her audiences' expectation that she would show herself to be either a monster, a whore, or a madwoman:

My desire is to imitate that approved *Hannah* . . . who was in bitterness of soul, and prayed unto the Lord. . . . And if handmaids in these days pray and weep for their Lord . . . such praying cannot be borne by the inhabitants of this nation; there is such an evil spirit of misconstruing. . . . *England's* rulers and clergy do judge the Lords handmaid to be mad, and under the administration of evil angels, and a witch, and many other evil terms they raise up to make me odious, and abhorr'd in the hearts of good and bad, that do not know me.[52]

Perhaps Trapnel's ecstatic manner was an authentic attempt to imitate the behavior of the ancient Hannah. It may have also helped her to endure ridicule. 'And . . . there came many to see me,' she wrote, 'some out of goodwill . . . and others came to gaze, and others to catch at my words, so as to reproach me; but the Lord taught me how to speak before them all.'[53] Ironically, her behavior must have also helped reinforce the perception of many in her audience that she was indeed mad.

Given popular preconceptions about the acceptable directions of women's religious and political writing, it should not surprise us that visionary women's strong individual characters and divergent social backgrounds often appear to be submerged beneath the weight of symbolic baggage. The Belgian Catholic Antonia Bourignon and the Fifth Monarchist Mary Cary seem to have been thoroughly opposed both in temperament and in social position. Bourignon, an aristocrat who established her own community of disciples, was dictatorial, ascetic, and elitist, while Cary, a member of a radical sect composed largely of artisans and laborers, was compassionate and democratic. Yet both characterized themselves, and were described by their patrons, as passive and inadequate. Antonia Bourignon defended her right to preach by saying that 'they ought to let God speak by a woman, if it be his pleasure, since he spoke in former times to a prophet by a beast.' Cary, who presented a systematic program of social reform that dealt with the issues of wage ceilings, a postal service, and a proposed stamp tax, conveyed the same negative message, although in very different tones:

> If any shall hereby receive any light [from my prophecies], . . . let them bless the Lord for it . . . for I am a very weak, and unworthy instrument, and have not done this work by any strength of my own, but have often been made sensible, that I could do no more herein . . . of my self, than a pencil or pen can do, when no hand guides it; being daily made sensible of my own insufficiency to do anything, as of myself.[54]

Does this persistent self-deprecation imply that Antonia Bourignon or Mary Cary were merely parroting the behavior that had been imposed on them by a male-dominated culture? Or does it imply that *men* were the victims of cold-blooded manipulation by *women* who consciously used traditional language and behavior as a covert strategy of self-expression? Perhaps Katherine Chidley was being disingenuous when she challenged the Puritan Thomas Edwards to a formal debate, saying that, if defeated, she would submit gracefully: 'But if you [ministers] overcome me, your conquest will not be great, for I am a poor woman, and unmeet to deal with you. . . . This is my charity towards them, though I know them not by face, and I think I may boldly say that none of them knows me.'[55] In most other cases, however, I am inclined to believe in the sincerity of women's gestures of self-denial, for while these same women might have been verbally aggressive and physically brutal in collective acts of parish protest or in presenting petitions to magistrates, most were unaccustomed to individual public leadership of any kind. They may indeed have had to reach a state of near catatonia or hysteria in order to convince themselves, as well as others, that their inspiration was genuine.[56] The articulate Mary Cary surely spoke for many women when she wrote,

> Not but that there are many godly women, many who have indeed received the Spirit; but in how small a measure is it? How weak are they? and how unable to prophesy? . . . Indeed, they have tasted of the sweetness of the spirit; and having tasted, are longing for more, and are ready to receive from those few that are in any measure furnished with the gifts of the spirit for prophesying; but they are generally very unable to communicate to others, though they would do it many times in their families, among their children and servants; and when they would be communicating to others into whose company they come, though sometimes some dry sprinklings come from them, yet at other times they find themselves dry and barren.[57]

[. . .]

Perhaps even more inhibiting than fear of public exposure was the degree to which the thrust of women's spiritual creativity was deflected by social strictures on women as public figures. The visionary's spiritual transformation was often triggered by and nourished by her experience as mother or daughter, and the image of motherhood was one redolent of spiritual and moral authority. But this maternal authority had no relevance whatsoever to the authority of the political thinker or actor. Even Queen Elizabeth, who exploited maternal and virginal imagery to dramatize her fidelity and love for her country, tended to resort to masculine imagery when she presented herself as a head of state, an incarnation of the sacred principle of kingship. 'I have the body of a weak and feeble woman,' went her famous speech to the forces arrayed against the Spanish Armada, 'but I have the heart and stomach of a king, and of a king of England too.' She also referred to herself habitually as 'prince,' using the term 'princess' to refer to discredited female monarchs like Mary Queen of Scots. In a passage to Parliament in 1601, two years before Elizabeth's death, the speaker noted that 'she said her kingly prerogative (for so she termed it) was tender.'[58]

Thus, bypassing the true psychological roots of their own visionary impulses, women relied on the image of the good wife, not the mother, in their political writings, an image that connoted not authority but subordination, even when presented in highly positive terms, as in Mary Pocock's mystical tract: 'Here is now the soul in the body, the husband and wife, God and the man. This is the representative, king and parliament, whose happy condition is bound up in the enjoyment of each other, in the union of the manhood, in the power of the Godhead: And this is the glory of the king.'[59] When women came to justify the authority of their own religious movements vis-à-vis the state, they referred not to the straightforward moral authority of the mother but to the derivative authority of the wife as steward for the husband who is unavoidably absent. Thus, Katherine Chidley compared the autonomy of the Independent congregation to that of a wife who acts as a deputy husband:

> Yea, the power of the *keys* is as absolutely the *Church's*, which is *Christ's wife*, as the power of the keys of the *family* are the mistress's, to whom the *husband* giveth full power . . . and I think no reasonable man will affirm (if her husband give her sole power in his absence) that she is subordinate to any of her servants. Now . . . Christ . . . hath delivered the power to his *church*.[60]

Maternal imagery did appear in many women's writings, of course, but it was generally used in conjunction with abstractions like God or the church, rarely as a symbol of the prophet's own spiritual experience or authority. 'O the milk that runs through Christ's breasts!' wrote Anna Trapnel: 'Come sucklings take it in.'[61] Eleanor Davies also portrayed God and the church as female (though hardly feminine): 'the church of God being then with child, travailing in birth, crying and pained to be delivered of the man child, roaring like a lion, the whole forest ringing.'[62] When women did use maternal symbols in relation to their own works, they often emphasized the vulnerability of the baby and the passivity of the mother. Sarah Jones was positively lyrical when she described the righteous congregation, 'out of whose bellies flow rivers of waters of life . . . holy brethren such are made partakers of the divine nature,' but the birth of her own text is described thusly: 'I presume to *father* this naked child without scholastic phrases, or school learning to dress it and garnish it.' [. . .] And thus spoke Mary Pope:

> Now your unworthy handmaid in Christ, which hath been long in travail, yet now in hopes, that the time draweth near of her delivery, doth present to you (worthies) these lines. . . . For God hath given me faith to believe, that this child shall not be abortive, but shall . . . be born a goodly child. . . . God having made me a mother in Israel, I thought it my duty to put my helping hand, . . . and finding God over-powering my spirit, and as it were forcing of me on, for the improving of those talents he hath given me for His glory, and serving of my generation.[63]

Yet if women generally felt unable to apply positive images of cosmic motherhood to their own spiritual creativity, they also eschewed the image of the monster mother and her wretched, evil children. There are, of my knowledge, no passages in women's writings comparable to that of Abiezer Coppe, denying accusations that he was a Ranter:

> There are many spurious brats, lately born: and because their parents have looked upon me as a rich merchant they have took on them the

boldness to lay them at my door, etc. Some of them (indeed) look somewhat like my children. But however, to put all out of doubt, whether they are mine, or no: I will not be so full of foolish pity, as to spare them. I will turn them out of doors, and starve them to death. And as for those which I know are not mine own: I will be so holily cruel, as to dispatch them.[64]

Unlike the male minister, who might refer to himself while preaching as the breasts of God or the bride ravished by Christ, or the male sectarian, who might express his own religiosity in sexual metaphors and actions that were even more explicit, women visionaries did not draw attention to their own bodies as sources of either passion or nourishment. In fact, they rarely portrayed their bodies as metaphors at all. Rather, their passages of damnation and desire are merged with passages of bodily annihilation.[65] Sarah Wight, who was struck lame, mute, and blind through guilt over sins committed against her mother, felt her damnation as a fire that surrounded her: '*I felt myself, soul and body in fire and brimstone already. If all the fire and brimstone in London, and all the pitch and tar, should all be in one fire, and I walking in the midst of that fire, this was my condition.*' She later exhibited her body, wasted by seventy-five days of partial fasting, as the site of triumphant combat between the forces of good and evil, announcing to members of her congregation gathered around the bedside,

> Now I have been four days in the grave, with Lazarus, and now I am risen to live with Jesus Christ. . . . Now I have my desire; I desired nothing but a crucified Christ and I have him; a crucified Christ, a naked Christ; I have him and nothing else. . . . I am so full of the creator that I can take in none of the creature. . . . I do eat, but it's meat to eat that the world knows not of. . . . His words were found, and I did eat them.[66]

Elizabeth Avery affirmed herself 'more enabled to act by the spirit, when I am most straightened in the flesh.'[67]

[. . .]

Women visionaries both before and after the English Revolution, whose writings were chiefly apolitical or mystical, employed maternal and sexual imagery with much greater freedom. One example from the final decade of the century, Anne Bathurst's visionary diary, contains this account of her praying for the victims of an earthquake in Jamaica:

> And my spirit was at Jamaica lying on my face at prayer. . . . And I lay stretched out on the earth, licking the dust and then breathing in the earth as brooding over it for a new Creation. . . . I milked milk out of my breasts on the earth. . . . Still I see my spirit much on its face, with

my breasts touching the earth . . . and I feel the witness of fire on my breasts . . . in my left breast, brooding, hatching as't were and nourishing a flame to break forth. . . . O 'tis love's fire that burns and heals and warms! Warm, warm love, warm through blood. I am big and warm with expectations what this warm healing power will come to. . . . When it breaks open it will be as sun-shine after rain. I flame, and it satisfies most of my desires.[68]

Elsewhere she described herself waiting for night to come and bring with it a vision of God: '[I] hoped at night that I might lie in his arms as I had done the night before . . . there I held Him and would not let Him go, but that He would lie all night as a bundle of myrrh between my breasts, and He was willingly held.'[69] Women may well have had such visions during the Puritan revolution, but no one of them ever found the patronage, even within the radical sects, to enable her to publish it. Those few women who believed they had given birth to Jesus expressed themselves verbally or in private letters, and we know they existed only through hostile pamphlet literature or the reports of the magistrates who arrested them.[70] Even Mary Cary, the most radical woman prophet of the 1640s, took care that she was shielded by patrons who introduced her to the public as a virtuous and respectable gentlewoman.

Of course there was no barrier to the visionary's appropriation of *negative* female imagery, particularly maternal imagery, to castigate her enemies, especially the clergy (or 'clergy-puff,' as Anna Trapnel said), and women used this negative imagery more vividly and with greater energy than they did images of nurturing and fulfillment. Thus, Mary Cary affirmed the equality of women and men in rather pallid prose: 'That which is given to the Husband [Jesus], the wife must partake of: for there is nothing that he possesses, which She [the Saints] hath not a right unto.'[71] She was much less restrained in describing the feminine decadence of Rome, predicting that the people will hate her 'for her filthiness, and cursed lewdness . . . and make her naked . . . [and] they will not only make her naked, but will eat her flesh: will make her destitute, not only of her outward robes of pomp and glory, but will eat her very flesh.' Elizabeth Poole envisioned the weak and distressed state of the country as the body of a diseased woman, 'full of imperfection, crooked, weak, sickly, imperfect.' Eleanor Davies envisioned 'the blaspheming blasts of the little Horn, that had eyes like a man, and such a mouth as much to say, *that mouth speaking such great things, a woman's and no man's* . . . Jezebel by name . . . this bloodthirsty mistress of *charms* and *spells*.'[72] She also railed against Parliament, 'the nursing mother of *dragons*,' against 'that strumpet hag *Rome*,' and against the Anglican church, 'this indulgent witch, the mother of harlots.'[73]

[. . .]

Clearly, it was no easy task for women visionaries to navigate between the Scylla of their audiences' praise of them as mindless vessels and the Charybdis of their critics' attacks on them as aggressive or self-serving. The editor of Elizabeth Avery's treatise wrote flatteringly on her behalf, 'the power of God doth appear in [this work] in respect of the weakness and contemptibleness of the instrument whom he doth here employ; as formerly it hath been his course in doing great things by weakest means, and so by such foolishness he doth bring to nought the wisdom of the wise.' The published reply to the treatise, written by Avery's brother, barely mentioned the substance of her arguments but expressed shock at the fact that she had written a book at all. 'You seem to be lifted up,' he said, 'as if you were a goddess, as if all should bow unto you. . . . Your printing of a Book, beyond the custom of your sex, doth rankly smell, but the exaltation of your self in the way of your opinions, is above all.' One can readily empathize with Elizabeth Avery's own rather strained rejoinder: 'If I am mad . . . it is to God; and if I am in my right mind, it is for the benefit of others.'[74]

Conclusion: women out of time

[. . .]

Did the female prophet have a mind? Mary Cary, as even her critics recognized, had a very formidable mind.[75] So, some would argue, did Eleanor Davies, although she may have lost and regained hers as she passed in and out of prison and in and out of public favor. Clearly, visionary women differed in their individual temperaments and intellectual capacities as well as in their prophetic vocations. Mary Cary viewed herself as a minister and teacher, using language that was at once ardent and pragmatic; Lady Eleanor was a student of symbolism who lived at various inns called 'Angel' in memory of the angel who visited her in prison; Anna Trapnel was a mystic for whom the sight of a rock in a field might trigger a flood of singing on Peter as her rock and sustainer. Yet even Trapnel found a public voice that was as much the fruit of her own intelligence and political activism as it was the product of a disembodied trance state. Not only did women as prophets display an understanding of the economic and political issues of the time; they also turned visionary language into a form of political resistance. Thus, they distanced themselves from negative female stereotypes by applying those stereotypes to their male enemies; with other women they formed associations that sustained them in the pulpit and in prison; and they exercised pastoral as well as prophetic authority within their congregations, speaking to appreciative men as well as women.

Yet it remains true that, whatever the prophet's individual character and capacity, and however appreciative her audience, her presence in the public arena constrained her as firmly, in some ways more firmly, than the walls of the nunnery did the behavior of the Catholic visionary of the Middle Ages. It also placed her in a profoundly vulnerable position, for the status of visionary or prophet was not a fixed social definition analogous to that of the minister or magistrate; it was one end of a very slippery continuum, the other end of which was the polluted whore or witch. Depending on a host of factors – her own class position, the politics of the moment, the reactions of family members – she was liable to move back and forth along this continuum in the perception of her audience or readership; or, like Anna Trapnel, she might find herself simultaneously abused as a witch and defended as a prophet by the confused mob that jostled for position around her bed.[76] Moreover, the degree of reasonableness or maturity displayed in her writings was often in direct proportion to the degree of hostility she aroused. Katherine Chidley, the most rational and assertive of all preaching women, who organized debates with ministers, led her own Independent congregation, and wrote extensively on political and social issues, was vilified as 'a brazen-faced audacious old woman resembled unto Jael.' The prophet Elizabeth Poole, who was received as a respectable gentlewoman by members of Parliament, was also described as a 'virgin,' 'girl,' and 'monstrous witch full of all deceitful craft.' [. . .] No wonder Eleanor Davies's daughter Lucy, wanting to honor her mother as a sage after her death, adorned her grave with the tribute, 'In a woman's body, a man's spirit.'

Indeed, what we have seen in contemplating women as prophets, whether the astute social critic Mary Cary or the flamboyant and abstruse Lady Eleanor, is a collective mentality stretched to the limit, and occasionally past the limits of coherent expression, by the contradictions of their public positions as females venturing onto the forbidden planet of male political discourse. Women not only had access to a restricted spiritual vocabulary; they also experienced a conflict between their impulse to preach in the mode of ministers carrying an ethical message and the need to present themselves as sibyls, not teachers.

[. . .]

We have, I hope, attained some insight as to why so many observers have been convinced of the female prophet's emotional and intellectual instability. In terms of conventional definitions of lunacy, the men who insisted that they were incarnations of Jesus or specific messengers out of the Book of Revelation were surely no less demented than the women who claimed to be simple generic handmaids of God.[77] Men, however, were able to fashion a public persona that was at once more coherent and more individualized than women's, one in which the emotions that attended their religious conversions became an integral part of their prophetic discourse. Ironically, they had more access to feminine maternal and sexual symbolism than women did.[78] Indeed, the male mechanic preacher, however aberrant his message or behavior, was part of a cultural tradition reaching back to the long-haired charismatic carpenter's son known as Jesus or even further back, to the unlettered prophets of the Old Testament. Like the *topos* of the medieval hermit or that of the modern lonesome cowboy, he was entirely recognizable to himself and others in cultural terms, however isolated he might have felt himself to be in personal terms.

For most prophetic women, the final solution to the ambiguities of their position was to project their utopian visions of equality into a spiritual millennium outside normal life. Mary Cary and Eleanor Davies expected the natural order to end in their lifetime; the books of Daniel and Revelation were to be realized in their day. Elizabeth Avery was also concerned with the millennium, particularly the resurrection of the dead. This focus on a world without time, 'when the streets shall be filled with boys and girls' and men and women live to a great age, was surely liberating for women. It may have also reflected what some theorists have called 'women's time,' a sensibility to the cyclical and eternal aspects of existence, as opposed to the linear, organized march of time as it is seen in history.[79] In terms of winning a new position for women within the natural, historical order, it was clearly self-defeating.

A more heartening aspect of visionary women's public identity was their membership in religious congregations, where they were personally known and where their audiences were predisposed to view their visionary insights as credible. Almost every prophet of note preached as a member of an independent church or sect and relied on the physical, moral, and financial support of her spiritual 'family.' Indeed, the religious ecstasies of prophets like Sarah Wight were profoundly social events, often conducted in rooms crowded with congregational members who supported them in their spiritual 'illness' and who, in turn, experienced a kind of vicarious sanctification by their witness of the prophet's own spiritual labor. Women prophets also engaged in more general political activities along with other women, agitating against churching and presenting petitions to Parliament. Eleanor Davies was again the exception, pursuing an aristocratic life-style utterly distant from the ordinary men and women who constituted her audience, though even Lady Eleanor found a circle of women in Lichfield with whom she attended church and discussed religious matters.

In the end, however, the potential of even collective behavior was limited for prophetic women, for all organized congregations, even radical congregations, excluded women from positions of real leadership. Women spoke at Baptist meetings, but their authority to preach or to lead meetings was contested. No Leveler or Muggletonian tracts were ascribed to women, and despite the women's networks that must have existed in order to mobilize the thousands of signatures seen on petitions to the government, there is no record of women regularly attending the men's meetings. The Fifth Monarchist sect to which Mary Cary and Anna Trapnel belonged respected women as prophets and may even have tolerated separate women's meetings, but the agenda of those meetings was set by men, and much of women's public activity as church members was in support of these male leaders.[80] Mary Pocock, describing herself as a 'member of the body' of enlightened people, defended the minister John Pordage when he was accused of heretical doctrine. Anna Trapnel's first vision took place in Whitehall, where she had accompanied the Fifth Monarchist Vavasour Powell when he was accused of sedition. Katherine Chidley's last public act in 1653 was to lead a contingent of women to the doors of Parliament to present a petition, signed by six thousand women, on behalf of the Leveler leader John Lillburne.[81]

By the end of the 1640s, the age of independent female prophecy was over.[82] The atmosphere of free expression and potential equality that had temporarily obscured class barriers during the Interregnum had not been sufficiently powerful to obscure the gender barrier, perhaps because the leaders of even the radical sects were beginning to see a fundamental contradiction in the very notion of a rationally organized society energized by occult spiritual forces. Visionary men like Gerrard Winstanley or John Rogers might have been seen to resolve this contradiction by embodying both unrestrained spiritual energy and practical leadership. Visionary *women*, active in a period of extreme political upheaval and intense political consciousness, made the contradiction more explicit.

[. . .]

Notes

1 Alfred Cohen, 'Prophecy and Madness: Women visionaries during the Puritan Revolution,' *Journal of Psychohistory* 11 (1984): 411–30. David S. Lovejoy, *Religious Enthusiasm in the New World: Heresy to Revolution* (Cambridge, Mass. and London: Harvard University Press, 1985), 68. Christopher Hill, *The World Turned Upside Down: Radical Ideas during the English Revolution* (New York: Viking Press, 1972), Chap. 15, 'Base Impudent Kisses,' and Chap. 3, 'The Island of Great Bedlam.'

2 Lyle Koehler, *A Search for Power: The 'Weaker Sex' in Seventeenth-Century New England* (Urbana, Chicago, and London: University of Illinois Press, 1980), 217. See also Elaine Hobby, *Virtue of Necessity: English Women's Writing, 1649–88* (London: Virago Press, 1988), 27; Dorothy P. Ludlow, '"Arise and Be Doing": English "Preaching" Women, 1640–1660,' Ph.D. diss., Indiana University, 1978, 273.

3 Nigel Smith, *Perfection Proclaimed: Language and Literature in English Radical Religion, 1640–1660* (Oxford: Clarendon Press, 1989), 342–43. Surviving church lists show women outnumbering men (Bernard Capp, *The Fifth Monarchy Men: A Study in Seventeenth-Century English Millenarianism* [London: Faber and Faber, 1972], 82).

4 Mary Cary, *The Resurrection of the Witness: and Englands Fall from (the Mystical Babylon) Rome* (London, 1648), 65–67.

5 Anna Trapnel, *A Legacy for Saints, Being Several Experiences of the Dealings of God with Anna Trapnel, in, and after Her Conversion* (London, 1654), Introduction.

6 Cary, *The Resurrection of the Witness*, 'Epistle to the Reader.' Christopher Feake, who contributed a preface to her tract *The Little Horn's Doom and Downfall*, called her a 'gentlewoman.'

7 Eleanor Audeley, *A Warning to the Dragon and All His Angels* (1625), 90. (Audeley was Eleanor Davies's maiden name.)

8 On male ministers' depression and visionary tendencies, see Owen Watkins, *The Puritan Experiment: Studies in Spiritual Autobiography* (New York: Schocken Press, 1972), 93ff.

9 On Joan Drake, see John Hart, *The Firebrand Taken out of the Fire* . . . (London, 1654). On Sarah Wight, see Henry Jessey, *The Exceeding Riches of Grace Advanced*, 7th ed. (1658), 95–97, quoted in Barbara Ritter Dailey, 'The Visitation of Sarah Wight: Holy Carnival and the Revolution of the Saints in Civil War London,' *Church History* 55 (1986): 450.

10 Anna Trapnel, *The Cry of a Stone: Or a Relation of Something Spoken in Whitehall, by Anna Trapnel, Being in the Visions of God* (London, 1654), 3.

11 Jessey, *The Exceeding Riches*, 30, quoted in Smith, *Perfection Proclaimed*, 46. Dailey, 'The Visitation of Sarah Wight,' 444; she had lied to her mother about a lost hood that she told her was at a grandmother's house.

12 Jessey, *The Exceeding Riches*, 25, 30, 39, 130.

13 On Avery, see John Rogers, *Ohel or Beth-shemesh: A Tabernacle for the Sun* (London, 1653), 403. On Chidley, see *Biographical Dictionary of British Radicals in the Seventeenth Century* (hereafter DBR), ed. R.L. Greaves and R. Zaller (Brighton, 1982–4), 1:139.

14 Rogers, *Ohel or Beth-shemesh*; many women in Rogers's sect converted after the death of a child. On the Countess of Warwick, see Sara Heller Mendelson, *The Mental World of Stuart Women: Three biographies* (Amherst: University of Massachusetts Press, 1987), 81–82.

15 Hart, *The Firebrand Taken out of the Fire*. See also George Huntston Williams, 'Called by Thy Name, Leave Us Not: The Case of Mrs. Joan Drake, A Formative Episode in the Pastoral Career of Thomas Hooker in England,' *Harvard Library Bulletin* 16 (1968): 111–28, 278–300. Martha Hatfield's case was recounted in James Fisher, *The Wise Virgin, or, a Wonderfull Narration of the Hand of God* . . . (London, 1653).

16 Theophilus Philaleihes Toxander, *Vox Coeli to England, or England's Forewarning from Heaven* (London, 1646), 3–11.

17 *The Lady Eleanor Her Appeal. Present This to Mr. Mace the Prophet of the Most High, His Messenger* (1646), quoted in George Ballard, *Memoirs of Several Ladies of Great Britain Who Have Been Celebrated for Their Writings or Skill in the Learned Languages, Arts and Sciences* (1775), ed. Ruth Perry (Detroit: Wayne State University Press, 1985), 258. Trapnel, *Report and Plea*, 26, quoted in Hobby, *Virtue of Necessity*, 33.

18 On Chidley, see DBR, 1:139–40. On Hazzard, see Claire Cross, '"He-goats before the Flocks": A Note on the Part Played by Women in the Founding of Some Civil War Churches,' in *Popular Belief and Practice*, ed. G.J. Cuming and Derek Baker (Cambridge: Cambridge University Press, 1972), 195–203. Lady Eleanor, *Her Appeal*, 8–9, and Esther Cope, '*Handmaid of the Holy Spirit. Dame Eleanor Davies, Never Soe Mad a Ladie?*' (Ann Arbor, University of Michigan Press, 1992), 43.

19 On women's social backgrounds, see Ludlow, '"Arise and Be Doing,"' 41–42. On Trapnel, see DBR, 3:250. On Chidley, see DBR, 1:140. On Lady Eleanor, HEH, Hastings Manuscripts Correspondence, HA 2344, discussed in Cope, '*Dame Eleanor Davies*.'

20 Toxander, *Vox Coeli*, 6.

21 Pope, *Treatise of Magistracy* (1647), 130. Mary Cary, *The Little Horn's Doom and Downfall: Or a Scripture-Prophesie of King James, and King Charles, and of This Present Parliament, Unfolded* (London, 1651), Preface, A3v.

22 Trapnel, Report and Plea, 2, 7. On Elizabeth Poole, see Elizabeth Poole, *An(other) Alarum of War, Given to the Army* (1649), quoted in Hobby, *Virtue of Necessity*, 30,

and in Ludlow, '"Arise and Be Doing,"' 228ff.; Poole may have left the congregation for doctrinal reasons. She denied the accusations of immorality. On Jones, see Ludlow, '"Arise and Be Doing,"' 80 n. 103.

23 Smith, *Perfection Proclaimed*, 46, 48.
24 Toxander, *Vox Coeli*, 9. Grace Cary, 'Englands Fore-Warning or: A Relation of True, Strange and Wonderfull Visions, . . .' Add, 32. iv and D.d. 14.25. (3), Cambridge University Library, discussed in Margaret J.M. Ezell, *The Patriarch's Wife: Literary Evidence and the History of the Family* (Chapel Hill and London: University of North Carolina Press, 1987), 65.
25 Elizabeth Poole, *A Vision: Wherein Is Manifested the Disease and Cure of the Kingdome* (London, 1648), 7, and *An(other) Alarum of War*, 12, paraphrased in Ludlow, '"Arise and Be Doing,"' 210.
26 On Chidley, see Katherine Chidley, 'Good Counsell, to the Petitioners for Presbyterian Government That They May Declare Their Faith before They Build Their Church,' broadside (1645), and *The Justification of the Independent Churches of Christ* (London, 1641), 37–38; on Warren, see DBR, 3:293; on Pope, see Pope, *Treatise of Magistracy*, 123–24.
27 Cary, *The Little Horn's Doom and Downfall*, 46.
28 Mary Cary, *A New and More Exact Mappe or Description of New Jerusalems Glory* . . . (London, 1651), 56–57, 67.
29 Ibid., 238–39.
30 Mary Rande, *Twelve Proposals* . . . (1653), 4. Capp, *Fifth Monarchy Men*, 189. Mary Cary took the name Rande at this time.
31 Trapnel, *Report and Plea*, 14; Trapnel, *Cry of a Stone*, 6.
32 Cohen, 'Prophecy and Madness,' 424. Trapnel, *Cry of a Stone*, 40, discussed in Capp, *Fifth Monarchy Men*, 144. Venner was a Fifth Monarchist leader.
33 Cary, *A New and More Exact Mappe*, 289–90. See also *Resurrection of the Witness*, 173, and Capp, *Fifth Monarchy Men*, 184: Cary wanted toleration even for papists and atheists; most others disagreed.
34 Rande, *Twelve Proposals*, 4, 6. She was also concerned for the idle poor, advocating workhouses that would dispense small allowances. See Capp, *Fifth Monarchy Men*, 147.
35 Chidley, *The Justification of the Independent Churches of Christ*, 43; Petition of April 24, 4, quoted in Ludlow, '"Arise and Be Doing,"' 121. On Pope, see Ludlow, '"Arise and Be Doing,"' 216–17.
36 Ludlow, ' "Arise and Be Doing," ' 209.
37 On Gadbury, see H[umphrey] Ellis, *Pseudochristus: Or, a True and Faithful Relation of the Grand Impostures, Abominable Practices, Horrid Blasphemies, Gross Deceits* . . . (London, 1650).
38 Eleanor Davies, *To Parliament* (1641), 11.
39 Keith Thomas, *Religion and the Decline of Magic* (New York: Scribner's, 1971), 133–37. Hill, *World Turned Upside Down*, 160.
40 Hill, *World Turned Upside Down*, 254. Owen Watkins remarks that Trapnel's writing, 'shows a remarkable freedom from aggressive self-concern' (*The Puritan Experiment*, 93).
41 Letter of December 21, 1654, quoted by Champlin Burrage, in 'Anna Trapnel's Prophecies,' Rawlinson Manuscripts A. 21. 325, Bodleian Library, Oxford.
42 Claire Cross, 'The Church in England, 1646–1660,' in *The Interregnum: The Quest for Settlement, 1640–1660*, ed. G.E. Aylmer (Hamden: Archon Books, 1972), 116–17.
43 Rogers, *Ohel or Beth-shemesh*, quoted in Joyce Irwin, *Women in Radical Protestantism, 1525–1675* (New York and Toronto: Edwin Mellen Press, 1979), 176.
44 Rogers, *Ohel or Beth-shemesh*, 476–77, quoted in Ludlow, '"Arise and Be Doing,"' 23. In another Fifth Monarchist meeting, one Sister Harrison raised the issue of women speaking, causing a fierce dispute, after which ordinary women were given no rights at all, but a prophetess was allowed to speak, prophesy, and pray (Capp, *Fifth Monarchy Men*, 174; Ludlow, '"Arise and Be Doing,"' 20–24).
45 Thomas Edwards, *Gangraena: Or a Catalogue and Discovery of Many of the Errours, Heresies, Blasphemies and Pernicious Practices of the Sectaries of This Time* . . . (London, 1645), 86.

46 Pope, *A Treatise of Magistracy*, 42, 108.
47 Ibid., 32, 39.
48 Lady Eleanor, *The Restitution of Prophecy: That Buried Talent to Be Revived* (1651), Introduction, n.p. Cope interprets Lady Eleanor's obscure grammar differently, as a deliberate attempt to confuse the majority of readers ('*Dame Eleanor Davies*,' 15, 134).
49 Audeley, *A Warning to the Dragon and All His Angels*, 94–95. Another factor in her changed style may have been the fact that the more incoherent passage was written after her incarceration in Bedlam, while this tract was composed at the beginning of her career. (Cope, '*Dame Eleanor Davies*,' 10, 214.)
50 Trapnel, *Report and Plea*, 20, 57.
51 Ibid., 50.
52 Ibid., Preface, n.p.
53 Ibid., 15.
54 Cary, *The Little Horn's Doom and Downfall*, 'To the Reader.' For a different interpretation of this passage, see Hobby, *Virtue of Necessity*, 30. Cary's economic proposals are in her *Twelve Proposals*.
55 Chidley, *The Justification of the Independent Churches of Christ*, 80–81. Chidley made no systematic attempt to counter her adversary Thomas Edwards's attacks on women, although she was tireless in her arguments in every other respect.
56 On women and parish protest, see Ludlow, '"Arise and Be Doing,"' 48–64. Women beat Anglican priests, tearing their robes and scratching their faces. Joan Hoby said she did not 'care a pin nor a fart for my Lords Grace of Canterbury' but hoped to live to see him hanged (Ludlow, '"Arise and Be Doing,"' 49). Women also felt free to argue with priests on points of theology (53–54).
57 Cary, *A New and More Exact Mappe*, 237–38.
58 Leah Sinanoglou Marcus, 'Shakespeare's Comic Heroines, Elizabeth I, and the Political Uses of Androgyny,' in *Women in the Middle Ages and the Renaissance: Literary and Historical Perspectives*, ed. Mary Beth Rose (Syracuse: Syracuse University Press, 1986), 135–53. Marcus states that Elizabeth's masculine imagery surfaced most frequently in her public pronouncements (137).
59 Pocock, *The Mystery of the Deity in the Humanity* (1649), 16, quoted in Smith, *Perfection Proclaimed*, 211.
60 Chidley, *A New-Yeares-Gift, or a Brief Exhortation to Mr. Thomas Edwards* (London, 1645), 13.
61 S.1.42.th., 84, Bodleian Library, Oxford, quoted in Cohen, 'Prophecy and Madness,' 425.
62 Audeley, *A Warning to the Dragon*, 3.
63 Mrs. Sarah Jones, *This Is the Light's Appearance* (1650), n.p. (emphasis added). Pope, *A Treatise of Magistracy*, 'The Epistle Dedicatory, To the Christian Reader,' C2v. Eleanor Davies also referred to her pamphlets as 'babes' (*The Restitution of Prophecy*, sig. A3r, quoted in Smith, *Perfection Proclaimed*, 63).
64 *Coppes Return* (1651), quoted in J.C. Davis, *Fear, Myth, and History: The Ranters and the Historians* (Cambridge: Cambridge University Press, 1986), 56.
65 Nigel Smith emphasizes that women saw their bodies as maps of their spiritual experiences, but he does not analyze the specific forms of bodily expression women displayed as distinct from men (*Perfection Proclaimed*, 43, 47–48, 50, 80, 87).
66 Jessey, *The Exceeding Riches*, 27–30, and see Dailey, 'The Visitation of Sarah Wight,' 447, 448.
67 E[lizabeth] Avery, *Scripture-Prophecies Opened, Which Are to Be Accomplished in These Last Times, Which Do Attend the Second Coming of Christ* (London, 1647), 17.
68 Diary of Anne Bathurst, 1692, Rawlinson Manuscripts, D. 1262–63/480.
69 Ibid., fol. 45.
70 Mary Gadbury testified that she had given birth to the Spirit (Ellis, *Pseudochristus*, 39–40). Mary Adams claimed that she was pregnant with the Holy Ghost (*An Account of Mary Adams, The Ranters Monster* [London, 1652]). Mrs. Pordage wrote to Abiezer Coppe about a metaphoric birth: 'What though we are weaker vessels,

women etc. yet . . . we shall mount up with wings as Eagles, . . . when the *Man-Child Jesus* is brought forth *In Us*' (Abiezer Coppe, *Some Sweet Sips, of Some Spirituall Wine* [London, 1649], 40). A Warwickshire woman thought she was the 'mother of God and of all things living' (Capp, *Fifth Monarchy Men*, 33). A woman stripped naked in Whitehall to mock a sermon preached there and was chastised in David Brown's *The Naked Woman* (1652). Anne Hall was reported to have cohabited with two male lay preachers and to have expected to give birth to a child who spoke in tongues (T.J., *A Brief Representation and Discovery of the Notorious Falshood and Dissimulation Contained in a Book Styled, The Gospel-Way Confirmed by Miracles* [London, 1649]).

71 Cary, *A New and More Exact Mappe*, 54.

72 Ibid., 173; on Poole, see C.H. Firth, ed., *The Clarke Papers: Selections from the Papers of William Clarke*, 4 vols. (Westminster: Nichols and Sons, 1894), 151; Eleanor Davies, *From the Lady Eleanor, Her Blessing to Her Beloved Daughter, the Right Honorable Lucy, Countess of Huntingdon. The Prophet Daniel's Vision* (1644) (quoted in Cope, 'Dame Eleanor Davies'), 13–14.

73 Davies, *Her Blessing to Her Beloved Daughter*, 17; *A Warning to the Dragon*, 19–20, 28, 29.

74 Avery, *Scripture-Prophecies Opened*, Preface, n.p. *The Copy of a Letter Written by Mr. Thomas Parker* . . . (London, 1650), 13.

75 Hugh Peters's preface to Cary's *The Little Horn's Doom and Downfall* stated that Cary wrote so well and in so scholarly a fashion that 'you might easily think she plowed with anothers Heifer, were not the contrary well known.' A published critique questioned her biblical exegesis but acknowledged her intelligence: 'And truly it is a pity that a woman of her parts should build with so much confidence upon so rotten a foundation' (*The Account Audited, Or the Date of the Resurrection of the Witnesses, Pretended to Be Demonstrated by M. Cary a Minister* [London, 1649], 2).

76 For a general discussion of the instability of women as subjects in seventeenth-century culture, see Catherine Belsey, *The Subject of Tragedy: Identity and Difference in Renaissance Drama* (New York and London: Methuen, 1985), 150, 153.

77 William Franklin had a history of mental illness, wife-beating, and spiritual delusion. He was expelled from his congregation before teaming up with Mary Gadbury (Ellis, *Pseudochristus*, 6–7).

78 For several examples of male maternal visions see Smith, *Perfection Proclaimed*, 58, 60–61, 65, 81.

79 On linear time viewed as masculine, see Frieda Johles Forman, 'Feminizing Time: An Introduction,' in *Taking Our Time: Feminist Perspectives on Temporality*, ed. Frieda Johles Forman and Caoran Sowton (Oxford and New York: Oxford University Press, 1989), 4.

80 On women in the Levelers, see Ludlow, '"Arise and Be Doing,"' 243ff. On women in the Fifth Monarchy sect, see Capp, *Fifth Monarchy Men*, Biographical Appendix; Anne Laurence, 'A Priesthood of She-Believers: Women and Congregations in Mid-Seventeenth Century England,' *Women in the Church*, ed. W.J. Sheils and Diana Wood, *Studies in Church History* (Oxford: Basil Blackwell, 1990), 345–63.

81 On Pocock, see Smith, *Perfection Proclaimed*, 190, 211; on Chidley, see DBR, 1:140.

82 Fewer books by female prophets (excluding Quakers) were published after 1650 (Patricia Crawford, 'Women's Published Writings, 1600–1700,' in *Women in English Society, 1500–1800*, ed. Mary Prior [London and New York: Methuen, 1985], 211–82). Eleanor Davies died in 1653. Little is known about the later activities of Mary Cary, Katherine Chidley, and Anna Trapnel.

11

Immaculate and powerful: the Marian revival in the nineteenth century

BARBARA CORRADO POPE

The nineteenth century witnessed a popular and official resurgence in the veneration of Mary throughout the Catholic world. Indeed, so great was this revival that leaders of the church call the years between 1850 and 1950 the Marian Age. The papacy demarcated this era by defining two controversial dogmas about the Mother of Christ: the Immaculate Conception, in 1854, and the Assumption of the Virgin, in 1950. The many reported apparitions of the Virgin throughout southern and western Europe, some of which gained widespread fame and church approval, were another sign of the rise in Marian fervor. Among these visions were those in Paris (1830), LaSalette (1846), Lourdes (1858), and Pontmain (1871), all in France; Fátima, Portugal (1917); and Beauraing (1932) and Banneaux (1933) in Belgium. With few exceptions, these apparitions aroused great hopes and fears, and their sites eventually attracted pilgrims from all walks of life.

The French visions set the pattern for later events. The image of the Immaculate Conception that Sister Catherine Labouré saw and recorded became the dominant image of the Virgin throughout Europe and the United States. And Lourdes remains the most popular of all Christian shrines and the most important site of miraculous healing in the world. In each of the last few years, over four million people have traveled to this little town in the Pyrenees. Lourdes still attracts twice as many pilgrims as Mecca, although, unlike Mecca, it represents neither an obligation of religious practice nor a central focus of a world faith.

How, then, can we understand the rise and endurance of modern Marian devotion? Some faithful Roman Catholics might answer that the renaissance in Marian devotion was part of a divine plan, that the Mother of God intervened in human history to counsel us about the need for redemption. Some Jungians might see in these events the reassertion of the female principle, either supernaturally or in the minds of those open to the message that religion and culture had become too masculine. Neither of these responses is fully satisfactory. Reports of visions and apparitions have been endemic to

Catholicism. Some are approved, and attract great followings. Others are discouraged by the church, slighted and forgotten. I assume that at least part of the reason why these Marian apparitions took on such importance lies in their social, political, and cultural context, that is, in their purely human history.

An important part of that history is the onset of the modern French pilgrimage movement in 1873. The practice of journeying to a sacred place is common to Islam and Hinduism as well as to Christianity. In both ancient and medieval times, many Christians undertook long and arduous journeys to be cured of their spiritual or physical ills and to see and touch holy places and objects. But by the eighteenth century, most pilgrimages, at least in France, were local in character, and most of the practitioners were peasants following their village or 'folk' traditions. Since the Catholic Reformation of the sixteenth century, there had been an increasing division between the official, orthodox church, bent on 'purifying' the faith, and those who believed in extrasacramental miraculous powers.[1] Although pilgrimages were condemned as superstitious or pagan by some clergymen, many Catholics continued to journey to special holy places, where they could literally touch, or, in the case of fountains, immerse themselves in, the sacred powers, as their ancestors had done.

Frequently entire villages made annual treks to a nearby shrine, image, or fountain to offer sacrifices and pray for good crops, the health of their livestock, and cures for their own ills. Personal or national crises also induced people to participate in this form of sacrifice and prayer. Women, in particular, used pilgrimages for their own needs: to provide them with occasions for all-female sociability and to petition the Virgin or the local patron saint for aid with problems of sexuality and reproduction.[2] As Fatima Mernissi has shown in her work on contemporary Moslem saints' shrines in North Africa, these unorthodox traditions also offer women a sense of empowerment and autonomy.[3] It is not surprising that such activity could be seen as a danger to orthodox belief.

By 1873 the official attitude had changed, and the church had moved to tie these potentially subversive impulses to the sacramental system.[4] As we will see, the modern pilgrimage movement was an expression of political discontent as well as religious fervor, yet the sheer number of pilgrims involved reinforced the religious legitimacy of the new symbols. This new form of devotion was also an adaptation to an increasingly urban and industrial society. In the end it sapped the power of local French shrines and created a mass rather than 'folk' religious culture, a culture tied to national and international rather than local systems. This religious culture relied upon modern mass production while it condemned modern political ideology.[5]

That Mary should be the focus of this new devotion is not surprising. The Virgin is the embodiment of what patriarchal Catholic theology had always defined as 'good' feminine qualities: chastity, humility, and maternal forgiveness. At least since the late Middle Ages the faithful have seen her as the last resort, the intercessor between humanity and God who would help in times of direct need.[6] As nineteenth-century Catholics increasingly saw themselves in a state of siege against the modern world, they turned to those symbols that promised comfort. Further, Mary's supernatural role reflected what most French people knew in a more intimate way. In both the city and the country, women were the first teachers of moral lessons and religious stories. They were more often in charge of mediating dissension between paternal authority and their children.[7] Since religion and understanding were learned, so to speak, at mother's knee, it should not be surprising that the most readily seen and accepted visions took the form of a mediating mother.

The apparitions

In 1830 the Virgin of the Miraculous Medal appeared several times to an uneducated country nun living at the Sisters of Charity in the Rue du Bac. During the first apparition the Virgin spoke at great length to the humble Catherine Labouré and warned that troubles would soon beset France. She prophesied that the cross would be treated with contempt and that blood would flow. This was the explicitly political content of the vision, which later interpreters took to predict the French revolutions of 1830, 1848, and 1871.

Labouré's later visions brought a more explicitly religious message and gave her a mission. The Virgin appeared within an oval; standing on a globe. Her feet trod on a snake, which represented Satan. She was dressed in white with a blue mantle (the colors of innocence and purity, and of royalist France). Her arms were extended downward and out. Her fingers were covered with rings of precious stones. From them radiated rays that symbolized the graces the Virgin would grant her devotees. Around the top of the oval ran the words 'O Mary conceived without sin, pray for us who have recourse to thee.' The vision asked that a medal be struck in this image.

Père Aladel, Labouré's confessor, showed a drawing of the image and explained its origins to the archbishop of Paris, Quélen, who authorized the pressing of the medals. Within ten years, millions of these images in gold, silver, and cheaper metals had been distributed throughout the world.[8] Accounts of miraculous cures and, especially, of spectacular conversions helped to spread the fame of this medal and fostered belief in its efficacy.

This image did not add any new elements to the symbolism of the Virgin, but its popularity did make some aspects more important than others and promoted a uniform, even universal notion of what she looked like. Both Bernadette of Lourdes and the visionaries of Pontmain described one of the stances of their apparitions as 'like the Miraculous Medal, but without the rays.'[9] Since these descriptions come from children living in relatively remote regions of France, these comments indicate how widely the image had spread. The coloration of blue and white (or simply white in some reproductions) reappeared at Lourdes, Fátima, Beauraing, and Banneaux. This is in contrast to earlier depictions of the Virgin, which were often multicolored and followed local cults.

Symbolically, Labouré's image of the Virgin projected a double message of hope and warning. The Virgin's outreaching arms seemed to beckon the sick, the alienated, and the lonely as well as sinners. The other prevalent attitude of succeeding visions would find Mary with her eyes lifted and hands clasped in prayer. This posture demonstrated her compassionate concern for humanity and her maternal willingness to intercede for the afflicted. It also expressed the increasingly popular hope that the divine Son could not refuse to grant any wish of his loving Mother.

Mary's crushing of the snake was the most direct iconographic link to the dogma of the Immaculate Conception. It signified Mary's own triumph over evil and especially her unique status as the only one of God's creatures never touched, even at the first instant of conception, by Original Sin. This dogma asserted that the vessel of Christ would never have been tainted by sin or temptation, that she was 'pre-redeemed' in eternity before the coming of Christ in time.

According to church tradition, the most ancient proof of this special divine favor appeared in the third chapter of Genesis, when God told the ancient serpent, 'I will put enmities between thee and the woman, between thy seed and her seed.' The vision also recalled the woman and the dragon in the twelfth chapter of Revelation in the New Testament. Indeed earlier paintings of the Immaculate Conception had made the connection more explicit by depicting Mary as the woman of the Apocalypse, 'clothed with the sun' and 'with the moon at her feet.' This accounts for some of the apocalyptic hopes and fears that were aroused with each new announcement of Marian apparitions.

Mary's triumph over sin was not merely a personal victory. She was also identified as Mother Church, and in this interpretation she represented the triumph of the spiritual family of Christ over sin and worldliness. The crushing of the snake could also signify the defeat of special kinds of sin. More and more, as we shall see, this came to mean the sins of the modern world, which ranged from the popularity of romantic novels to political and social revolution to an overweening human pride in the efficacy of science, materialism, and rationality. This message became more explicit in holy cards and in illustrated pamphlets, which added little phrases and texts to the original depiction.[10]

Thus while the outstretched arms of the Immaculate Conception promised mercy to the faithful, the iconography of this most widely distributed of Marian images also projected a militant and defiant message that through Mary the church would defeat its enemies.

Despite the apparent contemporary significance of its message and the tremendous popularity of reproductions of the image, Labouré's vision was not really a public affair. Labouré kept her identity a secret until she was near death, and the Rue du Bac did not become a popular shrine. Later apparitions were public events, propelled by messages for the faithful, abetted by publicity, and subject to the investigatory powers of church and state.

The first of these spectacular happenings occurred near LaSalette, a small town in the French Alps. On September 19, 1846, two shepherds, fourteen-year-old Mélanie Calvat and eleven-year-old Maximin Giraud, awoke from a nap to see a dazzling light in a ravine. Upon a closer look, they discerned a woman weeping. She beckoned them to her. Speaking in French, then in patois, this beautiful woman warned them that crop failures and famines would strike if the people did not stop blaspheming, learn to pray, and attend mass regularly. She told them that she had suffered greatly for their sins and could no longer hold up the arm of her Son, which would fall on them in punishment. Then she took each child aside and told each a secret. As she floated up toward heaven, she asked them to make her warnings known to all. This sad, majestic lady was dressed in white and gold and wore a crown. A golden crucifix hung from her neck, as did a hammer and pincers, torture instruments of Christ's Passion.

What ensued set the pattern for a social drama that would be reenacted several times during the next century. The actors (at LaSalette, Lourdes, Fátima, Pontmain, Beauraing, and Banneaux) were the child-peasant visionaries, a skeptical church, and an even more skeptical and hostile civil authority. In each case the children were subjected to threats and long hours of questioning aimed at finding contradictions in their testimony and (at LaSalette, Lourdes, and Fátima) at discovering their 'secrets.' In each case, the children stood firm. Word of the events spread through newspaper accounts and pamphlet literature. Before the church could investigate and define its opinion, pilgrims arrived. When the church did authorize the cults, it moved to define the meaning of the apparitions and control the celebrations. Special missionary orders came to serve at pilgrimage sites. Before all major gatherings, the sacrament of penance was strongly suggested and readily available. During the celebrations priests said mass, making the Eucharist, the ritual coming of Christ, the climactic event.

LaSalette was in many ways a test case, and at first the church was fully united neither about the veracity of the visions nor about how to proceed. Even after an investigation and official approval, LaSalette remained somewhat problematic, in part because of the intractability of its visionaries. Mélanie, who spent her adult life wandering from one religious order to another, was a particular source of embarrassment. She spoke often of the spiritual necessity of suffering and everywhere wore a scapular of her own design, which featured a bleeding sacred heart torn by sharp instruments and set between a pincers and hammer.[11] In 1870, after years of leaked information, she finally published her full 'secret'. This turned out to be a long diatribe on the sins of European nations and Catholic priests, replete with specific predictions about the coming of Lucifer and the reign of the Anti-Christ. Such behavior appealed only to the radical fringes of the Catholic right. For them the emphasis on sin and suffering reinforced the basic image of LaSalette: that of the weeping Virgin, complaining about the sins of the modern world.

Lourdes was much more fortunate in its visionary, the stolid Bernadette Soubirous, and in the multidimensionality of its message. Bernadette, the asthmatic fourteen-year-old daughter of a pitifully poor family, first saw her vision in February 1858 while gathering wood with her sister and a friend. When she told her companions of seeing a beautiful lady, word quickly spread. Soon Bernadette was being interviewed by local officials, a doctor, and rich, pious ladies of the town. One of the most photographed personages of the mid-nineteenth century, Bernadette exhibited to the world a stalwart, brooding, and (in her peasant dress) rather exotic presence. It matters little whether her quiet steady gaze was the result of confidence, docility, or befuddlement; her stubborn faithfulness, shrewd humor, and discretion inspired confidence in those who saw her and wished to believe her words. This was important because the protracted happening became a major news event.

Bernadette saw her vision seventeen times during the next five months, often in front of thousands of witnesses. Throughout she remained the perfect child of faith. When the vision told her to drink the water, Bernadette clawed the dry ground and ate mud; when asked to pray for sinners, she fell upon the ground in supplication. Bernadette also conformed with exactitude to the wishes of local churchmen, insisting only upon the truth of her visions as she had seen them. Bernadette's Virgin was beautiful, simple, and young. She wore a white robe and veil and a blue sash, and had two gold roses resting on her bare feet. She carried a rosary.

What the vision told Bernadette combined the old and the new, hope and atonement. As old as medieval apparitions was the request for the building of a church and a procession and the obedience of the visionary to numerous commands. Older still was the identification of a supernatural being with a miraculous fountain. In the Pyrenees villages, people associated healing water not only with old local Marian shrines but also with spirits of Celtic, pre-Christian origin. What was startlingly new was the apparition's identity. 'I am,' she replied to Bernadette's repeated question, 'the Immaculate Conception.'

The vision asked Bernadette to pray for sinners, told her she would suffer in this world and be happy in the next, and spoke the word *penitence* three times. The hope of Lourdes has always been focused on the magically discovered spring and the Virgin's command to drink it and wash in its waters. From the first, contact with the spring catalyzed miraculous cures and conversions. In its multidimensionality then, the Lourdes vision had

much in common with Labouré's Virgin: it expressed both hope and warning, and stated a preference for a certain kind of symbolic representation,
that of the Immaculate Conception.

Lourdes inspired many other visions. None gained church approval until
Pontmain (1871), which occurred during the winter of the Franco-Prussian
war. The claims of five peasant children that they had seen a smiling Virgin
on a starry night in north-western France had the charming quality of a
fairy tale. The whole village gathered together at the news that a heavenly
lady had appeared. But only a few boys and girls could actually see the oval
containing the vision as it grew larger and drew nearer to earth. The lady
wore a deep blue robe covered with gold stars. On her head sat a black veil
and a gold crown. She held a crucifix. The children watched in amazement
as a message was slowly written out beneath her feet, 'But pray, my children.
God will answer you soon. My Son is letting himself be touched by compassion.'[12] When the town was not bombarded and all its soldiers returned
unharmed, the vision and its message seemed to be verified. She became
known as Our Lady of Hope, in contrast to the weeping woman of
LaSalette or the more complex symbolization of Lourdes.

As one might expect, not everyone accepted the visions or the messages at
face value. Skeptics scoffed; and the secular press denounced the apparitions
as delusions or hoaxes or, worse, the manipulations of a wily clergy. Certainly
not all Catholics accepted the truth of the visions, but many did. Against
the disbelief of those who doubted the testimony of young, poor, illiterate
peasants, they opposed the Christian paradox that the humble and ignorant
could see the truth far better than the educated and worldly. This defense of
the visions was in part an assault on the intellectual pretensions of the day, in
part an expression of deeply felt piety, awe, and gratitude. It was an attitude
that emanated from the very top of the hierarchy, the papacy itself.

The role of the papacy

[...]

Pius IX (1846–1878) and his successor, Leo XIII (1878–1903), were personally
devoted to the veneration of the Virgin. They approved coronations, whereby
old statues of Mary received crowns in impressive ceremonies. They also
confirmed the validity of new apparitions and miracles, and granted special
indulgences for mass pilgrimages. They thoroughly believed, as the doctrine
and popular icon of the Immaculate Conception indicated, that Mary could
help the church in its time of dire need. Every October for ten years, Leo XIII,
a pope generally reputed to have progressive political views, issued an ency-
clical exhorting the faithful to say the Rosary. In the first of these decrees

(*Supremi Apostolatus*, 1883), he reminded Catholics that this prayer had saved the church from heresy and from the Turks in the sixteenth century. He hoped that contemporary devotion to Mary would similarly help Catholics to defeat secularism and materialism.

Catholic France, which considered itself to be the home of the Sacred Heart vision and the special realm of Mary, was both the inspiration and recipient of much of this papal activity. From the first, the apparitions in France reinforced Pius's belief in the rightness of his own views and seemed to verify Catholicism's claim to be the one true faith. Labouré's visions in 1830 and the consequent popularity of the Miraculous Medal helped to convince Pius that the time was ripe to declare the Immaculate Conception to be a true dogma of the church.[13] Four years after the declaration, the Lourdes visions were, literally, for this pope, a heaven-sent verification. From the point of view of temporal politics, too, it is not surprising that the popes regarded with special tenderness the appeal of French bishops for recognition of shrines and apparitions. In its quarrels with Italian nationalism, the church frequently looked to its 'eldest daughter' for military aid. Rome also had an interest in shoring up traditional faith within the country that it considered to be the seedbed of modern revolutions. Thus the combined motives of faith and political sensitivity moved the papacy to confirm French Catholics' belief that they had been chosen by Mary.[14]

Catholic piety in the Third Republic

This sense of being chosen provided French Catholics with a national unifying symbol when they most needed it. The last third of the century was an age of fervent nationalism. Yet during this period many French Catholics became extremely alienated from their own government, the Third Republic, founded in 1870. The conflict was exacerbated by the fact that many Catholics were ardent monarchists and many Republicans were avowed anticlericals.

[. . .]

Among the chief protagonists in this struggle were the Augustinian Fathers of the Assumption, whose role in religion and politics was so crucial that the historian René Rémond has labeled the years from 1871 to 1901 the era of Assumptionist Catholicism.[15] In 1883 the Assumptionists founded a daily, *La Croix*, which brought into play all the defensive tactics of nineteenth-century Catholicism. Its writers accepted with pride the accusations made against the church by rationalists. More, they exulted in their differences. But their paper not only defended, it attacked. *La Croix* equated revolutions and the Republic with Satan and his legions, mocked politicians with vitriolic sarcasm, and consistently blamed all problems (including crime, poverty, disease, and natural disasters) on the secular state.

The Assumptionists published the paper *for* Catholics. Two primary goals were to promote religious fervor and to give church members a sense of solidarity and community in the increasingly hostile environment of the anticlerical Republic. What made the order so influential was its willingness to apply modern technological and organizational means to these ends. They exploited with élan the possibilities inherent in mass literacy, transportation, communication, and production. Although they did not approve of universal suffrage, their paper, with its short dramatic headlines, sensationalistic reporting, and hyperbolic prose, successfully met the challenge of shaping opinion in a newly democratic, industrialized, modern society. To a large extent the Assumptionists managed to reach the disparate and isolated elements in Catholic society. Subscriptions to their paper cut across class lines and included an estimated twenty-five thousand members of the lower clergy, who could be counted on to spread the word.[16] Further, *La Croix* was only the most important publication produced and promoted by the Assumptionists and their press. *Le Pèlerin*, a weekly newsletter on pilgrimages founded in 1873, echoed *La Croix*'s political and religious perspective. So did an estimated ninety-one regional newspapers.[17] In addition, *La Croix* and *Le Pèlerin* advertised and distributed mass-produced holy cards. The short, repeated dramatic phrases, satirical editorial cartoons, and holy images presented symbols or 'opinion molecules' rather than rational, factual arguments.[18] Taken together they promoted a symbolic consciousness that invited subscribers to discover layers of mystical meanings behind objects and events. For example, the large cross on the masthead not only pictured the suffering of Jesus but also symbolized the suffering church in Rome and ghettoized Catholics in France.

The treatment of Bastille Day and Marianne, contrasted with that of the Assumption and the Virgin, is a more relevant example of how *La Croix* elaborated symbols for its readers. The newspaper's reportage of the 'national orgy' on July 14 in Paris was always filled with sarcasm and predictions of doom. For days afterward, the paper would recount all the crimes or tragedies in the poor *quartiers*, claiming that these were caused either by drunkenness or barbaric celebration or the moral failures of Republican government. The paper was aroused to special fury in 1883 when a statue of Marianne was unveiled during the Bastille Day ceremony. Artists usually depicted this female symbol of the Republic as a brave warrior or a robust mother surrounded by children. *La Croix*'s front-page editorial derided her as 'neither a queen nor a cook,' compared her to the 'impure Venus' created by 'pagan demons,' and finally called her a nothing. But they concluded, 'she replaced something. She recalls Mary, queen of the Gauls' (July 16 and 17, 1883). This true queen had her feast on August 15. The real France, throne and altar France, had chosen the Assumption as its national holiday in the seventeenth century when Louis XIII dedicated his country to Our Lady. Front-page articles repeating this fact coincided with the onset of the yearly mass pilgrimages to Lourdes. Instead of disasters, the follow-up to this feast day featured miraculous cures and conversions.

The Assumptionists were eclectic in their use of symbols. They did not favor any subject of renewed devotion over others except insofar as some symbols had a national or historical significance that harmonized with their own sense of religious and political necessity. Thus they reported successful religious processions and fêtes, crownings at Marian shrines, and the legends of statues and saints. But their greatest and most consistent efforts were to instill a love for and familiarity with the cross, with Mary, and with the Sacred Heart of Jesus. Each May and June the paper ran stories to celebrate the months of Mary and the Sacred Heart. Pilgrimages and the church calendar were major news events for the Assumptionists and their readers because current events, like history, had a natural and supernatural realm and meaning.

The Assumptionists made their greatest contribution to establishing the realm of Mary in France by orchestrating a yearly cycle of pilgrimages. Leadership fell to them in 1872 when the order was asked to help with a large penitential pilgrimage to LaSalette. The next year the site was Lourdes, which drew a mere 492 people.[19] Ten years later, an estimated twenty thousand journeyed to Lourdes during August.

[...]

The meaning and power of Lourdes

Despite the defiant tone found in much of the Assumptionists' work, it should be obvious that the Lourdes pilgrimage was not built upon political discontent and antimodernism alone. The Assumptionist monks, like their followers, were motivated by sincere religious belief and spiritual hope. They were fortunate that, almost by accident, Lourdes and not LaSalette became the pilgrimage site. Because the LaSalette vision mirrored the Assumptionist temperament so well, any mass pilgrimages based on it would have been permanently tied to aggressive antimodernism. Even the Pontmain apparition was more closely tied to a specific time, place, and mood than was Lourdes. Bernadette envisioned a truly polyvalent symbol that could evoke different emotional and intellectual responses. Her Immaculate Conception was simple and beautiful, yet she left a variety of messages that could lend themselves to many interpretations.

Because of the immediate political context, the Lourdes vision evoked new interpretations of old litanies. Mary, refuge of the sick and sinners, could also be Mary the refuge of Catholic France. In her Immaculate Conception, she vanquished not only Satan but also his Republican legions and materialistic ideas. Queen of heaven, she was also Queen of France, or at least the symbol of the 'true France.' Yet in her youth and simple clothes she could also be identified with the young, the poor, and the humble. Mary was truly a unifying symbol that could help French people overcome their class, regional, and local differences.

But even for the most politically motivated pilgrim, the Lourdes vision was something more. She was powerful, a miracle worker. The sources of these thaumaturgic powers were two: a belief in the special 'privileges' accorded to Mary in Catholic ideology (her virginity, maternity, immaculate conception, and physical assumption) and the *communitas* the pilgrims en masse created at her shrine.

The most immediate attraction of Lourdes, of course, was the belief that Mary, Mother of God, had come there eighteen times. The belief in nineteenth-century apparitions is so strong that they were considered then, as now, 'facts.'[20] The 'fact' of LaSalette or Lourdes is supported by the popular belief that Mary was physically assumed into heaven.[21] This tenet of faith makes the possibility of her reappearance more real. An actual physical presence is something to behold, to touch, and to feel. Pilgrims came and continue to come to Lourdes to feel Mary's presence.

The privilege of physical assumption is, in turn, connected to Mary's motherhood, virginity, and immaculate conception. There is a vast psychological and anthropological literature describing how both virginity and maternity confer powers on a person.[22] Virginity is a special condition of integrity or intactness. Within Catholicism, virginity is almost exclusively identified with sexual purity, a holy state that confers the power to transcend physical corruptibility. Mary's physical assumption is one sign of this empowerment; her ability to cure humanity's physical ills is another.

Motherhood, too, in myth and legend signifies the power over life and death. In a Catholic interpretation more directly informed by human experience, Mary as the mother of Jesus had the right to expect or ask him for favors. One of these favors was the preredemption of the Immaculate Conception, which Archbishop Dupanloup described as a privilege every son would give his mother if he could![23] As the mother of humanity, Mary could mitigate the effect of divine judgment upon the children who came to her with their spiritual ills and abrogate the harsh laws of nature for those who sought a cure for their physical ailments.

It is this interpretation of Mary's maternity that has infuriated Protestant critics. Writing in 1855 (to protest the dogmatic definition of the Immaculate Conception), E. de Pressensé accused Catholics of a kind of neopaganism for their worship of a deity 'made in their own [human] image' and for their adoration of 'the gracious symbols of a feminized cult.'[24] He wrote his pamphlet to recall Christians to their true symbol, the bloody cross. Giovanni Miegge made a strikingly similar analysis almost one hundred years later, just after the Assumption became an official dogma. Mary's compassion, he wrote, is outside the ethical, like the maternal instinct that without discrimination is always on the side of the son however depraved, and covers the guilt with indulgent complicity.

Calling the Mary cult merely 'humanity's pity for itself,'[25] Miegge accused Catholics of not understanding that Jesus was the true intermediary between harsh patriarchal divine laws and humanity.

Both Pressensé and Miegge were wrong, I think, in their assertions that Catholics did not understand Christ's compassion and suffering. *La Croix*'s crucifix and the widely distributed holy cards and statues of the red Sacred Heart of Jesus were highly honored and beloved symbols in Catholic France. Yet these two Protestant critics were correct in perceiving the unique attraction of the Marian cult at Lourdes. Even though the Sacred Heart was supposed to embody Christ's love for his people, in Third Republic France this symbol almost exclusively signified the need to atone for the modern sins that caused Jesus to bleed and suffer.[26] The 'gracious femininity' of the Lourdes visions, then, did seem to promise a more indulgent forgiveness and compassion.

It was in this promise that the faithful placed their hope and trust as they approached the shrine. According to newspaper reports and Émile Zola's long realistic novel *Lourdes* (1894), most pilgrims came to Lourdes quite unencumbered by the niceties of dogmatic belief and definition. Again and again in *La Croix* and in Zola's book, sojourners referred to Mary quite simply as 'the good Mother' or 'the good' or 'holy Virgin.' By their rich description of the great Assumptionists' pilgrimages, these sources help us to understand how the believers themselves activated the miraculous powers of the symbol of the Immaculate Conception at Lourdes.

Each August, trains full of pilgrims traveled from Paris and other major cities, converging at Lourdes within days and hours of each other. Each train had a set of white hospital cars, where the 'poor sick' were taken care of by the Sisters of the Assumption, volunteer doctors, *dames hospitalières*, and male *brancardiers* or stretcher-bearers. Using specially prepared manuals, priests and nuns took the pilgrims through a schedule of prayers and meditations. As the journey progressed, expectations mounted. Sometimes, as a July 1887 edition of *La Croix* put it, 'the Virgin in her impatience to work miracles, healed sick pilgrims en route.'[27]

At the site, a combination of ritual and social organization served to release the pilgrims from the mundane. For its actors, Lourdes, like all liminal experiences, was radically equalizing – so radical that it turned the world upside down. Here the sick and the poor, who were ordinarily shunted off to the margins of society, became the center of attention. The child with the misshapen limbs, the woman with the unsightly running sores, the coughing, grizzled tubercular man, were no longer despised, but served by the healthy and the rich. In *Lourdes*, Zola wrote of stretcher-bearers and volunteer nurses who came from every social class and practiced three days of real communalism every year; he told of aristocrats who took special pleasure in working long days and eating common meals that cost only three sous a day. For the sick, Lourdes represented at best the possibility of cure, and at the very least a means of overcoming isolation and alienation.[28] For the rich and healthy, it was the opportunity to fulfill a mission of perfect Christian charity. These role reversals helped to engender the religious experience that pilgrims sought, and gave them a taste of heaven, where all would equally join Mary in singing God's praises. In simple terms, the pilgrimage drew devotees closer to the divine.

So did the vigils, the outdoor and indoor masses, and the nightly candle-lit parade that spectacularly revealed the numbers of those who believed in the powers and mercy of Jesus and his mother. The sick looked forward most to the immersions at the bathhouses and the outdoor Benediction ceremonies, at which the Eucharist was paraded through the crowds. Almost all of the proclaimed miracles took place during these two events, when pilgrims could feel and see sacred objects. At the bathhouses the *brancardiers* and the sick all prayed to the Virgin as each patient was immersed in the waters of the fountain. During the outdoor Benedictions, the Son upstaged the Mother. The sick and the well spread out their arms in the characteristic Lourdes stance of supplication and prayer. Those who were able fell to their knees as the Eucharist passed. All asked for mercy and for miracles. Often during this rite, people would at last hear the long hoped-for cry, 'I am cured.' When this happened the pilgrims could feel, perhaps more dramatically than at any other time in their life, that they had been touched by divine power. With or without a total cure for their physical and spiritual ills, they gained something by experiencing Mary's realm at Lourdes.

The heritage of Marian apparitions

Lourdes has endured because of the fame of its miracles and its message of hope. The conservative nationalism that partly motivated its first great pilgrimages is no longer apparent. Lourdes is now an international shrine. Like much of the rest of the world, it is more commercialized, more bureaucratized, and more sanitized than in the past. But the Lourdes pilgrimage still provides believers with a sense of *communitas* and Mary's presence.[29]

But what is the legacy of Lourdes and the other apparitions for those who will never visit the shrine? Can we see in the Marian revival a resurgence of the 'feminine principle' or a 'feminization' of religion or culture?

The most famous treatment of the feminization of religion in the nineteenth century is Ann Douglas's *The Feminization of American Culture* (1977). In her discussion of American Protestantism one can distinguish three aspects or stages of feminization: a growing preponderance of women in congregations; the power that this preponderance gave women over religious life; and a 'softening' of theology and religious symbolism that followed as a consequence. One does not necessarily have to accept the logic of her argument to make use of these distinctions. In the French Catholic experience, only the first and third aspects of feminization hold true.

Historians of France have long noted that religious practice fell more and more to women throughout the nineteenth century. This was true in the countryside as well as in the city, where a bourgeois ideology common to France, England, and America assumed that women were 'naturally' more religious, whereas men were more 'rational.'

In contrast to Douglas's description of the American experience, however, this trend did not lead to a female ideological ascendancy in the Catholic church. The male hierarchy, as we have seen, not only maintained but extended control of religious life by validating and popularizing certain affective religious practices and by tying them to the sacramental system.

The revival of the Marian cult can be and has been interpreted as a 'softening' of religious symbolism or a 'resurgence of the feminine.'[30] But it should be clear that this female symbolism has long been shaped and defined by men. By the time of the modern apparitions, over sixteen hundred years of Catholic theology had defined Mary as both Virgin and Mother. This depiction presented real women with a complex ideal of womanhood that they could not fulfill. For some women, it had the effect of denying female power, or the positive power of sexuality in human life. At the same time, the Virgin Mother provided a male, celibate clergy with a 'safe' object of contemplation and adoration.

This does not mean that women did not respond to Mary. On the contrary, religious women enthusiastically took up her cause as it was defined by the newspapers, books, and holy images of their day. They admired Mary, the most powerful and ideal of mothers, because she knew the glories and tragedies of maternity without having had to experience its painful, impure, or bloody realities. Besides, a special identity between women and Mary was the product of a lifelong cultivation. Many girls had been told to model themselves after their Blessed Mother. Virtuous bourgeois convent students usually joined her sodality, the Children of Mary, and wore its special livery, the Miraculous Medal, for the rest of their lives.[31] As adults some still signed *Enfant de Marie* after their name. Mary's high position in the church was obviously a source of female pride. But as powerful as Mary was, her male-defined cult had serious limitations, particularly for women. These become clear when we consider what the nineteenth-century Virgin did *not* represent.

This Virgin had no connection with fertility and sexuality, the two most obvious attributes of any symbol of female divinity. This connection could only belong to an underground interpretation of the Good Mother's role. Although the connection was recognized and utilized in village rituals and local cults, it went unrecognized (officially at least) in the cults of the famous black Virgins, some of whom may have gotten their coloration from their connection with the earth and with pre-Christian goddesses.[32] From the perspective of these earlier images, the blue and white Virgin seems not only immaculate but also bloodless and disconnected from the earth and from the experiences of most women.

The Virgin, who did not have any control over fertility, also had little autonomy within 'her' church. In official interpretations all evidences of her independence were slighted. But they were there. At Pontmain the vision's robes and headdress could be interpreted as priestly. At LaSalette the Lady (who never identified herself) made remarkable statements: '*I* gave you six days' work. *I* have reserved the seventh for *myself*.' (Italics mine.) Certainly there was no suggestion that God was a woman! In fact, leaders of the church were not at all troubled by this lapse. They either ignored the first-person pronouns or dismissed them as a common means found often in the Hebrew Bible, whereby God spoke through his prophets.[33]

The Virgin of the apparitions is not the Mary of the Bible, who had doubts and hesitations during her life. Although she usually appeared alone, she was always cast as an intermediary, who had been given her privileges by a loving Son and prescient Father. Her *active* cooperation was not stressed. She was a vessel rather than the first disciple, who willingly acted out of faith.[34]

This is not surprising. In nineteenth-century Catholicism, discipleship and its historical successor, priesthood, belonged exclusively to males. A female model for sacramental and public leadership roles seemed inconceivable. Any official and public version of the apparitions would have to suit a celibate priesthood's sense of fitness. Mary the pure and passive vessel was an important part of the inherited interpretation.

Finally, if the apparitions had a prophetic mission, it only struck one social and political note. Although the visions appeared to the humble, they never carried a message of social transformation or suggested that the realm of Mary or the coming of Christ meant the overcoming of exploitation or oppression.[35] The political direction they augured was always backward rather than forward: in favor of kings and the old social order, and fearful of change.

This defensive antimodernism may be the most distinct legacy of the church-defined Marian cult of the nineteenth century. Major Marian apparitions still have a highly political and defensive function. The visions seen by the three children at Fátima (1917) echoed the warnings of the Lady of LaSalette. When Fátima's secret messages were revealed in the 1930s, their political spirit also recalled the earlier vision. This time, however, it was not famine or the Anti-Christ that threatened the church, but the spread of Russian Communism. Belief in these messages helped to inform Marian piety with an aggressive Cold War anti-Communism in the years preceding Vatican II. The Blue Army of Our Lady, formed in 1947 to fulfill the command of Fátima, at one time enrolled twenty million, who by their prayers hoped to vanquish the 'red army of atheists.'[36] The Rosary said against the Turks in the sixteenth century and against impiety in the nineteenth, was being recited in the 1950s over the radio for the conversion of Russia.

Now apparitions have turned against the changes within the church itself. In places as culturally diverse as Garabandal in rural Spain and Bayside in New York City, Mary has appeared as the defender of the old pre-Vatican II faith.[37] Neither of these series of visions has been approved. But they draw large crowds and are only the most famous of similar happenings.

The Second Vatican Council (1962–65) signaled a break with the spirit of defensiveness and deemphasized certain kinds of piety. Even some of the mass-produced statues and holy cards brought into vogue during the nineteenth century have disappeared from the churches. Much of the attention of Catholic theologians is now focused on the search for resolutions to the problems of nuclear war, sexual politics, racism, economic exploitation, and the Third World. Pope John Paul II is deeply devoted to the Virgin and her apparitions. Unfortunately this piety may very well be related to his conservative attitudes on the issues of birth control, sexuality, and women's roles. Some liberation and feminist theologians have attempted to redefine Mary's role in the church.[38] But most of these progressive Catholics are at present more committed to redefining living women's roles than to rehabilitating a symbol weighed down by a heritage of defensive conservatism and male projection. This article suggests that the old saying, 'As Mary goes, so goes the Church,'[39] should be reversed. Rather we have learned: 'As the Church goes, so goes Mary.'

Notes

1 Thomas A. Kselman, *Miracles and Prophecies in Nineteenth-century France* (New Brunswick, N.J.: Rutgers University Press, 1983), p. 28.
2 Michael Marrus, 'Cultures on the Move: Pilgrims and Pilgrimages in Nineteenth-century France,' *Stanford French Review* 1 (1977): 206–212; Eugen Weber, *Peasants into Frenchmen: The Modernization of Rural France, 1870–1914* (Stanford: Stanford University Press, 1976), pp. 332–355.
3 Fatima Mernissi, 'Women, Saints, and Sanctuaries,' *Signs* 3 (1977): 101–112.
4 This is a major theme of Kselman's excellent book.
5 Marrus, 'Cultures on the Move,' pp. 205–206, 218.
6 Lawrence Cunningham, *Mother of God* (New York: Harper and Row, 1982), pp. 67–68.
7 Gerard Cholvy, 'Le Catholicism populaire en France au xixe siècle,' in Bernard Plongeron and Robert Pannet, eds., *Le Christianisme populaire. Les dossiers de l'histoire* (Paris: Centurion, 1976), pp. 201–202.
8 Père Aladel, *The Miraculous Medal*, trans. P. S. (Baltimore: John B. Piet, 1880), p. 71.
9 René Laurentin, *Lourdes. Histoire authentique*, vol. 3 (Paris: Lethielleux, 1962), p. 186, n. 25; René Laurentin and A. Durand, *Pontmain. Histoire authentique*, vol. 3 (Paris: Apostolat des Editions, 1970), p. 38.
10 A jubilee card on the tenth anniversay showed the sins of the world coming out in licks of flames under the serpent. Among the sins were errors, lies, impiety, and

sacrilege. Another card, obviously for young girls, mentioned novels as a specific danger. I viewed these cards and much rare pamphlet literature at the Marian Library, University of Dayton, Dayton, Ohio. I am grateful to Brother William Fackovec for his kind assistance.

11 There is a picture of this scapular in G. LaFoy, 'Le Secret de LaSalette,' *Revue illustré*, October 5, 1908.

12 The actual words were: 'Mais priez, mes enfants. Dieu vous exacera en peu du temps. Mon fils se laisse toucher.'

13 Cunningham, *Mother of God*, p. 71; William McSweeney, *Roman Catholicism: The Search for Relevance* (Oxford: Basil Blackwell, 1980), p. 44.

14 McSweeney, *Roman Catholicism*, pp. 45–47.

15 René Rémond, *The Right Wing in France from 1815 to de Gaulle*, trans. J. Laux (Philadelphia: University of Pennsylvania Press, 1966), pp. 185–186.

16 Judson Mather, '*La Croix* and the Assumptionist Response to Secularization in France, 1870–1900' (Ph.D. diss., University of Michigan, 1971), p. 28.

17 Joseph Grenier, 'To Reach the People: *La Croix*, 1883–1890' (Ph.D. diss., Fordham University, 1976), p. 140.

18 Mather, '*La Croix*,' p. 30.

19 Grenier, 'To Reach the People,' p. 413.

20 For example, Louis Bassette's *Le Fait de la Salette, 1846–1854* (Paris: Cerf, 1965).

21 Edith Turner and Victor Turner, *Image and Pilgrimage in Christian Culture: Anthropological Perspectives* (New York: Columbia University Press, 1978), pp. 154–155.

22 For example, on virginity see John A. Saliba, 'The Virgin-Birth Debate in Anthropological Literature: A Critical Assessment,' *Theological Studies* 36 (1975): 428–454; Joyce E. Salisbury, 'Fruitful in Singleness,' *Journal of Medieval History* 8 (1982): 97–106; Clarissa Atkinson, '"Precious Balsam in a Fragile Glass": The Ideology of Virginity in the Later Middle Ages,' *Journal of Family History* 8 (1983): 131–143; Kirsten Hastrup, 'The Semantics of Biology: Virginity,' in Shirley Ardener, ed., *Defining Females* (New York: John Wiley and Sons, 1978). On motherhood, see especially Erich Neumann, *The Great Mother: An Analysis of the Archetype*, trans. Ralph Manheim (New York: Pantheon, 1955), and the introduction and essays in James J. Preston, ed., *Mother Worship: Themes and Variations* (Chapel Hill: University of North Carolina Press, 1980).

23 Félix-Antoine-Philibert Dupanloup, 'Mandement et Instruction Pastorale de Monseigneur l'Eveque d'Orléans sur l'Immaculée Conception de la Très-Sainte Vierge' (Orleans, 22 Jan. 1855), p. 50.

24 E. de Pressensé, *L'Immaculée Conception. Histoire d'un dogme catholique-romain ou comment l'hérésie devient un dogme* (Paris: Ch. Meyrueis et cie., 1855), p. 16.

25 Giovanni Miegge, *The Virgin Mary: The Roman Catholic Marian Doctrine*, trans. Waldo Smith (Philadelphia: Westminster Press, 1955), pp. 153, 155.

26 Rémond, *The Right Wing*, pp. 185–186.

27 Grenier, 'To Reach the People,' p. 415.

28 Kselman, *Miracles*, pp. 62–79, and Henri Bernard, *Le Pelerinage: Une Response a l'aliénation des malades et infirmes* (Montreal: Oratoire Saint-Joseph du Mont-Royal, 1975).

29 For a recent description see Patrick Marnham, *Lourdes: A Modern Pilgrimage* (New York: Coward, McCann and Geoghegan, 1980).

30 This is a major thesis of Miegge's book. See especially chapter 7, 'The Compassionate Mother,' and 'Conclusion: Mary in Dogma and Devotion.'

31 Bonnie G. Smith, *Ladies of the Leisure Class: The Bourgeoises of Northern France in the Nineteenth Century* (Princeton: Princeton University Press, 1981), pp. 109–110; Aladel, *The Miraculous Medal*, pp. 272–273.

32 Leonard W. Moss and Stephen C. Cappannari, 'In Quest of the Black Virgin: She Is Black Because She Is Black,' in Preston, *Mother Worship*, pp. 53–72.

33 Bassette, *Le Fait de la Salette*, pp. 132–144 and Abbé Rousselot, *Manuel du pèlerin a Notre-Dame de la Salette* (Grenoble, 1848).

34 Victor Branick, 'Mary: Model of the Charismatic as Seen in Acts 1–2, Luke 1–2, and John,' in Branick, ed., *Mary, the Spirit of the Church* (Ramsey, N.J.: Paulist Press, 1980), pp. 28–43.

35 This is liberation theology's recent interpretation of the Gospel of Luke, which presents Mary as praising God for the divine favor he has shown her and for the new revolutionary order that her cooperation in redemption will help make possible. See, for example, Rosemary Radford Ruether, *Sexism and God-Talk* (Boston: Beacon Press, 1983), p. 153, and Robert M. Brown, *Theology in a New Key: Responding to Liberation Themes* (Philadelphia: Westminster Press, 1978), pp. 98–100.
36 'The Blue Army of Our Lady,' *The Marian Era* (1965), VI, pp. 47ff.
37 See Joseph A. Pelletier, *Our Lady Comes to Garabandal* (Worcester, Mass.: Assumptionist Press, 1971), and 'Faithful Reproductions: The Miraculous Photos of Bayside,' *Boston Phoenix*, November 10, 1981.
38 See notes 34 and 35.
39 Turner and Turner, *Image and Pilgrimage*, p. 171.

POLITICS

Introduction

Politics is the conventional subject matter of history and, as such, has been most marked by the 'great men' school of writing. Biographies, political memoirs, accounts of wars, cabinet meetings and diplomatic incidents documented an area of life in which it was assumed that, until very recently, women had no part and gender no relevance. Even the rise of social history in the 1960s and 1970s, with its burgeoning interest in 'low politics', did little to change the situation. Labour history became identified with the history of trade unions and socialist parties and, even though it was broadly associated with the political left, historians from across the political spectrum proved very resistant to gender analysis when, they claimed, women simply were not there. For historians working before the modern period, the problem was exaggerated by the elite nature of political activity. Not only were women excluded, apart from the richest and the most royal, but so too were most men.

Some work, of course, was done. The participation of men and women in popular protest – notably but not exclusively bread riots – in both early modern and modern Europe was well documented. Such actions, often reviled by contemporaries as violent and unfeminine, reflected women's role as providers and household managers, as well as their involvement, at least as customers, in local markets. It is, however, hard to disentangle immediate economic motives from wider political ones in explaining female involvement in rioting, although women, like children, retained a strong symbolic status when complaining about poverty and the absence of food.[1]

Natalie Zemon Davis's 'Women on Top', which begins this Section, is a classic study of festive rituals and popular protest in early modern France. She illustrates the use of a gendered discourse to sanction riot and popular disturbance and, in her examination of language and symbolism, foreshadows an approach to political history which gender historians were to find extremely fruitful. If the study of gender and politics were not to confine itself to exceptional movements, such as feminist groups or the British Suffragettes, and, largely, to the twentieth century, the language of politics had to be examined. For the period since 1789 this has really crystallized around the discourse of citizenship, as suggested in the essay by Siân Reynolds reproduced below.

The French Revolution was among the first 'great events' to be re-evaluated by gender historians. Much early work was dedicated to recovering the presence of women in the events which shook France from 1789. Despite a famous complaint that no-one's understanding of the Revolution was changed by knowing that women were involved in it, it soon became apparent that, during true revolutionary moments, when everything was in flux and there was no clear sense as to the society or polity which might emerge, the dispossessed and invisible could stake a claim in the revolution's outcome. Yet, women's presence, even more than that of the poor, often served to confirm rather than advance the limits of revolutionary activity and ideology. As revolutionary gains became institutionalized, so women took less and less part in them.[2] The French Revolution provided modern Europe with abiding notions of popular sovereignty, the rights of man and 'universal' citizenship. Yet, as Reynolds shows, the Republican tradition that developed in post-Revolutionary France was deliberately and self-consciously masculine: both citizenship and political office were reserved for the Revolution's male heirs.

Political systems subject to evolutionary rather than revolutionary change were not immune from these debates. The Chartist movement in Britain, for example, showed how both men and women were concerned as to how citizenship should be defined, even though Chartism came to be dominated by men and a masculine discourse (see pp. 10–11 of the Introduction). Similarly, studies of left-wing politics in the later nineteenth and early twentieth centuries mapped both the impact of explicitly feminist ideologies and the resilient male dominance of both socialist and anarchist groups, though far less work was done on how and why certain political creeds appealed specifically to men *as men*.[3] The implicit assumption of a male political norm was still far too easy.

Although no European women won the vote before the First World War and many were subject to the paternalist view of the 'head of the family' laid down in the Napoleonic law code, they were still, of course, political subjects. Full citizenship was usually reserved to men, but women had both a civic role and civic duties while individuals of both sexes held political opinions. Such opinions were often informed by religious conviction and, in the area of moral campaigning, women were often welcomed, essentially because of the greater moral strength and religious virtue widely attributed to them. Throughout nineteenth-century Europe, articulate middle-class women complemented philanthropic work by campaigning against slavery, for prison or hospital reform, in favour of the redemption of prostitutes or the better care of orphans and the mentally infirm. As such women became involved in organized, structured campaigns, so they influenced the strategies and goals adopted by established pressure groups, often fundamentally changing their nature.[4]

Such female involvement in political campaigns was part of a wider development taking place in modern Europe, which was the creation and designation of a space known simply as 'the social'. Like the women philanthropists themselves, those concerns designated 'social' crossed public and private boundaries, and this idea of an intermediate, female-dominated area may prove a rewarding way to reconfigure ideas of 'separate spheres'. Education and family policy joined a burgeoning list of social concerns, which, as Koven and Michel's article in this Section shows, contributed directly to the changing ideas of the role of the state being formulated in twentieth-century Europe. The development of the welfare state drew directly on women's political experience, both in their active role as campaigners and expertise as social workers, and in their creation of a distinct sociopolitical agenda. A wide body of work now exists on this topic, which, in its consideration of the role and nature of the state, directly addresses a central concern of political historians and state theorists.[5]

The association between women and the social persisted after European adults had been given full and equal electoral rights, in part because of the various ways in which women's claims to political rights were legitimated. While the feminist claim to equality posited on a belief in human rather than manhood rights was particularly strong in the Anglo-American world, women in other traditions claimed a unique expertise, generally on the basis of their status as mothers. Perhaps strongest among conservative women and in Catholic cultures, ideas of maternalism provided a distinct validation for female suffrage and helped to maintain an identification between women and 'the social' which has persisted during the broadening of full democratic rights which has taken place among both sexes and throughout western Europe since the end of the Second World War.[6]

Notes

1 See E. P. Thompson, 'The Moral Economy of the English Crowd in the Eighteenth Century', *Past and Present* 50 (1971), pp. 76–136; John Bohstedt, 'Gender, Household and Community Politics: Women in English Riots 1790–1810', *Past and Present* 120 (1988), pp. 88–122; and Thompson's reply to Bohstedt in his *Customs in Common* (London, 1991), ch. 5.

2 Joan B. Landes, *Women and the Public Sphere in the Age of the French Revolution* (Ithaca, NY, and London, 1988); William H. Sewell Jr, '*Le citoyen/la citoyenne*: Activity, Passivity and the Revolutionary Concept of Citizenship' in Colin Lucas (ed.), *The French Revolution and the Creation of Modern Political Culture* (2 vols.: Oxford, 1988), II, pp. 105–21; Olwen Hufton, *Women and the Limits of Citizenship in the French Revolution* (Toronto, 1992). There are comparable analyses for later European revolutions, notably Russia 1917 and Spain 1936: cf. Beryl Williams, 'Kollontai and After: Women in the Russian Revolution' in Siân Reynolds (ed.), *Women, State and Revolution* (Brighton, 1986), pp. 60–80; Frances Lannon, 'Women and Images of Woman in the Spanish Civil War', *Transactions of the Royal Historical Society* (Sixth Series: 1991), pp. 213–28 and Mary Nash, *Defying Male Civilization: Women in the Spanish Civil War* (Denver, CO, 1996).

3 See Barbara Taylor, *Eve and the New Jerusalem: Socialism and Feminism in the Nineteenth Century* (London, 1983); Charles Sowerwine, *Sisters or Citizens? Women and Socialism in France since 1876* (Cambridge, 1982); Karen Offen, 'Defining Feminism: A Comparative Historical Approach' repr. in Gisela Bock and Susan James (eds), *Beyond Equality and Difference: Citizenship, Feminist Politics and Female Subjectivity* (London and New York, 1992); Martha Acklesberg, *Free Women of Spain: Anarchism and the Struggle for Women's Emancipation* (Bloomington, IN, 1991). Jon Lawrence, 'Class and Gender in the Making of Urban Toryism, 1880–1914', *English Historical Review* 100 (1993), pp. 629–52 looks specifically at appeals to men.

4 Clare Midgley, *Women against Slavery: The British Campaigns, 1780–1870* (London, 1992).

5 Denise Riley, *'Am I That Name?'* (London, 1988), ch. 3; Seth Koven and Sonya Michel (eds), *Mothers of a New World: Maternalist Politics and the Origins of Welfare States* (London and New York, 1993); Gisela Bock and Pat Thane (eds), *Maternity and Gender Politics: Women and the Rise of the European Welfare States 1880s–1950s* (London and New York, 1991); Theda Skocpol, *Protecting Soldiers and Mothers: The Political Origins of Social Policy in the United States* (Cambridge, MA, and London, 1992).

6 Susan Pedersen, *Family, Dependence and the Origins of the Welfare State: Britain and France 1914–45* (Cambridge, 1993); Mary Vincent, 'The Politicisation of Catholic Women in Salamanca, 1931–6' in Frances Lannon and Paul Preston (eds), *Elites and Power in Twentieth-Century Spain* (Oxford, 1990), pp. 107–26. Post-war political behaviour by women and men has been extensively studied: see further Bock and James, *Beyond Equality and Difference*.

12
Women on top
NATALIE ZEMON DAVIS

I

The female sex was thought the disorderly one par excellence in early modern Europe. '*Une beste imparfaicte,*' went one adage, '*sans foy, sans loy, sans craincte, sans constance.*' Female disorderliness was already seen in the Garden of Eden, when Eve had been the first to yield to the serpent's temptation and incite Adam to disobey the Lord. To be sure, the men of the lower orders were also believed to be especially prone to riot and seditious unrest. But the defects of the males were thought to stem not so much from nature as from nurture: the ignorance in which they were reared, the brutish quality of life and conversation in the peasant's hut or the artisan's shop, and their poverty, which led to envy.[1]

With the women the disorderliness was founded in physiology. As every physician knew in the sixteenth century, the female was composed of cold and wet humors (the male was hot and dry), and coldness and wetness meant a changeable, deceptive, and tricky temperament. Her womb was like a hungry animal; when not amply fed by sexual intercourse or reproduction, it was likely to wander about her body, overpowering her speech and senses. If the Virgin Mary was free of such a weakness, it was because she was the blessed vessel of the Lord. But no other woman had been immaculately conceived, and even the well-born lady could fall victim to a fit of the 'mother,' as the uterus was called. The male might suffer from retained sexual juices, too, but (as Doctor François Rabelais pointed out) he had the wit and will to control his fiery urges by work, wine, or study. The female just became hysterical. In the late seventeenth century, when vanguard physicians were abandoning humoral theories of personality in favor of more mechanistic notions of 'animal spirits' and were beginning to remark that men suffered from emotional ills curiously like hysteria, they still maintained that the female's mind was more prone to be disordered by her fragile and unsteady temperament. Long before Europeans were asserting flatly that the 'inferiority' of black Africans was innate, rather than the result, say, of climate, they were attributing female 'inferiority' to nature.[2]

The lower ruled the higher within the woman, then, and if she were given her way, she would want to rule over those above her outside. Her disorderliness led her into the evil arts of witchcraft, so ecclesiastical authorities claimed; and when she was embarked on some behavior for which her allegedly weak intellect disqualified her, such as theological speculation or preaching, that was blamed on her disorderliness, too. The rule of a queen was impossible in France by the Salic law, and mocked by the common proverb '*tomber en quenouille*.' For Pastor John Knox it was a 'monstrous regimen,' 'the subversion of good order . . . all equitie and justice,' whereas the more moderate Calvin 'reckoned it among the visitations of God's anger,' but one that should be borne, like any tyranny, with patience. Even a contemporary defender of queenship, John Aylmer, still had to admit that when he thought of the willfulness of women, he favored a strong role for Parliament. As late as 1742, in the face of entomological evidence to the contrary, some apiologists pretended that nature required the rule of a King Bee.[3]

What were the proposed remedies for female unruliness? Religious training that fashioned the reins of modesty and humility; selective education that showed a woman her moral duty without enflaming her undisciplined imagination or loosing her tongue for public talk; honest work that busied her hands; and laws and constraints that made her subject to her husband.[4]

In some ways, that subjection was gradually deepening from the sixteenth to the eighteenth centuries as the patriarchal family streamlined itself for more efficient property acquisition, social mobility, and preservation of the line, and as progress in state-building and the extension of commercial capitalism were achieved at a cost in human autonomy. By the eighteenth century, married women in France and England had largely lost what independent legal personality they had formerly had, and they had less legal right to make decisions on their own about their dowries and possessions than at an earlier period. Propertied women were involved less and less in local and regional political assemblies. Working women in prosperous families were beginning to withdraw from productive labor; those in poor families were increasingly filling the most ill-paid positions of wage labor. This is not to say that females had no informal access to power or continuing vital role in the economy in these centuries; but the character of those relations was in conflict.[5]

Which side of the conflict was helped by the disorderly woman? Since this image was so often used as an excuse for the subjection of women, it is not surprising to find it opposed by one strain in early feminist thought, which argued that women were *not* by nature more unruly, disobedient, and fickle than men. If anything it was the other way around. 'By nature, women be sober,' said the poet Christine de Pisan, 'and those that be not, they go out of kind.' Women are by nature more modest and shamefaced than men, claimed a male feminist, which is demonstrated by the fact that women's privy parts are totally covered with pubic hair and are not handled by women the way men's are when they urinate. Why, then, did some men maintain that women were disorderly by nature? Because they were misogynists – vindictive, envious, or themselves dissolute.[6]

These claims and counterclaims about sexual temperament raise questions not merely about the actual character of male and female behavior in preindustrial Europe, but also about the varied uses of sexual symbolism. Sexual symbolism, of course, is always available to make statements about social experience and to reflect (or conceal) contradictions within it. At the end of the Middle Ages and in early modern Europe, the relation of the wife – of the potentially disorderly woman – to her husband was especially useful for expressing the relation of all subordinates to their superiors, and this for two reasons. First, economic relations were still often perceived in the medieval way as a matter of service. Second, the nature of political rule and the newer problem of sovereignty were very much at issue. In the little world of the family, with its conspicuous tension between intimacy and power, the larger matters of political and social order could find ready symbolization.

Thus, Jean Calvin, himself a collapser of ecclesiastical hierarchies, saw the subjection of the wife to the husband as a guarantee of the subjection of both of them to the authority of the Lord. Kings and political theorists saw the increasing legal subjection of wives to their husbands (and of children to their parents) as a guarantee of the obedience of both men and women to the slowly centralizing state – a training for the loyal subject of seventeenth-century France or for the dutiful citizen of seventeenth-century England. 'Marriages are the seminaries of States,' began the preamble to the French ordinance strengthening paternal power within the family. For John Locke, opponent of despotic rule in commonwealth and in marriage, the wife's relinquishing her right of decision to her husband as 'naturally . . . the abler and stronger' was analogous to the individual's relinquishing his natural liberties of decision and action to the legislative branch of government.[7]

Indeed, how could one separate the idea of subordination from the existence of the sexes? Gabriel de Foigny's remarkable fictitious land of Australie (1673), a utopia of hermaphrodites, shows how close the link between the two was perceived to be. The Australian, in whom the sexes were one, could not understand how a conflict of wills could be avoided within the 'mutual possession' of European marriage. The French traveler answered that it was simple, for mother and child were both subject to the father. The hermaphrodite, horrified at such a violation of the total autonomy that was the sign of complete true 'men,' dismissed the European pattern as bestial.[8]

The female's position was used to symbolize not only hierarchical subordination but also violence and chaos. Bruegel's terrifying *Dulle Griet*, painted during the occupation of the Netherlands by Spanish soldiers, makes a huge, armed, unseeing woman, Mad Meg, the emblem of fiery destruction, of brutal oppression and disorder. Bruegel's painting cuts in more than one way, however, and shows how female disorderliness – the female out of her place – could be assigned another value. Next to Mad Meg is a small woman in white on top of a male monster; it is Saint Margaret of Antioch tying up the devil. Nearby other armed women are beating grotesque animals from Hell.[9]

Bruegel's Margarets are by no means alone in preindustrial Europe. In hierarchical and conflictful societies that loved to reflect on the world-turned-upside-down, the *topos* of the woman-on-top was one of the most enjoyed. Indeed, sexual inversion – that is, switches in sex roles – was a widespread form of cultural play in literature, in art, and in festivity. Sometimes the reversal involved dressing and masking as a member of the opposite sex – the prohibitions of Deuteronomy 22, Saint Paul, Saint Jerome, canon law, and Jean Calvin notwithstanding.[10] Sometimes the reversal involved simply taking on certain roles or forms of behavior characteristic of the opposite sex. Women played men; men played women; men played women who were playing men.

It is the uses of sexual inversion, and more particularly of play with the image of the unruly woman in literature, in popular festivity, and in ordinary life, that will be the subject of the rest of this essay. Evidently, the primary impulse behind such inversion in early modern Europe was not homosexuality or disturbed gender identity. Although Henri III expressed special wishes of his own when he and his male 'mignons' masked as Amazons in the 1570s, and although the seventeenth-century Abbé de Choisy, whose mother had dressed him as a girl through adolescence, had special reasons for using a woman's name and wearing female clothes until he was thirty-three,[11] still most literary and festive transvestism at this time had a wider psychosexual and cultural significance than this.

Anthropologists offer several suggestions about the functions of magical transvestism and ritual inversion of sex roles. First, sexual disguise can ward off danger from demons, malignant fairies, or other powers that threaten castration or defloration. Second, transvestism and sexual reversal can be part of adolescent rites of passage, either to suggest the marginality of the transitional state (as when a male initiate is likened to a menstruating woman) or to allow each sex to obtain something of the other's power (as in certain initiation and marriage customs in early Greece). Third, exchange of sex can be part of what Victor Turner has called 'rituals of status reversal,' as when women in certain parts of Africa usurp the clothing, weapons, or tasks of the superior males and behave in lewd ways to increase the chance for a good harvest or to turn aside an impending natural catastrophe. Finally, as James Peacock has pointed out, the transvestite actor, priest, or shaman can symbolize categories of cosmological or social organization. For instance, in Java the transvestite actor reinforces by his irregularity the importance of the categories high/low, male/female.

However diverse these uses of sexual inversion, anthropologists generally agree that they, like other rites and ceremonies of reversal, are ultimately sources of order and stability in a hierarchical society. They can clarify the structure by the process of reversing it. They can provide an expression of, and a safety valve for, conflicts within the system. They can correct and relieve the system when it has become authoritarian. But, so it is argued, they do not question the basic order of the society itself. They can renew the system, but they cannot change it.[12]

Historians of early modern Europe are likely to find inversions and reversals less in prescribed rites than in carnivals and festivities. Their fools are likely to escape the bounds of ceremony,[13] and their store of literary sources for inversion will include not only the traditional tales of magical transformation in sex, but also a variety of stories in which men and women *choose* to change their sexual status. In addition, there are comic conventions and genres, such as the picaresque, that allow much play with sexual roles. These new forms offered increased occasions and ways in which topsy-turvy could be used for explicit criticism of the social order. Nevertheless, students of these festive and literary forms have ordinarily come to the same conclusion as anthropologists regarding the limits of symbolic inversion: a world-turned-upside-down can only be righted, not changed. To quote Ian Donaldson's recent study *Comedy from Jonson to Fielding*: 'The lunatic governor . . . , the incompetent judge, the mock doctor, the equivocating priest, the hen-pecked husband: such are the familiar and recurrent figures in the comedy of a society which gives a general assent to the necessity of entrusting power to its governors, judges, doctors, priests, and husbands.'[14]

I would like to argue, on the contrary, that comic and festive inversion could *undermine* as well as reinforce that assent through its connections with everyday circumstances outside the privileged time of carnival and stage-play. Somewhat in contradistinction to Christine de Pisan and the gallant school of feminists, I want to argue that the image of the disorderly woman did not always function to keep women in their place. On the contrary, it was a multivalent image that could operate, first, to widen behavioral options for women within and even outside marriage, and, second, to sanction riot and political disobedience for both men and women in a society that allowed the lower orders few formal means of protest. Play with the unruly woman is partly a chance for temporary release from the traditional and stable hierarchy; but it is also part of the conflict over efforts to change the basic distribution of power within society. The woman-on-top might even facilitate innovation in historical theory and political behavior.

II

Let us begin with a review of the major types of sexual inversion we find in literary sources – sources sober and comic, learned and popular. Then we will consider the disorderly woman in more detail. What kinds of license were allowed through this turnabout? First of all, we have stories of men who dress as women to save themselves from an enemy or from execution, to sneak into the opponent's military camp, or to get into a nunnery or women's quarters for purposes of seduction. In all of these cases, the disguise is not merely practical but exploits the expected physical frailty of women to prevent harm to the male or to disarm his victim. A more honorable trickery is ventured by Pyrocles in Sidney's *Arcadia*, by Marston's Antonio, and by d'Urfé's Céladon, for they dress as brave Amazons or as a Druid priestess in order to have access to the women they wish to woo. Here no more than in the first case does the inversion lead to criticism of social hierarchy. Rather Pyrocles is rebuked by his friend for 'his effeminate love of a woman,' for letting his 'sensual weakness' rebel against his manly reason.

Only with the male fool or clown do we find literary examples of male transvestism serving to challenge order. In the seventeenth-century *commedia dell'arte*, a black-faced Harlequin dolls himself up as a ridiculous Diana, goddess of the chase, replete with crescent-moon ruff, fancy clothes, and a little bow. The result is so absurd that not only are boundaries between high and low effaced, but, as William Willeford has suggested, reality itself seems to dissolve.[15]

The stories, theater, and pictorial illustration of preindustrial Europe offer many more examples of women trying to act like men than vice versa, and more of the time the sexual inversion yields criticism of the established order. One set of reversals portrays women going beyond what can ordinarily be expected of a mere female; that is, it shows women ruling the lower in themselves and thus deserving to be like men. We have, for instance, tales of female saints of the early Church who lived chastely as male monks to the end of their lives, braving false charges of fathering children and withstanding other tests along the way. Five of these transvestite ladies appear in Voragine's *Golden Legend*, which had wide circulation in manuscript and printed editions in both Latin and the vernacular.[16]

Other uncommon women changed their roles in order to defend established rule or values associated with it. Disguised as men, they prove fidelity to lovers whom they wish to marry or, as in the case of Madame Ginevra in Boccaccio's tale, prove their chastity to doubting husbands. Disguised as men, they leave Jewish fathers for Christian husbands and plead for Christian mercy over base Jewish legalism. Disguised as men, they rescue spouses from prison and the family honor from stain. For example, in *The French Amazon*, one of Mademoiselle l'Héritier's reworkings of an old French tale, the heroine maintains her father's connections with the court by fighting in the place of her slain and rather incompetent twin brother. She, of course, ultimately marries the prince. Along with Spenser's Britomart, Tasso's Clorinda, and others, the French Amazon is one of a line of noble women warriors, virtuous viragos all, magnanimous, brave, and chaste.[17]

To what extent could such embodiments of order serve to censure accepted hierarchy? They might reprove by their example the cowardice and wantonness of ordinary men and women. But they used their power to support a legitimate cause, not to unmask the truth about social relationships. By showing the good that could be done by the woman out of her place, they had the potential to inspire a few females to exceptional action and feminists to reflection about the capacities of women (we will see later whether that potential was realized), but they are unlikely symbols for moving masses of people to resistance.

It is otherwise with comic play with the disorderly woman, that is, inversion that can be expected of the female, who gives rein to the lower in herself and seeks rule over her superiors. Some portraits of her are so ferocious (such as Spenser's cruel Radagunde and other vicious viragos) that they preclude the possibility of fanciful release from, or criticism of, hierarchy. It is the same with those tales, considered humorous at the time, that depict a savage taming of the shrew, as in the fabliau of *La Dame escoillée*, where the domineering lady is given a counterfeit but painful 'castration' by her son-in-law, and in the sixteenth-century German cartoon strip *The Ninefold Skins of a Shrewish Woman*, which are stripped off one by one by various punishments. The legend of the medieval Pope Joan also has limited potential for mocking established order. As told by Boccaccio, it is a hybrid of the transvestite saint and the cruelly tamed shrew: Joan wins the papacy by her wits and good behavior, but her illicit power goes to her head, or rather to her womb. She becomes pregnant, gives birth during a procession, and dies wretchedly in the cardinals' dungeon.[18]

There are a host of situations, however, in which the unruly woman is assigned more ambiguous meanings. For our purposes we can sort out three ways in which the multivalent image is used. First, there is a rich treatment of women who are happily given over to the sway of their bodily senses or who are using every ruse they can to prevail over men. There is the wife of Bath, of course, who celebrates her sexual instrument and outlives her five husbands. And Rabelais' Gargamelle – a giant of a woman, joyously and frequently coupling, eating bushels of tripe, quaffing wine, joking obscenely, giving birth in a grotesque fecal explosion from which her son Gargantua somersaults shouting 'Drink, drink.' Then the clever and powerful wife of the *Quinze joies de mariage* – cuckolding her husband and foiling his every effort to find her out, wheedling fancy clothes out of him, beating him up, and finally locking him in his room. Also Grimmelshausen's Libuschka, alias Courage, one of a series of picaresque heroines – fighting in the army in soldier's clothes; ruling her many husbands and lovers; paying them back a hundredfold when they take revenge or betray her; whoring, tricking, and trading to survive or get rich. Husband-dominators are everywhere in popular literature, nicknamed among the Germans St. Cudgelman (Sankt Kolbmann) or Doktor Siemann (she-man). The point about such portraits is that they are funny and amoral: the women are full of life and energy, and they win much of the time; they stay on top of their fortune with as much success as Machiavelli might have expected for the Prince of his political tract.[19]

A second comic treatment of the woman out of her place allows her a temporary period of dominion, which is ended only after she has said or done something to undermine authority or denounce its abuse. When the Silent Wife begins to talk and order her husband about in Ben Jonson's *Epicoene*, she points out that women cannot be mere statues or puppets and that what her husband calls 'Amazonian' impudence in her is simply reasonable decorum. When the Woman-Captain of Shadwell's comedy puts aside her masculine garb and the sword with which she has hectored her jealous and stingy old husband, she does so only after having won separate maintenance and £400 a year. The moral of the play is that husbands must not move beyond the law to tyranny. In *As You Like It*, the love-struck Rosalind, her tongue loosed by her male apparel and her 'holiday humor,' warns Orlando that there is a limit to the possession he will have over a wife, a limit set by her desires, her wit, and her tongue. Though she later gives herself to Orlando in marriage, her saucy counsel cannot be erased from the real history of the courtship.

The most popular comic example of the female's temporary rule, however, is Phyllis riding Aristotle, a motif recurring in stories, paintings, and household objects from the thirteenth through the seventeenth centuries. Here Aristotle admonishes his pupil Alexander for his excessive attention to a certain Phyllis, one of his new subjects in India. The beautiful Phyllis gets revenge before Alexander's eyes by coquettishly persuading the old philosopher to get down on all fours and, saddled and bridled, carry her through the garden. Here youth overthrows age, and sexual passion, dry sterile philosophy; nature surmounts reason, and the female, the male.[20]

Phyllis' ambiguous ride brings us to a third way of presenting the woman-on-top, that is, where the license to be a social critic is conferred on her directly. Erhard Schoen's woodcuts (early sixteenth century) portray huge women distributing fools' caps to men. This is what happens when women are given the upper hand; and yet in some sense the men deserve it. Erasmus' female Folly is the supreme example of this *topos*. Stultitia tells the truth about the foibles of all classes and defends the higher folly of the Cross, even though paradoxically she's just a foolish gabbling woman herself.[21]

These varied images of sexual topsy-turvy – from the transvestite male escaping responsibility and harm to the transvestite fool and the unruly woman unmasking the truth – were available to city people who went to the theater and to people who could read and afford books. They were also familiar to the lower orders more generally in both town and country through books that were read aloud and through stories, poems, proverbs, and broadsheets.[22]

In addition, popular festivals and customs, hard though they are to document, show much play with switches in sex roles and much attention to women-on-top. In examining these data, we will notice that sexual inversion in popular festivity differs from that in literature in two ways. Whereas the purely ritual and/or magical element in sexual inversion was present in literature to only a small degree, it assumed more importance in the popular festivities, along with the carnivalesque functions of mocking and unmasking the truth. Whereas sexual inversion in literary and pictorial play more often involved the female taking on the male role or dressing as a man, the festive inversion more often involved the male taking on the role or garb of the woman, that is, the unruly woman – though this asymmetry may not have existed several centuries earlier.

The ritual and/or magical functions of sexual inversion were filled in almost all cases by males disguised as grotesque cavorting females. In sections of Germany and Austria, at carnival time male runners, half of them masked as female, half as male, jumped and leaped through the streets. In France it was on St. Stephen's Day or New Year's Day that men dressed as wild beasts or as women and jumped and danced in public (or at least such was the case in the Middle Ages). The saturnalian Feast of Fools, which decorous doctors of theology and prelates were trying to ban from the French cathedrals in the fifteenth and sixteenth centuries, involved both young clerics and laymen, some of them disguised as females, who made wanton and loose gestures. In parts of the Pyrénées at Candlemas (February 2), a Bear Chase took place involving a lustful bear, costumed hunters, and young men dressed as women and often called Rosetta. After an amorous interlude with Rosetta, the bear was killed, revived, shaved, and killed again.[23]

In England, too, in Henry VIII's time, during the reign of the Boy Bishop after Christmas some of the male children taken from house to house were dressed as females rather than as priests or bishops. The most important English examples of the male as grotesque female, however, were the Bessy and Maid Marian. In the northern counties, a Fool-Plough was dragged about the countryside, often on the first Monday after Epiphany, by men dressed in white shirts. Sword dances were done by some of them, while old Bessy and her fur-clad Fool capered around and tried to collect from the spectators. Maid Marian presided with Robin Hood over the May games. If in this capacity she was sometimes a real female and sometimes a disguised male, when it came to the Morris Dance with Robin, the Hobby Horse, the dragon, and the rest, the Marian was a man. Here again the Maid's gestures or costume might be licentious.[24]

All interpreters of this transvestism see it, like the African example mentioned earlier, as a fertility rite – biological or agricultural[25] – embedded into festivities that may have had other meanings as well. In the European context the use of the female garb was especially appropriate, for it drew not merely on the inevitable association of the female with reproduction, but on the contemporary definition of the female as the lustier sex. Did it also draw on other features of sexual symbolism in early modern Europe, e.g. the relation of the subordinate to the superior? Did it (as with our transvestite Harlequin of the *commedia dell'arte*) suggest to peasants or city folk the blurring or reversing of social boundaries? Perhaps. When we see the roles that the woman-on-top was later to play, it is hard to believe that some such effect was not stimulated by these rites. In the urban Feast of Fools, in any case, the fertility function of the transvestism was already overshadowed by its carnivalesque derision of the celibate priestly hierarchy.

Along with these instances of festive male transvestism, we have some scanty evidence of a more symmetrical switch. During the Twelve Days of Christmas or on Epiphany, mummers and guisers in northern England, the Scottish Lowlands, and northern France might include men *and* women wearing the clothes of the opposite sex. At Fastnacht in fifteenth-century Nuremberg men dressed as women and women as men, and the same was the case at Shrovetide in sixteenth-century England and perhaps at Mardi Gras in early modern France. Possibly here too there is some old relation to fertility rites, but the exchange may well be connected with the more flexible license of carnivalesque inversion. At least in the case of 'goose-dancing' at Eastertime on the Scilly Islands in the mid-eighteenth century, we know the license was used to tell the truth: 'the maidens are dressed up for young men and the young men for maidens: thus disguised they visit their neighbours in companies, where they dance, and make jokes upon what has happened on the island; when everyone is humorously told their own without offense being taken.'[26]

The truth-telling of Europe's male festive societies was much less gentle than that of the Scilly geese. These organizations were the Kingdoms and Abbeys of Misrule.[27] (In England and Scotland we have Lords of Misrule and Abbots of Unreason, though the exact character of their bands remains to be studied.) Among other roles in town and countryside, the Abbeys expressed the community's interest in marriages and their outcome much more overtly than the cavorting Bessy or Rosetta. In noisy masked demonstrations – charivaris, scampanate, katzenmusik, cencerrada, rough music, and the like – they mocked newlyweds who had not produced a baby soon enough and people marrying for the second time, especially when there was a gross disparity in age between bride and groom. Indeed, any local scandal might be made the target for their pots, tambourines, bells, and horns.

The unruly woman appeared in the Abbey's plays in two forms. First as officers of Misrule. In rural areas, these were usually called Lords and Abbots; in the French cities, however, they took all kinds of pompous titles. Among these dignitaries were Princesses and Dames and especially Mothers: we find Mère Folle in Dijon, Langres, and Chalon-sur-Saône; Mère Sotte in Paris and Compiègne; and Mère d'Enfance in Bordeaux. In Wales, though I know of no female festive titles, the men who conducted the *ceffyl pren*, as the local rough music was called, blackened their faces and wore women's garb.[28] In all of this there was a double irony: the young villager who became an Abbot, the artisan who became a Prince directly adopted for their Misrule a symbol of licit power; the power invoked by the man who became Mère Folle, however, was already in defiance of natural order – a dangerous and vital power, which his disguise made safe for him to assume.

The unruly woman not only directed some of the male festive organizations; she was sometimes their butt. The village scold or the domineering wife might be ducked in the pond or pulled through the streets muzzled or branked or in a creel.[29] City people from the fifteenth to the eighteenth centuries were even more concerned about husband-beating, and the beaten *man* (or a neighbor playing his part) was paraded through the streets backward on an ass by noisy revelers. In the English Midlands the ride was known as a Skimmington or a Skimmety, perhaps from the big skimming ladle sometimes used by women in beating their husbands. In northern England and Scotland, the victim or his stand-in 'rode the stang' (a long hobbyhorse), and a like steed was used in the *ceffyl pren* in Wales. In some towns, effigies of the offending couple were promenaded. In others, the festive organization mounted floats to display the actual circumstances of the monstrous beating: the wives were shown hitting their husbands with distaffs, tripe, sticks, trenchers, water pots; throwing stones at them; pulling their beards; or kicking them in the genitalia.[30]

With these last dramatizations, the Misrule Abbeys introduced ambiguities into the treatment of the woman-on-top, just as we have seen in the comic literature. The unruly woman on the float was shameful, outrageous; she was also vigorous and in command. The mockery turned against her martyred husband. And the message of the urban carnival was mixed: it both exhorted the henpecked husband to take command and invited the unruly woman to keep up the fight.

Real women in early modern Europe had less chance than men to initiate or take part in their *own* festivals of inversion. To be sure, a female fool named Mathurine flourished at the courts of Henri IV and Louis XIII and, dressed as an Amazon, commented on political and religious matters; but there is no sign of festive organizations for young women. Confraternities for young unmarried women, where they existed at all, stayed close to religious devotion. Queens were elected for special occasions, such as Twelfth Night or Harvest, but their rule was gentle and tame. The young May queens in their flowers and white ribbons begged for money for dowries or for the Virgin's altar, promising a mere kiss in return. Some May customs that were still current in early modern Europe, however, point back to a rowdier role for women. In rural Franche-Comté during May, wives could take revenge on their husbands for beating them by ducking the men or making them ride an ass; wives could dance, jump, and banquet freely without permission from their husbands; and women's courts issued mock decrees. (In nearby Dijon by the sixteenth century, interestingly enough,

Mère Folle and her Infanterie had usurped this revenge from the women; May was the one month of the year when the Misrule Abbey would chari-vari a man who had beaten his wife.) Generally, May – Flora's month in Roman times – was thought to be a period in which women were powerful, their desires at their most immoderate. As the old saying went, a May bride would keep her husband in yoke all year round. And in fact marriages were not frequent in May.[31]

In Nuremberg it was at carnival time that women may have assumed some kind of special license in the sixteenth and seventeenth centuries. Illus-trated proclamations in joking pompous language granted every female with 'a wretched dissolute husband' the right to deny him his freedom and to beat him till 'his asshole [was] roaring.' Another decree, issued by Foem-inarius, the Hereditary Steward of Quarrel and Dispute Valley, gave three years of Privileges to the suffering Company of Wives so that they might rule their husbands: they could bear arms, elect their own mayor, and go out and entertain as they wished while their spouses could buy nothing or drink no wine or beer without the wives' permission. And, of course, the men did all the housework and welcomed any bastards that the wives might bear.[32]

III

The relationship between real marriages and May license, between real preg-nancy and Fastnacht games returns us to the question posed earlier in this paper. What were the overall functions of these festive and literary inversions in sex roles? Clearly they filled in part the role attributed to them by anthro-pologists and historians of literature: they afforded an expression of, and an outlet for, conflicts about authority within the system; and they also provided occasions by which the authoritarian current in family, workshop, and polit-ical life could be moderated by the laughter of disorder and paradoxical play. Accordingly, they served to reinforce hierarchical structure.

Indeed, in the early modern period, up to the late eighteenth century, the patriarchal family is not challenged as such even by the most searching critics of relations between the sexes. The late seventeenth-century feminists François Poullain de La Barre and Mary Astell believed the submission of the wife to her husband not to be justified by any natural inferiority of females, but to be necessary nonetheless. As Astell said, 'There can be [no] Society great or little, from Empires down to private Families, without a last Resort, to determine the Affairs of that Society by an irresistible sentence. . . . This Supremacy must be fixed somewhere.' The best they could imagine was an impossible hermaphroditic utopia or a primitive state of equality between the sexes, now irrevocably lost (perhaps the experience of festive role-reversals at least helped keep this egalitarian dream alive, as Victor Turner has suggested in another connection). The best they could hope for and recommend, like

Shadwell's Woman-Captain, were ways to prevent husbandly tyranny: better education for women or a better choice of marriage partners. The only countermodel for the family they had come to recognize by the mid-eighteenth century was the equally hierarchical one of matriarchy.[33]

Thus, this study does not overturn the traditional theory about rites and festivities of inversion; but it does hope to add other dimensions to it. Rather than expending itself primarily during the privileged duration of the joke, the story, the comedy, or the carnival, topsy-turvy play had much spillover into everyday 'serious' life, and the effects there were sometimes disturbing and even novel. As literary and festive inversion in preindustrial Europe was a product not just of stable hierarchy but also of changes in the location of power and property, so this inversion could prompt new ways of thinking about the system and reacting to it.

Let us begin with a historical reflecton about the family. Europeans of the fifteenth to eighteenth centuries found it remarkably difficult to conceive of the institution of the family as having a 'history,' of changing through time. Its patriarchal form went back either to the Garden of Eden, where the woman's subjection to the man was at least a gentle one, or to the first moment in human history, when monogamous marriage set mankind off from the promiscuous horde. Political forms might follow each other in a predictable cyclical fashion; economic, religious, and cultural systems might change along with them (as Vico thought). But the family stayed the same. To be sure, curious sexual customs were noted in the New World, but they were used merely to satirize European abuses or dismissed as products of savagery or degeneration. Play with the various images of woman-on-top, then, kept open an alternate way of conceiving family structure. Ultimately, when the Jesuit Lafitau found an order in the strange family patterns (matrilineal and matrilocal) that he had observed among the Iroquois and heard about in the Caribbean, he was able to refer back to legends of the Amazons and to the Lycians, whom he had read about in Herodotus. Lafitau's new theory of 'gynaecocracy,' as he called the matriarchal stage, was published in 1724 in his *Moeurs des sauvages ameriquains, comparées aux moeurs des premiers temps*. It owed something to the unruly woman.[34]

Play with the exceptional woman-on-top, the virtuous virago, was also a resource for feminist reflection on women's capacities. Although she did not argue that men and women should change the separate offices to which God had ordained them, nevertheless Christine de Pisan was glad to use examples of ancient female conquerors, stock figures in the legends about Amazons and in the stories and proverbs about women's rule, to show that 'in many women there is . . . great courage, strength, and hardiness to undertake all manner of strong things and to achieve them as did . . . great men and solemn conquerors.' Subsequent writers on 'Women Worthies' almost always included some viragos, readily incorporating Joan of Arc into the company. By the early eighteenth century, speculation about virtuous

Amazons could be used not only to praise the wise rule of contemporary lawful queens (as it had been already in Elizabeth I's day), but also to hint at the possibility of a wider role of citizenship for women.[35]

Furthermore, the exceptional woman-out-of-her-place enriched the fantasy of a few real women and might have emboldened them to exceptional action. Marie Delcourt has argued convincingly that Joan of Arc's male garb, to which she clung obdurately to the end, was not the product of mere practical military considerations, but was inspired by the example of the transvestite saints of the *Golden Legend*. The unusual seventeenth-century mystic Antoinette Bourignon started her career by fleeing from an impending marriage in the clothes of a male hermit. Among her later visions was that of humankind created originally as androgynous, a state of whole perfection to which it would return at the resurrection of the dead. The Recusant Mary Ward, founder of an innovating unenclosed teaching order for women with no male superior but the pope, was taking the Jesuits as her model but may also have received encouragement from traditions of sexual inversion. Galloping over the countryside in the vain effort to reconvert the English to Holy Mother Church, she and the members of her Company struck observers as 'apostolic Amazons.'[36]

Two of these women ultimately went to prison; the third narrowly escaped arrest. The virtuous virago could be a threat to order after all. But what about the majority of unexceptional women living within their families? What could the woman-on-top mean to them?

Girls were brought up to believe that they ought to obey their husbands; and boys were brought up to believe that they had the power of correction over their wives. In actual marriage, subjection might be moderated by the common causes of economic support, to which they both contributed, of sexual need, of childrearing, or of shared religious interest. It might be reversed temporarily during the lying-in period, when the new mother could boss her husband around with impunity. And subjection might be aggravated by the husband's repeated beatings of his wife. Some women accepted these arrangements. Some women got around them by sneaky manipulations that made their husbands fancy themselves the sole decision-makers. Still other wives rebelled, told their husbands to go to the devil, badgered them, thrashed them. Many circumstances might produce a wife of the third type. Here I wish only to speculate that the ambiguous woman-on-top of the world of play made the unruly option a more conceivable one within the family.[37]

Ordinary women might also be disorderly in public. In principle, women could pronounce on law and doctrine only if they were queens, had unusual learning, or fell into an ecstatic trance. Virtually never were they to take the law into their own hands. In fact, women turn up telling off priests and pastors, being central actors in grain and bread riots in town and country, and participating in tax revolts and other rural disturbances. In England in the early seventeenth century, a significant percentage of the rioters against enclosures and for common rights were female. In Calvinist Edinburgh in 1637, the resistance to Charles I's imposition of the Book of Common Prayer was opened by a crowd of 'rascally serving women' at Saint Giles' Church, who drowned out the Dean's reading, threw stools at the Bishop of Edinburgh, and when evicted, stoned the doors and windows. The tax revolt at Montpellier in 1645 was started by women, led down the streets by a virago named la Branlaïre, who shouted for death for the tax-collectors who were taking the bread from their children's mouths.[38]

There are several reasons for this female involvement that we cannot consider here, but part of its background is the complex license accorded the unruly woman. On the one hand, she was not accountable for what she did. Given over to the sway of her lower passions, she was not responsible for her actions; her husband was responsible, for she was subject to him. Indeed, this 'incapacity' was embodied in varying degrees in English law and in some French customary law. In England, in most felonious acts by a married woman to which her husband could be shown to be privy or at which he was present, the wife could not be held entirely culpable. If indicted, she might be acquitted or receive a lesser sentence than he for the same crime. In Normandy and Brittany, the husband might have to answer for her crimes in court, and everywhere the *sexus imbecillus* might be punished less severely. The full weight of the law fell only on the ruling male. Small wonder that the husbands sometimes thought it safer to send their wives out to do the rioting alone. And small wonder that the Star Chamber grumbled in 1605 that some women who had torn down enclosure fences were 'hiding behind their sex.'[39]

On the other hand, sexual inversion also gave a more positive license to the unruly woman: her right as subject and as mother to rise up and tell the truth. When a great pregnant woman at the front of a crowd curses grain-hoarders or cheating authorities, the irreverent Gargamelle is part of her tradition. When Katherine Zell of Strasbourg dares to write an attack on clerical celibacy in the 1520s and claims 'I do not pretend to be John the Baptist rebuking the Pharisees. I do not claim to be Nathan upbraiding David. I aspire only to be Balaam's ass, castigating his master,' then Dame Folly is part of her tradition.[40]

It turns out, however, that Dame Folly could serve to validate disobedient and riotous behavior by men, too. They also could hide behind that sex. Much has been written by historians on the ideals, traditions, symbols, and solidarities that legitimated the numerous rural and urban uprisings of early modern Europe. Among these traditions was the carnival right of criticism and mockery, which sometimes tipped over into real rebellion. In 1630 in Dijon, for instance, Mère Folle and her Infanterie were part of an uprising in masquerade against royal tax officers. In fact, the donning of female clothes by men and the adopting of female titles for riots were surprisingly frequent, beginning (so our still scanty data suggest) in the seventeenth century. In many of these disturbances, the men were trying to protect traditional rights against change; in others, it was the rioters who were pressing for innovation. But in all cases, they were putting ritual and festive inversion to new uses.

So in the Beaujolais in the 1770s, male peasants blackened their faces and dressed as women and then attacked surveyors measuring their lands for a new landlord. In the morning, when the police agents came, the peasants' wives knew nothing, and said the attackers were 'fairies' who came from the mountains from time to time. Among the market women who marched to Versailles in October 1789, it is very likely there were men in female garb. And in 1829–30, the 'War of the Demoiselles' took place in the Department of Ariège in the Pyrénées. The peasants dressed themselves in long white shirts, suggesting women's clothes, wore women's hats, and defended their much-needed rights to wood and pasturage in the forests, then being threatened by a new Forest Code.[41]

In England we find the same thing. In 1451, in the wake of Cade's rebellion, blackfaced 'servants of the Queen of the Fairies' broke into the Duke of Buckingham's park in Kent and took his bucks and does. In 1629, 'Captain' Alice Clark, a real female, headed a crowd of women and male weavers dressed as women in a grain riot near Maldon in Essex. In 1641, in the dairy and grazing sections of Wiltshire, bands of men rioted and leveled fences against the king's enclosure of their forests. They were led by men dressed as women, who called themselves 'Lady Skimmington.' In May 1718, Cambridge students followed 'a virago, or man in woman's habit, crowned with laurel' to assault a Dissenting meeting house. Two years later, laborers in Surrey rioted in women's clothes, and at mid-century country men disguised as women tore down the hated tollbooths and turnpike gates at the Gloucestershire border. In April 1812, 'General Ludd's Wives,' two weavers dressed as women, led a crowd of hundreds to smash steam looms and burn a factory at Stockport.[42]

In Wales and Scotland, too, there were uprisings in female disguise. The *ceffyl pren*, with its blackfaced transvestite males, gave way in the 1830s and 1840s in west Wales to the Rebecca riots against the detested turnpike tolls and other sources of agrarian complaint. They were led by one 'Rebecca' and noisy men in women's clothes. And in 1736 in Edinburgh, the Porteous Riots, which were sparked by a hated English officer, oppressive customs laws, and resistance to the union of Scotland with England, were carried out by men disguised as women and with a leader known as Madge Wildfire.[43]

Finally, in Ireland, where old stories told of the ritual killing of the king at Samhain by men dressed as animals and as women, and where the funeral wakes involved fertility rites with women dressed as men, we have the most extensive example of disturbances led by men disguised as women. For about a decade, from 1760 to 1770, the Whiteboys, dressed in long white frocks and with blackened faces, set themselves up as an armed popular force to provide justice for the poor, 'to restore the ancient commons and redress other grievances.' They tore down enclosures, punished landowners who raised the rents, forced masters to release unwilling apprentices, and fought the gouging tithe-farmers mercilessly. Those who opposed their rule they chastised and ridiculed. They sometimes said they acted under 'sanction of being fairies,' and a favorite signature on their proclamations was Sieve Outlagh (or Sadhbh Amhaltach) – 'Ghostly Sally.' Ultimately they were suppressed by the armed might of the gentlemen and magistrates, but not before they had left a legacy for the Molly Maguires and the Ribbon Societies of the nineteenth century.[44]

The female persona was only one of several folk disguises assumed by males for riots in the seventeenth and eighteenth centuries, but it was quite popular and widespread. Our analysis of sexual symbolism and of the varieties of sexual inversion should help us understand why this was so. In part, the black face and female dress were a practical concealment, and readily at hand in households rarely filled with fancy wardrobes. More important, however, were the mixed ways in which the female persona authorized resistance. On the one hand, the disguise freed men from full responsibility for their deeds and perhaps, too, from fear of outrageous revenge upon their manhood. After all, it was mere women who were acting in this disorderly way. On the other hand, the males drew upon the sexual power and energy of the unruly woman and on her license (which they had long assumed at carnival and games) – to promote fertility, to defend the community's interests and standards, and to tell the truth about unjust rule.

The woman-on-top was a resource for private and public life in the fashions we have described only so long as two things were the case: first, so long as sexual symbolism had a close connection with questions of order and subordination, with the lower female sex conceived as the disorderly lustful one; second, so long as the stimulus to inversion play was a double one – traditional hierarchical structures *and* disputed changes in the distribution of power in family and political life. As we move into the industrial period with its modern states, classes, and systems of private property and its exploitation of racial and national groups, both symbolism and stimuli were transformed. One small sign of the new order is the changing butt of domestic charivaris: by the nineteenth century, rough music in England was more likely to be directed against the wife-beater than against the henpecked husband, and there are signs of such a shift in America and even in France.[45]

The woman-on-top flourished, then, in preindustrial Europe and during the period of transition to industrial society. Despite all our detail in this essay, we have been able to give only the outlines of her reign. Variations in sexual inversion from country to country or between Protestants and Catholics have been ignored for the sake of describing a large pattern over time. Cultural play with sex roles intended to explore the character of sexuality itself (Where did one sex stop and the other begin?) has been ignored to concentrate on hierarchy and disorder. The timing and distribution of transvestite riots, and the nature of play with sex roles before the fourteenth century, need to be investigated. (Is it not likely that there were female transvestite rituals in areas where hoeing was of great consequence? Can the unruly woman have been so much an issue when sovereignty was less at stake?) The asymmetry between male and female roles in festive life from the fifteenth through the eighteenth centuries remains to be explored, as do some of the contrasts between literary and carnivalesque inversion. What has been established are the types of symbolic reversal in sex roles in early modern Europe and their multiple connections with orderliness in thought and behavior. The holiday rule of the woman-on-top confirmed subjection throughout society, but it also promoted resistance to it. The Maid Marian danced for a plentiful village; the Rosetta disported with the doomed old bear of winter; the serving women of Saint Giles threw stools for the Reformed Kirk; Ghostly Sally led her Whiteboys in a new kind of popular justice. The woman-on-top renewed old systems, but also helped change them into something different.

Notes

1 Pierre Grosnet, *Les motz dorez De Cathon en francoys et en latin . . . Proverbes, Adages, Auctoritez et ditz moraulx des Saiges* (Paris, 1530/31), f. F. vii[r]. Claude de Rubys, *Les privileges franchises et immunitez octroyees par les roys . . . aux consuls . . . et habitans de la ville de Lyon* (Lyon, 1574), p. 74. Christopher Hill, 'The Many-Headed Monster in Late Tudor and Early Stuart Political Thinking,' in C.H. Carter, ed., *From the Renaissance to the Counter-Reformation, Essays in Honour of Garrett Mattingly* (London, 1966), pp. 296–324.
2 Laurent Joubert, *Erreurs populaires au fait de la medecine* (Bordeaux, 1578), pp. 161ff. François Poullain de La Barre, *De l'excellence des hommes contre l'egalité des sexes* (Paris, 1675), pp. 136ff., 156ff. Ilza Veith, *Hysteria, The History of a Disease* (Chicago, 1965). Michael Screech, *The Rabelaisian Marriage* (London, 1958), chap. 6.
3 Heinrich Institoris and Jacob Sprenger, *Malleus Maleficarum* (ca. 1487), trans. M. Summers (London, 1928), Part I, question 6: 'Why it is that Women are chiefly addicted to Evil Superstitions.' Florimond de Raemond, *L'histoire de la naissance, progrez et decadence de l'hérésie de ce siècle* (Rouen, 1623), pp. 847–48, 874–77. Fleury de Bellingen, *L'Etymologie ou Explication des Proverbes françois* (La Haye, 1656), pp. 311ff. James E. Phillips, Jr., 'The Background of Spenser's Attitude toward Women Rulers,' *Huntington Library Quarterly* 5 (1941–42): 9–10. [John Aylmer], *An Harborowe for Faithfull and Trewe Subiectes, agaynst the late blowne Blaste, concerninge the Government of Wemen* (London, 1559). J. Simon, *Le gouvernement admirable ou la République des Abeilles* (Paris, 1742), pp. 23ff. John Thorley, in *The Female Monarchy. Being an Enquiry into the Nature, Order and Government of Bees* (London, 1744), still finds it necessary to argue against those who cannot believe in a queen bee (pp. 75–86).
4 See, for instance, Juan Luis Vives, *The Instruction of a Christian Woman* (London, 1524), and François de Salignac de la Mothe Fénelon, *Fénelon on Education*, trans. H.C. Barnard (Cambridge, 1966).

5 P.C. Timbal, 'L'esprit du droit privé,' *XVIIe siècle* 58–59 (1963): 38–39. P. Ourliac and J. de Malafosse, *Histoire du droit privé* (Paris, 1968), 3: 145–52, 264–68. L. Abensour, *La femme et le féminisme avant la Révolution* (Paris, 1923), Part 1, chap. 9. Alice Clark, *The Working Life of Women in the Seventeenth Century* (London, 1919; reprint 1968). E. Le Roy Ladurie, *Les paysans de Languedoc* (Paris, 1966), pp. 271–80 and *Annexe* 32, p. 859.

6 Christine de Pisan, *The Boke of the Cyte of Ladyes* (a translation of *Le Tresor de la Cité des Dames*, 1405; London, 1521), f. Ee iᵛ. Henry Cornelius Agrippa of Nettesheim, *Of the Nobilitie and Excellencie of Womankynde* (translation from the Latin edition of 1509; London, 1542), f. B iv^r–v.

7 Jean Calvin, *Commentaries on the Epistles of Paul The Apostle to the Corinthians*, trans. J. Pringle (Edinburgh, 1848), 1: 353–61 (1 Cor. 11:3–12). William Gouge, *Domesticall Duties*, quoted in W. and M. Haller, 'The Puritans Art of Love,' *Huntington Library Quarterly* 5 (1941–42): 246. John G. Halkett, *Milton and the Idea of Matrimony* (New Haven, 1970), pp. 20–24. Gordon J. Schochet, 'Patriarchalism, Politics and Mass Attitudes in Stuart England,' *Historical Journal* 12 (1969): 413–41. Catherine E. Holmes, *L'éloquence judiciaire de 1620 à 1660* (Paris, 1967), p. 76. Ourliac and de Malafosse, *Droit privé*, 3: 66 ('*L'époque des rois absolus est aussi celle des pères absolus.*'). John Locke, *The Second Treatise of Government*, ed. T.P. Peardon (Indianapolis, Ind., 1952), chap. 7, par. 82; chap. 9, pars. 128–31.

8 [Gabriel de Foigny], *Les avantures de Jacques Sadeur dans la découverte et le voyage de la terre australe* (Amsterdam, 1732), chap. 5, especially pp. 128–39.

9 Robert Delevoy, *Bruegel* (Lausanne, 1959), pp. 70–75.

10 Deut. 22:5; 1 Cor. 11:14–15. Saint Jerome, *The Letters of Saint Jerome*, trans. C.C. Mierow (London, 1963), 1: 161–62 (Letter 22 to Eustochium). Robert of Flamborough, *Liber Penitentialis*, ed. J.F. Firth (Toronto, 1971), Book 5, p. 264. Jean Calvin, 'Sermons sur le Deutéronome,' in *Ioannis Calvini opera quae supersunt omnia*, ed. G. Baum, E. Cunitz, and E. Reuss (Brunswick, 1863–80), 28: 17–19, 234 (hereafter cited as *Calvini opera*). Vern Bullough, 'Transvestites in the Middle Ages,' *American Journal of Sociology* 79 (1974): 1381–94.

11 Pierre de l'Estoile, *Mémoires-journaux*, ed. Brunet et al. (Paris, 1888–96), 1: 142–43, 157, 180. François-Timoléon de Choisy, *Mémoires*, ed. G. Mongrédien (Paris, 1966), pp. 286–360.

12 Max Gluckman, *Order and Rebellion in Tribal Africa* (New York, 1963), Introduction and chap. 3. Victor Turner, *The Forest of Symbols, Aspects of Ndembu Ritual* (Ithaca, N.Y., 1967), chap. 4. *Idem, The Ritual Process. Structure and Anti-Structure* (Chicago, 1968), chaps. 3–5. Gregory Bateson, 'Culture Contact and Schismogenesia,' *Man* 35 (Dec. 1935): 199. J.C. Flügel, *The Psychology of Clothes* (London, 1930), pp. 120–21. Marie Delcourt, *Hermaphrodite. Myths and Rites of the Bisexual Figure in Classical Antiquity* (London, 1956), chap. 1. James Peacock, 'Symbolic Reversal and Social History: Transvestites and Clowns of Java,' in Barbara Babcock-Abrahams, ed., *The reversible world: symbolic inversion in art and societies* (Ithaca, New York, 1978).

13 William Willeford, *The Fool and his Scepter* (Evanston, Ill., 1969), especially pp. 97–98.

14 Ian Donaldson, *The World Upside-Down, Comedy from Jonson to Fielding* (Oxford, 1970), p. 14.

15 Stith Thompson, *Motif-Index of Folk Literature* (rev. ed.; Bloomington, Ind., 1955–58), K310, K514, K1321, K1836, K2357.8. Sir Philip Sidney, *The New Arcadia*, Book I, chap. 12. Honore d'Urfé, *Astrée* (1609–19). John Marston, *The History of Antonio and Mellida* (1602). Willeford, *The Fool*, pp. 58–62.

16 Delcourt, *Hermaphrodite*, pp. 84–102. John Anson, 'The Female Transvestite in Early Monasticism: The Origin and Development of a Motif' *Viator* 5 (1974), 1–32.

17 Thompson, *Motif-Index*, K3.3, K1837. A. Aarne and Stith Thompson, *The Types of the Folktale* (2d rev. ed.; Helsinki, 1964), 88A, 890, 891A. Giovanni Boccaccio, *Decameron*, Second Day, Story 9. William Shakespeare, *The Merchant of Venice*, Act II, scenes 4–6; Act IV, scene 1. M.J. L'Héritier de Villandon, *Les caprices du destin ou Recueil d'histoires singulieres et amusantes. Arrivées de nos jours* (Paris, 1718), *Avertissement* and tale 'L'Amazone Françoise.' Celeste T. Wright, 'The Amazons in

Elizabethan Literature,' *Studies in Philology* 37 (1940): 433–45. Edmund Spenser, *The Faerie Queen*, Book III, Canto 1.

18 Spenser, *Faerie Queene*, Book V, Cantos 4–5; Wright, 'Amazons,' pp. 449–54. 'The Lady Who Was Castrated,' in Paul Brians, ed. and trans., *Bawdy Tales from the Courts of Medieval France* (New York, 1972), pp. 24–36. David Kunzle, *The Early Comic Strip. Narrative Strips and Picture Stories in the European Broadsheet from 1450 to 1825* (Berkeley and Los Angeles, 1973), pp. 224–25. Giovanni Boccaccio, *Concerning Famous Women*, trans. G.G. Guarino (New Brunswick, N.J., 1963), pp. 231–34.

19 Chaucer, *The Canterbury Tales*, 'The Wife of Bath's Prologue.' François Rabelais, *La vie très horrifique du Grand Gargantua, père de Pantagruel*, chaps. 3–6. Mikhail Bakhtin, *Rabelais and His World* (Cambridge, Mass., 1968), pp. 240–41. *Les quinze joies de mariage*, ed. J. Rychner (Geneva, 1963). H.J.C. von Grimmelshausen, *Courage, The Adventuress and the False Messiah*, trans. Hans Speier (Princeton, 1964). Johannes Janssen, *History of the German People at the Close of the Middle Ages*, trans. A.M. Christie (London, 1896–1925), 12: 206, n. 1. Kunzle, *Early Comic Strip*, p. 225. *Mari et femme dans la France rurale* (catalogue of the exhibition at the Musée national des arts et traditions populaires, Paris, September 22–November 19, 1973), pp. 68–69.

20 Ben Jonson, *Epicoene*, Act IV. See Donaldson, *World Upside-Down*, chap. 2, and Edward B. Partridge, *The Broken Compass* (New York, 1958), chap. 7. Thomas Shadwell, *The Woman-Captain* (London, 1680). William Shakespeare, *As You Like It*, Act IV, scene 1. Henri d'Andeli, *Le Lai d'Aristote de Henri d'Andeli*, ed. M. Delboville (Bibliothèque de la Faculté de Philosophie et Lettres de l'Université de Liège, 123; Paris, 1951). Hermann Schmitz, *Hans Baldung gen. Grien* (Bielefeld and Leipzig, 1922), Plate 66. K. Oettinger and K.-A. Knappe, *Hans Baldung Grien und Albrecht Dürer in Nürnberg* (Nuremberg, 1963), Plate 66. Kunzle, *Early Comic Strip*, p. 224.

21 *Erasmus en zijn tijd* (Catalogue of the exhibition at the Museum Boymans–van Beuningen, Rotterdam, October–November 1969), nos. 151–52. Willeford, *The Fool*, Plate 30, drawing by Urs Graf. Erasmus, *The Praise of Folly*.

22 See, for instance, John Ashton, ed., *Humour, Wit and Satire in the Seventeenth Century* (New York, 1968; republication of the 1883 ed.), pp. 82ff. John Wardroper, ed., *Jest upon Jest* (London, 1970), chap. 1. Aarne and Thompson, *Folktale*, 1375, 1366A. Kunzle, *Early Comic Strip* pp. 222–23.

23 S.L. Sumberg, *The Nuremberg Schembart Carnival* (New York, 1941), especially pp. 83–84, 104–5. Maria Leach, ed., *Funk and Wagnalls Standard Dictionary of Folklore, Mythology and Legend* (New York, 1949–50), 'Schemen.' Jean Savaron, *Traitté contre les masques* (Paris, 1608), p. 10. M. du Tilliot, *Mémoires pour servir à l'histoire de la Fête des Foux* (Lausanne and Geneva, 1751), pp. 8, 11–12. Arnold Van Gennep, *Manuel du folklore français* (Paris, 1943–49), 1.3: 908–18. Violet Alford, *Pyrenean Festivals* (London, 1937), pp. 16–25. Curt Sachs, *World History of the Dance* (New York, 1963), pp. 335–39.

24 Joseph Strutt, *The Sports and Pastimes of the People of England* (new ed.; London, 1878), pp. 449–51, 310–11, 456. C.L. Barber, *Shakespeare's Festive Comedy* (Princeton, 1951), p. 28. Leach, *Dictionary of Folklore*, 'Fool Plough,' 'Morris.'

25 Leach, *Dictionary of Folklore*, 'Transvestism.' Willeford, *The Fool*, p. 86. Van Gennep, *Manuel*, 1.8: 910. Alford, *Festivals*, pp. 19–22. Sachs, *Dance*, pp. 335–39.

26 Henry Bourne, *Antiquitates Vulgares; or the Antiquities of the Common People* (Newcastle, 1725), pp. 147–48. Roger Vaultier, *Le Folklore pendant la guerre de Cent Ans* (Paris, 1965), pp. 93–100. J. Lefebvre, *Les fols et la folie* (Paris, 1968), p. 46, n. 66. A. Holtmont, *Die Hosenrolle* (Munich, 1925), pp. 54–55, Donaldson, *World Upside-Down*, p. 15. Van Gennep, *Manuel*, 1.3: 884. Strutt, *Sports*, p. 125.

27 For full documentation and bibliography on this material, see Natalie Zemon Davis, *Society and Culture in Early Modern France* (Stanford, 1975), Chap. 4, 'The Reasons of Misrule,' and E.P. Thompson, ' "Rough Music": Le Charivari anglais', *Annales ESC* 27 (1972): 285–312.

28 P. Sadron, 'Les associations permanentes d'acteurs en France au moyen-age,' *Revue d'histoire de théâtre* 4 (1952): 222–31. Du Tillot, *Mémoires*, pp. 179–82. David

Williams, *The Rebecca Riots* (Cardiff, 1955), pp. 53–54. Willeford, *The Fool*, pp. 175–79.

29 See Davis, 'The Reasons of Misrule,' n. 34. J.W. Spargo, *Juridical Folklore in England Illustrated by the Cucking-Stool* (Durham, N.C., 1944).

30 In addition to the sources given in n. 28, see Hogarth's illustration of a Skimmington Ride made about 1726 for Samuel Butler's *Hudibras* ('Hudibras encounters the Skimmington').

31 Enid Welsford, *The Fool, His Social and Literary History* (London, 1935), pp. 153–54. Van Gennep, *Manuel*, 1.4: 1452–72, 1693–94. Lucienne A. Roubin, *Chambrettes des Provençaux* (Paris, 1970), pp. 178–79. Davis, 'The Reasons of Misrule,' n. 13. Jean Vostet, *Almanach ou Prognostication des Laboureurs* (Paris, 1588), f. 12^{r-v}. Erasmus, *Adagiorum Chiliades* (Geneva, 1558), col. 135, 'Mense Maio nubunt malae.' Gabriel Le Bras, *Etudes de sociologie religieuse* (Paris, 1955), 1: 44.

32 Kunzle, *Early Comic Strip*, pp. 225, 236.

33 Poullain de La Barre, *De l'excellence des hommes*, Preface, especially his discussion of Saint Paul. *Idem, De l'égalité des deux sexes* (Paris, 1676), pp. 16–22. Mary Astell, *Some Reflections upon Marriage* (4th ed.; London, 1730), pp. 99–107. Turner, *Ritual Process*, chap. 5 (cited in n. 12).

34 Jean Calvin, *Commentaries on Genesis*, trans. J. King (Edinburgh, 1847), 1: 172 (Gen. 3: 16). Giambattista Vico, *The New Science*, trans. T.G. Bergin and M.H. Fisch (Ithaca, New York, 1968), nos. 369, 504–7, 582–84, 671, 985–94. J.F. Lafitau, S.J., *Moeurs des sauvages ameriquains, comparées aux moeurs des premiers temps* (Paris, 1724), 1: 49–90.

35 Christine de Pisan, *Cyte of Ladyes*, ff.Ff. v^r–Hh ii^r. Thomas Heywood, *Gynaikeion, or Nine Bookes of Various History, concerninge Women* (London, 1624). Discussion of the Amazons by Pierre Petit in *De Amazonibus Dissertatio* (2d ed.; Amsterdam, 1687) and by Claude Guyon in *Histoire des Amazones anciennes et modernes* (Paris, 1740) tries to find plausible arguments to account for their bravery and successful rule. By the time Condorcet and Olympe de Gouges make a plea for the full citizenship of women in the early years of the French Revolution, the argument is being waged in terms of rights.

36 Delcourt, *Hermaphrodite*, pp. 93–96. Salomon Reinach, *Cultes, mythes et religions* (Paris, 1905), 1: 430, 453–56. M.C.E. Chambers, *The Life of Mary Ward, 1585–1645* (London, 1882).

37 On the husband's power of correction over the wife, see William Blackstone, *Commentaries on the Laws of England* (Oxford, 1770), Book I, chap. 15; and Ourliac and de Malafosse, *Droit privé*, 3: 133, 140 (cited in n. 5). Evidence here comes from examination of diaries, criminal cases, and the records of the Geneva Consistory. See, for instance, Charles de Ribbe, *Les familles et la société en France avant la Révolution* (Paris, 1874), 2: 85–87. On wives being beaten, *Journal de Gilles de Gouberville pour les années 1549–1552*, ed. A. de Blangy (Rouen, 1892), 32: 195. For women beating their husbands, in addition to charivaris against them, see E. de la Poix de Fréminville, *Traité de la police generale des villes, bourgs, paroisses et seigneuries de la campagne* (Paris, 1758).

38 E.P. Thompson, 'The Moral Economy of the English Crowd in the Eighteenth Century,' *Past and Present* 50 (Feb. 1971): 115–17. Olwen Hufton, 'Women in Revolution, 1789–96,' *Past and Present* 53 (Nov. 1971): 95 ff. Patricia Higgins, 'The Reactions of Women,' in Brian Manning, ed., *Politics, Religion and the English Civil War* (London, 1973), pp. 179–222. John Spalding, *The History of the Troubles and Memorable Transactions in Scotland and England from 1624 to 1648* (Edinburgh, 1828), 2: 47–48. S.R. Gardiner, *The Fall of the Monarchy of Charles I, 1637–1649* (London, 1882); 1: 105–12. Le Roy Ladurie, *Les paysans*, p. 497.

39 Margaret Ruth Kittel, 'Married Women in Thirteenth-Century England: A Study of Common Law' (unpublished Ph.D. dissertation, University of California at Berkeley, 1973), pp. 226–33. Blackstone, *Commentaries* (1770), Book IV, chap. 2; Book I, chap. 15. Ourliac and de Malafosse, *Droit privé*, 3: 135–36. On how husbands and wives jointly manipulated their diverse roles for their mutual benefit, see N. Castan, 'La criminalité familiale dans le ressort de Parlement de Toulouse, 1690–1730,' in A.

Abbiateci *et al., Crimes et criminalité en France, 17e–18e siècles* (Cahier des Annales, 33; Paris, 1971), pp. 91–107. Harvard Law School, Ms. 1128, no. 334, *Page vs. Page*, Nov. 13, 1605 (communicated by Thomas Barnes).
40 Roland Bainton, 'Katherine Zell,' *Medievalia et Humanistica*, n.s., 1(1970): 3.
41 Henri Hours, 'Les fayettes de Saint Just d'Avray. Puissance et limites de solidarité dans une communauté rural en 1774,' prepared for a forthcoming issue of the *Bulletin de l'Académie de Villefranche* (manuscript kindly shown me by M. Hours). John Merriman, 'The Demoiselles of the Ariège, 1829–1830,' in John M. Merriman, ed., *1830 in France.*
42 F.R.H. Boulay, *Documents Illustrative of Medieval Kentish Society* (Ashford, Eng., 1964), pp. 254–55. William A. Hunt, 'The Godly and the Vulgar: Religion, Rebellion and Social Change in Essex, England, 1570–1688' (Harvard University, 1974). Eric Kerridge, 'The Revolts in Wiltshire Against Charles I,' *The Wiltshire Archaeological and Natural History Magazine* 57 (1958–60): 68–71. Historical Manuscripts Commission, *Report on the Manuscripts of . . . the Duke of Portland* (London, 1901), 7: 237–38 (reference kindly communicated by Lawrence Stone). Surrey Quarter Sessions, sessions roll 241, Oct. 1721 (kindly communicated by John M. Beattie of the University of Toronto). *Ipswich Journal*, Aug. 5, 1749 (kindly communicated by Robert Malcolmson, Queen's University, Kingston, Ont.). A.W. Smith, 'Some Folklore Elements in Movements of Social Protest,' *Folklore* 77 (1967), 244–45. 'Memorial of the Inhabitants of Stockport and Vicinity' (Public Record Office, HO 42/128).
43 Williams, *Rebecca Riots*. Thompson, 'Rough Music,' pp. 306–7. Daniel Wilson, *Memorials of Edinburgh in the Olden Time* (2d ed.; Edinburgh and London, 1891), 1: 143–45. Sir Walter Scott, *The Heart of Midlothian*, chap. 7.
44 G.F. Dalton, 'The Ritual Killing of the Irish Kings,' *Folklore* 81 (1970): 15–19. Vivian Mercier, *The Irish Comic Tradition* (Oxford, 1962), pp. 49–53. Arthur Young, *Arthur Young's Tour in Ireland, 1776–1779*, ed. A.W. Hutton (London, 1892), 1: 81–84; 2: 55–56. W.E.H. Lecky, *A History of Ireland in the Eighteenth Century* (New York, 1893), 2: 12–44.
45 Thompson, 'Rough Music,' especially pp. 296–304. For examples of charivaris against wife-beaters in France in the early nineteenth century, see Cl. Xavier Girault, 'Etymologie des usages des principales époques de l'année et de la vie,' *Mémoires de l'Académie Celtique* 2 (1808): 104–6; J.A. Du Laure, 'Archeographe au lieu de La Tombe et de ses environs,' *Mémoires de l'Académie Celtique* 2 (1808): 449; Van Gennep, *Manuel*, 1.3: 1073.

13

Marianne's citizens? Women, the Republic and universal suffrage in France

SIÂN REYNOLDS

That Marianne should be the symbol of the French Republic is not merely an irony long ago noted by feminists: her inspiring figure actually masks the

Reprinted from S. Reynolds (ed.), *Women, State and Revolution* (Harvester, 1986). Reprinted by permission of the author.

masculinity of the republican tradition and of republican discourse as it has survived into the late twentieth century.

[. . .]

The First French Republic (1793 Constitution) had introduced the principle of universal manhood suffrage. The Second Republic (1848–51) effectively enacted it. All adult French men were enfranchised in 1848 (an event often referred to by historians as the introduction of 'universal suffrage' to France). Manhood suffrage, albeit with some modifications, remained in place throughout the Second Empire (1852–70) and the Third Republic (1870–1940). French women had to wait until the end of the Second World War before they could vote. An ordinance approved by the Provisional French government in Algiers on 21 April 1944, outlining arrangements for post-Liberation France, contained as Article 17 'Women will vote and be eligible in the same way as men'. Women actually cast votes for the first time in 1945. These dates have consequently been seen as important for women, but in most general histories of twentieth-century France, they appear almost in parenthesis, if at all. Behind the construction of 1944–5 as a significant date for women, but not particularly significant for the Republic, lies a perception of history, and in particular of universal suffrage under the Republic, which has become a sort of orthodoxy by default.

The republican orthodoxy tends to explain the non-enfranchisement of women during the hundred years between 1848 and 1944 very largely in terms of how women might use their votes. Michelet told his audience in the Sorbonne in 1850 that giving women the vote would mean 'giving thousands of votes to the priests'. Assumptions of this kind continued to alarm anti-clerical republican politicians of the Third Republic. Fears of clerical influence over women, particularly voiced in the Senate between the wars, are generally held to explain why France lagged behind other European countries in allowing women to exercise their political rights. Much was also made of the apparent lack of militancy on the question by most French women. When eventually women did enter the 'city', the reason often cited is women's participation in the Resistance during the war, thus seen as 'earning' them the vote.

[. . .]

From the place they are accorded in mainstream history, neither the decree of 21 April 1944 nor the first votes in 1945 are regarded as major changes to the Republic. They are referred to as 'giving women the vote', rather than 'the institution of universal suffrage'. An anomaly (which had persisted for reasons not entirely unworthy, it is suggested) was being rectified; citizenship was being extended to a previously excluded group. For women, it is assumed, the decision was unequivocally a good thing: admission at last to the city. What is not suggested is that the city was receiving anything of value, let alone half its long-vaunted claim to universalism. If anything, rather the reverse: before long, since early studies of post-war voting showed women abstaining more often than men, they were being chided for 'poor citizenship'. All in all, however, it seemed that their admission to the city had not changed anything very much.

[. . .]

The point is not so much to argue that the republican orthodoxy is 'wrong': most people, myself included, have tended to accept that it contains at least elements of a convincing explanation. But it is perhaps possible to ask whether it has got in the way of looking at the same history from a different and more feminist perspective. This might start from Mary Wollstonecraft's observation that both men and women are in some way damaged by the domination of one over the other. What the French republican tradition has never acknowledged is that the Republic was as flawed by its exclusion of women as it would have been by its exclusion (say) of working-class men. The latter, if they had not been enfranchised in 1848, would never have been invisible in the same way women are in the unthinking discourse on universal suffrage. But there is more to it than this. Women were not left out of the Republic by some sort of oversight. On the contrary, the Republic was in many ways created and forged into a myth against them, not merely without them. In a necessarily very brief outline of this argument, what follows will concentrate on three points of reference: the creation of the Jacobin Republic after 1792; the republican tradition as it solidified in the late nineteenth century under the Third Republic; and the way many historians and political scientists write about women in a political context today.

1789 did not bring a Republic to France; it was the failure of constitutional monarchy with the king's flight to Varennes which precipitated the declaration of the Republic in 1792 and the drafting of a republican constitution the following year. What is most relevant to our question is the extent to which, at this phase of the revolution, members of the assemblies went back to reading their Montesquieu and Rousseau, and also to renewed interest in the models of antiquity, particularly Rome and Sparta. Interpreting the influence of the Enlightenment or of antiquity on the French Revolution is fraught with risks, but it does seem that on the question of women and citizenship at least some general points can be made.

In the minds of many revolutionaries, women were associated with weakness, corruption, frailty and specifically with the court and the *ancien régime*, as Mary Wollstonecraft pointed out. Indeed under the *ancien régime*, certain privileged women of all three estates took part in the preliminary voting for the Estates General of 1789 (Hause and Kenney, 1984, p. 3). At court they were associated with the 'occult power' traditionally exercised by the king's consort, favourites or female relatives. In short they stood for every-thing that was the opposite of republican virtue. Neither Montesquieu nor Rousseau was as crudely misogynist as they are sometimes assumed to be, but they certainly provide encyclopedic reference for women as capricious, indiscreet, petty and above all weak.[1] The index entry for 'women' in *L'Esprit des Lois* (1748) in the Pléiade edition runs to several columns, hardly any of the references favourable. It could be argued that Rousseau's much pub-licised views on women draw on the same tradition: his solution in his political writing to the frightening power of Eve, frail and corrupting, amounts to an attempt to contain and imprison the threat she represented by turning her (ideally) into a Spartan mother.

The source for almost everything eighteenth-century (or indeed twenti-eth-century) readers knew about Sparta was Plutarch's *Life of Lycurgus*, which Rousseau heard at his father's knee and which was read by virtually all French schoolboys and a few girls (such as Manon Phlipon, later Madame Roland). The two points many readers remembered concerning women were first that young girls shared all physical exercise with boys and danced naked at gymnastic displays; and second that since Sparta was a mil-itary society where men served for long periods in the army, Spartan matrons ran the household. Remembered out of context, these contributed to the view of Sparta as a licentious society where women held great power. But this was to misread Plutarch, and both Rousseau and the Jacobin Saint-Just (who admired Sparta this side of idolatry) correctly drew the inference intended by Plutarch that the education of girls was designed specifically to produce healthy bodies capable of bearing strong children (preferably boys who would fight for the fatherland, an image which had particular relevance to the beleaguered French Republic of the Year II). 'Spartan mother' paint-ings depicting a stern matron instructing her son with the famous words 'Come back with your shield or on it', appeared in the Salons of the 1790s (Rawson, 1969, p. 286). It was the role of the Spartan mother to indoctri-nate her children with virtue. She was not a citizen, but she was the chief source of civic education.

This is the image behind Rousseau's famous reference to women in the 'Dedication to the Citizens of Geneva' which precedes his *Discourse on the Origins of Inequality* (1755):

> I must not forget that precious half of the Republic, which makes the happiness of the other; and whose sweetness and prudence preserve its tranquility and virtue. Amiable and virtuous daughters of Geneva, it will always be the lot of your sex to govern ours. Happy are we so long as your chaste influence, solely exercised within the limits of conjugal union, is exerted only for the glory of the State and the happiness of the public. It was thus that the female sex commanded at Sparta . . . It is your task to perpetuate, by your insinuating influence and your

innocent and amiable rule, a respect for the laws of the State and harmony among the citizens . . . It is your task . . . to correct . . . those
extravagances which our young people pick up in other countries
whence they bring home hardly anything besides . . . a ridiculous
manner acquired among loose women.

(Rousseau, 1973 edn, pp. 36–7)

When Rousseau calls women 'the precious half of the Republic', he means
the half without citizenship. In the terminology of the *Social Contract*,
women are 'subjects' not 'citizens'.[2] Thus Eve can be recuperated and
recruited as a transmitter of republican virtue, without being called upon to
exercise political rights in person.

Neither Rousseau nor Montesquieu left women out of their writings as
irrelevant: on the contrary, they feared and in a way respected them as a
potentially destructive force. Antiquity provided a model of corrective training in the shape of the Spartan (or Roman) matron. While these views came
to be shared by many of the men who made the French Revolution, it is
worth pointing out that it *was* possible for men of the eighteenth century to
think otherwise, to regard women not as Eve, Marie Antoinette, the Virgin
Mary or the Spartan mother, but as human beings with rights. Condorcet,
the philosopher and mathematician who was also a member of the revolutionary assemblies, voiced this opinion in his article 'On admitting women
to the city', arguing on quite classic individualist grounds that women
should be granted citizenship on the same terms as men. It was a thought,
in other words, perfectly thinkable in the 1790s.

The rights of men derive entirely from their status as sentient beings,
capable of acquiring moral ideas and reasoning about those ideas. So
women having the same qualities necessarily have the same rights.
Either no individual of the human race has any real rights, or all have
the same. And one who votes against the rights of another, whatever
their religion, colour or sex, has by so doing abjured his own.[3]

Condorcet's feminism as well as that of women feminists of the time was
marginal and has no place in the tradition which sees the Republic as having
been forged in the heat of battle, symbolised by the citizen-army that fought
at Valmy. Women themselves entered into the patriotic role of the Spartan
mother, giving both their ardour and their children to the revolution. Effectively, the Republic was built on a set of principles which wrote women out of
the small share of public life they had previously been allotted and firmly
back into private life (principles endorsed by Napoleon I, the republican general who as Emperor personally supervised the drafting of the Civil Code).
The sinful female body was to become a virtuous republican body, bearing
sons who would be soldier-citizens. (French women could confer citizenship
on their sons by bearing them and on their foreign husbands by marriage.)

When in 1793, the Jacobin Chaumette closed down the women's political clubs, he said, 'the sans-culotte had a right to expect his wife to run the home while he attended public meetings: hers was the care of the family, this was the full extent of her *civic* duties' (Hufton, 1971, p. 102, my italics).

If one accepts that the Republic was constructed as much against women as without them, the development into a major issue of the clerical question in the nineteenth century can be seen as a development and consolidation of male republicanism rather than as something specific to the religious quarrels of the Third Republic (as contemporaries seem to have believed). There were certainly reasons to connect women with religion. We know (Hufton, 1971; Sutherland, 1985) that women were prominent in the religious reaction of the later 1790s. And it is certainly the case that before the 1850s, the education of girls in France was almost entirely in the hands of the Catholic authorities, mostly religious orders – as indeed was that of many boys in rural areas. By the time the embryonic feminist movement was gaining strength around 1900, the clerical/anticlerical division was at its height, exacerbated by the Dreyfus affair. But not even the fiercest republicans seriously suggested depriving churchgoers of their vote. It was because women had originally been excluded from the Republic that it was easy to convert an argument about rights into an argument about the putative result of giving women the vote.

It is not easy to discover hard facts about religious observance in nineteenth-century France. Twentieth-century surveys undoubtedly show that church attendance is higher, by a significant margin, among women overall than among men overall, and that the earlier the figures the greater the gap. Anyone who has been inside a French church will know that the congregation has a majority of women, often elderly, and the same was true in the nineteenth century. But that is not the same thing as saying that most women attend church. Already in the last century, church attendance was falling fast, and there was a considerable difference between many industrial areas and big cities, where the working class was virtually dechristianised with neither men nor women attending church regularly, and certain rural areas (Brittany for instance) where both men and women were devout Catholics. To have suggested disenfranchising Brittany on such grounds would of course have been quite unthinkable as an infringement of republican indivisibility and 'universality', but the continued exclusion of women on rather less clear evidence posed no problem. Unverified hypotheses about women and the strength of their religious convictions as a sex, and about the links between religious observance and voting behaviour were complemented in positivist thought by biological arguments.

Hypothesis for hypothesis, it is arguable that republican politicians, who were mostly middle-class town-dwellers, were generalising from their own experience. In the urban bourgeoisie, it was not uncommon for a husband to be free-thinking and anticlerical, while his wife, with at least his tacit consent, went to church and supervised the religious upbringing of the children. The case of the socialist Jean Jaurès (censured by his party for allowing his daughter to take communion) is typical. Indeed, some of his colleagues urged him to dictate to his wife over religion. Behind the claim that women would vote as their confessors told them to lay an unvoiced fear that they would *not* vote as their husbands told them to.

Despite the nuances introduced by recent scholarship (e.g. McMillan, 1981), the clerical/anticlerical debate is usually presented starkly in French republican historiography as being between obscurantism, reaction and superstition on one hand and progress, justice and freedom on the other. Neither participant could recognise any of its own values on the other side. But without holding any brief for the French Catholic hierarchy, it might be argued that in one respect at least, the Republic's universalism was less than that of the Church. When the Republic said 'universal suffrage' it meant 'unisexual suffrage', a term coined by French feminists (Hause and Kenney, 1984). When it said fraternity, it really meant brotherhood. The citizens of its heavenly city were all male.

In the Church on the other hand, where admittedly in the Middle Ages there had been debates about whether women had souls, the debate had at least been resolved in women's favour. It would be absurd of course to argue that women had anything much in the way of power and influence in a Church of which the hierarchy was and is male, and with a theology that powerfully reinforced sexual subordination. But at least all souls whether male or female were capable of salvation; women as much as men could be elevated to beatitude or sainthood; in short, all human beings 'capable of acquiring moral ideas' in Condorcet's words, whatever the shape of their bodies, were acceptable in the eyes of the Church and could aspire to fulfilment within it. Indeed this was precisely the ambition of a great number of French women, whose education as we have noted was within clerical schools and convents. Historians have increasingly pointed out in recent years how the work of women's religious orders, educational or charitable, and of lay organisations connected with the Church, provided many women with an outlet for energies denied a place in republican public life and gave them an opportunity, however limited in scope, to exert some initiative and leadership (cf. Smith, 1981; Bouchardeau, 1977; Langlois, 1985).

For the Republic, while regarding the Church's emphasis on 'the family' as a unit as reactionary, nevertheless saw women as best suited to the domestic sphere. In 1904 it celebrated with some pomp the centenary of the Civil Code, which enshrined many clauses depriving married women of a whole range of individual civil rights and which was being fiercely challenged by the feminists of the day (Hause and Kenney, 1984, pp. 75 ff). Even when the Republic tried to win women away from the Church, it did so with the intention that they should act as Rousseau had exhorted the women of Geneva to do. Behind the provisions for girls' education in the Jules Ferry laws of the

1880s, which undoubtedly brought durable benefits for French women, lay the aim not of making women citizens, but of making them the major repositories of republican values for the benefit of their sons. Like the Spartan mothers, they would act as a transmission belt for values that excluded themselves. When a reporter attended a prizegiving at a state girls' school in the 1880s, he professed admiration of both the physical and the moral superiority of the pupils compared to the girls in the Church school down the road:

> How clear it is that the young girls whom Madam H. is preparing for the struggle of life will one day be valiant citizens (*de vaillantes citoyennes*) who will be able to bring up their children in respect for justice and hatred of prejudice. (Ozouf, 1963, p. 108)

We are not far from Rousseau's vision of Sparta here.

One could pursue that Spartan parallel even further in the post-1918 period, when concern for the birth-rate produced an official discourse directed at encouraging women to have large families, while still refusing them rights within the city. The rhetoric too of the various republican 'catechisms' produced during the Third Republic, has a Spartan, military quality.[4] The origins of the Republic thus seem to have combined with the clerical/anticlerical debate to consolidate women's position as subjects not citizens and to confine them within the family unit under a Republic which asked many things of women (taxes and children to name but two) but offered little or nothing in return. That by comparison the church did not seem to be an entirely negative pole has increasingly been suggested by historians. Hause and Kenney (1984) have stressed the importance of the Catholic feminist movement, and a full discussion of the contradictions and convergances of clerical and anticlerical positions on the issue of women's rights is provided by McMillan's very well documented article (1981).

What the republican orthodoxy tends to do, when discussing this period, is to mask the extent to which republicans used the clerical threat (which was by no means imaginary) to bolster a long-standing, inherited view of the Republic in which women had a clearly-defined role. The result is to validate retrospectively the universalist discourse of the Republic (about democracy, the people, universal suffrage), while retrospectively invalidating (as sectional) the Church's universalist discourse (about human souls and salvation). Women are either absent from the picture, or are viewed as powerless objects of the debate. That they may have had good reason to oppose the Republic, that in many cases they sought alternative channels for political energies, or even that they may have been torn between the republican values they received in school and their exclusion from political rights, are questions which do not therefore have to be confronted.

That the traditional version of the story tends to excuse rather than explore the Republic's unwillingness to admit women, may help to explain the survival of a universalist republican language which sometimes seems to be unaware of its masculinist assumptions. The men of the Third Republic were after all the prisoners of a cultural tradition of great strength, and French feminism, though no doubt underestimated by historians, was not in a position to make much impact on that tradition. Less explicable is the failure of present-day writers, especially in France, to absorb the findings of what is by now a large body of literature in women's/feminist history into their analysis of the Republic. Sometimes (Nicolet, 1982) it is still a matter simply of silence. But other writers pay lip-service to modern feminism in a way that suggests that they have accepted its premises. Thus they include blanket condemnations of the past as 'sexist' (something the present presumably is not) within an analysis of the past in much the same terms as before.

Let two examples stand for the rest. Maurice Agulhon, an otherwise admirable historian, is guilty of this practice in his fascinating book on Marianne as a symbol of the Republic. He remarks that the nineteenth century, 'which we would call phallocratic', was a period 'marked by extreme inequality of the sexes' (Agulhon, 1981, p. 185). Yet throughout the book there is hardly any reference to the difficult paradox that real women were excluded from the Republic whose imagery was so overwhelmingly female, and the term 'universal suffrage' is used for the system introduced in 1848 without batting an eyelid (ibid., p. 161). Similarly, J.G.A. Pocock in *The Machiavellian Moment* (Princeton and London, 1975) writing of republican theory in an earlier period (not only in France), after 450 pages with no mention of women, has a single reference to a woman – significantly as the capricious buyer of a dress which may create work for commerce – in a context where the debate is precisely about commerce versus republican virtue. Again the writer feels obliged to pay lip-service to feminism by commenting that the example illustrates the 'rather prominent sexism found in Augustan social criticism' (p. 465). In other words, writing an important and respected book on republican theory in which this is virtually the only reference to women cannot be remotely construed as 'sexism', prominent or otherwise. Such writers – and the examples are deliberately chosen from eminent historians whose work I would not wish unduly to disparage – while adopting a sort of post-feminist discourse, do no seem to recognise that the omission of gender from their discussion of the Republic is itself a problem.

If the problem for historians describing the Republic before 1945 is a failure to register the masculinity of their own perspective, the tendency of political scientists writing since 1945 has been to categorise women as unworthy of the Republic. In the voting studies of the 1950s, much was made of the higher abstention rates shown by women: having been told all their lives that they were not supposed to vote, women were now being criticised if they chose not to. A note of disapproval (since most French political scientists are of the centre-left) crept into commentaries on the higher proportions of women voters for religious or right-wing parties. Slightly conflicting with this finding was another which indicated that married couples often voted for the same party – a finding writers sometimes liked to interpret as evidence that women voted as they were bidden by their husbands.

In more recent years, a more sophisticated 'revisionist' account takes the form of excusing these forms of electoral behaviour on the grounds that the generation under observation in the first twenty years or so after 1945 contained an unusually high proportion of elderly women who either never acquired the habit of voting (not having done so before the war) or who like men of their own generation, voted more often for the right than for the left. This is the starting point for the recent very thorough study by Janine Mossuz-Lavau and Mariette Sineau (1983) of the political attitudes of women in France today. From a middle-of-the-road feminist position, they accept the analysis of their predecessors: their concern however is to show that 'women have changed' since 1945, using as a major criterion paid employment outside the home and concluding that there is every indication that Frenchwomen, who now make up over 40 per cent of the active population, take more interest in politics and vote in roughly the same proportions as men for parties of left or right.[5]

The point at issue here is not so much to support or deny the empirical findings of political scientists as to question the assumption behind all the studies, however sympathetic to women's rights their authors may be, and however scrupulous about interpreting the results, that somehow women are 'at fault' in abstaining from voting for instance; that they are – or were – 'poor citizens' in Alain Duhamel's words; and that at best this behaviour can be excused by finding that other factors besides sex are 'to blame'. Women have been only too ready to admit that they have felt inadequate in the political arena. But political scientists are no more inclined than historians to contemplate the possibility that the Republic was imperfect and in a very profound sense invalid when it was created and sustained without women.

So it is understandable that radical feminists in France have simply ignored the Republic, despite the formal admission of women, as irrelevant and illegitimate. But this is not a satisfactory position to maintain over time. The first step towards a different stance must surely be a less triumphalist historiography of the Republic and more explicit exposure of it as single-sexed until 1945. That is not of course to suggest that if there was a problem then 1945 resolved it. The occulting of 1945 as a republican landmark, and the survival intact of the republican legend makes 1945 part of the problem rather than its resolution. It serves only to make it more invisible. France comes off no better than countries without a republican tradition. Part of the explanation is surely that women could hardly feel other than alienated from the male political world whose rule had been devised expressly to disqualify them. It is significant that there were more women in the French Assembly in 1945 than there have been at any time since: the Resistance generation was used to playing by the emergency rules of wartime. As in times of revolution, women were more likely to participate than when the traditional political culture reasserted itself.

Feminist history should have a part to play in opening up this blind abscess. There are signs (cf. Faure, 1985; Fraisse, 1983, 1984) that this is beginning to happen. But in France more than in Britain and America, the language of 'la grande histoire' and the discourse of everyday politics remain extremely resistant to what must surely be the aim of feminist history – to force a revaluation of the past as a whole, not just women's past. It is true that since 1974 there has been a ministry responsible for the improvement of women's rights and status in France. Although feminists may be divided in their attitudes towards it, it has a list of impressive concrete achievements to its credit, especially when viewed from across the Channel. But significantly, it is in the political arena that the ministry has made least impact: its plans for introducing a quota of women candidates in elections were quashed by the Constitutional Council and in 1985, the minister herself was moved to protest at the shabby treatment of women in the distribution of winnable seats within her own party in the run-up to the 1986 election.[6]

Among the various explanations suggested for this, vague accusations of 'sexism' seem the least adequate, or at any rate the least susceptible of analysis. More satisfactory would be an explanation in terms of the continued masculinity, well into the 1980s, of the republican tradition, as most people perceive it. A good illustration was provided by a survey published in December 1984 by *Le Nouvel Observateur*, a left-wing Parisian weekly which is a reliable guide to fashionable sentiment. To mark the new prominence of republicanism, it asked a series of questions reminiscent of the republican catechisms of the nineteenth century ('Would you be prepared to fight for the Republic?').[7] When they were asked which of a select list of living politicians were 'good republicans', those questioned evidently found this a difficult label to apply to the only woman on the list, former Health Minister, Simone Veil. She received only 4 per cent of mentions, although she might be assumed to be at least as attached to republican values as Raymond Barre (the former prime minister who, like herself, was not a career politician, but who received 33 per cent of mentions) if understandably scoring less than President Mitterrand (44 per cent). Since Simone Veil was at the time a very *popular* politician as measured by straight 'approval' opinion polls, it is simply as if 'republican' did not seem the right word to apply to her as a woman. This impression was reinforced by the accompanying statements from public figures about what the Republic meant to them. Madame Veil (again the only woman asked) gave a noticeably less clearly defined list of republican symbols than her seven male colleagues for whom republicanism was firmly rooted (whatever their politics) in two periods above all: the Jacobin Republic and the early years of the Third Republic. Valmy, the Marseillaise and the *école Jules Ferry* received several mentions. The reply of the socialist Minister of Education, Jean-Pierre Chévènement, is particularly striking:

> My republican ideal is the school (i.e. the *école Jules Ferry*). It is the crucible of the Republic. It arouses the intelligence, gives access to knowledge, sharpens the critical spirit, in short it shapes the *free men and citizens (les hommes libres et les citoyens)* of whom the Republic has most need. (my italics)

For him – and one suspects for many French people, including women – the symbolic apparatus of the Republic is thus one from which women are strikingly absent, yet the absence is rarely remarked. Similarly, and with even less justification, the minister's view of the primary school appeared from all the literature surrounding the 1985 reforms, to be dominated by the classic figure of *le maître*, the schoolmaster, the *instituteur* of the Third Republic. This, in an education system where 100 per cent of nursery school teachers and 62 per cent of primary school teachers are women (so that quotas have recently been introduced to protect the 'mixity' of the profession). The schoolmistress of today is almost as absent in republican discourse as the non-voting women of the past. Since women do not have a republican past, it is not surprising if they find it difficult to construct a republican present in terms of participating in a world built to exclude them (not to mention more material obstacles). Liberty on the barricades is from time to time reproduced as Marianne on French postage stamps and bank notes. Just as she is usually assumed by art historians to be an allegory or a figure representing the proletariat, without noticing the sexual power at the heart of Delacroix's painting, so the Republic she often symbolises is seen as a universal or sometimes as a class triumph, not as a system in which sexual power, that of men over women, has been enshrined.

Notes

1 Space prevents more than the sketchiest reference to the 'Enlightenment debate on women'; for full discussion see Tomaselli (1985) and Faure (1985).
2 'Those who are associated . . . take collectively the name of people and severally are called citizens as sharing in the sovereign authority, and subjects as being under the laws of the State', Rousseau, *Social Contract* (1973 edn, I, vi, p. 175).
3 Condorcet, 'On the Admission of Women to the City', in *Oeuvres de Condorcet* (1847 edn, vol. X, p. 122, my translation).
4 Cf. for example Charles Renouvier (ed. M. Agulhon), *Manuel Républicain de l'Homme et du Citoyen, 1848* (Garnier, Paris, 1981).
5 Their views are published in English in their contribution to Lovenduski and Hills (1981), which also summarises the earlier debate.
6 Cf. Christiane Chombeau's articles in *Le Monde*, 8/9 December 1983; cf. articles in the *Sunday Times*, 1 December 1985, and the *Guardian*, 7 January 1986.
7 'Hourra pour la République', *Le Nouvel Observateur*, 7 December 1984.

References

Agulhon, Maurice (1981), *Marianne into Battle: Republican Imagery and Symbolism in France 1789–1880*, trans. J. Lloyd (Cambridge: Cambridge University Press).

Bouchardeau, Huguette (1977), *Pas d'histoire les femmes* (Paris: Syros).

Faure, Christine (1985), *La Démocratie sans les femmes, essai sur le libéralisme en France* (Paris: Presses Universitaires de France).

Fraisse, Geneviève (1983), 'Droit naturel et question de l'origine dans la pensée féministe au XIXe siècle', in *Stratégies des femmes* (Paris: Tierce).

Fraisse, Geneviève (1984), 'Singularité féministe: historiographie critique de l'histoire du féminisme en France', in Michelle Perrot (ed.), *Une histoire de femmes est-elle possible?* (Marseilles: Rivages).

Hause, Steven, with Kenney, Anne (1984), *Women's Suffrage and Social Politics in the French Third Republic* (Princeton, NJ: Princeton University Press).

Hufton, Olwen (1971), 'Women in Revolution 1789–1796', *Past and Present* 53.

Langlois, Claude (1985), *Le Catholicisme au féminin* (Paris: Editions du Cerf).

Lovenduski, Joni, and Hills, Jill (eds) (1981), *The Politics of the Second Electorate, Women and Public Participation* (London).

McMillan, James F. (1981), 'Clericals, anticlericals and the women's movement in France under the Third Republic', *Historical Journal* 24: 2.

Mossuz-Lavau, Janine, and Sineau, Mariette (1983), *Enquête sur les femmes et la politique en France* (Paris: Presses Universitaires de France).

Nicolet, Claude (1982), *L'Idée républicaine en France 1789–1924* (Paris: Gallimard).

Ozouf, Mona (1963/1982), *L'Ecole, l'église, la république, 1870–1914* (Paris: Seuil (1963) and Cana (1982)).

Rawson, Elizabeth (1969), *The Spartan Tradition in European Thought* (Oxford: Clarendon Press).

Rousseau, Jean-Jacques (1973), *The Social Contract and Discourses*, trans. G.D.H. Cole (London: Dent, Everyman edn).

Smith, Bonnie (1981), *Ladies of the Leisure Class: The Bourgeoises of Northern France in the Nineteenth Century* (Princeton, NJ: Princeton University Press).

Sutherland, Donald (1985), *France 1789–1815: Revolution and Counter-Revolution* (London: Fontana).

Tomaselli, Sylvana (1985), 'The Enlightenment Debate on Women', *History Workshop Journal* 20.

14

Womanly duties: maternalist politics and the origins of welfare states in France, Germany, Great Britain, and the United States, 1880–1920

SETH KOVEN AND SONYA MICHEL

The emergence of large-scale state welfare programs and policies coincided with the rise of women's social action movements in France, Germany, Great Britain, and the United States in the late nineteenth and early twentieth centuries.[1] Despite their concurrence, historians have, until quite recently, studied these two great historical trends separately. But a new and voluminous body of scholarship in welfare-state history and women's history has uncovered the deep and intricate connections between them. Women's reform efforts and welfare states not only coincided in time, place, and sometimes personnel but also reinforced and transformed one another in significant and enduring ways. Women in all four countries succeeded, to varying degrees, in shaping one particular area of state policy: maternal and child welfare. It was in this area, closely linked to the traditional female sphere, that women first claimed new roles for themselves and transformed their emphasis on motherhood into public policy. During the years 1880 to 1920, when state welfare structures and bureaucracies were still rudimentary and fluid, women, individually and through organizations, exerted a powerful influence on state definitions of the needs of mothers and children and the designs of institutions and programs to address them.

In this period, women in France, Germany, Great Britain, and the United States developed grass-roots organizations as well as national and international lobbying groups to press for maternal and child welfare benefits. Many, but by no means all, used their authority as mothers to campaign for the expansion of women's rights in society. While resisting these demands for expanded citizenship rights, male bureaucrats, politicians, and propagandists encouraged women in their welfare work. Since the turn of the century, the din of male voices – Catholic and Protestant, liberal, socialist, and conservatist – demanding that women take up their sacred duties has, ironically, obscured women's own initiatives in this area. The subsequent rejection of

Reprinted from *American Historical Review* 95:4 (1990). Reprinted by permission of the authors.

motherhood and maternalism as incompatible with female emancipation
has led some historians to minimize women's influence on the formation of
welfare states; this essay offers a reevaluation of the early history of 'maternalist' politics and welfare states.

Maternalists not only concerned themselves with the welfare and rights
of women and children but also generated searching critiques of state and
society. Emilia Kanthack, a midwife and lecturer on infant welfare in St.
Pancras, London, observed that 'the chain reaches farther and farther back
– from baby to mother, from mother to father, from father to existing social
conditions swaying the labor market, which in turn result from economic
conditions of supply and demand.'[2] Some maternalists believed that their
values should be applied universally to transform the very foundations of
the social order. As early as 1885, French feminist Hubertine Auclert posed
the choices confronting the French people in stark terms: the state could
either devour its citizens, like the Minotaur (*état minotaur*), to satisfy its
martial appetites, or mother its citizens to health and productivity in peace
(*état maternel*).[3] In 1904, German utopian feminist Ruth Bré exalted motherhood as the fundamental, life-sustaining social labor and called for the
radical restructuring of society on the basis of matriarchal family units.[4]

Late nineteenth and early twentieth-century maternalists envisioned a
state in which women displayed motherly qualities and also played active
roles as electors, policymakers, bureaucrats, and workers, within and outside
the home. Before 1919, women in all four countries lacked full citizenship
rights and necessarily operated in the interstices of political structures. The
same men who applauded women's work on behalf of children were often
openly antagonistic to women's aspirations to use their welfare activities to
promote their own political and economic rights. The interests of children –
the nation's future workers and soldiers – came before the rights of mothers.
Even groups of men ostensibly committed to raising women's status, like the
fledgling Labour party in Great Britain and the Parti Ouvrier Français in
France, expected women to subordinate their gender-specific demands to
male-controlled political and economic agendas. That the women and movements we explore in this essay ultimately lacked the political power to
refashion the state according to their own visions does not diminish the
importance of those visions, their accomplishments, or their legacy.

Our account focuses primarily on the political initiatives of middle-class
women who were free from domestic drudgery and had the educational and
financial resources to campaign for social welfare programs and policies. In
the name of friendship and in the interests of the health of the family and
the nation, these reformers claimed the right to instruct and regulate the
conduct of working-class women. The shared concerns of family brought
together different groups of women, but, at the same time, conflicts over
control of the workplace and household divided them along class, race, and
ethnic lines.[5]

Other patterns also characterized maternal and child welfare in the four countries under consideration here. First, the growth of welfare bureaucracies between 1880 and 1920 led to the expansion of care-taking professions dominated by women: social work, health visiting, and district nursing. Both as professionals and as volunteers, women entered into new relationships with the state, which, in turn, sharpened their political awareness and expanded the rank and file of a wide range of women's movements and movements of women.[6]

Second, maternalist discourses – often competing – lay at the heart of debates about the social role of women, children, and the family among philanthropists, legislators and bureaucrats, employers and workers, men and women. The invocation of maternalism by so many different social actors compels us to reevaluate its meanings and uses. We apply the term to ideologies that exalted women's capacity to mother and extended to society as a whole the values of care, nurturance, and morality.[7] Maternalism always operated on two levels: it extolled the private virtues of domesticity while simultaneously legitimating women's public relationships to politics and the state, to community, workplace, and marketplace. In practice, maternalist ideologies often challenged the constructed boundaries between public and private, women and men, state and civil society.[8]

Finally, in all four countries, women were usually the first to identify the social welfare needs of mothers and children and respond to them through a wide array of charitable activities.[9] States relied on the initiatives of private-sector, largely female organizations and, in many instances, subsequently took over the funding and management of their welfare programs.[10] Such activities thus constituted an important (but often overlooked) site of public policy and, ultimately, state formation. Yet a comparative examination of maternalists' achievements in the four countries leads to an awkward and disconcerting conclusion: the power of women's social action movements was inversely related to the range and generosity of state welfare benefits for women and children. 'Strong states,' defined as those with well-developed bureaucracies and long traditions of governmental intervention, allowed women less political space in which to develop social welfare programs than did 'weak states,' where women's voluntary associations flourished.[11]

For example, the United States, with the most politically powerful and broadly based female reform movements and the weakest state, yielded the least extensive and least generous maternal and child welfare benefits to women. To a lesser degree, the same pattern prevailed in Great Britain. Germany, with the strongest state, had politically ineffective women's movements but offered the most comprehensive programs for women and children; the experience of France was similar. While the degree of state strength affected the extent and character of women's movements, it cannot explain their subsequent political successes and failures. Female reformers using maternalist arguments alone could seldom compel states to act. They were more likely to be effective when their causes were taken up by male political actors pursuing other goals, such as pro-natalism or control of the labor force. The decades before World War I were supercharged with nationalist agendas and anxieties concerning depopulation, degeneration, and efficiency, as states vied for military and imperial preeminence. These issues, and then the war itself, prompted legislators to establish many programs that might not have received state support under other conditions.[12] But the programs, in turn, owed their very existence to the models, organization, and momentum created by female activists.

In seeking to uncover the affinities and reciprocal impact of women's movements and welfare states, we need first to look at the existing theoretical and empirical literature on these subjects. From the late 1880s, men and women throughout Europe and North America vigorously debated the proper role of the state in regulating the lives of its citizens. In the name of widely divergent causes, they lobbied the state to stand between them and the callous forces of the market. The impulse behind state welfare policies was sometimes conservative, as in Bismarck's introduction of social insurance in 1881; sometimes liberal or radical, as with the social reforms that accompanied the rise to prominence of British radical Lloyd George after 1906. In France and the United States as well, the 'rediscovery' of poverty in the late nineteenth century by social scientists and policymakers focused attention on the breakdown of social and familial institutions in the great cities of the industrial world. Not surprisingly, many turned to the state as the sole institution with the resources needed to restore the health of the nation and to remedy the ills of modernity afflicting the family and its members.

The vast historiography of welfare states mirrors the complexity of its subject and the diversity of views expressed by contemporaries. Historians working outside a feminist perspective have offered a range of explanations for the emergence of welfare states: the process of modernization, the rise of new social forces and groups, and the internal dynamics and momentum of the state itself. Modernization theorists see the welfare state as a response to economic development, industrialization, and labor force differentiation.[13] They naturalize the welfare state as a logical response to the increasing complexity of a mature industrial society. Society-centered theorists fall into two categories. Social-democratic analysts attribute welfare-state development to the efforts of working-class leaders who translated their newly won political power into state programs designed to enhance the social and economic conditions of the workplace and home.[14] Neo-Marxists take a much less benign view. They point to the rise of professionals and corporate managers seeking to stabilize and control the work force. State welfare in such accounts is seen as a kind of bribe intended to coopt the legitimate (conflictual) political aspirations of the working class.[15] Finally, state-centered theorists stress the initiatives of bureaucrats and the imperatives of governmental machinery in explaining the expanded scope and role of the state in the twentieth century.[16] Some also advocate what they call an 'institutional-political process perspective,' in which 'political struggles and policy outcomes are presumed to be jointly conditioned by the institutional arrangements of the state and by class and other social relationships.'[17]

Each of these models explains important aspects of the emergence of state welfare programs and policies, but none pays sufficient attention to the impact of organized women's movements and gender issues on the process. In all four countries, factors such as the 'anomie' of modernity, the social consequences of rapid industrial and urban growth, and the growing power of class-based movements threatened the foundations of bourgeois civil societies and created political climates that were receptive to social welfare initiatives. Without this long-term change in attitudes toward the relationship of the state to civil society, women's successes in shaping social welfare programs and in lobbying for a variety of legislative enactments would not have been possible. However, though a necessary condition, the shift toward collectivist policies and greater state intervention in regulating home and workplace does not account for the forms of women's organizations and their causes.

From the perspective of women's history, the operative concepts and definitions of nonfeminist models seem too restrictive. For example, most nonfeminist theorists define the welfare state in terms of work-related pensions, general medical care, and old-age benefits, without examining the ways in which their models either include or exclude women or affect relationships between men and women in families. They pay little attention to the aspects of state welfare policy that most directly and explicitly affected women, namely, sex-based protective labor legislation and maternal and child welfare programs. Like the policymakers themselves, they take as their paradigm the regularly employed male wage earner. All too often, this paradigm renders women workers invisible, for it ignores differences and variations in their labor patterns created by domestic and family responsibilities. Employers' and politicians' perceptions of these responsibilities produced distinctions in their treatment of male and female workers and in the social policies devised to ensure workers' welfare. Nonfeminists have also overlooked the role of women in shaping policy. Despite abundant historical evidence pointing to women's presence in the early stages of welfare-state formation, state-centered theorists have, until recently, restricted their inquiries to the period when state welfare structures had already emerged and to the male-dominated administration of the official state and the political parties vying for its control.[18] By construing the geographical and chronological boundaries of welfare-state development so narrowly, they fail to capture those women's activities in the voluntary or civic sector that often preceded state formation.

Similarly, modernization and society-centered theorists obscure women's impact on state development by taking male patterns of political activity as the norm. Women were absent from or marginal to male-dominated parties, trade unions, and fraternal associations. In nineteenth-century France and Germany, they were prohibited by law from joining political parties. Disenfranchisement made clear the limits of female citizenship within the boundaries of the official, male-controlled state.[19] Yet these forms of exclusion did not render women inactive as workers or as political lobbyists. Without access to the venues for political mobilization restricted to men, women came together in other ways and around other issues. In the United States and Great Britain, for example, women formed cross-class labor organizations to promote the growth of women's trade unionism and represent the interests of women workers.[20] In France at the turn of the century, some women built upon their traditionally close ties with the church to establish Social Catholic organizations and lobbying groups including L'Action Sociale de la Femme founded by Jeanne Popinel Chenu and the Maisons Sociales established by Mercedes Le Fer de La Motte.[21] Arenas of mobilization clearly affected the types of policies each group sought to promote. In the United States, for example, Julia Lathrop, Grace Abbott, and other 'federal maternalists' sought to translate the ethos of the settlement house into a distinct political mode and agenda. Voluntary organizations and the many institutions they spawned for women and children figured importantly in women's political education by training them to create and work through bureaucracies, research and write policy statements, and raise funds and prepare budgets.

In drawing out the gender implications of supposedly sex-neutral policies, women's historians and feminist theorists have necessarily adopted new approaches to the study of the welfare state and redefined the state itself. However, just as nonfeminist scholars have ignored the impact of welfare states on gender relations (and vice versa), many feminists have also been one-sided, focusing exclusively on the state's instrumentality in perpetuating patriarchy. Some argue that state welfare programs are intended primarily to regulate women's productive and reproductive lives. Capitalist states use welfare policies to impose a 'family ethic' on women, just as they use other measures to impose a 'work ethic' on men.[22] Elizabeth Wilson's provocative study *Women and the Welfare State* (1977) claimed that 'the difference between the policeman's and the social worker's role . . . illustrates the difference between the directly repressive State and the ideological repression of the State. In either case, the function of police and social welfare agencies is to repress.' The welfare state defined women as 'above all Mother,' which, Wilson asserted, equals 'submission, nurturance and passivity.' Many other feminists concur with Wilson that welfare states situated women as clients and dependents in order to limit them to their 'primary task' of 'reproducing the work force.'[23] Despite its insights into the power of welfare states to control behavior, such scholarship tends to produce narratives of loss and victimization, in which women appear as passive, disorganized, and helpless in the face of the encroaching male power of the state.[24] It obscures women's roles as autonomous actors and agents, in large part because here, too, the political process is conceived as a male domain.[25] If, under patriarchy, motherhood always entails dependency on a husband or father, or on the state serving *in loco patris*, it is difficult to conceive that claiming maternal identity could help women gain autonomy and political power.[26]

Recently, scholars have begun to revise social welfare history, insisting on clients' activism, even at the individual level, within the penumbra of the state. For example, Linda Gordon, in her study of family violence, while clearly aware of the discriminatory aspects of many policies, stresses the ways in which female clients of both voluntary and state agencies shaped policies and institutions to suit their own needs.[27] The history of middle-class women's activities on behalf of women and children, like that of Gordon's working-class heroes, does not support the equation of motherhood with dependence or the depiction of women as victims. Many middle-class women viewed motherliness not as their special burden or curse but as a peculiar gift that encouraged them and justified their efforts to gain some measure of personal and political autonomy.

The roots of maternalist movements lie in the early nineteenth century, when women in Western countries began to organize in the name of social reform, reclamation, and moral purity. Essential to this mobilization was the rise of domestic ideologies that stressed women's differences from men, humanitarian concerns for the conditions of child life and labor, and the emergence of activist interpretations of the gospel (which varied from country to country and included evangelicalism, Christian Socialism, Social Catholicism, and the social gospel).[28] Women's moral vision, compassion, and capacity to nurture came increasingly to be linked to motherliness. Once embedded within an ideological and political framework, these private qualities became the cornerstone of the public, political discourses we identify as maternalism.

Such discourses linked religious activism and domesticity to one another in a curiously unstable matrix of mutually reinforcing yet contradictory values. On the one hand, women were enjoined to cultivate their womanhood within the home; but, on the other, they were urged to impress Christian values on their communities through charitable work. Inevitably, the practice of some women's lives as charitable workers conflicted with the dictates of domesticity. Maternalist discourses were marked not only by national histories but also by their specific political and rhetorical contexts. Maternalism was and remains an extraordinarily protean ideology capable of drawing together unlikely and often transitory coalitions between people who appeared to speak a common language but had opposing political commitments and views of women.

Maternalism grew out of a variety of nationally specific constructions of domesticity. In the United States, for example, nineteenth-century women activists could draw on a rich legacy of domestic ideologies that historians have named 'the cult of true womanhood' and 'republican motherhood' in constructing maternalist visions of women and the state.[29] Working in organizations that were sex-segregated by choice, female reformers initially sought to avoid any association with politics, which, they feared, would compromise their putative moral purity and hence undermine the rationale for their womanly mission.[30] But some quickly realized that they would be more effective if they could mobilize the powers of the state on their own behalf. [...] Yet, even as they moved further onto the political stage, women continued to claim for themselves a kind of moral superiority rooted in their differences from men. As late as the Progressive Era, the noted reformer Florence Kelley insisted that women possessed special insights into issues of social justice and social welfare and were, at the same time, entitled to special protection.[31]

Not all American maternalists believed it was the federal government's responsibility to aid and protect women. The noted Boston Brahmin and anti-suffragist Elizabeth Lowell Putnam called upon her home state to pass pure milk laws but opposed any form of federal programs on behalf of women and children. She claimed that the U.S. Children's Bureau, established at the behest of women activists in 1912, 'is merely a clever way, because appealing, of granting power to the federal government and taking it away from individual states, which is the great way in which the Soviet government works in getting control of its people, particularly the young – by putting the many in the control of the few.'[32]

The British case also illustrates the ways in which women joined notions about their motherly social tasks to different political agendas. Although Millicent Garrett Fawcett, a leading constitutional suffragist, was committed to John Stuart Mill's vision of formal equality between the sexes, she believed that women's private and voluntary philanthropy and welfare work was 'the most womanly of women's duties.'[33] Her adversaries, the women who signed the 'Appeal against Female Suffrage' of 1889, also believed that social reform and reclamation were women's special province. The signatories, who included such prominent female leaders as Beatrice Webb and Mary Augusta (Mrs Humphry) Ward, contended that the parliamentary franchise would pollute women by implicating them in the violent business of wars and empire. They urged women, however, to extend their housekeeping out into the municipal arena by seizing opportunities to serve in local government as elected and appointed officials and social welfare organizers and workers.[34]

While it is not surprising to find anti-suffrage women invoking a maternalist vision of women's sex-specific social obligations, it is noteworthy to find such views in the writings of leading socialist feminists and Labour party women. In 1907, Margaret MacDonald, a founder of the Women's Labour League, appealed to that 'great majority of women whose first duty and responsibility is to their home and children but who are learning that they cannot thoroughly fulfill their charge without taking part in the civic life which surrounds and vitally affects their home life.'[35] MacDonald's plea was part of a larger platform that included women's suffrage, women's freedom to choose to work inside or outside the home, higher wages for male heads of households, and extensive benefits for mothers.

In French Third Republic, anxieties over depopulation and the perception of military weakness in the aftermath of crushing defeat in the Franco-Prussian War made the contest to control maternalist political rhetoric exceptionally intense. Maternalism took many forms among French women, depending on whether it was linked to conservative Catholic ideologies, the philanthropic traditions of the active-but-small Protestant minority, republicanism, socialism, or one of the late nineteenth-century variants of feminism. Until the 1880s, two groups of Catholic women had traditionally dominated the care of mothers and children within their communities: Catholic nuns and well-to-do Catholic lay women. Bonnie Smith's study of the bourgeoises of the Nord argues that these women saw charity as an organic and natural extension of their domestic roles as mothers and as Catholics.[36] Subscribing to an anti-modern, anti-capitalist world view, these *dames patronnesses* established crèches, kindergartens, and maternal aid societies. Such women lived very public lives but refused to see themselves as engaged in politics.

[...]

In the 1880s, the leaders of the Third Republic, as part of their struggle against the church, actively sought to undermine the hold of Catholic women on social welfare. Abandoning the moralistic prejudices against unmarried mothers that had characterized the work of Catholic maternalists, advocates of this new, modern ideology recognized all mothers and children as vital resources for the Republic.[37] Their efforts not only increased intervention by male professionals pursuing scientific, bureaucratic initiatives but also created an opening for women committed to advancing motherhood within a context of republican ideology and female emancipation.[38] This did not, however, lead to professional opportunities for women, for male republicans continued to stress the importance of women's contributions as 'the natural agents of ... charity.'[39]

Catholic women, though marginalized during this period, continued to promote maternal and child welfare, reemerging as a vocal and potent political group in the early twentieth century with La Ligue Patriotique des Femmes Françaises (the Patriotic League of French Women). Unlike their Catholic predecessors, league women felt compelled to enter politics, even as

they sought to uphold women's traditional subordination to men. At approximately the same time, a cadre of elite, moderately feminist Protestant French
women laid the foundations for the interdenominational Conseil National
des Femmes Françaises (National Council of French Women) by recruiting
members from associations 'that concerned themselves with the lot of
women or of children.'[40] Thus French women who openly opposed one
another on fundamental issues such as suffrage or married women's wage
labor often found themselves in agreement over the need to expand and
improve maternal and child welfare.

Maternalism was perhaps the most significant thread tying together the
disparate women's movements in Germany from the 1880s until the 1920s.
Ann Taylor Allen cogently argues that the 'overwhelming majority of feminist leaders during the nineteenth century' embraced the concept of 'spiritual motherhood.' Allen aptly insists that, 'far from the reactionary
affirmation of traditional subservience which some feminist historians have
denounced, the nineteenth-century glorification of motherhood was initially a progressive trend.'[41] Shortly after the 1848 Revolution, Henriette
Breymann, a leader of the kindergarten movement, wrote, 'I foresee an
entirely new age dawning for women when she will be the center of the
home and when she . . . will bring to the broader community a quality
which until now has been entirely lacking – the spirit of motherhood in its
deepest meaning and in its most varied forms.'[42]

[. . .]

Breymann could not have predicted the varied meanings and forms
'motherhood' would take in Germany over the next seventy years. By the
end of the century, maternalist women had linked it to sex reform, socialist
reconstruction of the state and society, suffrage, and a wide range of state
welfare policies and programs. Alice Salomon, who, along with Jeannette
Schwerin, pioneered the development of professional social work in Germany, literally built on the foundations laid by Breymann by establishing the
first Soziale Frauenschule (Social Work School for Women) in Breymann's
Pestalozzi-Fröbel Haus in Berlin.[43] Salomon demanded the vote and aggres-
sively pushed for state intervention: 'We asked not for privileges, for prefer-
ential laws, but for an adjustment to women's greater vulnerability arising
from specific organic functions imposed upon them by nature.'[44] Salomon's
maternalism was inextricably bound up with her consensual vision of social
relations. The daughter of a wealthy, assimilated Jewish family, she envisioned a motherly state that aimed not to transform class relations but to
transcend the conflicts between classes through the bonds of motherhood.

Socialist women, while divided among themselves, denounced Salomon
and the bourgeois feminist movement as collaborators with an exploitative
system.[45] Women's emancipation could never be acheived, nor the rights of

mothers and children secured, without transforming the relationship between working-class clients and middle-class female social reformers. Lily Braun, a renegade from the aristocracy and a leader of the ethical-socialist Bund für Mutterschutz (League for the Protection of Motherhood), enunciated a passionate brand of maternalism that challenged the male-centered foundations of her society. Braun insisted that women – as women, not only as socialists and workers – had essential contributions to make to society. She argued that just as women received 'the seed' from men in creating life, so, too, male-dominated societies needed to receive the seed of women's distinctive gifts to civilization.[46] Although Bebel's *Women under Socialism* was the bible of socialist women, and the Sozialdemokratische Partei Deutschlands (SPD) was the most powerful political advocate for women's emancipation in pre-World War I Germany, Braun believed that even the German socialist movement was implicitly part of the 'hitherto purely masculine culture' she sought to feminize.

Activist women in all four countries regarded motherhood as empowering, not as a condition of dependence and weakness. They saw the home – domestic and maternal duties – as the locus of their power within the community. Yet, although maternalism offered women a common platform that transcended differences in religious affiliation, political inclinations, and nationality, their commitment to it could not conceal conflicts among them. When Alice Salomon traveled to London for the Quintennial Meeting of the International Council of Women in 1899, she happily anticipated sharing the platform on 'Protective Labor Legislation for Women' with Beatrice Webb, the renowned Fabian socialist and expert on social welfare and social policy. [. . .] But Salomon discovered that Webb 'thought in different categories from feminists and social workers.'[47] Salomon's revelation underlines an important point: maternalist women, while actively seeking to improve the conditions of women, were not necessarily feminists – some, in fact, deliberately refused to so define themselves.

Maternalism proved a fragile foundation on which to build coalitions. Women were divided among themselves on many key issues, and they lacked the political power to maintain control over maternalist discourses and policies. Although male politicians used maternalist rhetoric, it was often merely a cloak for paternalism. Their interests seldom lay in promoting women's rights or even strengthening the family as a goal in itself. From the mid-nineteenth century onward, legislators passed a variety of measures that singled out women for special protection by the state. Protective legislation limited or prohibited women's labor force participation by dictating hours, wages, and working conditions. Despite the humanitarian and maternalist language that accompanied the passage of such bills, 'limiting legislation' effectively diminished women's earnings by barring them from employment without compensatory benefits. As feminist scholars have noted, the men who led the campaigns for limiting legislation such as the

Mines Act of 1842 in Great Britain and the 1892 labor legislation in France 'protected' women in order to reduce the threat of competition from female workers, shore up the family wage, and compel women to remain within their homes.[48] Female activists, by contrast, typically demanded 'redistributive' welfare measures that compensated women for lost wages and provided direct medical and social services. Such measures left open the possibility of maternal employment. For working women, the differences between 'limiting' and 'redistributive' welfare measures were stark. Limiting legislation buttressed the gender-based, dual labor market, while redistributive forms mitigated some of its worst consequences.[49]

By the early twentieth century, many male politicians had become aware of the inefficacy of limiting legislation, and they too began to call for redistributive measures. But they tended to do so not for women themselves but on behalf of infants, the race, and the nation. Emile Rey, during debates in the French Sénat over mandatory maternity leaves, echoed Frédéric Le Play's conservative prescriptions for women even as he argued for radically redistributive policies.[50] He insisted that the French state should offer non-contributory and universal allowances to all needy women, not just those who were wage workers, for performing the labor of producing and nurturing children. But Rey was not motivated by generous concern for women. Instead, he wished to prevent those who were not already employed outside the home from abandoning the *foyer* for the workshop merely to gain benefits. Rey equated women's work outside the home with 'immorality.'[51]

Did it make sense for women to support men like Rey, who, despite their explicit paternalism, promised to redistribute substantial resources to mothers? In 1915, American feminist Katharine Anthony advised her fellow feminists to heed the example of their German counterparts and take a pragmatic or opportunistic approach to maternalist politics. The great expansion of benefits to mothers in Germany, she confessed, 'relied in great measure upon good masculine reasons which the masculine mind will understand. The spectacle of official diplomacy working out official reasons for granting a feminist demand is an exhibition from which watchful feminists may learn a great deal, if indeed it doesn't make them too furious to think.'[52] What were the implications of the trade-off suggested by Anthony between gaining feminist demands in the area of child and maternal welfare and accommodating the 'masculine mind'? Were the stakes of conceding control over maternalist discourses to men higher in terms of women's long-term political power than Anthony imagined? What were the tangible results of women's activism on their political identities, on maternal and child welfare policies and programs, and, more generally, on the state itself?

In Britain, France, Germany, and the United States, female maternalists used their private voluntary associations to develop social welfare programs for working-class women and their children. But just as women's movements varied in strength, so too did the extent and influence of their voluntary associations. Theda Skocpol and other state-centered theorists have argued that weak states – that is, those with decentralized or undeveloped bureaucracies (less rationalized, in Weberian terms) – will produce or be accompanied by strong private sectors.[53] Skocpol, along with Kathryn Kish Sklar, advances an important and suggestive corollary: it is also in such situations that women's quasi-state social welfare activities burgeon.[54] During periods preceding the build-up of the state administration and in social spaces outside of government – in civic, confessional, and voluntary arenas – women's groups mobilize resources and work effectively to pursue social goals.

Skocpol highlights the strength of the British state and labor movement in comparison to those of the United States.[55] However, when placed within a broader framework of welfare policies and programs, the American and British states both appear relatively weak compared to those of France and Germany – and the political prominence of American and British women appears greater. In the United States, where organized labor had little political power, Sklar argues that female activists 'used gender-specific means . . . to ameliorate class inequities.'[56] American women claimed the political space occupied by state agencies, churches, and bureaucrats in France and Germany to transform their voluntary charity into a shadow welfare state, an entity that Sara Evans has dubbed 'the maternal commonwealth.'[57]

In contrast to the loose, decentralized 'state of courts and parties' that characterized the American polity in the last quarter of the nineteenth century,[58] the private-sector maternal commonwealth became increasingly centralized during this period. [. . .] Although independent and firmly based in the private sector, women's organizations frequently lobbied local and state governments for improved services to needy and dependent groups, and many received public funding for the services they themselves offered. The more progressive groups turned to state governments for permanent support. The General Federation of Women's Clubs, along with the National Congress of Mothers, was a key player in campaigns for mothers' and widows' pensions during the first two decades of the twentieth century.[59] By 1920, forty states had passed such measures.[60]

While local chapters drew thousands of family-based married women into political activity during this period, single, educated women of the same and subsequent generations were attracted to the newly established urban settlement houses, which offered them myriad opportunities to participate in reform. Institutions like Hull House [. . .] served as staging areas for campaigns on a range of maternalist issues, particularly protective labor legislation and health programs. These campaigns soon moved from the local to the state level. With the establishment of the U.S. Children's Bureau in 1912, Hull House and its informal affiliates across the country gained a base in Washington and adapted their political strategies accordingly.[61]

The very existence of the Children's Bureau testifies to the unusual power and vigor of women's higher education and women's movements in the United States and, more generally, to their authority as social policy experts.[62] But their bureaucratic power was isolated and did not translate readily into a federal program of redistributive maternal and child welfare benefits. [. . .] In 1921, Congress did pass the bureau-sponsored Sheppard–Towner maternal and infant health bill but refused to renew it in 1929. Another bureau-supported measure, the Child Labor Amendment, passed Congress in 1924 but could not garner adequate state support for ratification. Ironically but not surprisingly, the absence of federal redistributive infant and maternal welfare laws in the United States coincided with the presence of the only female-controlled state bureaucracy in the world. Despite these affronts to the Children's Bureau and its maternalist allies, American women became entrenched in several branches of the federal bureaucracy, on state boards of charity, and in local and state welfare agencies, where they were able to campaign successfully for state-level maternalist policies.

Although the British state was somewhat stronger and more centralized than its American counterpart, both societies shared an enduring distrust of centralized government and a traditional reliance on local and private forms of welfare provision. Women's voluntary associations in Great Britain were also extraordinarily broad-based and influential.[63] But British women never matched the success of their American counterparts in gaining an exclusive foothold in the central state, even though both the Majority and Minority Reports of the Poor Law Commission of 1909 called for the creation of a children's ministry, which, presumably, would have been run by female activists.[64] Throughout the nineteenth century, British women reformers developed welfare programs in the private sector. Many of these women saw voluntary activities as a means to test new ideas free from the constraints of public scrutiny and interference.[65] Armed with proof of their success, they then lobbied for public subsidies and legislative support on the municipal or state level.[66]

Women's settlements in England, like their more celebrated American counterparts, also functioned as 'borderlands' between the state and civil society where women developed social welfare programs and policies.[67] For example, Mrs. Humphry Ward, in conjunction with the Women's Work Committee of the Passmore Edwards Settlement House, established influential programs for handicapped children as well as after-school and recreation programs for the children of working mothers. Ward was quite clear about the role that women's voluntary associations should play in shaping public policy. Addressing the Victoria Women's Settlement in Liverpool at the turn of the century, she sketched her vision of women's settlements and voluntary associations in England.

These irregular individualistic experiments are the necessary pioneers
and accompaniments with us of all collective action. We don't wait for
Governments; we like to force the hand of Governments . . . [68]

Ward's child welfare schemes drew increasing subsidies from the London
County Council in the years before World War I. Ultimately, it was the
strains of war, with its double demand for women's labor as mothers and
factory workers, that led the president of the board of education, H.A.L.
Fisher, to approve a national and state-funded system of after-school recreation programs based on Ward's model in 1916. [69]

The maternal and child welfare scheme developed in the Yorkshire textile
town of Huddersfield illustrates the close links between women's voluntary
associations and the state, partnerships between activist male doctors and
politicians and women, as well as women's increasing power as paid and
unpaid officials. Championed by the mayor, Benjamin Broadbent, and
headed by a progressive male Medical Officer of Health, Dr. Samson G.H.
Moore, the scheme was explicitly modeled on French precedent and provided the blueprint for the Notification of Births Act of 1907. The Assistant
Medical Officers of Health who oversaw the system were salaried medical
women who saw their positions as 'steppingstones' to careers in the expanding area of maternal and child welfare. [70] Each district in the town was in
turn supervised by one to three unpaid Lady Superintendents. Approximately one hundred 'Lady Helpers' followed up on the official visit by the
Assistant Medical Officers of Health and Lady Superintendents by offering
personal advice and assistance to mothers.

In Huddersfield and elsewhere, the expansion of public welfare was
accompanied by increasing power and opportunities for women, who were
enlisted to execute policies. By the 1890s, an estimated 500,000 British
women were engaged in public social welfare work, 20,000 in salaried positions like the Assistant Medical Officers of Health in Huddersfield. [71] In the
years before World War I, these numbers continued to grow. Barbara
Hutchins, a feminist and early historian of female labor, argued that the
expansion of state and public welfare services was made possible by and in
turn encouraged the growth of women's professions, which then opened up
new social and political opportunities for women. [72] While some working-
class mothers resented the intrusion of both volunteers and professionals,
their presence did not automatically lead to greater social control on the
part of the middle class. In Huddersfield, for example, it was, at least in theory, up to the client to decide whether or not to admit the visitors.

[. . .]

Compared to British and American women, French women's power to
shape social policy was more circumscribed. To an extraordinary degree, the
French regarded family matters as a public concern, far too important in the

eyes of men to be left to women. Male politicians often initiated social welfare policies for women and children, and typically they headed private as well as public social welfare agencies. In an important study of women and protective labor legislation in France, Mary Lynn Stewart concludes that 'feminists played a peripheral role in the campaign for hours standards.'[73]

On the grass-roots level and in a wide range of organizations, however, French women did participate in public and private social welfare provision. Their activities in voluntary associations, unlike those of their British and American counterparts, were more often subsidized by public funds and regulated by government officials from the central state (in the case of parochial activities, the church provided funds), as well as from progressive *départements* such as the Seine and communes such as Villiers-le-duc. Well into the twentieth century, French women were far more likely to participate in maternalistic activities than join feminist organizations, even though maternalism did not necessarily further their emancipation as a sex. While some historians estimate that feminists before the turn of the century probably numbered no more than a few thousand,[74] the conservative Ligue Patriotique rapidly became the most powerful organization for women in the country, with over 400,000 members by World War I.[75] Léonie Chaptal, along with other committed Social Catholic women, established anti-tuberculosis clinics in the slums of Paris and developed pioneering childbirth and infant-care programs. The Paris branch of the Maternité Mutuelle, like so many other maternal and child welfare agencies in France, was established by a man but relied on a large corps of well-to-do patronesses to implement its directives.

Pointing to the reduced infant mortality rates resulting from the organization's excellent services to employed working women, legislators cited the Maternité Mutuelle of Paris as a model for the kind of programs envisioned by the Strauss Law of 1913.[76] This measure, which mandated a four-week post-partum period for working mothers to rest and care for their infants, also stressed the importance of creating an army of 'women of good standing in their communities' to offer person-to-person advice to working mothers about the virtues of breastfeeding and proper infant hygiene.

German women in the late nineteenth century, like those of the other three nation states, drew on a legacy of private charitable work in maternal and child welfare. But their freedom to initiate policy was profoundly limited by a strongly entrenched state bureaucracy and a system of education that made it difficult for women to acquire necessary skills and training.[77] The precocious development of state welfare programs under Bismarck and the mandarin workings of the exclusively male civil service that it sheltered narrowed the range of issues and power available to German women.[78]

Yet the work of Christoph Sachsse suggests that the middle-class German woman's movement played a key role in establishing the programmatic foundations of *Sozialfürsorge* (social relief), which, unlike alms and private charity, was based on the social rights of citizens and was preventive in aim.[79] As a wide range of new social problems confronted the rapidly expanding urban centers of Germany, middle-class feminists called for female emancipation based on women's motherly roles as welfare providers in society. They not only organized the national Bund Deutscher Frauenvereine (League of German Women's Associations) but also initiated policies and programs through organizations like the Mädchen-und-Frauengruppen für Sozialhilfsarbeit (Girls' and Women's Groups for Social Assistance Work). [80]

The socialist women who founded the Bund für Mutterschutz (The League for the Protection of Motherhood) called for a new sexual ethics and for birth control to give women direct control over their reproductive labors. The Bund demanded a wide range of redistributive state programs including maternity insurance, [81] extended terms of indemnified and mandatory leave from work before and after parturition, child care, and legal advice for mothers. It even succeeded in its campaign to have state maternity rights extended to unmarried mothers. [82]

While by no means exhaustive, these examples demonstrate that women in all four countries contributed substantially to the development of private, voluntary, maternal and child welfare programs, some of which served as models for state programs and others of which were themselves taken over by the state. But there were important and enduring differences among women's gains in terms of tangible benefits and political power, differences highlighted by two sets of comparisons. The first examines concrete benefits such as the provision of state-subsidized crèches, maternity leaves and nursing bonuses. The second evaluates women's success in achieving power within state and local bureaucracies as inspectors and officers of health.

A comparative survey of day nurseries and crèches in France, Germany, and Great Britain undertaken in 1904 revealed striking contrasts. In Great Britain, all of the day nurseries responding to the survey were charitable undertakings that relied entirely on private subscriptions. While not included in the survey, the United States presented a similar picture. In France and Germany, a majority of the crèches and *Krippen* were subsidized by a combination of local, state, and private resources, with the exception of parochial charities staffed, funded, and controlled by churches.

By the turn of the century, the sixty-six crèches in Paris alone received £1,468 from the minister of the interior, £67,045 from the Ville de Paris and £1,376 from the Conseil Général des Départements. While we do not have fully comparable statistics for Germany, the evidence strongly suggests that *Krippen* and 'waiting schools' (generally for children between two and six years old) were even more widespread and better funded than in France. In Berlin, as in Paris, there were sixty-six crèches in 1904, although the population of Paris was nearly 30 percent greater. By contrast, London, with more than twice the population of Berlin, had only fifty-four crèches, none of which were publicly subsidized or licensed. [83] New York City, with a population almost equal to London's, had ninety-two day nurseries, but these, too, lacked public support or regulation.[84] Outside the capital cities, the differences were even more marked. There were only nineteen provincial crèches in all of England, compared to 322 in France. In the United States, by 1916, there were approximately 700 nurseries in operation, but only a few received partial funding from municipal subsidies.[85]

With public funding came greater regulation. In both France and Germany, state and municipal-level authorities established detailed requirements for the management of all crèches and *Krippen* – both public and private – including minimum room temperatures, daily registers, and guides to weighing children and preparing pure milk. The French women who ran the crèches were closely supervised by officers of the ministry of the interior, who had the right to inspect nurseries to ensure that they conformed with codes.[86] By comparison, in Britain and the United States, standards were largely the concern of voluntary authorities. In Britain, regulation was left up to individual managers, while in the United States, where only a few states and cities required nurseries to obtain permits, the National Federation of Day Nurseries urged members to meet certain standards.

The British and American women who ran and staffed day nurseries were free from the scrutiny of male officials, but they also had to make do with less generous funding. As a result, their nurseries tended to be less well staffed. French crèches, for example, had large female staffs including directors, wardens, cooks, and laundry maids, who were assisted by well-to-do women, appointed by the mayor to serve as managers or *dames patronnesses*. Doctors, almost always men, visited the crèches daily and helped set up Schools for Mothers. The appointment of salaried crèche personnel typically required official approval by the prefect or mayor.[87] In Britain and the United States, women in similar positions were either privately employed or volunteers, and the slender budgets of the charitable nurseries kept staff wages and numbers to a minimum. It might be argued that American and British women had more autonomy in the field of child care – as elsewhere – but they also had to make do with scantier public subsidies and other kinds of governmental support.

The inability of American and British maternalists to gain more generous benefits for the women and children of their countries appears all the more ironic when one compares their bureaucratic and political power to that of women in France and Germany. In these latter countries, women had trouble gaining footholds in the state itself, even at the lowest levels of the civil service. Denied *Beamte* status (full membership in the civil service, which carried permanent job security) because they lacked the necessary qualifications, German women inspectors were viewed as little more than functionaries and had no police authority.[88] British women factory inspectors had full powers to prosecute offenders and did so themselves.[89] Their reports were published separately and often commended for their particular thoroughness and insight, while those of German women inspectors were usually published under the name of the (male) head inspector. The position of French *inspectrices* resembled that of their German counterparts: they were often denied powers to investigate conditions or to enforce codes, and their authority and discretionary powers were severely limited. Because of educational and other bureaucratic requirements, they were unlikely to be promoted.[91]

German and French women's restricted avenues to the civil service also denied them political leverage, with the result that they had little voice in the legislative process.[92] Nonetheless, concrete measures were passed on their behalf. British and American women were far more vocal. They served as expert witnesses and members of public boards and commissions, and used their positions as factory, health, and school board inspectors to organize female workers and more generally promote women's trade unionism. In addition to highly visible positions within the Children's Bureau, American women worked not only as factory inspectors but as statisticians and analysts in state labor bureaus, where they gathered data vital to their public reform campaigns.

[. . .]

In the development of maternal and child welfare legislation in the four countries, Germany and France repeatedly led the way in the range and amount of benefits they provided mothers and children. From 1883 onward, German women received assistance (*Wochengeld*, or confinement money) from the state to compensate for their lost earnings during mandatory maternity leaves. The length of these leaves and the categories of women eligible to receive them were expanded several times between 1880 and World War I, eventually reaching eight weeks and covering agricultural laborers as well as factory workers. Beginning in 1893, French women had the right to free medical treatment during confinement and, after 1911, paid maternity leave and a nursing bonus.[93]

British women received fewer benefits, and what they had often took the form of limiting rather than redistributive protective legislation. From 1891 until 1911, Britain alone prohibited postnatal employment for four weeks, but it offered no compensatory payments. In 1911, the wives of insured workers and women insured in their own right were finally granted a lump-sum payment, usually 30 shillings at confinement, to address this hardship. Initially, the benefit was paid to the husband, but after strenuous lobbying by groups including the largely working-class Women's Cooperative Guild, mothers gained direct control over these funds.[94] Confusion and skepticism over what constituted genuine incapacity to work due to pregnancy intensified deeply engrained objections to public support for maternal welfare in Britain. For several years after the Insurance Act was passed, the Approved Societies charged with administering it, fueled by the anxieties of their male

rank and file as well as a looming fiscal crisis caused by an actuarial miscalculation of the extent of women's perinatal illness, usually denied women's
claims for sickness benefits during pregnancy.[95]

The United States provided neither federal maternity benefits nor medical care for mothers and children. Under the Sheppard–Towner Act of 1921,
public health nurses could offer maternal and infant health education but
no direct services. The United States was, however, the first country to offer
widows' and mothers' pensions (albeit only at the state level until 1935).
Since payment levels in most states were calculated to support children but
not their mothers, these early pension plans did not prohibit maternal
employment; this restriction came later, when the federal government took
over provisions as Aid to Dependent Children under the Social Security Act
of 1935.

Although British and American maternalists were often stymied in
attempts to use their bureaucratic positions to institute and control maternal and child welfare programs in their own countries, they sometimes had
the peculiar experience of seeing them taken up in France and Germany.
With some bitterness, Margaret McMillan, a British child-welfare advocate,
noted that 'Germany never despised any advance in English social life.' In
1896, McMillan had spearheaded 'an agitation for school baths' in Brad-
ford, where she sat as an elected Independent Labour party representative
on the school board. As she tells it, 'A leaflet on Hygiene and Cleanliness
was sent out into the schools. It has been carefully and tactfully written.
England ignored the whole effect, but not so Germany. She [Germany] had
the leaflet translated and circulated in her schools, and she started to build
school baths by the thousand.'[96] While British women had the political and
social space and power to develop innovative schemes like school baths,
German bureaucrats transformed isolated pioneering efforts into widespread and publicly financed programs.[97]

Once established, the German and French state welfare systems, through
direct programs and indirect subsidies, offered mothers and children more
and better resources than did those of the United States and Britain. However, French and German women generally had much less control than did
their British and American counterparts over the formulation and administration of policy. In all four countries, women often lost control over maternalist discourses when they were debated in male-dominated legislatures or
became linked with other causes.[98] This sequence of events was most dramatic in Germany. The middle-class feminists who established the first
Soziale Frauenschule on the moral and non-partisan foundations of 'spiritual motherhood' endured the transformation of their schools into tools of
national socialism. The Prussian ministry of education decreed in 1934 that
Salomon's Frauenschulen should be renamed Schulen für Volkspflege
(Schools for Training Officials for the People's Welfare), with the aim of
planting 'the ideas of National-Socialism deeply in the mind of the stu-

dents' through instruction in subjects such as race theory and 'Adolph Hitler and the history of the National-Socialist Party.'[99]

A review of current research demonstrates that welfare-state development was deeply influenced by female activists and their philosophies, commitments, and experiments in social welfare. Maternalist women put an unmistakable stamp on emerging welfare administrations. But their success was always qualified by prevailing political conditions and tended to be inversely proportionate to the strength of women's movements. Without maternalist politics, welfare states would surely have been less responsive to the needs of women and children, for maternalists raised issues – or highlighted them in specific ways – that seldom occurred to male politicians. Indeed, many men felt that only women could identify and respond to these needs. Yet women activists were compelled to rely on male politicians to gain state support for their programs and often had to wait until a national crisis such as war or class conflict created an opening for their initiatives.[100]

To different degrees, depending on the availability of political space in the four nations we have examined, maternalism served women as an important avenue into the public sphere. Female reformers demonstrated that a strong commitment to motherhood did not necessarily limit or weaken their political participation but instead transformed the nature of politics itself. Paula Baker's observation about the United States holds true for France, Germany, and Great Britain: by identifying and insisting on issues of gender-based needs, women challenged the male monopoly on public discourse and opened it up to discussions of private values and well-being.[101] It was not the case that male political actors, unsolicited, instigated state encroachments on family life; rather, female political actors demanded that states take up the concerns of women and children.

Nevertheless, for female activists and clients alike, the political process that culminated in the passage of protective and welfare legislation for women and children functioned, in an exaggerated fashion, as a Weberian 'iron cage': they found dissonance between means and ends, their own motives and ultimate policy outcomes. The translation of maternalist measures into state policy meant that poor and working-class women, initially at a disadvantage because they lacked direct representation in philanthropically based social services, were even further removed from the sites of policy making. As social work and related health fields became professionalized and services moved into state-run agencies, middle-class women carved out niches for themselves within the state. In these new positions, however, women frequently found themselves at the bottom of organizational hierarchies, their voices diminished in policy discussions with male bureaucrats, physicians, and politicians. To offset their liability to marginalization, the younger generation of American activists consciously jettisoned maternalism, which they characterized as unsystematic and unscientific.[102]

In the United States and Great Britain, women used their authority as experts in maternal and child welfare to forge political identities. These identities, in turn, helped some to build a wide range of women's political and social action organizations and movements. By the end of World War I, significant groups of women in both countries achieved full citizenship rights. But, because their positions in mainstream political parties and within the central government remained peripheral for decades, female activists could not make legislative gains on their own. The need for male political allies often forced them into difficult compromises and concessions.

French and German women were even weaker politically. Though granted more generous benefits, they were unable to convert welfare programs into political currency. In France, maternal and infant legislation existed in what was otherwise a political wasteland for women, who were, legally, appendages of their husbands until after World War II. German women won employment rights and the vote after World War I, but these gains were vitiated during the Weimar Republic and under the Third Reich. Abetted by conservative women's organizations, the Nazi regime perverted the meaning of maternalism as it condemned women to producing children for the state.

Despite these outcomes, the weight of the new research compels revision of historical conceptualizations of maternalist activities, state development, and the relationships between them in the late nineteenth and early twentieth centuries. When viewed from the perspective of maternalist politics, women's charitable institutions and organizations take on new significance as components of networks of benevolence as well as sites of state welfare program and policy formulation, experimentation, and implementation. Women's campaigns for maternal and child welfare emerged at approximately the same time in all four nation states, sometimes in concert with one another, and drew attention to the special needs of women and children in an industrializing world. Joining humanitarian appeals to thorough research and investigation, they contributed to the political momentum needed for reform. Maternalist women not only played important roles in promoting the growth of publicly funded welfare programs but were quick to exploit the new opportunities that statutory agencies offered them. The interactions between women's movements, states, and national political cultures from 1880 to 1920 affected the subsequent course of both women's history and the history of welfare states. The traces of these interactions remain distinctly perceptible today.

Notes

1 This observation holds true for many advanced industrial societies. We focus on these four because the rich secondary literature for each permits meaningful comparisons.
2 Emilia Kanthack, *The Preservation of Infant Life* (London, 1907), 28.

3 Hubertine Auclert, "Programme électoral des femmes," *La Citoyenne*, August 1885, as cited in Edith Taïeb, ed., *Hubertine Auclert: La Citoyenne, 1848–1914* (Paris, 1982), 41.

4 Ruth Bré outlined her vision in *Das Recht auf Mutterschaft* (Leipzig and Berlin, 1904). For a discussion of this work and its relationship to the socialist Bund für Mutterschutz (League for the Protection of Motherhood), see Ann Taylor Allen, 'Mothers of the New Generation: Adele Scheiber, Helene Stocker, and the Evolution of a German Idea of Motherhood, 1900–1914,' *Signs*, 10 (Spring 1985): 418–38.

5 Scholars like Jane Lewis have rightly pointed out that interpersonal forms of welfare are often based on the assumption that the individual is morally culpable for her or his poverty; see Lewis, *The Politics of Motherhood: Child and Maternal Welfare in England, 1900–1939* (London, 1980), 18–19. The female founders of social work rejected this equation, at least in theory. While they complained about working-class mothers' neglect of their children, reformers were often acutely aware of the burdens faced by working women. The opening of Carolyn Steedman's autobiographical *Landscape for a Good Woman: A Story of Two Lives* (New Brunswick, N.J., 1987), highlights the class-divided nature of social welfare as women's work in Britain. The psychological violence a female health visitor inflicted on Steedman's mother becomes Steedman's own 'secret and shameful defiance'; 2. Racial and ethnic divisions between reformers and clients were most common in the United States, although most minority groups made concerted efforts to care for 'their own.'

6 By women's movements, we mean those expressly aimed at shaping and changing the conditions of women's lives, sometimes but not always sympathetic with the goals of political feminism. By movements of women, we refer to organizations and campaigns initiated and managed by women that did not seek to change women's status.

7 Our definition is similar to those that Karen Offen gives for 'familial feminism' in 'Depopulation, Nationalism, and Feminism in Fin-de-Siècle France,' *American Historical Review*, 89 (June 1984): 654, and for 'relational feminism' in 'Defining Feminism: A Comparative Historical Approach,' *Signs*, 14 (Autumn 1988): 119–57.

8 We have used the categories public and private to highlight their permeability. Other feminist scholars have pointed out that the strict gender division between public and private that many social theorists take as a given is, in fact, a social construction. For the evolution of this dichotomy, see Jean Bethke Elshtain, *Public Man, Private Woman: Women in Social and Political Thought* (Princeton, N.J., 1984), chap. 4: and Joan Landes, *Women and the Public Sphere in the Age of the French Revolution* (Ithaca, N.Y., 1988).

9 See Nancy Fraser, 'The Struggle over Needs: Outline of a Socialist-Feminist Critical Theory of Late Capitalist Political Culture,' in *Unruly Practices: Power, Discourse, and Gender in Contemporary Social Theory* (Minneapolis, Minn., 1989), 161–87; for a specific comparative case study, see Jane Jenson, 'Paradigms and Political Discourse: Protective Legislation in France and the United States before 1914,' *Canadian Journal of Political Science*, 20 (June 1989): 235–58.

10 States also relied on other forms of private-sector welfare initiatives, including those emanating from churches and business. On the role of business in the French welfare system, see Laura Lee Downs, 'Between Taylorism and *Dénatalité*: Women, Welfare Supervisors, and the Boundaries of Difference in French Metalworking Factories, 1917–1935,' in D.O. Helly and S.M. Reverby, eds, *Gendered Domains: rethinking public and private in women's history* (Ithaca, N.Y., 1992).

11 We use the terms 'strong' and 'weak' states here to designate domestic, policing, and welfare mechanisms, not external functions such as the financing and waging of war. See John Brewer, *The Sinews of Power: War, Money, and the English State, 1688–1783* (New York, 1989), xvii–xxii.

12 Deborah Dwork captured the irony of this political fact in the title of her book, *War Is Good for Babies and Other Young Children: A History of the Infant and Child Welfare Movement in England, 1898–1918* (London, 1987). On Britain, see also Anna Davin, 'Imperialism and Motherhood,' *History Workshop*, 5 (1977): 9–65. Alisa Klaus offers a useful comparison of the impact of similar ideologies in 'Depopulation and Race Suicide: Pronatalist Ideologies in France and the United States,' in

Seth Koven and Sonya Michel, eds, *Mothers of a New World: Maternalist Politics and the Origins of Welfare States* (London and New York, 1993); see also Offen, 'Depopulation, Nationalism, and Feminism.' On the inadequacy of provisions in Germany, see Karin Hausen, 'The German Nation's Obligations to the Heroes' Widows of World War I,' in Margaret Higonnet, *et al.*, eds, *Behind the Lines: Gender and the Two World Wars* (New Haven, Conn., 1987), 126–40.

13 See, for example, Gaston V. Rimlinger, *Welfare Policy and Industrialization in Europe, America and Russia* (New York, 1971); and Peter Flora and Arnold J. Heidenheimer, eds, *The Development of Welfare States in Europe and America* (New Brunswick, N.J., 1981).

14 For a comprehensive discussion of this group of theorists, see Michael Shaley, 'The Social Democratic Model and Beyond: Two Generations of Comparative Research on the Welfare State,' *Comparative Social Research*, 6 (1983): 315–51.

15 For the United States, see, for example, Edward Berkowitz and Kim McQuaid, *Creating the Welfare State: The Political Economy of Twentieth-Century Reform*, 2nd edn (New York, 1988); and Gwendolyn Mink, *Old Labor and New Immigrants in American Historical Development* (Ithaca, N.Y., 1986), esp. part. 3.

16 See Hugh Heclo, *Modern Social Politics in Britain and Sweden* (New Haven, Conn., 1974); Roger Davidson, 'Llewellyn Smith, the Labour Department, and Government Growth, 1886–1909,' in Gillian Sutherland, ed., *Studies in the Growth of Nineteenth-Century Government* (Totowa, N.J., 1972), 227–62; and Peter Evans, Dietrich Rueschemeyer, and Theda Skocpol, eds, *Bringing the State Back In* (New York, 1985).

17 Margaret Weir, Ann Shola Orloff, and Theda Skocpol, 'Understanding American Social Politics,' in Weir, Orloff, and Skocpol, eds, *The Politics of Social Policy in the United States* (Princeton, N.J., 1988), 3–27.

18 Strongly indebted to Max Weber, state-centered theorists have assimilated his restrictive definition of the state: '[L]ike the political institutions historically preceding it, the state is a relation of men dominating men, a relation supported by means of legitimate [that is, considered to be legitimate] violence'; 'Politics as a Vocation,' in *From Max Weber*, ed. and trans. by Hans Gerth and C. Wright Mills (New York, 1946), 78. Although Weber was using the word 'men' generically here, he was, in fact, describing a bureaucracy and political system occupied exclusively by men.

19 In this sense, women were following the pattern of disenfranchised Englishmen in the eighteenth and early ninteenth centuries who turned to charitable and civic work to gain political expertise and power. See John Brewer, 'Commercialization and Politics,' Part 2, in Neil McKendrick, John Brewer, and J.H. Plumb, *Birth of a Consumer Society* (Bloomington, Ind., 1982), 227; and R.J. Morris, 'Voluntary Societies and British Urban Elites,' *Historical Journal*, 26 (1983): 95–118. For men's charity work and voluntary associations, see also Leonore Davidoff and Catherine Hall, *Family Fortunes* (Chicago, 1989), chap. 10; on men's associations more generally, 73. For a comparative perspective, see Ira Katznelson, 'Working-Class Formation and the State: Nineteenth-Century England in American Perspective,' in Evans, Skocpol, and Rueschemeyer, *Bringing the State Back In*, 270–74. According to Katznelson, it was 'in the voluntary organizations created in the "free space" of communities separated from work spaces [that] English workers learned to put claims to their employers and to the state in a rhetoric and idiom of class'; 270.

20 See Elizabeth Payne, *Reform, Labor and Feminism: Margaret Dreier Robins and the Women's Trade Union League* (Urbana, Ill., 1988).

21 Henri Rollet, *L'Action social des catholiques en France: 1871–1914*, 2 vols. (Paris, 1958), 2: 34–36, 116–25.

22 Mimi Abramovitz, *Regulating the Lives of Women: Social Welfare Policy from Colonial Times to the Present* (Boston, 1988), 36–40.

23 Elizabeth Wilson, *Women and the Welfare State* (London, 1977), 14, 7–8. See also Abramovitz, *Regulating the Lives of Women*.

24 Gillian Pascall made a similar critique of reifying or monolithic feminist theories of patriarchy in *Social Policy: A Feminist Analysis* (London, 1986). A parallel criticism has been made of Marxist social control theorists who set up a binary opposition

between bourgeois and working-class culture that assigns thrift and sobriety to the former, leaving, by implication, shiftlessness and insobriety to the latter.

25 Nonfeminists simply take this for granted, while some feminists make it the explicit point of their critique.

26 Carole Pateman calls this 'Wollstonecraft's Dilemma.' While viewing women's political participation in a patriarchal state as problematic, she points out that women's growing economic importance has drawn attention to the inequities of their political status and believes that women can achieve equality if there is a shift from welfare states to welfare societies; Pateman, 'The Patriarchal Welfare State: Women and Democracy,' in Amy Gutman, ed., *Democracy and the Welfare State* (Princeton, N.J., 1988), esp. 250–60. For a more pessimistic view, see Catharine McKinnon, *Toward a Feminist Theory of the State* (Cambridge, Mass., 1989).

27 Women exerted what Linda Gordon, borrowing from Elizabeth Janeway, calls 'the powers of the weak' to use these agencies as resources to enlist middle-class visitors and social workers as their allies in efforts to protect themselves and their children; see *Heroes of Their Own Lives: The Politics and History of Family Violence* (New York, 1988), 251. Gordon has also written that '[w]elfare not only replaced men as the object of women's dependence; it also subverted women's dependence on men'; 'What Does Welfare Regulate?' *Social Research*, 55 (Winter 1988): 630.

28 Dorothy George linked this phenomenon, which she called the 'new humanitarianism,' to her optimistic assessment of early industrial capitalism in Britain. See *England in Transition: Life and Work in Eighteenth-Century England* (London, 1931). On the impact of evangelicalism on women's position, see Jane Rendall, *The Origins of Modern Feminism: Women in Britain, France and the United States, 1780–1860* (New York, 1984), chap. 3.

29 The term 'cult of true womanhood' was first used by Barbara Welter in her essay by the same name, 'The Cult of True Womanhood, 1820–1860,' *American Quarterly*, 18 (Summer 1966): 151–74. For the ideology of republican motherhood, see Linda Kerber, *Women of the Republic: Intellect and Ideology in Revolutionary America* (Chapel Hill, N.C., 1980), chap. 5.

30 Maternalist ideologies were closely linked to new notions of respectability, which, according to George Mosse, arose with the nationalisms of late eighteenth and early nineteenth-century Europe. See Mosse, *Nationalism and Sexuality: Middle-Class Morality and Sexual Norms in Modern Europe* (Madison, Wis., 1985), chap. 1.

31 See Florence Kelley, 'Should Women Be Treated Identically with Men by the Law?,' *American Review*, 3 (May–June 1923): 277.

32 Elizabeth Lowell Putnam, 'Note on the Children's Bureau' (n.d. [1929?]), box 3, folder 57, Elizabeth Lowell Putnam Papers, Schlesinger Library, Radcliffe College. Putnam's remark draws attention to the fact that anti-Soviet backlash was particularly strong in the United States and contributed to the overall hostility to federal welfare measures.

33 Mrs. Henry [Millicent Garrett] Fawcett, *Some Eminent Women of Our Times* (London, 1889), 1.

34 'An Appeal against Female Suffrage,' *Nineteenth Century*, 25 (June 1889): 781–88.

35 Women's Labour League, *Annual Report* (1907), 9.

36 Bonnie Smith, *Ladies of the Leisure Class: The Bourgeoises of Northern France in the Nineteenth Century* (Princeton, N.J., 1981), chaps. 4, 8; see also Margaret H. Darrow, 'French Noblewomen and the New Domesticity, 1750–1850,' *Feminist Studies*, 5 (1979): 41–65.

37 Feminists like Marie Deraismes linked women's emancipation to the protection of the family and the Republic; see Claire Goldberg Moses, *French Feminism in the Nineteenth Century*, Albany, N.Y., 1984), chap. 9.

38 Moses, *French Feminism*, chaps. 8–9; Steven Hause with Anne R. Kenney, *Women's Suffrage and Social Politics in the French Third Republic* (Princeton, N.J., 1984), chap. 2.

39 Klaus, 'Depopulation and Race Suicide.'

40 Hause with Kenney, *Women's Suffrage and Social Politics*, 38.

41 Ann Taylor Allen, 'Spiritual Motherhood: German Feminists and the Kindergarten Movement, 1848–1911,' *History of Education Quarterly*, 22 (1982): 319–20.

42   Henriette Schrader-Breymann, quoted in Allen, 'Spiritual Motherhood,' 323–24.

43   See Alice Salomon, *Sozialfrauenbildung* (Leipzig, 1908).

44   Alice Salomon, 'Character Is Destiny,' typescript autobiography, 66–67.

45   For socialist women in Germany, see Jean Quataert, *Reluctant Feminists in German Social Democracy, 1885–1917* (Princeton, N.J., 1979).

46   Lily Braun, 'The Female Mind,' in Alfred G. Meyer, ed. and trans., *Selected Writings on Feminism and Socialism by Lily Braun* (Bloomington, Ind., 1987), 188.

47   Salomon, 'Character Is Destiny,' 67.

48   See Jane Humphries, 'Protective Legislation, the Capitalist State and Working Class Men: The Case of the 1842 Mines Regulation Act,' *Feminist Review*, 7 (1981): 1–33; Mary Lynn Stewart, *Women, Work and the French State: Labour Protection and Social Patriarchy, 1879–1919* (Kingston, 1989), 202; Jean Quataert, 'Social Insurance and the Family Work of Oberlausitz Home Weavers in the Late Nineteenth Century,' in John C. Fout, ed., *German Women in the Nineteenth Century: A Social History* (New York, 1984), 270–89.

49   Examples of redistributive legislation include the 30 shillings maternity allowance in Britain that was part of Lloyd George's 1911 social insurance scheme, the 1913 Strauss Law in France, and the various state-level mothers' and widows' pension measures passed in the United States from 1906 on.

50   On the byzantine debates and political machinations over this issue, see Mary Lynn McDougall [Stewart], 'Protecting Infants: The French Campaign for Maternity Leaves, 1890s–1913,' *French Historical Studies*, 13 (Spring 1983): 79–105; and Jane Jenson, 'Gender and Reproduction: Or, Babies and the State,' *Studies in Political Economy*, 20 (Summer 1986): 9–46.

51   Emile Rey, Minutes of the Sénat, *Journal officiel*, March 8, 1912.

52   Katharine Anthony, *Feminism in Germany and Scandinavia* (New York, 1915), 132.

53   The concepts of 'strong' and 'weak' states were first introduced in J.P. Nettl, 'The State as a Conceptual Variable,' *World Politics*, 20 (1968): 559–92: see also the critical discussion by Peter B. Evans, Dietrich Rueschemeyer, and Theda Skocpol, 'On the Road toward a More Adequate Understanding of the State,' in Evans, Rueschemeyer, and Skocpol, *Bringing the State Back In*, 350–51.

54   In so doing, Skocpol and Sklar are expanding the concept of the private sector, which, in this context, is usually thought to include business, trade unions, and (male) voluntary associations. See Skocpol, *Protecting Soldiers and Mothers: The Political Origins of Social Policy in the United States* (Cambridge, Mass. and London, 1992); and Kathryn Kish Sklar, 'Explaining the Power of Women's Political Culture in the Creation of the American Welfare States, 1890–1930,' in Koven and Michel, *Gender and the Origins of Welfare States*.

55   Theda Skocpol and Gretchen Ritter, 'Gender and the Origins of Modern Social Policies in Britain and the United States' (forthcoming).

56   Sklar, 'Explaining the Power of Women's Political Culture.'

57   Sara Evans, *Born for Liberty: A History of Women in America* (New York, 1989), chap. 6.

58   The phrase is Skowronek's: see Stephen Skowronek, *Building the New American State: The Expansion of National Administrative Capacities, 1877–1920* (New York, 1982), part 2.

59   See Skocpol, 'An Unusual Victory for Public Benefits: The "Wildfire Spread" of Mothers' Pensions,' *Protecting Mothers and Soldiers*, chap. 7.

60   U.S. Children's Bureau, *Laws Relating to 'Mothers' Pensions' in the United States, Canada, Denmark and New Zealand*, U.S. Children's Bureau Publication no. 63 (Washington, D.C., 1919).

61   Molly Ladd-Taylor, 'Hull-House Goes to Washington: Mothers, Child Welfare and the State,' paper presented at the meeting of the American Historical Association, Cincinnati, Ohio, December 1988; Robyn L. Muncy, 'Creating a Female Dominion in American Reform, 1890–1930' (PhD. dissertation, Northwestern University, 1987), chap. 2.

62   Lela Costin, *Two Sisters for Social Justice: A Biography of Grace and Edith Abbott* (Urbana, Ill., 1983); Ellen Fitzpatrick, *Endless Crusade: Women Social Scientists and*

Progressive Reform (New York, 1990); and Muncy, 'Creating a Female Dominion,' chap. 3.

63 See Anne Summers, 'A Home from Home – Women's Philanthropic Work in the Nineteenth Century,' in Sandra Burman, ed., *Fit Work for Women* (London, 1979), 33–63.

64 See Jane Lewis, 'The Place of Social Investigation, Social Theory, and Social Work in the Approach to Late Victorian and Edwardian Social Problems: The Case of Beatrice Webb and Helen Bosanquet,' in Martin Bulmer, Kevin Bales, and Kathryn Kish Sklar, eds, *The Social Survey in Historical Perspective 1880–1940.* (Cambridge, 1991).

65 For example, Elizabeth Fry's voluntary work in the 1820s and 1830s for the insane and for criminal women and Mary Carpenter's institutional experiments in juvenile reformatories in the 1840s and 1850s paved the way for parliamentary legislative reform.

66 See Madeline Rooff's *Voluntary Societies and Social Policy* (London, 1957).

67 See Martha Vicinus, *Independent Women, Work and Community for Single Women, 1850–1920* (London, 1985), chap. 6; and Seth Koven, 'Borderlands: Women's Voluntary Associations and the Welfare State in Great Britain,' in Koven and Michel, *Gender and the Origins of Welfare States.*

68 Typescript, Liverpool Speech, delivered at Victoria Women's Settlement (n.d. [ca. 1899]), Passmore Edwards Settlement Papers, Mary Ward House, London.

69 See Janet Ward Trevelyan's account of this in *Evening Play Centres for Children* (New York, 1920), 56–57; for the effects of the war on other maternal and child welfare programs in Great Britain, see Dwork, *War Is Good for Babies.* Wartime demands increased the scope of welfare benefits elsewhere, but the topic is too large to take up here.

70 Ironically, the Vigilance Committee of the National Federation of Women Doctors blacklisted the posts in 1909 because the salaries were too low and because they feared that the work too closely resembled that of nurses. See Medical Women's Federation Collection, SA/MWF/C57, Contemporary Medical Archives, Wellcome Institute, London.

71 Louisa Hubbard, 'Statistics of Women's Work,' in Angela Burdett-Coutts, ed., *Women's Mission: A Series of Congress Papers on the Philanthropic Work of Women by Eminent Authors* (London, 1893), 364.

72 See Barbara [Elizabeth] Leigh Hutchins, *Conflicting Ideals: Two Sides of the Woman's Question?* (London, 1913).

73 Stewart, *Women, Work and the French State*, 96. For an alternative interpretation, see Alisa Klaus, *Every Child a Lion: The Origins of Infant Health Policy in the United States and France 1890–1920* (Ithaca, N.Y., 1993), chap. 3.

74 See Hause with Kenney, *Women's Suffrage*, 28–29.

75 Anne-Marie Sohn, 'Catholic Women and Political Affairs: The Case of the Patriotic League of French Women,' in Judith Friedlander, *et al.*, eds, *Women in Culture and Politics: A Century of Change* (Bloomington, Ind., 1986), 237.

76 Minutes of the Sénat, *Journal officiel*, March 8, 1912.

77 See works by James C. Albisetti, 'The Reform of Female Education in Prussia, 1899–1908: A Study in Compromise and Containment,' *German Studies Review*, 8 (February 1985): 11–41; 'Could Separate be Equal? Helene Lange and Women's Education in Imperial Germany,' *History of Education Quarterly*, 22 (Fall 1982): 301–17; and *Schooling German Girls and Women: Secondary and Higher Education in the Nineteenth Century* (Princeton, N.J., 1989).

78 See Fritz Ringer, *The Decline of the German Mandarins: The German Academic Community, 1890–1933* (Cambridge, Mass., 1969), esp. chap. 3.

79 See Christoph Sachsse and Florian Tennstedt, *Geschichte der Armenfürsorge in Deutschland*, 2 vols. (Stuttgart, 1980, 1988), vol. 2: *Fürsorge und Wohlfahrtspflege 1871–1929*; Sachsse, *Mütterlichkeit als Beruf* (Frankfurt, 1986); and Young Sun Hong, 'Femininity as a Vocation: Gender and Class Conflict in the Professionalization of German Social Work,' in Geoffrey Cocks and Konrad H. Jarausch, eds, *German Social Work, 1880–1950* (New York, 1990), 232–37.

80 Sachsse, 'Social Mothers, Feminism and Welfare State Formation in Germany, 1890–1929,' in Koven and Michel, *Gender and the Origins of Welfare States.*
81 See Lily Braun, *Die Mutterschaftsversicherung* (Berlin, 1906).
82 Anthony, *Feminism in Germany and Scandinavia*, 139.
83 Mrs Townshend, 'The Case for School Nurseries,' Fabian Tract 145 (September 1909), in Sally Alexander, ed., *Women's Fabian Tracts* (London, 1985).
84 Association of Day Nurseries of New York City, *Annual Report* (1910).
85 Emily D. Cahan, *Past Caring: A History of U.S. Preschool Care and Education for the Poor, 1820–1965* (New York, 1989), 13.
86 For example, see the proposed texts for a presidential decree and ministerial order adopted by the High Council for Public Assistance, *Revue philanthropique*, 1 (May 15, 1897): 117–19. According to the law of June 27, 1904, *inspectrices* were allowed to visit and inspect crèches.
87 It is important to recognize that the degree of official control, even in France and Germany, varied locally.
88 See Jean Quataert, 'A Source Analysis in German Women's History: Factory Inspectors' Reports and the Shaping of Working Class Lives, 1878–1914,' *Central European History*, 16 (June 1983): 99–121.
89 See Mary Drake McFeely, *Lady Inspectors: The Campaign for a Better Workplace 1893–1921* (Oxford, 1988), esp. chap. 7.
90 Quataert, 'Source Analysis,' 103–05.
91 Stewart, *Women, Work and the French State*, 89–93.
92 See Klaus, 'Depopulation and Race Suicide.'
93 French women were also given a nursing bonus for the first twelve weeks. In addition to a maximum of eight weeks of paid pre-partum and post-partum maternity leave, they received half a franc per day of nursing for four weeks.
94 The guild was also responsible for the initial inclusion of a maternity benefit in the 1911 Insurance Act. Under the leadership of Margaret Llewelyn Davies, the guild was the largest and most politically adept organization representing working-class mothers in England. The lobbying of women's groups like the Women's Co-operative Guild and Women's Labour League forced the government to acknowledge the sex-based distribution of resources within the family and to pay mothers directly.
95 This miscalculation was, in fact, an artifact of women's own underreporting of illness during the period when they were not covered and felt compelled to work, no matter what the state of their health. Once benefits were available, they acknowledged their illnesses more openly. See Margaret Bondfield, *The National Care of Maternity: A Scheme Put Forward as a Basis for Discussion* (London, 1914), 9.
96 Margaret McMillan, *The Camp School* (London, 1919), 18.
97 This incident suggests that the exchange between Britain and Germany did not always follow the usual pattern, which went in the opposite direction; see, for example, E.P. Hennock, *British Social Reform and German Precedents: The Case of Social Insurance, 1880–1914* (New York, 1987).
98 A striking example of such a turnabout is described by Susan Pedersen in 'Gender, Welfare, and Citizenship in Britain during the Great War,' *American Historical Review*, 95 (October 1990): 983–1006.
99 See Alice Salomon, *Education for Social Work: A Sociological Interpretation Based on an International Survey* (Zurich, 1937), esp. 21–36.
100 On the impact of class on French welfare policy, see Klaus, 'Depopulation and Race Suicide.'
101 Paula Baker, 'The Domestication of Politics: Women and American Political Society, 1780–1920,' *American Historical Review*, 89 (June 1985): 620–47.
102 This shift was led by Julia Lathrop, Grace and Edith Abbott, and Sophonisba Breckinridge; see Muncy, 'Creating a Female Dominion,' 102–03.

SECTION VI

WORK

IV

Introduction

Work was one of the earliest and most significant of the topics covered by women's historians, but much less has been written, from the point of view of gender, about men's work. Like many other areas of their lives, men's work has been assumed to be the norm, and what was seen to be of significance were the (relatively few) aspects of the topic where women entered this male domain. This perspective is reinforced by the nature of the documentary evidence, which often misleadingly tends to assign to men a single, stable occupational identity, while failing to record many types of women's waged labour (not to mention their unpaid labour in the household).[1] Consequently, the most common problem investigated has been the obstacles which have prevented women from engaging in the same employments as men. Reflecting the social scientific perspective of early gender historians, research focused initially on the economic changes (such as industrialization) and institutional obstacles (imposed by guilds, unions and the state) which excluded women (and less skilled or low status men) from many occupations. As the theoretical perspectives of gender historians have changed, however, their explanations have shifted to prioritize ideological factors. Deborah Valenze, for example, has ascribed women's exclusion from many jobs during the English industrial revolution to the growing influence of the values of productivity and rationality, which were perceived to be inherently masculine. In explaining the exclusion of women from skilled occupations in the nineteenth century, others have pointed to the influence of arguments that men should be paid a 'family' or 'breadwinning' wage, which privileged skilled work and that which took place in workshops over that which took place in the home. In the twentieth century, what was emphasized was men's technical competence.[2] These arguments shed important light on the conceptions of masculinity which were marshalled in support of men's privileged access to skilled jobs.

A common assumption in this historiography is that things got worse for women: that women in earlier times had more varied opportunities to work. The problem of change and continuity in the history of women's work has much exercised historians, ever since the classic works of Alice Clark and Ivy Pinchbeck introduced the argument that, in England, women's work opportunities were far more equal to men's before fundamental changes in the structure of the economy (the spread of capitalism in the seventeenth century, according to Clark, and the industrial revolution, according to Pinchbeck) pushed them out.[3] While such arguments continue to be influential, they have been rejected by some historians, who have stressed the continuities in women's exclusion from the more prestigious jobs, arguing that the so-called 'golden age' of women's work posited by Clark and Pinchbeck never existed. In a survey of women's work in Europe between 1200 and 1900, Judith Bennett claimed that, despite changes in the specific tasks performed by women, 'women were as clustered in low-skilled, low-status, and low-paying occupations in 1200 as in 1900', and this conclusion is reinforced by Part II of Amanda Vickery's survey of English women's historiography reproduced in Section III of this reader.[4]

As the article by Katrina Honeyman and Jordan Goodman reproduced below suggests, however, the fact that there has not been any linear change in gendered work patterns over several hundred years does not mean that no changes have taken place. Change could occur cyclically, with periods of greater overlap in the work performed by men and women alternating with periods of women's exclusion from better paid and more skilled jobs. While Honeyman and Goodman focus on the periods of exclusion, during what they call periods of 'gender conflict', Maxine Berg has outlined one important period when the number of women working and the types of jobs they performed expanded: the early stages of the industrial revolution in England. Arguing that historians have been misled by the deficiencies of their sources into underplaying the amount of work performed by women, Berg suggests that the late eighteenth and early nineteenth centuries witnessed a significant expansion in the female workforce, which contracted after around 1850. Since this implies that the industrial revolution in England was a more revolutionary process than is currently thought by economic historians, it is a good example of how introducing gender into history can significantly alter our understandings of formative historical events.[5]

The history of men and women at work is thus one of fluctuating and contested boundaries. What gender historians therefore need to understand is what makes these boundaries move, either to expand or to contract opportunities for each sex. As Berg's article suggests, changes in levels of demand for labour and in the types of labour required clearly played an important role; it is necessary to examine the changing requirements of employers, in terms of levels of skill and flexibility required and the location of employment, all of which were stimulated by structural changes in the economy such as protoindustrialization and industrialization. But historians of the sexual division of labour also need to examine broader changes in conceptions of masculinity and femininity which shape the types of work acceptable for each sex, such as the association of men with rationality from the seventeenth century and of women with moral domesticity from the eighteenth century. Honeyman and Goodman's article investigates all these factors, by examining the economic, institutional and ideological factors which restricted women's work in two periods of European history. None the less, it has been criticized for focusing almost exclusively on urban economies, and for paying insufficient attention to the role played by economic development in stimulating changes in the workforce which led to gender conflict.[6] It is worth considering whether rural protoindustrialization, or any other periods of expansion of women's work (such as wars), gave rise to similar conflicts. The article also reasserts the utility of patriarchy as an explanatory concept for gender historians.[7]

Notes

1 Robert B. Shoemaker, *Gender in English Society, 1650–1850: The Emergence of Separate Spheres?* (London, 1998), pp. 148–50.

2 Deborah Valenze, *The First Industrial Woman* (Oxford, 1995); Sonya Rose, 'Gender Antagonism and Class Conflict: Exclusionary Strategies of Male Trade Unionists in Nineteenth-Century Britain', *Social History* 13 (1988), pp. 191–208; Wally Seccombe, 'Patriarchy Stabilized: The Construction of the Male Breadwinner Wage Norm in Nineteenth-Century Britain', *Social History* 11 (1986), pp. 53–76; Joan Scott, 'Work Identities for Men and Women: The Politics of Work and Family in the Parisian Garment Trades in 1848', in her *Gender and the Politics of History* (New York, 1988), pp. 93–112; Pamela Radcliffe, 'Elite Women Workers and Collective Action: The Cigarette Makers of Gijón, 1890-1930', *Journal of Social History* 27:1 (1993), pp. 85–108; Michael Roper, 'Yesterday's Model: Product Fetishism and the British Company Man, 1945–85' in Michael Roper and John Tosh (eds), *Manful Assertions: Masculinities in Britain since 1800* (London, 1991), pp. 190–211.

3 Alice Clark, *Working Life of Women in the Seventeenth Century* (London, 1919); Ivy Pinchbeck, *Women Workers and the Industrial Revolution* (London, 1930).

4 Judith Bennett, '"History That Stands Still": Women's Work in the European Past', *Feminist Studies* 14 (1988), p. 278. Her arguments are more fully developed in 'Medieval Women, Modern Women: Across the Great Divide' in D. Aers (ed.), *Culture and History, 1350–1600: Essays on English Communities, Identities, and Writing* (London, 1992), pp. 147–75. The earlier article has been criticized in Bridget Hill, 'Women's History: A Study in Change, Continuity or Standing Still', *Women's History Review* 2 (1993), pp. 5–22, with a reply from Bennett on pp. 173–84. Support for Bennett's argument can be found in Peter Earle, 'The Female Labour Market in London in the Late Seventeenth and Early Eighteenth Centuries', *Economic History Review*, 2nd series, 42 (1989), pp. 328–47.

5 Maxine Berg, 'What Difference did Women's Work Make to the Industrial Revolution?', *History Workshop Journal* 35 (1993), pp. 22–44.

6 Hill, 'Women's History', pp. 14–15.

7 See Introduction, above, pp. 3–4.

15

Women's work, gender conflict, and labour markets in Europe, 1500–1900

KATRINA HONEYMAN AND JORDAN GOODMAN

The position of women in the labour markets of Europe from the middle ages to the beginning of the twentieth century has been the subject of a substantial and vital research effort in recent years. In this area of enquiry, as so often in the social sciences, greater certainty surrounds what happened than why it happened. The central problem in the history of women's work is to explain the nature of and changes in the gender division of labour and the persistence of women in the lowest paid, least stable, and most unrewarding occupations[1]. A wealth of detail is presented in recent research on working women in the past which suggests a framework for its analysis. The three main features of this framework can be identified as follows. The first involves an escape from the periodization prevalent in social and economic history which is inappropriate to the history of women's work and has previously resulted in faulty and misleading assumptions. The most serious of these misconceptions has been the attempt to explain the origins of women's oppression within the context of the emergence of industrial capitalism. The best research of recent years has clearly revealed that labour markets in which women face discrimination are of very long standing and were not the creation of the forces of industrialization.[2]

The second component suggests an emphasis on periods of gender conflict as of crucial importance. It is by focusing on such crisis periods, which might arise for a number of reasons, that a clearer appreciation of the causes of a particular gender division of labour can develop. Two particularly intense periods of gender conflict in the workplace were manifest in Europe: from the late fifteenth to the end of the sixteenth century, and from the early nineteenth century.[3] Both episodes apparently occurred because artisans and other skilled men believed their position of economic strength and thus patriarchal power to be under threat. The outcomes in both cases included a more clearly specified gendering of jobs, new restrictions on the employment of women, and a reduction in the value placed on women's work associated with a greater emphasis on their domestic position in the family.

Reprinted from *Economic History Review* 44:4 (1991), pp. 608–28. Copyright 1991 Economic History Society. Reprinted by permission of Blackwell Publishers Ltd.

The third feature of this framework concerns the nature of patriarchy and its institutions especially in times of exceptional crisis.[4] It is now more readily accepted than in the past that the economic, political, and social subordination of women has been at least partly determined by patriarchal forces, although too general a usage of patriarchy as an explanation has weakened its potential as a tool of analysis. Patriarchy can be defined as a pervading societal system or set of institutional arrangements which accept, reinforce, or structure male hegemony. There is nothing 'natural' about this system. Patriarchy is a construct, real and imagined. What is relevant in the present context is that patriarchy may seem inevitable because for long periods its forces are inactive and apparently invisible (and sometimes even denied), and its presence is affirmed only when threatened. It is at this point of 'active' patriarchy that its characteristics become open to examination.

By considering the recent contributions to the literature within the framework as outlined, it is hoped to show that significant progress has been made towards an understanding of the long-established gender division of labour and to indicate how it may be extended by further empirical investigations.

I

In early modern European cities occupational categories for men and women were already differentiated and there was a dual or segmented labour market.[5] Men's work comprised the primary labour market. Jobs were skilled, or perceived as such; they conferred a high degree of status and they were well rewarded both financially and in non-monetary ways. In workshop production, the locus of artisanal labour, wages formed the lesser part of the payment for work; of greater importance were customary rights to advanced payments and credit, widespread systems of subcontracting, and payments in food and lodgings. Social rewards, status, esteem, independence of supervision, dignified treatment, and mobility were part and parcel of this world.[6] Craftsmen more often resembled independent businessmen than workers. In the building industry in early modern England, for example, craftsmen not only supplied their own raw materials, but earned a significant proportion of their income from a variety of economic sources.[7] Evidence from Parisian workshops in the eighteenth century points to a similar conclusion.[8]

The characteristics of women's work already conformed to those of a secondary labour market where employment was largely unskilled, of low status, poorly paid, casual, seasonal, and irregular. Working women operated within a narrow occupational structure, were generally more prone than men to long periods of underemployment and unemployment, and enjoyed few of the security buffers built into men's work. In industrial activities women were more dependent upon monetary wage payments than were men. With little other compensation, women workers were particularly vulnerable to the vagaries of the early modern economy. This reinforced the irregular rhythm of work.

Although a dual labour market clearly existed in the early modern economy, its origin is difficult to trace. It seems clear, however, that while the nature of men's work remained constant, fundamental changes in women's employment patterns occurred in the late middle ages. We turn, therefore, to the mechanisms by which women's position in the labour market became secondary. The transformation of women's work began in towns where women became excluded from crafts and skilled work and were relegated to low paid and low productivity employment. Prior to this subordination, medieval urban women were relatively well represented in a variety of high status occupations, though the pattern of their work was by no means uniform across Europe.[9] In some northern European cities, such as Bruges, Leiden, and Douai, women figured prominently in the manufacture of high-quality woollen cloth, filling managerial and other esteemed occupations. In other cities, however, such as Cologne, Florence, and Paris, women were less conspicuous in such positions or were entirely barred from them. Similarly, women participated in long-distance trade and in craft activities in London and Cologne but not in Paris and Venice. The explanation for this disparity is not entirely clear, but it is certain that medieval guilds were not always hostile to women; girls were apprenticed and women occupied official positions in many guilds. In Paris and Cologne, moreover, some guilds were run exclusively by women though membership was open to both sexes.[10]

In northern European cities, women appear to have occupied high status positions in the labour market chiefly in those economic activities where production was organized on the basis of family units; that is, where family members shared in the production of goods and services for the market rather than selling their labour.[11] High status derived mainly from the independence associated with access to raw materials and control over distribution. As the family production unit began to lose its hold over market production in Leiden, Cologne, Douai, and Frankfurt from the late fifteenth century, the position of women in the labour market declined noticeably. Organizational changes in the economy of these cities weakened the family production unit as it strengthened other modes of production, notably small commodity production and capitalist production. The main victims of these changes were women who, finding their access to high status positions increasingly restricted, retreated from market production altogether. Economic forces were clearly at work, but they were not the primary cause of the changes in women's work experience. The patriarchal order, increasingly under threat from the participation of women in market production, ensured that these economic changes were distributed differentially between men and women. The exclusion of women from high status positions in turn served to reinforce patriarchy within changed economic circumstances.[12]

Organizational changes in industrial production were certainly responsible for some changes in the working experiences of women but a much more gender-inspired movement was on its way led by urban craft guilds. Their strategy was to attack women directly as workers. This onslaught took several forms. Some guilds chose to pursue a policy of barring women from participation in their affairs. In some cities, this exclusion was achieved in incremental stages while in others, women were simply forced out. In fifteenth-centry Leiden, for example, women were completely excluded and the guilds became male preserves. In Cologne, where women had actively participated in the guilds during the middle ages, their passage into marginality was less direct and immediate yet equally effective. By the late fifteenth century, almost all of the city's guilds had become male preserves with the exception of a few whose activities, such as needlework, embroidery, and belt-making were becoming defined as women's work.[13]

Another recourse was the imposition of a gender identification of work activities within individual guilds. In early modern German towns, for example, it became common for the tailors' guild to restrict the kind of work that seamstresses were allowed to do. In general, seamstresses were relegated to working with old, used, or cheap cloth while male tailors reserved the right to all other types. The bleaching and dyeing trades also distinguished minutely between men's and women's work, the latter being confined to small or used articles. In hatting, male guild members sought to bar women totally from making hats but when this failed, they settled for a compromise whereby women were confined to the least prestigious work of veil making, and hat repair.[14]

Evidence from a number of European economies, however, indicates that the most common form of attack was completely to close women's access to particular trades. Wherever this happened the result was the same: the range of occupations open to women became severely restricted; and because those that were available became defined as women's work, they normally ceased to be attractive to men. In Geneva, the marginality of women in the city's guild system had become well established by the mid sixteenth century. Few women remained in the skilled trades; their work identity was generally weak and their wages were particularly low. Apprenticeships for girls were confined to a narrow range of trades, such as those of laundress and seamstress and, overall, girls accounted for only a small proportion of the total number of apprentices. Women were found in domestic service, watchmaking, textile production, and working as seamstresses and laundresses, but rarely elsewhere.[15] In Frankfurt, Strasbourg, Nuremburg, Meningen, Stuttgart, and Munich, women were also excluded from a large number of crafts and, more generally, from the world of work. Male workers attempted to reduce competition for jobs by singling out and removing women. Journeymen demanded restrictions on women's work, even in instances where this worked against their own economic interests. Wives were prevented from earning decent wages and widows, who had been given unrestricted rights to carry on their former husband's shop in early German guild ordinances, found these curtailed.[16] In Augsburg, for example, widows were not permitted to keep apprentices, and in general, there was a growing hostility towards women operating independently of their men.[17]

Guilds did not, however, confine themselves simply to restricting the kinds of work women could practise; they also sought to define the proper spheres of productive and unproductive work in gender terms alone. In central Europe during the seventeenth and eighteenth centuries, conflict arose between guilds and household production units over the definition of productive work.[18] Guildsmen feared that rural household production, which could produce goods at lower cost than urban artisans, would undermine their monopoly position. Guilds had previously been hostile to rural production, but after the middle of the seventeenth century, their attack was directed as much at women as producers as at rural household production. Guildsmen, therefore, sought to debar the household from the market economy and, thereby, women from productive work. Gender, rather than industrial organization, became the determining factor. In future, esteemed productive work was to be a male sphere and domestic duties a female and less respected one.

The identification of gender as the criterion in deciding work values is also evident in the rhetoric of guilds and city councils in early modern Germany. Prohibitions on women's work were argued on the ground of gender alone. Some city councils seem to have been unashamedly hostile to women workers but were restrained in their desire to exclude women from the labour market altogether because of the likelihood of their becoming a burden. Low paid casual occupations were tolerated for this reason. Journeymen, too, took advantage of the chorus of anti-female rhetoric by successfully appropriating productive tasks which had previously been the responsibility of the master's wife and daughter.[19]

The origins of the guilds' hostility to women are still very poorly understood. That it was part of a complex process is beyond doubt, but its precise location is unclear. Guilds, for example, were involved in an intense political struggle with the state and guild monopolies over a wide variety of industrial work were themselves being attacked. On the other hand, women were also the target of both spiritual and secular authorities; institutions such as marriage and the family were subject to profound transformation. Whatever the explanation for the hostility, its impact on working women was straightforward. Some urban women retreated from the labour market altogether, and presumably found some refuge in the home; others, however, swelled the casual and irregular labour market and gravitated towards the distributive trades as well as towards large-scale, non-artisanal industrial production.[20] In the Florentine wool and silk industries, for example, women formed the majority of the workforce, appropriating tasks such as weaving which had earlier been male preserves; in the Bolognese silk industry all of the weavers were women. In both cases, the preponderance of women workers can be explained by the exclusion of women from artisanal trades and by the fact that the output of these industries consisted of simple cloths requiring little skill or capital.[21] By contrast, the silk industries in Lyons, Genoa, and Venice produced rich and complicated cloths and the vast majority of weavers were male.[22]

There was nothing inherently female or male about any activity, nor were the categorizations static; what identified gender and work was the intersection of the economic and gender systems. In the period from the late fifteenth century to the middle of the seventeenth, guilds, and through them, male artisans, were instrumental in creating an altered ideology of gender and work. The idea and reality of a female artisan which was common in the middle ages became untenable in the early modern period. The privileges, the work identity, and the customary rights, trappings of artisanal work values, became the exclusive domain of skilled men. By setting artisanal work apart from work in general, guildsmen were also equating women with the unskilled – a critical signpost for the future. It is true, of course, that many working women were in occupations unrepresented by guilds, but the important point is that it was the guild which provoked gender conflict in the workplace.

The exclusion of women from a wide range of industrial occupations was an urban phenomenon. The countryside seems to have been devoid of the kind of hostility towards working women that existed in the towns.[23] The boom in the demand for rural industrial labour beginning in the late sixteenth and early seventeenth centuries swelled the number of women working in industrial production.[24] It is very likely that women's labour was critical to the expansion of rural industrial production, especially that of textile manufacture.[25]

By the late seventeenth century, women's work in urban Europe had settled into a new pattern. No longer associated directly with the artisanal trades, women were now confined to a narrow band of industries consisting primarily of textile manufacture and the clothing trades. Outside industry, the chief areas of women's work were retailing and domestic service.

II

Despite the changes in industrial organization that occurred in nineteenth-century Europe with their attendant pressures on employment patterns, the position of women in the labour market remained fundamentally the same.

The functions performed by men and women within the pre-factory manu-facturing sector persisted in the nineteenth century but not without inter-vening upheaval. The possibility of restructuring gender relations in the labour market was momentarily indicated by changes in production meth-ods, but ultimately men retained their monopoly of the more rewarding occupations.[26] Female labour played a critical role in the expansion of the various processes of industrial capitalist production.[27] While the factory was the most striking feature of nineteenth-century industrial transforma-tion and depended heavily on women workers, cheap female labour was also used in the expansion of domestic service,[28] as the basis of some new urban and rural trades, and in the proliferating urban sweatshops of late nine-teenth-century Europe.[29] Women, therefore, provided much-needed flexibil-ity within the context of innovation, while men steadfastly maintained their domination of better-paid occupations and traditional crafts.[30]

From as early as the 1820s, but also during the later nineteenth century, gender relations in the labour market were temporarily disrupted. Anti-female sentiments, akin to those prominent in early modern guild politics, resurfaced. While the rhetoric and the exclusionary strategies were redolent of an earlier age, the gender conflict of the nineteenth century embraced novel social concerns. The marital status of women took on a new signifi-cance as protective legislation, the cult of the family wage, and the ideology of domesticity interacted to emphasize gender inequality in the labour mar-ket and to establish a hierarchical structure of employment that persists to the present. Thus, in nineteenth-century European labour markets, as mar-ried women became more overtly marginalized, young women and single women predominated in the visible urban trades. In the textile factories, for example, they commonly accounted for the bulk of the unskilled work-force,[31] and they dominated domestic service occupations and some sectors of garment-making in the towns and cities of England, France, Italy, and Germany.[32]

Later in the nineteenth century, the service sector provided new openings, particularly for unmarried women. Single women found work in the depart-ment store, which appeared in the larger European cities in response to the growth of consumerism. These new retail outlets provided employment on a grand scale; the Bon Marché in Paris, for example, employed 2,500 sales assistants in the 1880s and the Louvre, 3,500–4,000 in 1900.[33] Although some men were employed in these stores, women were much preferred because of their cheapness, because they were sober and polite, and because they were considered to be docile. The work was unskilled and low paid, and for women was usually curtailed on marriage.[34] The introduction of the typewriter in the last quarter of the nineteenth century restructured clerical occupations and also provided new opportunities for women. Male workers gained from this change, however, for, while women were allocated low sta-tus secretarial jobs, men moved into high status office work in banks and insurance companies.[35] The majority of female clerical occupations were reserved for the unmarried, and in most European offices, a marriage bar operated until well into the twentieth century.[36]

Married women's employment followed an altogether different pattern. The precise nature of their work is, however, difficult to ascertain. Many married women did not enter the official statistics (or other records) precisely because of their location in the secondary labour market and because their work was irregular, casual, and sometimes only semi-legal.[37] In many parts of industrial Europe, women tended to withdraw from the more visible areas of waged work – the factory and the workshop – upon marriage, and seek employment that could accommodate household responsibilities.[38] In Britain and Germany, this trend began before the mid nineteenth century, while in France the social and political pressures discouraging the gainful employment of married women began to emerge later in the century.[39]

Married women workers in nineteenth-century Europe were so concentrated in urban domestic industry that it is no exaggeration to speak of its feminization as one of the principal components of European industrialization.[40] They clustered in the clothing industry, in various forms of retail trading, and in menial occupations (like laundressing) that resembled household chores, a pattern reminiscent of the early modern period. The making of clothes, for example, had long been an important component of women's work and in most large cities of industrial Europe, the practice of the handicraft trades of plain sewing, shirtmaking, and button stitching apparently proved the salvation of women with family responsibilities in need of an income.[41] Plenty of such work existed and it was rare to find a clothing firm that did not employ many women at home in addition to those in the factory or workshop.

From the 1830s onwards, the numerous occupations subsumed within the general description of clothing employed thousands of women in the major European cities. Sweated labour either in the home or in what were euphemistically termed family workshops (sweatshops) prevailed in all the needleworking trades, where women worked irregularly for little reward.[42] The greater part of this workforce consisted of married women. In Berlin in 1887, for example, 75 per cent of all homeworkers were married, widowed, or separated women,[43] with an identical proportion of these categories employed as outworkers in Hamburg in 1913.[44] The introduction of the sewing machine considerably extended the possibilities for sweatshop and homeworking employment for women. Not only did it allow women to reconcile domestic functions with wage earning, and to comply with the late nineteenth-century moralists' feminine ideal, but it permitted the clothing manufacturers to make full use of a cheap and flexible labour force at a time when the expansion in the demand for ready-to-wear clothing placed great pressure on existing methods of production and suggested greater subdivision of tasks.[45]

The garment industries of Paris, Hamburg, and London were typically organized on the basis of outwork (or a refined putting-out system) making use of the large female labour force available in the fast expanding cities.[46] The system was capable not only of mass output, but also of the rapid expansion and contraction crucial in a trade where extreme seasonal fluctuations in demand occurred.[47] This was the case in the clothing industry generally and in women's fashions in particular. The women who dominated the labour force in this sector suffered very irregular employment.[48]

A clear, yet complex gender division of labour existed in the nineteenth-century European garment trades which distinguished workers both by the tasks they performed and by the location in which they performed them. The vast majority of outworkers were women, and those men that did enter the sweating sector did so as managers and middlemen.[49] Men monopolized such skilled work as remained within the scope of the generally unskilled ready-to-wear sector. Specializing in tailoring and the production of outer-wear, men worked in small workshops and abhorred the practice of home-working.[50] Women, by contrast, operated mainly in the mass production sector, at home, making women's garments, underwear, millinery, and standard workmen's clothes.[51] Outwork and homework also interacted with larger scale production in other sectors of the clothing trade. In the Parisian flowermaking trade, for example, which was partially mechanized, a large part of the production process was carried out in the homes of individual workers or in small workshops. As in other trades, a clear division of labour existed, whereby men were responsible for the dyeing and cutting, while women specialized in shaping and branching that required more manual dexterity.[52]

While homeworking suited the needs of many women, it did not end men's antipathy towards low-paid female labour. Indeed, in some instances, particularly in the early nineteenth century, skilled craftsmen were angered by the competition of cheaper and less skilled female domestic labour. In the early 1820s, tailors in the Saxon city of Naumburg an der Saale believed their families' livelihoods to be threatened and their own training undermined by the work of seamstresses engaged in dressmaking in their own homes.[53] Similarly, journeymen tailors in London in the 1830s accused sweatshop women of undercutting their product and of lowering their living standards.[54]

The expansion of domestic work, an integral component of nineteenth-century European industrial development, was the result both of married women's need to find socially and politically acceptable employment and of the increasing subdivision of tasks within factory production. Mechanization in one part of the work process, for example, often generated the growth of homework in another;[55] and the growth of large factories could give rise to a division of labour that included (unskilled) tasks that could be performed easily by hand or by small machines at home. By making use of

a plentiful supply of cheap female labour in a domestic setting, the capitalists not only reduced their labour costs by 25–50 per cent on factory levels,[56]
but also diluted the power of the artisan by interfering in the continuous
struggle between men and women for job recognition. Thus the greater division of labour served to intensify the gender segregation of the workforce
and further confirmed the position of the primary and secondary labour
markets.[57]

Working women were therefore employed, as before, in less skilled and
lower paid occupations than the majority of men irrespective of the nature
and location of their work. Thus, young single women who performed sim-
iliar tasks to their male counterparts in factories were as disadvantaged as
their married sisters who operated from home or in domestic-like environments in occupations that were almost exclusively 'female'. That women's
position in the labour market remained subordinate in the context of economic and industrial change was by no means automatic, but was more the
result of a number of powerful interacting forces that emphasized women's
domestic role and men's position as family breadwinners. These forces were
patriarchal in character, and include the ideology of domesticity,[58] state protective legislation, the widespread demand for the family wage, and the
craftsman's successful efforts to monopolize technology and skill.

III

The hierarchical division of labour was confirmed in the nineteenth century
after a brief interlude when, in some industries, notably textiles, greater
employment opportunities were created for women by changes in the organization and technology of production and were supported by capitalist
interests.[59] As artisans had used their control over the guilds in the late
medieval and early modern period to resist women's encroachment on
skilled and well-paid occupations, so skilled men in nineteenth-century
Europe, fearful of an erosion of their position at work and at home,
employed a range of restrictive practices for similar ends. Their actions
included the manipulation of the very techniques that might potentially
have undermined their own position: the deskilling implicit in the new technology itself was compounded by the threatened introduction of cheap and
'less skilled' female labour. Through the activities of the trade unions to
which skilled men had enforced a restricted entry from the beginning of the
century, they achieved control over the use of technical innovations, enhanc-
ing their own position and extending the inequality between men's work
and women's work. One of the results of their actions was a 'gendering' of
machinery: particular technologies commonly became associated with one
sex only.[60] Men monopolized the bulk of nineteenth-century inventions,[61]
while some machines, such as the typewriter, and to a lesser extent the

sewing machine, became the preserve of women. Integral to the gendering of technology was a gendering of skill, such that skilled work became associated only with male machines, while 'women's machines' were confined to low-paid, unskilled, and exploitative occupations.[62] Thus, by restructuring notions of skill, craftsmen both avoided much of the deskilling potential of the new technology and further strengthened the perception of their own work as skilled and that of women as unskilled.

This general pattern (subject to variation among industries and techniques) was the outcome of a series of individual struggles between men and women for control over technology and thus of skilled employment. The most widely cited examples of such struggles, over the mule in cotton spinning,[63] and the compositing machine in the printing industry,[64] reveal the mechanisms by which machines were monopolized and skill was reconstructed within a novel framework. The introduction of the self-actor in the 1830s removed all technical barriers to the use of unskilled labour on the mule, but despite the efforts of many cotton factory masters to introduce willing female labour, the mule craft unionists closed ranks and succesfully repelled the challenge to their position.[65] Among other tactics they persuaded the employers that they would relieve them of some of the task of controlling the labour force.

By careful redefinition, mule spinning remained a skilled job, largely entrusted to male hands. Although the new spinning system required a different range of tasks, skilled craft status persisted, not for technical reasons (though sometimes mechanical adjustment was required) but because the operator assumed responsibility for the management of the labour process and for quality control.[66] The ability to supervise had earlier been established as a skill to which only men had access, and by arguing that this was an essential component of the new system, the craftsmen retained control over employment. In cotton spinning, a hierarchical gender division of labour was established where mule spinning was male and skilled, while women, using older techniques, performed the unskilled work. The gender of the actor, more than the technology itself, determined the status of work.[67]

Gender conflict within the traditionally male-dominated printing trade similarly inverted the potential impact of technical development. The late nineteenth-century introduction of an American invention represented a major leap forward in compositing which both removed the physical restraints on the employment of women in this stage of the production process and reduced the necessary level of skill. The male printers' antipathy towards the proposed introduction of cheaper female labour was revealed in both France and Britain through the immediate and concerted actions of the male craft unions.[68] In France, the Couriau affair (a dispute in the printing industry) illustrated both the level of hostility aroused and the effectiveness of male solidarity;[69] while in Britain, the eventual monopoly of the new technology and the retention of skill by the male printers was facilitated by the poor organization of the print manufacturers.[70] Neither women nor employers resisted the long-established might of the craftsmen and, despite the temporary appearance of female compositors in Scotland, their proportion ultimately changed little in either Britain or France.[71]

Whatever the gender association of a new technology, it served to raise the level of male skill relative to that of women. The sewing machine was quickly identified with women and the growth of unskilled, casual sweated labour, and homeworking.[72] It exemplified the position of women, especially married women, in late nineteenth-century industrial Europe.[73] It provided women with the opportunity to integrate wage earning with domestic functions and thus to conform to the ideology of domesticity; and as a domestic technology, it served to emphasize the hierarchical gender division of labour and especially women's position as marginalized and casual workers.[74] Women's monopoly of the use of the typewriter forced a restructuring of skilled activities and a heightening of the gender division of labour within clerical work. Categories previously occupied by men became filled by women and redefined as unskilled, as men moved into newly created skilled jobs.[75]

Nineteenth-century technology was far from neutral in its influence on gender division in the workplace. Through machinery, jobs were constructed with the gender of their occupants in mind, ensuring that women were crowded into low-paid jobs which emphasized their previously established gender role as supplementary wage earners.[76] The process was frequently activated by skilled male unionists responding to a perceived threat of cheap female competition with its potential for weakening patriarchal authority. The institutional environment supported the male cause, as the ultimate goal of the skilled men – the removal of women from the labour market – found a parallel in the concerns of other social groups. Patriarchal forces underpinned women's subordinate position in the labour market and were particularly manifest in the actions of the state.

IV

The proletarianization of female labour in nineteenth-century Europe provoked extensive debate about the position of women in the economy. In Britain in the 1840s and in France and Germany towards the end of the century, the visible participation of women in the labour market was considered a problem both morally and because it challenged patriarchal power.[77] A range of possible solutions was discussed, including the total elimination of women's wage labour, equal pay, and sex segregated spheres of work. The most popular answer, however, was protective legislation which attempted to restrict female and child labour in factories and mines. Such legislation was introduced in Britain in 1842, in Germany in 1891, and in France in 1892.[78] It was designed to reinforce the position of women as wives and mothers and certainly helped further to marginalize women's position in the labour market.[79] German factory inspectors at the turn of the twentieth century, for example, waxed lyrical at the success of their labour legislation in returning women to the home.[80] Thus, as women were squeezed out of employment in the public arena, they were forced either into purely domestic activities or into homeworking or sweatshop employment. Though it has been argued that domestic work was a means by which factory owners in late nineteenth-century France could avoid the restrictions imposed by the law, it is as likely that the legislation itself provided the capitalist with the opportunity to remove women from the factory into the more economical environment of the sweatshop.[81] Although protective legislation established a precedent for improved working conditions for all workers, it was more significant in driving a wedge between men's work and women's work in industry. It excluded women from competition in important arenas of production and offered them little alternative but to work in unprotected places where gender conflict was minimal.[82]

The marginalization of female labour, an essential factor in the making of the modern family, was compounded by the persistent advocacy of the family wage.[83] That the norm of a breadwinner wage did not become a reality before 1914, does not detract from its significance in the nineteenth century as a principle that tended to undermine women's position in the labour market.[84] The idea of an individual male breadwinner earning sufficient to maintain a wife and children emerged in most parts of Europe during the course of the nineteenth century in parallel with an emphasis on women's domestic role, reducing their economic value and encouraging the diffusion of the 'ideal' bourgeois family form. This family wage was an unrealistic goal for the majority of working people, yet it was supported by most – women as well as men – and became a plank of male union wage demands. Men believed that with the introduction of a breadwinner wage, women's involvement in the labour market would be reduced. They would thus be less likely to compete for scarce jobs and to drive down the price of labour. As a result, men's position in the labour market would be greatly improved, not only absolutely but also in relation to the power of the employers.[85] The attainment of the family wage would also strengthen patriarchy, since a dependent and full-time housewife provided men with power and privileges in both the home and the workplace.[86]

The concept of the family wage, which originated with skilled workmen, also found support in the state, among capitalists, and in the middle class.[87] Pressure for its introduction grew in Britain from early in the nineteenth century, but emerged on the continent only from 1850. In France, where more women remained in paid employment upon marriage than in most other industrial European economies, the perception of working women as a problem and of the threat of their labour to the skilled working man arose relatively late.[88] It was not until the 1880s and 1890s that male unionists began to press for a family wage,[89] and middle-class concern over the well-being of children heightened demands for women to return to home duties with the financial support of a breadwinning husband.[90]

From the early nineteenth century the concept of the breadwinner wage and the bourgeois family gained currency, aided by changes in work practices, of which the most important was the decline of family hiring and sub-contracting.[91] Consequently, women became employed as individuals, competing with men in the labour market and earning an independent wage.[92] This threat to the job security of skilled workers was antithetical to the patriarchal environment that had existed virtually unchallenged since the earlier period of upheaval in the sixteenth century. The pressure placed on patriarchy by nineteenth-century industrial developments reawakened the need to reinforce – if not redefine – patriarchal structures. In the nineteenth century, patriarchy became associated with many separate but related issues which, as they undermined women's economic role and emphasized their domestic responsibilities, strengthened the power of fathers and husbands both in the labour market and at home.[93] The growth of feminism, of anti-feminism, and of the politics of fertility control, all of which became central issues in the late nineteenth and twentieth centuries, need to be seen in this context.

By the outbreak of the First World War, European working women were burdened by actions of the state and by a pernicious domestic ideology which confined them to traditional areas of employment. Occupations in the new industries of the late nineteenth and early twentieth centuries, such as engineering, car manufacture, steel, chemicals, and electricity, which had grown directly out of the anti-female artisanal sector, were effectively closed to women.[94]

V

In recent years it has become clear that such periods of transition in European history as the Reformation, the industrial revolution, and the rise of capitalism are of limited relevance to historians of women's work.[95] While industrialization affected the structure of the gender division of labour, it was not responsible for instigating women's subordinate position in the labour market.

The most profitable current approach to an analysis of this subordination stems from Hartmann's pathbreaking discussion of the relationship between patriarchy and capitalism. She identified two systems underlying the pattern of women's work – the economic and what has been called the sex-gender system.[96] Historically, these systems have interacted, sometimes in opposition and confrontation, at others in unison, to create a specific gender division of labour. Economic forces influence the nature of women's employment within a particular sex-gender system.

The sex-gender system and its principal component, patriarchy, remain in the background so long as changes within the economic system do not impinge on the operation of the system. But when changes in women's economic position threaten to upset the equilibrium of the sex-gender system, the response of the patriarchal component is to establish a new set of rules defining the acceptable gender division of labour in the workplace. The momentous historical episodes of confrontation between these systems have been few but protracted. Only two have occurred between the middle ages and the twentieth century.

One of the main conclusions to emerge from recent publications is that female work patterns and domestic preoccupations – the dialectic of production and reproduction – were not solely or primarily determined by economic forces but by complex relationships between patriarchy and economic materialism. Pleas for further research into the nature and operation of patriarchy are commonplace, but it must be emphasized that patriarchy should be examined within historically specific situations.[97] The most rewarding of these are likely to be major periods of confrontation when actions determined by patriarchy were most clearly revealed.[98] There may indeed be, as Bennett suggests, 'many histories of many patriarchies',[99] but this would not preclude the identification of the most salient features of patriarchal forces and the deconstruction of the sex-gender system.

Notes

1 This article focuses on the literature on women in industrial occupations. The problem of women in agricultural work has been largely excluded on the grounds that to do it justice would require a far longer essay. Notes 23–5 refer to some of the literature on this.
2 Bennett, 'History'; Thomas, 'Women'.
3 Gender conflict in the workplace can be argued to be a continuous feature of the politics of work. By isolating two momentous instances of such conflict, we are not denying this, but it is during these episodes only that fundamental changes in the pattern of women's employment occurred.
4 An approach supported by, among others, Bennett, 'Feminism', pp. 263–4.
5 There is a large literature on dual labour markets and labour market segmentation but nothing which explicitly treats the subject historically. See for example Sullivan, *Marginal workers*; Reich, Gordon, and Edwards, 'A theory'; Cain, 'Challenge'.
6 An assessment of the various forms of labour payments and their change over time is needed. Useful insights are, nevertheless, available. See, for example, Sonenscher, *Work and wages*; *idem*, 'Journeymen'; *idem*, 'Weavers'; *idem*, 'Work and wages'; Rule, *Labouring classes*; Hobsbawm, *Labouring men*, pp. 344–70.
7 Woodward, 'Wage rates'.
8 Sonenscher, 'Work and wages'.

9 The use and meaning of status in occupations is discussed in Howell, *Women, production*, p. 24.
10 Howell, 'Women, the family', p. 200; Wensky, 'Women's guilds'.
11 Howell, *Women, production*, pp. 24, 27–8. Howell uses the term 'family production unit' with a similar meaning to the 'family economy' as defined by Tilly and Scott, *Women, work and family*, p. 12.
12 Howell, *Women, production*, pp. 174–83.
13 Howell, 'Women, the family', pp. 202–13.
14 Wiesner, *Working women*, pp. 178–80.
15 Monter, 'Women in Calvinist Geneva', pp. 199–204.
16 Wiesner, *Working women*, pp. 3, 157.
17 Roper, 'Work, marriage and sexuality', pp. 62–81.
18 The following is based upon Quataert, 'Shaping of women's work', pp. 1122–35.
19 Wiesner, *Working women*, pp. 11–35, 194–8.
20 Wiesner Wood, 'Paltry peddlers'; Wiesner, 'Spinsters and seamstresses', pp. 203–5; *idem*, 'Women's work', pp. 67–9.
21 Brown and Goodman, 'Women and industry'; Poni, 'Proto-industrialization', p. 313; Goodman, 'Tuscan commercial relations', pp. 337–8.
22 Davis, 'Women in the crafts'; Garden, *Lyon et les lyonnais*, pp. 225–8; Massa, *La 'Fabbrica'*; Rapp, *Industry and economic decline*, p. 28.
23 This is partly explained by the absence of guild control over rural industrial production. Historians disagree, however, over the precise nature of gender divisions in rural industrial production. See for example, Berg, *Age of manufactures*, pp. 129–58; Hufton, 'Women and the family'; *idem*, 'Women without men'; Gullickson, 'Sexual division of labor'; *idem*, *Spinners and weavers*, pp. 52–3; Snell, 'Agricultural and seasonal unemployment'; Roberts, 'Sickles and scythes', pp. 18–9; Wrigley, 'Men on the land', p. 336; Boxer and Quataert, *Connecting spheres*, pp. 42–4. These stress the existence of clear divisions. Medick, 'Proto-industrial family economy', pp. 61–3 and Quataert, 'Combining agrarian and industrial livelihood', p. 151 argue for a neutral situation. Much work remains to be done.
24 There is now an enormous literature on the expansion of rural industry in early modern Europe. The field is surveyed in Clarkson, *Proto-industrialization*. For market conditions and background to these developments see Goodman and Honeyman, *Gainful pursuits*. Agricultural regions most favoured for the expansion of industrial production were those with a large landless or land-poor population. See Gullickson, 'Agriculture and cottage industry'; Quataert, 'New view'; Gullickson, *Spinners and weavers*; Holmes and Quataert, 'Approach to modern labor'; Quataert, 'Combining agrarian and industrial livelihood'. Many young women who would earlier have migrated to towns in search of industrial work and apprenticeships, now remained at home contributing to the family economy. See Snell, 'Apprenticeship of women'; Berg, *Age of manufactures*, p. 155; Monter, 'Women in Calvinist Geneva', p. 200; Carmona, 'Economia toscana', p. 38.
25 The best account is given by Gullickson in *Spinners and Weavers*, pp. 46–85; *idem*, 'Agriculture and cottage industry'; *idem*, 'Proto-industrialization'.
26 This pattern is still not fully accepted. Although early or more traditional historians strongly believed that new opportunities, or even emancipation for women, accompanied nineteenth-century industrial change (for example George, *England in transition*; Pinchbeck, *Women workers*; and Landes, *Unbound Prometheus*), the weight of opinion is now on the side of those (like Richards, 'Women in the British economy') who argue for a decline in women's economic position. Many of this latter group also favour the notion that before the capitalist era, women had enjoyed a golden age of economic opportunity, as suggested by the work of Clark, *Working life*. On the golden age see Hanawalt, *Women and work*, pp. vii–xviii and Bennett, 'History that stands still'.
27 For the use of women's labour and the persistence of hand and intermediate techniques as an alternative to or in association with mechanization see Berg, *Age of manufactures*, pp. 145–51 and *idem*, 'Women's work', pp. 76–7.
28 Tilly, 'Paths of proletarianization'; *idem*, 'Family, gender and occupations'.

29 Schmiechen, *Sweated industries*.
30 They continued to use the apprenticeship system, but, increasingly, they prevented women gaining access to the newest technology, and thus, commonly, to the best jobs; Rule, 'Property of skill'; Humphries, 'Sexual division of labor'.
31 Richards, 'Women in the British economy', p. 346; Tilly and Scott, *Women, work and family*, p. 82. The preponderance of young, unmarried females in cotton factories is also indicated in Hall, 'Home turned', pp. 24–5.
32 Scott and Tilly, 'Women's work', p. 39.
33 McBride, 'A woman's world', p. 665.
34 Ibid., pp. 670–1, 679.
35 Davies, 'Woman's place'; Zimmeck, 'Jobs for the girls', pp. 159–60.
36 It was the mid 1930s before married women were employed in the British Civil Service; see Zimmeck, 'Strategies and stratagems', pp. 903–4, 922–4.
37 This feature of under-recording in the official sources is illustrated in many studies, including Alexander, *Women's work*, pp. 11–4, 49–64; Roberts, *Women's work*, pp. 17–22; Scott and Tilly, 'Women's work', p. 40; John, *Unequal opportunities* introd., pp. 36–41.
38 Typically at home and frequently jobs like sewing or clothes washing that resembled household chores.
39 According to Offen, 'Feminism, antifeminism', p. 183, 40 per cent of the female French labour force in 1901 were married.
40 Franzoi, '. . . With the wolf', pp. 149, 154; Boxer and Quataert, eds., *Connecting spheres*, p. 101. See also Boxer, 'Protective legislation', pp. 47–51; Jordan, 'Exclusion of women'.
41 Franzoi, '. . . With the wolf', pp. 149–50.
42 Alexander, *Women's work*, pp. 30–40; Boxer, 'Protective legislation', pp. 45–7.
43 Hauser, 'Technischer Fortschritt', p. 163.
44 Dasey, 'Women's work', p. 243.
45 Perrot, 'Femmes et machines', pp. 12–3.
46 Hohenberg and Lees, *Urban Europe*, pp. 175–247.
47 Dasey, 'Women's work', pp. 232–4.
48 Ibid., pp. 238, 243; Hauser, 'Technischer Fortschritt', p. 163.
49 Hauser, 'Technischer Fortschritt', p. 160 and Dasey, 'Women's work', p. 235, although this was not true of the male immigrant workers, mostly Jews, in late nineteenth-century British cities who tended to be confined to, or often associated with sweated, unskilled work; see Schmiechen, *Sweated industries*, pp. 32–7, 189; Bythell, *Sweated trades*, p. 175.
50 Scott, 'Men and women', p. 70.
51 Dasey, 'Women's work', p. 235.
52 Boxer, 'Women in industrial homework'.
53 Quataert, 'Shaping of women's work', pp. 1122–3.
54 Alexander, *Women's work*, pp. 31–2; Taylor, *Eve*, pp. 101–17.
55 A widely recorded phenomenon; see for example, Rendall, *Origins of modern feminism*, pp. 171–3; Tilly and Scott, *Women, work and family*, pp. 123–36.
56 Boxer, 'Protective legislation', p. 49.
57 Rendall, *Origins of modern feminism*, pp. 155–8.
58 Boxer, 'Protective legislation', p. 47; Hall, 'Early formation'. See also Rose, 'Proto-industry', p. 191.
59 There is little doubt that the majority of capitalists preferred to employ women (and would have done so to a greater extent in the absence of male resistance).
60 Rose, '"Gender at work"', p. 119 and *idem*, 'Gender segregation', pp. 172–3 make explicit reference to the gendering of machines in the English midlands hosiery industry in the nineteenth century and it is implicit in much other writing on nineteenth-century capitalism. Such allocation of machines to particular genders may well have existed before the nineteenth century, but very little evidence on this subject is available.
61 Most notably the self-acting mule in cotton spinning and the compositing machine in the printing trade which will be discussed below.

62 Except where they were used by men, for example, when skilled male tailors used the sewing machine.
63 Most of the detailed research on this has focused on Britain, but evidence indicates parallels elsewhere; Lazonick, 'Industrial relations'; Freifield, 'Technological change'; Valverde, 'Giving the female'.
64 See Cockburn, *Brothers* and *Machinery of dominance*, pp. 15–43 for an overview.
65 Until the early nineteenth century, women and men had commonly engaged together in union activity. Beginning in the 1820s, women were denied access to unions as skilled male unionists practised exclusionary tactics; Rose, 'Gender antagonism'; Jordan, 'Exclusion of women'.
66 Freifield, 'Technological change'; Rose, 'Gender segregation', pp. 173–4. The monopoly of supervision by men had been generally established well before the nineteenth century, although there is some evidence that in France, it was not unusual to see women supervising men at the end of the eighteenth century; Perrot, 'Femmes et machines', p. 8.
67 This is discussed by Lazonick, 'Industrial relations'; Freifield, 'Technological change'; Valverde, 'Giving the female', pp. 621–5.
68 Boxer, 'Foyer or factory', p. 192.
69 Sowerwine, 'Workers and women', pp. 427–41.
70 Cockburn, *Brothers*, pp. 28–9.
71 Ibid., pp. 23, 26–31; Sowerwine, 'Workers and women', p. 415.
72 While higher, indeed skilled, status was accorded to work performed by men using the sewing machine.
73 Perrot, 'Femmes et machines', pp. 7, 12–3, 15–7; Hauser, 'Technischer Fortschritt', pp. 157–63; Offen, '"Powered by a woman's foot"'; Offen, 'Feminism, antifeminism', p. 183; Dasey, 'Women's work', p. 228.
74 It even became an 'instrument of women's servitude' as suggested by Boxer, 'Protective legislation', p. 49.
75 Davies, 'Woman's place', pp. 248–59; Zimmeck, 'Jobs for the girls', pp. 159–60.
76 Rose, '"Gender at work"', pp. 118–28.
77 Implicit in a good deal of the literature; Boxer, 'Protective legislation', pp. 45–7; Hilden, *Working women*, p. 165; and Seccombe, 'Patriarchy stabilized'.
78 John, 'Colliery legislation'; Boxer, 'Protective legislation'.
79 Ibid.; Rose, 'Proto-industry', p. 191; Seccombe, 'Patriarchy stabilized', pp. 63–4, 73–4.
80 Quataert, 'Source analysis', p. 120.
81 Boxer, 'Protective legislation', pp. 49–50.
82 Ibid., p. 55.
83 Ibid., p. 47.
84 Mark-Lawson and Witz, 'From "family labour"', p. 154.
85 Seccombe, 'Patriarchy stabilized', p. 55.
86 Ibid., pp. 58–9; Rose, '"Gender at work"', pp. 125–6.
87 Seccombe, 'Patriarchy stabilized', pp. 65–74. Murray, 'Property and "patriarchy"', however, considers that the historical structuring of property along gender lines (for reasons of kinship) would have given rise to the male breadwinner ideology.
88 Hilden, *Working women*, pp. 278–9.
89 This coincided with the death of feminism in socialism which had occurred in Britain in the 1830s; Boxer, 'Foyer or factory', p. 199. See also Offen, 'Depopulation, nationalism'; *idem*, 'Defining feminism'.
90 Offen, 'Feminism, antifeminism', p. 183.
91 The exclusion of women from the workplace was often argued on economic grounds, that is that women competed for jobs with men and drove down the wages for all; Boxer, 'Foyer or factory', pp. 196–8.
92 Seccombe, 'Patriarchy stabilized', p. 66.
93 Including skilled male unionism, the family wage, a domestic ideology, the notion of the bourgeois family, and protective legislation.
94 See for example, Jordan, 'Exclusion of women'; Stockmann, 'Gewerbliche Frauenarbeit'; Wecker, 'Frauenlohnarbeit'; Burdy et al., 'Rôles, travaux et métiers'. A useful survey of women's work in Germany can be found in Fout, 'Working-class women's work'.

95 See the comments by Thomas, 'Women and capitalism'; also Shorter, 'Women's work'; Bennett, 'History that stands still'.
96 Hartmann, 'Capitalism, patriarchy'.
97 The best discussion of the trouble with patriarchy can be found in Walby, *Patriarchy at work*, pp. 22–37. The most recent historical work which stresses this approach can be found in Howell, *Women, production*.
98 Bennett, 'Feminism', pp. 263–4.
99 Ibid., p. 262.

References

Alexander, S., *Women's work in nineteenth-century London: a study of the years 1820–50* (1983).

Bennett, J.M., 'History that stands still: women's work in the European past', *Feminist Stud.*, XIV (1988), pp. 269–83.

Bennett, J.M., 'Feminism and history', *Gender & Hist.*, I (1989), pp. 251–72.

Berg, M., *The age of manufactures, 1700–1820* (1985).

Berg, M., 'Women's work, mechanisation and the early phases of industrialisation in England', in P. Joyce, ed., *The historical meanings of work* (Cambridge, 1987), pp. 64–98.

Boxer, M.J., 'Foyer or factory: working class women in nineteenth century France', *Proc. Western Soc. French Hist.*, II (1975), pp. 192–206.

Boxer, M.J., 'Women in industrial homework: the flowermakers of Paris in the Belle Epoque', *French Hist. Stud.*, XII (1982), pp. 401–23.

Boxer, M.J., 'Protective legislation and home industry: the marginalization of women workers in late nineteenth-century France', *J. Soc. Hist.*, XX (1986), pp. 45–65.

Boxer, M.J. and Quataert, J.H., eds., *Connecting spheres* (New York, 1987).

Brown, J.C. and Goodman, J., 'Women and industry in Florence', *J. Econ. Hist.*, XL (1980), pp. 73–80.

Burdy, J.-P., Dubesset, M., and Zancarini-Fournel, M., 'Rôles, travaux et métiers de femmes dans une ville industrielle: Saint-Étienne, 1900–1950', *Le Mouvement social*, 140 (1987), pp. 27–53.

Bythell, D., *The sweated trades* (1978).

Cain, G.G., 'The challenge of segmented labor market theories to orthodox theory: a survey', *J. Econ. Lit.*, XIV (1976), pp. 1215–57.

Carmona, M., 'Sull'economia toscana del cinquecento e del seicento', *Archivio Storico Italiana*, CXX (1962), pp. 32–46.

Clark, A., *Working life of women in the seventeenth century* (1919).

Clarkson, L., *Proto-industrialization: the first phase of industrialization?* (1985).

Cockburn, C., *Brothers: male dominance and technological change* (1983).

Cockburn, C., *Machinery of dominance* (1985).

Dasey, R., 'Women's work and the family: women garment workers in Berlin and Hamburg before the First World War', in R.J. Evans and W.R. Lee, eds.,

The German family: essays on the social history of the family in nineteenth and twentieth century Germany (1981), pp. 221–55.

Davies, M., 'Woman's place is at the typewriter: the feminization of the clerical labor force', in Z. Eisenstein, ed., *Capitalism, patriarchy and the case for socialist feminism* (New York, 1978), pp. 248–66.

Davis, N.Z., 'Women in the crafts in sixteenth-century Lyon', *Feminist Stud.*, VIII (1982), pp. 47–80.

Fout, J.C., 'Working class women's work in imperial Germany', *Hist. Eur. Ideas*, 8 (1987), pp. 625–32.

Franzoi, B., '" . . . With the wolf always at the door . . . ": women's work in domestic industry in Britain and Germany', in M.J. Boxer and J.H. Quataert, eds., *Connecting spheres* (New York, 1987), pp. 149–54.

Freifeld, M., 'Technological change and the "self-acting" mule: a study of skill and the sexual division of labour', *Soc. Hist.*, XI (1986), pp. 319–43.

Garden, M., *Lyon et les lyonnais au xviiième siècle* (Paris, 1975).

George, D., *England in transition* (Harmondsworth, 1931).

Goodman, J., 'Tuscan commercial relations with Europe, 1550–1620: Florence and the European textile market', in *Firenze e la Toscana dei Medici nell'Europa del'500*, 3 vols. (Florence, 1983), I, pp. 327–41.

Goodman, J. and Honeyman, K., *Gainful pursuits: the making of industrial Europe, 1600–1914* (1988).

Gullickson, G.L., 'The sexual division of labor in cottage industry and agriculture in the Pays de Caux: Auffay, 1750–1850', *French Hist. Stud.*, XV (1981), pp. 177–99.

Gullickson, G.L., 'Proto-industrialization, demographic behavior and the sexual division of labor in Auffay, France, 1750–1850', *Peasant Stud.*, IX (1982), pp. 106–18.

Gullickson, G.L., 'Agriculture and cottage industry: redefining the causes of proto-industrialization', *J. Econ. Hist.*, XLIII (1983), pp. 831–50.

Gullickson, G.L., *Spinners and weavers of Auffay* (Cambridge, 1986).

Hall, C., 'The early formation of Victorian domestic ideology', in S. Burman, ed., *Fit work for women* (1979), pp. 15–32.

Hall, C., 'The home turned upside down? The working class family in cotton textiles, 1780–1850', in E. Whitelegg, ed., *The changing experience of women* (Oxford, 1982), pp. 17–29.

Hanawalt, B., ed., *Women and work in pre-industrial Europe* (Bloomington, 1986).

Hartmann, H., 'Capitalism, patriarchy, and job segregation by sex', *Signs*, I (1976), pp. 137–69.

Hauser, K., 'Technischer Fortschritt und Frauenarbeit im 19. Jahrhundert: zur Sozialgeschichte der Nähmaschine', *Geschichte und Gesellschaft*, IV (1978), pp. 148–69.

Hilden, P., *Working women and socialist politics in France, 1880–1914: a regional study* (Oxford, 1986).

Hobsbawm, E.J., *Labouring men* (1964).

Hohenberg, P.M. and Lees, L.H., *The making of urban Europe, 1000–1950* (Cambridge, Mass., 1985).

Holmes, D.R. and Quataert, J.H., 'An approach to modern labor: worker peasantries in historic Saxony and the Friuli region over three centuries', *Comparative Studies in Society and History*, XXVIII (1986), pp. 191–216.

Howell, M.C., 'Women, the family economy and the structure of market production in cities in northern Europe during the late middle ages', in B. Hanawalt, ed., *Women and work in pre-industrial Europe* (Bloomington, 1986), pp. 198–222.

Howell, M.C., *Women, production and patriarchy in late medieval cities* (Chicago, 1986).

Hufton, O., 'Women and the family economy in eighteenth-century France', *French Hist. Stud.*, IX (1975), pp. 1–22.

Hufton, O., 'Women without men: widows and spinsters in Britain and France in the eighteenth century', *J. Fam. Hist.*, IX (1984), pp. 255–76.

Humphries, J., '" . . . The most free from objection . . . ": the sexual division of labor and women's work in nineteenth-century England', *J. Econ. Hist.*, XLVII (1987), pp. 929–49.

John, A.V., 'Colliery legislation and its consequences: 1842 and the women miners of Lancashire', *Bull. John Rylands Lib.*, LXI (1978), pp. 78–114.

John, A.V., ed., *Unequal opportunities* (Oxford, 1986).

Jordan, E., 'The exclusion of women from industry in nineteenth-century Britain', *Comparative Studies in Society and History*, XXXI (1989), pp. 273–96.

Landes, D., *The unbound Prometheus* (Cambridge, 1969).

Lazonick, W., 'Industrial relations and technical change: the case of the self-acting mule', *Cambridge J. Econ.*, III (1979), pp. 231–62.

McBride, T., 'A woman's world: department stores and the evolution of women's employment, 1870–1920', *French Hist. Stud.*, X (1978), pp. 664–83.

Mark-Lawson, J. and Witz, A., 'From "family labour" to "family wage"? The case of women's labour in nineteenth-century coalmining', *Soc. Hist.*, XIII (1988), p. 151–74.

Massa, P., *La 'Fabbrica' dei velluti genovesi* (Genoa, 1981).

Medick, H., 'The proto-industrial family economy', in P. Kriedte, H. Medick, and J. Schlumbohm, eds., *Industrialization before industrialization* (Cambridge, 1981), pp. 38–73.

Monter, E.W., 'Women in Calvinist Geneva (1550–1800)', *Signs*, VI (1980), pp. 189–209.

Murray, M., 'Property and "patriarchy" in English history', *J. Hist. Sociol.*, 2 (1989), pp. 303–27.

Offen, K., 'Depopulation, nationalism and feminism in fin-de-siècle France', *Amer. Hist. Rev.*, LXXXIX (1984), pp. 648–76.

Offen, K., 'Defining feminism: a comparative historical approach', *Signs*, XIV (1988), pp. 119–57.

Offen, K., '"Powered by a woman's foot": a documentary introduction to the sexual politics of the sewing machine in nineteenth-century France', *Women's Stud. Internat. Forum*, XI (1988), pp. 93–101.

Offen, K., 'Feminism, antifeminism and national family politics in early Third Republic France', in M.J. Boxer and J.H. Quataert, eds., *Connecting spheres* (New York, 1987), pp. 177–86.

Perrot, M., 'Femmes et machines au XIXe siècle', *Romantisme*, XLI (1983), pp. 5–17.

Pinchbeck, I., *Women workers in the industrial revolution* (1930).

Poni, C., 'Proto-industrialization, rural and urban', *Review*, IX (1985), pp. 305–14.

Quataert, J.H., 'A new view of industrialization: "protoindustry" or the role of small-scale, labor-intensive manufacture in the capitalist environment', *Internat. Labor & Working-Class Hist.*, 33 (1988), pp. 3–22.

Quataert, J.H., 'A source analysis in German women's history: factory inspectors' reports and the shaping of working-class lives, 1878–1914', *Central Eur. Hist.*, 16 (1983), pp. 99–121.

Quataert, J.H., 'Combining agrarian and industrial livelihood: rural households in the Saxon Oberlausitz in the nineteenth century', *J. Fam. Hist.*, X (1985), pp. 145–62.

Quataert, J.H., 'The shaping of women's work in manufacturing: guilds, households and the state in central Europe, 1648–1870', *Amer. Hist. Rev.*, XC (1985), pp. 1122–48.

Rapp, R.T., *Industry and economic decline in seventeenth century Venice* (Cambridge, Mass., 1976).

Reich, M., Gordon, D.M., and Edwards, R.C., 'A theory of labor market segmentation', *Amer. Econ. Rev.*, LXIII (1973), pp. 359–65.

Rendall, J., *The origins of modern feminism: women in Britain, France and the United States, 1780–1860* (1985).

Richards, E., 'Women in the British economy since about 1700: an interpretation', *Hist.*, LXIX (1974), pp. 337–57.

Roberts, E., *Women's work, 1840–1940* (1988).

Roberts, M., 'Sickles and scythes: women's work and men's work at harvest time', *Hist. Workshop*, VII (1979), pp. 3–29.

Roper, L.A., 'Work, marriage and sexuality: women in Reformation Augsburg' (unpub. PhD. thesis, Univ. of London, 1985).

Rose, S.O., '"Gender at work": sex, class and industrial capitalism', *Hist. Workshop J.*, XXI (1986), pp. 113–31.

Rose, S.O., 'Gender segregation in the transition to the factory: the English hosiery industry, 1850–1910'. *Feminist Stud.*, 13 (1987), pp. 163–84.

Rose, S.O., 'Gender antagonism and class conflict: exclusionary strategies of male trade unionists in nineteenth-century Britain', *Soc. Hist.*, XIII (1988), pp. 191–208.

Rose, S.O., 'Proto-industry, women's work and the household economy in the transition to industrial capitalism', *J. Fam. Hist.*, 13 (1988), pp. 181–93.

Rule, J., *The labouring classes in early industrial England, 1750–1850* (1986).

Rule, J., 'The property of skill in the period of manufacture', in P. Joyce, ed., *The historical meanings of work* (Cambridge, 1987), pp. 99–118.

Schmiechen, J., *Sweated industries and sweated labour* (1984).

Scott, J.W. and Tilly, L.A., 'Women's work and the family in nineteenth-century Europe', *Comparative Studies in Society and History*, XVII (1975), pp. 36–64.

Scott, J.W., 'Men and women in the Parisian garment trades: discussions of family and work in the 1830s and 1840s', in P. Thane et al., eds., *The power of the past* (Cambridge, 1984), pp. 67–93.

Seccombe, W., 'Patriarchy stabilized: the construction of the male breadwinner wage norm in nineteenth-century Britain', *Soc. Hist.*, XI (1986), pp. 53–76.

Shorter, E., 'Women's work: what difference did capitalism make?', *Theory & Soc.*, III (1976), pp. 513–27.

Snell, K.D.M., 'Agricultural and seasonal unemployment, the standard of living and women's work in the south and east, 1690–1860', *Econ. Hist. Rev.*, 2nd ser., XXXIV (1983), pp. 407–37.

Snell, K.D.M., 'The apprenticeship of women', in *idem, Annals of the labouring poor: social change and agrarian England, 1660–1900* (Cambridge, 1985), pp. 270–319.

Sonenscher, M., 'Weavers, wage-rates and the measurement of work in eighteenth-century Rouen', *Textile History*, 17 (1986), pp. 7–18.

Sonenscher, M., *Work and wages* (Cambridge, 1989).

Sonenscher, M., 'Work and wages in Paris in the eighteenth century', in M. Berg, P. Hudson, and M. Sonenscher, eds., *Manufacture in town and country before the factory* (Cambridge, 1983), pp. 147–72.

Sonenscher, M., 'Journeymen, the courts and the French trades, 1781–1791', *Past and Present*, 114 (1987), pp. 77–109.

Sowerwine, C., 'Workers and women in France before 1914: the debate over the Couriau affair', *J. Mod. Hist.*, LV (1983), pp. 411–41.

Stockmann, R., 'Gewerbliche Frauenarbeit in Deutschland, 1875–1980: zur Entwicklung des Beschäftigtenstruktur', *Geschichte und Gesellschaft*, II (1985), pp. 447–75.

Sullivan, T.A., *Marginal workers, marginal jobs* (Austin, 1978).

Taylor, B., *Eve and the New Jerusalem* (1983).

Thomas, J., 'Women and capitalism: oppression or emancipation?', *Comp. Stud. Soc. & Hist.*, XXX (1988), pp. 534–49.

Tilly, L.A., 'Paths of proletarianization: organization of production, sexual division of labor, and women's collective action', *Signs*, VII (1981), pp. 400–17.

Tilly, L.A., 'Family, gender and occupations in industrial France: past and present', in A.C. Rossi, ed., *Gender and the life course* (New York, 1985), pp. 193–212.

Tilly, L.A. and Scott, J.W., *Women, work and family* (New York, 1978).

Valverde, M., '"Giving the female a domestic turn": the social, legal and moral regulation of women's work in British cotton mills, 1820–1850', *J. Soc. Hist.*, 21 (1988), pp. 619–34.

Walby, S., *Patriarchy at work* (Cambridge, 1986).

Wecker, R., 'Frauenlohnarbeit – Statistik und Wirklichkeit in der Schweiz an der Wende zum 20. Jahrhundert', *Schweizerische Zeitschrift für Geschichte*, 34 (1984), pp. 346–56.

Wensky, M., 'Women's guilds in Cologne in the later middle ages', *J. Eur. Econ. Hist.*, xi (1982), pp. 631–50.

Wiesner, M.E., 'Spinsters and seamstresses: women in cloth and clothing production', in M.W. Ferguson, M. Quilligan and N.J. Vickers, eds., *Rewriting the Renaissance: the discourses of sexual difference in early modern Europe* (Chicago, 1986), pp. 191–205.

Wiesner, M.E., *Working women in Renaissance Germany* (New Brunswick, 1986).

Wiesner, M.E., 'Women's work in the changing city economy, 1500–1650', in M.J. Boxer and J.H. Quataert, eds., *Connecting spheres* (New York, 1987), pp. 64–74.

Wiesner Wood, M., 'Paltry peddlers or essential merchants: women in the distributive trades in early modern Nuremberg', *Sixteenth Century J.*, xxi (1981), pp. 3–13.

Woodward, D., 'Wage rates and living standards in pre-industrial England', *Past and Present*, 91 (1981), pp. 28–46.

Wrigley, E.A., 'Men on the land and men in the countryside: employment in agriculture in early nineteenth-century England', in L.M. Bonfield, R.M. Smith, and K. Wrightson, eds., *The world we have gained* (Oxford, 1986), pp. 295–336.

Zimmeck, M., 'Jobs for the girls: the expansion of clerical work for women, 1850–1914', in A.V. John, ed., *Unequal opportunities* (Oxford, 1986), pp. 153–77.

Zimmeck, M., 'Strategies and stratagems for the employment of women in the British Civil Service, 1919–1939', *Hist. J.*, xxvii (1984), pp. 901–24.

Index

Abbott, Grace 324
Abrams, Philip 85, 100
Adler, L. 140
Africa, Africans 80, 138, 261, 285, 288
agency 10, 55
    men's 88
    women's 3, 11, 234
agricultural work 57, 211, 212
Agulhon, Maurice 314
Aladel, Père 262
Albistur, Maïté 25
Albucasis 124
Alexander, Sally 52–3, 81
Amazons 297
America *see* United States
Amussen, Susan 219
anal intercourse 162–3
    see also sodomy
anarchists 59–60, 282
Anatomie of the Body of Man, The (Vicary)
    124
Anglicanism, Anglicans 181, 186, 235, 240,
    242, 251
Anthony, Katherine 330
anthropology 56, 57, 67, 86, 204, 288
    cultural 149, 150
anti-semitism 38
anti-slavery movement 182, 184–5, 194
Appeal on One-Half the Human Race, An
    (Wheeler and Thompson) 131–2
Araeteus the Cappadocian 117
Arcadia (Sidney) 290
Arendt, Hannah 32, 36
aristocracy 183, 185, 202, 272, 329
Aristotle 116, 120, 292
art history 58
As You Like It (Shakespeare) 292
Assumptionists 267–9
Astell, Mary 215, 296
Auclert, Hubertine 320
Augsburg 74, 156, 357
Augustan period 215, 216, 314

Austria 293
Avery, Elizabeth 236, 240, 250, 252, 254
Avicenna 116–17, 118
Aylmer, John 286

Babington, Thomas 191
bachelors 68, 74, 76
Baden-Powell, Robert 73, 80
Baer, Karl Ernst von 134
Baker, Paula 339
Baker, Thomas 165
Baptist church, Baptists 236, 239, 243–4, 254
Barre, Raymond 316
Barrell, John 80
Barrett, Michèle 49–50
Barrows, Susanna 127
Bastille Day 268
Bathurst, Anne 250–1
Bauhin, Caspar 122–3
beaus 166–7
Bebel, Ferdinand 329
Behn, Aphra 163, 164
Belgium 260
Benjamin, Jessica 49
Bennett, Judith 4, 212, 349, 367
Benson, Mary 79
Berg, Maxine 350
Berlin 335, 360
Bernadette of Lourdes (Bernadette Soubirous)
    269
Bessy, the 293
binary opposition(s) 9, 11, 53–4, 55, 60, 151
biology
    men's neglected 67
    rejected by gender theorists 11, 23, 29–33,
        45
    see also body
Bischoff, Theodor L. W. 135, 137, 142
Bismarck, Otto Edward Leopold von 322, 334
black Virgins 273–4
Blumenbach, Johann Friedrich 134–5, 137
Boccaccio, Giovanni 290, 291

Bock, Gisela 11, 12, 23
Bodin, Jean 58
body
    female identified with biology 31
    gendered meanings assigned to 86–7, 89, 94
    importance in sexual difference 152, 158
    mortified by triumph of the spirit 250
    relationship to the psychic 13, 153–8
    scientific/ medical understandings of 11–12,
        14, 107–8, 111–48, 151, 152, 285
    signs of prophecy or witchcraft 234
Boerhaave, Herman 118
Bonald, Louis de 59
Bonaparte, Marie 124
Borie, Jean 138
Bourdieu, Pierre 57
bourgeoisie, bourgeois 73, 177, 181, 184, 185,
    194, 195, 206, 210, 214, 230, 273, 311, 327,
    366
Bourignon, Antoinette 298
Bourignon, Antonia 247
boys 5–6, 16, 67, 90–1, 311
    men's sexual relations with 58, 161, 162–5,
        166–7, 168
Branca, Patricia 201
Braun, Lily 329
Brazilian Indians 117
Bré, Ruth 320
breadwinner wage 68, 93, 349, 365–6
Breymann, Henriette 328
Britain 150
    citizenship 10–11, 93, 127, 282
    colonialism 57
    Marxist feminists 2, 49
    nineteenth-century masculinity 6, 67–81,
        95–9
    welfare state origins 319–46
    women and work 68, 69, 77, 93, 97, 324,
        330, 333, 336–7, 360, 363–4, 364–5
    writers' use of gender 57
    see also England; Ireland; Wales
Brittain, Vera 200
Broadbent, Benjamin 333
Browne, Thomas 120–2
Bruegel, Pieter 287–8
Bruges 355
buggery 162–3
Bulstrode, Whitelocke 163
Bund für Mutterschutz 335
Burke, Edmund 58
Burleigh, Michael 5
Butler, Judith 150, 151
Butler, Samuel 183, 200
Bynum, Caroline Walker 57–8
Byron, Lord 205

Calvat, Mélanie 264–5
Calvin, Jean 286, 287, 288
Calvinism 239, 299

Canon (Avicenna) 116
capitalism, capitalists 27, 181, 184, 188, 194,
    197, 210–11, 212, 213–14, 219, 286, 324,
    349, 353, 362, 365
    interaction with patriarchy 48, 366–7
Caribbean 80, 297
Carlyle, Thomas 71, 73
Cary, Grace 237, 238, 239
Cary, Mary 235, 236, 239, 240–1, 241–2, 247,
    248, 251, 252, 254, 255
Castlehaven, Lord 164
Catherine de Medici 58
Catholic feminism 313
Catholicism, Catholics 156–7, 229, 230, 247,
    253, 283, 311, 327–8
    Marian revival 260–77
ceffyl pren 294, 295, 300
Channel, Elinor 237, 238
Chaptal, Léonie 334
charitable work/philanthropy 92, 193, 208,
    209, 230, 282, 321, 325, 327
Charles I 238, 239, 240, 242, 299
Chartism 10–11, 72, 73, 282
Chaumette, Pierre 310–11
Chenu, Jeanne Popinel 324
Chereau, Achilles 136
Chévènement, Jean-Pierre 317
Chidley, Katherine 236, 238, 239, 240, 242,
    247, 249, 253, 255
childhood 5–6, 16, 90–1
Children's Bureau (US) 331–2, 337
Childs, Fenela 216
Chinn, Carl 72
Chodorow, Nancy 50, 51
Choisy, Abbé de, 288
Christian feminism 177
Christian Observer 182
Christianity, Christians 6, 27, 161, 162, 183, 185,
    193, 199, 229, 231, 261, 266, 270, 290, 325
church
    attitude to pilgrims 261
    and Evangelicalism 183, 184, 186
    as female 249
    female saints of early 290
    and Marian cult 263–4, 266–7, 275
    social action groups 324
    women's opportunities within 231, 312
    see also religion
Church of England *see* Anglicanism
Cibber, Colly 171
citizenship
    men's 97, 98
    women's 11, 93, 98, 127, 209, 211, 217,
        281–2, 298, 306–18, 319, 320, 324, 340
Civil War (America) 70
Civil War and Interregnum (England) 230,
    233–59

Clapham Sect 177, 181–95, 207
Clark, Alice 211, 213, 215, 300, 349
Clark, Anna 10–11, 72
Clarke, Charlotte 171
class 1, 43–4, 66, 99, 320, 323
  and education 193
  and gender 3, 8, 10, 37, 60, 73, 199–200,
    204–5
clitoris 111–12, 123–4, 125
clothing, changes in male 96
Cobbe, Frances Power 74
Cobbett, William 69, 71, 188
Coelebs (More) 189, 191–2, 193
Cohen, Alfred 233
Coleman, D. C. 216
Coleridge, Samuel Taylor 90
Colley, Linda 208, 209
Cologne 355, 356
Colombus, Renaldus 123, 124
colonialism 57, 60, 79–81
commedia dell'arte 290, 294
communion 155
Communism 274–5
Conan Doyle, Arthur 71
Condorcet, Marquis de 111, 310, 312
Connell, R.W. 75
conservatism, conservatives 202, 283, 322, 334
Cooper, John (Princess Seraphina) 169, 170
Coppe, Abiezer 242–3, 249–50
Cott, Nancy 198
Courtney, Edward 169
Cowper, Lady 168
Cowper, William 187, 188, 198–90, 205
crèches 335–6
Cromwell, Oliver 240, 241
Crooke, Helkiah, 124
Cruickshank, William 134
Culpepper, Nicholas 124
cultural history 16

Dalton, James 169
Daniel, Book of 235
Davidoff, Leonore 8, 14, 23, 73, 177, 178,
  204–6, 206–7, 208–10, 219
Davies, Eleanor 235, 237–8, 240, 242, 245,
  249, 251, 252, 254
Davies, Lucy 253
Davis, Natalie Zemon 4, 7, 15, 57, 66, 230,
  281
de Foigny, Gabriel 287
de Graaf, Regnier 112, 134
De humani corporis fabrica (Vesalius) 120
de Lauretis, Teresa 52
de Pisan, Christine 286, 289, 297
de Quincey, Thomas 80
deconstruction 2, 9–10, 53–4, 150
Defoe, Daniel 215
Delacroix, Ferdinand 317

Delcourt, Marie 298
Democritus 116
Denmark 25
Derrida, Jacques 9, 53
Deuteronomy, Book of 288
Dickens, Charles 71, 183
Dictionary of Modern English Usage (Fowler)
  42
Dictionnaire de la langue française 43
Diderot, Denis 130
difference
  among women 26, 27
  bodily aspects 48, 57, 113–14, 125–33, 140,
    144, 152, 158, 179, 285
  'different voices' 36, 53
  French psychoanalytic theorists of 12–13
  and individualism 89–90, 93
  vs equality 2, 127–8
  vs hierarchy 29
discipline 156
Discourse on the Origins of Inequality
  (Rousseau) 128, 129, 309
discourse theory 9–11, 149, 150, 152, 158–9
divorce legislation (French Revolution) 59
Donaldson, Ian 289
domestic ideology 56, 71, 96, 108, 131, 133,
  177, 178, 181–96, 199, 203, 216, 220, 325,
  326, 359, 362, 364
domestic violence 73
  husband beating 295
  wife beating 74, 301
Donne, John 165
Douai 355
Douglas, Ann 272–3
Douglas, Mary 114
Drake, Joan 236, 237
Duhamel, Alain 315
Duncan, Mathews 137
Dunton, John 167, 168
Dupanloup, Archbishop 270
Duval, Jacques 124

Earle, Peter 213, 217
economic factors 7, 48–9, 206, 210–11,
  213–14, 216–17, 322, 349, 355, 361–2,
  366–7
education 16, 56, 193, 201, 241, 286, 309, 311,
  312–13, 317
Edwards, Thomas 247
effeminacy 165–7
Eisenstein, Zillah, 132
Elias, Norbert 154
Elizabeth I 58, 248, 298
Ellis, Sarah 131, 133, 199
Elshtain, Jean 127
Emile (Rousseau) 129
Emily, Duchess of Leinster 207
Employers and Workmen's Acts (1870s) 97

Engels, Friedrich 48, 210–11
England 58, 60, 287
  Anglo-American psychoanalytic theory 47, 50
  early formation of domestic ideology 181–96
  homosexuality (1660–1750) 162–72
  language 31
  national identities 80
  sexual inversion and disorder 293, 294, 295, 298–9, 300, 301
  women prophets 233–59
  women's history 197–225
  women's work 188, 195, 210–14, 216–17, 238, 286, 349, 350
Enlightenment 111, 125, 126, 130, 308
Enquiries into Vulgar and Common Errors (Browne) 120
Epicoene (Jonson) 292
equality
  and appearance of the molly 171–2
  between men 187
  and gender 60
  and physical difference 31
  vs difference 2, 127–8
  woman's pleas for 187, 242, 251, 254, 283
  see also inequality
Erasmus 292
ethnic minorities 37–8
ethno-/Euro-centrism 29
Evangelicalism, Evangelicals 68, 91, 181–95, 199, 207, 325
Evans, Arise 238
Evans, Sara 331
exorcism 156–7
Ezekiel, the prophet 235

Factory Acts 95
Fair Quaker of Deal, The (Shadwell) 166
family and household 62, 91
  and acquisition of gender identity 16, 51, 77–9
  alternative conceptions of 297
  Evangelical view of 187–94
  homeworking 360–1
  men and 67–8, 70–2
  patriarchal 68, 230, 286, 296, 297
  as peripheral 99
  state intervention in 59, 95
  units of production 68, 212–13, 216, 355, 357
  women and 68, 72, 181, 187–94, 195, 197, 198–210, 214–16, 312–13, 353
Family Fortunes: Men and Women of the English Middle Class (Davidoff and Hall) 8, 23, 73, 177, 204–6, 206–7, 210
Family, Sex and Marriage (Stone) 35
fathers and fatherhood 36, 38

  as family supporters 93
  parental role 51, 79, 193
Fátima visions 274–5
Fawcett, Millicent Garrett 326
Female Reader (Wollstonecraft) 132
femininity 1, 15–16, 51–2, 153
  colonial projection of 80
  idea attacked by Wollstonecraft 187
  and the market place 91
  men's suppression of their own 78, 79
  and middle-class identity 199
  as natural and moral 15, 89
  of non-labour 93
  ovaries as essence of 136
  and political power 58, 59, 60
  possessed 157
  and sexuality 94, 171
  and social relations 57–8
  and types of work 350
  unchanging contradictions of 150
  Victorian ideal 199
feminism, feminist 1, 5, 62, 98, 187, 191, 200, 204, 210, 220, 282, 286–7, 291, 296, 310, 366
  anthropology 67
  and biology 32, 111, 126–7, 128, 141, 144, 152
  Catholic 313
  Christian 177
  and the French Republic 310, 311, 312, 313, 314, 315, 316
  historiography 2, 3–4, 7, 9, 26–7, 43, 44, 45, 46–54, 66, 85, 86, 87, 149–50, 177, 197, 229, 316, 324–5, 333
  literary criticism 215
  Marxist 2–3, 48–50, 99
  and maternalism 320, 324–5, 326–7, 328, 329, 330, 334, 335, 338
Feminist Studies 1980 symposium 53
Feminization of American Culture, The (Douglas) 272–3
Fifth Monarchist sect 235, 237, 240, 241, 244, 247, 255
Filmer, Robert 58
Firestone, Shulamith 47
First World War (Great War) 35, 98–9, 200, 282, 322, 333, 334, 337, 340, 366
Fisher, H.A.L. 333
Florence 27, 355
fops 165–7
Foucault, Michel 49, 52, 55, 58, 107, 214
Fox-Genovese, Elizabeth 2
France 58, 60, 74, 130–1, 230
  historiography 35–6, 37, 177–8, 314–16
  language 12, 43
  Marian revival 260–77
  popular protest 57, 281, 285–306

France *cont.*
  psychoanalytic theory 12–13, 47, 50
  Third Republic 127, 267–9, 307, 311–14,
    316–17, 327–8
  welfare state origins 319–46
  women's citizenship 306–18
  women's work 23, 359, 360, 363, 364, 365–6
Franklin, William 242
Frederick the Great 118
French Revolution 44, 58, 59, 127, 184, 185,
  186, 187, 207, 281–2, 308, 310
Freud, Sigmund 13, 50, 154
Froude, J.A. 71
Fry, Miles 242

Gadbury, Mary 242
Galen 112, 113, 114–17, 118, 120, 124
Gallagher, Catherine 131
Ganong, W.F., 144
Gardner, Augustus 136
garment industry 360–1
Garnier, Germain (formerly Marie) 122
Garrick, David 165
Geertz, Clifford 54
gender
  as an analytical category 28–33, 42–65,
    149–50
  and class 3, 8, 10, 37, 60, 73, 199–200,
    204–5
  conflict 52–3, 350, 353, 356–8, 359, 361,
    362–4
  defined 1, 55–8
  dichotomy with sex 1, 11–13, 28, 33, 43, 46,
    150–2
  domains in history and sociology 85–104
  historiography of 1–16, 28–9, 34–5, 35–6,
    43–54
  medical/scientific conceptions of 11–12, 14,
    107–8, 111–48, 151, 152, 285
  religious conceptions of 56, 58, 229–30,
    261–2, 272–3, 312, 313
  as social, cultural, historical relations 33–8
  and visionary expression 243–52
Gender and the Politics of History (Scott) 23
General Federation of Women's Clubs 331
Genesis 263
Geneva 356
Germany 30, 150, 178, 293
  body imagery in early modern 13, 108,
    155–6
  language 12, 28, 30, 31
  Nazi regime 3, 5, 11, 23, 32, 37–8, 59, 340
  welfare state origins 319–46
  women's work 356, 359, 360, 364, 365
Geschichtliche Grundbegriffe 28
Gilligan, Carol 36, 50, 53
Gillis, John 95
Giraud, Maximin 264

Girdwood, G.F., 139
girls 5, 16, 67, 91, 193, 201, 286, 309, 311,
  312–13
Gisborne, Thomas 182, 192
Gissing, George 209
Gladstone, William Ewart 43
Godelier, Maurice 57
Godwin, William 131, 186
Golden Legend (Voragine) 290
Goodman, Jordan 350
Gordon, Linda 4, 13, 325
Gordon, Thomas 170
Gosse, Edmund 200
Gray, Robert 92
Great War *see* First World War
Greece, early 58, 288
Greenblatt, S. 215
Grimmelshausen, Hans 291
Guest, Lady Charlotte 203
guilds 355, 356–8
Guilham, William 168

Haggard, Rider 71–2
Haighton, John 134
Halévy, E 192
Hall, Catherine 8, 14, 23, 73, 80, 177, 204–6,
  206–7, 208–10, 230
Hall, Jacqueline 56
Haller, Albrecht von 117–18, 125–6, 137
Hambleton, Lord Marquis of 238
Hamburg 360, 361
Hammerton, A.J. 4, 68, 76
Handbuch der Physiologie (Herman) 136
Harriman, Anna 243
Hartmann, Heidi 48, 366–7
Hatfield, Martha 237
Hause, S. 313
Havelock Ellis, Henry 125, 141
Hazzard, Dorothy 238
Heape, Walter, 140, 141
Henri III 288
Henry IV 295
Hensen, V 135–6
Herman, L 136
hermaphrodites 164–5, 287
Henrietta Maria, Queen 239
Herodotus 297
Herophilus 112
Hill, Christopher, 233
Hill, Mary 56
Hinduism 261
Hippocrates 117
Historisches Wörterbuch der Philosophie 28
History of Sexuality (Foucault) 107
Hitchen, William 168–9, 170
Hitschmann, F. 140
Hobbes, Thomas 126, 128, 133
Holder, Margaret 170

homosexuality 6, 58, 61, 70, 74, 76, 78, 107, 161–73
Honeyman, Katrina 350
Houghton, Walter 199
household *see* family and household
Hoyle, John 163–4
Huddersfield 333
Huften, Olwen 211–12
Huggins, William 167–8
Hutchins, Barbara 333
Hutchinson, Anne 233
Huxley, Aldous 133

identity *see* sexual/gender identity
Immaculate Conception 260, 263, 265, 266, 267, 269, 270, 271
imperialism 8, 76–7, 79–81
India 57, 80, 182
individuality 89–91
industrial revolution 206, 349, 350, 366
industrialization 212, 322, 349, 353, 360, 366
inequality
    ignored in object-relations theory 51
    and patriarchy 47–8
    see also equality
Insurance Act (1911) 337–8
Iran 59
Ireland 186, 300–1
Irigaray, Luce 12–13, 61
Iroquois 297
Islam, Islamic 57, 58, 261
Italy 25, 163, 166, 359
    language 12, 31
    women's incarceration in early modern 27

Jacobi, Mary Putnam 141–3
Jacobinism, Jacobins 59, 186, 309, 310
Jaeger, Muriel 199
Jameson, Mrs 191
Jaurès, Jean 311–12
Java 288
Jerome, St 288
Jesuits 298
Jesus Christ 155, 241, 242, 249, 250, 254, 272
Jews 3, 37, 290
Joan, Pope 291
Joan of Arc 297, 298
John Paul II, Pope 275
Jones, Sarah 239, 249
Jonson, Ben 292
Jordanova, Ludmilla 107

Kanthack, Emilia 320
Kelley, Florence 326
Kelly, Joan 1, 48–9
Kenney, A. 313
Kerber, Linda 177, 198–9
Khomeni, Ayatollah 59

kinship systems 56, 99
kissing, amongst men 166
Klein, Melanie 154, 155
Knox, John 286
Koven, Seth 282
Kristeva, Julia 13, 155

la Branlaïre 299
La Croix 267–9, 271
La Pèlerin 268
Labouchere, Henry 74
Labour party 320, 326–7
Labouré, Catherine 260, 262, 264
Labouvie, Eve 153
Lacan, Jacques 50, 51, 52, 214
Lacanian theory 12, 51–3, 56
Ladies Magazine 218
Lafitau, J.F. 297
Laget, Mireille 30
Lancet 136
language
    and body images 154–5
    of Christian thought 229
    and construction of meaning 9–11, 14–15
    and subjective identity 50, 51, 153
Laqueur, Thomas 14, 11–12, 107–8, 151, 178
Larpent, Anna 218
LaSalette visions 264–5, 269, 274
Lathrop, Julia 324
Laud, Archbishop 235, 239
Lawrence, T.E. 80
Le Fer de la Motte, Mercedes 324
Le Nouvel Observateur 316
Le Play, Frédéric 330
Lee, Nathaniel 164
Leeds Intelligencer 218
Legacy for Saints, A (Trapnel) 235
Legates, Marlene 216
Leiden 355, 356
Leigh Smith, Barbara 203
Leo XIII, Pope 266–7
Leonardo da Vinci 120
lesbianism 107, 171
L'Esprit des Lois (Rousseau) 309
Levelers 240, 242, 254, 255
Lewis, Jane 204
l'Héritier, Mademoiselle 290
liberalism, liberals 127, 131, 132, 194, 322
Life of Lycurgus (Plutarch) 309
Ligue Patriotique des Femmes Françaises 327–8, 334
Lilburne, John 255
linguistic theory 2, 8–11, 15
Lloyd George, David 322
Locke, John 58, 287
London 73, 74, 151, 161, 162, 186, 213, 217, 335, 355, 361
London Medical Dictionary 112

London Working Men's Association 72
Lords of Misrule 294–5
Louis XIII 269, 295
Lourdes (Zola) 271–2
Lourdes 260, 265–6, 267, 269–72
Lovejoy, David 233

Macaulay, Zachary 182, 185, 191
MacDonald, Margaret 327
Machiavelli, Niccolò 292
Machievellian Moment, The (Pocock) 314
Mack, Phyllis 14, 230
MacKinnon, Catherine 47
'Maid Marian' 293, 302
Majority Finds Its Past, The (Lerner) 28
Making of the English Working Class, The
   (Thompson) 205
*Making Sex: Body and Gender from the
   Greeks to Freud* (Laqueur) 107
Malthus, Thomas 131
Manful Assertions (Roper and Tosh) 66
manliness 6, 78–9, 87
Maria Theresa, Princess 125
Marian devotion 260–77
Marianne 268, 306–7, 314, 317
Marie-Antoinette 58
market, the 91–2
Marlowe, Christopher 171
marriage 95, 96, 230, 286, 296–7, 298
   Evangelical model 191–2
   homosexual 169
   and legitimate sexual activity 6, 161, 162
   married women's employment 195, 359,
      361, 365–6
   men's cruelty censured 4
   as metaphor for piety 245–6, 248–9
   political analogies 58, 59, 240, 248–9, 287
   strong women and weak men 201–2, 291–2
   as symmetrical union 177
   and transition to adult life 68
   women's reform campaigns 74, 76
   and women's subjecthood 90
Marston, John 290
Martin, Biddy 56
Marx, Karl 44, 47
Marxism, Marxists 9, 44, 47, 205–6, 322
Marxist feminists 2–3, 48–50, 99
Mary, Countess of Warwick, 236
Mary, Virgin 157, 285
   visions of 230, 260–77
   see also Immaculate Conception
Mary, Queen of Scots 248
Mary, Queen of the Gauls 268
masculinity 1, 6, 15–16
   and agency 88
   hegemonic 6, 75, 76
   historiography of 4–7, 65–7
   and the individual 89–90

and middle-class identity 199
and monarchy 248
and political power 58, 59, 60
as rational and scientific 15, 88–9, 349, 350
of the republican tradition 307, 316
and sexuality 94, 162, 171
and social relations 57–8, 67–77, 87–100
subjective identity 51–2, 77–81, 153
and war 35, 60, 98–9
maternalism 283, 319–46
Mathurine 295
Matrimonial Causes Act (1978) 74
May customs 295–6
McClelland, Keith 75
McDougall, Joyce 155
McMillan, J.F., 313
McMillan, Margaret 338
medical/scientific understandings of the body
   11–12, 14, 107–8, 111–48, 151, 152, 285
medieval spirituality 57–8
men
   all-male associations 69–70, 70–2, 98
   appeal of certain political creeds to 282
   biological analogies with women 112,
      113–14, 114–25
   biology ignored 67
   citizenship 97, 98
   disguised as women 290, 293–4, 294–5,
      299–301
   Evangelical view of 189, 190, 191
   in the family and household 67–8, 70–2
   homosexuality 6, 58, 61, 70, 74, 76, 78, 107,
      161–73
   ministers and prophets 234, 235, 242–3,
      244, 249–50, 253–4, 255
   'man' as category 61, 99
   manipulated by women 247
   monarchs 58
   morality of 89
   new economic 206, 214
   as part of gender studies 2, 35–6, 45, 66
   popular protest by 281, 299–301
   and the private sphere 70–1, 99, 178
   and property 93
   and the public sphere 3, 15, 69, 70–1, 78, 90,
      99, 177, 189, 190, 217
   rationality of 15, 88–9, 349, 350
   reaction to women prophets 237–9, 244, 255
   relationships among 34
   and religion 91, 273, 311–12
   sexuality 89, 93–4, 114–15, 116, 118–20, 285
   subordination of other men 6, 74
   subordination of women 3–4, 13, 47–8, 59,
      85–6, 192, 286, 287, 320, 324–5, 354
   unconfined by gender 5, 11, 30–1, 67, 129
   victims of domestic violence 295
   victims of Nazism 3
   and war 35, 60, 98–9

men *cont.*
  and work 3, 68–9, 70–2, 73, 93, 95–7, 211,
    212–13, 349, 354, 359, 361, 362–4,
    365–6
  see also masculinity; patriarchy
men's history 5, 66, 25–6, 27, 35–6
men's movement 5
men's studies 35–6
menstruation 117–18, 136–41, 142
Mernissi, Fatima 261
Methodism, Methodists 181, 182, 183, 184,
  207
Michel, Sonya 282
Michelet, Jules 117, 135, 141, 307
Middle Ages 253, 262, 287, 293, 312, 355, 358
middle class 365, 366
  belief in separate spheres 177, 199, 207, 208,
    209
  constitutive role of gender 8, 199, 204–5
  depiction of working class as feminine 60
  and the Evangelical movement 184–6,
    186–7, 188, 194, 207
  men 68–9, 70, 71–2, 73, 77, 78–9, 87, 95–6,
    98, 311–12
  women 78–9, 93, 181, 201, 210, 214, 219,
    282, 311–12, 320, 325, 329, 333, 334–5,
    338, 339
  see also bourgeois, bourgeoisie
Miegge, Giovanni 270–1
military history 35
Mill, James 111, 131
Mill, John Stuart 326
Millar, John 130
Mitterand, François 316
modernization theorists 322
mollies 165–6, 168–72
monarchs 58, 248, 286
Montagu, Mary Wortley 42, 207
Montaigne, Michel de 117
Montesquieu, Charles de 308–9, 310
Moore, John 242
Moore, Samson G. H. 333
morality
  Evangelical 181–95
  and the market 92
  men's 89
  women's 89, 128–33, 138–9, 190–1, 216,
    229–30, 282, 326
More, Hannah 131, 182, 183, 187, 188, 189, 190,
  191–2, 193, 199, 205, 206
Moreau, Thérèse 141
Moreau de la Sarthe, Jacques 113
Mosse, George 6
Mossuz-Lavau, Janine 315
motherhood, mothers
  conflation with biology 32
  and Marian visions 262, 270
  maternal imagery 157, 158, 249–50, 250–1

maternalism 283, 319–46
parental role 78–9, 193, 309
and spiritual transformation 236, 248
Muggleton, Lodowijk 242
Muller, Johannes 135, 138

Naissances (Laget) 30
Napoleon I 310
National Congress of Mothers 331
National Socialism 30, 32, 38, 338–9
'nature vs. nurture' debate 30, 33
Nazi regime 3, 5, 11, 23, 32, 37–8, 59, 340
Nemesis of Faith, The (Froude) 71
Nemesius, Bishop 112
New Left Review 49
New Poor Law (1834) 95
New Woman, the 76, 202, 209
Nightingale, Florence 203
Norton, John 167
Nuremberg 294, 296, 356

Oakley, Ann 1, 11
object-relations theory 50, 51
O'Brien, Mary 47
Oedipus and the Devil (Roper) 108
On the Seed (Galen) 114
On the Usefulness of the Parts of the Body
  (Galen) 114
orgasm
  female 111–12, 116–17, 118, 119–20, 125–6
  male 116, 118
Origin of the Distinctions of Ranks (Millar)
  130
Origins of the Family (Engels) 48
otherness 32, 89–90, 99
  colonial 80–1
  women's 2, 32
Otway, Thomas 164
ovaries, ovulation 112, 113, 134–44

Paine, Thomas 187
papacy 266–7
Pare, Ambroise 119, 122
Paris 161, 334, 335, 354, 355, 359, 361
Parkes, Bessie 203
Parliament 74, 189, 237, 238, 239, 240, 241,
  255, 286
Parti Ouvrier 320
Pateman, Carole 89
Patmore, Coventry 71, 199, 202
patriarchy 3–4, 13, 47–8, 261, 350, 354
  in the family and household 68, 230, 286,
    296, 297
  and gender division of labour 48, 355–6,
    362, 364, 365, 366–7
  interaction with capitalism 48, 366–7
  and masculinity 67–77, 81
  state perpetuation of 324–5

Paul, St 192, 209, 288
Peacock, James 288
Pechey, John 123
Pepys, Samuel 163, 215
Peterson, Jeanne 201, 202
Pfluger, E.F.W. 141
philanthropy/charitable work 92, 193, 208, 209, 230, 282, 321, 325, 327
Phlipon, Manon (later Madame Roland) 309
Physiology (Haller) 137
pilgrimage 261, 269–72
Pinchbeck, Ivy 188, 211, 349
Pitt, William 185
Pius IX, Pope 266, 267
Plato 129
Pliny 117, 120, 137
Plutarch 309
Pocock, J.G.A. 314
Pocock, Mary 248, 255
politics 7, 56, 206–7, 279–346
    citizenship 11, 93, 97, 98, 209, 211, 217, 281–2, 298, 306–18, 319, 320, 324, 340
    content of the Marian visions 262, 269–70, 274–5
    gender and political theory 15, 58–62, 111, 125–33
    popular protest 281, 285–306
    and religion 185, 267–9
    and women prophets 237, 238, 239–43, 248–50, 252, 254–5
    women's activity in nineteenth and early twentieth century 74, 200, 203, 204, 319–46
Pontmain visions 262, 266, 269, 274
Poole, Elizabeth 238, 239–40, 251, 253
Pope, Barbara Corrado 14, 230
Pope, Mary 236, 238–9, 240, 242, 244–5, 249
Poplet, Mary 170
Pordage, John 255
Porteous Riots 300
postmodernism 8–11, 150, 229
    see also discourse theory, deconstruction
poststructuralists 50, 54, 150
Pouchet, F.A. 135, 138, 142
Poullain de La Barre, François 296
Powell, Vavasour 255
power relations 6, 9, 10, 29, 31–2, 55, 57, 58–62
Powers of Desire (Snitow, Stansell and Thompson) 49
Practical Christianity (Wilberforce) 183, 186, 190
Pressensé, E. de 270
printing trade 363–4
private sphere
    men and 70–1, 99, 178
    woman and 3, 15, 87, 90, 92, 99, 127, 177, 178, 189, 190, 199, 200, 298, 310–11, 312–13

projection 79–80
property 92–3
prophets and visionaries 230, 233–59
prostitutes 161, 167, 168
Protestantism, Protestants 229, 230, 270–1, 272–3, 327, 328
psychoanalytic theory 5, 12–13, 15, 16, 47, 50–4, 56, 77–8, 108, 154, 155
public sphere(s) 86, 204
    men and 3, 15, 69, 70–1, 78, 90, 99, 177, 189, 190, 217
    women and 76, 90, 200, 209–10, 217–18, 248, 253, 298–9, 339
Pugh, Martin 202–3
Puritanism, Puritans 193–4, 195, 233, 235, 236, 239, 247, 251
Putnam, Elizabeth Lowell 326

Quélen, archbishop of Paris 262
Question of Rest for Women During Menstruation, The (Jacobi) 141–3
Quinlan, Maurice 199

Rabelais, François 285, 291
race 3, 8, 31–2, 43–4, 285, 320
Racial State, The (Burleigh and Wippermann) 5
Raciborski, Adam 142
racism 31–2, 37–8, 79–80
radicalism, radicals 10, 181, 184, 188, 203–4, 239, 240, 241, 251, 322
rakes 162–5
Ramsden, Bessy 218
Ranters 242, 249
rationality 15, 88–9, 153, 349, 350
Rebecca riots 300
Reeve, John 242
Reform Act (1832) 95
Reformation 155, 156, 230, 366
religion 37, 58, 95, 227–77
    debate on communion 155
    Marian devotion 260–77
    men and 91, 273, 311–12
    women and 56, 132, 190–1, 208, 229–31, 233–59, 272–3, 282, 311–12, 325
    see also Evangelicalism
Remak, Robert 137–8
Rémond, René 267
Renaissance 1
    medicine 111–12, 117–25
Rendall, Jane 203–4
republicanism 306–17
Restoration 163, 164, 165, 171, 214, 215
Revelation 263
Review of Medical Physiology (Ganong) 144
Rey, Emile 330
Reynolds, Siân 7, 15, 281
Richardson, Samuel 188

Rigby, Captain 166–7
Riley, Denise 2, 53
Rochester, Lord 163
Roderick Random (Smollett) 166
Rogers, John 242, 244, 255
Romance languages 12, 30
Rome, ancient 308
Roper, Lyndal 13, 74, 108
Roper, Michael 66
Rosaldo, Michelle Zimbalist 34, 55, 67
Rose, Sonya 75
'Rosetta' 293, 302
Ross, Ellen 72
Rousseau, Jean-Jacques 30, 67, 128–30, 132,
　　133, 308, 309–10, 312, 313
Roussel, Pierre 112
Rubin, Gayle 56
Rueff, Jacob 118–19
ruling classes 73, 97, 186
rural industry 212–13, 358
Ruskin, John 199, 202, 209
Russia 274–5

Sachsse, Christoph 334
Sade, Marquis de 111, 133
Sadler, John 119
Saint-Just, Louis 309
Salomon, Alice 328, 329
Savile, Henry 163
Schiebinger, Londa 152
Schoen, Erhard 292
Schreber, Daniel Paul 154
Schwerin, Jeanette 328
scientific/medical understandings of the body
　　11–12, 14, 107–8, 111–48, 151, 152, 285
Scilly Islands 294
Scotland 294, 295, 299, 300, 364
Scott, Joan 7, 8–9, 10–11, 23, 99, 149–50
Scott, Walter 207
Scout movement 72, 73
Scouting for Boys (Baden-Powell) 80
Second Vatican Council 275
Second World War 35, 283, 307, 340
Sedgwick, Eve 70
Sedley, Charles 163
Seed, The 116
Segalen, Martine 177–8
separate spheres 14, 45, 46, 70–1, 175–225,
　　282, 321
　　notion questioned 177–8, 178–9, 197–225
'Seraphina, Princess' 169, 170
servants 91, 97, 98
settlement houses 331–2
sex, dichotomy with gender 1, 11–13, 28, 33,
　　43, 46, 150–2
sex-gender system 367
sexism 31–2, 38, 314, 316
sexual/gender identity 12–13, 15–16, 50–4,

　　56–7, 77–81, 94, 149, 150, 151–2, 153,
　　158–9
sexual imagery 157–8, 250–1
sexual inversion 288–96
sexual symbolism 287
sexuality
　　denied by depictions of Virgin Mary 273
　　men's 89, 93–4, 114–15, 116, 118–20, 285
　　and power relations 47, 49, 57
　　and racism 38
　　Victorian attitudes to 202, 207
　　women's 89, 93–4, 111–12, 114–15, 116–17,
　　　118–20, 123–4, 125–6, 131, 132, 137–8,
　　　139, 142, 143, 216, 234, 285
　　see also homosexuality; lesbianism
Shackleton, Elizabeth 218
Shadwell, Charles 166
Shadwell, Thomas 292, 297
Shakespeare, William 171
Sharp, Jane 123
Shelley, Lady 184
Sheppard–Towner Act (1921) 332, 338
Sherwood, Mrs 199
Shevelow, Kathryn 214
Showalter, Elaine 76
Sidney, Philip 290
Simeon, Charles 182
Simmel, Georg 85–6, 88
Sineau, Mariette 315
Sklar, Kathryn Kish 56, 331
Skocpol, Theda 331
Smith, Bonnie 177, 327
Smollett, Tobias 166
Social Catholics 334
Social Contract (Rousseau) 310
Social Security Act (US, 1935) 338
social and social scientific history 8, 9, 14, 16,
　　45–6, 86, 229, 281, 353
socialism, socialists 48, 59–60, 94, 131, 229,
　　282, 311, 328–9, 335
socialist feminists 326
society-centred theorists 322
sociology 85, 88, 95, 99–100
sodomy 157, 161–73
Soranus 114
Soubirous, Bernadette 262, 265
Sozialdemokratische Partei Deutschlands
　　(SPD) 329
Spain 275, 287
　　language 12
Sparta 308, 309, 313
Spenser, Edmund 290, 291
Spivak, Gayatri 57
Stalin, Joseph 59
Stansell, Christine 9, 10
state
　　well-ordered family as basis of 59, 287
　　see also welfare states

state-centred theorists 322–3, 331
Staves, Susan 165
Stead, W.T. 70
Stedman Jones, Gareth 10
Stephen, James 182, 188–9, 192
Stevenson, Robert Louis 71
Stewart, Mary Lynn 334
Stone, Lawrence 35, 37, 214
Strachey, Lytton 200
Strachey, Ray 200
Strauss Law (1913) 334
subject
  double meaning of 90
  Lacanian fixation on 52
suffrage
  men's 56, 98, 307
  universal 306–7
  women's 2, 127, 283, 306–18, 326–7
Sweden 25
Switzerland 25

Tabulae sex (Vesalius) 120
Tasso, Torquato 290
Taylor, Barbara 81, 96, 131, 132–3, 152
Taylor Allen, Ann 328
technology, gendering of 362–4
Teignmouth, Lord 182
Tennyson, Alfred Lord 199
textile industry 212–13, 362
Thackeray, William Makepeace 183
Thane, Pat 201
Third Reich *see* Nazi regime
Third Republic *see under* France
Thompson, E.P. 184, 205
Thompson, William 131–2
Thornton, Henry 182, 185
Thornton, John 182, 185
Tilly, Louise 9
Tiresias 114
Tocqueville, Alexis de 127
Toryism 184
Tosh, John 4, 5, 23
trade unions 362
transvestism 152
  female 171, 290, 288
  male 167, 170, 171, 288, 289, 290, 293–4,
    294–5, 299–301
Trapnel, Anna 235, 236, 237, 238, 239, 240,
  241, 243, 246–7, 249, 251, 252, 253, 255
Trimmer, Mrs 199
Trotulla 118
Trumbach, Randolph 107, 151
Tunbridge-Walks (Baker) 165
Turks 275
Turner, Victor 288, 296

United States of America 1, 260, 301
  Anglo-American psychoanalytic theory 47,
    50

'cult of true womanhood' 197, 326
democracy and patriarchy 127
ethnic minorities in 37
feminization of Protestantism 272–3
historiography 2, 3, 25, 177, 197, 198–9, 200
  Marxist feminists 49
  use of gender 43, 57
  welfare state origins 319–46
upper classes 181, 184, 214
  see also ruling class, aristocracy
Urfé, Honoré d' 290
uterus (womb) 115, 119, 126, 140–1, 142, 285
Utilitarianism 194

Valenze, Deborah 349
Vaughan, Thomas 168
Veil, Simone 316
Venice 355
Venn, John 182
Venner, Thomas 241
Vesalius, Andreas 120
Vicary, Thomas 124
Vicinus, Martha 202
Vickery, Amanda 177
Vico, Giovanni 297
Victorian era 4, 56, 67–81, 87, 91, 93, 94,
  95–9, 178, 181–96, 197–210, 219
Vindication of the Right of Woman
  (Wollstonecraft) 187
Virchow, Rudolph 141
virginity 270
Voragine, Jacobus de 290

Wales 294–5, 300
Wandering Whore 162, 164
war 35, 46, 60, 62, 98–9, 130
  see also Civil War and Interregnum; First
    World War; Second World War
'War of the Demoiselles' 300
Ward, Mary Augusta (Mrs Humphrey) 298,
  326, 332–3
Ward, Ned 169
Warren, Elizabeth 238, 240
Webb, Beatrice 326, 329
Weber, Max 89, 233
welfare states 59, 282–3, 319–46
Welter, Barbara 197
Wesley, John 181
Wheeler, Anna 131–2
Whig history 181–2
White, William Hale 71
Whiteboys 300–1, 302
Whitle, George 169
Wight, Sarah 236, 239, 250, 254
Wilberforce, William 182, 183, 185, 186,
  188–9, 190, 207, 208
Wild, Jonathan 168–9, 170
Wilde, Oscar 70

Willeford, William 290
Willis, Paul 69
Wilson, Elizabeth 324
Winstanley, Gerrard 255
Wippermann, Wolfmann 5
witchcraft 13, 157–8, 234, 286
Wittie, Robert 164
Wives of England (Ellis) 133
Wolf, Christa 38
Wollstonecraft, Mary 131, 132–3, 152, 187, 308
womb *see* uterus
women
  biology 30–3, 111–44
  citizenship 11, 93, 98, 209, 211, 217, 281–2, 298, 306–18, 319, 320, 324, 340
  confined by gender 11, 30–1, 66–7, 89, 129
  descent into indolence 210–17
  differences among 26, 27
  essentialist notions of 53
  Evangelical view of 187–94, 195
  in the family and household 68, 72, 181, 187–94, 195, 197, 198–210, 214–16, 312–13, 353
  incarceration in early modern Italy 27
  incomes 37
  lesbianism 107, 171
  manipulation of men 247
  and the market 92
  men's thinking on 36
  monarchs 58, 248, 286
  morality of 89, 128–33, 138–9, 190–1, 216, 229–30, 282, 326
  mutual notion of self 94–5
  and origins of welfare states 282–3, 319–46
  pilgrims 261
  political insignificance 88, 89, 98
  and popular protest 281, 285–306
  and the private sphere 3, 15, 87, 90, 92, 99, 127, 177, 178, 189, 190, 199, 200, 298, 310–11, 312–13
  and property 92–3
  prophets 230, 233–59
  and the public sphere 76, 90, 200, 209–10, 217–18, 248, 253, 298–9, 339
  racism against 37–8
  relationships among 34
  and religion 56, 132, 190–1, 208, 229–31, 272–3, 282, 311–12, 325
  sexuality 89, 93–4, 111–12, 114–15, 116–17, 118–20, 123–4, 125–6, 131, 132, 137–8, 139, 142, 143, 216, 234, 285

  subordination by men 3–4, 13, 47–8, 59, 85–6, 192, 286, 287, 320, 324–5, 354
  support for female prophets 239
  thinkers 36
  victims and perpetrators of Nazism 3, 32
  victims of domestic violence 74, 301
  and war 35, 98–9, 130
  'woman' as category 2, 3, 7, 61, 99, 151
  and work 3, 7, 68, 69, 77, 87, 93, 97, 188, 195, 210–14, 216–17, 230–1, 238, 286, 323, 324, 329–30, 333, 334, 336–7, 337–8, 349–50, 353–76
  see also femininity
Women and the Welfare State (Wilson) 324
Women under Socialism (Bebel) 329
Women Workers and the Industrial Revolution (Pinchbeck) 211
'women's culture' 50, 53
women's history 1–3, 4–5, 7–8, 25–7, 34–5, 43, 44, 45, 66, 149, 197–225
women's movement 1, 30, 200
women's studies 32, 43, 66, 201
'women's time' 254
Woolf, Virginia 111, 200
work 14, 347–76
  men's 3, 68–9, 70–2, 73, 93, 95–7, 211, 212–13, 349, 354, 359, 361, 362–4, 365–6
  women's 3, 7, 68, 69, 77, 87, 93, 97, 188, 195, 210–14, 216–17, 230–1, 238, 286, 323, 324, 329–30, 333, 334, 336–7, 337–8, 349–50, 353–76
working class
  church attendance 311
  conflict with Clapham Sect 186
  contribution to welfare state development 322
  men 11, 68, 69, 72, 73, 75–6, 93, 96–7
  shaped by task of surviving 10
  subordination of 6
  women 11, 68, 72, 69, 94–5, 97, 98, 320, 329, 331, 333, 339
Working Life of Women in the Seventeenth Century (Clark) 211
World Turned Upside Down, The (Hill) 233
Wright-Mills, C. 100
Wrightson, Keith 198

Zell, Katherine 299
Zola, Émile 271–2

PERSONAL COPY. PLEASE TAKE CARE.

DATE DUE

This Library charges fines on overdues.			
Jan 10 -	11:51		
Jan 12	15:52		
Jan 17	11:57		
17 -	7:50		
Jan 19	14:02		
Feb 28	17:57		
Feb Mar 1	11:53		
March 3 -	16:43		
4 -	12:38		
11	17:28		
11	22:03		